JavaScript

Complete Concepts and Techniques

Gary B. Shelly
Thomas J. Cashman
William J. Dorin
Jeffrey J. Quasney

COURSE TECHNOLOGY
ONE MAIN STREET
CAMBRIDGE MA 02142
Thomson Learning™

SHELLY CASHMAN SERIES®

Australia • Canada • Denmark • Japan • Mexico • New Zealand • Philippines
Puerto Rico • Singapore • South Africa • Spain • United Kingdom • United States

Printed in the United States of America

For more information, contact:

Course Technology
One Main Street
Cambridge, Massachusetts 02142, USA

or find us on the World Wide Web at: www.course.com

Asia (excluding Japan)
Thomson Learning
60 Albert Street, #15-01
Albert Complex
Singapore 189969

Japan
Thomson Learning
Palaceside Building 5F
1-1-1 Hitotsubashi, Chiyoda-ku
Tokyo 100 0003 Japan

Australia/New Zealand
Nelson/Thomson Learning
102 Dodds Street
South Melbourne, Victoria 3205
Australia

Latin America
Thomson Learning
Seneca, 53
Colonia Polanco
11560 Mexico D.F. Mexico

South Africa
Thomson Learning
Zonnebloem Building,
Constantia Square
526 Sixteenth Road
P.O. Box 2459
Halfway House, 1685
South Africa

Canada
Nelson/Thomson Learning
1120 Birchmount Road
Scarborough, Ontario
Canada M1K 5G4

UK/Europe/Middle East
Thomson Learning
Berkshire House
168-173 High Holborn
London, WC1V 7AA United Kingdom

Spain
Thomson Learning
Calle Magallanes, 25
28015-MADRID
ESPANA

PHOTO CREDITS: *Project 1, pages J 1.2-3* Mountain lake, twisting road, Courtesy of PhotoDisc, Inc.; boulders, dirt road, Courtesy of Digital Stock; road sign, Courtesy of KPT Metatools; BMW, web site, ©1999 BMW of North America, Inc. used with permission. The BMW name and logo are registered trademarks; *Project 2, pages J 2.2-3* Piggy bank, checkbook, calculator, money, man working at computer, Courtesy of PhotoDisc, Inc.; computer monitor, Courtesy of KPT Metatools; *Project 3, pages J 3.2-3* Barbie® doll, Barbie Web site, Ruth Handler, Courtesy of Mattel, Inc.; Barbie and associated trademarks are owned by and used with permission from Mattel, Inc. ©1998 Mattel, Inc. All Rights Reserved. All screens shown © Mattel. Fashion Avenue is a trademark of Newport News, Inc. a member of the Spiegel Group; *Project 4, pages J 4.2-3* Asphalt road texture, Courtesy of KPT Metatools; circuit board texture, Courtesy of PhotoDisc, Inc.; *Project 5, pages J 5.2-3* Pentium III, Courtesy of Intel Corporation; Iomega Zip Drive, Courtesy of Iomega Corporation; Sound Blaster Live! sound card, Courtesy of Creative Labs, Inc.; Altec Lansing speakers, Courtesy of Altec Lansing Technologies; Dell computer, Michael Dell, Courtesy of Dell Computer Corporation; Viper V770 Ultra video card, Courtesy of Diamond Multimedia.

ISBN 0-7895-5642-1

1 2 3 4 5 6 7 8 9 10 BC 04 03 02 01 00

JavaScript

Complete Concepts and Techniques

CONTENTS

INTRODUCTION

INTRODUCTION TO JAVASCRIPT PROGRAMMING

PROJECT ONE

INTEGRATING JAVASCRIPT AND HTML

PROJECT TWO

CREATING POP-UP WINDOWS, ADDING SCROLLING MESSAGES, AND VALIDATING FORMS

Preface

In the several years since its birth, the World Wide Web, or Web for short, has grown beyond all expectations. During this short time, the Web has increased from a limited number of networked computers to more than twenty-five million computers offering hundreds of millions of Web pages on any topic you can imagine. Schools, businesses, and the computing industry all are taking advantage of this new way of delivering information and they are using JavaScript to bring their Web pages to life by adding dynamic content and interactive elements.

Objectives of This Textbook

JavaScript: Complete Concepts and Techniques is intended for a two-unit course on using JavaScipt to add functionality to Web pages. This book also is suitable for use in a distance education or a continuing education course. Specific objectives of this book are as follows:

- To expose students to adding functionality to Web pages
- To teach students how to use JavaScript
- To acquaint students with the proper procedures to create dynamic Web Pages suitable for course work, professional purposes, and personal use
- To illustrate common Web page interactivity
- To encourage students to use their creativity in developing Web pages
- To develop an exercise-oriented approach that allows students to learn by example
- To encourage independent study and help those who are learning how to enhance Web pages in a distance education environment

Organization of This Textbook

JavaScript: Complete Concepts and Techniques is comprised of an introduction to JavaScript section and five projects that step students through enhancing Web pages. This book assumes students have a working knowledge of HTML. Each project begins with a statement of Objectives. The topics in the project are presented in a step-by-step, screen-by-screen manner. Each project ends with a Project Summary and a section titled What You Should Know. Questions and exercises are presented at the end of each project. Exercises include Test Your Knowledge, Use Help, Apply Your Knowledge, In the Lab, and Cases and Places. The projects are organized as follows:

JavaScript

Take an Order

Unordinary Dell Directs Online Computer Sales

Michael Dell was not an ordinary kid. When he was 8-years-old, he applied for a high school General Equivalency Diploma. When he was 9, he applied for his own checking account. When he was 12, he earned $2,000 creating a 12-page catalog and conducting a national mail order stamp auction. When he was 13, he invested successfully in stocks, gold, and silver.

As a freshman biology major at the University of Texas in 1983, Michael Dell had a vision: to sell computers directly to consumers without using dealers or stores. He started assembling computers in his dormatory, much to the chagrin of his parents and

Introduction to JavaScript Programming The Introduction provides an overview of JavaScript. The differences between Java and JavaScript and between JavaScript and VB Script are discussed. This section presents the basic concepts of JavaScript variables, conditionals, functions, objects, properties, methods, event handlers, forms, frames, and arrays.

Project 1 - Integrating JavaScript and HTML In Project 1, students are introduced to integrating JavaScript into an HTML file. Topics include placing JavaScript tags and comments within HTML; placing HTML tags within JavaScript statements; using the document object; setting the background colors property; extracting the system date; setting the substring property; defining variables; writing user-defined functions; and using the setTimeout() and Alert() functions.

1. Press ALT+F, S

How Cookies Are Stored

Cookies are stored in special files by a browser. It is possible to find these files and read their contents on your computer. For more information about how cookies are stored, visit www.scsite.com/js/p4.htm and then click How Cookies Are Stored.

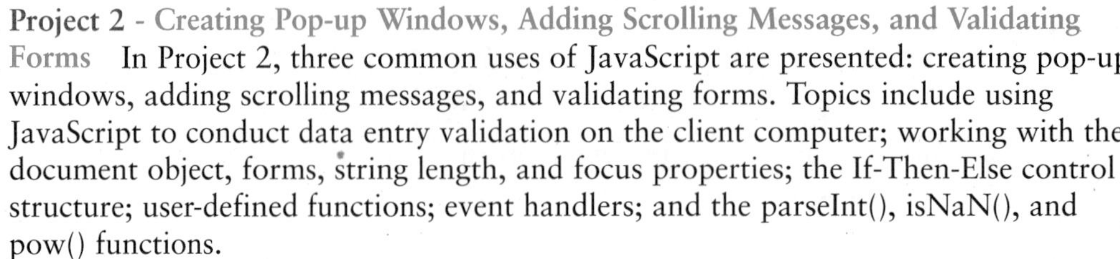

Project 2 - Creating Pop-up Windows, Adding Scrolling Messages, and Validating Forms In Project 2, three common uses of JavaScript are presented: creating pop-up windows, adding scrolling messages, and validating forms. Topics include using JavaScript to conduct data entry validation on the client computer; working with the document object, forms, string length, and focus properties; the If-Then-Else control structure; user-defined functions; event handlers; and the parseInt(), isNaN(), and pow() functions.

Project 3 - Enhancing the Use of Image and Form Objects In Project3, students learn more about functions and the common objects used in JavaScript. Topics include writing a function that calculates the number of days to a future date; changing graphic images; using the index from a select list in an If-Then-Else control structure; passing a value to a function that sets a value in a text box; and calculating an estimated cost for services.

Project 4 – Cookies, Arrays, and Frames In Project 4, students learn how to create and manipulate data in cookies. Topics include creating a cookie; reading a cookie; setting the expiration date of a cookie; deleting a cookie; creating an array of custom objects; use of the new operator; use of the this keyword; and writing information from one form to another.

Project 5 – Using Objects to Create a Shopping Cart Application In Project 5, students build on their knowledge of JavaScript by learning more about objects, frames, and windows. Topics include creating a shopping cart application using hidden frames; using objects to store complex data; writing methods for objects; using the With statement; using the For-in loop; using the history object; writing HTML from one window to another; using the navigator object; and detecting keystrokes in a browser.

End-of-Project Student Activities

A notable strength of the Shelly Cashman Series Internet books is the extensive student activities at the end of each project. Well-structured student activities can make the difference between students merely participating in a class and students retaining the information they learn. These activities include all of the following sections.

- What You Should Know A listing of the tasks completed within a project together with the pages where the step-by-step, screen-by-screen explanations appear. This section provides a perfect study review for students.
- Test Your Knowledge Four or five pencil-and-paper activities designed to determine students' understanding of the material in the project. Included are true/false questions, multiple-choice questions, and two short-answer exercises.
- Use Help Any user of JavaScript must recognize the importance of the JavaScript Web sites that discuss JavaScript and illustrate algorithms. Therefore, this book contains two Help exercises per project that have students visit JavaScript Web sites. These exercises alone distinguish the Shelly Cashman Series from any other set of instructional materials.
- Apply Your Knowledge A substantive exercise intended to be completed in a few minutes that provides practice with project skills.
- In the Lab Several assignments per project that require students to apply the knowledge gained in the project to solve problems.
- Cases and Places A set of unique case studies allow students to apply their knowledge to real-world situations.

Shelly Cashman Series Teaching Tools

A comprehensive set of Teaching Tools accompanies this textbook in the form of a CD-ROM. The CD-ROM includes an electronic Instructor's Manual and teaching and testing aids. The CD-ROM (ISBN 0-7895-4695-7) is available through your Course Technology representative or by calling one of the following telephone numbers: Colleges and Universities, 1-800-648-7450; High Schools, 1-800-824-5179; Career Colleges, 1-800-477-3692; Canada, 1-800-268-2222; and Corporations and Government Agencies 1-800-340-7450. The contents of the CD-ROM are listed below.

- **Instructor's Manual** The Instructor's Manual is made up of Microsoft Word files that include lecture notes, solutions to laboratory assignments, and a large test bank. The files allow you to modify the lecture notes or generate quizzes and exams from the test bank using you own word processor. The Instructor's Manual includes the following for each project: project objectives; project overview; detailed lesson plans with page number references; teacher notes and activities; answers to the end-of-project exercises; test bank of 110 questions (50 true/false, 25 multiple-choice, and 35 fill-in-the-blank); transparency references; and selected transparencies. The transparencies are available on the Figures in the Book described below. The test bank questions are numbered the same as in Course Test Manager. Thus, you can print a copy of the project and use the printed test bank to select your questions in Course Test Manager.

- **Figures in the Book** Illustrations for every figure in the textbook are available. Use this ancillary to create a slide show from the illustrations for lecture or print transparencies for use in lecture with an overhead projector.
- **Course Test Manager** Course Test Manager is a powerful testing and assessment package that enables instructors to create and print tests from the large test bank. Instructors with access to a networked computer lab (LAN) can administer, grade, and track tests online. Students also can take online practice tests, which generate customized study guides that indicate where in the textbook students can find more information for each question.

- **Lecture Success System** The Lecture Success System is a set of files that allows you to explain and illustrate the step-by-step, screen-by-screen development of a project in the textbook. The Lecture Success System requires that you have a copy of Notepad, a browser, a personal computer, and a projection device.
- **Instructor's Lab Solutions** Solutions and required files are available for all the Apply Your Knowledge and In the Lab assignments at the end of each project and the projects themselves.
- **Student Data Files** All the files that are required by students to complete the projects and the Apply Your Knowledge exercises are included. See the section titled JavaScript Data Disk on the next page.
- **Interactive Labs** Eighteen hands-on interactive labs that take students from ten to fifteen minutes to step through help solidify and reinforce computer concepts. Student assessment requires students to answer questions about the contents of the interactive labs.

JavaScript Data Disk

The JavaScript Data Disk is required for some of the projects and exercises. Students can obtain a copy of the JavaScript Data Disk by following the instructions on the inside back cover of this book. The Shelly Cashman Series Teaching Tools CD-ROM contains a copy of the files that comprise the JavaScript Data Disk.

Shelly Cashman Online

Shelly Cashman Online is a World Wide Web service available to instructors and students of computer education. Visit Shelly Cashman Online at www.scseries.com. Shelly Cashman Online is divided into four areas:

- Series Information History of the Shelly Cashman Series, technology news, and more
- Teaching Resources Product catalog, Teaching Tools, companion products, and electronic aids
- Community Pressbox, Summer Institute, and more
- Student Resources Data Disk downloads, careers, and links to the Shelly Cashman Series instructional Web sites

Acknowledgments

The Shelly Cashman Series would not be the leading computer education series without the contributions of outstanding publishing professionals. First, and foremost, among them is Becky Herrington, director of production and designer. She is the heart and soul of the Shelly Cashman Series, and it is only through her leadership, dedication, and tireless efforts that superior products are made possible. Becky created and produced the award-winning Windows series of books.

Under Becky's direction, the following individuals made significant contributions to these books: Doug Cowley, production manager; Ginny Harvey, series specialist and developmental editor; Ken Russo, senior Web designer; Mike Bodnar, associate production manager; Mark Norton, Web designer; Stephanie Nance, graphic artist and cover designer; Marlo Mitchem, Chris Schneider, Hector Arvizu, and Kenny Tran, graphic artists; Jeanne Black and Betty Hopkins, Quark experts; Nancy Lamm, copyeditor/proofreader; Cristina Haley, indexer; Sarah Evertson of Image Quest, photo researcher; and Susan Sebok and Ginny Harvey, contributing writers.

Special thanks go to Richard Keaveny, managing editor; Jim Quasney, series consultant; Lora Wade, product manager; Meagan Walsh, associate product manager; Francis Schurgot, Web product manager; Tonia Grafakos, associate Web product manager; Scott Wiseman, online developer; Rajika Gupta, marketing manager; and Erin Bennett, editorial assistant.

Finally, a special thanks to our reviewers Ravi Singh, Jeffrey Popyack, Larry Manning, Abul Sheikh, and Dwight Watt, and to Judy Knapp, Elyn Rykken, Andrea Dorin, and Caroline Ruhs for reading the manuscript and providing valuable comments.

Gary B. Shelly
Thomas J. Cashman
William J. Dorin
Jeffrey J. Quasney

JavaScript

Introduction to JavaScript Programming

OBJECTIVES

You will have mastered the material in this project when you can:

- Describe JavaScript
- Define HTML and explain the use of HTML tags
- Define attribute
- Differentiate between JavaScript and VBScript
- Define JavaScript cookies and variables
- Describe string, numeric, and Boolean JavaScript variable types
- Discuss the rules for naming variables
- Differentiate between variables and literals
- Discuss special codes and how they are used in a literal
- Discuss the advantages and disadvantages of using JavaScript
- Define expression and describe the arithmetic operators
- Discuss the order of precedence in an expression
- Define concatenation
- Define conditionals and the use of If and While statements
- Discuss the use of JavaScript functions
- Discuss If, If . . . Else, and While statements and loops
- Define objects, properties, methods, and events
- Describe how event handlers and forms are used
- Define frames and arrays

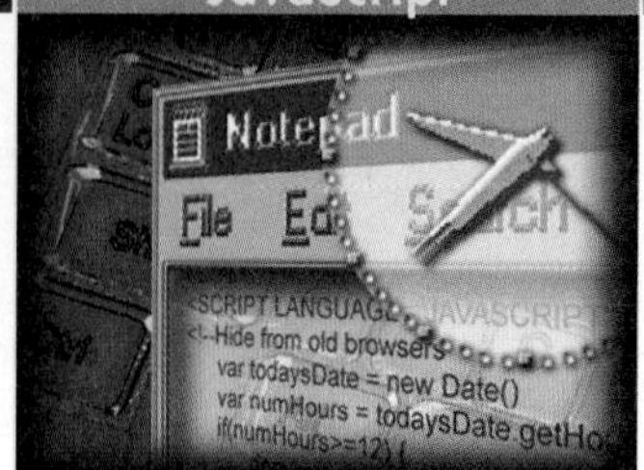

JavaScript

Introduction to JavaScript Programming

INTRODUCTION

I

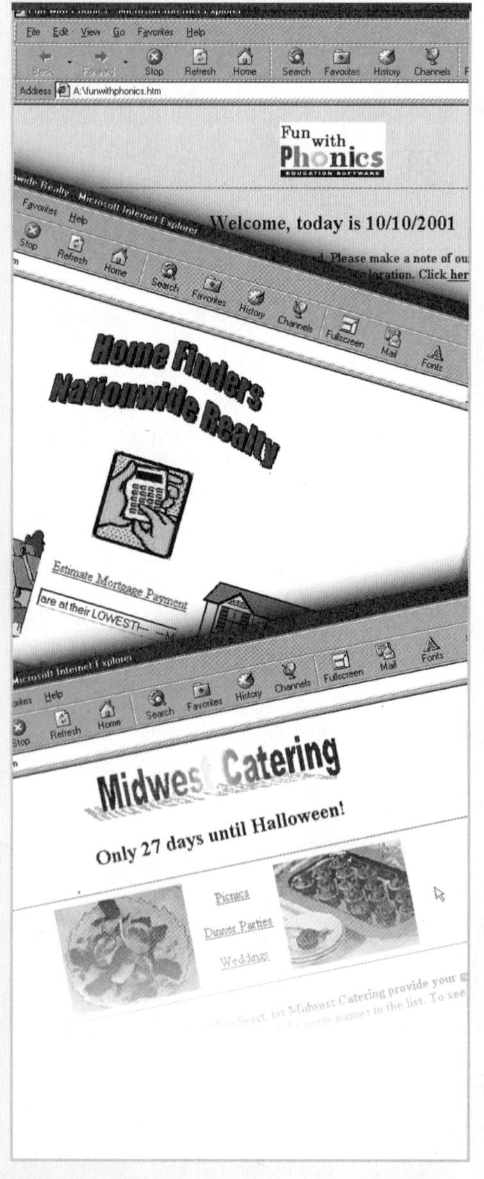

Introduction

JavaScript is a programming language that allows you to add functionality to your Web pages by inserting code within an HTML document. Whereas **HTML (hypertext markup language)** tells your browser how to display text and images, set up lists and option buttons, and establish hyperlinks, JavaScript brings your Web page to life by adding dynamic content and interactive elements. Using JavaScript, you can enhance a Web page by adding items such as:

- scrolling messages
- animations and dynamic images
- data input forms
- pop-up windows
- interactive quizzes

JavaScript is a product of a joint venture between Sun Microsystems and Netscape Communications Corporation. Netscape originally began development of a script language called *LiveScript*, while Sun was trying to simplify its *Java* programming language. Today, JavaScript is endorsed by a number of software companies. It is an open language that anyone can use without purchasing a license. JavaScript thus allows you to improve the appearance of your Web pages without spending a large amount of money or learning a high-level programming language.

Several other programming languages allow you to add functionality to Web pages. One such language is Sun Microsystems's **Java**, which is a full-fledged, object-oriented programming language. Java is similar to more traditional compiler programming languages such as C or COBOL, in that you can use it to create stand-alone applications. Java also is used to create a special type of mini application, called an applet. An **applet** is a small program designed to execute within another application. Unlike a JavaScript statement, which is embedded in the HTML document, an applet is sent to the browser as a separate file alongside an HTML document. The applet adds functionality, such as an interactive animation or game, to a Web page. To write a Java program or applet, you must use the Java Developer's Kit (JDK) from Sun Microsystems or Microsoft's Visual J++.

Although it shares many of the features of the full Java language, JavaScript is a simpler language that supports less functionality. You cannot use JavaScript, for example, to create applets or stand-alone applications. In its most common form today, JavaScript resides inside HTML documents and can provide interactivity to otherwise static HTML documents.

Unlike Java, JavaScript is an interpreted language, meaning it does not end up as an executable file (like a typical program). Instead, the code runs only on a JavaScript interpreter built into your browser. The **interpreter** translates each line of a language and converts it into machine code line by line as it is executed. When you request a Web page, your browser retrieves and reads the page from top to bottom, displaying the results of the HTML code and executing JavaScript statements as it goes.

Because the interpreter is a built-in feature of the browser, the version of JavaScript you use depends on the version of your browser. JavaScript is supported by recent browsers from Netscape and Microsoft. Because Internet Explorer supports additional features, Microsoft calls its version *Jscript.* Many older browsers are unable to handle newer JavaScript codes.

JavaScript and HTML Tags

Tags and Attributes

HTML tags and attributes are not case sensitive. Some browsers do not recognize lowercase or mixed-case tags and attributes. If an error occurs and the syntax is correct, try changing the tag and attributes to all uppercase characters.

This book assumes you have a basic knowledge of HTML (hypertext markup language). You can build very sophisticated Web pages with the WYSIWYG (what you see is what you get) editors such as Netscape Composer, Microsoft FrontPage, Corel Web Designer, and others without knowing any HTML. A basic understanding of HTML is important because it allows you to correct errors and bugs that may occur in the coding of the page.

The script code is embedded within the HTML tags. A **tag** is an instruction that is surrounded by less than (<) and greater than (>) symbols. As the browser reads the HTML file and encounters these tags, it formats the page according to the instructions given by the tags. These instructions are called attributes. **Attributes** are characteristics of a tag that have values assigned to them. Figure I-1 shows a typical BODY tag with two attributes: text (for text color) and background (to name the image used for a background). In general, these attributes instruct in formatting text, placing headings, paragraphs, images, links, and creating and establishing tables and frames to format the page layout. In this book, attributes and tags are shown as all uppercase. The example figures show mixed case to demonstrate that tags and attributes are not case sensitive.

```
<BODY Text = "00008B" Background = "image.gif">
```

FIGURE I-1

In HTML, you use tags in pairs. You must have a beginning tag and an ending tag or formatting will be incorrect. For example, to make text display bold on a Web page, start with a <B> tag, enter the text, and then end with a </B> tag. The bold tags are simple and do not use any attributes. Others, such as the INPUT tag, have attributes associated with the tag.

Figure I-2 shows the INPUT tag for a text box found on the typical form for data entry. Type, name, and size are all attributes of the INPUT tag. In this example, the TYPE attribute indicates whether a text box, option button, check box, image, SUBMIT button, or RESET button is created. The NAME attribute assigns a name or variable (PhoneNumber) to the text box. This variable stores the data entered until it is needed. In addition, you will use the variable name later in the JavaScript code to validate the data entered into that text box. You may assign an initial or default value to the VALUE attribute on the form. For example, in Figure I-2, a blank value is being assigned to the text object of the form. The SIZE attribute indicates the size of the text box, which is based on the number of characters to be placed in a text box.

```
<INPUT Type = "text" Name = "PhoneNumber" Value = " " Size = 17>
```

FIGURE I-2

SCRIPT Tags

To use JavaScript, or any scripting language, in the HTML code, the browser needs to be told that a script language is being used. Most Web page designers place an initial SCRIPT tag in the heading of the HTML document. This initial script includes the various JavaScript functions that will be defined. In addition, a SCRIPT tag must be used again in order to place JavaScript code in other areas on the Web page. Every time you use the SCRIPT tag, it is recommended an HTML comment is used to hide the code from the user's browser in case it does not support JavaScript. Figure I-3 shows the code for the SCRIPT tag to identify JavaScript.

```
<SCRIPT LANGUAGE = "JavaScript">
<!-- Hide from old browsers
place your JavaScript code here
//-->
</SCRIPT>
```

FIGURE I-3

One of the attributes for the SCRIPT tag is LANGUAGE. In the **LANGUAGE** attribute, the word, JavaScript, with no version number indicates version 1.0. To indicate a different version, you must add the version number to the JavaScript value. For example, JavaScript1.1, indicates version 1.1 and, JavaScript1.2, indicates version 1.2. The version of JavaScript to use depends on which browser the users are expected to have.

Scripting Languages

In Microsoft documentation, JavaScript is called JScript. NASA's Jet Propulsion laboratory developed Perl, which stands for practical extraction and report language.

JavaScript Versus VBScript

Because of the popularity of its Visual Basic programming language, Microsoft has developed a script language called **VBScript** (VB stands for Visual Basic). JavaScript follows syntax similar to the programming language C, while VBScript uses syntax similar to Visual Basic. For example, you write functions with JavaScript (as in C), and you write subroutines with VBScript (as in Visual Basic). In JavaScript, functions begin and end with braces ({}), while in VBScript, a subroutine begins with the word, SUB, followed by the words, END SUB. As of this writing, version 4 or higher of Microsoft Internet Explorer executes JavaScript, but Netscape Navigator does not execute VBScript.

Why Use JavaScript?

Using JavaScript enhances a Web page by adding interactivity to HTML. Users can be provided instant feedback without complicated CGI (Common Gateway Interface) scripts and languages. A **CGI** script is any program that runs on a Web server for the purpose of processing data. The Web page sends the data to the server that processes the data and may return a result to the Web page. CGI scripts are powerful tools useful in searching databases or processing purchase orders for companies doing mainstream business on the Internet.

CGI scripts are a waste of resources, however, when the needed task can be processed on the user's computer. For example, with JavaScript, you can validate a data entry form, such as a purchase request, immediately on the user's computer. The need to send the data back to the server for validation is eliminated. The user receives feedback instantaneously and is not waiting for a response during heavy Internet traffic times.

CGI Scripts

The CGI script specifies the communication between the server and Web browser. Many functions of CGI scripts can be accomplished through ActiveX controls and Java applets.

JavaScript Cookies

Forms are not the only types of data a Web browser handles. Some generated data is not part of an HTML defined object, such as a data file. One type of data is the cookie file. **Cookies** are pieces of data sent and stored in files on the user's computer. Web developers use these pieces of data to track a user's preferences while visiting a Web site. Navigator stores cookies in the cookies.txt file. Internet Explorer stores cookies as separate files in the Cookies folder.

Internet Explorer and Netscape Navigator use cookies to help users build personal start pages. Companies use cookies to remember what a person wants to buy. If you have shopped for items on the Internet, then you have used a cyber-shopping cart, which is a cookie. You collect things in the cart and then pay for them when you check out. Cookies also help Web developers identify dead-end paths. **Dead-ends** are sections on the Web site a user visits, which apparently cause them to leave the Web site for lack of interest. Advertisers like to use cookies to profile your interests. Certain advertisements record cookies. Clicking certain advertisements eventually will determine what type of advertisement you will see in the future.

Cookies

For more information on cookies, visit www.scsite.com/js/int.htm and then click cookies.

JavaScript cookies cannot get data from the user's hard drive, read e-mail, or steal other sensitive information. The JavaScript code limits access to the user's hard disk for security reasons. JavaScript only has one way to write cookies, which the browser controls through a predetermined cookie location. Because the cookie information is embedded in the data sent to the browser, the browser can block cookies. Some sites give limited access if the cookie information is blocked, however.

JavaScript Basics — Variables, Literals, and Expressions

Much of the processing with forms or functions you will perform requires the use of variables. A **variable** represents a value stored in memory for use by the script. The more common types of values stored in the variable are numbers, words, or a combination of both. Values that hold numbers are called **numeric** and values that hold words or combinations of letters and numbers are called **strings**. JavaScript also uses **Boolean** type variables that represent a state or condition as being True or False (Yes or No).

Unlike many other programming languages, when you define a variable in JavaScript you do not have to indicate its type. The variable assumes its type depending on the type of data it stores. This flexibility means you can use a variable for one type of value in one instance, and then use the variable again for another type of value in a different instance. This practice is unwise, however, because it can lead to confusion. As in other programming languages, it is best to use unique variable names in developing JavaScript pages.

Reserved Words

Reserved words are the names of built-in objects, functions, and methods used by JavaScript. Using these words as variable names would create confusion for the interpreter. For more information on reserved words, visit www.scsite.com/js/int.htm and then click reserved words.

Rules for Naming Variables

Various names may be used for a variable, but adhere to the following simple rules:

- The name must begin with a letter or an underscore.
- The rest of the name is made up of letters, numbers, or underscores.
- Avoid naming variables with reserved words. **Reserved words** are predefined words that have special meaning to JavaScript.
- Do not place any spaces or punctuation in the name.

The reason that a period cannot be used in a variable name is that periods separate objects, properties, and methods. Table I-1 shows examples of valid and invalid variable names. In addition, remember that in JavaScript, variable names are case sensitive. **Case sensitive** means that if you create a form and use mixed-case spelling, such as State, as a variable name, and later use the uppercase spelling, STATE, as a variable name, JavaScript will determine these spellings as two different variable names.

Table I-1

VALID	INVALID
idnumber	id number (space)
Cust_ID	Cust.ID (period)
Major	*Major (does not start with a letter)
Year2000	2000 (does not start with a letter)
Passwd	Password (reserved word)
_Continue	Continue (reserved word)

Variables are declared the first time they are used by inserting the word, var, before the variable name, followed by an equal sign (=), and then the value. For example, if you type, var gpa, this name will declare a variable named, gpa, with no value assigned. Current versions of Netscape Navigator and Internet Explorer display the word, undefined, on the screen for the variable value if it is used without a value having been assigned to it.

Literals

While a variable is used to store data or values, a literal is a constant value that does not change. A **literal** is an actual number or character text, rather than a calculated result or value input from a keyboard. If the literal is a number, it is called a numeric literal. Character or text values are called string literals. Figure I-4 shows how to define a variable with a numeric literal value.

Case Sensitive

Unlike HTML tags and attributes, which can be mixed case, JavaScript commands and variable names are case sensitive. However, JavaScript objects, properties, methods, and event handler names are mixed case.

```
var width = 3
```

FIGURE I-4

The numeral three (3) cannot be changed and always will remain the same. The value of width can be changed from three (3) to some other number either through a calculation or through reassigning it another value.

A **string literal** is text enclosed in pairs of quotation marks. Figure I-5 shows how to assign a string literal to a variable. With string literals the text must be placed inside a pair of quotation marks. Numeric digits may be placed inside quotation marks, but they will be treated as a string, not as a number. Think of the characters between quotation marks as a sequential group of characters, one after the other, forming a continuous string.

```
var browserType = "Netscape"
```

FIGURE I-5

If the characters are not enclosed inside quotation marks, JavaScript will try to interpret the characters as having some other meaning. JavaScript might show an error message that says it cannot find the undefined variable, or it might interpret the characters as an object or function.

In addition, JavaScript string literals can use certain special characters or codes. This feature is borrowed from the C programming language, and is convenient if you need to insert quotation marks in the middle of a string. For example, to place quotation marks within a string, use a slash and a quotation mark (\"), placed at the location you want the quotation marks to display. In Figure I-6, a quotation from Shakespeare is placed in a variable called Shakespeare. The \" keeps the quotation marks around the string so they will display if the value of Shakespeare is ever displayed.

```
var Shakespeare = "\"To be or not to be, that is the question!\" Hamlet."
```

FIGURE I-6

A number of these special codes exist and are explained in Table I-2. The user, however, must be warned that some symbols act differently depending on the operating system in use. For example, a script needs the \r\n for a carriage return, line feed in the Microsoft Windows environment, but only the \n in the UNIX environment. You may find it easier to use the HTML tags of <P> or <BR> in the write() method for a new line. The **write()** method is associated with the Document object and is used to write text to the Web page. These tags work the same in the JavaScript write() method, as they do in any HTML document, but these tags cannot be used in the alert() method. The **alert()** method is used to display messages in a dialog box. Both of these statements will be discussed in more detail in Project 1. Remember the maximum number of characters in a string is 255. This limit is based on the older browsers, so the developer always must account for them.

Table I-2

CODE	SYMBOLS
Backslash	\\
Single quotation	\'
Double quotation	\"
Tab	\t
Carriage return	\r
Backspace	\b
Form feed	\f
New line	\n

Expressions and Operators

An **expression** is a formula or a way to assign values to variables. The JavaScript expression uses a combination of variables and literals to derive other values. Figure I-7a shows an expression that might be used in a simple math problem. This example assumes that the sum has been defined previously in the JavaScript code. Figure I-7b demonstrates how to initialize a variable to zero (0). This practice is used widely in programming to insure that no unusual values are in the Count variable, which might cause an error in the result.

```
average = totalValue/Count
```

FIGURE I-7a

```
var Count = 0
```

FIGURE I-7b

An expression operates by taking the values to the right-hand side of the equal sign, performing the arithmetic operation, and then storing the result in the variable on the left-hand side of the equal sign. The action in Figure I-7b on the previous page still is an expression because the value on the right-hand side of the equal sign is assigned to the variable on the left-hand side. In most uses of expressions, you probably will use variables instead of literals.

For example, imagine you have a Web page where you sell used musical compact disks (CDs). Your Web page displays pictures and titles of the CDs with a price. A person browsing your Web site may pick a certain CD with a price of $7.99. This value is stored in a variable called Cost. You ask the user to enter the number of CDs they want to purchase, which will be stored in a variable called Quantity. To calculate the sale price and store it in a variable called SalePrice, you multiply the Quantity by the Cost (SalePrice = Quantity * Cost).

JavaScript uses the same basic arithmetic operators as other programming languages or application software packages. The **arithmetic operator** is the symbol that instructs the expression what to do. Table I-3 describes the arithmetic operators with an example.

More About

Modulus

Modulus operations return the remainder of a division. For example, 7 % 2 equals 1 because 7 divided by 2 equals 3 with a remainder of 1.

Table I-3

SYMBOL	DESCRIPTION	EXAMPLE
=	Assign values	counter = counter + 1
+	Addition	sum = 4 + 5
-	Subtraction	difference = most - least
*	Multiplication	pay = hours * rate
/	Division	percent = totalAmt / portion
%	Modulus - returns the remainder only in division	remainder = 27 % 12
++	Increments the variable by one	j++, ++j
--	Decrements the variable by one	j--, --j

JavaScript uses the increment (++) and decrement (--) operators borrowed from the C programming language. The use of these operators needs some explanation because j++ is not the same as ++j. The difference can be seen in how the operator is used in an expression. Avoid using this operator until you fully understand how it works. Table I-4 shows how the different expressions are evaluated. The initial values of m and x are equal to seven.

Table I-4

m	x	EXPRESSION	RESULT	EXPLANATION
7	7	m = x++	m = 7, x = 8	m is assigned first, then x is incremented
7	8	m = ++x	m = 9, x = 9	x is incremented, then m is assigned
9	9	m = x--	m = 9, x = 8	m is assigned first, then x is decremented
9	8	m = --x	m = 7, x = 7	x is decremented, then m is assigned

Like the programming language C, JavaScript allows expressions like x + = y. This expression is the same as writing x = x + y. Table I-5 shows how this style of expression is written with other arithmetic operators. Writing expressions in this format can be confusing. Using expressions you understand is recommended. By writing expressions in an easily understood format, the JavaScript code will be easier to debug in the event of problems.

In addition, the mathematical order of precedence is used in evaluating an expression in JavaScript. Table I-6 shows the order of precedence for the operators discussed thus far.

Proceeding in a left to right order, the first thing evaluated is anything inside the parentheses. If more than one set of parentheses exists, the innermost set is evaluated first. Any increment and decrement symbols are evaluated, followed by multiplication, division, or modulus operators and finally, the addition or subtraction operators are evaluated. The other symbols and levels to the order of precedence are not discussed in this book.

The plus sign (+) is used in another operation called concatenation. **Concatenation** is used to join string literals or variables together as one variable. Figure I-8 is an example of combining two string variables to create a message. The end result is that completeMsg now contains the contents of Message1 and Message2.

Table I-5

EXPRESSION	*SAME AS*
a + = b	a = a + b
a - = 1	a = a - 1
x * = x	x = x * x
n / = m	n = n / m
remainder % = d	remainder = remainder % d

Table I-6

SYMBOLS	*OPERATORS*
( )	Parentheses, with innermost parentheses first
++ and --	Increment and decrement
*, /, and %	Multiplication, division, and modulus
+ and -	Addition and subtraction

```
var Message1 = "You can only put so many letters in a string"
var Message2 = "before you run out of space."
var completeMsg = Message1+" "+Message2
```

FIGURE I-8

More About

Concatenation

Concatenation sequentially joins string data. The result of the JavaScript statement, *var answer* = "3" + "2", is not 5, but "32".

This technique is useful because older browsers have a limitation on how many characters you can place in a string. You will learn the use of concatenation in Project 1.

Conditionals

One of the advantages to using JavaScript is the capability to validate data entered into a form. To validate data, you compare or test the data entered to a desired value. This test is called a **conditional,** and the result of the test is either True or False. Based on the result of the test, you execute different JavaScript code.

Remember, the test only has two possible outcomes: True or False. JavaScript uses conditionals with If and While statements, to compare or test the values stored in variables (Table I-7 on the next page). The function of the **If** statement is to select and execute alternative sections of code. The function of the **While** statement is to initiate a loop. Notice in the table that the conditions are enclosed in a pair of parentheses, as they would appear in JavaScript code.

Table I-7

OPERAND	EXAMPLE	RESULTS
= =	(a = = b)	true if a equals b
!=	(a != b)	true if a does not equal b
>	(a > b)	true if a is greater than b
<	(a < b)	true if a is less than b
>=	(a >= b)	true if a is greater than or equal to b
<=	(a <= b)	true if a is less than or equal to b
&&	(a = = b) && (x < y)	true if both a equals b and x is less than y
||	(a != b) || (x >= a)	true if either a does not equal b or x is greater than or equal to a

If and If...Else Statements

The first part of the If statement is written as *If (conditional)*. Place the JavaScript code to be executed if the result of the conditional test is True, inside a set of braces ({ }) as illustrated in Figure I-9.

```
var todaysDate = new Date()
var numHours = todaysDate.getHours()
if (numHours>=12) {
   document.write("Good Afternoon")
   }
else {
   document.write("Good Morning")
   }
the rest of your code...
```

FIGURE I-9

The use of the **Else** clause indicates which code should be executed when the result of the test is False. Though you will not understand some of the statements, Figure I-9 illustrates a way to test the time of day and display a message whether it is morning or afternoon. Not every condition test needs an Else clause. Do not make the mistake of placing code after the Else clause brace that you need to execute, regardless of the results of the conditional.

While Loop

A **loop** is a set of JavaScript codes that are to be executed repeatedly. The **While loop** tests a condition at the beginning of the loop. If the condition is True, the loop is executed. If the condition is False, the code after the closing brace (}) is executed. The basic form of the While statement is shown in Figure I-10. You will learn more about While loops in Project 2.

```
while (condition) {
       the JavaScript code to be executed while the condition is True
       }
the JavaScript code to be executed when the loop is finished
```

FIGURE I-10

Functions

A **function** is a way to write several lines of script and use them repeatedly as needed. Functions are defined by starting with the keyword function followed by a set of parentheses. Figure I-11 shows a sample function, which displays a message using the alert() method.

The instructions or code for the function are written inside a set of braces ({ }). The left-hand brace indicates the beginning of the function and the right-hand brace indicates the ending of the function. Notice the placement and direction of the braces in Figure I-11.

```
function Greetings() {
      alert("Hello, this is a friendly message.")
      }
```

FIGURE I-11

The function name is, Greetings, and it will display a dialog box with the words, "Hello, this is a friendly message." The alert() method displays a dialog box with an OK button. The browser waits for the user to click the OK button and then closes the box. The browser then will continue executing the next set of script codes. You can use the function Greetings() instead of typing the code *alert("Hello, this is a friendly message.")* every time you need to display this message.

By slightly changing the Greetings() function, you can make it an all-purpose message display function. Figure I-12 shows how to pass a value using a variable to a function. By passing a value to the function, the message changes as needed, using the same Greetings() function.

```
messageStr = "This is a customized message."
function Greetings(messageStr) {
      alert(messageStr)
      }
```

FIGURE I-12

Objects, Properties, and Methods

Object-Oriented Programming

For more information on object-oriented programming, visit www.scsite.com/js/int.htm and then click object-oriented.

An **object** is a real-world entity. Your book, car, pets, and friends are all objects. JavaScript makes use of objects in its association with Web browsers. This technique is called **object oriented** (**OO**). When it refers to programming it is called **Object-Oriented Programming** (**OOP**). The development of OOP provides a way to represent the world in conceptual terms that is understood easily. People understand their everyday objects and can understand easily that objects have properties and behaviors.

An object is described by its properties. **Properties** are attributes that help differentiate one object from another. For example, a car has a color, a certain body style, and a certain type of interior. These are all properties of the car that can be used to describe it. You separate an object and its property with a period. For example, you would write, car.color = "red", to indicate the car is the object and color is the property. Red is the value of the property.

A behavior is called a method. A **method** is a function or action you want the object to perform. You either can write your own functions, or use the built-in methods supplied with JavaScript. Methods associated with car, pet, and friend objects might be drive, feed, and talk, respectively. Thus, for a drive() method, it is written, car.drive().

Some methods require what is called an argument. An **argument** is a value given to the method. The argument is the message used in a method that is passed to the object. For example, you might have the cat object and the feed() method, written, cat.feed("Tuna"). The argument, "Tuna", is a message describing what to feed the cat. Just as in the statement document.write("this is an example"), the document is the object, write() is the method, and "this is an example" is what is to be written to the document.

Arguments can be variables or literals. The argument must match the method. This means, the method must be able to use the argument. For example, in the write() method you can add regular HTML tags for special formatting. You must include the tags in quotation marks as shown in Figure I-13.

```
document.write("<CENTER><B>PLEASE READ THE FOLLOWING</B></CENTER>")
```

FIGURE I-13

Although JavaScript uses objects, it is not to be considered a complete OOP language. JavaScript provides many built-in objects, even though you can define and create your own. The objects that you define and create are object instances. An **object instance** is the actual object used. For example, instructions for building a backyard shed are an object, but the actual shed is an instance.

The built-in objects include the Date, Arrays, windows, and forms, along with the items on a form such as a text box, a check box, or an option button. One rule about defining objects is to assign unique and meaningful names. For example, it is acceptable to name a form, form1, but not very meaningful.

It makes more sense to name the form based on its activity. A registration form, might be called, regForm, while an order form might be called, ordForm. This naming style easily differentiates the order form from the registration form, especially if several months pass and you need to make a change to the Web page. The form1 name may not have meaning by then.

The confusion about the entire set of objects in JavaScript is that some objects can be properties of another object. For example, a **document** is an object on it own, but it also can be a property of the Window object. The **Window** object is the top-level object in the hierarchy. By using the various properties and methods associated with the Window object, you can manipulate your document. In Figure I-13, the Document object was used with the write() method. The statement could have been written as window.document.write("<CENTER><B>Good Morning</CENTER ></B>"). Because of the hierarchy of the JavaScript object, the Window object is assumed. Figure I-14 shows a small portion of the object hierarchy in JavaScript.

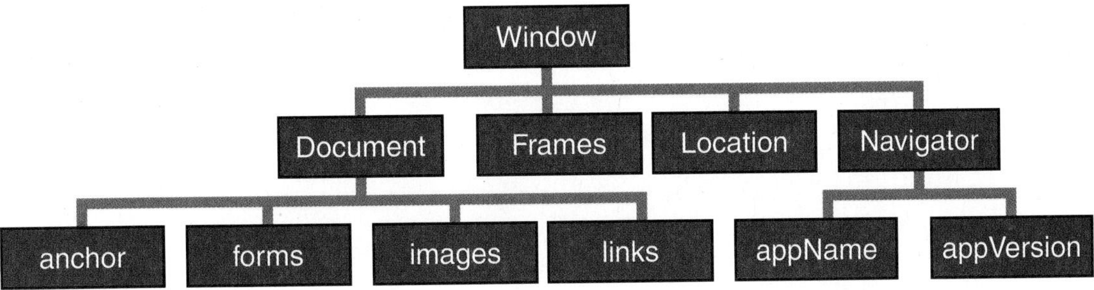

FIGURE I-14

Events

Many applications today require that you do something before an action takes place. These actions are called **events**. In a word processor, you click a toolbar or property button to save the document, print the document, or run the spell check. These buttons actually represent events. The document will not print until you click the Print button, or a new document cannot be opened until you click the Open button.

Table I-8 lists the basic event handlers and their descriptions. Netscape recommends that all event handlers be written in lowercase.

As users read the Web page, they may click a button or move the mouse pointer over an image or a link. By using one of the event handlers, the JavaScript code associated with the event is executed. When you execute the code associated with an event handler shown in Table I-8, you are **triggering** the event.

Table I-8

EVENT HANDLER	*DESCRIPTION*
onfocus	Used to draw attention to an object when the insertion point moves to it.
onblur	Removes attention when the insertion point moves off the object.
onselect	Used when the user highlights text.
onchange	Does something when the user changes the value of the object, and moves off.
onsubmit	Action performed when the user clicks the SUBMIT button.
onclick	Action performed when the user clicks any button.
onmouseover	Action performed when the user moves the mouse over something.
onmouseout	Action performed when the mouse moves off of something.
onload	Action performed when a document is loaded.
onunload	Action performed when the user leaves a page.
onabort	Action performed when the user clicks Stop to interrupt loading a page.
onerror	Action performed when an error occurs in the script.
onreset	Used to clear values when the user clicks the RESET button.
ondragdrop	Action performed when the user drags and drops an object in a window.
onkeydown	Action performed when the user presses a designated key.
onkeypress	Action performed when the user holds a key (preceded by onkeydown).
onkeyup	Action performed when the user releases a designated key.
onmousedown	Action performed when the user presses a mouse button.
onmousemove	Action performed when the user moves the mouse.
onmouseup	Action performed when the user releases the mouse button.
onmove	Action performed when the user moves a window or frame.
onresize	Action performed when the user resizes a window or frame.

Forms

Because many of the event handlers work with forms, you need to know how the HTML tags work for forms. If you have ever filled out a request for information on a Web site, you have worked with a **form**. The form may have text boxes, option buttons, check boxes, and other buttons. Many Web sites use forms to collect data and transmit it back to the main Web server. These sites might use CGI to submit the data on the form to the server. Then the server runs a program that may validate the values in the text boxes. If a problem is found, an error message is sent back to the user.

Perl

For more information on Perl, visit www.scsite.com/js/int.htm and then click Perl.

To use CGI in this fashion requires fairly extensive programming capability. One of the more popular CGI languages is **Perl**, which is primarily a UNIX-based language. Users of Microsoft Windows NT servers can use C or Visual Basic as their language of choice. With JavaScript, however, the Web page user's browser window can validate the form before the data is sent to the server. The JavaScript code can keep the user on the form until the data is entered correctly to the satisfaction of the Web page author.

Using event handlers in forms is quite simple. For example, suppose you have a form with a dark background color such as dark gray. Knowing that users might have video display units that make it difficult to read the text on this kind of background, you can create a button to change the background color to white or another lighter color. Figure I-15 illustrates the code to change the background color to white.

```
<INPUT TYPE = "Button" Value = "White" onclick = "document.bgColor = 'White'">
```

FIGURE I-15

Onclick is the event handler. When the user clicks the button that displays, the background color will turn white. To execute a function with an event handler, simply place the function name between the quotation marks after the equal sign associated with the event handler. For example, in Figure I-16, suppose you wanted to display an image of the sun for someone viewing the Web page in daytime, and an image of the moon if the page is viewed at night. You create a function called timeLine(), which would test the clock and determine whether to display the sun or moon image in a certain location when the Web page is loaded.

```
<BODY bgColor = "White" onload = "timeLine()">
```

FIGURE I-16

Many of the event handlers (such as onfocus, onblur, onchange, onsubmit, and onreset) described in Table I-8 on the previous page, usually are used with the INPUT tag. Clicking a form's text box, check box, or option button gives that object the focus. **Focus** means that a text box, check box, or option button has attention drawn to it. For example, a text box that has the focus contains the insertion point. Thus, you would use the onfocus event handler to trigger the script associated with this object.

An object no longer has the focus when you click another part of the form or another object. In JavaScript, when an object loses focus, it is said to blur. **Blur** means that the attention has moved from the object; for example, the user clicks a text box to move the insertion point to the new text box. Thus, you can use the onblur event handler to execute a function to perform a task. JavaScript is capable of knowing when the value of the text box, option button, or check box has changed. You can use the onchange event handler to trigger a function.

Finally, many forms have Submit and Reset buttons. The onsubmit event is the event handler triggered when you point to and click the Submit button. Usually, you will have an action that will transmit the form either to a CGI program or e-mail it to an intended receiver. The Reset button allows you to trigger an event handler that clears the form and allows the user to start over and reenter the data. Figure I-17 shows how the HTML tag creates a Submit button with a JavaScript function set to an onclick event handler. This INPUT tag has several attributes, with an onclick event handler. The function associated with the onclick event handler will be triggered when the user clicks the Submit button.

```
<INPUT TYPE = "Button" Name = "SubmitText" Value = "Submit" onclick = "Transmit()">
```

FIGURE I-17

Frames and Arrays

A **frame** is a feature that allows a browser window to be split into smaller units. These units are not windows. You need to think of the frame as similar to the windows in a house. Some windows are all one large sheet of glass, similarly to picture windows. Others are broken down into smaller pieces called panes. In a browser you might see one large window, or it might be broken into smaller frames.

Frames actually are created with the HTML tags <FRAMESET> and </FRAMESET>. The FRAMESET tag actually takes the place of the <BODY> tag. The FRAMESET tag has one set of attributes, which is used to create columns or rows depending on the attributes used. Each frame created with a FRAMESET tag has its own HTML source page, which is identified by the SRC attribute. The **SRC attribute** identifies the HTML document you want to load. A sample FRAMESET tag is shown in Figure I-18. The figure shows a 25/75 split in the window, with the left-hand side being narrower than the right-hand side. The left-hand side will display a table of contents, while the right-hand side will display the first page.

A concern with frames in JavaScript is that each frame is an object. As such, JavaScript applies properties and methods to the frame object to provide dynamic controlling of the browser window.

> **More About**
> **Frames**
> Netscape Navigator 2.0 introduced frames. Each frame represents a separate document. A common practice uses a frame on the left to serve as a table of contents for multiple Web pages or sites.

```
<FRAMESET COLS = "25%,75%">
   <FRAME SRC = "TOC.HTML">
   <FRAME SRC = "MAINPAGE.HTML">
</FRAMESET>
```

FIGURE I-18

Arrays

To understand and use some aspects of frames, you must understand how an array works. An **array** is a collection of data items that is identified by a singular name. This singular name is used in place of the many different variables that would have to be used if JavaScript did not have the capability of using arrays. JavaScript arrays were introduced with Netscape Navigator 3.0, although an array can be simulated in earlier versions. Creating arrays will be discussed in Project 3.

In the latest versions of JavaScript, arrays are true objects. To define an array, you use the built-in Array object (Figure I-19). Notice in the figure that an argument is used in the object array's parentheses. This value is called the length. The **length** actually represents the number of items stored, not how many characters are being stored. The individual items or elements in the array are indicated by a subscript in square brackets.

```
var currMonth = new Array(13)
currMonth[1] = "January"
currMonth[2] = "February"
.
.
currMonth[12] = "December"
```

FIGURE I-19

Notice that the number of elements is 13 and not 12, to match the number of months in a year. As with most other programming languages, JavaScript's first array element is [0]. As mentioned earlier, however, you can simulate an array in JavaScript version 1.0. The problem is that in the older browsers and JavaScript versions, the [0] element contains the size of the array. In the newer versions, which use the built-in Array object, the first element can be used for storing any data. It is recommended always to leave element [0] empty and start with element [1].

Unique to JavaScript arrays is that you can add more items to the array than originally defined. By assigning any value to the intended item, JavaScript extends the size of the array. Netscape Navigator and Internet Explorer display the word, undefined, if you attempt to display an array element outside the original size that does not have data stored in it. Be aware that with this feature, JavaScript does not provide error messages. If you use an undefined array element in a mathematical expression, you can have serious errors that are difficult to find. Therefore, it is imperative you keep data defined to the initial size of the array and do not arbitrarily add elements.

Summary

This introduction provided an overview of JavaScript and its components: attributes, tags, variables, expressions, operators, codes, functions, objects (Window, Document), properties, methods, events, event handlers, frames, and arrays. This overview provides the basic concepts on how HTML tags are used and how to incorporate JavaScript into HTML code. As you work through the projects that follow you will learn the power of JavaScript. You will learn how to begin developing more interesting, dynamic, and interactive Web pages.

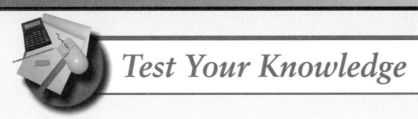

Test Your Knowledge

1 True/False

Instructions: Circle T if the statement is true or F is the statement is false.

T F 1. JavaScript is a product of a joint venture between Microsoft and Sun Microsystems.
T F 2. Microsoft Internet Explorer can execute JavaScript but Netscape Navigator will not execute VBScript.
T F 3. A variable is a name given to a value that is stored for use by the script.
T F 4. You can change the value of a literal with the <var> tag.
T F 5. In the order of precedence, addition is evaluated before multiplication.
T F 6. A property is something that describes an object.
T F 7. In object-oriented languages, methods are used to associate built-in functions with objects.
T F 8. In JavaScript, an event is a function.
T F 9. Including the latest version of JavaScript, you can choose from 22 total event handlers.
T F 10. You cannot mix JavaScript event handlers with HTML tag properties.

2 Multiple Choice

Instructions: Circle the correct response.

1. _________ is a programming language developed by Sun Microsystems to be the standard for the Internet.
   a. VBScript b. J++ c. Java d. C++
2. Netscape originally started developing a script called _________.
   a. LiveWire b. HotWire c. LiveScript d. VBScript
3. An HTML _________ is an instruction surrounded by less than and greater than sign symbols (< >).
   a. tag b. instruction c. file d. object
4. A _________ is a name given to a value that is stored in memory for use by the script.
   a. function b. tag c. variable d. frame
5. Values or variables that hold numbers are called _________ variables.
   a. numeric b. string c. Boolean d. array
6. A variable name must begin with a(n) _________ or a(n) _________.
   a. letter, number
   b. letter, underscore
   c. number, pound sign (#)
   d. uppercase letter, number
7. The reason that a(n) _________ cannot be used in a variable name, is that they are used to separate objects, properties, and methods.
   a. underscore
   b. comma
   c. period
   d. slash

(continued)

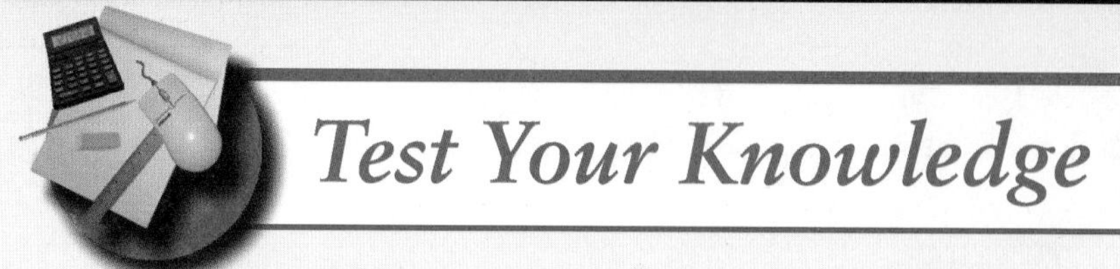

Test Your Knowledge

Multiple Choice *(continued)*

8. One limitation of string variables is they can hold a maximum of _________ characters.
   a. 40
   b. 90
   c. 128
   d. 255
9. Which conditional operand requires that the results of two conditions both be True in order for the whole conditional test to be True?
   a. **
   b. //
   c. &&
   d. ||
10. A(n) _________ requires that the user do something before an action takes place.
   a. event
   b. method
   c. property
   d. subroutine

3 Understanding Variables Names and Types

Instructions: In the examples below, the first column contains a series of var statements or arithmetic expressions used to define variable names. In the spaces provided in the second column, indicate whether the bold variable name in the first column is valid or invalid. In the spaces provided in the third column, indicate the variable type as string, numeric, or Boolean.

VARIABLE OR EXPRESSION	VALID	TYPE
1. var **userName** = "Fred"	_______________	_______________
2. var **status** = True	_______________	_______________
3. var **Count** = Count + 1	_______________	_______________
4. **_address** = "10 Downing St"	_______________	_______________
5. **end of file** = "False"	_______________	_______________
6. **cap_size** = 7.5	_______________	_______________
7. var **1k** + = 1	_______________	_______________

Test Your Knowledge

4 Understanding Arithmetic Expressions

Instructions: In the examples below, the first column contains one or more variables and their current values. In the second column, the variables are used in an expression. In the spaces provided, determine the value of the expression shown in the second column and enter the result in the third column.

VARIABLE	EXPRESSION	RESULT
1. m = 3	m = m + 1	________
2. Cost = 0, Price = 3.00, Units = 5	Cost = Price * Units	________
3. Total_Cost = 33.00, Cost = 15.00	Total_Cost = Total_Cost + Cost	________
4. j = 5	j++	________
5. Sum = 9	--Sum	________
6. counter	counter = counter + 1	________
7. t = 5	t * = t	________
8. a = 15, b = 4, c = 0	c = a % b	________
9. n = 5, x = 2, t = 2	t = (n + 1) * x	________
10. dist = 0, speed = 55, time = 3	dist = speed * time	________

Apply Your Knowledge

1 Add a Greeting to a Web Page Based on the Time of Day

Instructions: Start your browser and Notepad. Open the Web page carboncopy.htm on the JavaScript Data Disk. If you did not download the Data Disk, see the inside back cover for instructions for downloading the JavaScript Data Disk or see your instructor. The Web page has a generic greeting. Modify the Web page by adding the JavaScript code that reads the system time. If the hour is between 4:00 A.M. and noon, add the lines, `Good Morning. Have a rush job for the afternoon? We can handle it!` (see Figure I-20 on the next page). If the hours are between noon and 6:00 P.M., then add the lines, `Good Afternoon. We can get that print job ready by tomorrow morning.` If the hours are between 6:00 P.M. and 11:00 P.M., then add the lines, `Good Evening. We will be here all night if you need us!` Finally, if the hours are between midnight and 4:00 A.M., then add the line, `Yes, we are working at this hour!` (*Hint*: the system type is in European time, so you must compare the hour appropriately. For example, 4:00 P.M. is 16 hours.) Perform the tasks on the next page.

(continued)

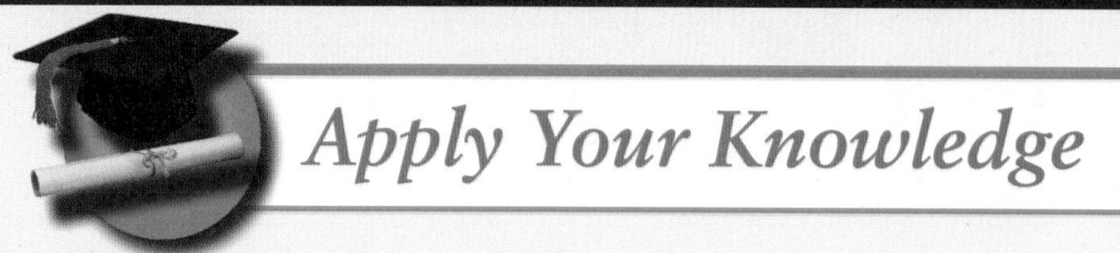

Add a Greeting to a Web Page Based on the Time of Day *(continued)*

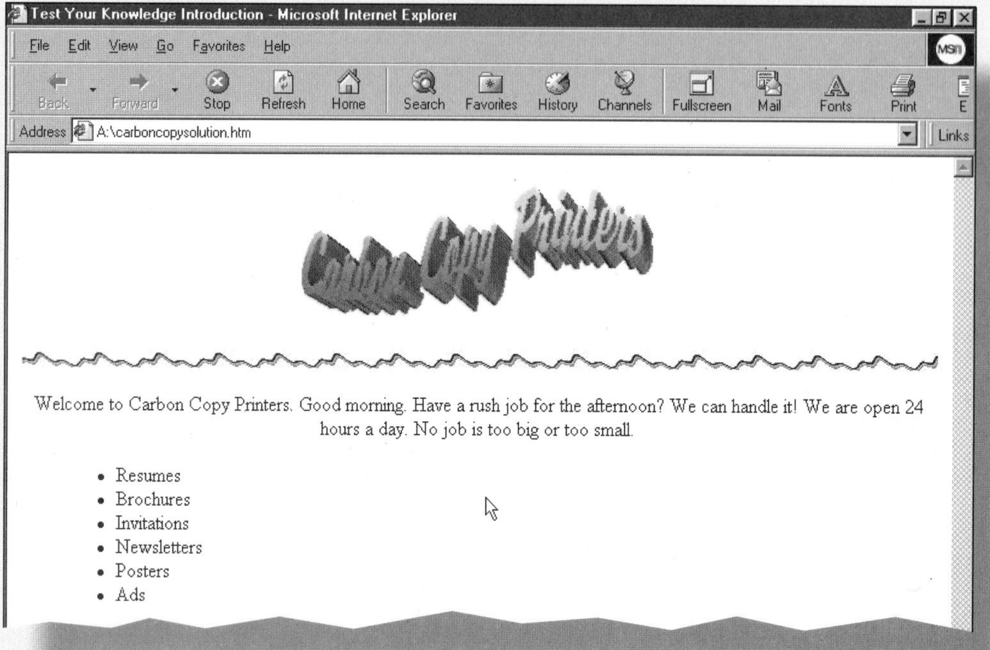

FIGURE I-20

1. Start Notepad. Open a:\carboncopy.htm.
2. Scroll down to the blank line (line 14) right above the statements, *We are open 24 hours a day. No job is too big or too small.</p>*
3. Position your insertion point on the blank line.
4. Type the following JavaScript code on separate lines. Be sure to enter a space after the if. Press the SPACEBAR to indent as shown.

```
<SCRIPT LANGUAGE="JAVASCRIPT">
<!-- Hide the script from old browsers --
   today = new Date()
   if ((today.getHours() >=4) && (today.getHours() <=12)){
     document.write("Good Morning. Have a rush job for the afternoon? We can handle it!")
   }
   if ((today.getHours() >12) && (today.getHours() <=18)){
      document.write("Good afternoon. We can get that print job ready by tomorrow
morning.")
   }
   if ((today.getHours() >18) && (today.getHours() <=23)){
      document.write("Good evening. We will be here all night if you need us!")
   }
   if ((today.getHours() >=0) && (today.getHours() <4)){
      document.write("Yes, we are working at this hour!")
   }
// -- End hiding here -->
</SCRIPT>
```

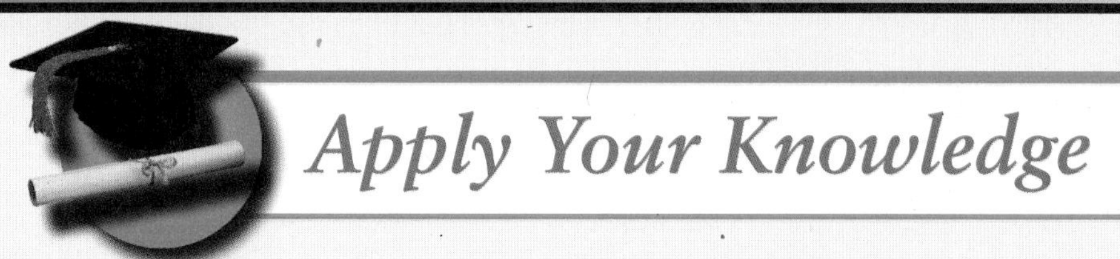

Apply Your Knowledge

5. Save the revised Web page using the file name, carboncopysolution.htm, on the floppy disk in drive A.
6. To test your Web page, start your browser, and then open the a:\carboncopysolution.htm file.
7. If an error occurs, go back to Step 4 and double-check your spelling, quotation marks, parentheses, and relational operators. Make corrections in the Notepad text file. You must click the Refresh button on your toolbar to reload the Web page and view your corrections.
8. If correct, use your browser to print the carboncopysolution.htm Web page and then print the HTML file using Notepad. Hand in the printouts to your instructor.

In the Lab

1 Using Mouse Event Handlers to Show Images

Problem: One of the advantages of using JavaScript is the ability to change an image in a given placeholder. You can use the mouse event handlers to accomplish tasks by calling a function that assigns a new graphic file to the image location in the HTML code. The Pine Wood Country Club and Golf Course would like to add an image on their Web page that displays when the user points to a link and then another image that displays when the mouse pointer is moved from the link (Figure I-21).

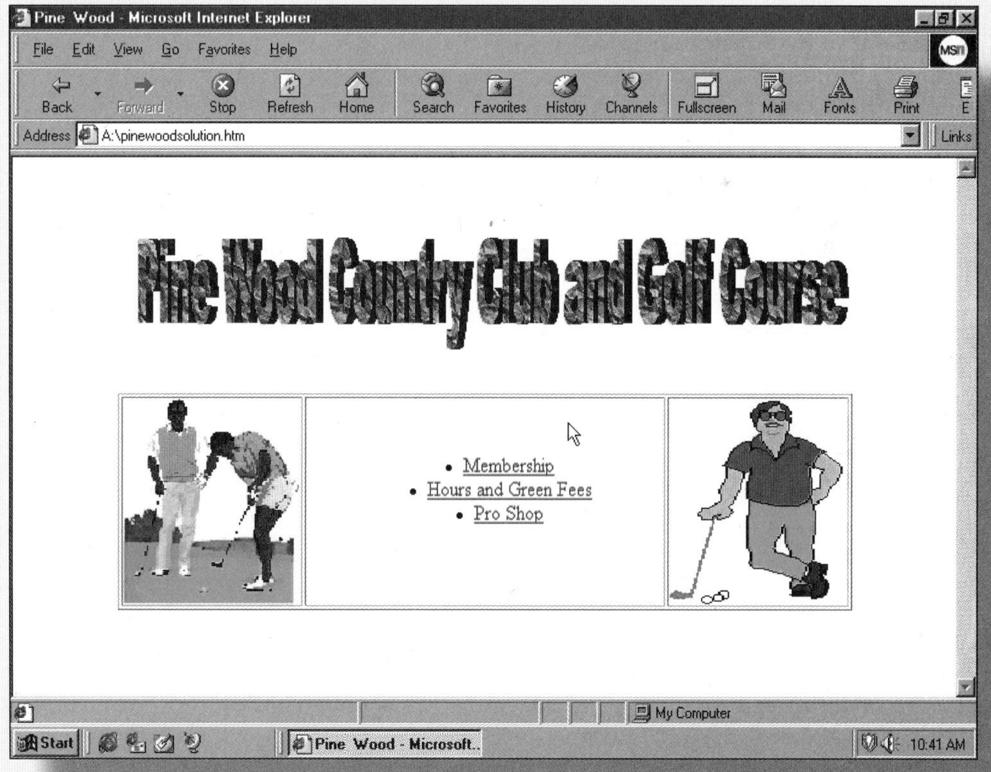

FIGURE I-21

(continued)

Using Mouse Event Handlers to Show Images *(continued)*

Instructions: Start Notepad. Open the pinewood.htm Web page on the JavaScript Data Disk. If you did not download the Data Disk, see the inside back cover for instructions for downloading the JavaScript Data Disk or see your instructor. Add a function similar to the LeftSide() function called by the onmouseover event handler. Perform the following tasks.

1. Locate the function RightImage() in the first SCRIPT tag.
2. Position the insertion point under the t in the word function (line 10).
3. Type `document.RightSide.src="golfer1.jpg"` and then press the ENTER key.
4. Find the HREF for the Membership link.
5. Position the insertion point after the onmouseover="LeftImage()" statement.
6. Type `onmouseout="RightImage()"` as the statement.
7. Do not press the ENTER key.
8. Save the Web page using the file name, pinewoodsolution.htm, on the floppy disk in drive A.
9. Start your browser and then open the pinewoodsolution.htm file.
10. Test the Web page by placing the mouse pointer over the Membership link. An image of two golfers should display on the left. Move the mouse pointer off the Membership link and an image of a golfer should display to the right.
11. Print the Web page. Click the Notepad button on the taskbar and then print the pinewoodsolution.htm file. Hand in the printout to your instructor.

2 Displaying a Message when a Web Page Is Opened

Problem: Not all Web pages are placed on the Internet. Many companies use in-house Intranets to provide employees with critical information and access to databases. The Little PC Company places all company information on an Intranet for their sales and technical support staff. As the Webmaster, the Human Resources department has asked you to display important employee messages when the Web page loads. They want the following message, *Please remember to update your employee benefit forms by the end of this month. Thank you. Human Resources.* You decide to accommodate the Human Resources department by writing a function that uses the built-in alert() function to display the message in a dialog box (Figure I-22). This approach allows you to change the message easily in the future.

Instructions: Insert the JavaScript Data Disk in drive A. Start Notepad. Open the littlepc.htm Web page, and add a function that is triggered by an onload event handler. Perform the following tasks.

1. Write a function, called HRMsg, which displays a message in a dialog box. Position the insertion point on line six in the SCRIPT section and enter the following code:

```
function HRMsg() {
  alert("Please remember to update your employee benefit forms by the end of this month.
Thank you. Human Resources.")
}
```

2. Locate the <BODY> tag (about line 14). Position the insertion point between the Y and the > symbol.
3. Type `onload="HRMsg()"` and do not press the ENTER key.
4. Save the Web page using the file name, littlepcsolution.htm, on the floppy disk in drive A.
5. Start your browser and then open the littlepcsolution.htm file to test the Web page.
6. Print the littlepcsolution.htm from Notepad. (*Note*: You will not be able to print the Web page while the dialog box is on the screen.) Hand in the printout to your instructor.

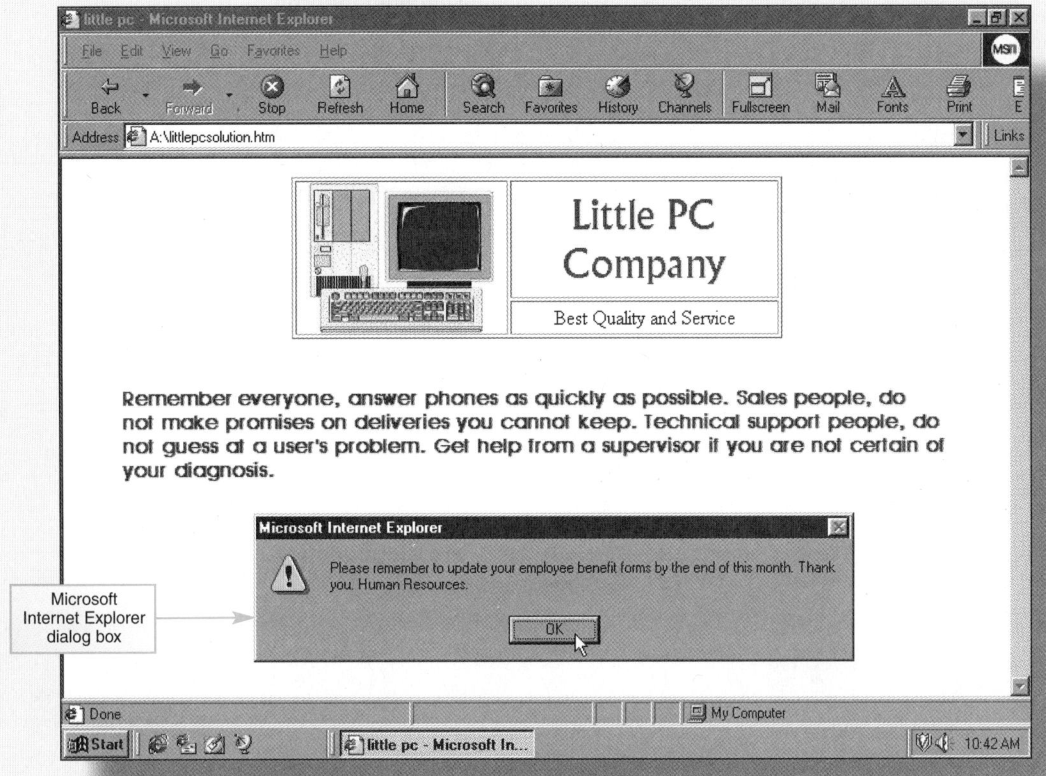

FIGURE I-22

3 Correcting the Errors on a JavaScript Web Page

Problem: Paul's Painting estimate Web page has a form button that when clicked displays an Explorer User Prompt dialog box that asks for the number of square feet to be painted (Figure I-23a on the next page). When the user enters a value, however, and clicks the OK button, an error occurs. The regular Webmaster is sick today and your boss has asked you to fix the error. (*Hint*: The spelling of variables and function names is important.) The corrected Web page displays in Figure I-23b on the next page.

Instructions: Perform the following tasks to correct the errors.

1. Insert the JavaScript Data Disk in drive A. Start your browser. Click the Address text box and enter `a:\paulspaint.htm` to open the Web page.
2. Click the Paint Estimate button.
3. Use Notepad to correct the errors.
4. After correcting the errors, save the file using the file name, paulspaintsolution.htm, on the floppy disk in drive A.
5. Test the Web page by opening the paulspaintsolution.htm in your browser.

(continued)

Correcting the Errors on a JavaScript Web Page *(continued)*

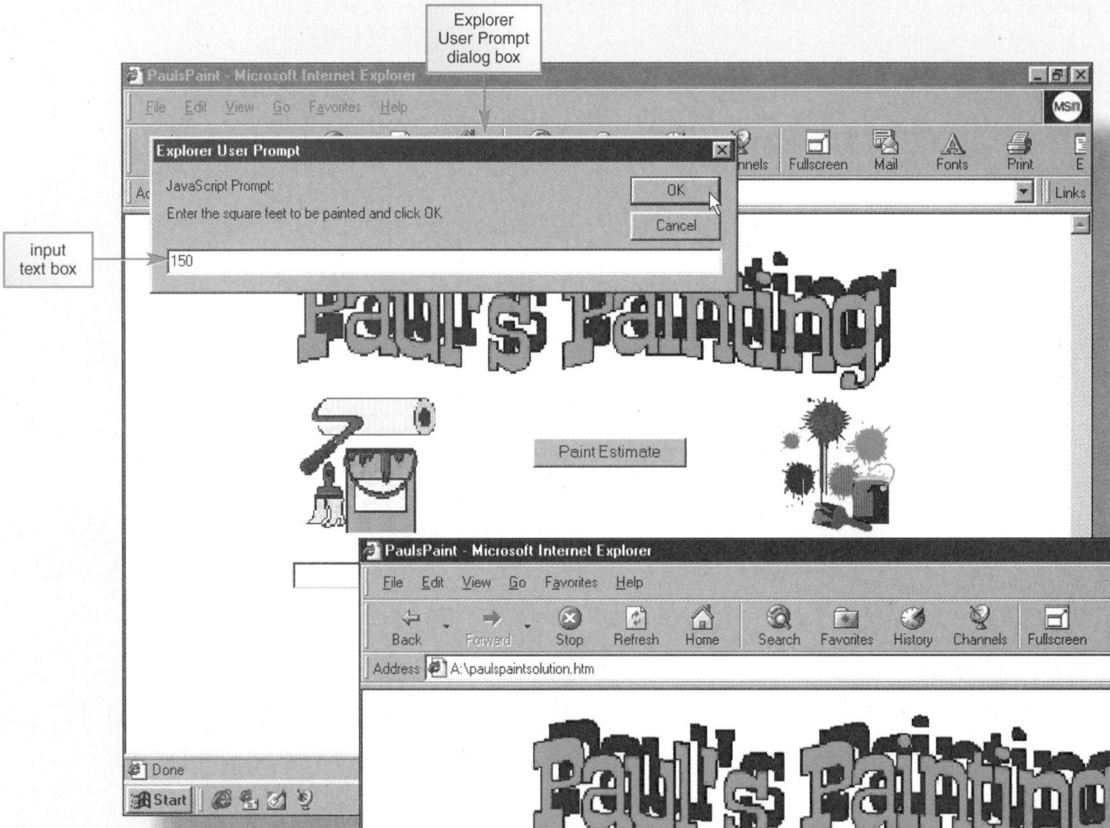

FIGURE I-23a

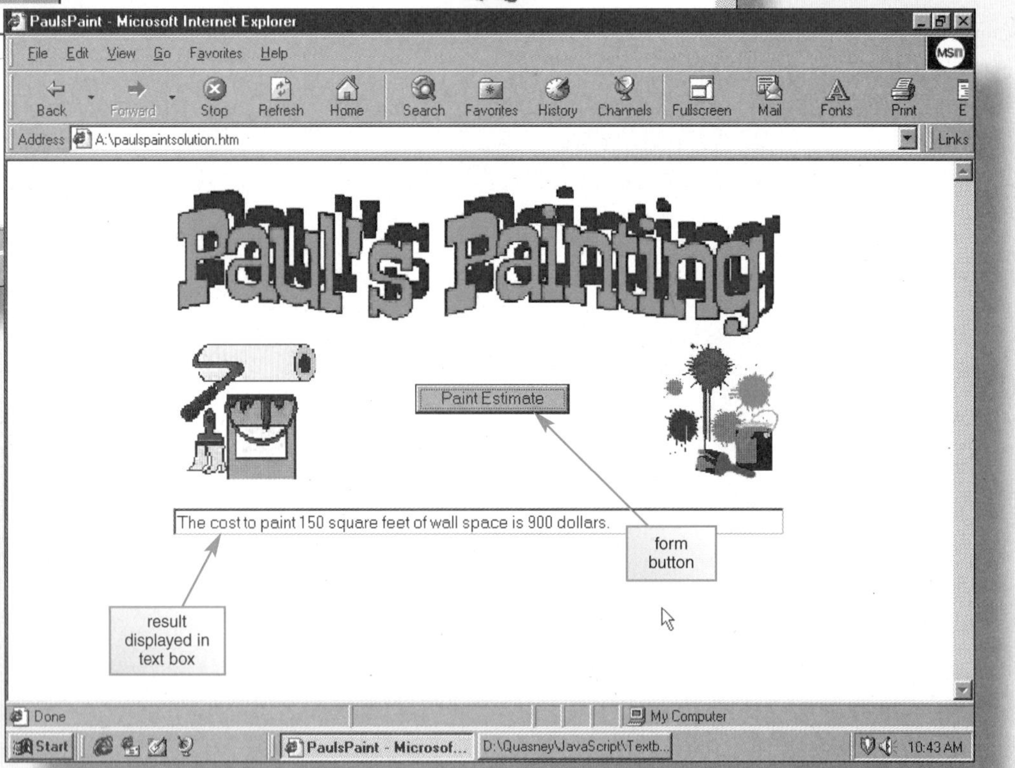

FIGURE I-23b

6. If an error still exists, open paulspaintsolution.htm in Notepad and check the spelling and wording of all variables and functions. Repeat Steps 4 through 6 until all errors are corrected.
7. Print the Web page and the Notepad file. Hand in the printouts to your instructor.

JavaScript

Integrating JavaScript and HTML

OBJECTIVES

You will have mastered the material in this project when you can:

- Discuss how to integrate JavaScript and HTML
- Insert SCRIPT tags on a Web page
- Write beginning and ending SCRIPT tags
- Define and use flickering to draw attention
- Describe the background color property of the document object
- Set the background color of a Web page using JavaScript
- Save the HTML file
- Test the Web page
- Discuss JavaScript variables
- Extract the system date
- Use several variables to construct a message
- Describe the write() method of the document object
- Write a user-defined function that displays a message and links viewers to a new site
- Describe how the setTimeout() method works
- Use the lastModified property to display the last modified document date
- Print an HTML Notepad file

Ready, Set, Stop

BMW's Driving School *Brakes* New Ground

While driving to class, you start thinking about your math test and weekend plans. Suddenly, a car pulls out in front of you. You jam on your brakes, swerve to the left, and narrowly avoid the collision.

Braking, cornering, and accident avoidance skills are required to face the rigors of sharing the road with today's aggressive drivers. BMW, the German carmaker known for its commitment to safety and performance, is driving home the need for driver training with its Ultimate Driving Experience.

The two-hour event held in major cities across the United States features an intensive, defensive driving course with classroom and racetrack components. Participants start the day by attending a *chalk talk* and learning driving dynamics. Then they divide into small groups and hit the road. With professional drivers at their sides, they maneuver BMW's 3 Series sedans through a winding track and learn the rudiments of accelerating, turning, and stopping.

After several trial runs, they are ready to put their split-second reactions to the test. Drivers are grouped into teams to face the ultimate challenge: using their newly honed skills to swerve through the track as quickly as possible. This timed auto-cross race allows drivers to gain confidence and compare their driving abilities.

After competing in the race, drivers can wind down by test driving other BMW models, viewing historic BMW vehicles, or purchasing exclusive BMW accessories.

Realizing that teenagers have extraordinarily high accident records, the automaker developed a separate program for drivers ages 15 to 21. This four-hour segment motivates these inexperienced motorists to develop lifelong defensive driving skills.

While the Ultimate Driving Experience helps drivers maneuver successfully on today's highways, BMW has found a home on another highway – the information superhighway. Its Web site, www.bmwusa.com, features a multitude of interactive components.

For example, would you like to design your dream Z3 roadster? Just click Z3 roadster, then Build Your Own Z3, and let your creativity soar. How about a metallic fern green exterior with a two-tone sand leather interior? Or bright red with black upholstery? Do you prefer the 2.8 liter in-line six-cylinder or the 1.9 in-line four? Your configurations display in vivid detail in front of your eyes, complete with technical specifications, warranty and maintenance information, and features on BMW's engineering marvels.

The Web site's functionality is enhanced with JavaScript, the object-based language you will explore in this textbook. In each project in this book, you will use the Web page development cycle to define a problem, analyze the situation, and then develop the solution. Likewise, BMW's Web page developers used these design principles to create an effective interactive site. For example, their pages feature information on lease and financing options. You can obtain an estimated monthly payment for each car you design. If the figures look good, you can apply for credit online.

Just as BMW's Web site uses JavaScript to steer driving enthusiasts through its features effectively, its Ultimate Driving Experience uses defensive driving skills to help drivers navigate the roadways safely.

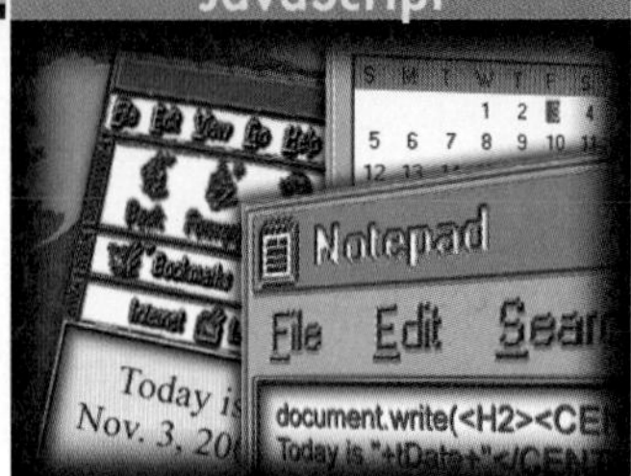

JavaScript

Integrating JavaScript and HTML

CASE PERSPECTIVE

You are a summer intern in the Online Development Group at Fun with Phonics. At a general development group meeting, Mandy Senicott, the Webmaster, announces a contract has been signed with a new Internet service provider (ISP), which means the Web home page will be moved.

Mandy is concerned about the users who have links pointing to the old domain address in their bookmarks. The old ISP contract will not expire for two months, so Mandy asks you to create a Web page that announces the move and automatically forwards users to the new Web site.

Mandy informs you the Web page must meet the following criteria: the Web page must flicker to gain the reader's attention, then display a message about the move, and include a link to the new location. The page automatically displays a message that informs the reader they now will be linked to the new site after 15 seconds.

Introduction

Many companies build and use Web sites, primarily to market and sell their products and services. Since 1996, many companies have developed and gained a substantial market edge using e-commerce (electronic commerce). **E-commerce** is business activity that takes place using networked computers and the Internet. For example, Auto-By-Tel, Dell Computers, Cisco Systems, and E-Trade all boast of market improvements because of their Web presence.

As a marketing tool, a good Web site must attract users and keep their attention. Marketing experts state that you have six to seven seconds to attract and retain someone's attention. This principle also applies to a well-designed Web page. You want a surfer to hit your page and stay, especially if you have a product or service to sell. Once users are on the page, you want them to stay and peruse it. If you are selling products or services, the page must convince them to make a purchase.

To gain a share of the cyber marketplace, many companies and individuals purchase their own domain names. In e-commerce, companies with easy to remember domain names are more likely to have repeat visitors to their Web sites. Because of the competition among Internet service providers, and the growth in users, many Web site locations are moved constantly. A Navigator bookmark or Internet Explorer favorite Web page a few months ago may no longer be valid now.

Unfortunately, when a Web site moves the user often encounters the error message: 404 Object not found. This error message does not tell you if the site has moved, has a new domain name, or if the site no longer exists on the Internet. Some organizations, however, leave a forwarding message at the old location or domain name when they move. This message informs you of the new domain name or address, and allows you to click a link to the new location. Unfortunately, HTML does not allow automatic links to domain addresses, the user must click a reference link.

One way Web developers solve this problem is to use JavaScript. JavaScript is an object-based language. An **object-based** language uses built-in objects, but is not capable of creating classes of objects or using inheritance features of object-oriented languages such as C++ or Java. In addition, JavaScript has predefined properties, methods, and event handlers.

As discussed in the Introduction to JavaScript Programming, an **object** is a person, place, or thing. **Properties** are attributes of objects and describe some aspect about the object.

You assign a property to an object by writing objectname.property=value. Spaces around the equal signs are optional.

Methods are actions, such as write, or function calls, such as Date("July 4, 2001"). You perform a method by writing objectname.method(parameters), where parameters are items or instructions the method uses.

Table 1-1 contains a short description of four commonly used objects with sample properties and methods.

Table 1-1

OBJECT	SAMPLE PROPERTIES AND METHODS
window	The window object is the main object. Many of the window-object properties are objects in their own right (i.e., document, frame, and location). The window object is not needed in many statements because it is assumed. For example; To link to a new site location = "www.scsite.com" To open another window open("win1.htm", "window1", "toolbar = yes") To cause a script to be executed after a specified period of time setTimeout("chngSite(s)", 15000)
document	The document object is one of the more often-used objects derived from the window object. A few of its properties and methods are fgColor, cookie, and write. For example; To set a document foreground color use the fgColor property document.fgColor = "white" To read the information stored in a cookie text file use the cookie property var cookieInfo = document.cookie To display the date the Web page was last modified, combine with the write() method document.write("The date last modified"+document.lastmodified)
math	The math object provides the capability to perform calculations PI is a property and represents the value of PI (3.14159). pow() is a method, which means to raise to the power. For example; pow(value, exponent) To calculate the area of a circle you would write var area = PI * pow(radius,2)
navigator	The navigator object determines which browser the user is running. For example; appName is a property that contains the browser's code name var browser = navigator.appName appVersion is a property that provides browser's release version var browserVer = navigator.appVersion

More About

E-commerce

Internet technology enables companies to recap the benefits of electronic trading. In an *Information Week* survey on Internet usage, 81 percent of the companies deploy e-commerce systems to improve customer services, and 77 percent stated e-commerce improved business processes. For more information on e-commerce, visit www.scsite.com/js/p1.htm and then click e-commerce.

More About

Auto-by-Tel, Dell, and E-trade

Auto-by-Tel, Dell, and E-trade are very prominent Web sites. To find out how these companies incorporate graphics and interactivity to maintain a strong Web presence, visit www.scsite.com/js/p1.htm and then click Auto-by-Tel.

More About

Domain Names

To learn more about domain names, visit www.scsite.com/js/p1.htm and then click domain names.

Scripting Languages

Netscape's JavaScript and Microsoft's VBScript are the two main client side script languages used today. To read more about scripting languages and why many organizations want one common language platform, visit www.scsite.com/js/p1.htm and then click scripting languages.

An **event** is the result of a user's action. **Event handlers** are the way to associate that action with the set of JavaScript codes you want executed. The general form of an event handler is in Table 1-2.

Table 1-2 – Event Handler	
General form:	<TAG attribute eventHandler = "JavaScript code">
Comment:	where TAG is the HTML tag; an attribute is a characteristic of a tag that can have a value assigned to it; eventhandler is the name of the JavaScript event handler; and JavaScript code is the instruction to execute, normally in the form of a function name.
Example:	`<BODY onload = "displayWindow()">`

The Introduction to JavaScript Programming has a complete list of event handlers shown in Tables I-8 on page J I.13.

Project One — Fun with Phonics Web Page

You have determined the requirements for the Web page update and are ready to make the necessary changes. First, you will create a Web page (Figure 1-1a) that displays a message informing the user that the Web site location has been moved. Second, you will create a link to the new Web page location, so users may click the link and go directly to the Web site. The HTML code is in a file on the JavaScript Data Disk. Your job in this project is to add JavaScript code to the HTML file so the Web page displays as shown in Figures 1-1a and 1-1b. The HTML and JavaScript code is shown in Figure 1-1c.

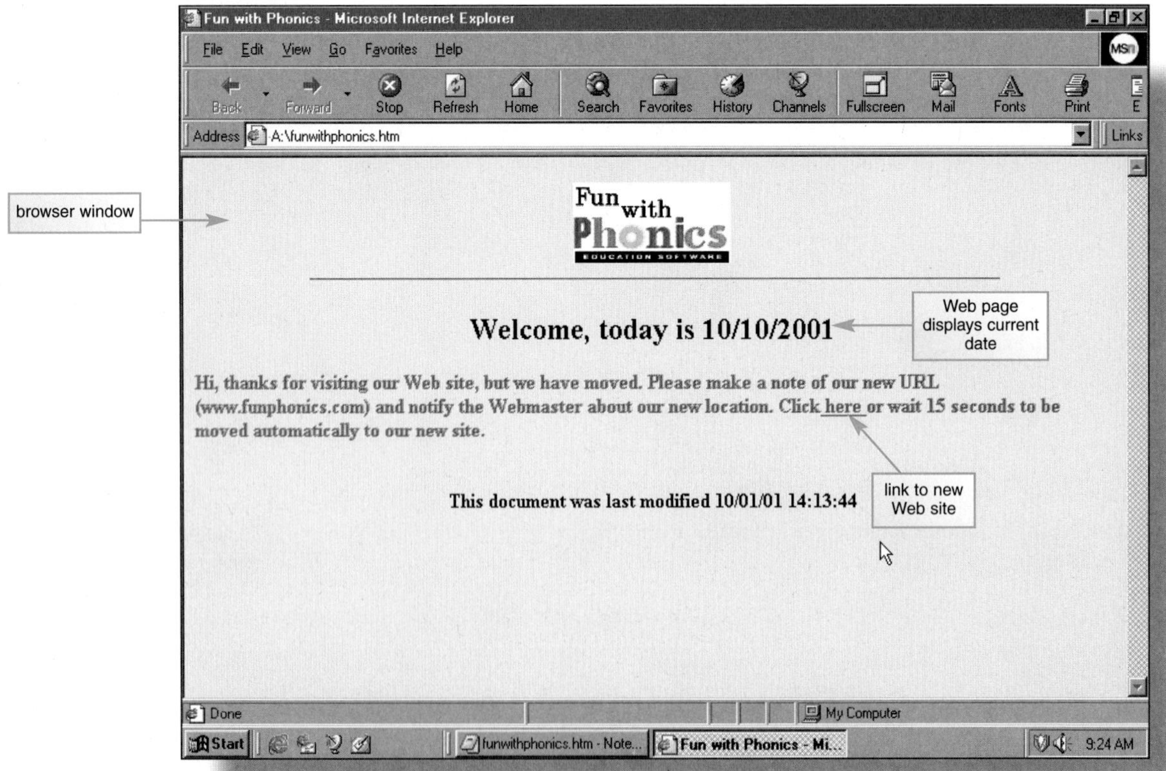
browser window
Fun with Phonics - Microsoft Internet Explorer
A:\funwithphonics.htm
Fun with Phonics
Welcome, today is 10/10/2001
Web page displays current date
Hi, thanks for visiting our Web site, but we have moved. Please make a note of our new URL (www.funphonics.com) and notify the Webmaster about our new location. Click here or wait 15 seconds to be moved automatically to our new site.
This document was last modified 10/01/01 14:13:44
link to new Web site

FIGURE 1-1a

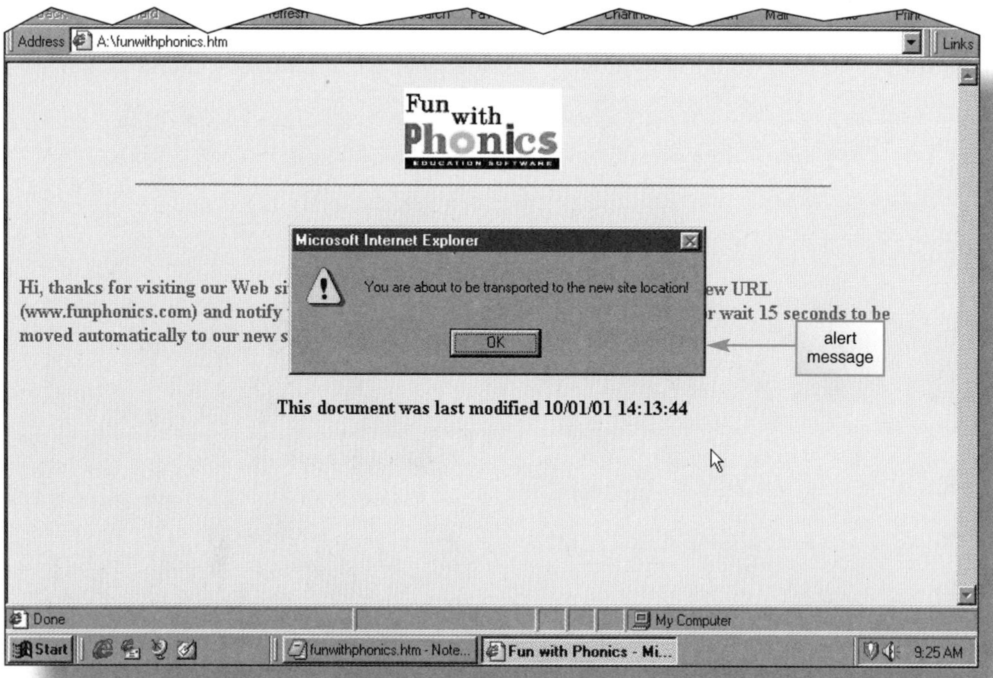

FIGURE 1-1b

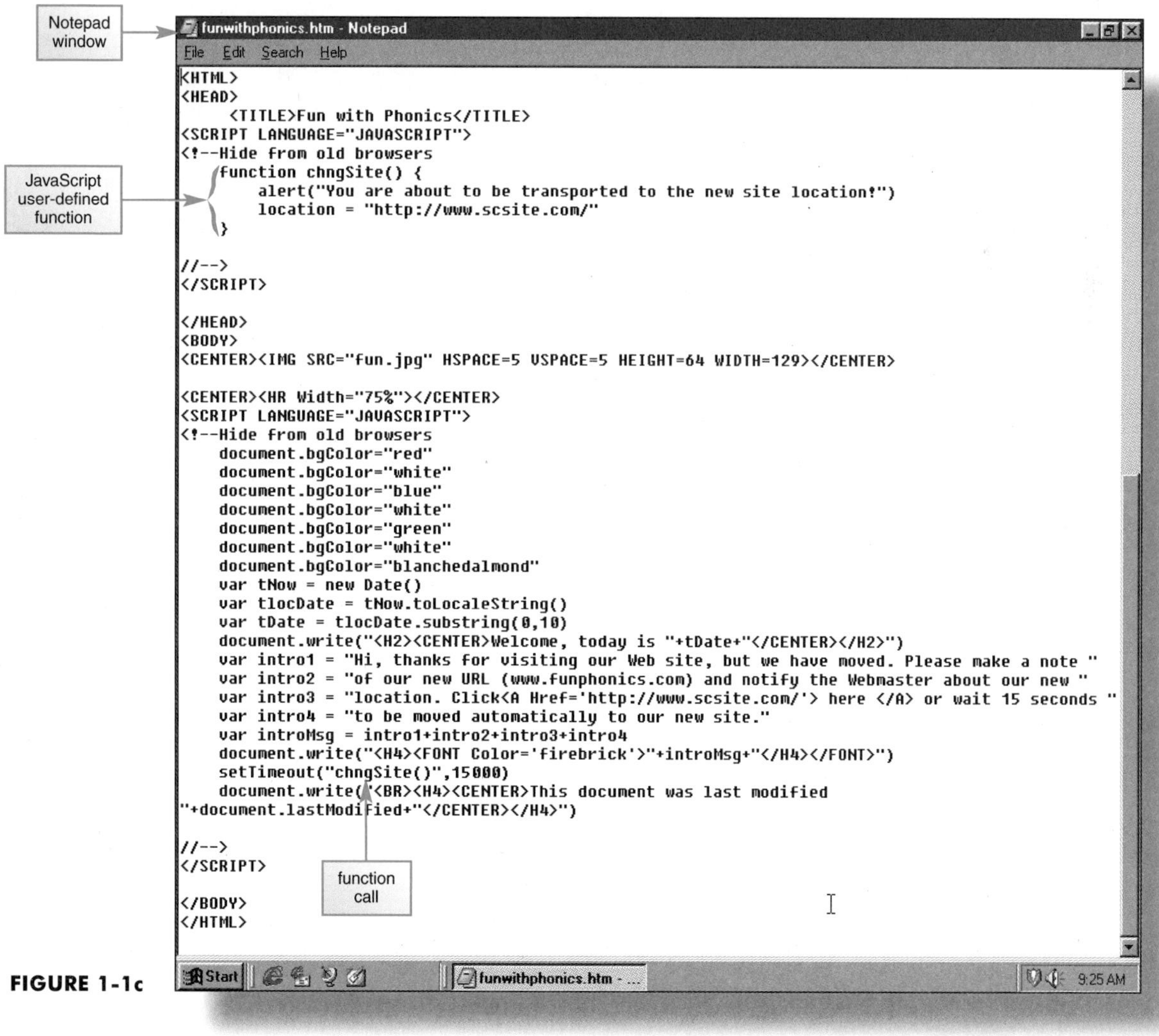

Notepad window

funwithphonics.htm - Notepad

File Edit Search Help

JavaScript user-defined function

function call

```
<HTML>
<HEAD>
     <TITLE>Fun with Phonics</TITLE>
<SCRIPT LANGUAGE="JAVASCRIPT">
<!--Hide from old browsers
     function chngSite() {
          alert("You are about to be transported to the new site location!")
          location = "http://www.scsite.com/"
     }

//-->
</SCRIPT>

</HEAD>
<BODY>
<CENTER><IMG SRC="fun.jpg" HSPACE=5 VSPACE=5 HEIGHT=64 WIDTH=129></CENTER>

<CENTER><HR Width="75%"></CENTER>
<SCRIPT LANGUAGE="JAVASCRIPT">
<!--Hide from old browsers
     document.bgColor="red"
     document.bgColor="white"
     document.bgColor="blue"
     document.bgColor="white"
     document.bgColor="green"
     document.bgColor="white"
     document.bgColor="blanchedalmond"
     var tNow = new Date()
     var tlocDate = tNow.toLocaleString()
     var tDate = tlocDate.substring(0,10)
     document.write("<H2><CENTER>Welcome, today is "+tDate+"</CENTER></H2>")
     var intro1 = "Hi, thanks for visiting our Web site, but we have moved. Please make a note "
     var intro2 = "of our new URL (www.funphonics.com) and notify the Webmaster about our new "
     var intro3 = "location. Click<A Href='http://www.scsite.com/'> here </A> or wait 15 seconds "
     var intro4 = "to be moved automatically to our new site."
     var introMsg = intro1+intro2+intro3+intro4
     document.write("<H4><FONT Color='firebrick'>"+introMsg+"</H4></FONT>")
     setTimeout("chngSite()",15000)
     document.write("<BR><H4><CENTER>This document was last modified
"+document.lastModified+"</CENTER></H4>")

//-->
</SCRIPT>

</BODY>
</HTML>
```

Start funwithphonics.htm - ... 9:25 AM

FIGURE 1-1c

Starting Notepad

To start Notepad, Windows must be running. Perform the following steps to start Notepad.

Steps To Start Notepad

1 Click the Start button on the taskbar and then point to Programs on the Start menu. Point to Accessories on the Programs submenu, and then point to Notepad.

Figure 1-2 shows the default menu structure for Accessories. Your system may have a different set of menus. Whenever you point to a menu name that has a right arrow following it, a submenu displays.

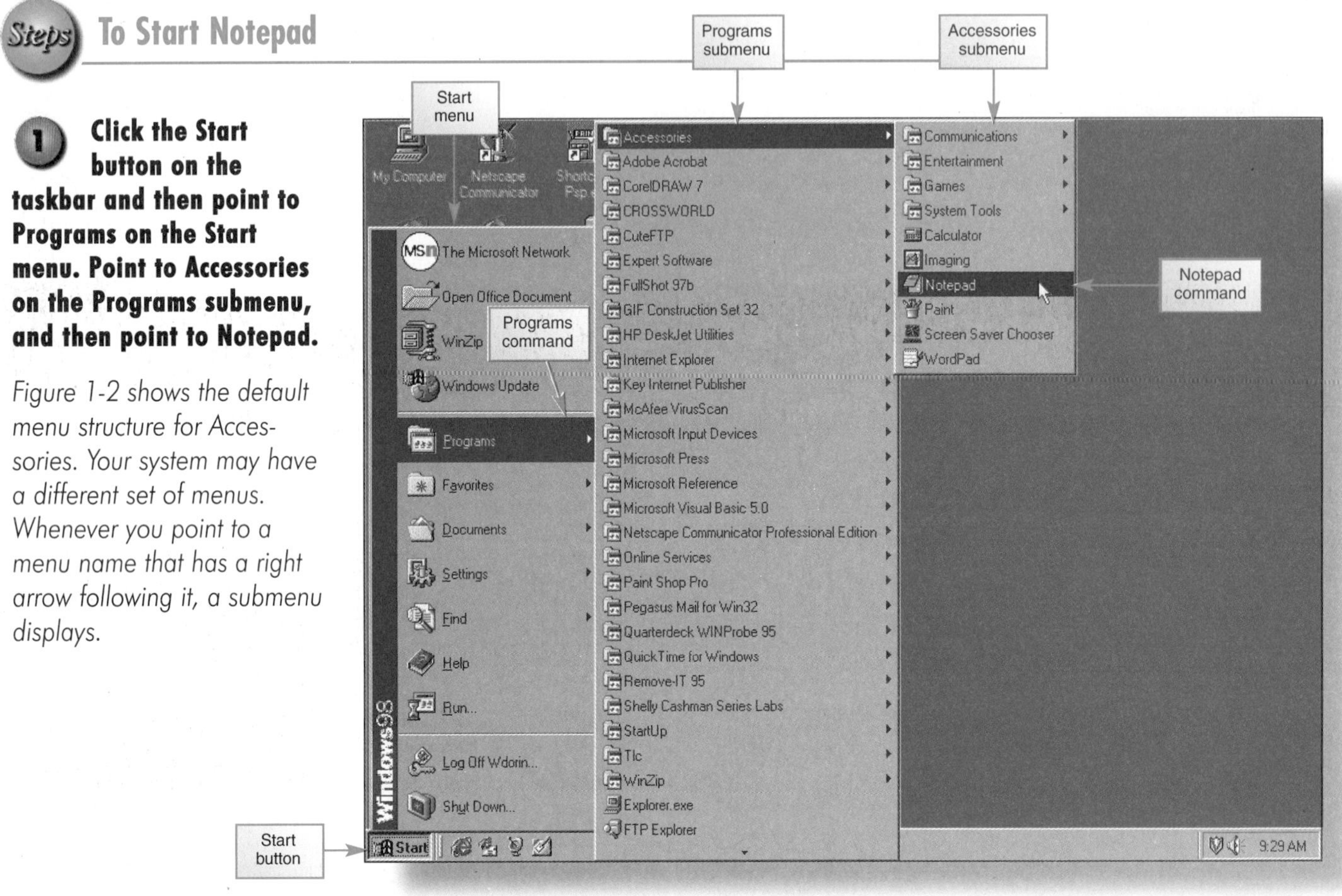

FIGURE 1-2

2 Click Notepad. When the Notepad window displays, click the Maximize button.

The maximized blank Notepad window displays (Figure 1-3).

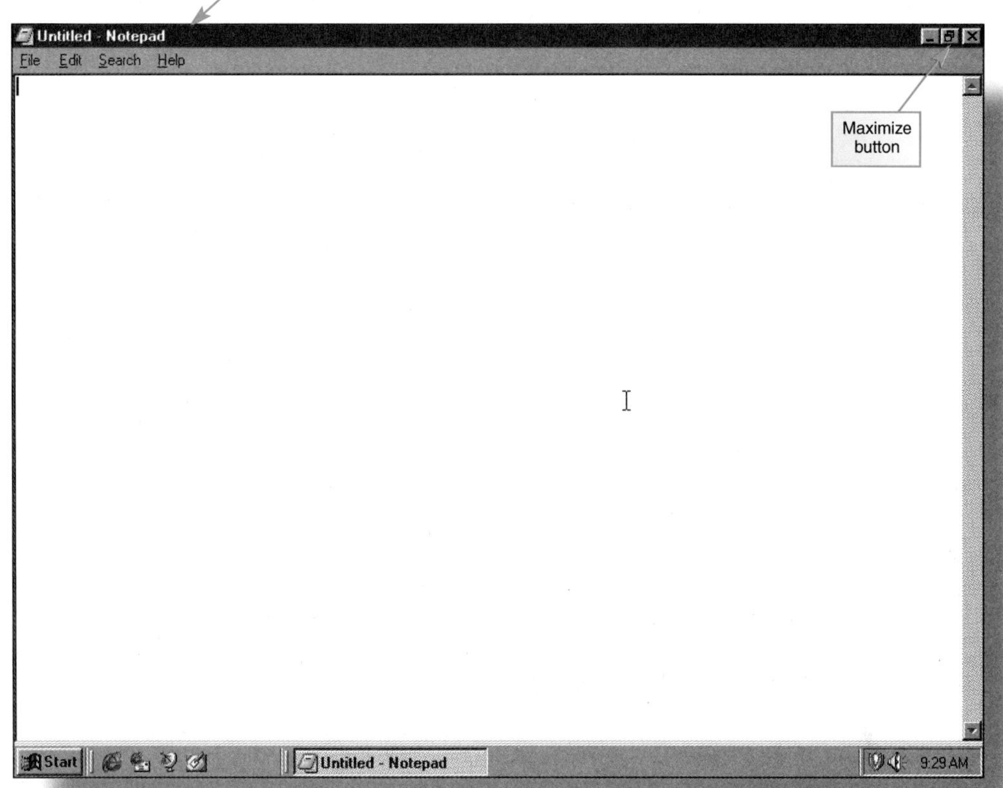

FIGURE 1-3

The Notepad application is a text editor. If you are familiar with any word processing application, many of the same concepts apply. Notepad can cut, copy, and paste text, as well as search and find text. You do not need to format any text in this project. The Windows 98 version of Notepad automatically wordwraps. If you are using the Windows 95 version, however, you may have to check Word Wrap on the Edit menu. To begin, you must open the Fun with Phonics Web page. To open the fun.htm file in Notepad, perform the steps on the next page.

To Open a Web Page Stored on the Data Disk

1 Insert the JavaScript Data Disk in drive A. If you do not have a copy of the JavaScript Data Disk, see the inside back cover for instructions for downloading the JavaScript Data Disk, or see your instructor. Click File on the menu bar and then click Open. When the Open dialog box displays, type `*.htm` **in the File name text box.**

The Open dialog box displays (Figure 1-4). Text Documents is the default Files of type. The file name extension is changed to .htm.

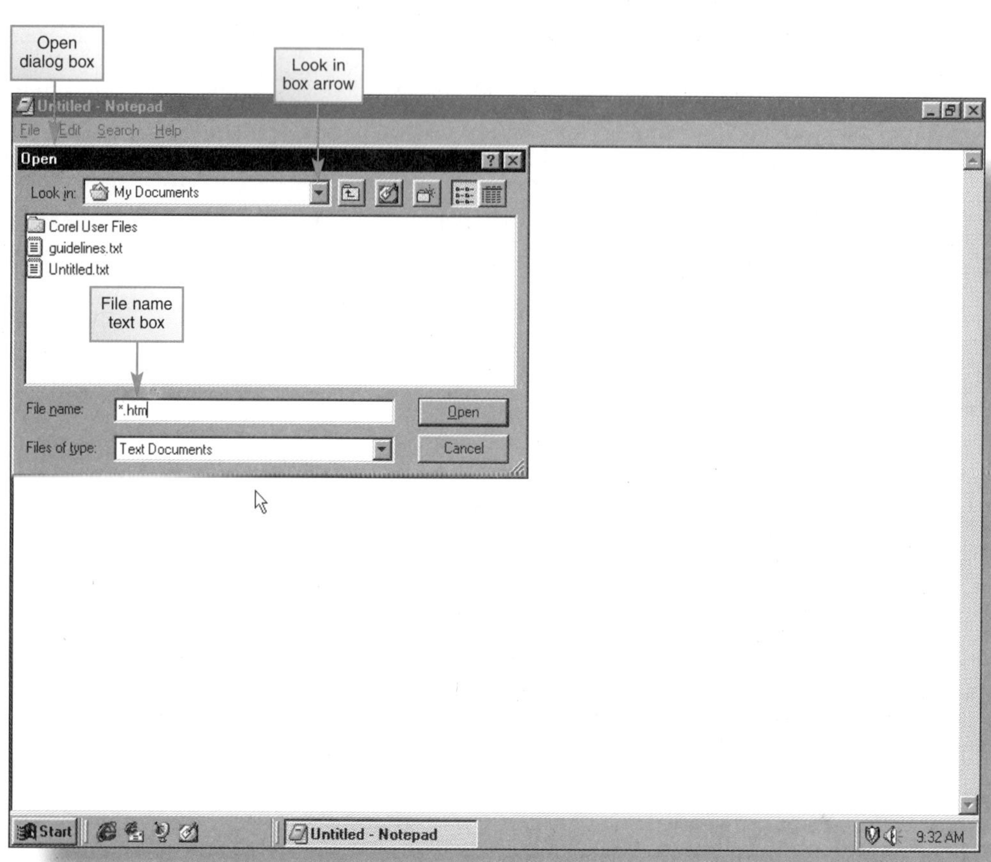

FIGURE 1-4

2 Click the Look in box arrow and then click 3½ Floppy (A:). Click fun.htm and then point to the Open button.

When you click the Look in box arrow, the Look in list displays (Figure 1-5). When you click 3½ Floppy (A:), a list of files displays with fun.htm highlighted.

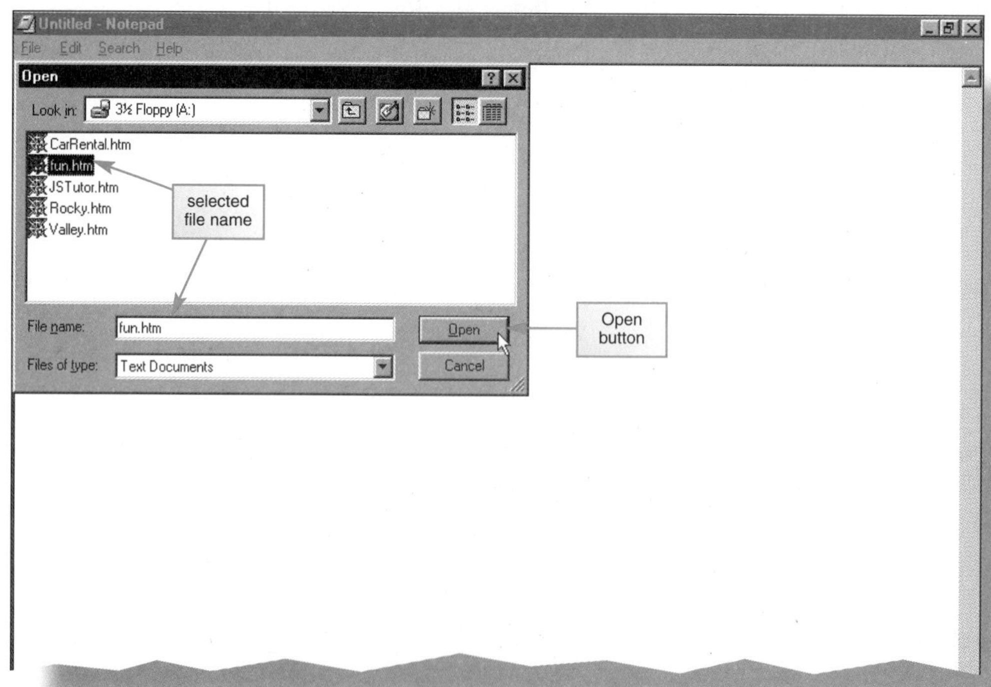

FIGURE 1-5

Click the Open button.

The fun.htm document opens in the Notepad window. The fun.htm file name displays on the title bar (Figure 1-6).

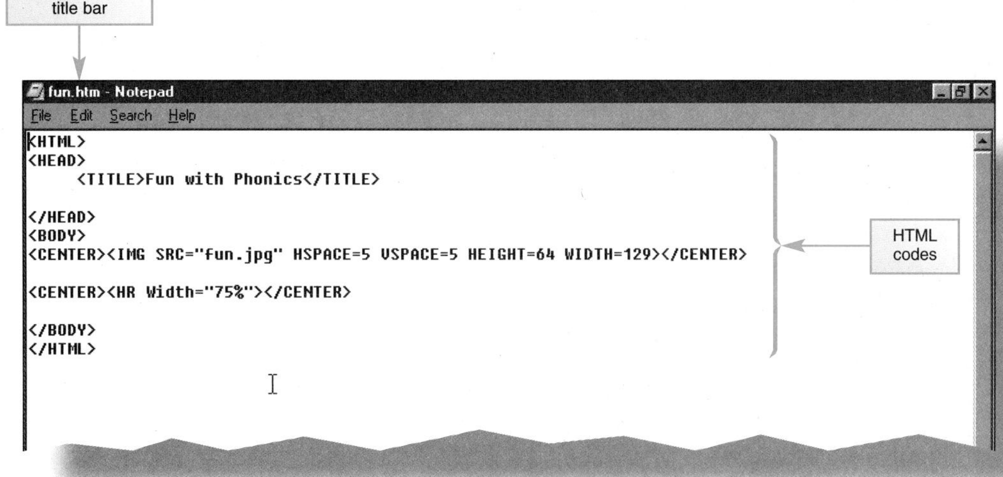
file name displays on Notepad title bar
fun.htm - Notepad
File Edit Search Help
<HTML>
<HEAD>
<TITLE>Fun with Phonics</TITLE>
</HEAD>
<BODY>
<CENTER><IMG SRC="fun.jpg" HSPACE=5 VSPACE=5 HEIGHT=64 WIDTH=129></CENTER>
<CENTER><HR Width="75%"></CENTER>
</BODY>
</HTML>
HTML codes

FIGURE 1-6

1. Press ALT+F, press O

The fun.htm HTML code displays in Notepad. The next step is to insert the JavaScript code in the BODY section to make the Web page flicker.

Inserting SCRIPT Tags on a Web Page

You can place JavaScript code anywhere in the HTML code. Most Web developers agree that the HEAD section should contain the user-defined JavaScript functions and the BODY section should contain the event handlers or other JavaScript code sections.

You always begin the JavaScript section with a SCRIPT tag, which indicates the language you are using. Similarly to other HTML tags, the JavaScript SCRIPT tag needs a beginning and ending tag. Some Web developers recommend inserting the beginning and ending tags immediately as you modify or construct the Web page. The important rule to remember is there must be a complete set of SCRIPT tags such as <SCRIPT> and </SCRIPT>.

JavaScript

To learn more about why JavaScript is used, visit www.scsite.com/js/p1.htm and then click JavaScript.

Writing the Beginning SCRIPT Tag

As discussed in the Introduction to JavaScript Programming, the SCRIPT tag has one attribute, which is LANGUAGE. You write the tag as <SCRIPT LANGUAGE = "JAVASCRIPT">. If you omit the LANGUAGE attribute, most browsers default to JavaScript.

Following the SCRIPT tag, Web developers commonly agree to add an HTML comment line. The HTML comment line hides any script language that a browser may not be able to interpret. As with all HTML tags, there must be a beginning and ending tag. To begin the JavaScript section you enter

```
<SCRIPT LANGUAGE="JAVASCRIPT">
<!--Hide from old browsers
```

In this project, you will use only JavaScript features that work in all versions of Internet Explorer or Netscape Navigator. To enter the beginning SCRIPT tag and comment to create a JavaScript section in the BODY section, perform the steps on the next page.

JavaScript Comment Lines

An HTML comment is a tag that begins with <! and ends with >. If you fail to close the HTML comment with a bracket (>), all your HTML code will be ignored. In JavaScript, the double slash (//) is used to indicate comments.

To Enter the Beginning SCRIPT Tag and Comment

1. **Click the blank line (line 10) above the </BODY> tag as shown in Figure 1-7.**

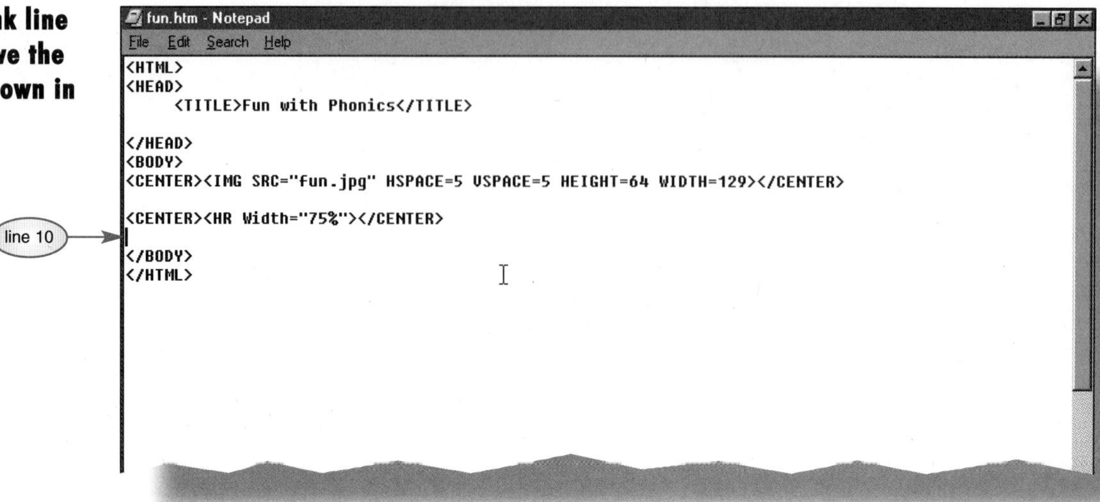

FIGURE 1-7

2. **Type** <SCRIPT LANGUAGE="JAVASCRIPT"> **and then press the ENTER key. Type** <!--Hide from old browsers **and then press the ENTER key.**

The beginning SCRIPT tag and comment display (Figure 1-8).

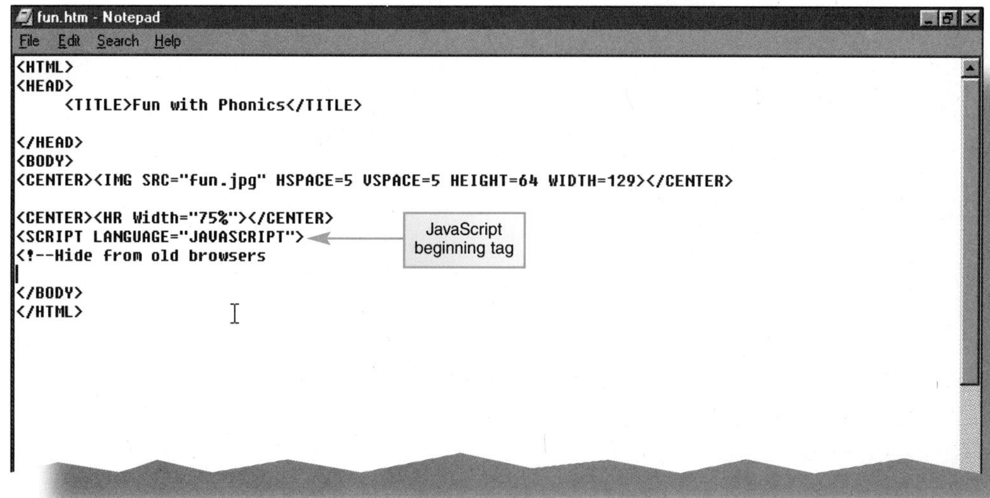

FIGURE 1-8

These lines begin the JavaScript section. Later, you will enter the ending tags before testing the Web page.

Using a Flicker on a Web Page to Draw Attention

You probably have had some experience waiting for a Web page that takes too long to display. The number of users on a Web server, the speed of your connection, the amount of traffic on the Internet, the size of the Web page, and the number of graphics the Web page contains have an impact on how long it takes to display. Users begin to *wonder* and quit paying attention to their screens. One way to grab users' attention is to make the page flicker. You can make the page flicker using JavaScript code to change the background color in rapid succession.

With HTML, you set the background color once in the <BODY> tag with the BGCOLOR attribute. Because Web pages have one BODY section, the background color can be set only once. With JavaScript, you can change the background color anytime using the document object and BGCOLOR property. As described earlier, the general form of an object and property is objectname.propertyname = value.

To set the background color of your document to red, you write the following JavaScript code:

```
document.bgColor="red"
```

To create the flickering effect, place several of these statements in sequence, alternating between a color background and a white background. You may enter the property name using all lowercase, uppercase, or mixed-case letters as shown below.

```
document.bgColor="red"
document.bgColor="white"
document.bgColor="blue"
document.bgColor="white"
document.bgColor="green"
document.bgColor="white"
```

When a visitor references the Web page with the above code, the document background colors change immediately and flicker. Perform the following steps to create flicker on the Web page.

More About

The Document Object

The document object is actually a property of the Window object. To learn more about the document object, visit www.scsite.com/js/p1.htm and then click document objects.

More About

Background Color Codes

Color codes can be identified as either hex properties or the actual color name. A hex number 00FFFF indicates the amount of red, green, and blue to display, respectively. To see a complete list of colors and hex codes, visit www.scsite.com/js/p1.htm and click background colors.

To Create Flicker on the Web Page

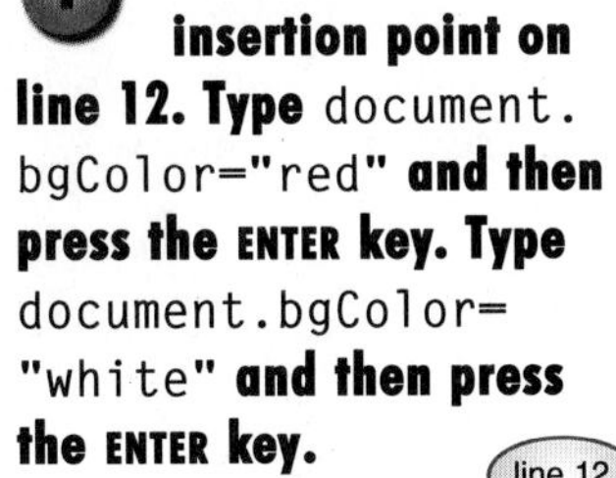

1 Position the insertion point on line 12. Type `document.bgColor="red"` **and then press the ENTER key. Type** `document.bgColor="white"` **and then press the ENTER key.**

Each line is indented four spaces for readability purposes (Figure 1-9).

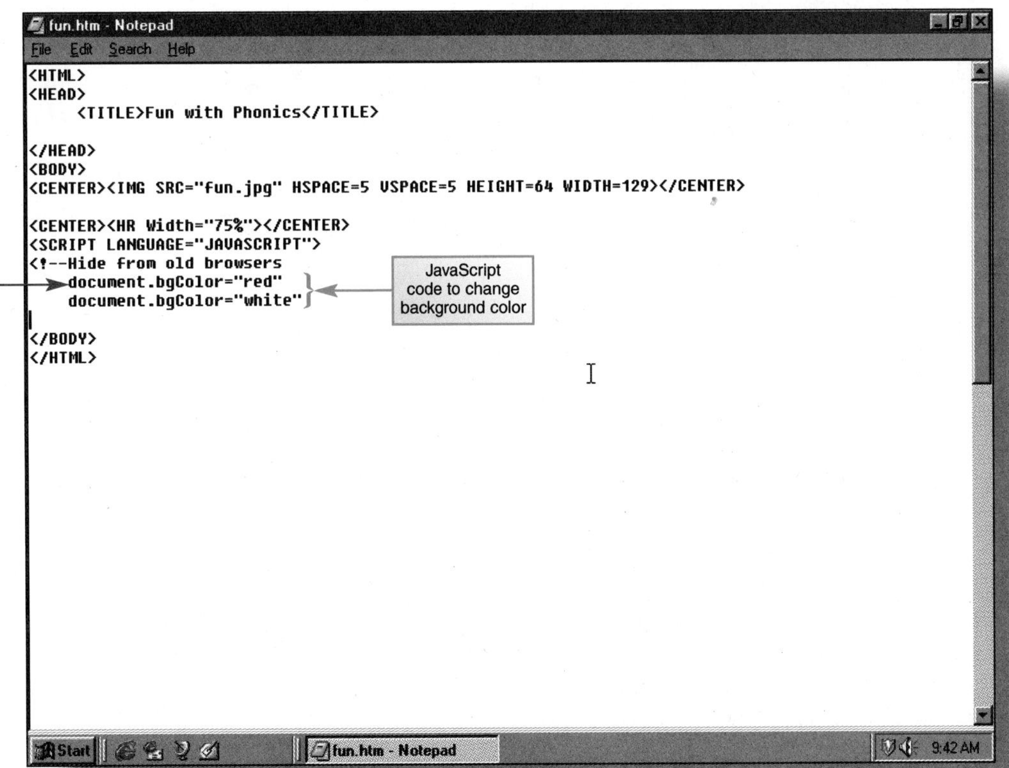

FIGURE 1-9

2 With the insertion point on line 14, enter the four lines of code as shown in Figure 1-10.

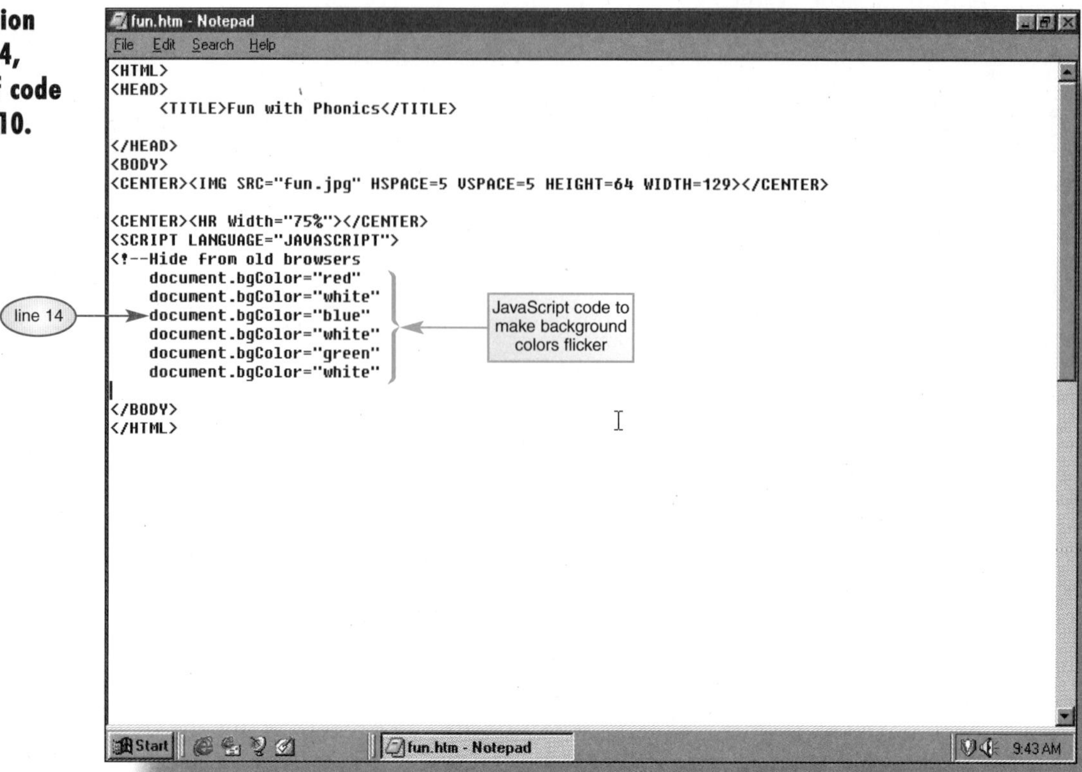
fun.htm - Notepad
File Edit Search Help
<HTML>
<HEAD>
<TITLE>Fun with Phonics</TITLE>
</HEAD>
<BODY>
<CENTER><IMG SRC="fun.jpg" HSPACE=5 VSPACE=5 HEIGHT=64 WIDTH=129></CENTER>
<CENTER><HR Width="75%"></CENTER>
<SCRIPT LANGUAGE="JAVASCRIPT">
<!--Hide from old browsers
document.bgColor="red"
document.bgColor="white"
document.bgColor="blue"
document.bgColor="white"
document.bgColor="green"
document.bgColor="white"
</BODY>
</HTML>
line 14
JavaScript code to make background colors flicker
Start
fun.htm - Notepad
9:43 AM

FIGURE 1-10

As you enter JavaScript code, be careful with the spelling and placement of quotation marks. The browser cannot interpret misspelled HTML tags and JavaScript commands. In addition, missing or unbalanced quotation marks cause the browser to misinterpret commands. These types of errors prevent the browser from loading and displaying the Web page properly. If users becomes confused or frustrated, they will abandon the Web page and look for another site.

Setting the Background Color to a Static Color

After making the page flicker to gain the user's attention, set the background color to the final color. The background and text colors should be pleasing to the eye and provide ample contrast to make reading the text easy. Perform the following step to set the background color to blanched almond.

To Set the Background Color to a Static Color

1 With the insertion point on line 18, type document.bgColor="blanchedalmond" **and then press the ENTER key.**

This statement sets the background color to blanched almond (Figure 1-11).

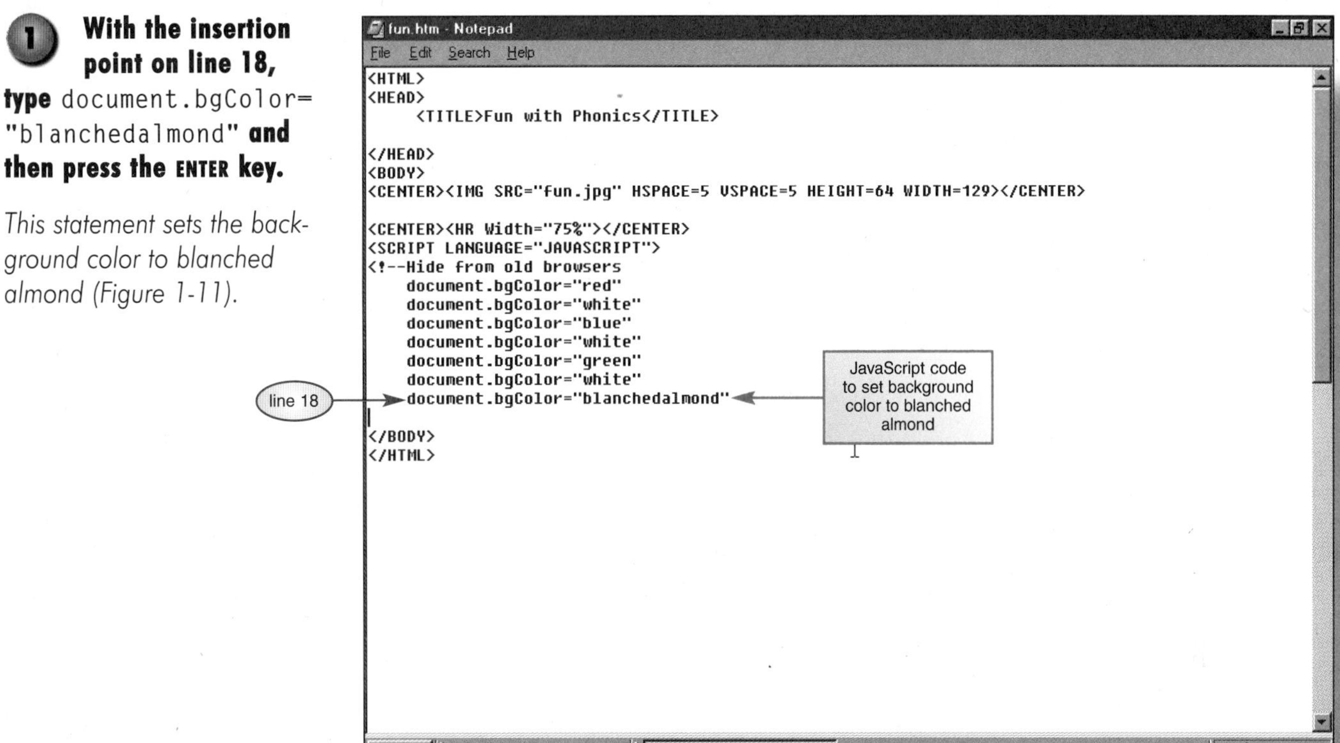
fun.htm - Notepad
File Edit Search Help
<HTML>
<HEAD>
<TITLE>Fun with Phonics</TITLE>
</HEAD>
<BODY>
<CENTER><IMG SRC="fun.jpg" HSPACE=5 VSPACE=5 HEIGHT=64 WIDTH=129></CENTER>
<CENTER><HR Width="75%"></CENTER>
<SCRIPT LANGUAGE="JAVASCRIPT">
<!--Hide from old browsers
document.bgColor="red"
document.bgColor="white"
document.bgColor="blue"
document.bgColor="white"
document.bgColor="green"
document.bgColor="white"
document.bgColor="blanchedalmond"
</BODY>
</HTML>
line 18
JavaScript code to set background color to blanched almond
Start
fun.htm - Notepad
9:43 AM

FIGURE 1-11

The six JavaScript statements entered on lines 12 to 17 make the page flicker. The last statement on line 18 sets the background color to a static blanched almond.

Completing the JavaScript Section

As discussed earlier, all HTML tags must have beginning and ending tags to separate them from other page elements. To complete this set of JavaScript codes, you must add the ending SCRIPT tags. You must close the comment in line 11 and the beginning SCRIPT tag in line 10 as follows:

```
//-->
</SCRIPT>
```

The JavaScript //--> closes the beginning comment, and <!--Hide from old browsers, encloses the JavaScript code within the comments. If the user has an old browser, the JavaScript code is hidden from the user. In addition, if you do not close the comment, the Web page may display nothing when loaded. The </SCRIPT> tag closes the JavaScript section. This ending tag also prevents the HTML code that follows from being interpreted as JavaScript code. Perform the steps on the next page to enter the ending tags.

To Enter the Ending SCRIPT Tag

1 If necessary, position the insertion point on line 19. Press the ENTER key to create another blank line.

2 With the insertion point on line 20, type //--> and then press the ENTER key. Type </SCRIPT> and then press the ENTER key.

The ending //--> and </SCRIPT> tags complete the JavaScript section (Figure 1-12).

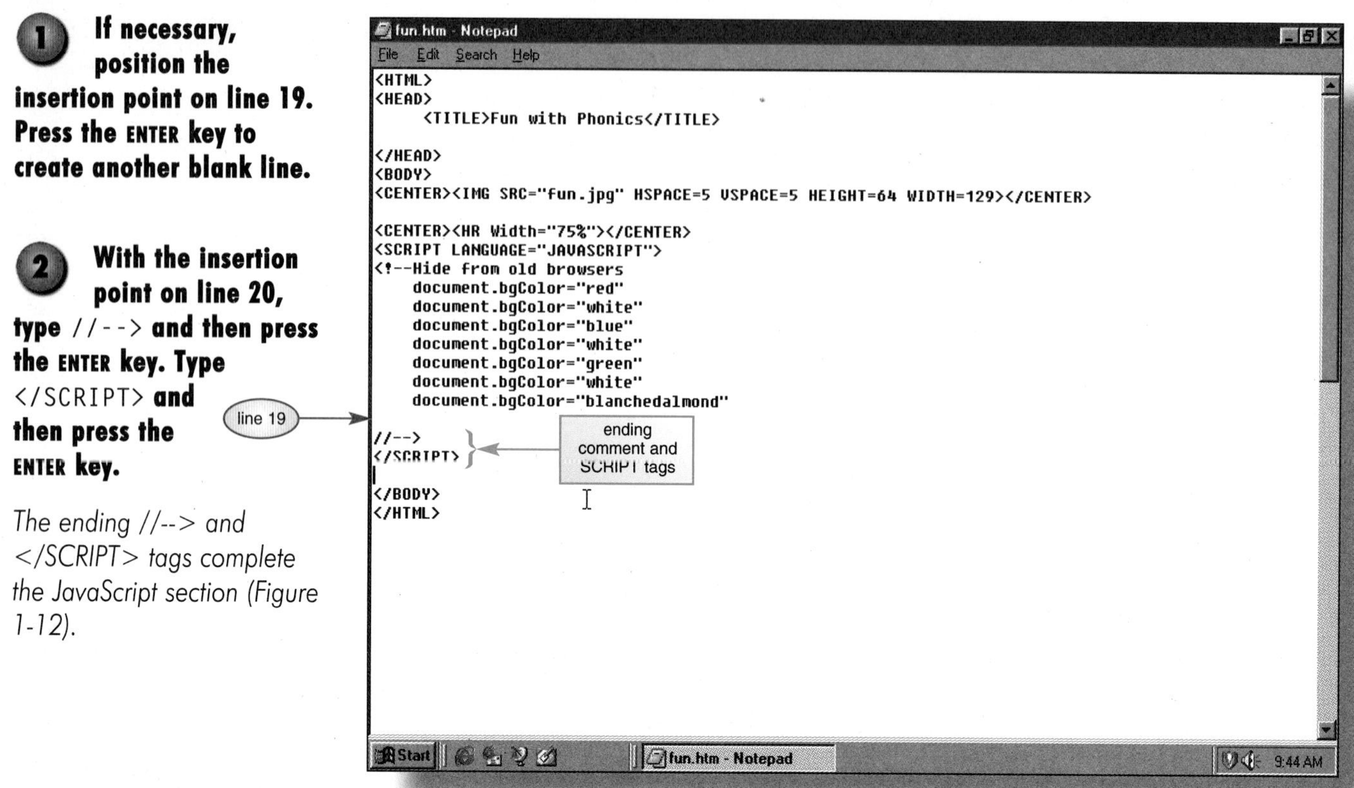
fun.htm - Notepad
File Edit Search Help
<HTML>
<HEAD>
<TITLE>Fun with Phonics</TITLE>
</HEAD>
<BODY>
<CENTER><IMG SRC="fun.jpg" HSPACE=5 VSPACE=5 HEIGHT=64 WIDTH=129></CENTER>
<CENTER><HR Width="75%"></CENTER>
<SCRIPT LANGUAGE="JAVASCRIPT">
<!--Hide from old browsers
document.bgColor="red"
document.bgColor="white"
document.bgColor="blue"
document.bgColor="white"
document.bgColor="green"
document.bgColor="white"
document.bgColor="blanchedalmond"
//-->
</SCRIPT>
</BODY>
</HTML>
line 19
ending comment and SCRIPT tags
Start
fun.htm - Notepad
9:44 AM

FIGURE 1-12

The JavaScript code to cause the Web page to flicker is complete. This is a good point to test the newly entered code. The HTML file must be saved on disk before it can be tested. You then can start your browser and display the saved file to check the flicker.

Saving the HTML File

Save the file using the Save As command on the File menu. You are required to add the .htm extension to the file name, because Notepad automatically saves all files with the default .txt extension. Perform the following steps to save the HTML file on the floppy disk as funwithphonics.htm. The file name is not case sensitive and can be entered in uppercase or lowercase characters.

To Save the File on the Floppy Disk

1 Make sure the floppy disk is in drive A. Click File on the menu bar and then click Save As.

The Save As dialog box displays (Figure 1-13). The File name text box contains the highlighted entry of the previously opened file (a:\fun.htm).

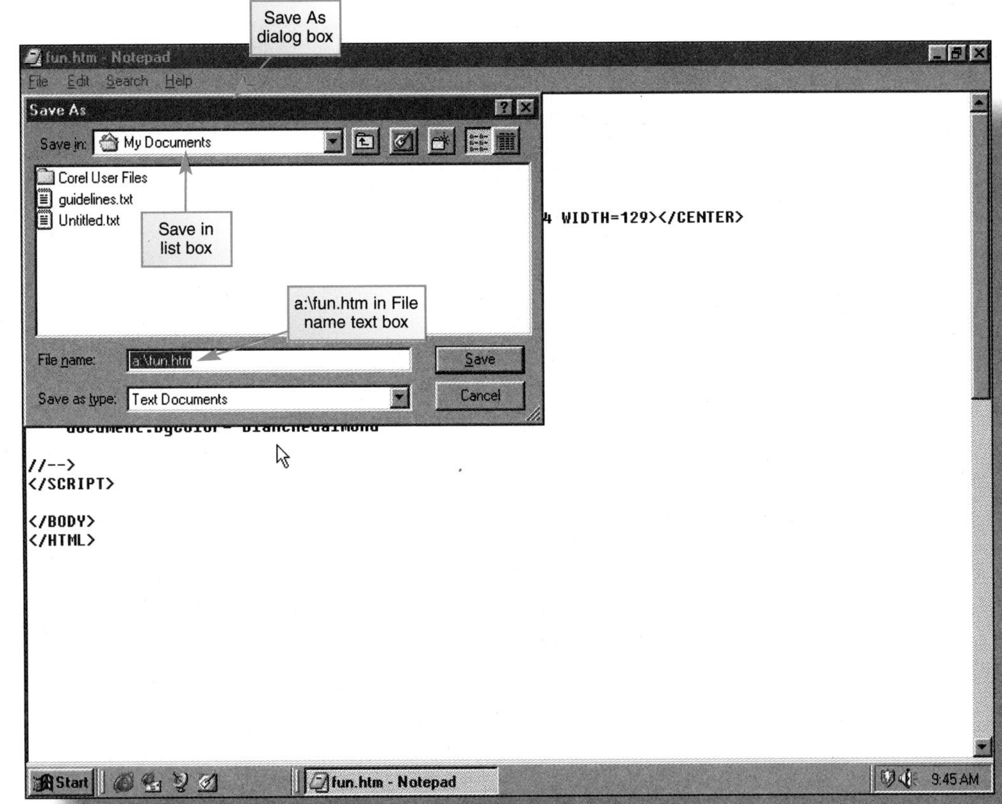

FIGURE 1-13

2 Type a:\funwithphonics.htm **in the File name text box (Figure 1-14).**

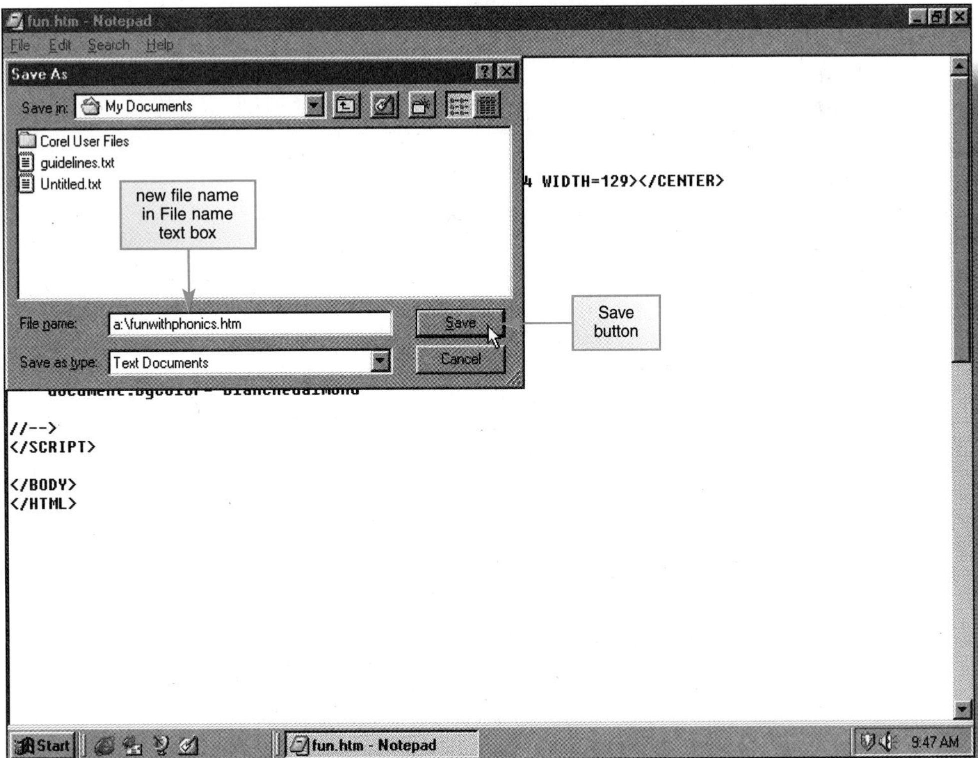

FIGURE 1-14

Click the Save button.

The dialog box closes, the file is saved, and the new file name displays on the Notepad title bar (Figure 1-15).

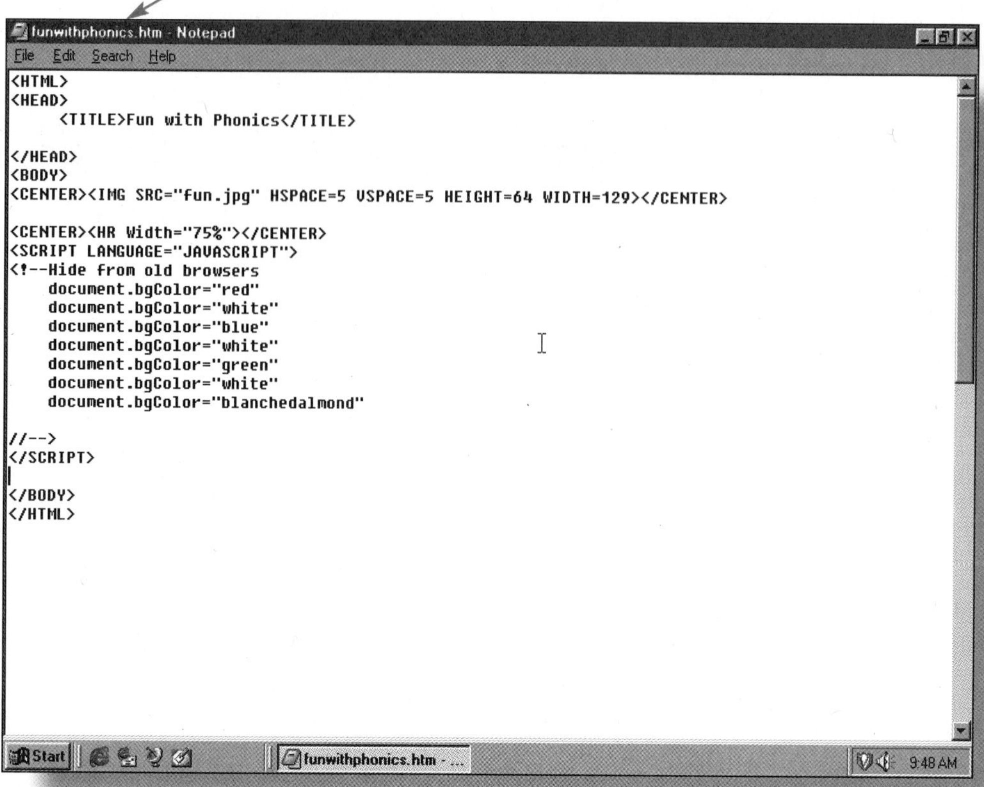


```
<HTML>
<HEAD>
      <TITLE>Fun with Phonics</TITLE>

</HEAD>
<BODY>
<CENTER><IMG SRC="fun.jpg" HSPACE=5 VSPACE=5 HEIGHT=64 WIDTH=129></CENTER>

<CENTER><HR Width="75%"></CENTER>
<SCRIPT LANGUAGE="JAVASCRIPT">
<!--Hide from old browsers
     document.bgColor="red"
     document.bgColor="white"
     document.bgColor="blue"
     document.bgColor="white"
     document.bgColor="green"
     document.bgColor="white"
     document.bgColor="blanchedalmond"

//-->
</SCRIPT>

</BODY>
</HTML>
```

FIGURE 1-15

Other Ways

1. Press ALT+F, A

You will need to remember the file name, funwithphonics.htm, when you test the file in the browser.

Testing the Web Page

The next step is to test your funwithphonics.htm Web page. Missing periods, quotation marks, or misspelled words will cause errors. If an error occurs, a dialog box displays with a message and indicates where the browser could not interpret the JavaScript code. To continue loading your Web page, click the OK button in the dialog box if an error message displays. The browser will cease to process any more JavaScript code, and load what it can of the remaining Web page. Perform the following steps to test the Web page.

To Test the Web Page

Start your browser.

Click the Address box. Type `a:\funwithphonics.htm` **and then press the ENTER key.**

The Fun with Phonics web page displays in the browser window. The JavaScript code causes the Web page to flicker. The Web page then displays the background color blanched almond (Figure 1-16).

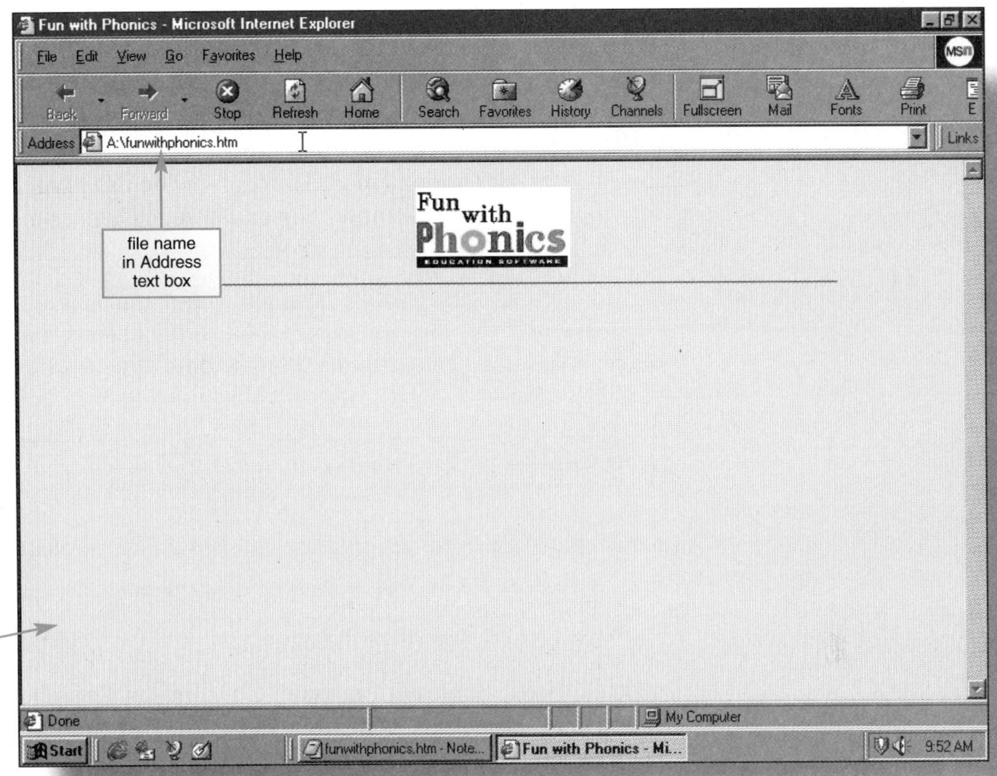

FIGURE 1-16

If your browser does not display the Web page correctly, close any error message, and click the Notepad button on the taskbar. Check your JavaScript code according to Figure 1-15. Correct any errors, save the file, activate the browser, and then click the Refresh button.

More About

Variable Names

JavaScript variables are temporary places to store data. Visit www.scsite.com/js/p1.htm and then click variable names. At the Netscape site, scroll through the JavaScript Guide Contents frame on the left side until you find the section on Value, Variables, and Literals, and then click Variables.

JavaScript Variables

As in other programming languages, JavaScript variables are used to store values temporarily. JavaScript variable naming conventions are similar to the naming conventions of variables in other programming languages such as C. For example, JavaScript variable names are case sensitive. Table 1-3 shows the rules for naming JavaScript variables.

Table 1-3

COMMENT	VALID NAMES EXAMPLE	INVALID NAMES EXAMPLE
Must begin with a letter or underscore	Months	9Months
Rest of name must be letters or underscores	Last_Name	Last-Name
Do not use spaces or other punctuation	ZipCode	Zip.Code
Avoid JavaScript objects, properties, and reserved words	xNow	Date

JavaScript variables are loosely typed. **Loosely typed** means you are not required to define the variable data types as either numeric or character in advance. JavaScript determines the data type from the data. This feature is an advantage, because variables are flexible and can store any data type. If you are not careful, however, you can change a variables' data type in the middle of JavaScript code and create an error. This type of error can be difficult to find.

String data types are variables that hold characters or a combination of letters, numbers, or symbols. Numeric data types hold numbers. Boolean data types contain logical data as *True* or *False*. To indicate the data type, define the variable by assigning the value to the variable. For example, assigning a string value to a variable as in

```
var LastName = "Simon"
```

makes the variable LastName a string data type. Assigning a numeric value to a variable as in

```
var pageCnt = 1
```

makes pageCnt a numeric data type. Assigning Boolean values to a variable as in

```
var Done = false
```

makes Done a Boolean data type. Conditional testing and loops use Boolean variables.

The var keyword is not required in the previous examples. Most Web developers and JavaScript programmers, however, recommend using the var keyword. If you display the value of a variable that you have not used previously in the program, JavaScript displays the term, undefined.

Extracting the System Date

The next step is to display the date as shown in Figure 1-1a on page J 1.6. Web developers use the built-in Date() object to manipulate the current system date and time by creating a new object instance. The *new* keyword creates the new object instance

var variable = new object

where object is a JavaScript built-in object. A **built-in object** is a JavaScript object that is not dependent on nor belongs to another object, such as the document or window.

The parentheses after the Date() means you can obtain the current system date and time, or pass a specific date to the new object instance. By placing a specific date between the parentheses, the variable stores that date. For example,

```
var birthDay = Date("Jul, 13, 1975")
```

returns July 13, 1975 to birthDay.
Whereas, the statement

```
var curDate = new Date()
```

returns the current system date and time information as a string as follows:

Fri Jul 13 08:41:44 Central Daylight Time 2001

To extract just the date from the object instance (curDate), you use the toLocaleString and substring() methods as described in Table 1-4.

Table 1-4

METHOD	EXPLANATION (In the examples below, assume the Date () object is nDate).
toLocaleString()	Converts nDate to a string using the default display format used by the user's computer. Use: var tempDate = nDate.toLocaleString() Result: the date and time as MM/DD/YYYY HH:MM:SS (Windows format) assigned to tempDate
substring(x,y)	Any object may use the substring() method. The method extracts the date only from the Date() object. Use: var todaysDate = tempDate.substring(0,10) Result: the date as MM/DD/YYYY assigned to todaysDate

To extract the current system date and use it in the format as MM/DD/YYYY, you write the following statements:

```
var tNow = new Date()
var tlocDate = tNow.toLocaleString()
var tDate = tlocDate.substring(0,10)
```

The first statement defines the new object for the date as tNow, which contains the day of the week, the month, day, time (in European time), the time zone, and the year as described earlier. The second statement uses the toLocaleString() method to extract the date and time and store it in tlocDate in the MM/DD/YYYY MM:HH:SS format. The third statement extracts only the date portion from the tlocDate variable.

The substring() method needs two parameters (x,y), where x is the starting point of the string and y is the location of the last character needed. Calculating these positions can be tricky because JavaScript uses relative addressing. **Relative addressing** means the location of any character in a string is calculated in relation to the first character in the string. Because the system identifies the first location address as zero (0), the first character position of a string is position 0. So in the string of data "MM/DD/YY HH:MM:SS" the first M is position 0. The last character you want is the second Y, which is at relative position 7 (Table 1-5). The substring() method, however, requires you to state the last position as one character more than the actual last position. Thus, 7 + 1 equals 8. The substring() method parameters are (0,8) for the first digit of the date and the last digit of the date.

Table 1-5

M	M	/	D	D	/	Y	Y		H	H	:	M	M	:	S	S
0	1	2	3	4	5	6	7	8	9	10	11	12	13	14	15	16

Perform the steps on the next page to activate Notepad and enter the JavaScript code that will extract the current system date from the computer using the Date() object.

The System Date

The way the system date displays in Netscape Navigator is different from the way the system date displays in Internet Explorer. Netscape extracts the date in the MM/DD/YY format. In Internet Explorer, the substring() method used to extract just the date is substring(0,8) not substring(0,10). The system date in Internet Explorer returns a string similar to Fri Jul 13 08:41:44 CDT 2001.

Extracting the System Date

Because of the difference in how Netscape Navigator and Internet Explorer return the system date, you always must check your relative addressing used in the substring() method.

To Extract the Current System Date Using the Date() Object

1 **Click the Notepad button on the taskbar to activate the Notepad window. Position the insertion point on line 19 beneath the document.bgColor= "blanchedalmond" statement.**

The Notepad window and the funwithphonics.htm file display (Figure 1-17).

line 19

```
funwithphonics.htm - Notepad
File  Edit  Search  Help
<HTML>
<HEAD>
      <TITLE>Fun with Phonics</TITLE>

</HEAD>
<BODY>
<CENTER><IMG SRC="fun.jpg" HSPACE=5 VSPACE=5 HEIGHT=64 WIDTH=129></CENTER>

<CENTER><HR Width="75%"></CENTER>
<SCRIPT LANGUAGE="JAVASCRIPT">
<!--Hide from old browsers
     document.bgColor="red"
     document.bgColor="white"
     document.bgColor="blue"
     document.bgColor="white"
     document.bgColor="green"
     document.bgColor="white"
     document.bgColor="blanchedalmond"

//-->
</SCRIPT>

</BODY>
</HTML>
```

depressed Notepad button

Start | funwithphonics.htm - ... | 9:55 AM

FIGURE 1-17

2 **Type** `var tNow = new Date()` **and then press the ENTER key. Type** `var tlocDate = tNow.toLocaleString()` **and then press the ENTER key. Type** `var tDate = tlocDate.substring (0,10)` **and then press the ENTER key.**

The three lines display (Figure 1-18).

```
funwithphonics.htm - Notepad
File  Edit  Search  Help
<HTML>
<HEAD>
      <TITLE>Fun with Phonics</TITLE>

</HEAD>
<BODY>
<CENTER><IMG SRC="fun.jpg" HSPACE=5 VSPACE=5 HEIGHT=64 WIDTH=129></CENTER>

<CENTER><HR Width="75%"></CENTER>
<SCRIPT LANGUAGE="JAVASCRIPT">
<!--Hide from old browsers
     document.bgColor="red"
     document.bgColor="white"
     document.bgColor="blue"
     document.bgColor="white"
     document.bgColor="green"
     document.bgColor="white"
     document.bgColor="blanchedalmond"
     var tNow = new Date()
     var tlocDate = tNow.toLocaleString()
     var tDate = tlocDate.substring(0,10)

//-->
</SCRIPT>
```

extracts the current system date

FIGURE 1-18

The three statements extract the current system date in the desired format. For example, if the system date is Fri Jul 13 08:41:44 Central Daylight Time 2001, then the system assigns tDate the date 7/13/01.

Displaying the Current System Date

You write directly to the Web page using the write() or writeln() methods. The general forms of the write() and writeln() methods are shown in Table 1-6.

Table 1-6 – write() and writeln() Method

General form:	document.write(message) document.writeln(message)
Comment:	where message is any combination of text variables, and HTML tags.
Examples:	document.write("<H1><CENTER>Welcome to our Web page</CENTER> </H1> ") document.writeln("Welcome to our Web page")

The only difference between write() and writeln() is that writeln() displays each message parameter on a new line. To display the contents of a variable with a text string, you concatenate the text and the variable. **Concatenate** means to join or link together. The symbol for concatenate is the plus sign (+). In this project, to display a simple welcome message with the current date, you write

```
document.write("<H2><CENTER>Welcome, today is "+tDate+"</CENTER></H2>")
```

You enclose the HTML codes in quotation marks within the message text. The plus signs (+) concatenate the tDate variable with the message and the ending HTML codes. The message and HTML codes within parentheses are enclosed in quotation marks. The variable name is not enclosed in quotation marks.

Perform the following step to display the current system date in the initial greeting.

writeln()

You can accomplish the same effect by inserting <P> or <BR> tags in the write() method.

To Display the Current System Date in the Initial Greeting

1 Position the insertion point on line 22. Type `document.write("<H2><CENTER>Welcome, today is "+tDate+"</CENTER></H2>")` **and then press the ENTER key.**

Figure 1-19 shows the embedded HTML code, which writes the date in heading 2 style and centers it on the page. You concantenate the tDate variable with the message to display within the string.

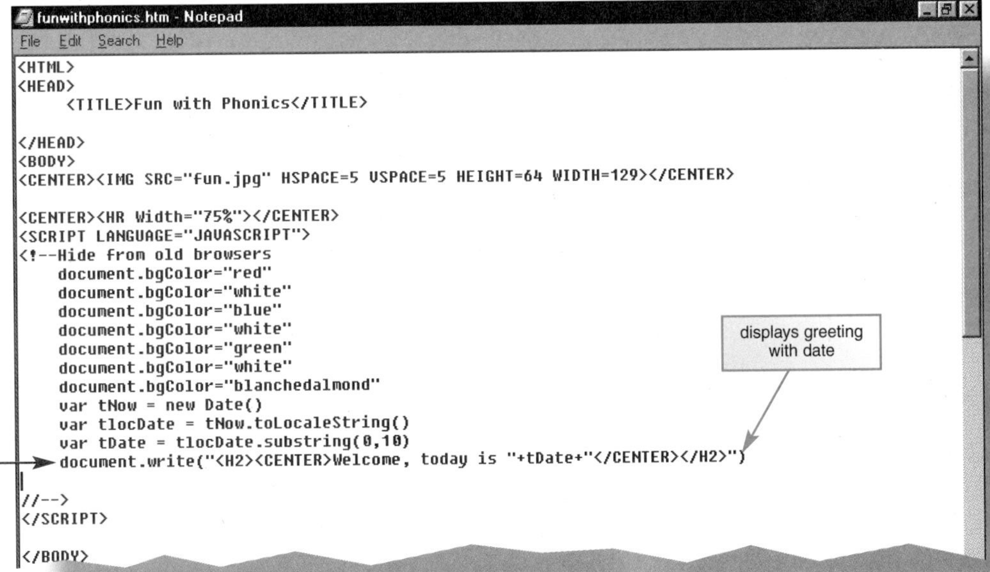
funwithphonics.htm - Notepad
File Edit Search Help
<HTML>
<HEAD>
<TITLE>Fun with Phonics</TITLE>
</HEAD>
<BODY>
<CENTER><IMG SRC="fun.jpg" HSPACE=5 VSPACE=5 HEIGHT=64 WIDTH=129></CENTER>
<CENTER><HR Width="75%"></CENTER>
<SCRIPT LANGUAGE="JAVASCRIPT">
<!--Hide from old browsers
document.bgColor="red"
document.bgColor="white"
document.bgColor="blue"
document.bgColor="white"
document.bgColor="green"
document.bgColor="white"
document.bgColor="blanchedalmond"
var tNow = new Date()
var tlocDate = tNow.toLocaleString()
var tDate = tlocDate.substring(0,10)
document.write("<H2><CENTER>Welcome, today is "+tDate+"</CENTER></H2>")
//-->
</SCRIPT>
</BODY>
displays greeting with date
line 22

FIGURE 1-19

Using Several Variables to Construct a Message

The next step is to incorporate the message that displays following the date (Figure 1-1a on page J 1.6). Older browsers have a limit of 255 characters to a line. Thus, it is recommended that you break up large groups of text by using several variables to construct a message. Perform the following steps to construct a long message using several JavaScript variables.

TO CONSTRUCT A MESSAGE USING SEVERAL VARIABLES

1. Position the insertion point on line 23. Type var intro1 = "Hi, thanks for visiting our Web site, but we have moved. Please make a note " and then press the ENTER key.
2. Type var intro2 = "of our new URL (www.funphonics.com) and notify the Webmaster about our new " and then press the ENTER key.
3. Type var intro3 = "location. Click<A Href='http://www.scsite.com/'> here </A> or wait 15 seconds " and then press the ENTER key.
4. Type var intro4 = "to be moved automatically to our new site." and then press the ENTER key.
5. Type var introMsg = intro1+intro2+intro3+intro4 and then press the ENTER key.

The four variables store several lines of text. Make sure you place a space before the closing quotation mark in the first three lines. Note the embedded HTML codes in intro3 for the new Web site reference. Also, when placing quotation marks inside of quotation marks use single quotation marks as in the intro3 variable. The five lines of code display (Figure 1-20).

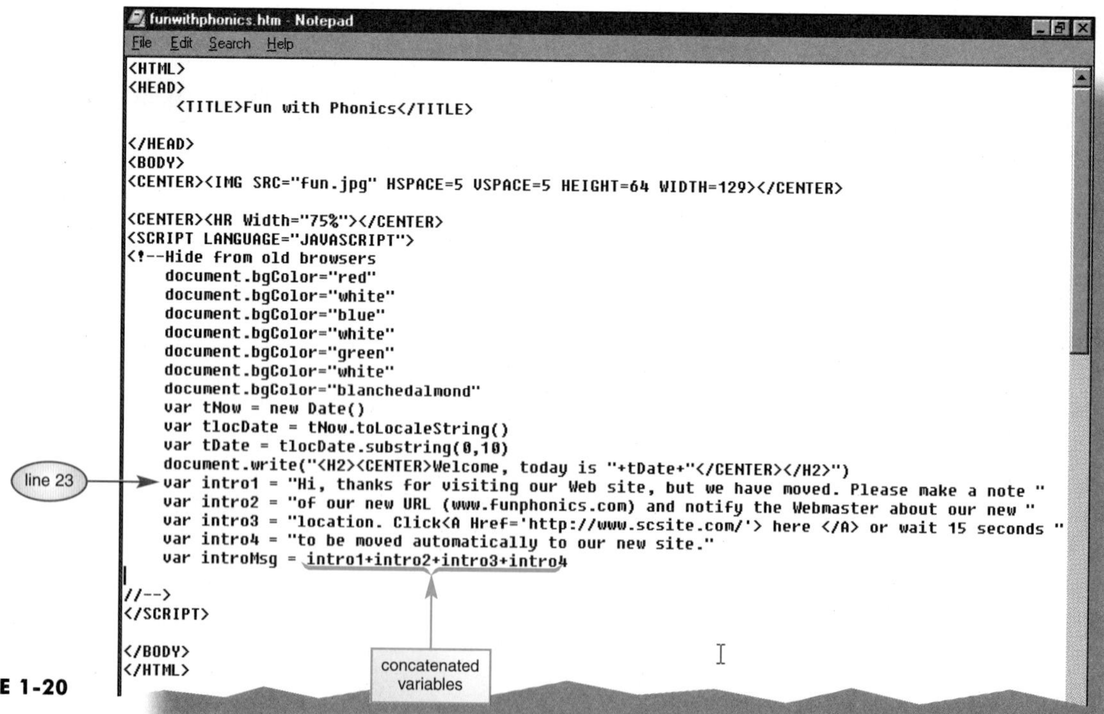

```
funwithphonics.htm - Notepad
File  Edit  Search  Help
<HTML>
<HEAD>
     <TITLE>Fun with Phonics</TITLE>

</HEAD>
<BODY>
<CENTER><IMG SRC="fun.jpg" HSPACE=5 VSPACE=5 HEIGHT=64 WIDTH=129></CENTER>

<CENTER><HR Width="75%"></CENTER>
<SCRIPT LANGUAGE="JAVASCRIPT">
<!--Hide from old browsers
    document.bgColor="red"
    document.bgColor="white"
    document.bgColor="blue"
    document.bgColor="white"
    document.bgColor="green"
    document.bgColor="white"
    document.bgColor="blanchedalmond"
    var tNow = new Date()
    var tlocDate = tNow.toLocaleString()
    var tDate = tlocDate.substring(0,10)
    document.write("<H2><CENTER>Welcome, today is "+tDate+"</CENTER></H2>")
    var intro1 = "Hi, thanks for visiting our Web site, but we have moved. Please make a note "
    var intro2 = "of our new URL (www.funphonics.com) and notify the Webmaster about our new "
    var intro3 = "location. Click<A Href='http://www.scsite.com/'> here </A> or wait 15 seconds "
    var intro4 = "to be moved automatically to our new site."
    var introMsg = intro1+intro2+intro3+intro4

//-->
</SCRIPT>

</BODY>
</HTML>
```


FIGURE 1-20

The last statement concatenates the four separate message variables into one message, which creates one continuous string of text. You need not worry about the length of the message.

Writing the Message on the Web Page

To display the message as part of the Web page, you use the write() method. Use the heading 4 style and the font color firebrick to format the line. Perform the following step to write the message on the Web page.

To Write the Message on the Web Page

Position the insertion point on line 28. Type `document.write("<H4><FONT Color='firebrick'>"+introMsg+"</H4></FONT>")` **and then press the ENTER key.**

The document.write statement will display the combined message variable in a continuous sequence as if it was written as one long string of characters. Figure 1-21 shows the placement of the command and how the HTML codes are used.

```
funwithphonics.htm - Notepad
File  Edit  Search  Help
<HTML>
<HEAD>
     <TITLE>Fun with Phonics</TITLE>

</HEAD>
<BODY>
<CENTER><IMG SRC="fun.jpg" HSPACE=5 VSPACE=5 HEIGHT=64 WIDTH=129></CENTER>

<CENTER><HR Width="75%"></CENTER>
<SCRIPT LANGUAGE="JAVASCRIPT">
<!--Hide from old browsers
    document.bgColor="red"
    document.bgColor="white"
    document.bgColor="blue"
    document.bgColor="white"
    document.bgColor="green"
    document.bgColor="white"
    document.bgColor="blanchedalmond"
    var tNow = new Date()
    var tlocDate = tNow.toLocaleString()
    var tDate = tlocDate.substring(0,10)
    document.write("<H2><CENTER>Welcome, today is "+tDate+"</CENTER></H2>")
    var intro1 = "Hi, thanks for visiting our Web site, but we have moved. Please make a note "
    var intro2 = "of our new URL (www.funphonics.com) and notify the Webmaster about our new "
    var intro3 = "location. Click<A Href='http://www.scsite.com/'> here </A> or wait 15 seconds "
    var intro4 = "to be moved automatically to our new site."
    var introMsg = intro1+intro2+intro3+intro4
    document.write("<H4><FONT Color='firebrick'>"+introMsg+"</H4></FONT>")

//-->
</SCRIPT>

</BODY>
</HTML>
```

line 28

JavaScript code to display message

Start | funwithphonics.htm - ... | Fun with Phonics - Microso... | 9:57 AM

FIGURE 1-21

The one document.write() statement on line 28 displays a short paragraph formatted in the font size and color you desire. When displaying text on the Web page using this concatenation technique, you can use just one set of beginning and ending HTML formatting codes.

Save and Test the Web Page

At this point, you should test the JavaScript code. Check your code for spelling errors, missing quotation marks, or parentheses. After you check for errors, save the file on the floppy disk in drive A, activate the browser, and then click the Refresh button. Perform the following steps to save the HTML file on the floppy disk in drive A.

Steps To Save a File

1 Make sure the JavaScript Data Disk is in drive A.

2 Click File on the menu bar and then click the Save command.

No dialog box displays (Figure 1-22). The file is saved using the same file name, funwithphonics.htm.

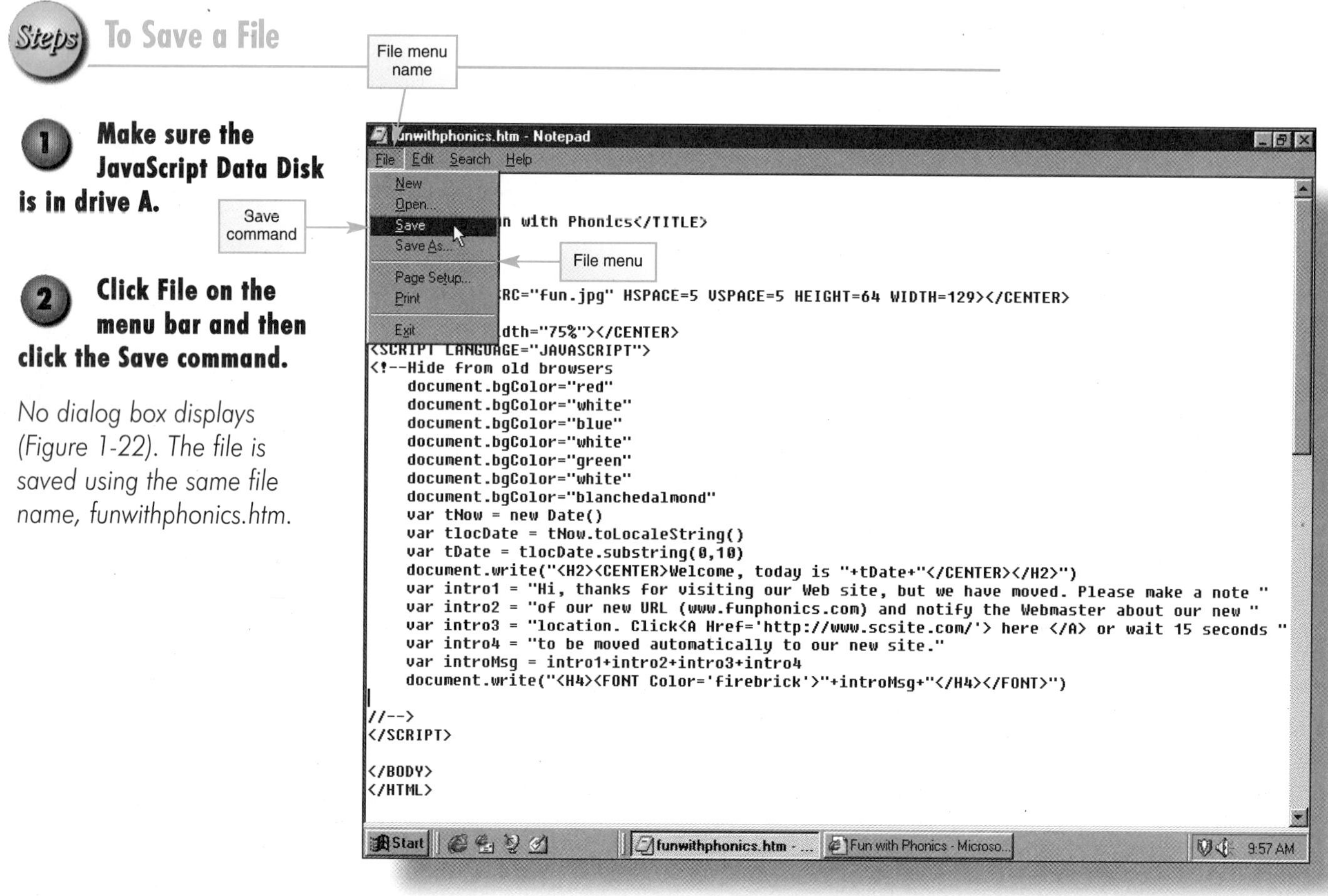
File menu name
Save command
File menu
funwithphonics.htm - Notepad
File Edit Search Help
New
Open...
Save
Save As...
Page Setup...
Print
Exit
n with Phonics</TITLE>
RC="fun.jpg" HSPACE=5 VSPACE=5 HEIGHT=64 WIDTH=129></CENTER>
dth="75%"></CENTER>
<SCRIPT LANGUAGE="JAVASCRIPT">
<!--Hide from old browsers
document.bgColor="red"
document.bgColor="white"
document.bgColor="blue"
document.bgColor="white"
document.bgColor="green"
document.bgColor="white"
document.bgColor="blanchedalmond"
var tNow = new Date()
var tlocDate = tNow.toLocaleString()
var tDate = tlocDate.substring(0,10)
document.write("<H2><CENTER>Welcome, today is "+tDate+"</CENTER></H2>")
var intro1 = "Hi, thanks for visiting our Web site, but we have moved. Please make a note "
var intro2 = "of our new URL (www.funphonics.com) and notify the Webmaster about our new "
var intro3 = "location. Click<A Href='http://www.scsite.com/'> here </A> or wait 15 seconds "
var intro4 = "to be moved automatically to our new site."
var introMsg = intro1+intro2+intro3+intro4
document.write("<H4><FONT Color='firebrick'>"+introMsg+"</H4></FONT>")
//-->
</SCRIPT>
</BODY>
</HTML>
Start
funwithphonics.htm - ...
Fun with Phonics - Microso...
9:57 AM

FIGURE 1-22

Other Ways

1. Press ALT+F, S

To test the Web page in the browser, perform the following step.

To Test the Web Page in the Browser

1 Click the Fun with Phonics button on the taskbar to activate the browser. Click the Refresh button.

The Fun with Phonics Web page displays (Figure 1-23). The browser is the active window. Clicking the Refresh button, reloads the current Web page.

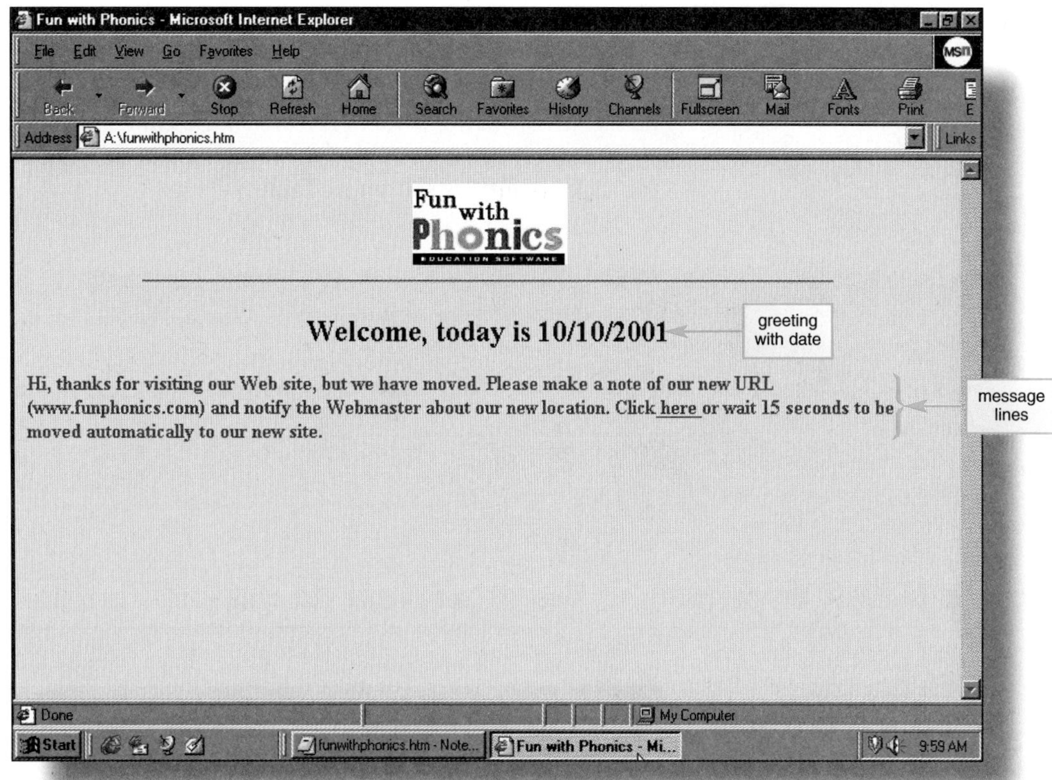

FIGURE 1-23

If the browser does not display the Web page correctly, close any error message, and then click the Notepad button on the taskbar. Check the JavaScript code against Figure 1-21 on page J 1.25. Correct any errors and save the file. Activate the browser and click the Refresh button.

After the test is complete, perform the following step to activate the Notepad window.

TO ACTIVATE THE NOTEPAD WINDOW

Click the Notepad button on the taskbar to activate the Notepad window.

Notepad becomes the active window on the desktop. You can continue to edit the Notepad file.

setTimeout()

To learn more about the setTimeout() method, visit www.scsite.com/js/p1.htm and then click setTimeout. At the Netscape site, locate the Navigator JavaScript reference and then click setTimeout.

Calling a JavaScript Function

JavaScript has two basic methods to call functions. One method to call functions is to use event handlers and object methods. The other method is to code the function name in a JavaScript section at the logical point of execution. The user-defined function you will write in this project will be called from the setTimeout() method. The setTimeout() causes a delay before an instruction is executed. The general form of the setTimeout() is shown in Table 1-7.

Table 1-7 – setTimeout() Method

General form:	setTimeout("instruction", time delay in milliseconds)
Comment:	where instruction is any valid JavaScript statement, and time delay is expressed in number of milliseconds
Example:	`setTimeout("chngSite()", 15000)`

The user-defined function, chngSite(), executes in 15 seconds (time delay). Fifteen seconds is written as 15000 milliseconds. The next step is to write the setTimeout() method that will execute the chngSite() function, which will be written later.

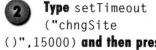

To Write the setTimeout() Method to Execute the chngSite() Function

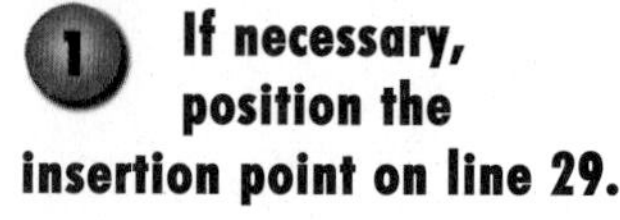

1. **If necessary, position the insertion point on line 29.**

2. **Type** `setTimeout("chngSite()",15000)` **and then press the ENTER key.**

The setTimeout method waits 15 seconds (15 x 1000 milliseconds) and then calls the chngSite() function (Figure 1-24). The chngSite() function will be added to the HEAD section later.

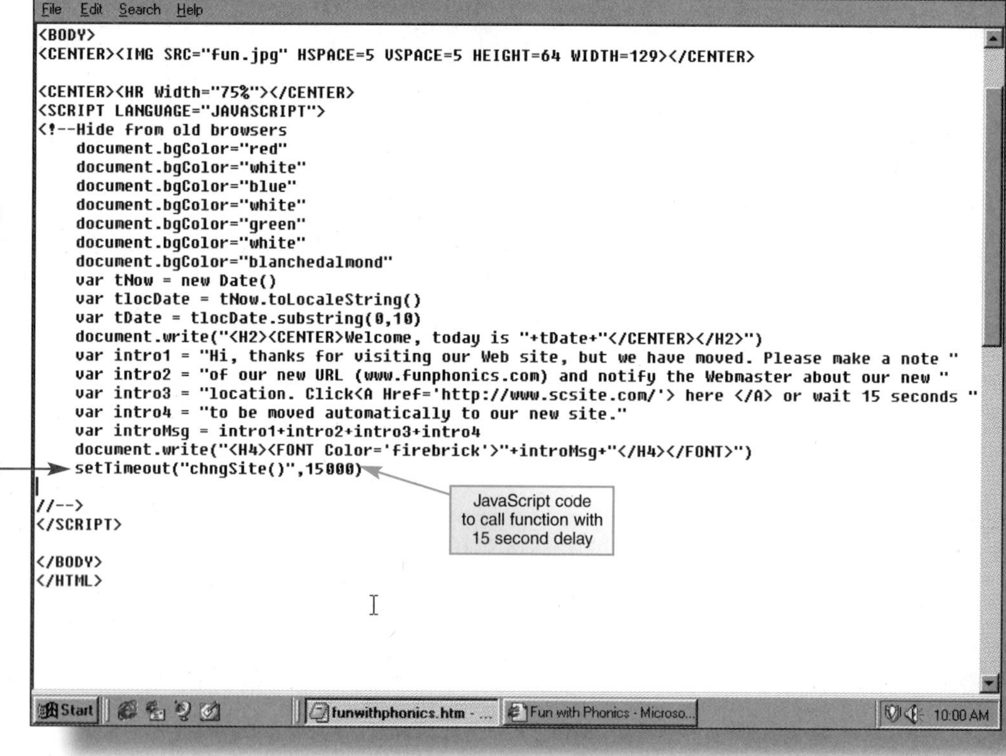
funwithphonics.htm - Notepad
File Edit Search Help
<BODY>
<CENTER><IMG SRC="fun.jpg" HSPACE=5 VSPACE=5 HEIGHT=64 WIDTH=129></CENTER>
<CENTER><HR Width="75%"></CENTER>
<SCRIPT LANGUAGE="JAVASCRIPT">
<!--Hide from old browsers
document.bgColor="red"
document.bgColor="white"
document.bgColor="blue"
document.bgColor="white"
document.bgColor="green"
document.bgColor="white"
document.bgColor="blanchedalmond"
var tNow = new Date()
var tlocDate = tNow.toLocaleString()
var tDate = tlocDate.substring(0,10)
document.write("<H2><CENTER>Welcome, today is "+tDate+"</CENTER></H2>")
var intro1 = "Hi, thanks for visiting our Web site, but we have moved. Please make a note "
var intro2 = "of our new URL (www.funphonics.com) and notify the Webmaster about our new "
var intro3 = "location. Click<A Href='http://www.scsite.com/'> here </A> or wait 15 seconds "
var intro4 = "to be moved automatically to our new site."
var introMsg = intro1+intro2+intro3+intro4
document.write("<H4><FONT Color='firebrick'>"+introMsg+"</H4></FONT>")
setTimeout("chngSite()",15000)
//-->
</SCRIPT>
</BODY>
</HTML>
line 29
JavaScript code to call function with 15 second delay
Start
funwithphonics.htm - ...
Fun with Phonics - Microso...
10:00 AM

FIGURE 1-24

Be careful about the amount of time you give users to read a page that is transfering them to another page.

Displaying the Last Modified Document Date

Most developers agree that you should display the date the Web page was last modified. The message displays at the bottom of the page, written with a small font to keep the message from distracting the user (Figure 1-1a on page J 1.6). JavaScript provides an easy way to display the date. The command is document.lastModified. You insert this command in a write() method with a message as follows:

```
document.write("<BR><H4><CENTER>This document was last modified
"+document.lastModified+"</CENTER></H4>")
```

Perform the following step to display the date last modified in a message.

To Display the Date Last Modified in a Message

1 **If necessary, position the insertion point on line 30, after the setTimeout() method. Type** `document.write("<BR><H4><CENTER>This document was last modified "+document.lastModified+"</CENTER></H4>")` **and then press the ENTER key.**

The lastModified property displays the date and time the file was saved on disk (Figure 1-25).

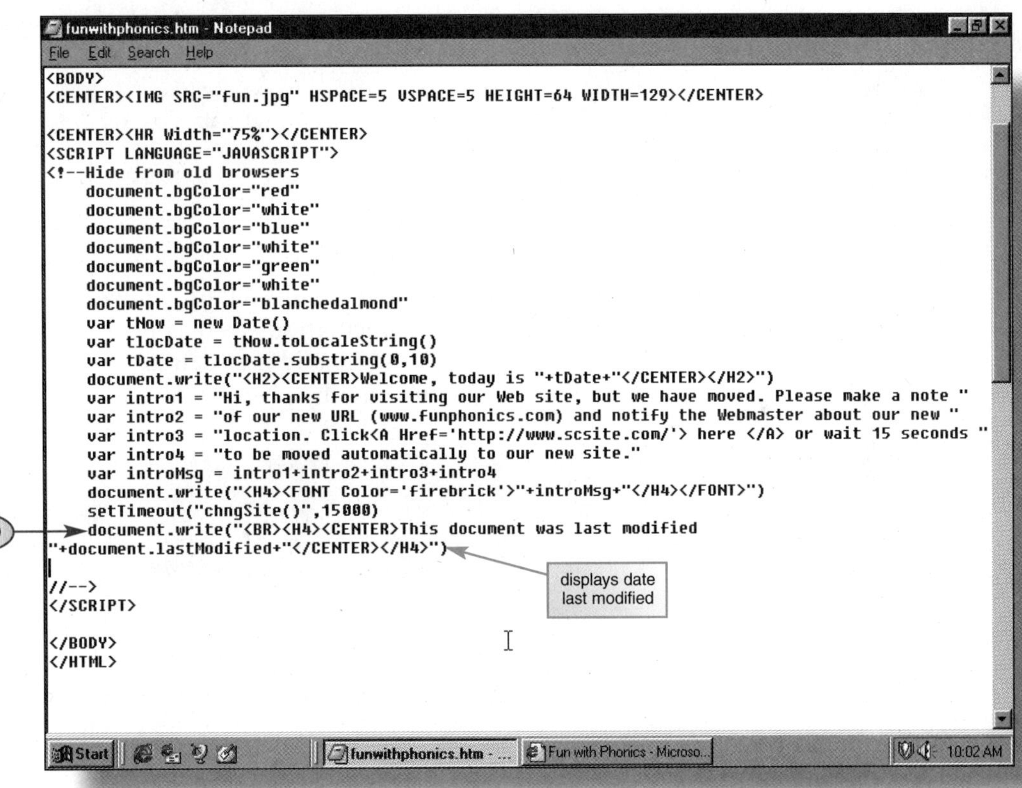
funwithphonics.htm - Notepad
File Edit Search Help
<BODY>
<CENTER><IMG SRC="fun.jpg" HSPACE=5 VSPACE=5 HEIGHT=64 WIDTH=129></CENTER>
<CENTER><HR Width="75%"></CENTER>
<SCRIPT LANGUAGE="JAVASCRIPT">
<!--Hide from old browsers
document.bgColor="red"
document.bgColor="white"
document.bgColor="blue"
document.bgColor="white"
document.bgColor="green"
document.bgColor="white"
document.bgColor="blanchedalmond"
var tNow = new Date()
var tlocDate = tNow.toLocaleString()
var tDate = tlocDate.substring(0,10)
document.write("<H2><CENTER>Welcome, today is "+tDate+"</CENTER></H2>")
var intro1 = "Hi, thanks for visiting our Web site, but we have moved. Please make a note "
var intro2 = "of our new URL (www.funphonics.com) and notify the Webmaster about our new "
var intro3 = "location. Click<A Href='http://www.scsite.com/'> here </A> or wait 15 seconds "
var intro4 = "to be moved automatically to our new site."
var introMsg = intro1+intro2+intro3+intro4
document.write("<H4><FONT Color='firebrick'>"+introMsg+"</H4></FONT>")
setTimeout("chngSite()",15000)
document.write("
<H4><CENTER>This document was last modified
"+document.lastModified+"</CENTER></H4>")
//-->
</SCRIPT>
</BODY>
</HTML>
line 30
displays date last modified
Start
funwithphonics.htm - ...
Fun with Phonics - Microso...
10:02 AM

FIGURE 1-25

Writing a JavaScript User-Defined Function

A **function** is JavaScript code that is written to perform certain tasks repeatedly. JavaScript comes with a number of built-in functions (Table 1-8 on the next page). Most of these functions actually belong to the Window object, but because the Window object is assumed, they are called built-in functions.

Table 1-8

FUNCTION	EXPLANATION
close()	closes an open window
open()	opens a new window
print()	prints the contents of the window
setTimeout()	causes a script to be executed after a time delay
stop()	stops a download (same as clicking the Stop button)

A **user-defined function** is one in which the Web developer writes the tasks to be performed. Functions replace large sets of JavaScript codes that are not able to fit within an HTML attribute. Most functions are associated with JavaScript event handlers, but can be written in any JavaScript section.

A function can have data passed to it, which is processed and a result is returned. This feature allows for flexibility in screen displays and interaction with the user. The code in the function is not executed until a JavaScript statement calls the function. To **call** a function means to have JavaScript execute the function.

The general form of a user-defined function is shown in Table 1-9.

Functions

To learn more about JavaScript user-defined functions, visit ww.scsite.com/js/p1.htm and then click functions. At the Netscape site, scroll down the left frame until you find the section on Object Model and then click Functions.

Table 1-9 – User-Defined Function

General form:	function FunctionName() {
	JavaScript code
	}

Comment:	where FunctionName is the name of the user-defined function, and JavaScript code is the code you want executed when the function is called.

Example:	`Function showBrowserName(){`
	`alert("You are using" + navigator.appName)`
	`}`

Naming conventions for functions are similar to those of variables. A function name must begin with a letter, may contain numerals and the underscore, but may not contain any spaces, punctuation (such as periods or commas), or reserved words. Table 1-10 shows valid and invalid user-defined function names. Values or parameters are passed to the function by placing a variable name between the parentheses.

Table 1-10

VALID FUNCTION NAMES	INVALID FUNCTION NAMES	REASON
verifyForm()	3Ddisplay()	starts with number
get_Cookie()	make.cookie	no periods allowed
calcPayment()	calc payment	space in middle of name
popWind()	pop-upWindow	no hyphens in name

The function you need to write in this project is called chngSite() and is written as shown below:

```
function chngSite() {
      alert("You are about to be transported to the new site location!")
      location = "http://www.scsite.com/"
}
```

The built-in alert() function displays a message notifying the viewer of the link. The alert dialog box displays. The user must click a button in the dialog box to continue. Table 1-11 describes other functions that use dialog boxes. Following the alert() function, the location statement executes the link to the new Web site.

Table 1-11

PROMPT AND CONFIRM DIALOG BOXES	
Prompt()	
Purpose:	To prompt the user for input
Use:	var response = prompt("What is your name?")
Explanation:	A dialog box displays with a text box, and an OK and Cancel button. The prompt displays above the text box, the user types in the text box, and then clicks OK or Cancel. OK returns the value in the text box to the variable response.
Confirm()	
Purpose:	To prompt the user for a yes, no answer.
Use:	var makeItSo = confirm("Do you really want to open another window?")
Explanation:	A dialog box displays the prompt, and an OK and Cancel button. If the user clicks OK, then a True value is returned to makeItSo. If the user clicks the Cancel button, a False value is returned to makeItSo.

Placing User-Defined Functions in the HEAD Section

Where you place the user-defined functions is important. Most Web developers agree the HEAD section is where to place user-defined functions. The main reason functions are placed in the HEAD section of the HTML code is the function must be defined and loaded into memory before it can be called by the other JavaScript code or event handlers. If the user accidentally executes an event handler as the page is loaded, and the event handler is associated with a function not yet defined, the action will generate an error.

Complete the following steps to enter the chngSite() user-defined function in the HEAD section.

To Enter the chngSite() User-Defined Function in the HEAD Section

1 Position the insertion point on the blank line (line 4) between the TITLE tags and the closing </HEAD> tag. Type `<SCRIPT LANGUAGE="JAVASCRIPT">` **and then press the ENTER key. Type** `<!--Hide from old browsers` **and then press the ENTER key (Figure 1-26).**

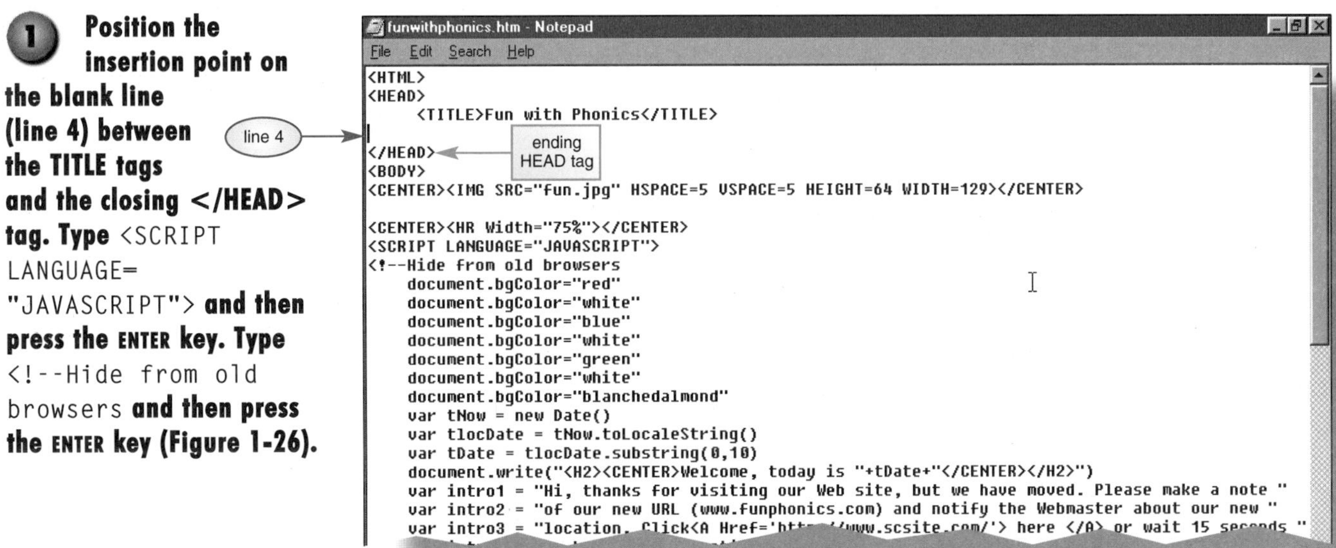
funwithphonics.htm - Notepad
File Edit Search Help
line 4
ending HEAD tag
<HTML>
<HEAD>
<TITLE>Fun with Phonics</TITLE>
</HEAD>
<BODY>
<CENTER><IMG SRC="fun.jpg" HSPACE=5 VSPACE=5 HEIGHT=64 WIDTH=129></CENTER>
<CENTER><HR Width="75%"></CENTER>
<SCRIPT LANGUAGE="JAVASCRIPT">
<!--Hide from old browsers
document.bgColor="red"
document.bgColor="white"
document.bgColor="blue"
document.bgColor="white"
document.bgColor="green"
document.bgColor="white"
document.bgColor="blanchedalmond"
var tNow = new Date()
var tlocDate = tNow.toLocaleString()
var tDate = tlocDate.substring(0,10)
document.write("<H2><CENTER>Welcome, today is "+tDate+"</CENTER></H2>")
var intro1 = "Hi, thanks for visiting our Web site, but we have moved. Please make a note "
var intro2 = "of our new URL (www.funphonics.com) and notify the Webmaster about our new "

FIGURE 1-26

2 **Type** `function chngSite() {` **and then press the ENTER key. Type** `alert("You are about to be transported to the new site location!")` **and then press the ENTER key. Type** `location = "http://www.scsite.com/"` **and then press the ENTER key. Type** `}` **and then press the ENTER key. Type** `//-->` **and then press the ENTER key. Type** `</SCRIPT>` **and then press the ENTER key.**

The chngSite() user-defined function displays (Figure 1-27).

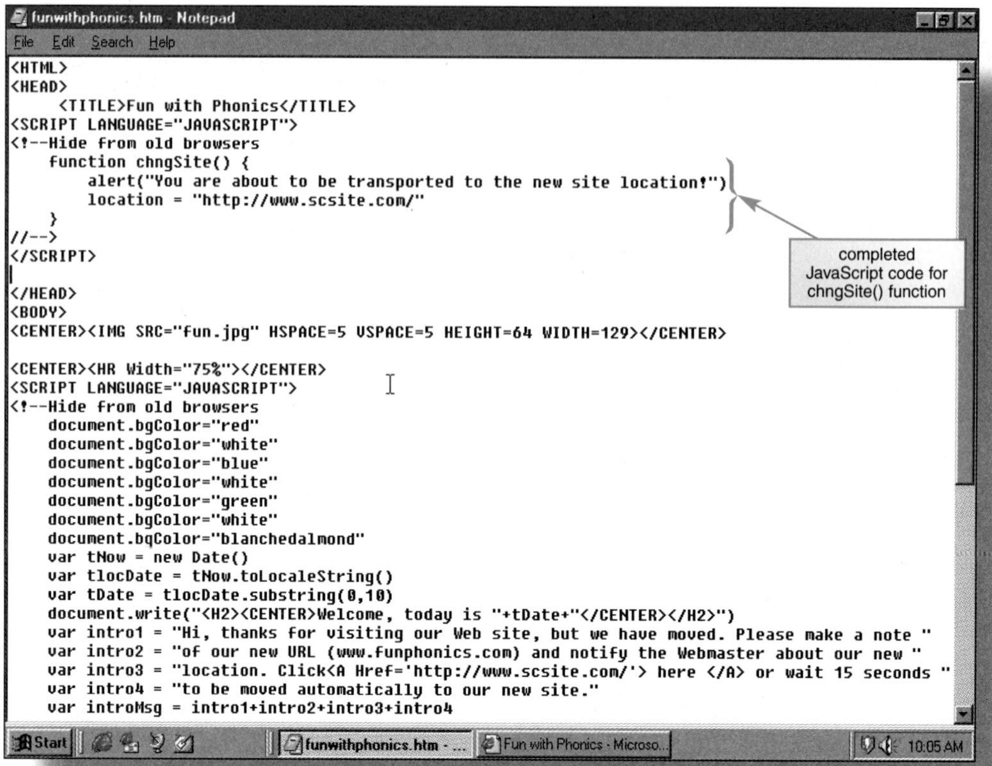

```
<HTML>
<HEAD>
    <TITLE>Fun with Phonics</TITLE>
<SCRIPT LANGUAGE="JAVASCRIPT">
<!--Hide from old browsers
    function chngSite() {
        alert("You are about to be transported to the new site location!")
        location = "http://www.scsite.com/"
    }
//-->
</SCRIPT>

</HEAD>
<BODY>
<CENTER><IMG SRC="fun.jpg" HSPACE=5 VSPACE=5 HEIGHT=64 WIDTH=129></CENTER>

<CENTER><HR Width="75%"></CENTER>
<SCRIPT LANGUAGE="JAVASCRIPT">
<!--Hide from old browsers
    document.bgColor="red"
    document.bgColor="white"
    document.bgColor="blue"
    document.bgColor="white"
    document.bgColor="green"
    document.bgColor="white"
    document.bgColor="blanchedalmond"
    var tNow = new Date()
    var tlocDate = tNow.toLocaleString()
    var tDate = tlocDate.substring(0,10)
    document.write("<H2><CENTER>Welcome, today is "+tDate+"</CENTER></H2>")
    var intro1 = "Hi, thanks for visiting our Web site, but we have moved. Please make a note "
    var intro2 = "of our new URL (www.funphonics.com) and notify the Webmaster about our new "
    var intro3 = "location. Click<A Href='http://www.scsite.com/'> here </A> or wait 15 seconds "
    var intro4 = "to be moved automatically to our new site."
    var introMsg = intro1+intro2+intro3+intro4
```

funwithphonics.htm - Notepad

File Edit Search Help

completed JavaScript code for chngSite() function

Start | funwithphonics.htm - ... | Fun with Phonics - Microso... | 10:05 AM

FIGURE 1-27

The HEAD section contains the user-defined functions, which are called by other JavaScript code or from the embedded event handlers in the HTML tags. This function is called by the setTimeout() method in the BODY section. At this point, save the HTML file and test the Web page.

TO SAVE THE FILE ON THE FLOPPY DISK

1. Make sure the JavaScript Data Disk is in drive A. Click File on the menu bar.
2. Click Save on the File menu.

TO TEST THE WEB PAGE

1. Click the Fun with Phonics button on the taskbar.
2. Click the Refresh button.

The Web page displays (Figure 1-28a). After 15 seconds, a message displays (Figure 1-28b). You can click the OK button in the dialog box or wait 15 seconds. If you are connected to the Internet, you will be taken to the Shelly Cashman Series site (www.scsite.com). To return to the Web page in Figure 1-28a, click the Back button.

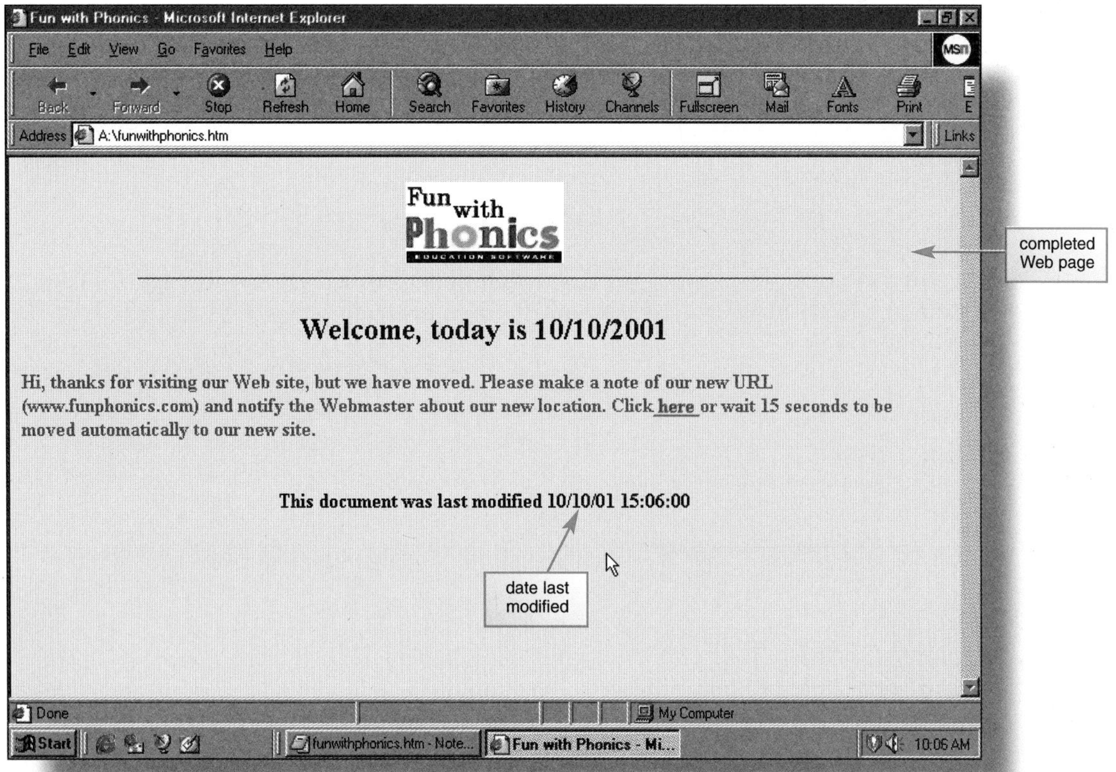

FIGURE 1-28a

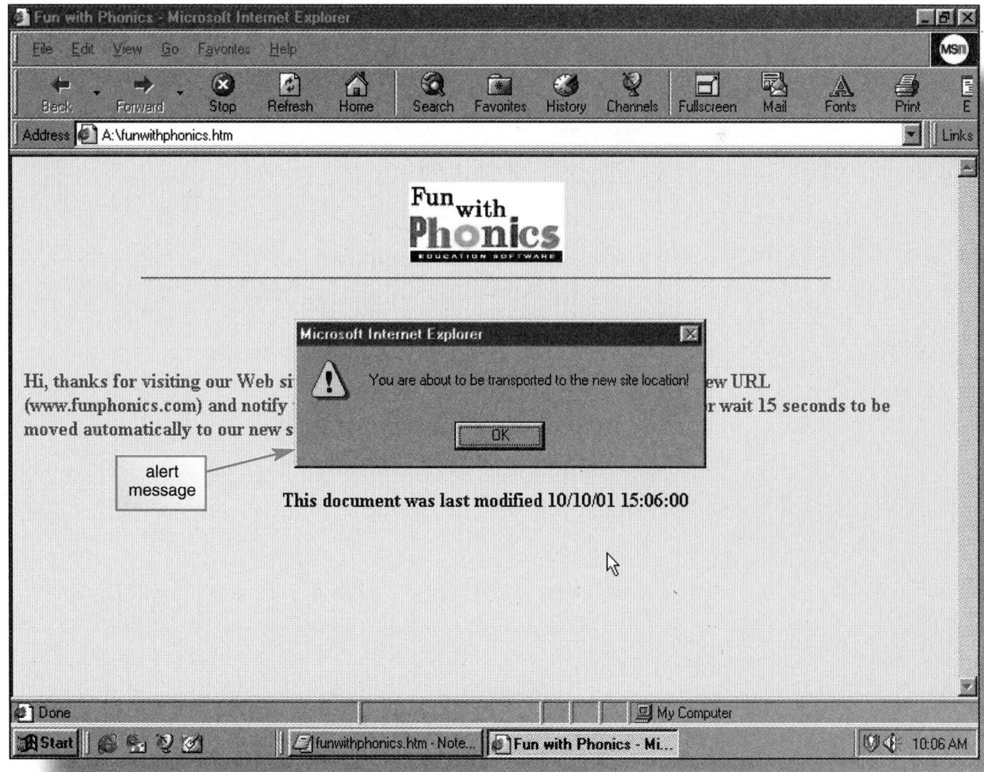

FIGURE 1-28b

If you encounter an error, make sure the variable and function names are consistent. Check the beginning and ending quotation marks on all strings, and the beginning and ending curly braces on the functions. Check that you have beginning and ending parentheses where needed.

Printing the HTML File Using Notepad

After you have completed and tested the Web page, you may want to print it. You can print the HTML file using Notepad. Perform the following steps to print the funwithphonics.htm file.

To Print the HTML File Using Notepad

1 **If necessary, click the Notepad button on the taskbar. Click File on the menu bar and then point to Print (Figure 1-29).**

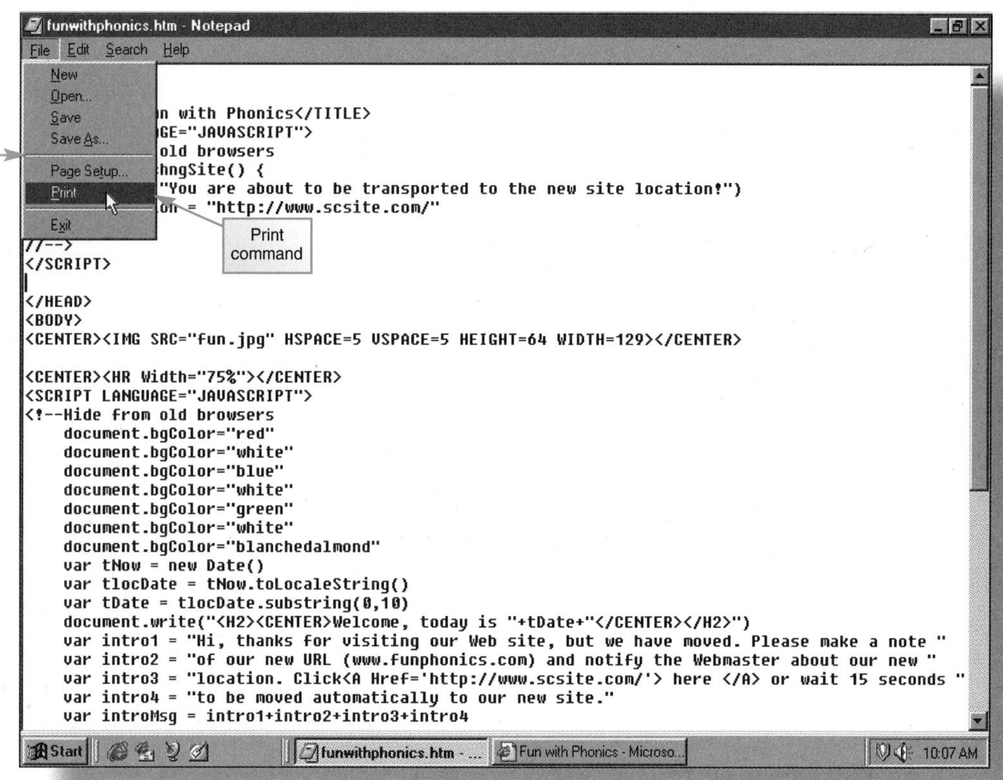

FIGURE 1-29

Click Print

The HTML with the JavaScript code prints (Figure 1-30).

```
funwithphonics.htm

<HTML>
<HEAD>
      <TITLE>Fun with Phonics</TITLE>
<SCRIPT LANGUAGE="JAVASCRIPT">
<!--Hide from old browsers
     function chngSite() {
          alert("You are about to be transported to the new site location!")
          location = "http://www.scsite.com/"
     }
//-->
</SCRIPT>

</HEAD>
<BODY>
<CENTER><IMG SRC="fun.jpg" HSPACE=5 VSPACE=5 HEIGHT=64 WIDTH=129></CENTER>

<CENTER><HR Width="75%"></CENTER>
<SCRIPT LANGUAGE="JAVASCRIPT">
<!--Hide from old browsers
     document.bgColor="red"
     document.bgColor="white"
     document.bgColor="blue"
     document.bgColor="white"
     document.bgColor="green"
     document.bgColor="white"
     document.bgColor="blanchedalmond"
     var tNow = new Date()
     var tlocDate = tNow.toLocaleString()
     var tDate = tlocDate.substring(0,10)
     document.write("<H2><CENTER>Welcome, today is "+tDate+"</CENTER></H2>")
     var intro1 = "Hi, thanks for visiting our Web site, but we have moved.
Please make a note "
     var intro2 = "of our new URL (www.funphonics.com) and notify the Webmaster
about our new "
     var intro3 = "location. Click<A Href='http://www.scsite.com/'> here </A> or
wait 15 seconds "
     var intro4 = "to be moved automatically to our new site."
     var introMsg = intro1+intro2+intro3+intro4
     document.write("<H4><FONT Color='firebrick'>"+introMsg+"</H4></FONT>")
     setTimeout("chngSite()",15000)
     document.write("<BR><H4><CENTER>This document was last modified
"+document.lastModified+"</CENTER></H4>")

//-->
</SCRIPT>

</BODY>
</HTML>

Page 1
```

FIGURE 1-30

Printing with Notepad

You can modify the header and footer in Notepad. Click File on the menu bar and then click Page Setup. In the Page Setup dialog box, type the desired Header and Footer. To learn more about Notepad codes, search Notepad Help for inserting headers and footers.

Project Summary

The Web page created in this project serves as a notice to Fun with Phonics customers indicating that the Web site has moved to a new location. The Web page meets the requirements of the Webmaster, Mandy Senicott. The Web page flickers to get the user's attention, sets the background color, displays a message, and allows the user to link manually to the new site if needed. After 15 seconds, a message notifies the user that the Web page will link automatically to the new site. The link executes when the user clicks the OK button in the message.

In creating this project, you learned how to modify a Web page using the Notepad text editor. You learned how and where to place JavaScript code in an HTML file. In adding the JavaScript code, you learned how to use the document object and write() method. The project introduced the concepts of creating new objects by defining variables. You learned the rules for naming variables. You learned about the Date() object and how to extract only the date from the user's computer system.

You learned how to write a user-defined function that calls the built-in alert function to display a message. You learned how to embed HTML codes within JavaScript code and to format displayed text. Using the setTimeout() method, you learned how to call the user-defined functions. Finally, you learned how to work with Notepad and test the Web page in your browser.

What You Should Know

Having completed this project, you should be able to perform the following tasks:

- Activate the Notepad Window *(J 1.27)*
- Create Flicker on the Web Page *(J 1.13)*
- Construct a Message Using Several Variables *(J 1.24)*
- Display the Current System Date in the Initial Greeting *(J 1.23)*
- Display the Date Last Modified in a Message *(J 1.29)*
- Enter the Beginning SCRIPT Tag and Comment *(J 1.12)*
- Enter the chngSite() User-Defined Function in the HEAD Section *(J 1.31)*
- Enter the Ending SCRIPT Tag *(J 1.16)*
- Extract the Current System Date Using the Date() Object *(J 1.22)*
- Open a Web Page Stored on the Data Disk *(J 1.10)*
- Print the HTML File Using Notepad *(J 1.34)*
- Save a File *(J 1.26)*
- Save the File on the Floppy Disk *(J 1.17, J 1.32)*
- Set the Background Color to a Static Color *(J 1.15)*
- Start Notepad *(J 1.8)*
- Test the Web Page *(J 1.19, J 1.32)*
- Test the Web Page in the Browser *(J 1.27)*
- Write the Message on the Web Page *(J 1.25)*
- Write the setTimeout() Method to Execute the chngSite() Function *(J 1.28)*

Test Your Knowledge

1 True/False

Instructions: Circle T if the statement is true or F if the statement is false.

T F 1. Since 1980, companies have developed and gained substantial marketing edge with e-commerce.
T F 2. Marketing experts will tell you that you have six to seven seconds to attract and retain someone's attention.
T F 3. One of the advantages to JavaScript is the capability to process data immediately on the user's machine.
T F 4. JavaScript cannot work with HTML codes.
T F 5. The SCRIPT tag can have three attributes.
T F 6. The exclamation point (!) is used to indicate HTML comments.
T F 7. To change Web page background colors dynamically, you use the BGCOLOR attribute in the <BODY> tag.
T F 8. You cannot view a Web page created and stored on a floppy disk. It must be posted to a Web server.
T F 9. To display text on the Web page with JavaScript, you use the document.write() object and method.
T F 10. In the setTimeout() method, the number of seconds that should lapse before a command is executed actually is stated in nanoseconds.

2 Multiple Choice

Instructions: Circle the correct response.

1. Marketing experts will tell you that you have __________ seconds to attract and retain someone's attention.
   a. 6 to 7
   b. 8 to 9
   c. 3 to 4
   d. 10 to 12
2. Notepad files have an automatic extension of __________.
   a. .DOC
   b. .HTM
   c. .TXT
   d. .HTML
3. You place JavaScript code in the __________ section(s) of a Web page.
   a. BODY
   b. HEAD and BODY
   c. HEAD
   d. TITLE

(continued)

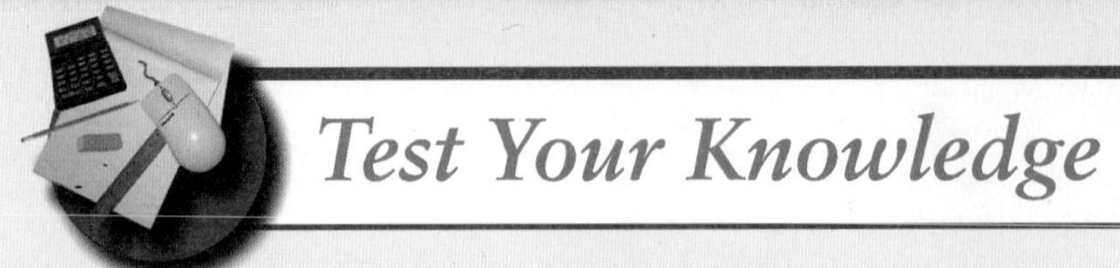

Test Your Knowledge

Multiple Choice *(continued)*

4. The <SCRIPT> tag defaults automatically to which script language?
   a. VBScript
   b. DHTML
   c. Java
   d. JavaScript
5. What is the document property for changing the background color in JavaScript?
   a. backgroundColor
   b. bgColor
   c. bkColor
   d. pageColor
6. To test a Web page with your browser, click __________ on the menu bar, and then either click Open File or Open Page.
   a. File
   b. Edit
   c. Favorites
   d. View
7. Which of the following is *not* a data type for JavaScript variables?
   a. Boolean
   b. floating point
   c. string
   d. numeric
8. When defining a JavaScript variable it is best to use the __________ statement.
   a. define
   b. DIM
   c. var
   d. DIM var
9. Which of the following is *not* contained in the Date() object?
   a. the day of the week
   b. the time zone
   c. the GMT
   d. the year
10. When using the substring() method to extract a string of data, you need to supply the relative position of the first character to be extracted and __________.
    a. the relative position of the last character
    b. the relative length of the characters extracted
    c. the relative position of the last character plus one
    d. the number of characters in the entire string

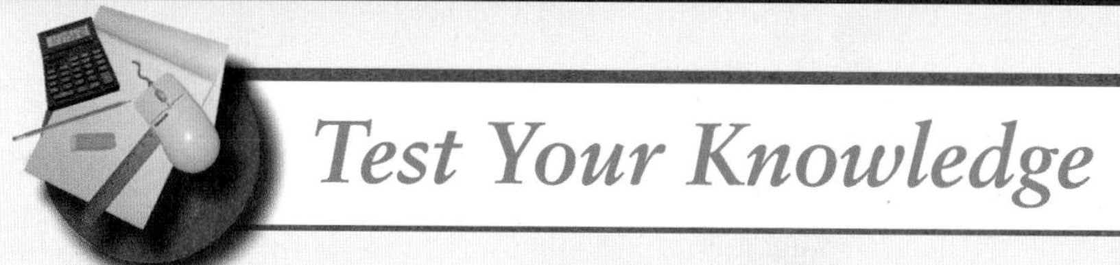
Test Your Knowledge

3 Understanding the Various Parts of a Web Page

Instructions: In Figure 1-31, arrows point to components of a Web page. Identify the various parts of the Web page in the spaces provided.

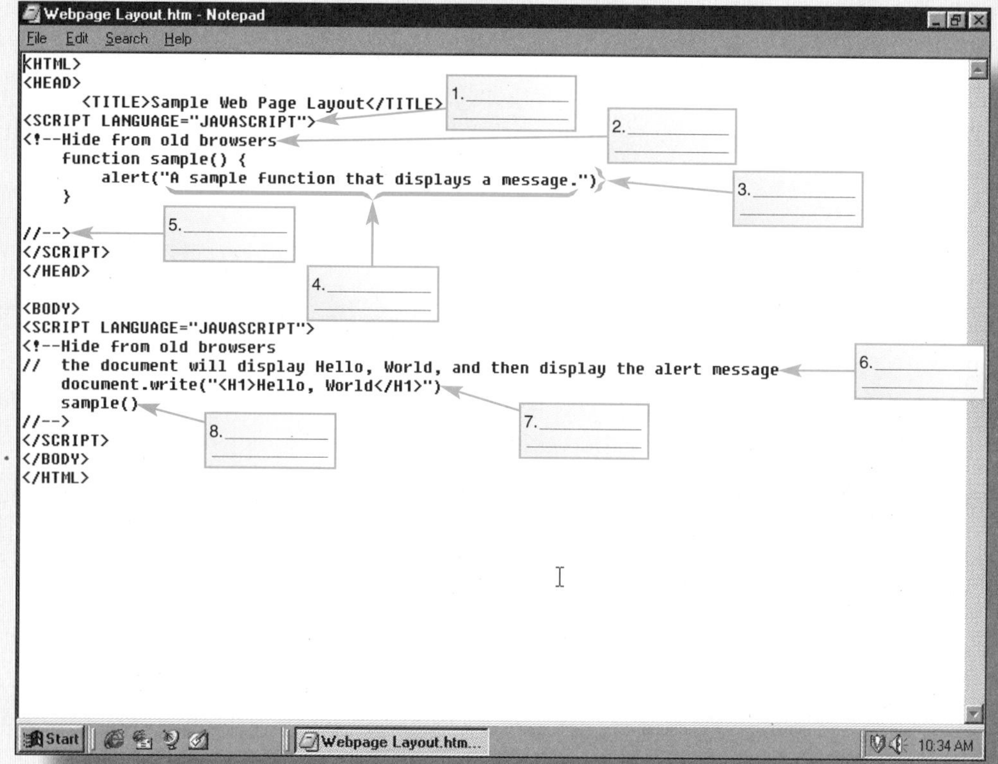
Webpage Layout.htm - Notepad
File Edit Search Help
<HTML>
<HEAD>
<TITLE>Sample Web Page Layout</TITLE>
<SCRIPT LANGUAGE="JAVASCRIPT">
<!--Hide from old browsers
function sample() {
alert("A sample function that displays a message.")
}
//-->
</SCRIPT>
</HEAD>
<BODY>
<SCRIPT LANGUAGE="JAVASCRIPT">
<!--Hide from old browsers
// the document will display Hello, World, and then display the alert message
document.write("<H1>Hello, World</H1>")
sample()
//-->
</SCRIPT>
</BODY>
</HTML>
1.
2.
3.
4.
5.
6.
7.
8.
Start
Webpage Layout.htm...
10:34 AM

FIGURE 1-31

4 Understanding Code Statements

Instructions: Carefully read each of the following descriptions. Write JavaScript code statements to accomplish these specific tasks. Number your answers to correspond to the code description. Record your answers on a separate sheet of paper. Hand in the answers to your instructor.

1. Write a JavaScript statement that will define a new variable object called OurTime. Assign it the Date() object.
2. Write a JavaScript statement that will define a new variable called LocOurTime. Assign it the toLocaleString() method with the new OurTime object described in Step 1.
3. Write a JavaScript statement that will set the background color to spring green.
4. Write a JavaScript statement that will concatenate three message variables (Msg1, Msg2, and Msg3) and assign to one variable called CompMsg.
5. Write a setTimeout method that calls a function newWindow() after 5 seconds.
6. Write the JavaScript statement that will display the following: This document was last changed on 10/31/01. (*Hint*: Assume the date has been extracted to a variable called curDate.)
7. Given the following: <Input Type="Button" Name="Continue" Value="Continue">, rewrite and add the event handler that executes a function called goNext() when the user clicks the button.

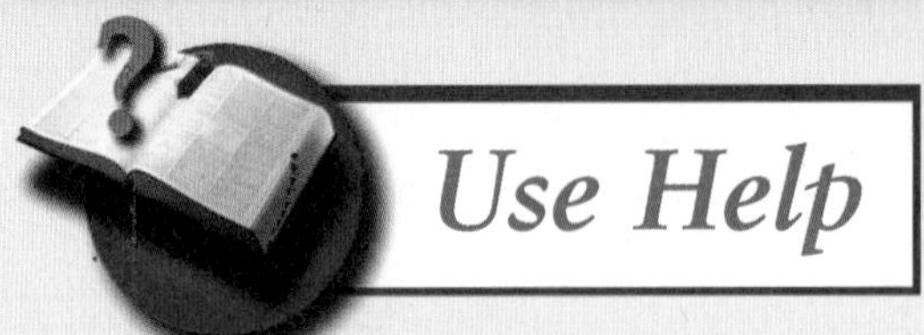

1 Exploring Online Documentation

Instructions: Start your browser. Type `www.scsite.com/js/p1.htm` in the Address text box and then click Project 1 Use Help 1. Using the Web site, answer the questions below.

1. Click Chapter 1 Getting Started in the left frame. What is JavaScript?
2. Scroll down the right frame until you locate Table 1-1. Answer the following questions:
   a. Which language is interpreted (not compiled)?
   b. Which language is object-oriented?
   c. Which language has classes and instances that cannot have properties or methods added dynamically?
   d. Which language's code is integrated with, and embedded in, HTML?
   e. Which language uses variable data types not declared (loose typing)?
3. Scroll down the same page to locate the heading, Using JavaScript Expressions as HTML Attribute Values. How can a JavaScript expression be used as an HTML attribute value?
4. Scroll down the same page to locate the heading, Specifying Alternate Content With the NOSCRIPT Tag. What purpose does the NOSCRIPT tag serve in JavaScript?
5. Scroll down the same page to locate the heading, Defining and Calling Functions. Answer the following questions:
   a. What are functions and list the basic parts?
   b. What is the difference between defining a function and calling a function?
   c. Why should you define functions in the HEAD section?
6. Scroll down the same page to locate the heading, Using the Write Method. Why is the write method one of the more often-used JavaScript methods?

2 Exploring Links to Other JavaScript Site Links

Instructions: Start your browser. Type `www.scsite.com/js/p1.htm` in the Address text box and then click Project 1 Use Help 2. Perform the following tasks.

1. Scroll down the left frame.
2. Click Chapter 1, The Message Box.
3. Read the entire section and click Let's Break it Down.
4. Read all the pages. After you have read the final page of Chapter 1, print the final page.
5. When you have completed Chapter 1, click On to Chapter 2, and then click the Red, Green, Blue, and White buttons to try the demonstration. Click Show me how to do it.
6. Read the Show me how to do it pages and print the last page. Hand in the printouts to your instructor.

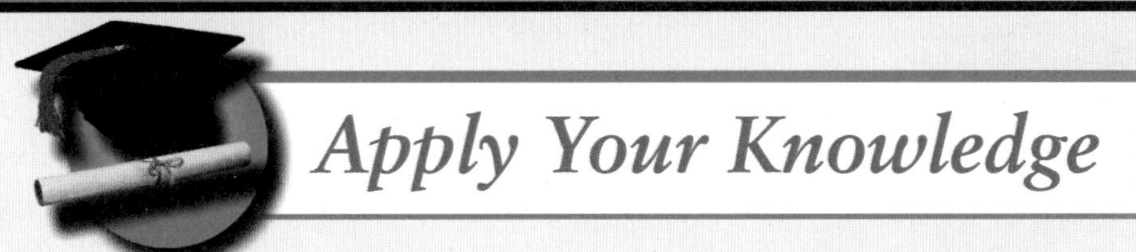

Apply Your Knowledge

1 Changing the Message and Linking to a New Web Site for an Initial Screen

Instructions: Start Notepad. Open carrental.htm on the JavaScript Data Disk. If you did not download the Data Disk, see the inside back cover for instructions for downloading the JavaScript Data Disk or see your instructor. This Web page is an initial screen a viewer might encounter while doing a search for a car rental office. This Web page automatically links to a new Web site after 15 seconds. Figure 1-32 shows the completed Web page. The function, which executes the link to the new Web site, already has been coded. Perform the following tasks.

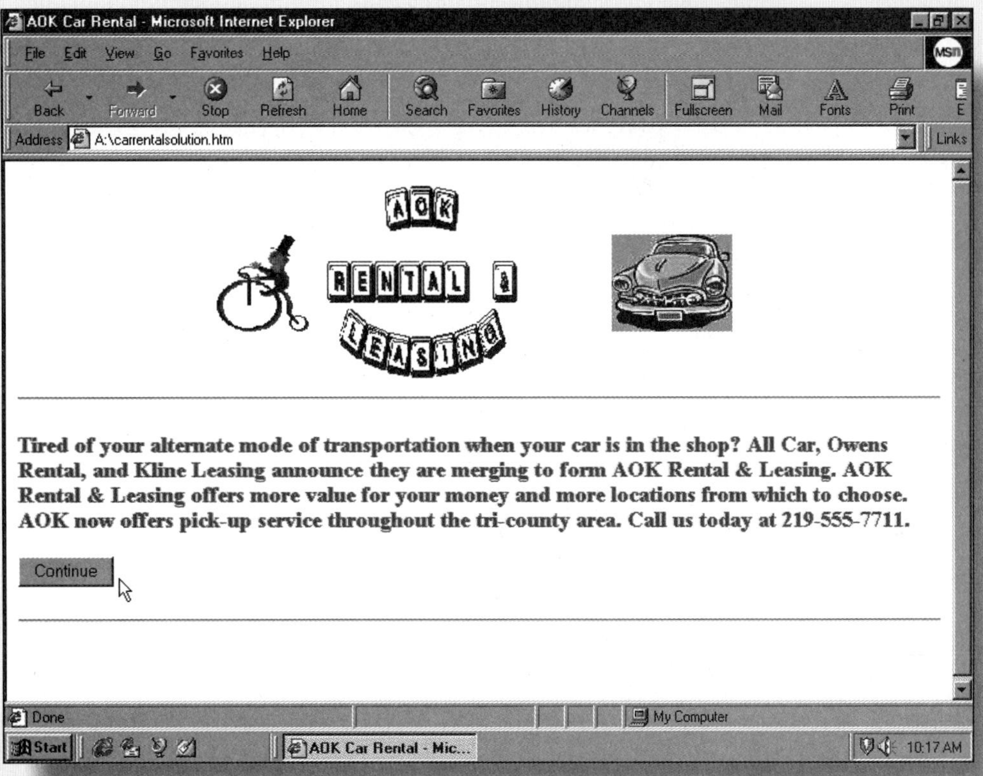

FIGURE 1-32

1. Locate the JavaScript tag after the images and horizontal line that contains the JavaScript comment, // build the message line & display.
2. Enter the following code:

```
var msgLine1="Tired of your alternate mode of transportation when your car is in the "
var msgLine2="shop? All Car, Owens Rental, and Kline Leasing announce they are merging "
var msgLine3="to form AOK Rental & Leasing. AOK Rental & Leasing offers more value for "
var msgLine4="your money and more locations from which to choose. AOK now offers pick-up "
var msgLine5="service throughout the tri-county area. Call us today at 219-555-7711."
```

3. Enter the following statement to concatenate the five variables into one variable called message:

```
var message = msgLine1+msgLine2+msgLine3+msgLine4+msgLine5
```

(continued)

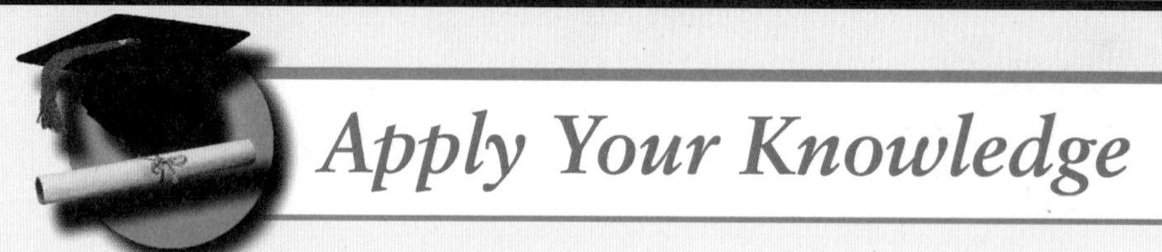

Changing the Message and Linking to a New Web Site for an Initial Screen *(continued)*

4. Display the message using the write() method as follows:
   document.write("<H3><FONT Color='darkgreen'><B>"+message+"</H3></FONT></B>").
5. Save the HTML file on the disk in drive A using the file name, carrentalsolution.htm.
6. Start your browser. Open the a:\carrentalsolution.htm Web page to test JavaScript code. If no errors occur, continue with Step 7. If an error occurs, activate Notepad and double-check your spelling in the HTML file. Save the file on the disk, and then click the Refresh button on the browser toolbar to retest.
7. Find the closing </SCRIPT> tag in the BODY section. Position the insertion point after the comment line that reads <!--Continue button>. Enter the following on separate lines:
```
<FORM>
<Input Type="Button" Name="Continue" Value="Continue" onClick="newSite()">
</FORM>
```
8. Locate the setTimeout() method in the SCRIPT section and delete it.
9. Save the Notepad file, activate your browser, and click the Refresh button on your browser's toolbar to test the Web page.
10. Print the Web page.
11. Return to Notepad and print the HTML text file. Hand in the printouts to your instructor.

1 Writing a Function that Changes Background Colors

Problem: You are teaching an introductory Web class at the local high school. You want to develop a Web page that allows your students to change the background color (Figure 1-33a) by clicking a button that is associated with a specific color. The Web page in Figure 1-33b has the azure background.

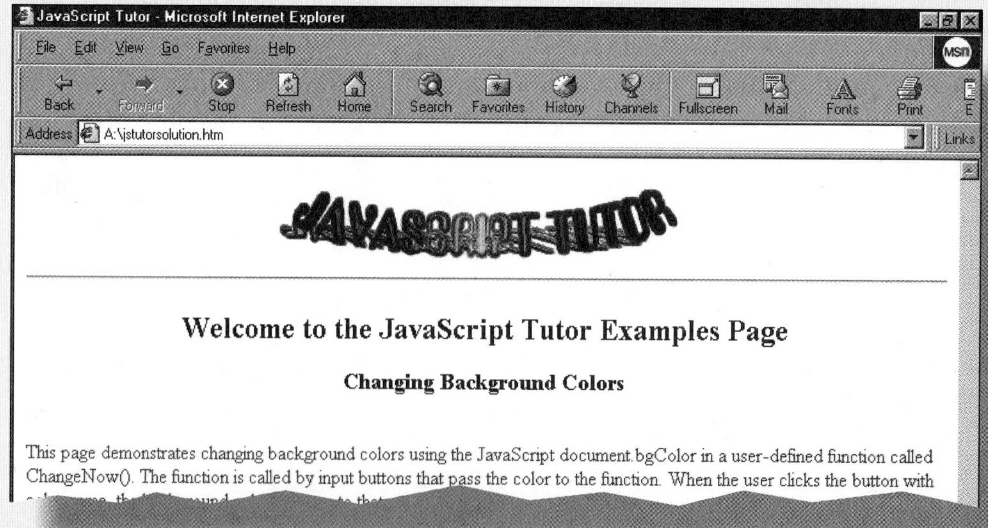

FIGURE 1-33a

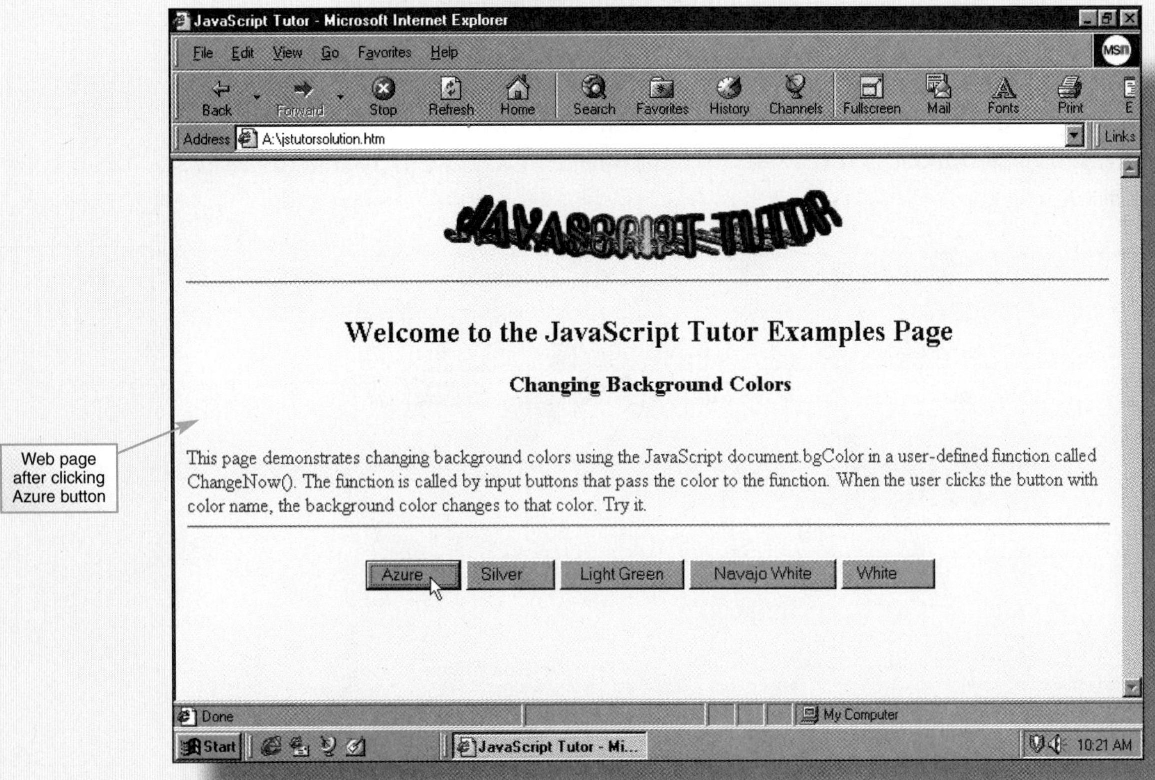

FIGURE 1-33b

Instructions: Start your browser and Notepad. Use Notepad to open jstutor.htm on the JavaScript Data Disk. If you did not download the Data Disk, see the inside back cover for instructions for downloading the JavaScript Data Disk or see your instructor. Perform the following tasks.

1. Locate the SCRIPT tag in the HEAD section.
2. On the line following the comment, // Change background color to color passed to function, enter the following:
```
function ChangeNow(color) {
   document.bgColor=color
}
```
3. Locate the form that creates the five input buttons with the color names in the BODY section.
4. For each button, insert the onclick event handler to call the ChangeNow() function and pass the associated color. Use the actual color name as the passed value that matches the button value as shown in the code for the Azure and Silver buttons.
   <INPUT Type="button" Name="ChngRed" Value="Azure" onclick="ChangeNow('azure')">
   <INPUT Type="button" Name="ChngRed" Value="Silver" onclick="ChangeNow('silver')">
5. Save the Notepad file on the disk in drive A using the file name, jstutorsolution.htm.
6. Activate the browser and open a:\jstutorsolution.htm in the browser to test your JavaScript code.
7. If any errors occur, double-check Steps 2 through 4 and test the file again. If no errors occur, print the Web page, activate Notepad, and print the HTML file. Hand in the printouts to your instructor.

2 Adding Alert Messages to Display a Factoid before Executing a Link

Problem: You are an intern at Valley Recycling and the Webmaster, Juan Garcia, wants you to modify the current Welcome page (Figure 1-34a) to add a factoid to each of the four links. The factoid should display a message before the link is executed (Figure 1-34b). In addition, Juan requests that you add the date and time the document was last modified.

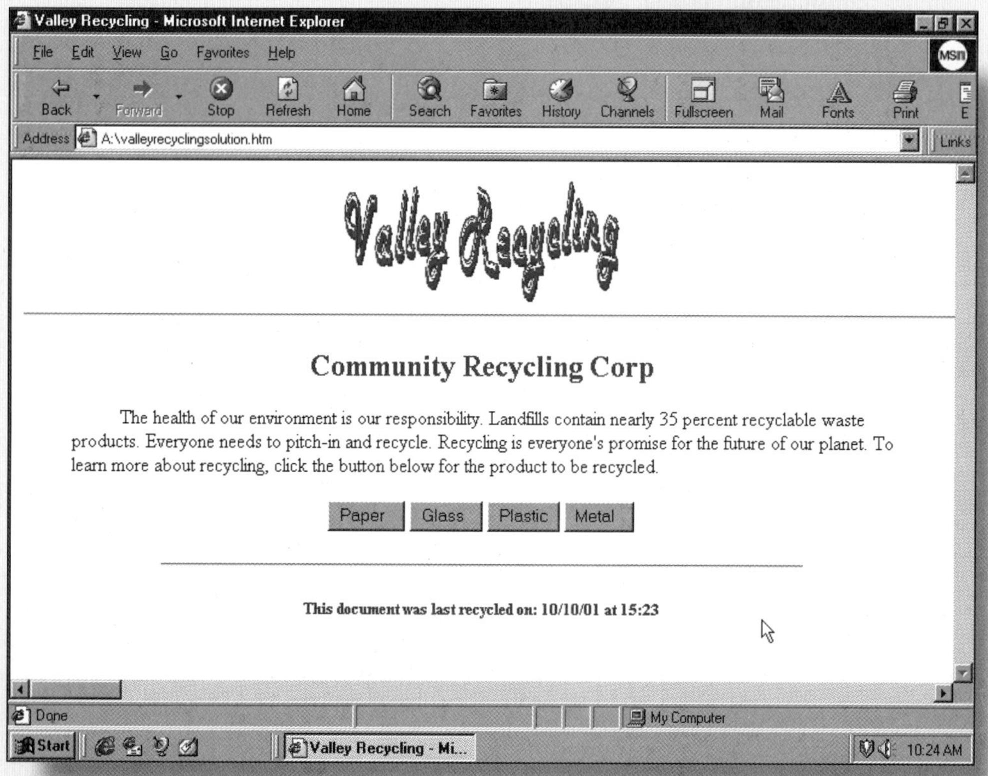

FIGURE 1-34a

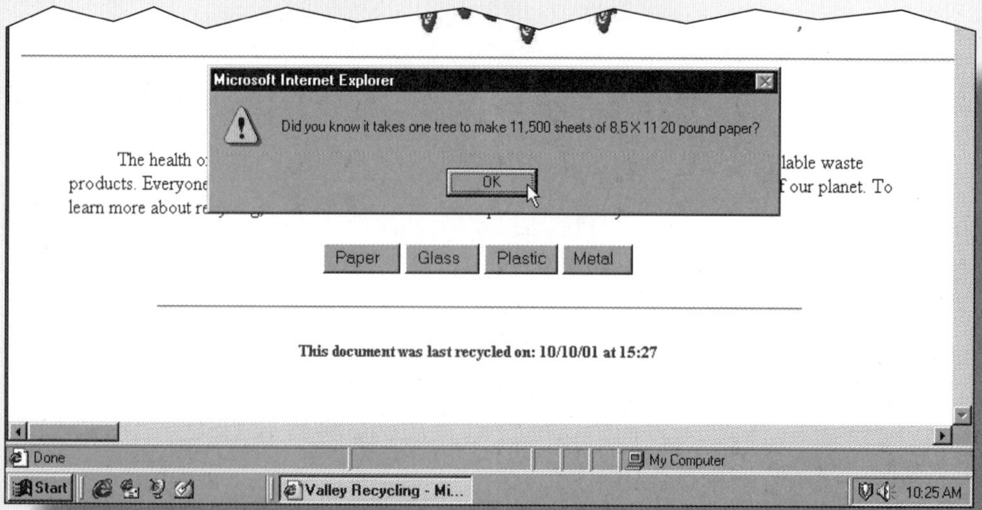

FIGURE 1-34b

In the Lab

Instructions: Start your browser and Notepad. Use Notepad to open valley.htm on the JavaScript Data Disk and then perform the following tasks.

1. Locate the first SCRIPT tag in the HEAD section of the Web page. The first function for the Paper button has been written. Using this function as a model, write three more functions, one for each of the remaining buttons (Glass, Plastic, Metal).
2. Type the remaining functions beneath the Paper() function. Press the SPACEBAR to indent in the same manner as the Paper() function.
3. The function for the Glass button is Glass().
   a. Assign the following factoid to a variable: Recycling glass containers saves 9 gallons of fuel oil for every ton of recycled glass.
   b. Display the variable with the factoid using the alert() function.
   c. Enter `location = "http://www.scsite.com/"` as the location command.
   d. Enter } (the closing brace).
4. The function for the Plastic button is Plastic().
   a. Assign the following factoid to one variable: Styrofoam is neither plastic nor recyclable.
   b. Assign the following factoid to another variable: Styrofoam still will be in your landfill 500 years from now. Is that what you want?
   c. Concatenate the two variables into one.
   d. Display the new variable with the factoid using the alert() function.
   e. Enter `location = "http://www.scsite.com/"` as the location command.
   f. Enter } (the closing brace).
5. The function for the Metal button is Metal().
   a. Assign the following factoid to one variable: For every ton of metal recycled, 2.5 tons of iron ore,
   b. Assign the following to another variable: .5 tons of coal, and 40 pounds of limestone are saved.
   c. Concatenate the two variables into one.
   d. Display the new variable with the factoid using the alert() function.
   e. Enter `location = "http://www.scsite.com/"` as the location command.
   f. Enter } (the closing brace).
6. Locate the HTML comment, <!--Date last modified>, towards the bottom of the document before the SCRIPT section.
7. Within the SCRIPT section, display the date and time the document was last modified. Separate the two pieces of data using the substring() method as follows: `document.write("This document was last recycled on: "+document.lastModified.substring(0,8)+" at " + document.lastModified.substring(8,14))` and then add the HTML codes to center the message. Make the font color firebrick.
8. Save the HTML file on the disk in drive A using the file name, valleysolution.htm.
9. Activate the browser. Open the a:\valleysolution.htm Web page to test your JavaScript code.
10. If any errors occur, double-check Steps 2 through 7 and test again. If no errors occur, print the Web page, activate Notepad, and print the HTML file. Hand in the printouts to your instructor.

3 Creating a Welcome Page that Displays Information in an Alert Message

Problem: You are the Webmaster at Rocky Mountain Steel Credit Union. The current Welcome page is very plain (Figure 1-35a). The credit union board chairperson, Terry Russell, wants you to add the day and time to the greeting and display an informative message when users click a link. The message informs users about specials relating to the linked page. For example, a message about the current loan rates displays when a user clicks the Loans link (Figure 1-35b). Terry suggests you add the date the document was last modified. Because you know that the message will change often, you decide to use the document.lastModified property to display the last modified date.

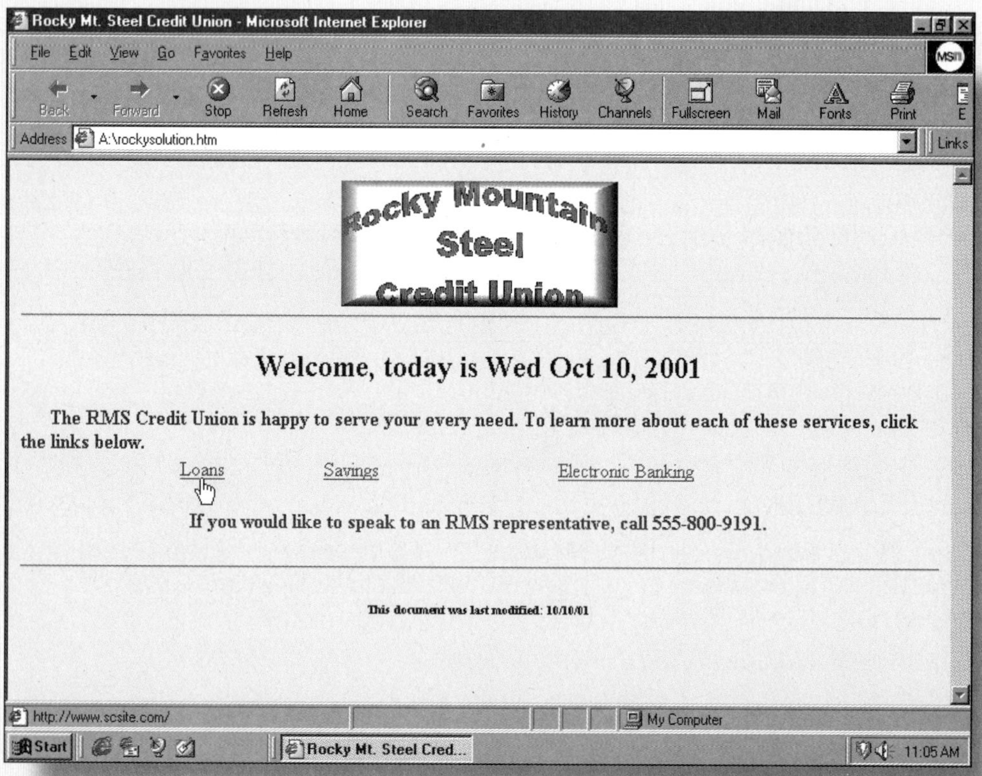

FIGURE 1-35a

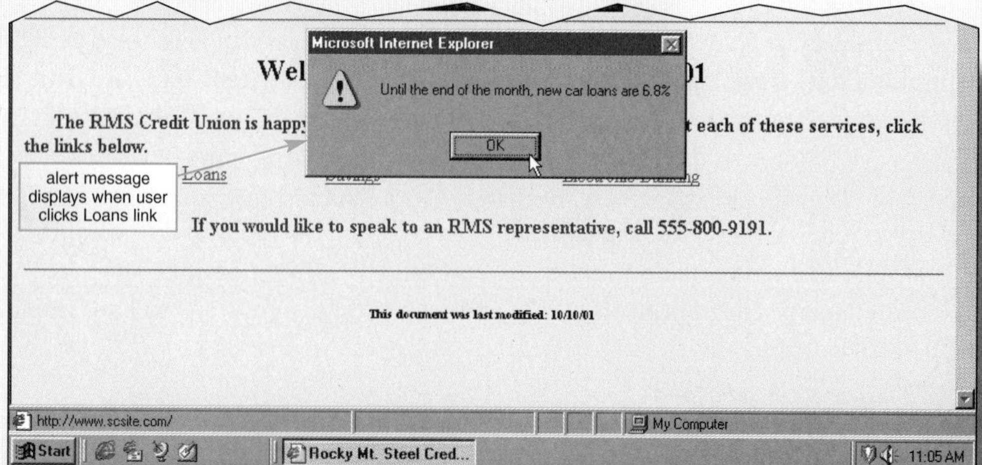

FIGURE 1-35b

In the Lab

Instructions: Start your browser and Notepad. Use Notepad to open Rocky.htm. Perform the following tasks.

1. Write the JavaScript code that will display a welcome message that includes the day of the week and the date. For example, Welcome, today is Fri Oct 5, 2001. Place this message beneath the credit union logo (Figure 1-35a). (*Hint*: use the Date() object and extract the day of the week, the date, and the year from the object. A sample output from the Date() object is

   Fri Oct 13 08:41:44 CDT 2001

   so you must count the position of the characters to use the substring() method to extract the day of the week, the date, and the year.
2. Write three functions that use the alert() function to display a message. Place them in the HEAD section (the SCRIPT section has been provided starting on the fourth line).
3. The first function name is showLoans(). It displays the message, Until the end of the month, new car loans are 6.8%.
4. The second function name is showSavings(). It displays the message, If you have more than $5,000 in savings, consider a CD.
5. The third function name is showEB(). It displays the message, Try our new BankAtHome software at the main branch.
6. Just before the </BODY> tag, insert another JavaScript section to display the date the document was last modified, but not the time. Include the HTML code <H6> to make the text small and centered between margins.
7. Save the Notepad file on the disk in drive A using the file name, rockysolution.htm.
8. Activate the browser. Open the a:\rockysolution.htm Web page to test your JavaScript code.
9. If any errors occur double-check Steps 1 through 6 and test again. If no errors occur, print the Web page, activate Notepad, and print the HTML file. Hand in the printouts to your instructor.

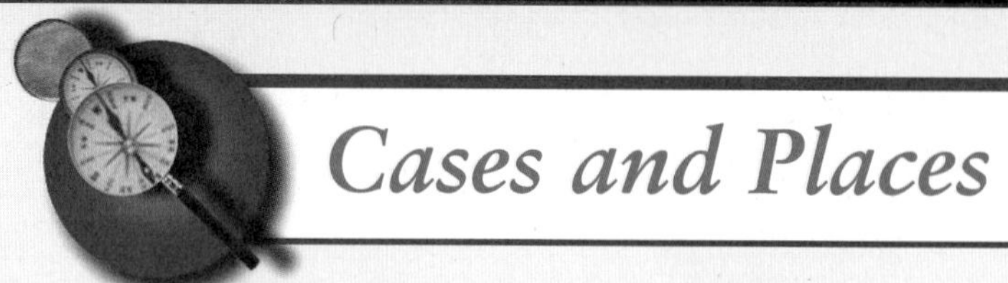

Cases and Places

The difficulty of these case studies varies:
◗ are the least difficult; ◗◗ are more difficult; and ◗◗◗ are the most difficult.

1 ◗ You have taken a summer job with Ace Carpet and Furniture Cleaning. The owner asks you to create a Web site for them. Because you have just finished your course in Web page design, you tell the owner it is important to have a first page that captures the viewer's attention. You suggest this page be simple in design, but direct in content information. After a few seconds, the page automatically transfers to the Web site main page. Use the concepts and techniques presented in this project to create the greeting page.

2 ◗ As part of your course credit in your marketing class, you must volunteer to work for a not-for-profit organization one hour a week. Because you like working with children, you volunteer for Kids Club. Kids Club has a Web page created by the Internet service provider they use. The provider, however, has informed Kids Club that the domain address will be changed. Kids Club will have use of the old domain address for three months before it is disabled. The director of Kids Club is aware of your computer skills and asks you to create a greeting page for the old domain address to notify viewers of the address change and automatically link users to the new domain address. Use the concepts and techniques presented in this project to create the greeting page.

3 ◗ Your father owns a heating and cooling business. He has a Web page with a local Internet service provider. The business will be carrying a new furnace and air conditioning unit starting in the fall. American Furnace and Air Conditioning (AFAC) only recognizes top heating and cooling businesses as distributors. Because this manufacturer is recognized nationally as one of the best, your father wants current viewers to be aware of the new line now. He asks you to create a new greeting page that has a link to the current Web page and a link to the AFAC Web page. Use the concepts and techniques presented in this project to create the greeting page.

4 ◗◗ You have a summer internship with the local ad and sales paper (*The Community Shopper*). At a general meeting, you suggest they start a Web site that contains ads, local announcements, community news, and other features. The editor is very impressed with your suggestion and states she was thinking about signing a contract with the local Internet service provider. You are instructed to create a greeting page with links to each of the shopper's features. The editor would like an input box that would prompt users for the name of their community. Once the user enters the name of the community, the user is linked automatically to Web ads and news associated with their community. Use the concepts and techniques presented in this project to create the greeting page.

5 ◗◗ Your sister recently graduated from Chiropractic College and is ready to open an office. She would like to start a Web site, but wants it to be more than an advertisement page. You suggest that she have a greeting page that has a list containing the top ten ailments treated by chiropractors. The viewer selects one of the ailments and then is linked to a page that explains the ailment, common causes, and common treatments. Use the concepts and techniques presented in this project to create the greeting page.

JavaScript

Creating Pop-up Windows, Adding Scrolling Messages, and Validating Forms

OBJECTIVES

You will have mastered the material in this project when you can:

- Explain the four basic components of a scrolling message
- Write a user-defined function to display a scrolling message in a form text box
- Describe the If statement
- Define conditionals and discuss the conditional operands
- Define recursion
- Describe the focus() method
- Write a user-defined function to calculate mortgage payments
- Validate data entry using a nested If...Else statement
- Describe the parseInt(), parseFloat(), and isNaN() built-in functions
- Describe the math pow() method
- Write a user-defined function to format output in currency format
- Discuss For and While loops
- Use the open() method to display another Web page in a pop-up window
- Use the lastModified property to display the date a Web page was last modified

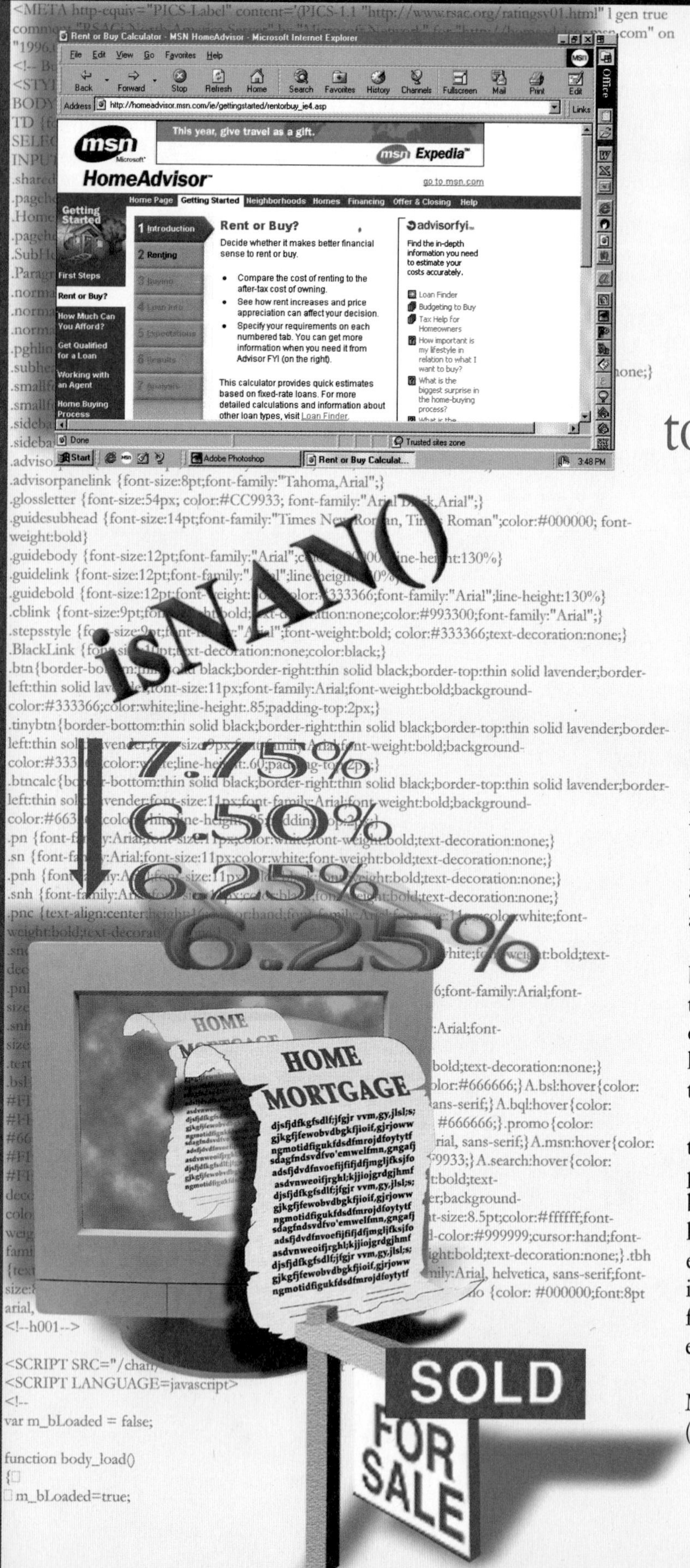

It Figures!

Mortgage Sites Are Keys to Home Ownership

The *American Dream* is owning a home. The dream can be yours once you save for the down payment and earn sufficient income. But how much do you need to save? And how much do you need to earn? Now you can find the answers easily by navigating the Internet.

Do you need to know how much house fits your budget? Various sites help you determine how much house you can afford, the amount you can borrow, and the amount of your monthly payments.

At these sites, you follow step-by-step instructions that prompt you to make choices, such as the number of years you plan to live in the house and input numbers, such as the amount you plan to borrow.

The Web page you will build in this project estimates a monthly payment based on the amount borrowed, the interest rate, and the length of the loan. As users enter each amount, JavaScript uses the isNaN() — Is Not a Number — function to evaluate the figures and ensure they are numeric.

Likewise, Microsoft's MSN HomeAdvisor Web site (homeadvisor.msn.com) offers a

finance page using JavaScript that prompts you for figures and then uses the isNaN() function to validate each amount. The program performs calculations and finds 50 lenders offering products that fit your needs. You can sort these products according to criteria such as the lowest interest rate or the smallest monthly payment.

If these monthly figures make you uncomfortable, the various sites offer options with calculators that work like gigantic spreadsheets and let you fiddle with the numbers. For example, you often can obtain a lower interest rate if you pay points, which are one percent of the loan amount. Or you can try another type of mortgage, such as an adjustable rate loan, that has a low interest rate for the first year or so.

Once you determine the right mortgage for your budget, the sites allow you to check current mortgage rates in your area. Some help you prequalify for a loan, which strengthens negotiating power when discussing prices with home sellers.

Others send e-mail messages alerting you when national mortgage rates move upward or downward by at least one-tenth of one percent, which can happen daily.

When you find the ideal property, you can apply for the cybermortgage online. Banks and various financial institutions in the United States lend $725 billion each year; online mortgage approvals are expected to cut into at least five percent of that amount in the next few years as more than 2,000 lenders with Web sites vie for mortgage dollars. By eliminating loan officers, you often can save money and add that sum to your down payment. Some sites promise approval in less than five minutes.

Various pages offer online appraisals. Others estimate the costs of homeowner's insurance, property taxes, closing costs, and private mortgage insurance, which often is needed if your down payment is less than 20 percent of the purchase price.

Using the Internet to explore the multitude of mortgage options can save time and money. Your efforts can open the door to financial flexibility, and to your new home. It figures!

JavaScript

Creating Pop-up Windows, Adding Scrolling Messages, and Validating Forms

CASE PERSPECTIVE

You have taken a part-time job with Home Finders Nationwide Realty to work on their Web site. Carrie Rayburn, the owner, dislikes their current Web page and wants the page to be more interesting. You suggest adding a simple, but eye-catching scrolling message box. Carrie likes the idea and suggests that the first message remind site visitors of current, low interest rates.

Carrie mentions that customers have asked for mortgage payment information. She suggests a page with a large table that lists various mortgage amounts, interest rates, the number of years for the mortgage, and the associated monthly payment. You recommend making the Web page more interactive by adding a mortgage payment calculator form. The form would allow customers to enter the mortgage loan amount, interest rate, and number of years, and then click a button to display the monthly mortgage payment. You also suggest that a notice about the mortgage payment calculator display in a pop-up window that opens each time a customer hits the Home Finders Nationwide Realty Web page. Carrie asks you to implement your suggestions.

Introduction

In Project 1, you learned how to integrate JavaScript and HTML. You learned how to use variables and objects to extract the current system date from the computer and to use several variables to construct a message. You further learned how to write a user-defined function that calls the built-in alert() function.

This project reinforces these topics and introduces new ones, including creating a scrolling message that uses the string length property and the If statement. You also will learn how to validate form text boxes using the If...Else statement and parseInt(), parseFloat(), and IsNaN() built-in functions. You will learn how to use the math object's pow() method in a formula, and how to format results as currency. Finally, you will learn to use the open() method to display messages in a pop-up window. These JavaScript techniques and statements allow you to improve the functionality of your Web pages.

Project Two — Home Finders Nationwide Realty

Before starting on the project, you meet with Carrie to summarize your planned modifications to the Web site. You state that you determine the following needs, data validation requirements, and calculations based on your discussion.

Needs: When the Web page first loads, a pop-up window displays a message informing users of the new mortgage payment calculator (Figure 2-1a). The Web page also includes a scrolling message that constantly displays, to remind visitors of the current low mortgage rates (Figure 2-1b). The mortgage payment form allows users to calculate their monthly payment based on the amount of mortgage, interest rate, and number of years for the mortgage (Figure 2-1c). Separate functions validate the data

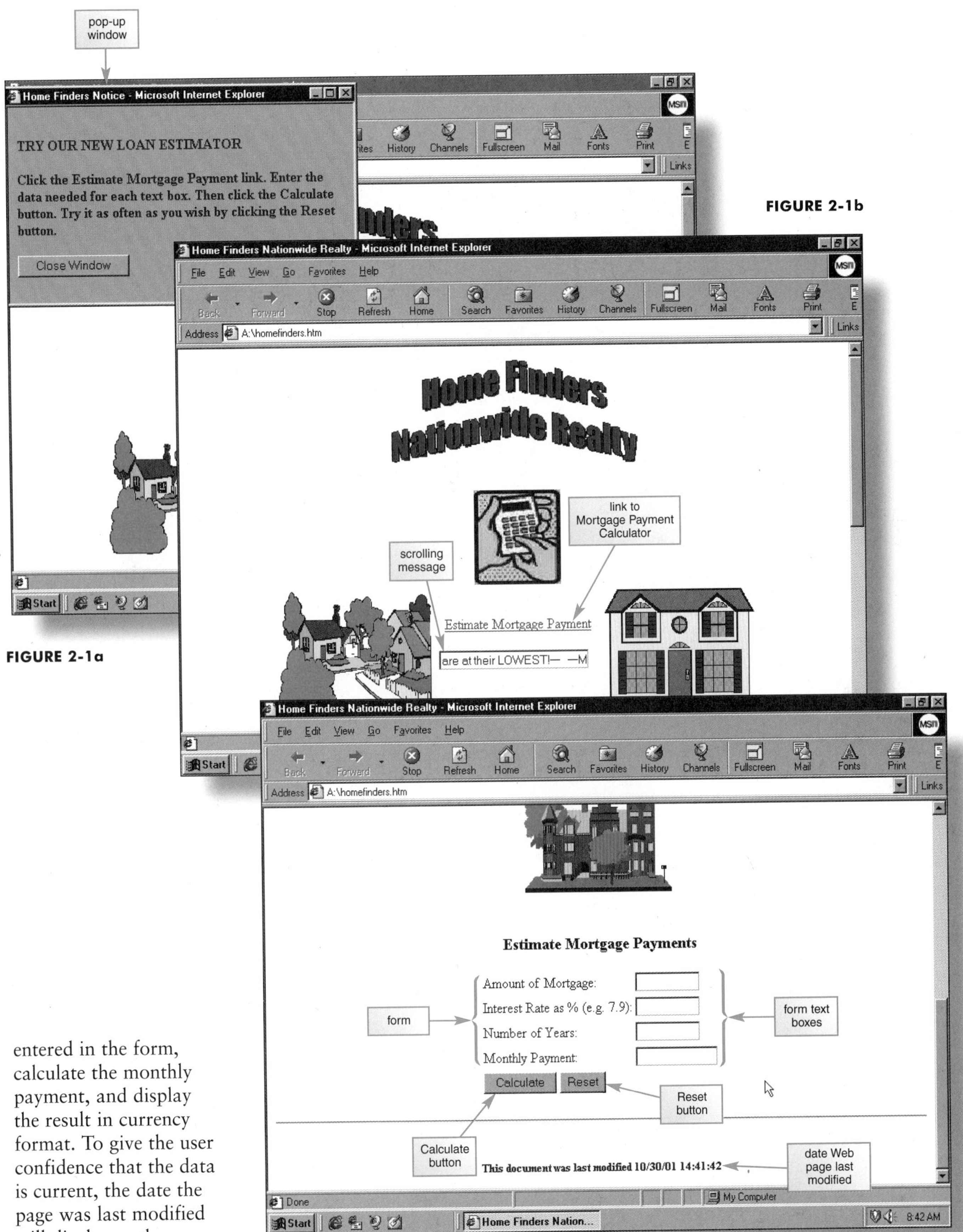

FIGURE 2-1a

FIGURE 2-1b

FIGURE 2-1c

entered in the form, calculate the monthly payment, and display the result in currency format. To give the user confidence that the data is current, the date the page was last modified will display at the bottom of the page.

Data validation requirements: The user enters the data (used in the mathematical calculation for the monthly payment) in the form text boxes (Figure 2-1c on the previous page). The data must not be blank and must be numeric. If the data is not valid, an alert message box notifies the user and positions the insertion point in the appropriate text box. Until all entries are valid, the formula will not attempt to calculate the monthly payment.

Calculations: The formula for calculating a monthly payment is

$$\text{monthly payment} = \text{loan} * \text{rate} / (1 - (1 / (1 + \text{rate})^{\text{payments}}))$$

where loan is the total amount of the mortgage, rate is the interest rate, and payments is the number of payments to be made. Because the interest rate is a percent, the function must convert the annual rate to a monthly rate. The formula also must convert the number of years into the total number of payments.

Starting Notepad and Opening the Home.htm File

Your first step is to open the HTML file to which you will add JavaScript code using Notepad. The HTML file for the Home Finders Nationwide Realty Web page is stored on the JavaScript Data Disk as a file named home.htm. See the inside back cover for instructions for downloading the JavaScript Data Disk or see your instructor for information on accessing the files required in this book. To start Notepad and open the home.htm file, perform the following steps.

TO START NOTEPAD AND OPEN A WEB PAGE STORED ON THE DATA DISK

1. Click the Start button on the taskbar. Click Programs on the Start menu. Click Accessories on the Programs submenu.
2. Click Notepad on the Programs submenu.
3. Insert the JavaScript Data Disk in drive A.
4. Click Open on the File menu.
5. Click 3½ Floppy (A:) in the Look in list box. Type `*.htm` in the File name text box and then press the ENTER key.
6. Double-click the document, home.htm.

The home.htm document displays in the Notepad window (Figure 2-2).

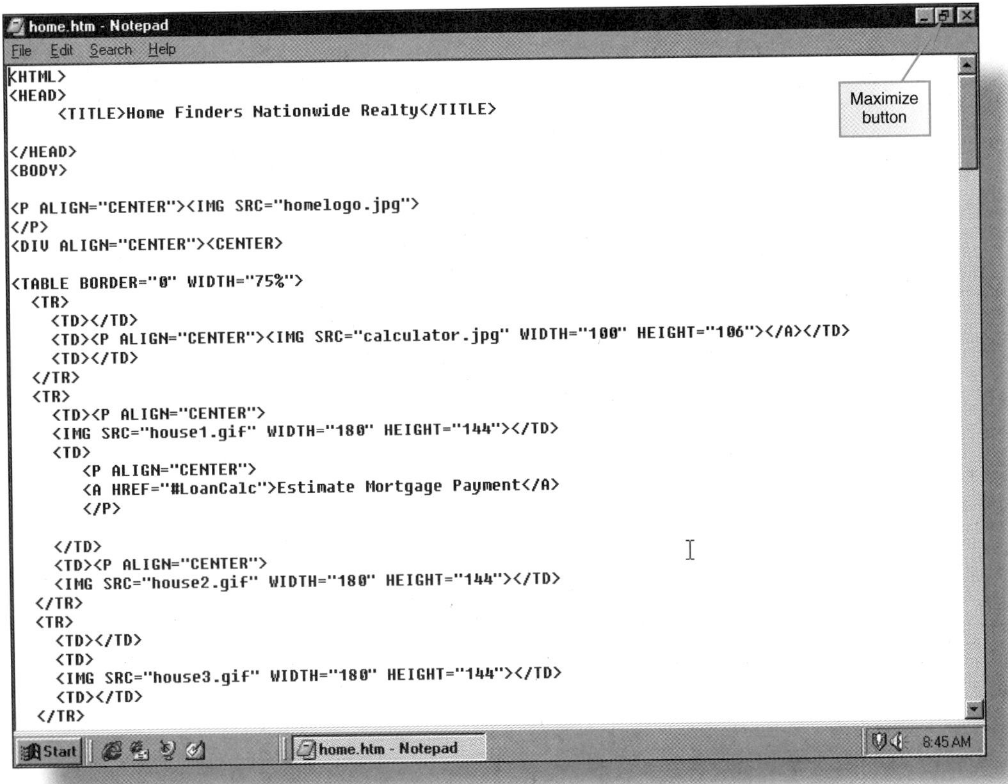


```
<HTML>
<HEAD>
     <TITLE>Home Finders Nationwide Realty</TITLE>

</HEAD>
<BODY>

<P ALIGN="CENTER"><IMG SRC="homelogo.jpg">
</P>
<DIV ALIGN="CENTER"><CENTER>

<TABLE BORDER="0" WIDTH="75%">
  <TR>
    <TD></TD>
    <TD><P ALIGN="CENTER"><IMG SRC="calculator.jpg" WIDTH="100" HEIGHT="106"></A></TD>
    <TD></TD>
  </TR>
  <TR>
    <TD><P ALIGN="CENTER">
    <IMG SRC="house1.gif" WIDTH="180" HEIGHT="144"></TD>
    <TD>
       <P ALIGN="CENTER">
       <A HREF="#LoanCalc">Estimate Mortgage Payment</A>
       </P>

    </TD>
    <TD><P ALIGN="CENTER">
    <IMG SRC="house2.gif" WIDTH="180" HEIGHT="144"></TD>
  </TR>
  <TR>
    <TD></TD>
    <TD>
    <IMG SRC="house3.gif" WIDTH="180" HEIGHT="144"></TD>
    <TD></TD>
  </TR>
```

FIGURE 2-2

With the home.htm HTML file open, the next step is to create the text box in the BODY section that will contain the scrolling message.

Inserting a Scrolling Message on a Web Page

A simple way to attract the attention of a site visitor is to add a scrolling message to your Web page. Companies often use scrolling messages on their Web sites to highlight breaking news, key products, or special promotions. The scrolling message displays either in a text box within the Web page or on the status bar in the browser window.

To make it easier to build scrolling messages, Microsoft developed the MARQUEE HTML tag. While Internet Explorer recognizes the MARQUEE tag, Netscape Navigator does not. By writing your own user-defined function, however, can you create a scrolling message that works with virtually any browser.

A scrolling message has four basic components: (1) the display object; (2) the message; (3) the position; and (4) the delay. The **display object** defines where the scrolling message displays, which is either on the status bar or in a form text box. The **message** is a text string assigned to a variable. The text string is what the user sees when the message displays. Netscape warns Web developers that large messages use memory inefficiently. In addition, large text strings may cause older Netscape browsers to crash. The **position** is the starting location in which the message first displays in the display object. The starting location can be either the left or right side of the display object. The **delay** is the length of time between when a message ends and when it starts to appear again.

More About

Scrolling Messages

Another reason to avoid assigning a scrolling message to the status bar is that the message can hide information the user needs to see relating the current or next page being loaded.

More About

The MARQUEE Tag

The MARQUEE tag is one of Microsoft's JScript statements. For more information on the MARQUEE tag, visit www.scsite.com/js/p2.htm and then click Marquee.

The Web page you create in this project includes a scrolling message in a form text box (Figure 2-1b on page J 2.5). The form you construct is a single text box. When creating the form text box, you must name the form and the text box objects. Later, the function you write uses these names to assign the text to the text box. Figure 2-3 shows the code for the form containing the single text box. The name of the form is msgForm, and the name of the text box is scrollingMsg.

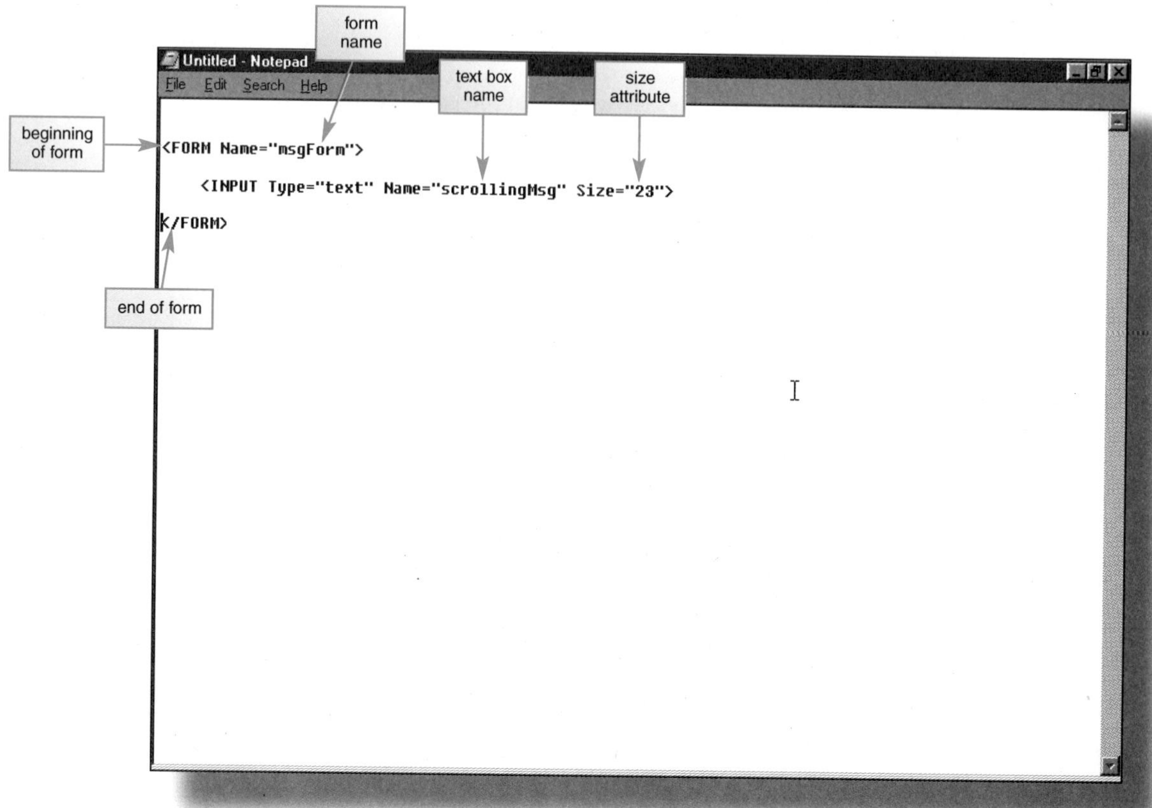

FIGURE 2-3

These names serve as variables in the JavaScript code when assigning the message string to the text box. The size attribute indicates the display width of the text box.

Creating a Form Text Box to Display a Scrolling Message

With JavaScript, you can assign a scrolling message to either the status bar or a text box. Because visitors to a Web page often do not look at the status bar, most Web developers agree that a scrolling message in a text box on the Web page is the better location.

The Web page for Home Finders Nationwide Realty uses a table to arrange and organize the graphics, links, and scrolling message (Figure 2-4). The center cell of the table contains a link to the mortgage payment form. You will place the form text box for the scrolling message in the same cell as this link. Perform the following steps to create a form text box to display a scrolling message.

To Create a Form Text Box to Display a Scrolling Message

1 Scroll down to the BODY section and position the insertion point on line 25 (beneath the paragraph </P> tag).

Place the insertion point as shown in Figure 2-4.

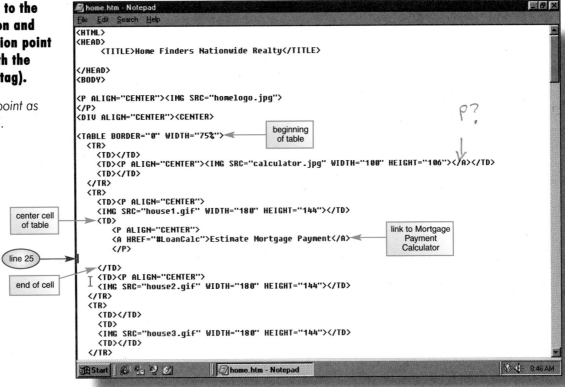

```
<HTML>
<HEAD>
    <TITLE>Home Finders Nationwide Realty</TITLE>

</HEAD>
<BODY>

<P ALIGN="CENTER"><IMG SRC="homelogo.jpg">
</P>
<DIV ALIGN="CENTER"><CENTER>

<TABLE BORDER="0" WIDTH="75%">
  <TR>
    <TD></TD>
    <TD><P ALIGN="CENTER"><IMG SRC="calculator.jpg" WIDTH="100" HEIGHT="106"></A></TD>
    <TD></TD>
  </TR>
  <TR>
    <TD><P ALIGN="CENTER">
    <IMG SRC="house1.gif" WIDTH="180" HEIGHT="144"></TD>
    <TD>
       <P ALIGN="CENTER">
       <A HREF="#LoanCalc">Estimate Mortgage Payment</A>
       </P>

    </TD>
    <TD><P ALIGN="CENTER">
    <IMG SRC="house2.gif" WIDTH="180" HEIGHT="144"></TD>
  </TR>
  <TR>
    <TD></TD>
    <TD>
    <IMG SRC="house3.gif" WIDTH="180" HEIGHT="144"></TD>
    <TD></TD>
  </TR>
```


FIGURE 2-4

2 Type <FORM Name="msgForm"> **and then press the ENTER key. Type** <INPUT Type="text" Name="scrollingMsg" Size="23"> **and then press the ENTER key. Type** </FORM> **and then press the ENTER key.**

The HTML code for the form and the input text box displays. Each line of the code is indented for readability purposes (Figure 2-5).

```
<HEAD>
    <TITLE>Home Finders Nationwide Realty</TITLE>

</HEAD>
<BODY>

<P ALIGN="CENTER"><IMG SRC="homelogo.jpg">
</P>
<DIV ALIGN="CENTER"><CENTER>

<TABLE BORDER="0" WIDTH="75%">
  <TR>
    <TD></TD>
    <TD><P ALIGN="CENTER"><IMG SRC="calculator.jpg" WIDTH="100" HEIGHT="106"></A></TD>
    <TD></TD>
  </TR>
  <TR>
    <TD><P ALIGN="CENTER">
    <IMG SRC="house1.gif" WIDTH="180" HEIGHT="144"></TD>
    <TD>
       <P ALIGN="CENTER">
       <A HREF="#LoanCalc">Estimate Mortgage Payment</A>
       </P>
       <FORM Name="msgForm">
          <INPUT Type="text" Name="scrollingMsg" Size="23">
       </FORM>

    </TD>
    <TD><P ALIGN="CENTER">
    <IMG SRC="house2.gif" WIDTH="180" HEIGHT="144"></TD>
  </TR>
  <TR>
    <TD></TD>
    <TD>
```


FIGURE 2-5

The form text box created by the HTML code serves as the display object for the scrolling message. The name of the form is msgForm, and the name of the text box is scrollingMsg. The Name attributes in the FORM tag and the INPUT tag become properties of the msgForm object in the user-defined function, scrollingMsg().

The next section describes the statements you need to write a user-defined function, scrollingMsg(), to display the scrolling message in the form text box.

Creating a User-Defined Function for a Scrolling Message

The **scrollingMsg() function** performs three tasks: (1) it assigns the message and a space to the display object (which, in this project, is the form text box); (2) it checks for the end of the message, and (3) it assigns the next character in the message to the text box, starting with the beginning of the message, in order to make the message scroll.

The scrollingMsg() function requires three variables: the message; a spacer; and the initialization of the beginning position of the message in the form text box. The variables are assigned initial values before the function statements, as follows:

```
var scrollMsg = "Mortgage Rates are at their LOWEST!"
var msgSpace = "---   ---"
var beginPos = 0
```

You assign the message text to the scrollMsg variable. Using the msgSpace variable, you define a space to place a break after a message. In this instance, the msgSpace variable contains three hyphens, three spaces, and three hyphens. The beginPos initial value is zero, which indicates that the message starts at the leftmost position in the text box. Recall from Project 1 that JavaScript uses relative addressing to determine locations, meaning that the first character position of a string is position 0.

The scrollMsg and msgSpace values are concatenated and assigned to the scrollingMsg text box using the statement

```
document.msgForm.scrollingMsg.value = scrollMsg.substring(beginPos,
scrollMsg.length)+msgSpace+scrollMsg.substring(0,beginPos)
```

The object, document.msgForm.scrollingMsg.value, is derived from the form object and the input object. Figure 2-6 illustrates the relationship between these objects and how the statement is derived.

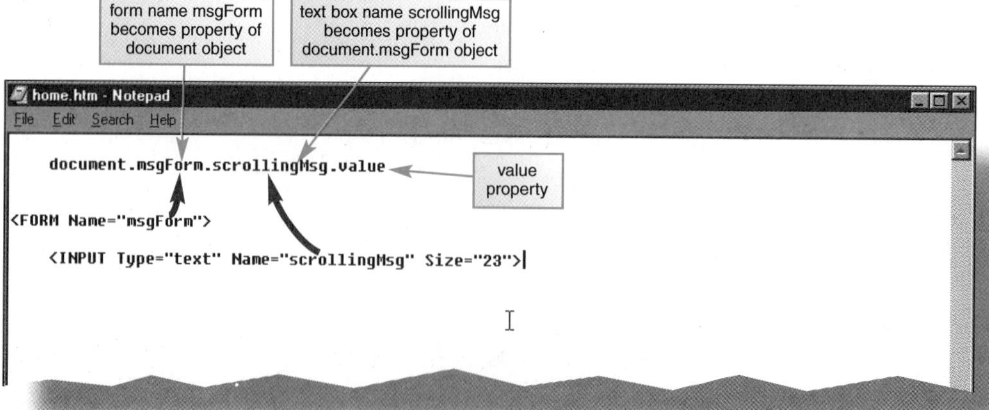

FIGURE 2-6

In this statement, the form object (msgForm) becomes an attribute of the document object, and the input text box object (scrollingMsg) becomes an attribute of the msgForm object. JavaScript assigns a value (the message) to the text box object, scrollingMsg, using the value attribute.

The remainder of the assignment statement concatenates the scrollMsg variable, the msgSpace variable, and the beginning of the scrollMsg. Recall that the scrollingMsg() function assigns the next character in the message to the text box, starting with the beginning of the message. The substring() method is used to return the beginning of the message. As you learned in Project 1, the substring() method needs two parameters (x,y), where x is the starting point of the string and y is the location of last character needed. To create the scrollingMsg() user-defined function and define its variables, perform the following steps.

To Create the scrollingMsg() User-Defined Function

1 Position the insertion point on line 4.

Line 4 is located in the HEAD section of the HTML code (Figure 2-7).

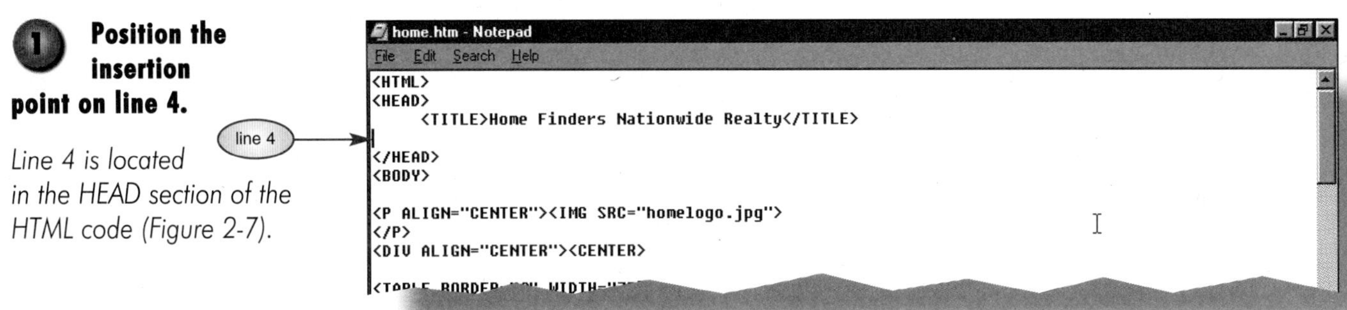

FIGURE 2-7

2 Type `<SCRIPT LANGUAGE="JAVASCRIPT">` **and then press the ENTER key. Type** `<!-- Hide from old browsers` **and then press the ENTER key. Type** `var scrollMsg = "Mortgage rates are at their LOWEST!"` **and then press the ENTER key. Type** `var msgSpace = "---    ---"` **and then press the ENTER key. Type** `var beginPos = 0` **and then press the ENTER key.**

Figure 2-8 shows the three variables and their assigned initial values.

```
home.htm - Notepad
File Edit Search Help
<HTML>
<HEAD>
    <TITLE>Home Finders Nationwide Realty</TITLE>
<SCRIPT LANGUAGE="JAVASCRIPT">
<!--Hide from old browsers
   var scrollMsg = "Mortgage rates are at their LOWEST!"
   var msgSpace = "---    ---"
   var beginPos = 0

</HEAD>
<BODY>

<P ALIGN="CENTER"><IMG SRC="homelogo.jpg">
</P>
<DIV ALIGN="CENTER"><CENTER>

<TABLE BORDER="0" WIDTH="75%">
  <TR>
    <TD></TD>
    <TD><P ALIGN="CENTER"><IMG SRC="calculator.jpg" WIDTH="100" HEIGHT="106"></A></TD>
    <TD></TD>
  </TR>
  <TR>
    <TD><P ALIGN="CENTER">
    <IMG SRC="house1.gif" WIDTH="180" HEIGHT="144"></TD>
    <TD>
       <P ALIGN="CENTER">
       <A HREF="#LoanCalc">Estimate Mortgage Payment</A>
       </P>
       <FORM Name="msgForm">
           <INPUT Type="text" Name="scrollingMsg" Size="23">
       </FORM>
    </TD>
    <TD><P ALIGN="CENTER">
    <IMG SRC="house2.gif" WIDTH="180" HEIGHT="144"></TD>
```


FIGURE 2-8

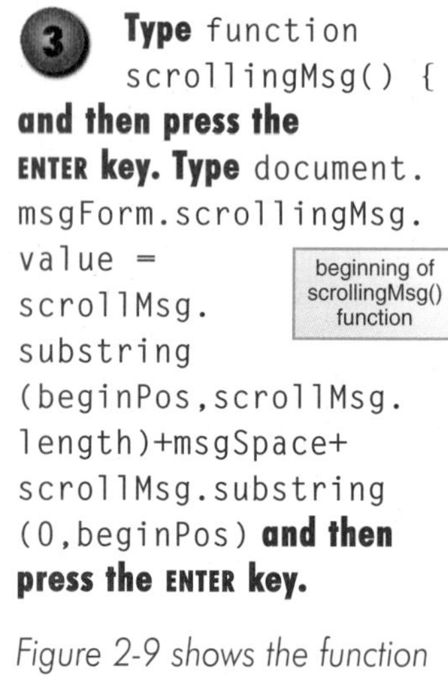

3 **Type** `function scrollingMsg() {` **and then press the ENTER key. Type** `document.msgForm.scrollingMsg.value = scrollMsg.substring(beginPos,scrollMsg.length)+msgSpace+scrollMsg.substring(0,beginPos)` **and then press the ENTER key.**

Figure 2-9 shows the function name and the statement to assign the message to the text box. The assignment statement wraps around to a second line, but consider this statement one line.

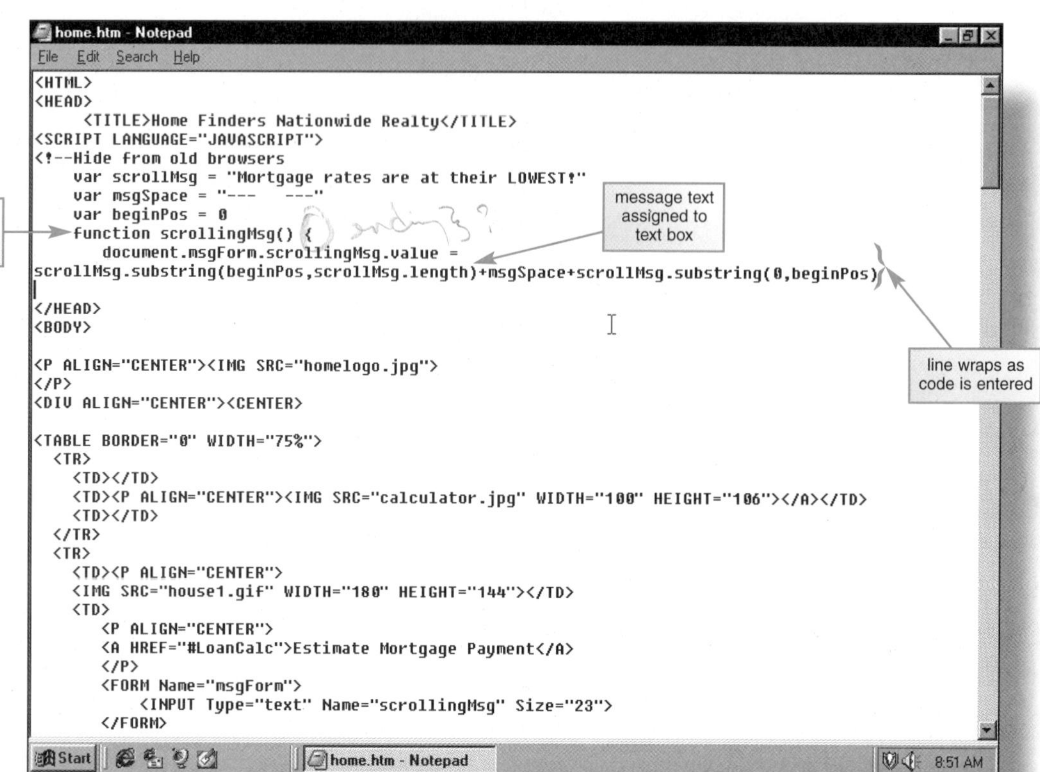

FIGURE 2-9

The JavaScript statements assign the message to the text box, append the spacer value, and start the message display with the first character. Be sure to count the assignment statement on line 10 as one line. The next steps are to increment the beginPos variable, and append the next character from the message string to the text box.

Incrementing the Position Locator Variable

To cause the message to scroll in the text box, you must increment the position locator variable by one. As discussed in the Introduction and shown in Table 2-1, JavaScript provides several ways to increment variables.

Table 2-1 – Incrementing a Variable

STATEMENT	EXPLANATION
variable++	adds 1 to variable
variable = + 1	adds number after plus sign to variable
variable = variable + 1	executes expression on right side of equal sign, and assigns the result to variable on left side

A good programming practice is to use statements easily understood by programmers familiar with other languages. To increment the beginPos locator, you write

```
beginPos = beginPos + 1
```

Once incremented, this new value of the position locator allows the substring() method to extract the next character in the message string and append it to the end of the message in the text box.

Entering an If Statement

After incrementing the position location variable (beginPos) by one, you must determine if the current value of beginPos exceeds the length of the message. To determine if the current value of the beginPos variable is greater than the length of the message, use the If statement. The general form of the If statement is shown in Table 2-2. The first part of the If statement is written as if (condition). You place the JavaScript code to be executed if the result of the conditional test is True within a set of curly braces. Figure 2-10 shows the flowchart that corresponds to an If statement.

Table 2-2 – If Statement

General form:	if (condition) {
	 JavaScript statements if condition true
	 }

Comment:	The condition is the comparison of values. If the result of the comparison is true, JavaScript executes the statements between the curly braces.

Example:	`if (beginPos > scrollMsg.length) {`
	 `beginPos = 0`
	 `}`

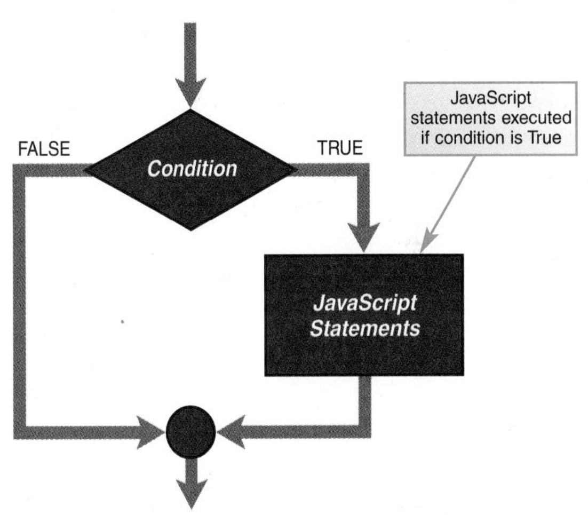

FIGURE 2-10

A **condition** is any expression that evaluates to True or False. When writing an If statement, you must place parentheses around the condition, but leave a space after the If statement so that JavaScript does not interpret the If statement as a function. Table 2-3 shows the conditional operands used for comparisons. For more information on conditionals, refer to page J I.10 of the Introduction.

Table 2-3 – Conditional Operands

OPERAND	EXAMPLE	RESULTS
= =	(a == b)	True if a equals b
!=	(a != b)	True if a does not equal b
>	(a > b)	True if a is greater than b
<	(a < b)	True if a is less than b
>=	(a >= b)	True if a is greater than or equal to b
<=	(a <= b)	True if a is less than or equal to b
&&	(a == b) && (x < y)	True if both conditions are true (a equals b and x is less than y)
||	(a != b) || (x >= a)	True if either condition is true (a does not equal b or x is greater than or equal to a)

More About

The If Statement

If statements are an integral part of script languages and Web pages. For more information on If statements, visit www.scsite.com/js/p2.htm and then click If statement.

More About

Conditional Operators

Conditional operators in JavaScript are similar to the operators used by other programming languages. For more information on conditional operators, visit www.scsite.com/js/p2.htm and then click conditional operators.

The flowchart shown in Figure 2-11 illustrates how the If statement compares the beginning position variable (beginPos) with the overall length of the message (scrollMsg.length).

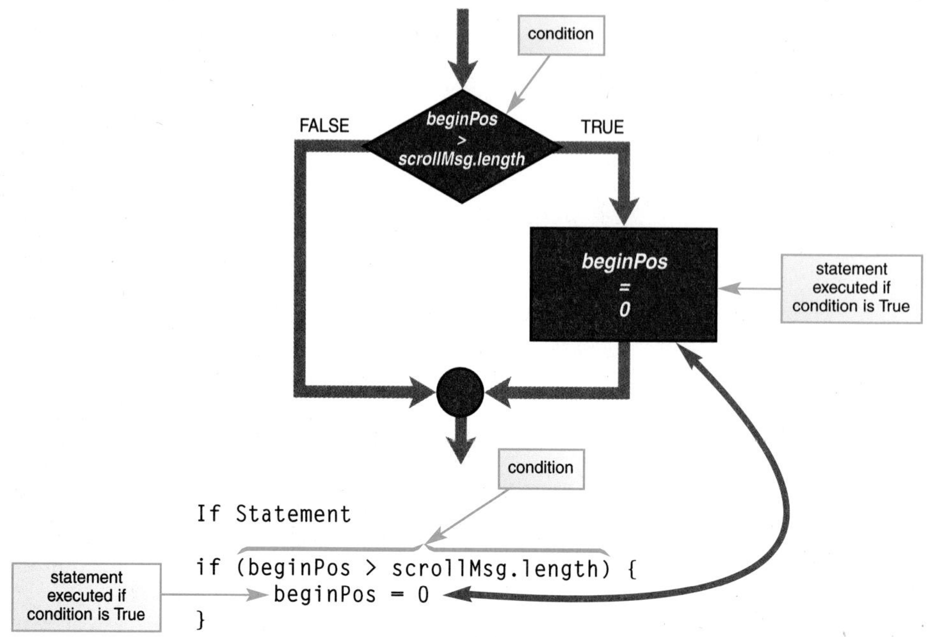

FIGURE 2-11

If the current value of beginPos variable exceeds the scrollMsg.length variable, the statement assigns the value zero to the beginPos variable. When you set the beginPos to zero, it sets the variable back to the first character position of the text string. Perform the following steps to enter an If statement.

To Enter an If Statement

1 **Position the insertion point on line 11. Type** `beginPos = beginPos + 1` **and then press the ENTER key.**

The expression used to increment the beginning position variable displays (Figure 2-12).

home.htm - Notepad

File Edit Search Help

```
<HTML>
<HEAD>
    <TITLE>Home Finders Nationwide Realty</TITLE>
<SCRIPT LANGUAGE="JAVASCRIPT">
<!--Hide from old browsers
    var scrollMsg = "Mortgage rates are at their LOWEST!"
    var msgSpace = "---    ---"
    var beginPos = 0
    function scrollingMsg() {
        document.msgForm.scrollingMsg.value =
scrollMsg.substring(beginPos,scrollMsg.length)+msgSpace+scrollMsg.substring(0,beginPos)
        beginPos = beginPos + 1

</HEAD>
<BODY>

<P ALIGN="CENTER"><IMG SRC="homelogo.jpg">
</P>
<DIV ALIGN="CENTER"><CENTER>

<TABLE BORDER="0" WIDTH="75%">
  <TR>
    <TD></TD>
    <TD><P ALIGN="CENTER"><IMG SRC="calculator.jpg" WIDTH="100" HEIGHT="106"></A></TD>
    <TD></TD>
  </TR>
  <TR>
```

line 11

increments position variable by 1

FIGURE 2-12

2 **Type** `if (beginPos > scrollMsg.length) {` **and then press the ENTER key. Type** `beginPos = 0` **and then press the ENTER key. Type** `}` **and then press the ENTER key.**

The If statement displays (Figure 2-13).

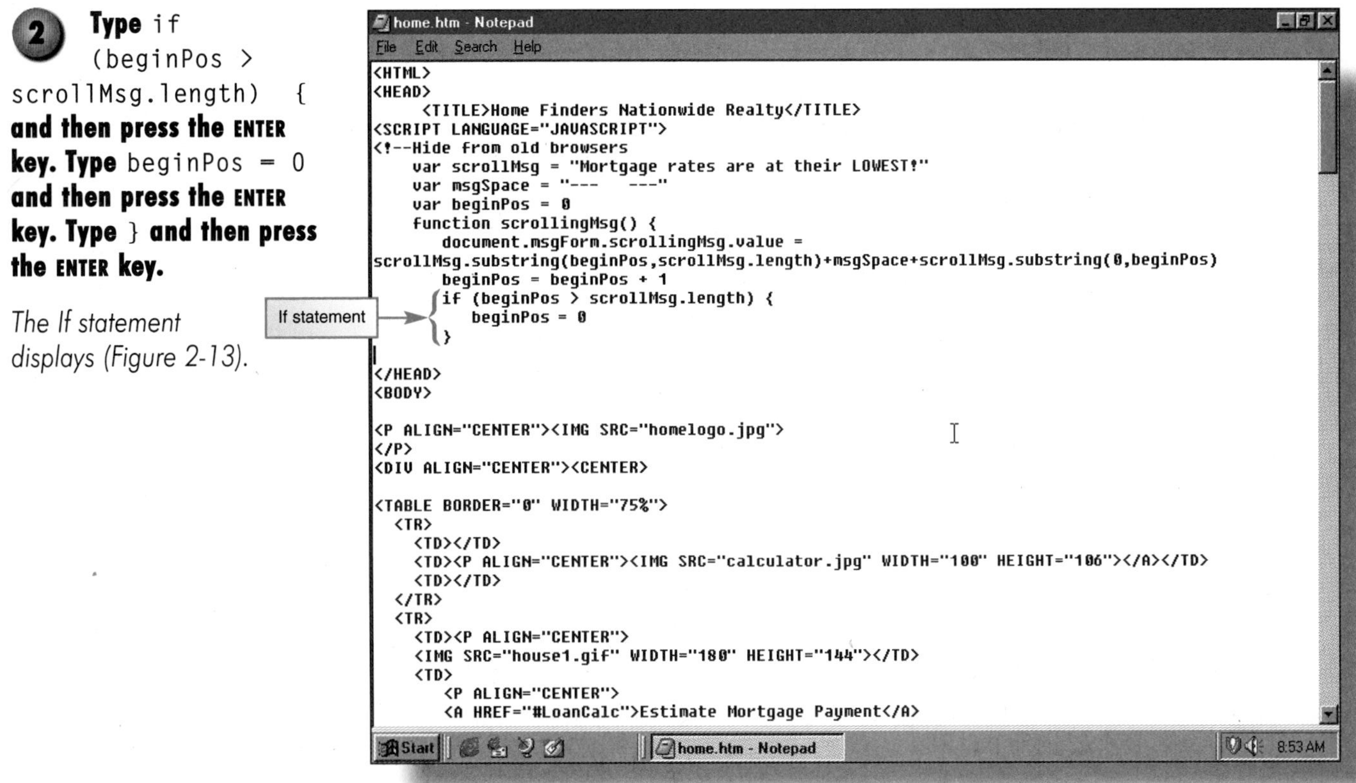


```
<HTML>
<HEAD>
      <TITLE>Home Finders Nationwide Realty</TITLE>
<SCRIPT LANGUAGE="JAVASCRIPT">
<!--Hide from old browsers
     var scrollMsg = "Mortgage rates are at their LOWEST!"
     var msgSpace = "---    ---"
     var beginPos = 0
     function scrollingMsg() {
        document.msgForm.scrollingMsg.value =
scrollMsg.substring(beginPos,scrollMsg.length)+msgSpace+scrollMsg.substring(0,beginPos)
        beginPos = beginPos + 1
        if (beginPos > scrollMsg.length) {
           beginPos = 0
        }

</HEAD>
<BODY>

<P ALIGN="CENTER"><IMG SRC="homelogo.jpg">
</P>
<DIV ALIGN="CENTER"><CENTER>

<TABLE BORDER="0" WIDTH="75%">
  <TR>
    <TD></TD>
    <TD><P ALIGN="CENTER"><IMG SRC="calculator.jpg" WIDTH="100" HEIGHT="106"></A></TD>
    <TD></TD>
  </TR>
  <TR>
    <TD><P ALIGN="CENTER">
    <IMG SRC="house1.gif" WIDTH="180" HEIGHT="144"></TD>
    <TD>
       <P ALIGN="CENTER">
       <A HREF="#LoanCalc">Estimate Mortgage Payment</A>
```

FIGURE 2-13

Using the setTimeout() Method to Create a Recursive Function Call

Recall from Project 1, the **setTimeout()** method calls a function or evaluates an expression after a specified amount of time has elapsed, which is measured in milliseconds. To complete the scrollingMsg() function, you need to add a setTimeout() method that pauses before calling the scrollingMsg() function again. This programming technique, called **recursion**, is used to call the same function from within the function. In this project, the recursive call to the scrollingMsg() function is what makes the message scroll in the text box continuously. Perform the steps on the next page to add the setTimeout() method to create a recursive call to the scrollingMsg() function.

Recursion

Recursive functions generally have a condition that eventually stops the function. For more information on recursion, visit www.scsite.com/js/p2.htm and then click recursion.

To Add the setTimeout() Method to Create a Recursive Function Call

With the insertion point on line 15, type window.setTimeout ("scrollingMsg()", 200) **and then press the ENTER key. Type** } **and then press the ENTER key three times.**

The setTimeout() method pauses the scrolling message for 200 milliseconds and then again calls the scrollingMsg function.

2 **Type** //--> **and then press the ENTER key. Type** </SCRIPT> **and then press the ENTER key.**

The end //--> and </SCRIPT> tags complete the JavaScript section (Figure 2-14).

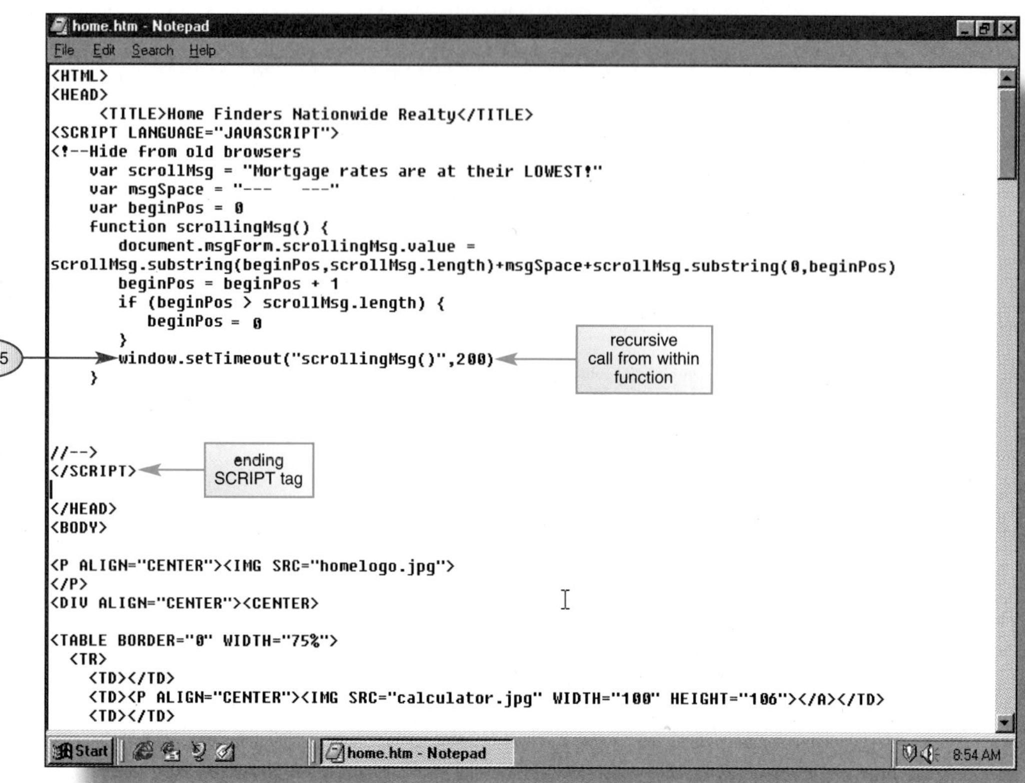

FIGURE 2-14

More About

Event Handlers

Event handlers are the primary technique for calling functions. To learn more about event handlers, visit www.scsite.com/js/p2.htm and then click event handlers.

The setTimeout() method calls the function scrollingMsg() every 200 milliseconds, which allows the message to scroll continuously through the text box. Web developers warn that recursive calls can create undesired results, such as infinite loops or stack overflows. You should use recursive functions carefully to avoid Web page failures.

Adding an Event Handler

The next step is to add an event handler to start the scrolling message when the Web page loads. Recall that an event is a user action. When the user performs an action, such as clicking a button, an event handler triggers associated JavaScript code. In this project, the onload() event handler is used to start the scrollingMsg() function. To have the function called when the page is loaded, you place the onload() event handler in the <BODY> tag. When you insert an event handler within an HTML tag, the statement takes the general form, as shown in Table 2-4.

Table 2-4 – Event Handler	
General form:	<TAG tag attributes eventhandlername = "JavaScript instruction">
Comment:	where TAG is the HTML tag; tag attributes are any HTML attributes; eventhandlername is any of the event handlers; and JavaScript instruction is any JavaScript code or function name.
Examples:	<A HREF = "#LoanCalc" onclick = "doMort()"> <INPUT Type = "Button" Name = "Calc" Value = "Calculate" onclick = "Calc()">

Event handler names are not case sensitive. The Netscape documentation warns that mixed case spellings may not work and strongly recommends Web developers to use all lowercase spellings. In addition, you cannot use all of the event handlers with all HTML tags and attributes. Table 2-5 shows some of the event handlers and the associated HTML attributes. For example, the onclick event handler triggers JavaScript code when used with buttons and links, while the onload event handler is used generally with BODY, FRAMESET, and IMG tags.

The onload event handler is used to trigger an action when a document is loaded into the browser window. In this project, the onload event handler calls the scrollingMsg() function, using the following statement:

Table 2-5

OBJECT	*EVENT HANDLER*
button	onclick
document	onload, onunload
form	onsubmit, onreset
hyperlink	onclick, onmouseover, onmouseout
image	onload, onabort
input box	onblur, onchange, onfocus
submit button	onclick
window	onload, onunload, onblur, onfocus

```
onload="scrollingMsg()"
```

where onload is the event handler and scrollingMsg is the handler text. The statement is entered directly after the beginning BODY tag. To enter the onload event handler to call the scrollingMsg() function, perform the following steps.

To Enter the Event Handler to Call the scrollingMsg() Function

1 **Locate the <BODY> tag on line 24. Position the insertion point directly between the word, BODY, and the > symbol. Press the SPACEBAR once.**

2 **Type** `onload="scrollingMsg()"` **and do not press the ENTER key.**

The onload() event handler displays within the BODY tag. The onload() event handler will call the user-defined function, scrollingMsg(), when the Web page loads (Figure 2-15).

home.htm - Notepad

File Edit Search Help

```
<HTML>
<HEAD>
     <TITLE>Home Finders Nationwide Realty</TITLE>
<SCRIPT LANGUAGE="JAVASCRIPT">
<!--Hide from old browsers
     var scrollMsg = "Mortgage rates are at their LOWEST!"
     var msgSpace = "---    ---"
     var beginPos = 0
     function scrollingMsg() {
          document.msgForm.scrollingMsg.value =
scrollMsg.substring(beginPos,scrollMsg.length)+msgSpace+scrollMsg.substring(0,beginPos)
          beginPos = beginPos + 1
          if (beginPos > scrollMsg.length) {
               beginPos = 0
          }
          window.setTimeout("scrollingMsg()",200)
     }

//-->
</SCRIPT>

</HEAD>
<BODY onload="scrollingMsg()">

<P ALIGN="CENTER"><IMG SRC="homelogo.jpg">
</P>
<DIV ALIGN="CENTER"><CENTER>

<TABLE BORDER="0" WIDTH="75%">
  <TR>
     <TD></TD>
     <TD><P ALIGN="CENTER"><IMG SRC="calculator.jpg" WIDTH="100" HEIGHT="106"></A></TD>
     <TD></TD>
```

onload event handler

line 24

Start | home.htm - Notepad | 8:55 AM

FIGURE 2-15

Saving the HTML File and Testing the Web Page

As you work on a document, you periodically should save your file. Save this file using the file name, homefinders.htm. As in Project 1, you must be sure to add the .htm extension to the file name when you save the file, because Notepad automatically saves all files with a .txt extension. Perform the following steps to save the HTML file on your JavaScript Data Disk using Notepad.

TO SAVE THE FILE ON THE DATA DISK

1. With your JavaScript Data Disk in drive A, click Save As on the File menu.
2. Type `a:\homefinders.htm` in the File name text box and then click the Save button in the Save As dialog box.

The file is saved to the JavaScript Data Disk in drive A. The new file name displays on the Notepad title bar.

While working on a project, save your file several times. After you have saved a file the first time, subsequent Save commands use the same file name. In addition, every time you need to test your Web page you also must save the HTML file by viewing it with your browser. In general, it is a good development practice to test the Web page several times during its development and a final time before posting it to your Web site. When site visitors encounter errors on a Web site, they often leave the Web site — meaning a potential customer is lost. To view and test your Web page using your browser, perform the following steps.

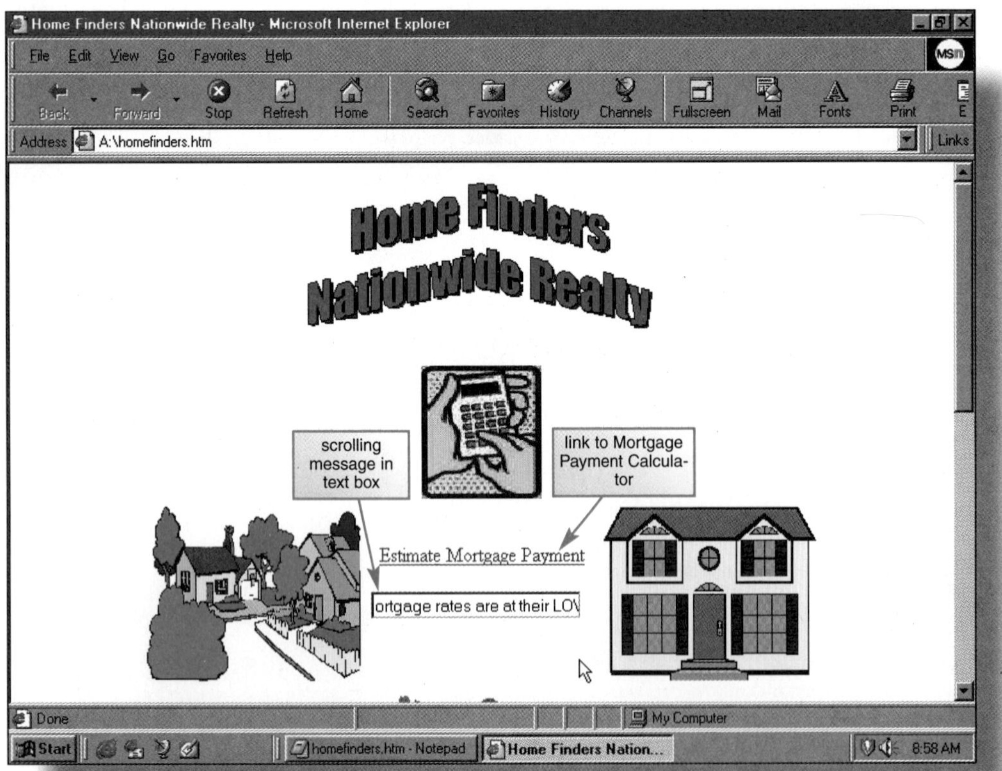

FIGURE 2-16

TO TEST THE WEB PAGE

1. Start your browser. If necessary, click the Maximize button.
2. Click the Address text box. Type `a:\homefinders.htm` and then press the ENTER key.

The Home Finders Nationwide Realty Web page displays with the scrolling message in the text box (Figure 2-16).

If your browser does not display the Web page correctly, close any error messages and then click the Notepad button on the taskbar. Check your JavaScript code according to Figures 2-7 through 2-15 on pages J 2.11 through J 2.17. Correct any errors, save the file, activate the browser, and then click the Refresh button. The next section discusses the mortgage payment calculator form.

The Mortgage Payment Calculator Form

The mortgage payment calculator form shown in Figure 2-17 allows user input. The form is created using HTML and JavaScript code that displays the form and the results (Figure 2-17). To assign a value to a text box object within a form, you must use the form name, the text box name, and the value attribute. Table 2-6 shows the general form of the JavaScript statement used to assign a value to a text box object within a form.

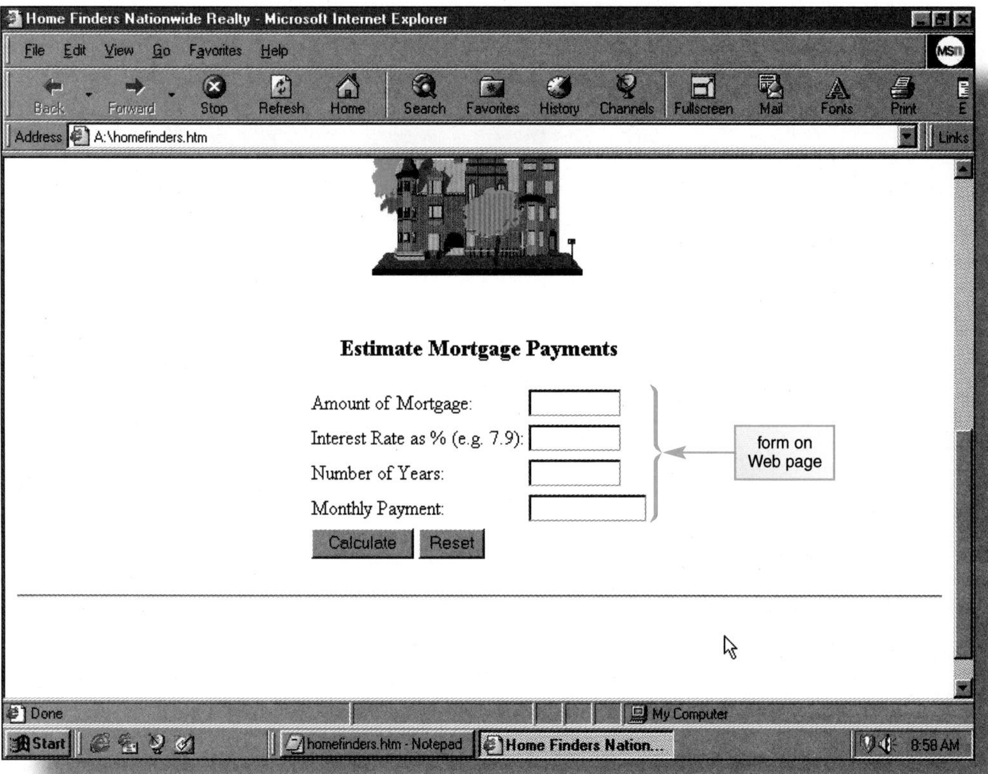

FIGURE 2-17

Table 2-6 – Assign Statement	
General form:	document.formname.textboxname.value = variable_or_literal
Comment:	where formname is the name of the form; textboxname is the name of a text box in the form; value is the attribute; and the variable_or_literal is the value assigned to the text box.
Examples:	`document.MortCalc.Amount.value = LoanAmt` `document.MortCalc.Amount.value = "12500"`

Inserting an Event Handler in an Anchor Tag

In this project, you insert an onclick event handler in an anchor tag to trigger a user-defined function when a user clicks the Estimate Mortgage Payment link. The **anchor** tag defines a target link. The Estimate Mortgage Payment link, for example, refers to an anchor located within the Home Finders page, directly above the mortgage payment calculator (Figure 2-16). When the user clicks the link, the browser scrolls to the anchor reference within the page to display the form used for the mortgage payment calculator.

An anchor tag begins with <A> within the HTML code. The onclick() event handler inside the anchor tag triggers the user-defined function called doMort() when the Estimate Mortgage Payment link is clicked. The doMort() user-defined function contains statements that clear the text boxes and then display the insertion point in the Amount of Mortgage text box. To insert an event handler in the anchor tag for the Estimate Mortgage Payment link, perform the following steps.

To Insert an Event Handler in an Anchor Tag

1 Make sure Notepad is the active window. Scroll down to the BODY section. Position the insertion point on line 41 between the last quotation mark and the > symbol of the <A HREF="#LoanCalc"> anchor tag.

Figure 2-18 shows the position of the insertion point.

line 41

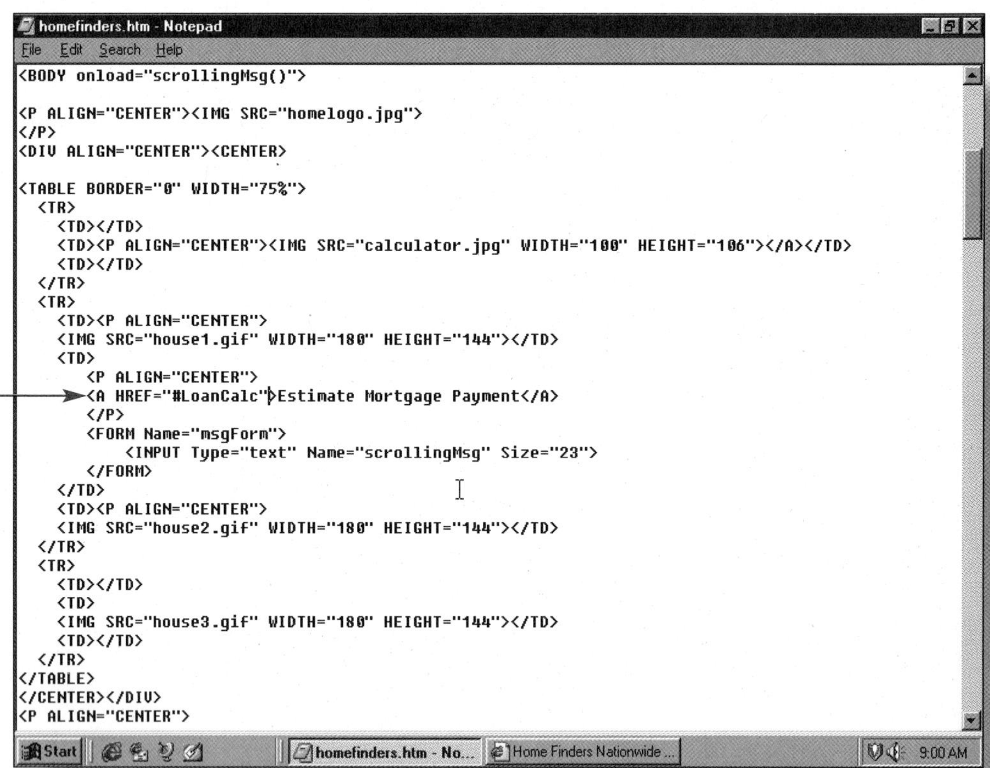


```
<BODY onload="scrollingMsg()">

<P ALIGN="CENTER"><IMG SRC="homelogo.jpg">
</P>
<DIV ALIGN="CENTER"><CENTER>

<TABLE BORDER="0" WIDTH="75%">
  <TR>
    <TD></TD>
    <TD><P ALIGN="CENTER"><IMG SRC="calculator.jpg" WIDTH="100" HEIGHT="106"></A></TD>
    <TD></TD>
  </TR>
  <TR>
    <TD><P ALIGN="CENTER">
    <IMG SRC="house1.gif" WIDTH="180" HEIGHT="144"></TD>
    <TD>
       <P ALIGN="CENTER">
       <A HREF="#LoanCalc">Estimate Mortgage Payment</A>
       </P>
       <FORM Name="msgForm">
           <INPUT Type="text" Name="scrollingMsg" Size="23">
       </FORM>
    </TD>
    <TD><P ALIGN="CENTER">
    <IMG SRC="house2.gif" WIDTH="180" HEIGHT="144"></TD>
  </TR>
  <TR>
    <TD></TD>
    <TD>
    <IMG SRC="house3.gif" WIDTH="180" HEIGHT="144"></TD>
    <TD></TD>
  </TR>
</TABLE>
</CENTER></DIV>
<P ALIGN="CENTER">
```

FIGURE 2-18

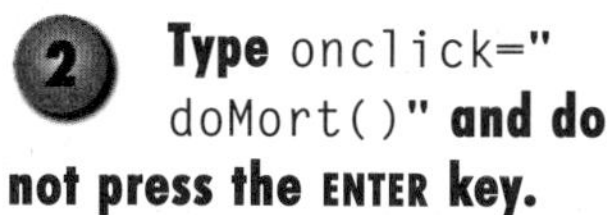

2 Type `onclick="doMort()"` **and do not press the ENTER key.**

The onclick() event handler is entered within the anchor tag (Figure 2-19).

```
homefinders.htm - Notepad
File  Edit  Search  Help
<BODY onload="scrollingMsg()">

<P ALIGN="CENTER"><IMG SRC="homelogo.jpg">
</P>
<DIV ALIGN="CENTER"><CENTER>

<TABLE BORDER="0" WIDTH="75%">
  <TR>
    <TD></TD>
    <TD><P ALIGN="CENTER"><IMG SRC="calculator.jpg" WIDTH="100" HEIGHT="106"></A></TD>
    <TD></TD>
  </TR>
  <TR>
    <TD><P ALIGN="CENTER">
    <IMG SRC="house1.gif" WIDTH="180" HEIGHT="144"></TD>
    <TD>
      <P ALIGN="CENTER">
      <A HREF="#LoanCalc" onclick="doMort()">Estimate Mortgage Payment</A>
      </P>
      <FORM Name="msgForm">
          <INPUT Type="text" Name="scrollingMsg" Size="23">
      </FORM>
    </TD>
    <TD><P ALIGN="CENTER">
    <IMG SRC="house2.gif" WIDTH=     ="144"></TD>
  </TR>
  <TR>
    <TD></TD>
    <TD>
```


FIGURE 2-19

When the viewer clicks the Estimate Mortgage Payment link, the onclick() event handler will execute the doMort() function. The next step is to code the doMort() user-defined function in the HEAD section, below the scrollingMsg() user-defined function.

Writing the doMort() User-Defined Function

Table 2-7

LINE	CODE
19	`function doMort() {`
20	`document.MortCalc.Amount.value=" "`
21	`document.MortCalc.Rate.value=" "`
22	`document.MortCalc.Years.value=" "`
23	`document.MortCalc.Payment.value=" "`
24	`document.MortCalc.Amount.focus()`
25	`}`

The doMort() function shown in Table 2-7 will clear all the text boxes in the form and set the focus to the Amount of Mortgage text box.

Setting the focus means giving attention to an object. When you set focus to a text box, the JavaScript statement automatically positions the insertion point in the text box. The general form of the focus() method is shown in Table 2-8.

Table 2-8 – focus() Method

General form:	document.formname.objectname.focus()
Comment:	where formname is the name of the form that contains the object; and objectname identifies the object to which focus should be set.
Example:	`document.MortCalc.Amount.focus()`

The user sees only the insertion point in the Amount of Mortgage text box and is not aware of the other commands. To clear each text box, you assign a blank to the value property of each object, as shown in lines 20 through 23 in Table 2-7. Line 24 shows setting the focus to the Amount text box. The spacing shown in the tables is for readability purposes. A good programming practice is to indent lines of code under functions, If, If...Else, and Loop statements. To enter the doMort() function to clear the text boxes and set focus to the Amount of Mortgage text box, perform the steps on the next page.

To Enter the doMort() Function

1. **Position the insertion point in the HEAD section on line 18.**

2. **Enter the JavaScript code as shown in Table 2-7 on the previous page.**

These statements cause the Web page to scroll down to the form when the user clicks the Estimate Mortgage Payment link. The doMort() function clears the text boxes and places the insertion point in the Amount of Mortgage text box (Figure 2-20).

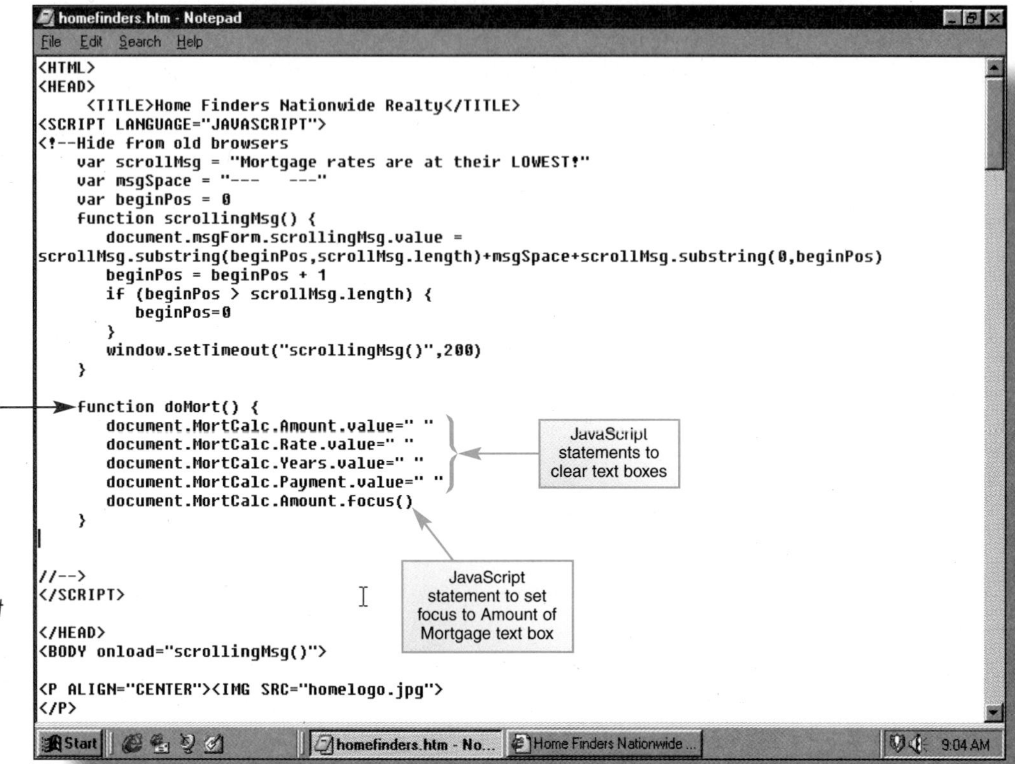

FIGURE 2-20

The focus() method in line 23 causes the Web page to scroll down and position the insertion point in the desired text box when the user clicks the Estimate Mortgage Payment link (Figure 2-16 on page J 2.18).

Saving and Testing the Web Page

Before continuing, you should double-check the spelling, special characters, and quotation marks in the code. The next steps are to save your file and test the Web page.

TO SAVE AND TEST THE WEB PAGE

1. With your JavaScript Data Disk in drive A, click File on the menu bar and then click Save on the File menu.
2. Click the browser button on the taskbar.
3. Click the Refresh button on the browser toolbar.
4. Click the Estimate Mortgage Payment link.

The Web page should display the mortgage payment calculator form with the insertion point in the Amount of Mortgage text box (Figure 2-21).

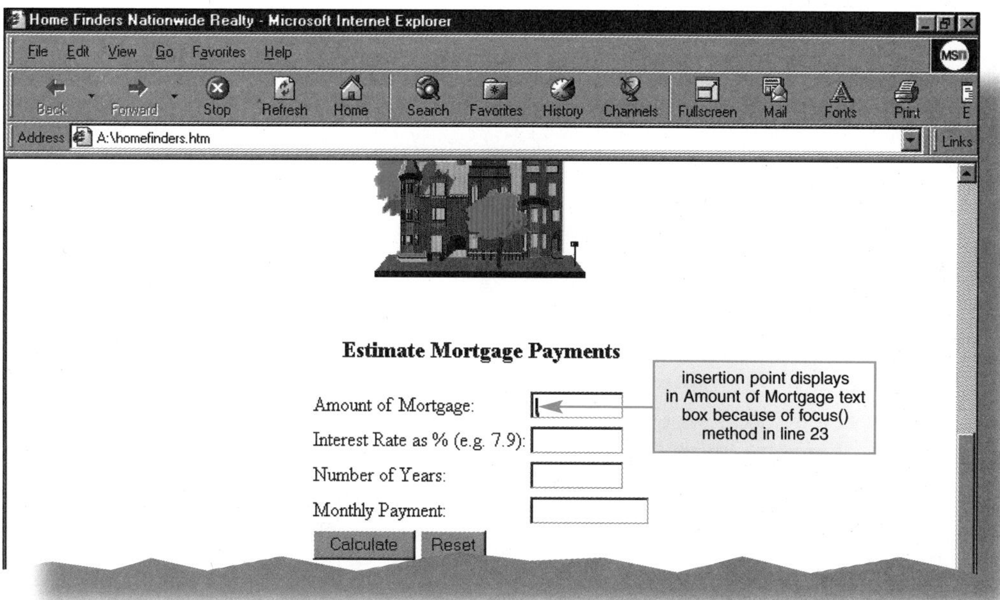

FIGURE 2-21

More About

Validation

Programmers also should write JavaScript code to test data for values that are negative or zero, and reject them as invalid. To keep things simple, the validation presented in this project only tests to ensure that all entered values are numeric. For more information, visit www.scsite.com/js/p2.htm and then click validation.

If your browser does not display the Web page correctly, close any error messages and then click the Notepad button on the taskbar. Check your JavaScript code against Figures 2-18 through 2-20 on pages J 2.20 through J 2.22. Correct any errors and save the file. Activate the browser and then click the Refresh button.

Validating the Mortgage Payment Calculator Form

Form validation is one of the most important features of JavaScript. With JavaScript, the validation procedure is completed on the user's computer instead of the Web server on which the Web page is stored. Along with form validation, JavaScript's math features allow immediate processing of the data. Form validation uses the If...Else statement, which is an extension of the If statement as shown in the flowchart in Figure 2-22.

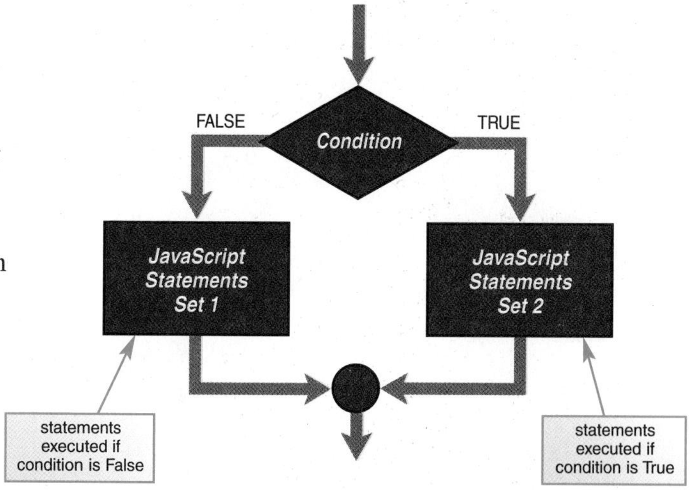

FALSE
Condition
TRUE
JavaScript Statements Set 1
JavaScript Statements Set 2
statements executed if condition is False
statements executed if condition is True

FIGURE 2-22

Validating Data Using the If...Else Statement

Much like the If statement, an If...Else statement tests a condition. If the condition is true, the statements between the curly braces after the If (condition) statement execute. The statements between the curly braces after the Else statement execute if the condition is false.

In this form, you will use the Calc() validation function to convert and store the text box values in temporary variables for validation. The Calc() validation function is placed within an If...Else statement, so that, if the value of a text box is invalid (a True condition), a message displays, the text box clears, and the insertion point is placed back in the text box. This occurs until the user enters valid data in the text box. If the value is valid (a False condition), the next text box is examined until all text boxes are validated. The validation process is shown in the flowchart in Figure 2-23 on the next page.

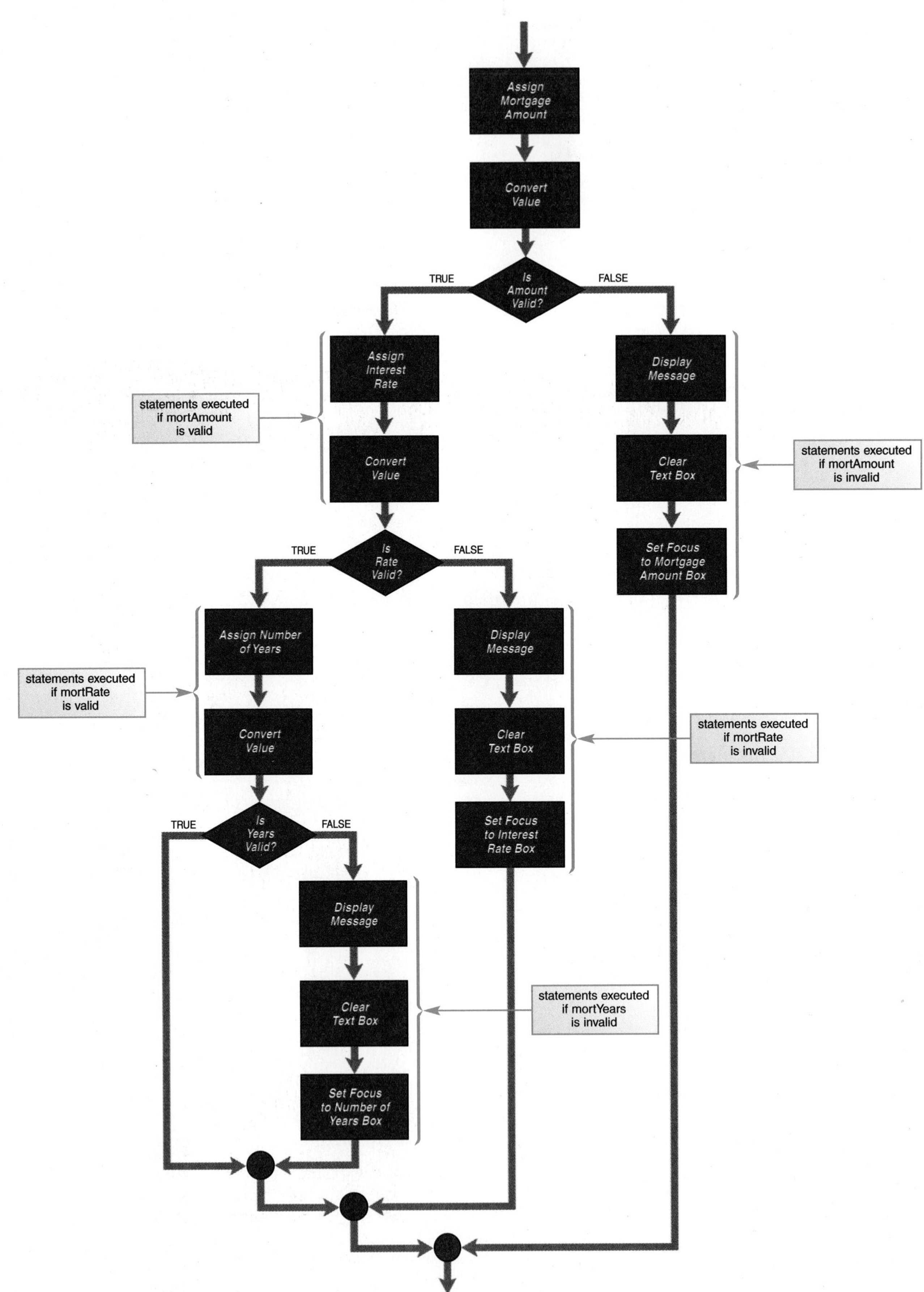
Assign Mortgage Amount
Convert Value
Is Amount Valid?
TRUE
FALSE
Assign Interest Rate
Convert Value
statements executed if mortAmount is valid
Display Message
Clear Text Box
Set Focus to Mortgage Amount Box
statements executed if mortAmount is invalid
Is Rate Valid?
TRUE
FALSE
Assign Number of Years
Convert Value
statements executed if mortRate is valid
Display Message
Clear Text Box
Set Focus to Interest Rate Box
statements executed if mortRate is invalid
Is Years Valid?
TRUE
FALSE
Display Message
Clear Text Box
Set Focus to Number of Years Box
statements executed if mortYears is invalid

FIGURE 2-23

This validation design is necessary because of the event-driven nature of JavaScript. When a user triggers an event that calls a function, processing stays within that function until all statements execute. Because all the statements execute in a function, the form validation routine uses nested If...Else statements to ensure each text box is validated correctly. By nesting If...Else statements, you can place another If...Else statement inside of another as shown in Figure 2-24. Using nested If...Else statements is one method to test multiple conditions.

Attempting to place separate If statements to validate a series of text boxes will not work with event driven programming logic as desired. Each If statement executes until all the statements in the function are complete. Processing continues through the entire set of If statements without terminating as may be desired; thus, the need for the nested If...Else statements. In addition, the placement of the curly braces is important to the logical processing and validation of the text boxes. The curly braces must enclose a complete block of If or Else statements. As shown in Figure 2-24, if the first condition is false, no other statements execute in this block of code. Most Web developers recommend writing nested If...Else statements with the indentation shown in Figure 2-24 for readability purposes.

Validating Forms

JavaScript programmers have developed several ways to validate forms. For more information about validating forms, visit www.scsite.com/js/p2.htm and then click validating forms.

More About

The parseInt() Function

The parseInt() function is one of the built-in functions of JavaScript. You can use the parseInt() function to convert integer numbers to binary, decimal, and hexadecimal form. For more information, visit www.scsite.com/js/p2.htm and then click parseInt().

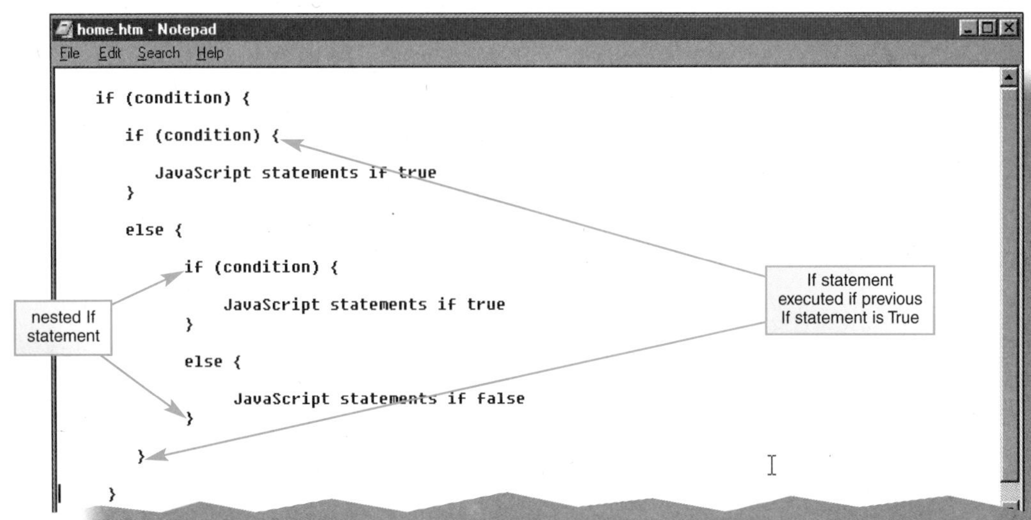

FIGURE 2-24

Validating Data Criteria Using Built-in Functions

When validating data, you may have to evaluate several criteria. You may want, for example, to ensure that a text box is not blank or that it contains numeric data (not text or characters). JavaScript accepts data entered into a text box as string data. You must convert the string values to a number before they can be tested or validated. Table 2-9 describes the built-in functions used for converting values.

Table 2-9

BUILT-IN FUNCTION	SAMPLE AND EXPLANATION
answer = eval(expression)	**Sample:** `answer = eval("1"+"2"+"3")` **Explanation:** converts string values to numbers and executes the expression
variable = parseInt(value, base)	**Sample:** `parseInt(mortAmount, 10)` **Explanation:** value is any string; base is the number base to which you want the string converted. A 2 means binary base number, an 8 means octal, and a 10 means decimal. Returns an integer value, stripping the value after the decimal point.
variable = parseFloat(value)	**Sample:** `parseFloat(mortAmount)` **Explanation:** returns the value as a floating-point number. A floating-point number is a number with a fractional or decimal value.
isNaN(value)	**Sample:** `isNaN(mortAmount)` **Explanation:** returns a Boolean condition of true or false. isNaN means is Not a Number.

The parseFloat() Function

The parseFloat() function is one built-in function. The parseFloat function parses a string argument and returns a floating-point number. If the first character cannot be converted to a number, it returns "NaN" (not a number). For more information on the parseFloat() function, visit www.scsite.com/js/p2.htm and then click parseFloat().

The isNaN() Function

The isNaN() built-in function is the only function that tests for numeric values. The test uses the NOT operator. For more information on the isNaN() function, visit www.scsite.com/js/p2.htm and then click isNaN().

In this project you create the Calc() user-defined function that converts and stores the text box values as integer or floating-point numbers in temporary variables. The function passes the value of the text box to a variable, uses the parseInt() function to convert the variable to a number, and then uses the isNaN() function to verify the value is a number. To pass the text box values to the function, you must place the name of the form (in this case, myform) in the parentheses of the user-defined function Calc() as shown in Figure 2-25.

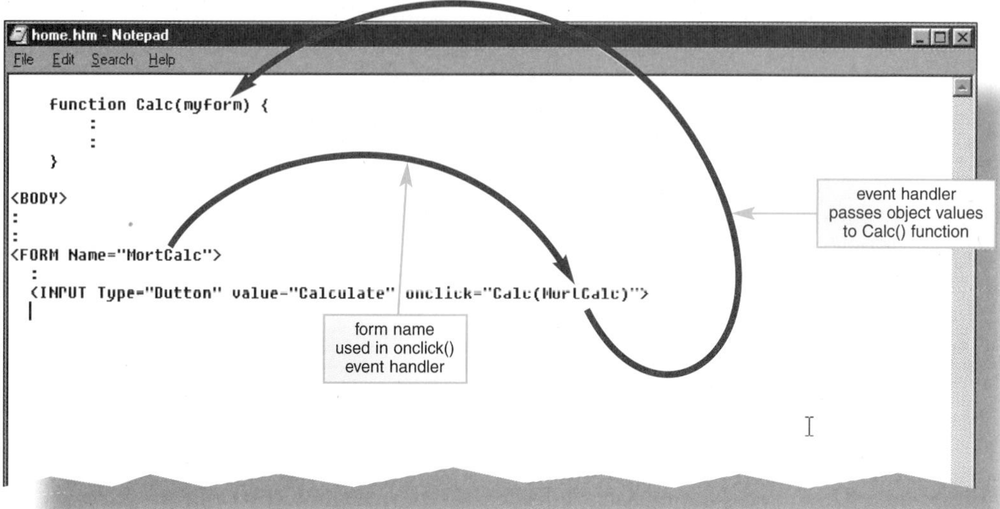

FIGURE 2-25

The If statement beginning in line 29 in Table 2-10 checks the condition to see if the value for the variable mortAmount is not a number. If the result of the condition is true (it is not a number) the function performs the following steps. It notifies the user with an alert message (line 30); it clears the text box entry (line 31); and then it sets the focus back to the Amount of Mortgage text box (line 32). The final curly brace in line 33 closes the If statement.

Table 2-10

LINE	CODE
26	`function Calc(myform) {`
27	`   var mortAmount=document.MortCalc.Amount.value`
28	`   var mortAmount=parseInt(mortAmount,10)`
29	`   if (isNaN(mortAmount)) {`
30	`      alert("The loan amount is not a number!")`
31	`      document.MortCalc.Amount.value=" "`
32	`      document.MortCalc.Amount.focus()`
33	`   }`

To enter the Calc() user-defined function that validates the value in the Amount of Mortgage text box, perform the following steps.

To Enter a Calc() User-Defined Function

1 If necessary, activate Notepad. Scroll up to the HEAD section. Position the insertion point on line 26.

2 Enter the JavaScript code as shown in Table 2-10.

The JavaScript statement passes the text box values to the Calc() function, which converts the Amount of Mortgage value to an integer. If the value is not a number, an alert message displays and the focus is reset to the Amount of Mortgage text box (Figure 2-26).

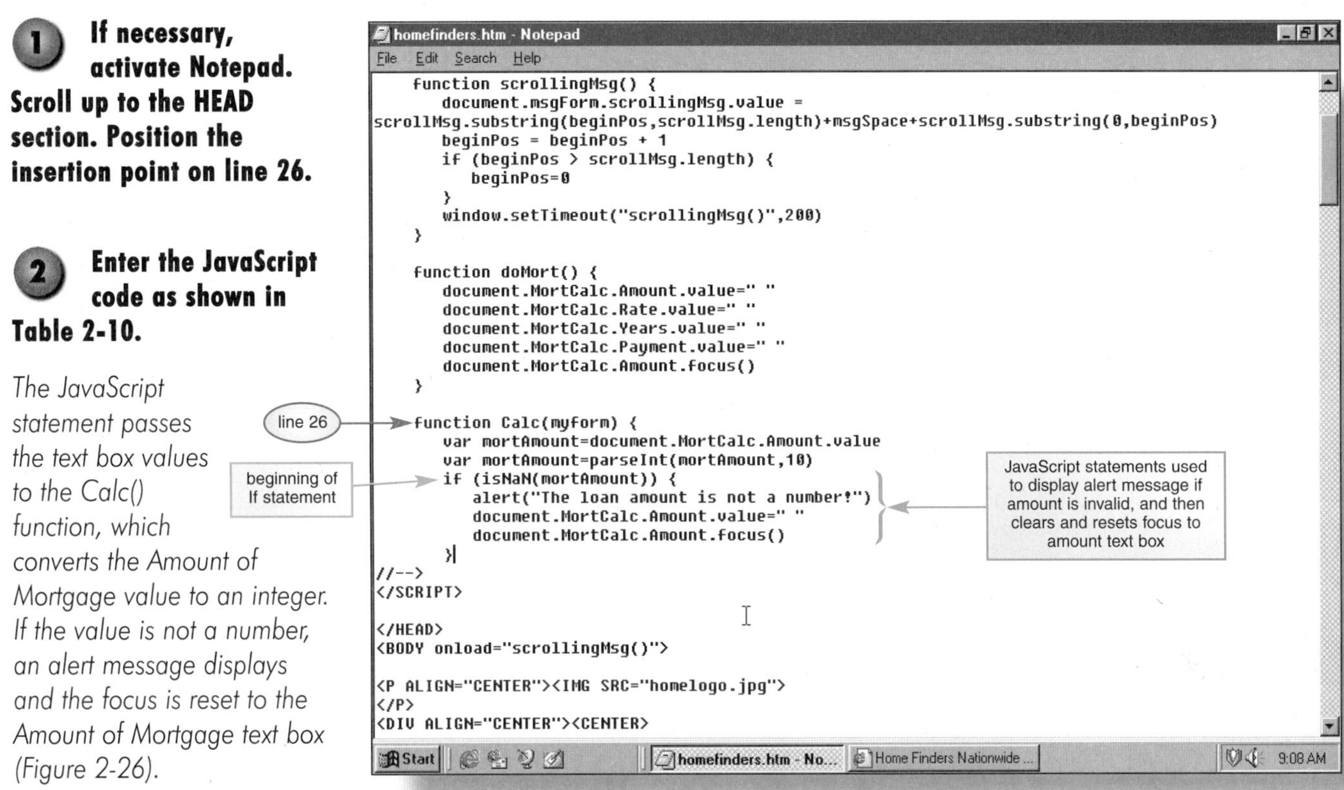

FIGURE 2-26

Because you have two more text boxes to validate in this form, you want the function to continue checking the text box values. The If...Else statement provides the control needed to test the remaining text boxes. Table 2-11 shows the code to validate the data entered in the Interest Rate as % text box. The interest rate validation is similar to that of the mortgage amount, except that you will use the parseFloat() function (line 36 in Table 2-11). Because the interest rate is a floating point number, it requires the parseFloat() function to keep the interest rate a floating number. Table 2-12 on the next page shows the code used to validate the data entered in the Number of Years text box.

Table 2-11

LINE	CODE
34	`else {`
35	`    var mortRate=document.MortCalc.Rate.value`
36	`    var mortRate=parseFloat(mortRate)`
37	`    if (isNaN(mortRate)) {`
38	`       alert("The interest rate is not a number!")`
39	`       document.MortCalc.Rate.value=" "`
40	`       document.MortCalc.Rate.focus()`
41	`    }`

Table 2-12

LINE	CODE

```
42              else {
43                   var mortYears=document.MortCalc.Years.value
44                   var mortYears=parseInt(mortYears,10)
45                   if (isNaN(mortYears)) {
46                      alert("The number of years is not a number!")
47                      document.MortCalc.Years.value=" "
48                      document.MortCalc.Years.focus()
49                   }
50              }
51          }
52     }
```

Perform the following steps to enter the Else portion of the nested If...Else statement that validates the data entered in the Interest Rate as % and Number of Years text boxes.

Steps To Enter the Else Portion of the Nested If...Else Statement

1 Position the insertion point on line 34.

2 Enter the JavaScript code as shown in Table 2-11 on the previous page.

The first Else statement displays (Figure 2-27).

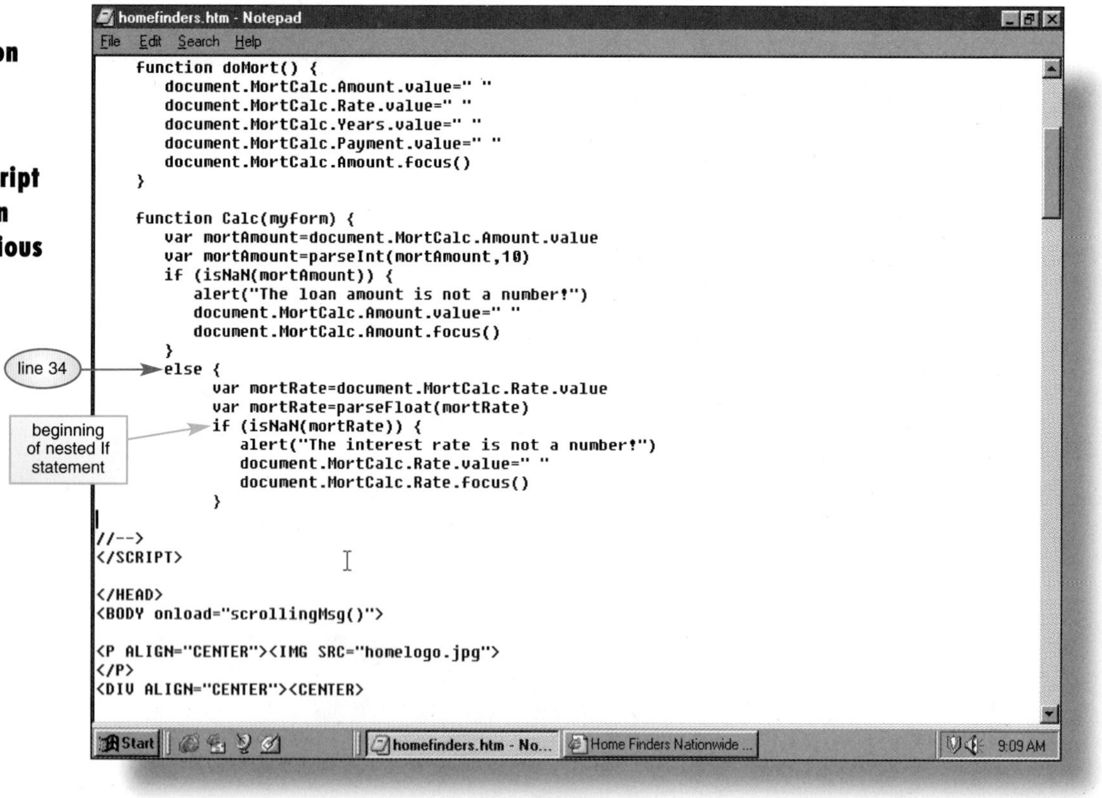

```
homefinders.htm - Notepad
File  Edit  Search  Help
   function doMort() {
      document.MortCalc.Amount.value=" "
      document.MortCalc.Rate.value=" "
      document.MortCalc.Years.value=" "
      document.MortCalc.Payment.value=" "
      document.MortCalc.Amount.focus()
   }

   function Calc(myform) {
      var mortAmount=document.MortCalc.Amount.value
      var mortAmount=parseInt(mortAmount,10)
      if (isNaN(mortAmount)) {
         alert("The loan amount is not a number!")
         document.MortCalc.Amount.value=" "
         document.MortCalc.Amount.focus()
      }
      else {
           var mortRate=document.MortCalc.Rate.value
           var mortRate=parseFloat(mortRate)
           if (isNaN(mortRate)) {
              alert("The interest rate is not a number!")
              document.MortCalc.Rate.value=" "
              document.MortCalc.Rate.focus()
           }

//-->
</SCRIPT>

</HEAD>
<BODY onload="scrollingMsg()">

<P ALIGN="CENTER"><IMG SRC="homelogo.jpg">
</P>
<DIV ALIGN="CENTER"><CENTER>
```

line 34

beginning of nested If statement

Start | homefinders.htm - No... | Home Finders Nationwide ... | 9:09 AM

FIGURE 2-27

3 **Position the insertion point on line 42.**

4 **Enter the JavaScript code as shown in Table 2-12.**

The second Else statement displays (Figure 2-28).

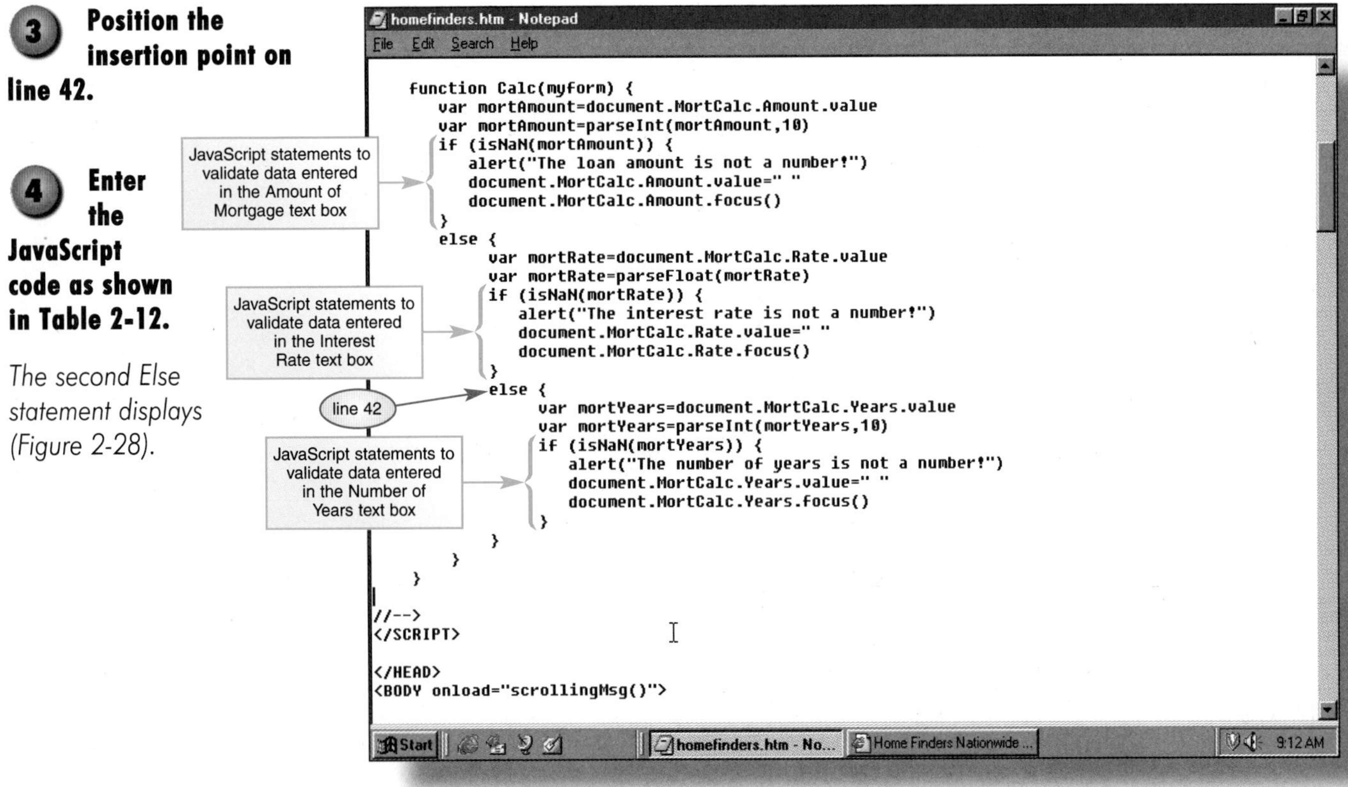


```
function Calc(myform) {
   var mortAmount=document.MortCalc.Amount.value
   var mortAmount=parseInt(mortAmount,10)
   if (isNaN(mortAmount)) {
      alert("The loan amount is not a number!")
      document.MortCalc.Amount.value=" "
      document.MortCalc.Amount.focus()
   }
   else {
        var mortRate=document.MortCalc.Rate.value
        var mortRate=parseFloat(mortRate)
        if (isNaN(mortRate)) {
           alert("The interest rate is not a number!")
           document.MortCalc.Rate.value=" "
           document.MortCalc.Rate.focus()
        }
        else {
             var mortYears=document.MortCalc.Years.value
             var mortYears=parseInt(mortYears,10)
             if (isNaN(mortYears)) {
                alert("The number of years is not a number!")
                document.MortCalc.Years.value=" "
                document.MortCalc.Years.focus()
             }
        }
    }
}

//-->
</SCRIPT>

</HEAD>
<BODY onload="scrollingMsg()">
```

FIGURE 2-28

Placing the If...Else statement within the Calc() function allows you to validate the three text boxes as the user enters data. If the user enters a non-numeric value in any text box, the validation will notify the user and place the insertion point back in that text box.

Adding an Event Handler to Call a Function

Once the user enters valid data in the three form text boxes, he or she can click the Calculate button to calculate the monthly payment. To calculate the monthly payment requires calling the Calc() function. To call the Calc() function by clicking the Calculate button, you must associate an event handler with the Calculate button. Perform the steps on the next page to enter the event handler to call the Calc() function.

To Enter the onclick Event Handler to Call the Calc() Function

1. **Scroll down to the BODY section inside the table. Position the insertion point on line 120, directly before the rightmost > bracket.**

2. **Press the SPACEBAR. Type** `onclick="Calc(MortCalc)"` **and do not press the ENTER key.**

The event handler associates the function Calc() and the Calculate button that is part of the mortgage payment calculator form (MortCalc) (Figure 2-29).

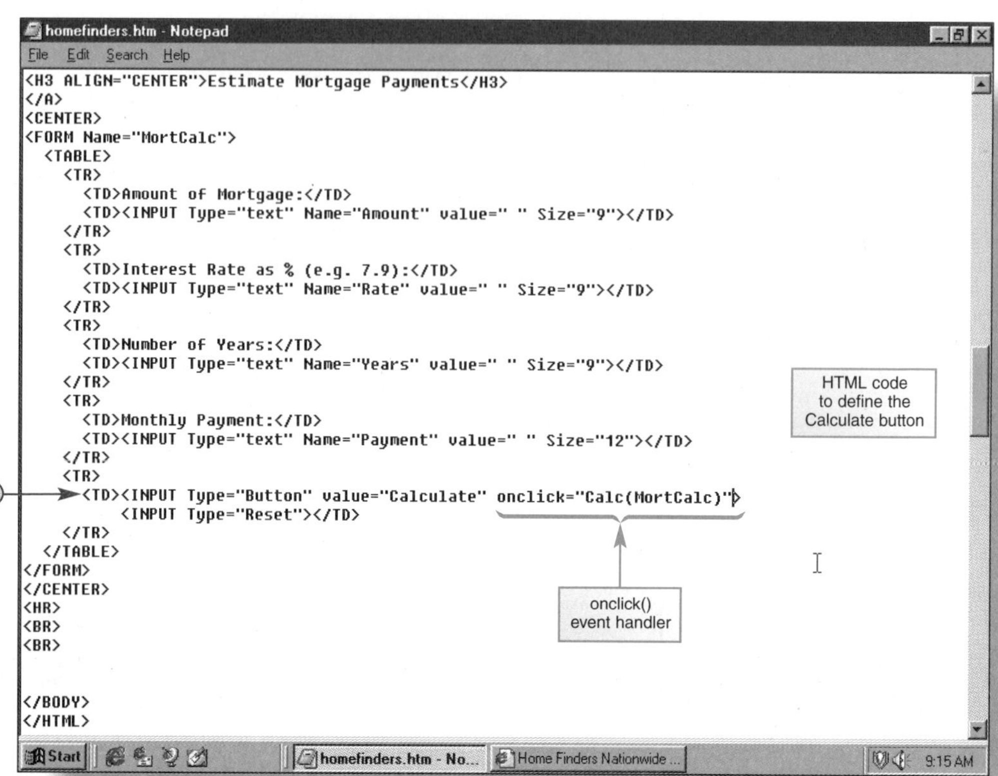

FIGURE 2-29

Saving and Testing the Web Page

The function will not yet calculate the monthly payment, but you can test your validation statements. Before continuing, double-check the spelling, special characters, and quotation marks. The next step is to save your file and test the JavaScript code using your Web browser. To save and test your Web page, perform the following steps.

TO SAVE AND TEST THE WEB PAGE

1. With your JavaScript Data Disk in drive A, click File on the menu bar and then click Save on the File menu.
2. Click the browser button on the taskbar.
3. Click the Refresh button on the browser toolbar.
4. When the Web page displays, click Estimate Mortgage Payment to display and set the focus to the Amount of Mortgage text box.
5. Enter test data set 1, as shown in Table 2-13. Press the TAB key to move the insertion point to the next text box.
6. When you have entered test data set 1, click the Calculate button.
7. When the message box displays, click the OK button.

8. Click the Reset button on the Web page.
9. Repeat steps 5 through 8, using test data sets 2, 3, and 4 (Table 2-13).

Table 2-13

TEST DATA SET	AMOUNT OF MORTGAGE	INTEREST RATE AS %	NUMBER OF YEARS	COMMENT
1		7.9	30	Amount of Mortgage blank
2	10000	A		Interest Rate invalid
3	25000	1	5	Valid
4	69000	7.9		Number of Years blank

The Web page displays the mortgage payment calculator with the insertion point in the Amount of Mortgage text box. When you enter test data set 4, an alert message displays to notify you that the data entered for Number of Years is invalid (Figure 2-30).

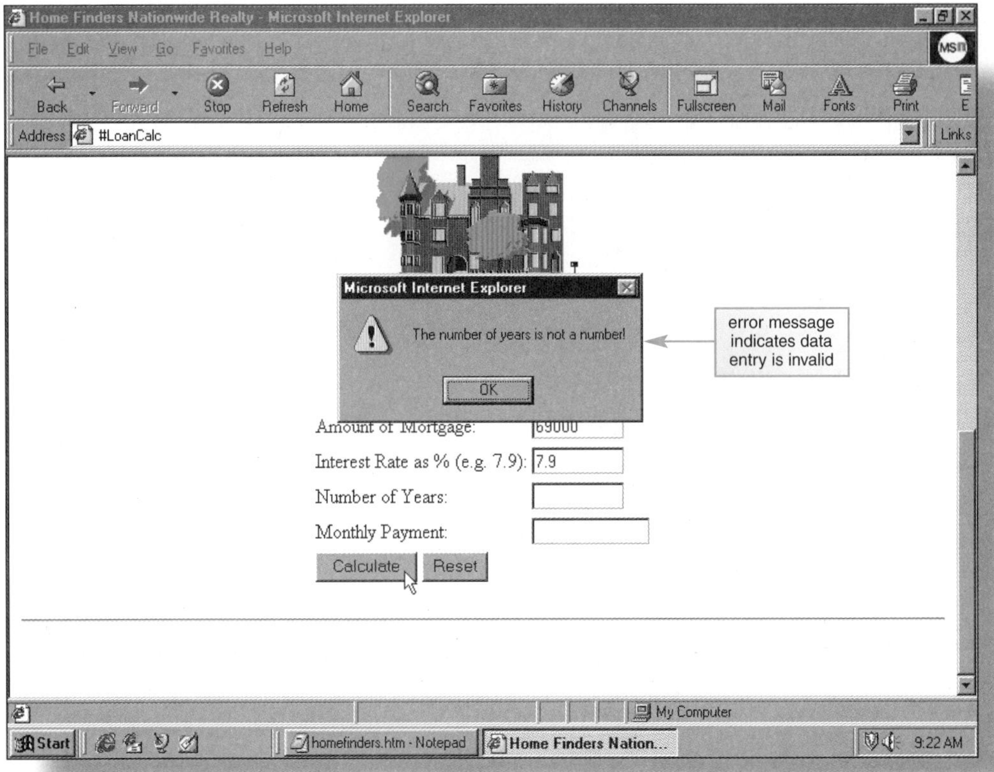

FIGURE 2-30

If your browser does not display the Web page correctly, close any error message windows, and click the Notepad button on the taskbar. Check your JavaScript code against Figures 2-26 through 2-29 on pages J 2.27 through J 2.30. Correct any errors and save the file. Activate the browser and then click the Refresh button.

Determining the Monthly Payment

The next statement in the Calc() function calls a user-defined function, named monthly(), that you will create to calculate the monthly payment. The monthly() function requires that valid data is entered in the Amount of Mortgage, Interest Rate as %, and Number of Years text boxes before it can calculate the monthly payment. Once the monthly() function calculates the monthly payment, it returns the result to the Monthly Payment text box.

The function call is inserted on line 52, before the last curly brace of the Calc() function. The function call is written as follows

```
document.MortCalc.Payment.value=monthly(mortAmount,mortRate,mortYears)
```

In this statement, MortCalc is the name of the form; Payment is the name of the Monthly Payment text box; and value is the value returned by the monthly() user-defined function. The variables mortAmount, mortRate, and mortYears are the values entered in the Amount of Mortgage, Interest Rate as %, and Number of Years text boxes.

Perform the following steps to enter a function call that passes the required values to the monthly() user-defined function.

To Pass Values to the monthly() User-Defined Function

1 Scroll up to the HEAD section. Position the insertion point on line 52. Press the ENTER key to insert a blank line. Position the insertion point on the blank line.

The insertion point displays on the blank line (Figure 2-31).

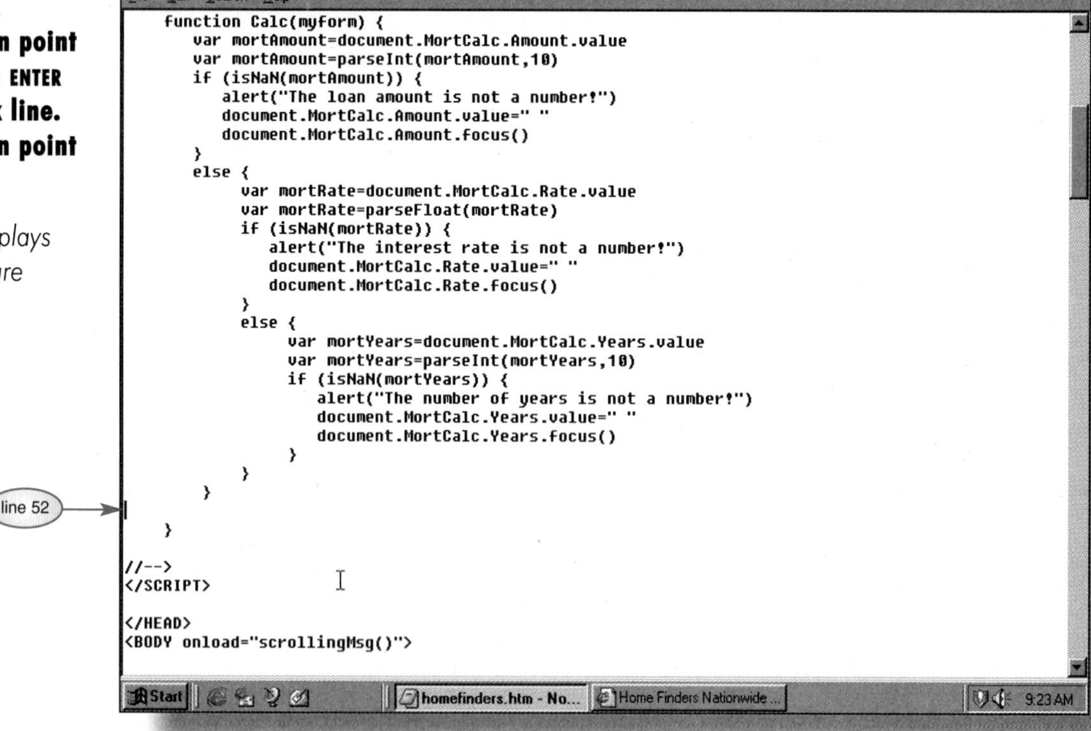

FIGURE 2-31

Type `document.MortCalc.Payment.value=monthly(mortAmount,mortRate,mortYears)` **and then press the ENTER key.**

The function call statement displays (Figure 2-32).

```
homefinders.htm - Notepad
File  Edit  Search  Help
    function Calc(myForm) {
       var mortAmount=document.MortCalc.Amount.value
       var mortAmount=parseInt(mortAmount,10)
       if (isNaN(mortAmount)) {
          alert("The loan amount is not a number!")
          document.MortCalc.Amount.value=" "
          document.MortCalc.Amount.focus()
       }
       else {
            var mortRate=document.MortCalc.Rate.value
            var mortRate=parseFloat(mortRate)
            if (isNaN(mortRate)) {
               alert("The interest rate is not a number!")
               document.MortCalc.Rate.value=" "
               document.MortCalc.Rate.focus()
            }
            else {
                 var mortYears=document.MortCalc.Years.value
                 var mortYears=parseInt(mortYears,10)
                 if (isNaN(mortYears)) {
                    alert("The number of years is not a number!")
                    document.MortCalc.Years.value=" "
                    document.MortCalc.Years.focus()
                 }
            }
        }
        document.MortCalc.Payment.value=monthly(mortAmount,mortRate,mortYears)

    }

//-->
</SCRIPT>

</HEAD>
<BODY onload="scrollingMsg()">
```

call to monthiy() function

FIGURE 2-32

If you were to test the Web page at this point, an error message would display because you have not yet entered the monthly() function into the HTML file.

Creating the monthly() Function

The monthly() function, which is used to calculate the monthly payment amount, requires three parameters: the mortgage amount (mortAmount), the interest rate (mortRate), and the number of years that the payments will be made (mortYears). The call statement entered in the previous set of steps passes the three variables — mortAmount, mortRate, and mortYears — to the monthly() function. The JavaScript code for the function is shown in Table 2-14.

Table 2-14

CODE
`function monthly(mortAmount,mortRate,mortYears) {`
`   var Irate=mortRate/1200`
`   var Pmts=mortYears*12`
`   var Loan=mortAmount`
`   return Loan * (Irate / (1 - (1 / Math.pow(1+Irate,Pmts))))`
`}`

You use the validated values in a mathematical expression or formula that calculates the monthly payment. The formula for calculating a monthly payment is shown in line 60. JavaScript does not use typical programming language symbols to represent exponentiation. To calculate the expression $(1 + \text{Irate})^{\text{payment}}$, JavaScript uses the pow() method associated with the Math object. Table 2-15 shows the general form of the pow() method.

Math Object Methods

The Math object has a number of helpful methods, including pow(). For more information on the Math object, visit www.scsite.com/js/p2.htm and then click Math object methods.

Table 2-15 – Math.pow() Method

General form:	Math.pow(number, exponent)
Comment:	where number is the value raised to the power of the exponent value. The pow() method accepts variables (X, n), constants (2, 3), or both (Sidelength, 2).

Example:	`Math.pow(2,3)`
	`Math.pow(X,n)`
	`Math.pow(Sidelength,2)`

Before the formula executes, however, you must convert two of the values. In line 57, the annual rate of interest must be converted to a monthly rate. In line 58, the number of years must be converted to the number of payments. To convert the monthly interest and shift the decimal point to the right two places, divide the annual rate by 1200 and store it in the variable Irate. To convert the total number of payments multiply the years by 12 and store it in Pmts. The following statements show how to convert the interest and years. To prevent the mortAmount from being changed accidentally, assign it to a temporary variable (Loan) as shown in line 59.

The return statement (line 60) tells the function to send the results of the expression back to the calling function. The value then displays in the Monthly Payment text box. Perform the following steps to enter the monthly() function.

Steps To Enter the monthly() Function

1 **Position the insertion point on line 56, the line directly above the //--> tag.**

2 **Enter the JavaScript code as shown in Table 2-14 on the previous page and then press the ENTER key.**

The monthly() function displays (Figure 2-33).

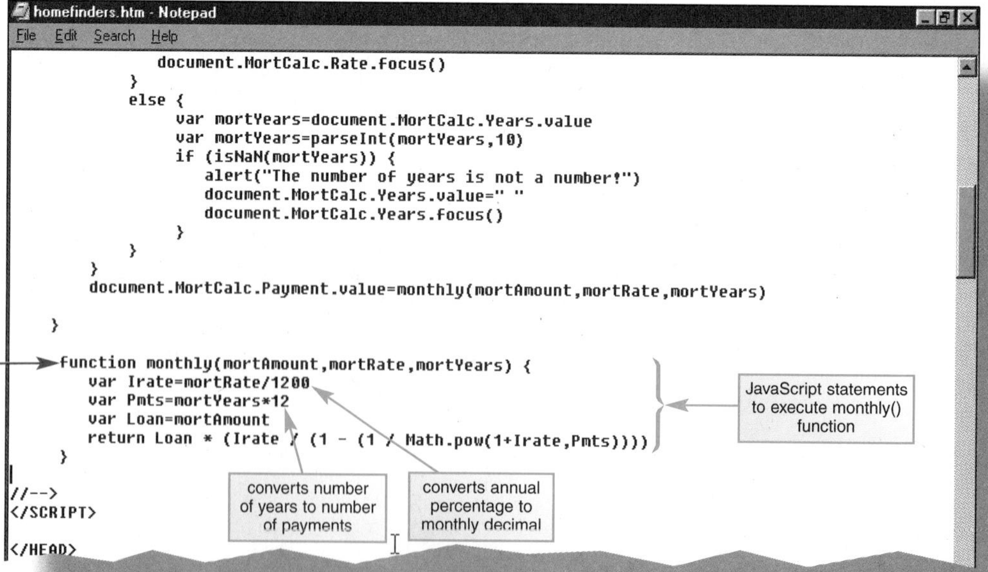

FIGURE 2-33

Before continuing, you should double-check the spelling, symbols, parentheses, curly braces, and quotation marks in the code. The next steps are to save your file and test the Web page using test data.

TO SAVE AND TEST THE WEB PAGE

1. With your JavaScript Data Disk in drive A, click File on the menu bar and then click Save on the File menu.
2. Click the browser button on the taskbar.
3. Click the Refresh button on the browser toolbar.
4. If necessary, click the Amount of Mortgage text box to place the insertion point in the text box.
5. Type `69000` in the Amount of Mortgage text box and then press the TAB key.
6. Type `7.9` in the Interest Rate as % text box and then press the TAB key.
7. Type `30` in the Number of Years text box and then click the Calculate button.

The amount of the monthly payment, 501.4957296230, displays (Figure 2-34).

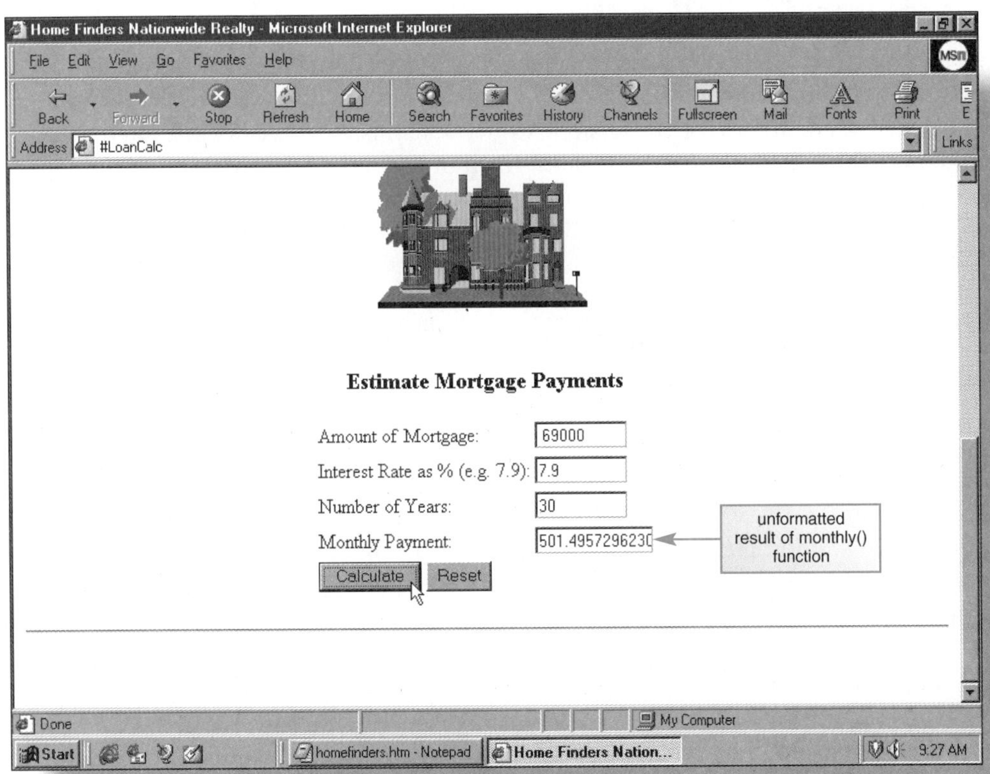

FIGURE 2-34

If your browser does not display the Web page correctly, close any error messages and then click the Notepad button on the taskbar. Check your JavaScript code against Figures 2-31 through 2-33 on pages J 2.32 through J 2.34. Correct any errors and save the file. Activate the browser, click the Refresh button, and then reenter the data listed in the previous steps.

Formatting the Monthly Payment Output as Currency

In the previous steps, the monthly payment amount calculated using the test data displayed as the value, 501.4957296230. To set the form to display the monthly payment amount in a currency format with two decimal places and a dollar sign, you need to enter a new function called dollarFormat(). First, you must enter a statement that passes the resulting string object of the monthly payment Calc() function to the dollarFormat() function. The dollarFormat() function then analyzes the string and adds commas and displays the number with a dollar sign and two decimal places.

To format the result, the dollarFormat() function performs these five basic steps. The function: (1) takes the string value and separates the dollars from the cents based on the position of the decimal point; (2) determines the location of the decimal point using the indexOf() method; (3) separates the value to the left of the decimal point as the dollar amount and the value to the right of the decimal point as the cents amount; (4) inserts commas every three positions in dollar amounts exceeding 999; and (5) reconstructs the string value with two decimal places, inserts a dollar sign immediately to left of the first digit without spaces, and then returns the completed formatted value.

More About

The indexOf() Method

The indexOf() method often is used in conjunction with other string methods to subdivide string values. For more information on the indexOf() method, visit www.scsite.com/js/p2.htm and then click indexOf().

Using the indexOf() Method

The indexOf() method is used to search a string for a particular value and returns the relative location of that value within the string. The indexOf() method searches the string object for the desired value, which is enclosed within the quotation marks. Table 2-16 shows the general form of the indexOf() method.

Table 2-16 – indexOf() Method	
General form:	var position = stringname.indexOf("c")
Comment:	where position is a variable; stringname is any string object; and "c" is the value for which the function searches.
Example:	`var decipos = valuein.indexOf(".")`

If the search value is found in the string object, the indexOf() method returns the relative position of the value within the string object. If the search value is not found, the indexOf() method returns a negative one (-1). In this project, the indexOf() method is used to search for a decimal point in the monthly payment amount. Figure 2-35 provides an example of how the indexOf() method works.

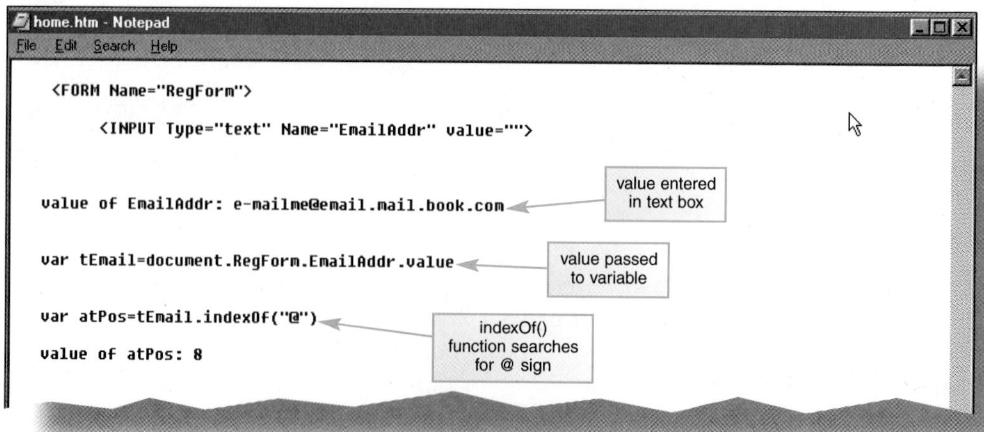

FIGURE 2-35

Determining the Dollars Portion

The dollarFormat() function initializes the variable that will return the formatted value and the variable used to manipulate the unformatted value. Most programmers agree it is a good programming practice to clear and initialize variables to ensure the data is valid. Table 2-17 shows the JavaScript code used to initialize the variables.

Table 2-17

LINE	CODE
63	`function dollarFormat(valuein) {`
64	`var formatStr=""`
65	`var Outdollars=""`
66	`var decipos=valuein.indexOf(".")`
67	`if (decipos==-1)`
68	`decipos=valuein.length`

Lines 64 and 65 clear the variables used to assemble the formatted output. The indexOf() method in line 66 returns a value indicating the location of the decimal point – a value stored as the decipos. The decipos value indicates at what position to concatenate the decimal values. Lines 67 and 68 test the decipos variable for a value greater than zero. If the value of decipos is zero, then the input value (valuein) is an integer. If the value of decipos is negative one, then decipos is set equal to the length of the string, as shown in line 68.

Perform the following steps to enter the dollarFormat() function and initialize the variables.

Steps To Enter the dollarFormat() Function

1. **Position the insertion point on line 63.**

2. **Enter the JavaScript code as shown in Table 2-17 and then press the ENTER key.**

The dollarFormat() function and the statements to initialize the variables display (Figure 2-36).

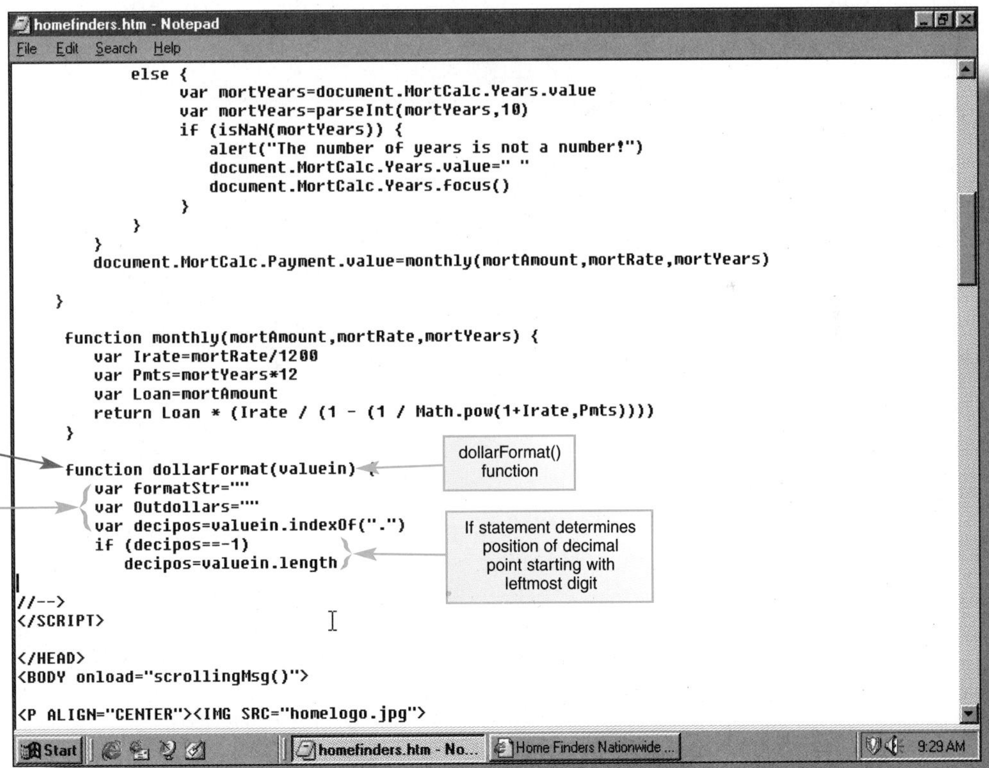

FIGURE 2-36

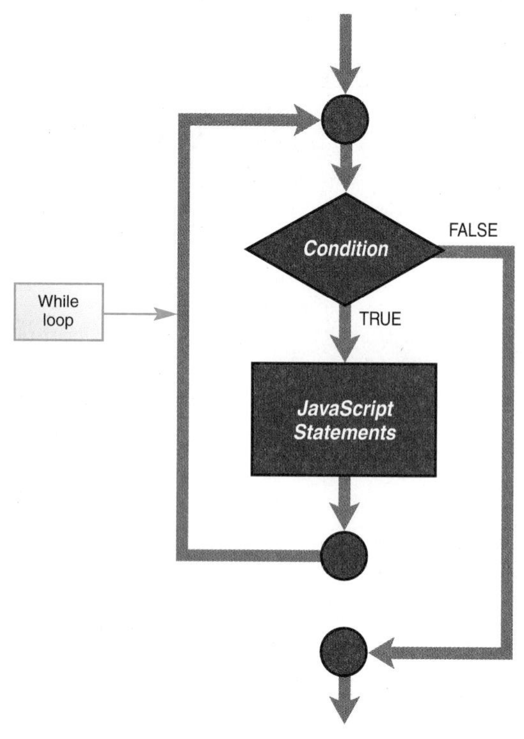

FIGURE 2-37

The first three statements initialize the variables that temporarily hold data during the formatting process. The indexOf() method determines the position of the decimal point and stores it in the variable decipos. The If statement verifies if a decimal point exists; if not, it sets the position to the length of the string.

Next, you enter statements that will format any dollar values greater than three digits with commas. To accomplish this task, you will use a While loop.

Using For Loops and While Loops

A **loop** is a series of statements that executes repeatedly until it satisfies a condition. JavaScript has two types of loops, the For loop and the While loop. Both the For loop and the While loop use the logic illustrated by the flowchart in Figure 2-37. Both loops first test a condition to determine if the instructions in the loop are to be executed.

The **For loop** relies on a conditional statement using numeric values and thus often is referred to as a counter-controlled loop. Table 2-18 shows the general form of the For loop.

Table 2-18 – For Loop	

General form:	for (start; stop; counter-control) {
	    JavaScript statements
	}

Comment:	where start is a variable initialized to a beginning value; stop is an expression indicating the condition at which the loop should terminate; and the counter-control is an expression indicating how to increment or decrement the counter. Semicolons separate the three variables.

Examples:	`for (j=1; j=5; j++) {`
	`for (ctr = 6; ctr < 0; ctr--) {`
	`for (item = 1; item = 100; item=+2) {`

The **While loop** relies on a conditional statement that can use either a numeric value or a string. Table 2-19 shows the general form of the While loop.

Table 2-19 – While Loop	

General form:	while (condition) {
	    JavaScript statements
	}

Comment:	where condition is either a numeric value or a string; and the JavaScript statements execute while the result of the condition is true.

Examples:	`while (ctr < 6) {`
	`while (isNaN(temp))  {`
	`while (Response != "Done") {`

Extracting the Dollars Portion and Inserting Commas

In this project, the While loop is used in formatting the dollar value of the Monthly Payment value. The dollars portion is represented by the digits to the left of the decimal point. If the dollars portion of the mortgage payment contains more than three digits, you need to insert commas. To determine how many digits are in the dollar portion of the monthly payment amount, you use an If...Else statement. Table 2-20 shows the JavaScript statements used to determine the length of the dollar value and placement of the commas.

Table 2-20

```
LINE  CODE
69    var dollars=valuein.substring(0,decipos)
70    var dollen=dollars.length
71    if (dollen>3) {
72       while (dollen>0) {
73             tDollars=dollars.substring(dollen-3,dollen)
74             if (tDollars.length==3) {
75                Outdollars=","+tDollars+Outdollars
76                dollen=dollen-3
77             } else {
78                    Outdollars=tDollars+Outdollars
79                    dollen=0
80                }
81       }
82    if (Outdollars.substring(0,1)==",")
83       dollars=Outdollars.substring(1,Outdollars.length)
84    else
85       dollars=Outdollars
86    }
```

The substring() method on line 69 uses the decipos value (the location of the decimal point) to extract the dollar value (the variable dollars). Next, a series of statements determine the length of the dollar value and then assign the length to the variable, dollen (line 70). Line 71 begins the If statement. Lines 72 through 81 use a While loop that places a comma every three digits, as needed. The statements insert a comma every three digits, while the length of the dollar value is greater than three digits. Line 73 extracts three digits starting from the right by subtracting 3 from the length of the dollar value (dollen). Line 74 verifies three digits and line 75 inserts a comma in the output string. Line 76 decrements the length of the dollar value to look for the next group of three digits. When no more groups of three digits exist, the length of dollen is set to zero (line 79) and the loop terminates at line 81. The statements in lines 82 through 86 prevent the code from inserting a comma if only three digits are to the left of the decimal point. Perform the steps on the next page to extract the dollar portion of the output and insert commas into the output, if needed.

To Extract the Dollar Portion of the Output and Insert Commas

1 Position the insertion point at line 69, the line directly below the statement, decipos=valuein. length.

2 Enter the JavaScript code as shown in Table 2-20 on the previous page and then press the ENTER key.

The code displays (Figure 2-38).

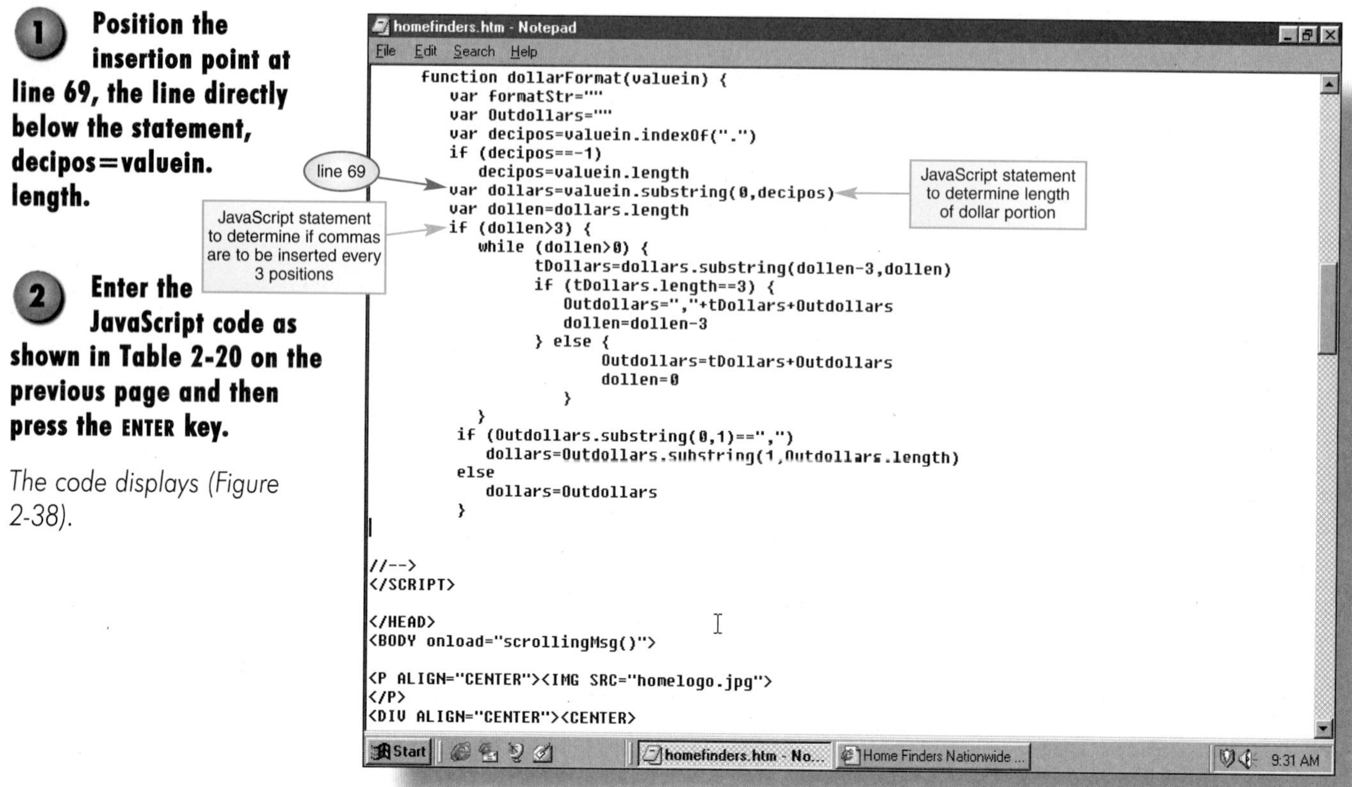
homefinders.htm - Notepad
File Edit Search Help
function dollarFormat(valuein) {
var formatStr=""
var Outdollars=""
var decipos=valuein.indexOf(".")
if (decipos==-1)
decipos=valuein.length
var dollars=valuein.substring(0,decipos)
var dollen=dollars.length
if (dollen>3) {
while (dollen>0) {
tDollars=dollars.substring(dollen-3,dollen)
if (tDollars.length==3) {
Outdollars=","+tDollars+Outdollars
dollen=dollen-3
} else {
Outdollars=tDollars+Outdollars
dollen=0
}
}
if (Outdollars.substring(0,1)==",")
dollars=Outdollars.substring(1,Outdollars.length)
else
dollars=Outdollars
}
//-->
</SCRIPT>
</HEAD>
<BODY onload="scrollingMsg()">
<P ALIGN="CENTER"><IMG SRC="homelogo.jpg">
</P>
<DIV ALIGN="CENTER"><CENTER>
line 69
JavaScript statement to determine length of dollar portion
JavaScript statement to determine if commas are to be inserted every 3 positions
Start
homefinders.htm - No...
Home Finders Nationwide ...
9:31 AM

FIGURE 2-38

Before continuing, you should double-check the spelling, special characters, and quotation marks in the code.

Extracting the Cents Portion and Defining the Decimal Amount

Recall that the mortgage payment amount should display with two decimal places to the right of the decimal point. After you have written JavaScript to extract the dollar portion of the string and place commas, as needed, you must write a statement to extract the cents portion from the valuein string. Table 2-21 shows the statement used to complete this task.

Table 2-21

LINE	CODE
87	`var cents=valuein.substring(decipos+1, decipos+3)`
88	`if (cents=="")`
89	`    cents="00"`

The statement at line 87 extracts two digits from the valuein string, starting at the calculated monthly payment decimal point position plus one. The value returned is tested to see if it is an integer (line 88). If it is — meaning the monthly payment is a dollar value like $432.00 or $51.00 — line 89 assigns two zeros to the cents string. If it is not, the statements in line 87 extract and store the first two decimal places as the cents portion of the monthly payment. Perform the following steps to enter the statements to extract the cents portion and define the decimal amount.

To Extract the Cents Portion and Define the Decimal Amount

1 Position the insertion point on line 87.

2 Enter the JavaScript code as shown in Table 2-21 and then press the ENTER key.

The code displays (Figure 2-39).

homefinders.htm - Notepad

File Edit Search Help

```
   function dollarFormat(valuein) {
      var formatStr=""
      var Outdollars=""
      var decipos=valuein.indexOf(".")
      if (decipos==-1)
         decipos=valuein.length
      var dollars=valuein.substring(0,decipos)
      var dollen=dollars.length
      if (dollen>3) {
         while (dollen>0) {
               tDollars=dollars.substring(dollen-3,dollen)
               if (tDollars.length==3) {
                  Outdollars=","+tDollars+Outdollars
                  dollen=dollen-3
               } else {
                     Outdollars=tDollars+Outdollars
                     dollen=0
                  }
         }
       if (Outdollars.substring(0,1)==",")
          dollars=Outdollars.substring(1,Outdollars.length)
       else
          dollars=Outdollars
       }
       var cents=valuein.substring(decipos+1,decipos+3)
       if (cents=="")
          cents="00"


//-->
</SCRIPT>

</HEAD>
<BODY onload="scrollingMsg()">
```

line 87

JavaScript statement to add zeroes to right of decimal point if no decimal value

Start | homefinders.htm - No... | Home Finders Nationwide ... | 9:31 AM

FIGURE 2-39

The JavaScript statements extract the first two digits to right of the decimal point and store them as the cents portion. For values that are blank or null, the JavaScript statements add two zeroes for the decimal amount. JavaScript does not have a function that rounds decimal values up or down to the next cent. Because the monthly payment is only an estimate, however, the mortgage payment calculator does not need to round the cents values.

Reconstructing the Formatted Output and Returning the Formatted Value

Next, you must write JavaScript statements to reconstruct (concatenate) the formatted dollars and cents output into a payment amount value, store the payment amount value in the formatStr variable, and return the formatStr value. Table 2-22 shows the statements needed to complete this task.

Table 2-22

LINE	CODE
90	`var formatStr="$"+dollars+"."+cents`
91	`return formatStr`
92	`}`

When you enter the JavaScript code as shown in Table 2-22, make sure you place a period between the quotation marks in line 90, as this represents the decimal point. Also be sure not to forget the final brace (line 92). Perform the following steps to reconstruct the formatted output and return the formatted value.

To Reconstruct the Formatted Output and Return the Formatted Value

1. **Position the insertion point on line 90.**

2. **Enter the JavaScript code as shown in Table 2-22.**

   The code displays (Figure 2-40).

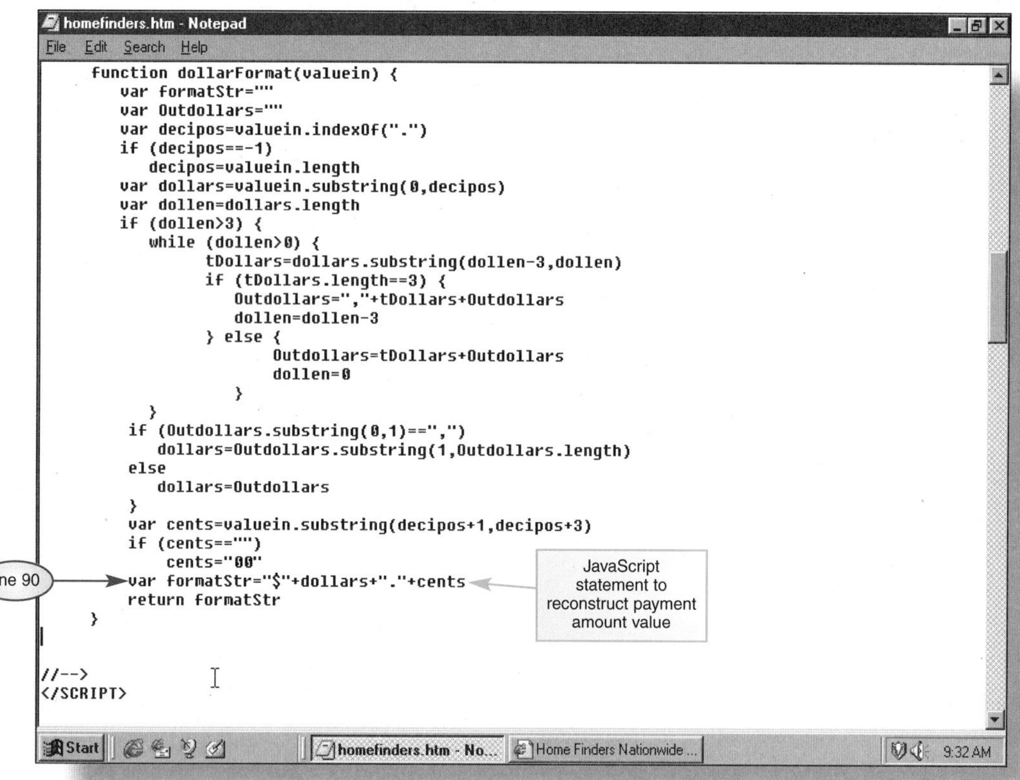
homefinders.htm - Notepad
File Edit Search Help
function dollarFormat(valuein) {
var formatStr=""
var Outdollars=""
var decipos=valuein.indexOf(".")
if (decipos==-1)
decipos=valuein.length
var dollars=valuein.substring(0,decipos)
var dollen=dollars.length
if (dollen>3) {
while (dollen>0) {
tDollars=dollars.substring(dollen-3,dollen)
if (tDollars.length==3) {
Outdollars=","+tDollars+Outdollars
dollen=dollen-3
} else {
Outdollars=tDollars+Outdollars
dollen=0
}
}
if (Outdollars.substring(0,1)==",")
dollars=Outdollars.substring(1,Outdollars.length)
else
dollars=Outdollars
}
var cents=valuein.substring(decipos+1,decipos+3)
if (cents=="")
cents="00"
var formatStr="$"+dollars+"."+cents
return formatStr
}
//-->
</SCRIPT>
line 90
JavaScript statement to reconstruct payment amount value
Start
homefinders.htm - No...
Home Finders Nationwide ...
9:32 AM

FIGURE 2-40

The JavaScript statements add the dollar sign and decimal point to the variable formatStr and display the monthly payment value in the currency format.

Passing the Monthly Payment Value to the dollarFormat() Function

To pass the monthly payment value to the function, you first must call the dollarFormat() function. The JavaScript statements used to call the dollarFormat() function use the same general form as the call to the monthly() function (see Figure 2-32 on page J 2.33). Perform the following steps to enter the JavaScript statements needed to pass the monthly payment as a string object to the dollarFormat() function.

To Pass the Monthly Payment Value to the dollarFormat() Function

1 **Position the insertion point line 53 (Figure 2-41).**

homefinders.htm - Notepad

File Edit Search Help

```
                alert("The interest rate is not a number!")
                document.MortCalc.Rate.value=" "
                document.MortCalc.Rate.focus()
            }
            else {
                var mortYears=document.MortCalc.Years.value
                var mortYears=parseInt(mortYears,10)
                if (isNaN(mortYears)) {
                    alert("The number of years is not a number!")
                    document.MortCalc.Years.value=" "
                    document.MortCalc.Years.focus()
                }
            }
        }
        document.MortCalc.Payment.value=monthly(mortAmount,mortRate,mortYears)

    }

    function monthly(mortAmount,mortRate,mortYears) {
        var Irate=mortRate/1200
        var Pmts=mortYears*12
        var Loan=mortAmount
        return Loan * (Irate / (1 - (1 / Math.pow(1+Irate,Pmts))))
    }

    function dollarFormat(valuein) {
        var formatStr=""
        var Outdollars=""
        var decipos=valuein.indexOf(".")
        if (decipos==-1)
            decipos=valuein.length
        var dollars=valuein.substring(0,deci...
```

line 53

FIGURE 2-41

2 **Type** document.MortCalc.Payment.value=dollarFormat(document.MortCalc.Payment.value) **as the statement.**

The statement displays directly below the statement that calls the monthly() function before the closing brace (Figure 2-42).

homefinders.htm - Notepad

File Edit Search Help

```
                alert("The interest rate is not a number!")
                document.MortCalc.Rate.value=" "
                document.MortCalc.Rate.focus()
            }
            else {
                var mortYears=document.MortCalc.Years.value
                var mortYears=parseInt(mortYears,10)
                if (isNaN(mortYears)) {
                    alert("The number of years is not a number!")
                    document.MortCalc.Years.value=" "
                    document.MortCalc.Years.focus()
                }
            }
        }
        document.MortCalc.Payment.value=monthly(mortAmount,mortRate,mortYears)
        document.MortCalc.Payment.value=dollarFormat(document.MortCalc.Payment.value)
    }

    function monthly(mortAmount,mortRate,mortYears) {
        var Irate=mortRate/1200
        var Pmts=mortYears*12
        var Loan=mortAmount
```

JavaScript statement to call to dollarFormat() function

FIGURE 2-42

This statement passes the unformatted monthly result as a string object to the dollarFormat() function, which then formats the result. Finally, the result displays in the Monthly Payment text box formatted as currency with the dollar sign and two decimal points.

Before continuing, you should double-check the spelling, special characters, and quotation marks in the code. The next steps are to save your file and test the Web page.

TO SAVE AND TEST THE WEB PAGE

1. With your JavaScript Data Disk in drive A, click File on the menu bar and then click Save on the File menu.
2. Click the browser button on the taskbar.
3. Click the Refresh button on the browser toolbar.
4. Enter the same test data in the text boxes: Mortgage Amount – `69000`; Interest Rate as % – `7.9`; and Number of Years – `30`.
5. Click the Calculate button.

The formatted result displays in the currency format, as $501.49 (Figure 2-43).

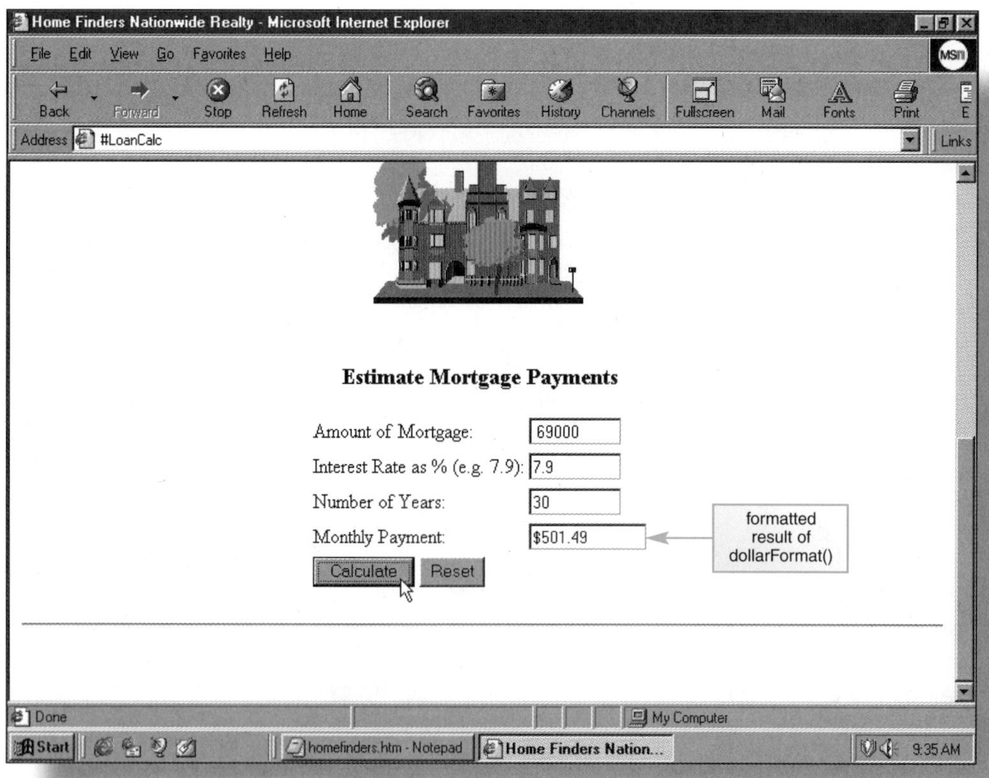

FIGURE 2-43

If your browser does not display the Web page correctly, close any error messages and then click the Notepad button on the taskbar. Check your JavaScript code against Figures 2-36 through 2-42 on pages J 2.37 through J 2.43. Correct any errors and save the file. Activate the browser and then click the Refresh button.

Adding a Pop-up Window

Recall from Project 1 that one way to display messages on a Web page is to use alert and confirm message boxes. These message boxes, however, only display text on a gray background. To create more visually interesting messages, you can use JavaScript to open and display another HTML file in a separate window that displays colors, graphics, animations, and other media. Such a window is called a **pop-up window**, because it displays over the previously opened browser window.

To create a pop-up window, you use the open() method. Table 2-23 shows the general form of the open() method. Table 2-24 describes the more commonly used pop-up window features.

Table 2-23 – open() Method

General form:	var windowname=open("window file name(URL)", "object name", "window features")
Comment:	where windowname is an optional name of a window object (required only if you need to refer to the pop-up window in any other Web page); window file name is the name of the HTML file; and window features describe how the window should display.
Examples:	`open("Adwindow.htm", "AdWin", "resize=off, titlebar=false")`

Table 2-24

FEATURE	DESCRIPTION	WRITTEN AS	COMMENTS
LOCATION	includes URL bar	"location"	
MENUBAR	includes menu bar	"menubar"	
RESIZE	allows user to resize	"resize=off"	default is on; if off, pop-up window is a fixed size
SCROLLBARS	includes scrollbars	"scrollbars"	
STATUS	includes status bar	"status"	
TITLEBAR	removes title bar	"titlebar=false"	default is true
TOOLBAR	includes toolbar	"toolbar=yes"	
WIDTH	states width in pixels	"width=220"	being replaced by innerWidth and outerWidth
HEIGHT	states height in pixels	"height=450"	being replaced by innerHeight and outerHeight

When adding the statement for a pop-up window, you should enclose all of the pop-up window features within one set of quotation marks. In this project, for example, to open the notice.htm file in a pop-up window, you enter

```
open("notice.htm", "noticeWin", "width=400, height=220")
```

The statement opens the notice.htm file in a pop-up window that is 400 pixels wide and 220 pixels high. Web developers usually enter the open() method in a user-defined function and call it with an onload event handler placed in the BODY section of the HTML file. Another way to execute JavaScript statements when a Web page loads is to place the user-defined function in the HEAD section.

Because this page already has an onload event handler for the scrolling message bar in the BODY section, you must insert the open() method statement in the HEAD section of the HTML file. To enter the open() method to open the notice.htm file in a pop-up window, perform the steps on the next page.

More About

Creating Pop-up Windows

In addition to using alert() message boxes, Web developers use pop-up windows to display messages. For more information on pop-up windows, visit www.scsite.com/js/p2.htm and then click pop-up windows.

To Enter the open() method to Open a Pop-up Window

1 **Position the insertion point on line 94, the line directly above the //--> tag (Figure 2-44).**

homefinders.htm - Notepad

File Edit Search Help

```
        if (dollen>3) {
           while (dollen>0) {
                 tDollars=dollars.substring(dollen-3,dollen)
                 if (tDollars.length==3) {
                    Outdollars=","+tDollars+Outdollars
                    dollen=dollen-3
                 } else {
                        Outdollars=tDollars+Outdollars
                        dollen=0
                    }
           }
        if (Outdollars.substring(0,1)==",")
           dollars=Outdollars.substring(1,Outdollars.length)
        else
           dollars=Outdollars
        }
        var cents=valuein.substring(decipos+1,decipos+3)
        if (cents=="")
            cents="00"
        var formatStr="$"+dollars+"."+cents
        return formatStr
    }

//-->
</SCRIPT>

</HEAD>
<BODY onload="scrollingMsg()">

<P ALIGN="CENTER"><IMG SRC="homelogo.jpg">
</P>
<DIV ALIGN="CENTER"><CENTER>

<TABLE BORDER="0" WIDTH="75%">
```

line 94

Start | homefinders.htm - No... | Home Finders Nationwide ... | 9:35 AM

FIGURE 2-44

2 **Type** `open ("notice.htm", "noticeWin", "WIDTH=400, height=220")` **and then press the ENTER key.**

Entering the open() method on the last line in the HEAD section means that it will execute as soon as the HEAD section of the Web page loads (Figure 2-45).

```
           while (dollen>0) {
                 tDollars=dollars.substring(dollen-3,dollen)
                 if (tDollars.length==3) {
                    Outdollars=","+tDollars+Outdollars
                    dollen=dollen-3
                 } else {
                        Outdollars=tDollars+Outdollars
                        dollen=0
                    }
           }
        if (Outdollars.substring(0,1)==",")
           dollars=Outdollars.substring(1,Outdollars.length)
        else
           dollars=Outdollars
        }
        var cents=valuein.substring(decipos+1,decipos+3)
        if (cents=="")
            cents="00"
        var formatStr="$"+dollars+"."+cents
        return formatStr
    }
    open("Notice.htm","noticeWin","WIDTH=400,HEIGHT=220")

//-->
</SCRIPT>

</HEAD>
<BODY onload="scrollingMsg()">

<P ALIGN="CENTER"><IMG SRC="homelogo.jpg">
</P>
<DIV ALIGN="CENTER"><CENTER>
```

JavaScript to open notice.htm in a pop-up window

Start | homefinders.htm - No... | Home Finders Nationwide ... | 9:37 AM

FIGURE 2-45

The WIDTH and HEIGHT features supplied in the open() method allow you to determine the size at which the pop-up window initially displays. Because the default value for the RESIZE feature is on, a user also can resize the pop-up window once it opens. The notice.htm file that opens in the pop-up window already has been created and is stored on the JavaScript Data Disk. Figure 2-46 shows the HTML and JavaScript code used in the notice.htm file.

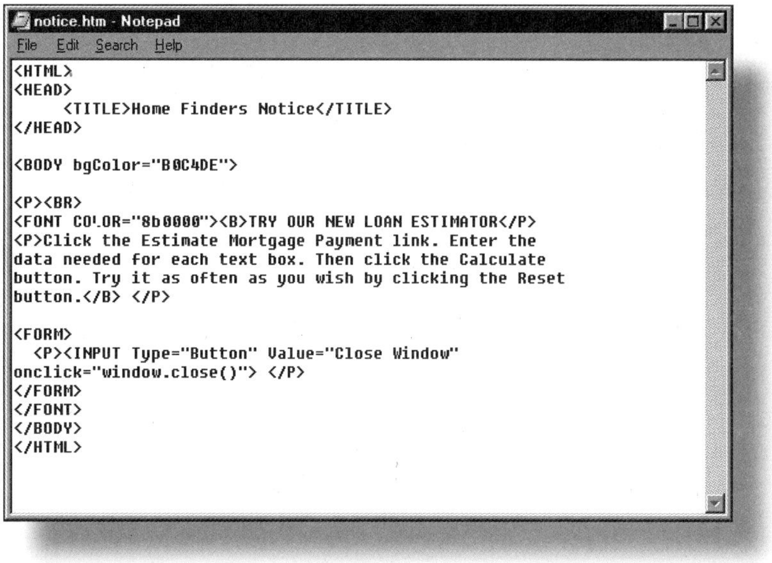

```
notice.htm - Notepad
File  Edit  Search  Help
<HTML>
<HEAD>
     <TITLE>Home Finders Notice</TITLE>
</HEAD>

<BODY bgColor="B0C4DE">

<P><BR>
<FONT COLOR="8b0000"><B>TRY OUR NEW LOAN ESTIMATOR</P>
<P>Click the Estimate Mortgage Payment link. Enter the
data needed for each text box. Then click the Calculate
button. Try it as often as you wish by clicking the Reset
button.</B> </P>

<FORM>
  <P><INPUT Type="Button" Value="Close Window"
onclick="window.close()"> </P>
</FORM>
</FONT>
</BODY>
</HTML>
```

FIGURE 2-46

Adding the Date Last Modified

As in the Fun with Phonics Web page in Project 1, you want to display the date the file was last modified at the bottom of the Home Finders Nationwide Realty Web page. To place this message at the bottom of the page, you will need to add a complete JavaScript section. To enter the JavaScript code to display the date the file was last modified, perform the following steps.

TO DISPLAY THE DATE LAST MODIFIED

1. Position the insertion point on line 171, the line directly above the closing </BODY> tag.
2. Type <SCRIPT LANGUAGE="JAVASCRIPT"> and then press the ENTER key.
3. Type <!-- Hide from old browsers and then press the ENTER key.
4. Type document.write("<CENTER><FONT COLOR='maroon'><H5>This document was last modified "+document.lastModified+"</H5></FONT></CENTER>") and then press the ENTER key.
5. Type //--> and then press the ENTER key.
6. Type </SCRIPT> and then press the ENTER key.

This completes the JavaScript section. The H5 tag makes the font small, so that the message is unobtrusive (Figure 2-47).

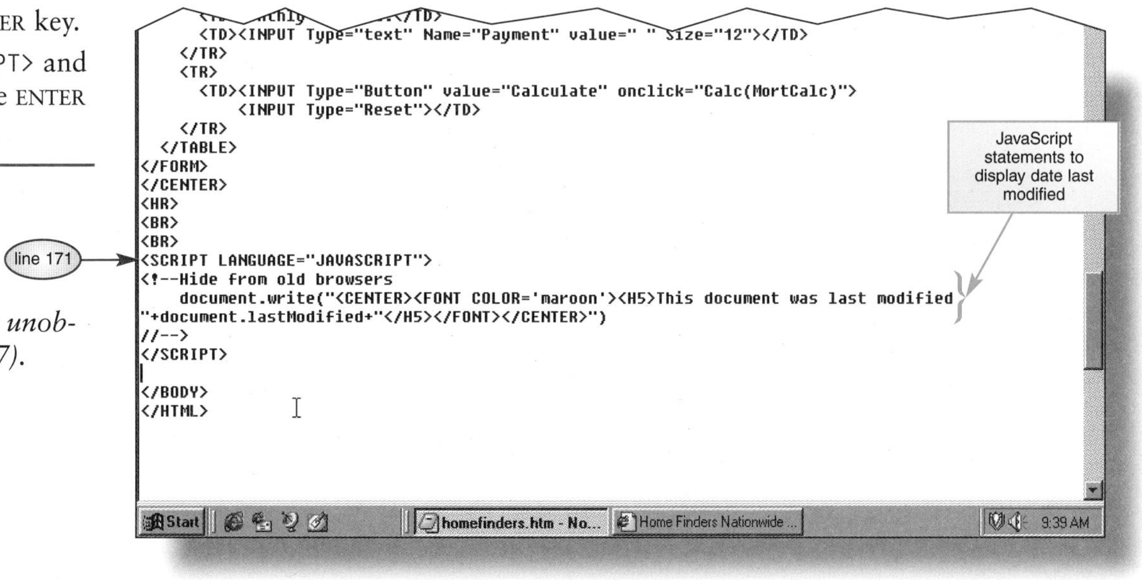

```
      <TD><INPUT Type="text" Name="Payment" value=" " Size="12"></TD>
    </TR>
    <TR>
      <TD><INPUT Type="Button" value="Calculate" onclick="Calc(MortCalc)">
          <INPUT Type="Reset"></TD>
    </TR>
  </TABLE>
</FORM>
</CENTER>
<HR>
<BR>
<BR>
<SCRIPT LANGUAGE="JAVASCRIPT">
<!--Hide from old browsers
    document.write("<CENTER><FONT COLOR='maroon'><H5>This document was last modified
"+document.lastModified+"</H5></FONT></CENTER>")
//-->
</SCRIPT>

</BODY>
</HTML>
```

line 171

JavaScript statements to display date last modified

Start | homefinders.htm - No... | Home Finders Nationwide ... | 9:39 AM

FIGURE 2-47

Saving and Testing the Finished Web Page

Before continuing, you should double-check the spelling, special characters, and quotation marks in the code. The next steps are to save your file and test the Web page.

TO SAVE AND TEST THE WEB PAGE

1. With your JavaScript Data Disk in drive A, click File on the menu bar and then click Save on the File menu.
2. Click the browser button on the taskbar.
3. Click the Refresh button on the browser toolbar.
4. Click the Close Window button to close the pop-up window.
5. Click the Close button to close the browser window.

The pop-up window displays. If necessary, scroll down to verify that the last line displays the date the page was last modified (the date and time the file was saved on disk) (Figure 2-48).

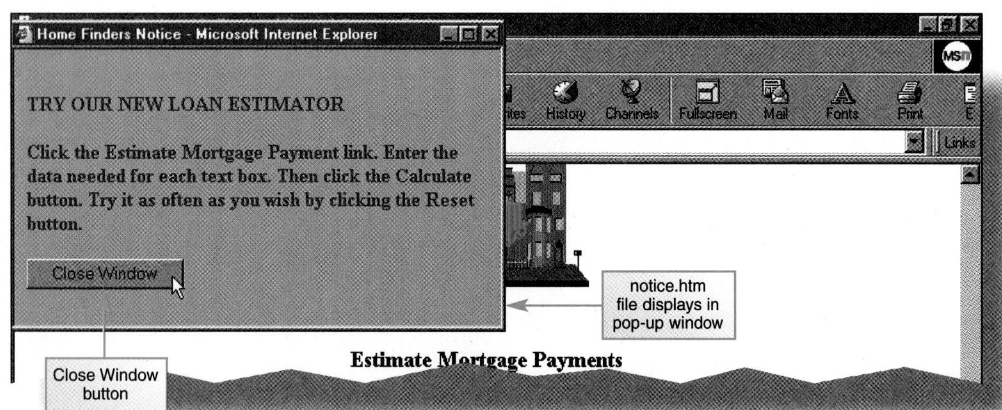

FIGURE 2-48

If your browser does not display the Web page correctly, close any error messages and then click the Notepad button on the taskbar. Check your JavaScript code against Figures 2-44 through 2-47 on pages J 2.46 through J 2.47. Correct any errors and save the file. Activate the browser and then click the Refresh button.

Printing the HTML File Using Notepad

After you have completed and tested your Web page, you may want to print it. You can print the HTML file with Notepad. Perform the following steps to print the homefinders.htm Notepad file.

TO PRINT THE HTML FILE USING NOTEPAD

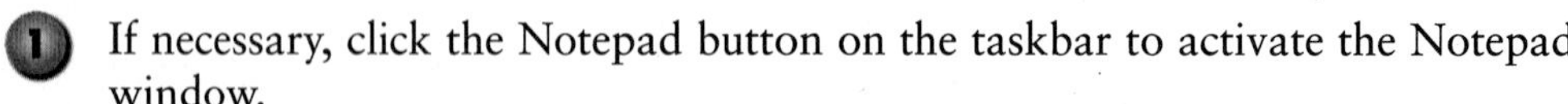

1. If necessary, click the Notepad button on the taskbar to activate the Notepad window.
2. Click Print on the File menu.

A Notepad Print dialog box briefly displays with a message that indicates the homefinders.htm file is being printed. The dialog box closes after the file has been sent to the printer. The HTML file with the JavaScript code prints (Figure 2-49).

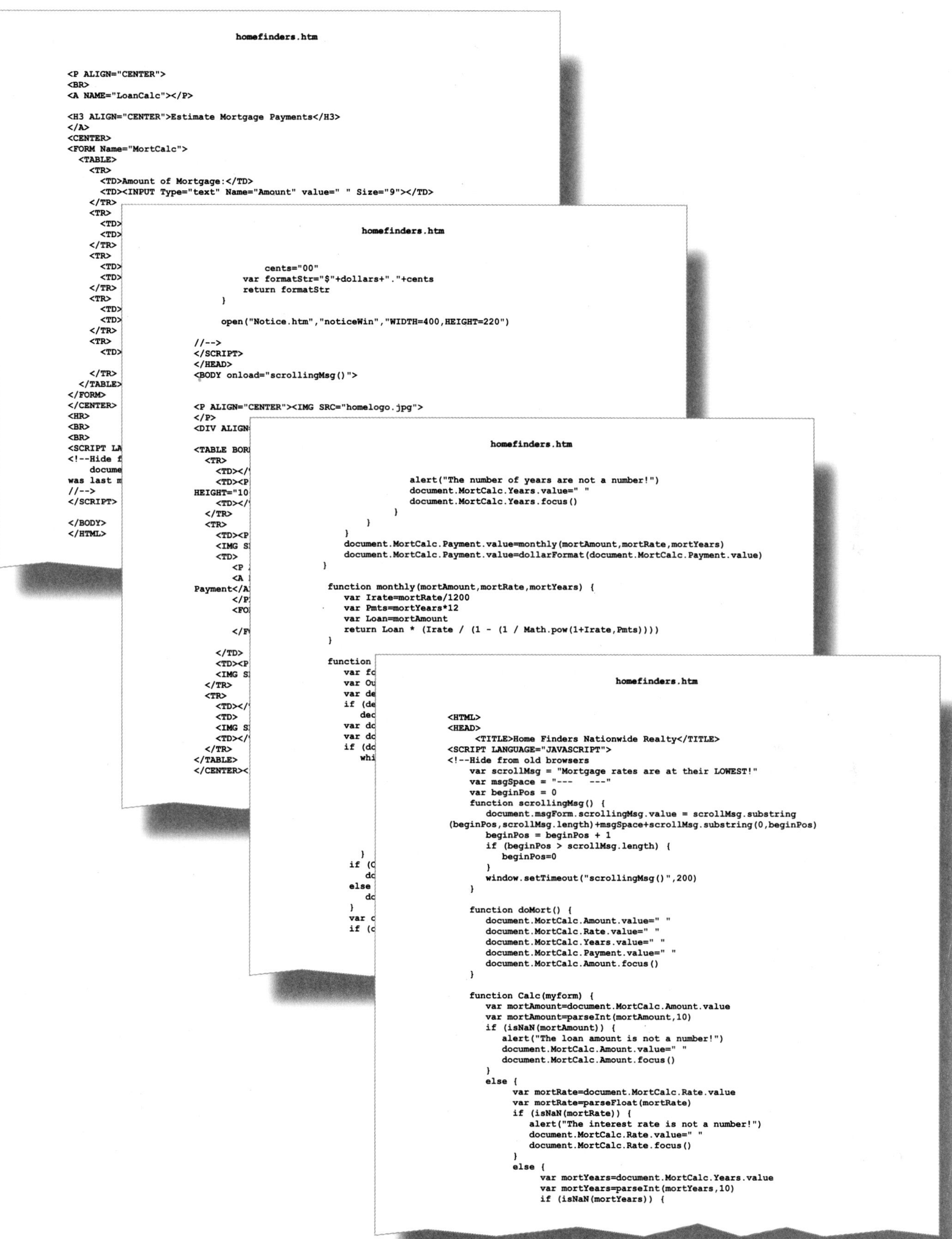

```
homefinders.htm

<P ALIGN="CENTER">
<BR>
<A NAME="LoanCalc"></P>

<H3 ALIGN="CENTER">Estimate Mortgage Payments</H3>
</A>
<CENTER>
<FORM Name="MortCalc">
  <TABLE>
    <TR>
      <TD>Amount of Mortgage:</TD>
      <TD><INPUT Type="text" Name="Amount" value=" " Size="9"></TD>
    </TR>
    <TR>
      <TD>
      <TD>
    </TR>
    <TR>
      <TD>
      <TD>
    </TR>
    <TR>
      <TD>
      <TD>
    </TR>
    <TR>
      <TD>

    </TR>
  </TABLE>
</FORM>
</CENTER>
<HR>
<BR>
<BR>
<SCRIPT LA
<!--Hide f
    docume
was last m
//-->
</SCRIPT>

</BODY>
</HTML>
```

```
homefinders.htm

                cents="00"
            var formatStr="$"+dollars+"."+cents
            return formatStr
        }

        open("Notice.htm","noticeWin","WIDTH=400,HEIGHT=220")

//-->
</SCRIPT>
</HEAD>
<BODY onload="scrollingMsg()">


<P ALIGN="CENTER"><IMG SRC="homelogo.jpg">
</P>
<DIV ALIGN

<TABLE BOR
  <TR>
    <TD></
    <TD><P
HEIGHT="10
    <TD></
  </TR>
  <TR>
    <TD><P
    <IMG S
    <TD>
       <P
       <A
Payment</A
       </P
       <FO

       </F

    </TD>
    <TD><P
    <IMG S
  </TR>
  <TR>
    <TD></
    <TD>
    <IMG S
    <TD></
  </TR>
</TABLE>
</CENTER><
```

```
homefinders.htm

                  alert("The number of years are not a number!")
                  document.MortCalc.Years.value=" "
                  document.MortCalc.Years.focus()
               }
            }
         }
         document.MortCalc.Payment.value=monthly(mortAmount,mortRate,mortYears)
         document.MortCalc.Payment.value=dollarFormat(document.MortCalc.Payment.value)
      }

      function monthly(mortAmount,mortRate,mortYears) {
         var Irate=mortRate/1200
         var Pmts=mortYears*12
         var Loan=mortAmount
         return Loan * (Irate / (1 - (1 / Math.pow(1+Irate,Pmts))))
      }

      function
         var fo
         var Ou
         var de
         if (de
            dec
         var do
         var do
         if (do
            whi






         }
         if (C
            do
         else
            do
         }
         var c
         if (c
```

```
homefinders.htm

<HTML>
<HEAD>
      <TITLE>Home Finders Nationwide Realty</TITLE>
<SCRIPT LANGUAGE="JAVASCRIPT">
<!--Hide from old browsers
      var scrollMsg = "Mortgage rates are at their LOWEST!"
      var msgSpace = "---    ---"
      var beginPos = 0
      function scrollingMsg() {
         document.msgForm.scrollingMsg.value = scrollMsg.substring
(beginPos,scrollMsg.length)+msgSpace+scrollMsg.substring(0,beginPos)
         beginPos = beginPos + 1
         if (beginPos > scrollMsg.length) {
            beginPos=0
         }
         window.setTimeout("scrollingMsg()",200)
      }

      function doMort() {
         document.MortCalc.Amount.value=" "
         document.MortCalc.Rate.value=" "
         document.MortCalc.Years.value=" "
         document.MortCalc.Payment.value=" "
         document.MortCalc.Amount.focus()
      }

      function Calc(myform) {
         var mortAmount=document.MortCalc.Amount.value
         var mortAmount=parseInt(mortAmount,10)
         if (isNaN(mortAmount)) {
            alert("The loan amount is not a number!")
            document.MortCalc.Amount.value=" "
            document.MortCalc.Amount.focus()
         }
         else {
               var mortRate=document.MortCalc.Rate.value
               var mortRate=parseFloat(mortRate)
               if (isNaN(mortRate)) {
                  alert("The interest rate is not a number!")
                  document.MortCalc.Rate.value=" "
                  document.MortCalc.Rate.focus()
               }
               else {
                     var mortYears=document.MortCalc.Years.value
                     var mortYears=parseInt(mortYears,10)
                     if (isNaN(mortYears)) {
```

FIGURE 2-49

Project Summary

In this project, you created a Web page that will allow Home Finders Nationwide Realty customers to calculate the amount of their monthly mortgage payment, based on the amount of mortgage, interest rate, and the number of years. The form validates the data as the user enters it and displays the resulting monthly payment amount using the currency format. Per the request of Home Finders owner, Carrie Rayburn, you also added a scrolling message to remind customers of low interest rates; you also added a pop-up window to display information on using the mortgage payment calculator.

In creating this Web page, you used and expanded on the JavaScript commands you learned in Project 1. To begin, you wrote a scrollingMsg() user-defined function to create a scrolling message that displays in the text box. The scrolling message used the substring() method and introduced the string length property. In addition, this function introduced the If statement and showed how to create a recursive call to the scrollingMsg() function.

You learned how to set the focus on a form text box; pass the form text box values to a function; and use the If...Else statement to validate data in a text box. The project introduces the concepts of validating data using the parseInt(), parseFloat(), and isNaN() built-in functions, as well as using the pow() method in the user-defined function Calc() to calculate the mortgage payment amount. You learned how to return values from a user-defined function and format string output results to appear as currency.

In creating a pop-up window on the Web page, you learned how to use the open() method to open a pop-up window and to set the features of this window. You then used the lastModified property to display the date the Web page was last modified. Finally, you saved the file and tested the Web page in your browser.

What You Should Know

Having completed this project, you now should be able to perform the following tasks:

- Add the setTimeout() Method to Create a Recursive Function Call *(J 2.16)*
- Create a Form Text Box to Display a Scrolling Message *(J 2.9)*
- Create the scrollingMsg() User-Defined Function *(J 2.11)*
- Display the Date Last Modified *(J 2.47)*
- Enter a Calc() User-Defined Function *(J 2.27)*
- Enter an If Statement *(J 2.14)*
- Enter the dollarFormat() Function *(J 2.37)*
- Enter the doMort() Function *(J 2.22)*
- Enter the Else Portion of the Nested If...Else Statement *(J 2.28)*
- Enter the onclick() Event Handler to Call the Calc() Function *(J 2.30)*
- Enter the monthly() Function *(J 2.34)*
- Enter the Event Handler to Call the scrollingMsg() Function *(J 2.17)*
- Enter the open() method to Open a Pop-up Window *(J 2.46)*
- Extract the Cents Portion and Define the Decimal Amount *(J 2.41)*
- Extract the Dollar Portion of the Output and Insert Commas *(J 2.40)*
- Insert an Event Handler in an Anchor Tag *(J 2.20)*
- Pass the Monthly Payment Value to the dollarFormat() Function *(J 2.43)*
- Pass Values to the monthly() User-Defined Function *(J 2.32)*
- Print the HTML File Using Notepad *(J 2.49)*
- Reconstruct the Formatted Output and Return the Formatted Value *(J 2.42)*
- Save and Test the Web Page *(J 2.22, J 2.30, J 2.35, J 2.44, J 2.48)*
- Save the File on the Data Disk *(J 2.18)*
- Start Notepad and Open a Web Page Stored on the Data Disk *(J 2.6)*
- Test the Web Page *(J 2.18)*

Test Your Knowledge

1 True/False

Instructions: Circle T if the statement is true or F if the statement is false.

T F 1. Microsoft's MARQUEE HTML tag also works with other browsers.
T F 2. A scrolling message has four basic components: the message, position, display object, and delay.
T F 3. To assign a value, such as a scrolling message, to a text box, you must name both the form and the text box.
T F 4. Web developers agree that the status bar is the best place for a scrolling message.
T F 5. A condition is any expression that evaluates to true or false.
T F 6. Recursion is a programming technique used to have a function call another function from within itself.
T F 7. When a JavaScript statement automatically positions the insertion point in the text box, the text box is considered "onfocus."
T F 8. The parseInt() method has two properties: the string value and base.
T F 9. The Math.pow() method returns the exponent power of a square root.
T F 10. The indexOf() method is used to search a string for a particular character and return the relative location of that character within the string.

2 Multiple Choice

Instructions: Circle the correct response.

1. Which of the following is not a basic component for a scrolling message?
   a. the message
   b. the position
   c. the window object
   d. the time delay
2. Programmers call placing attention on an object __________.
   a. setting the focus
   b. giving the focus
   c. losing the focus
   d. out of focus
3. In an If statement, the __________ is placed in parentheses directly after the word, If.
   a. function
   b. JavaScript command
   c. condition
   d. event handler

(continued)

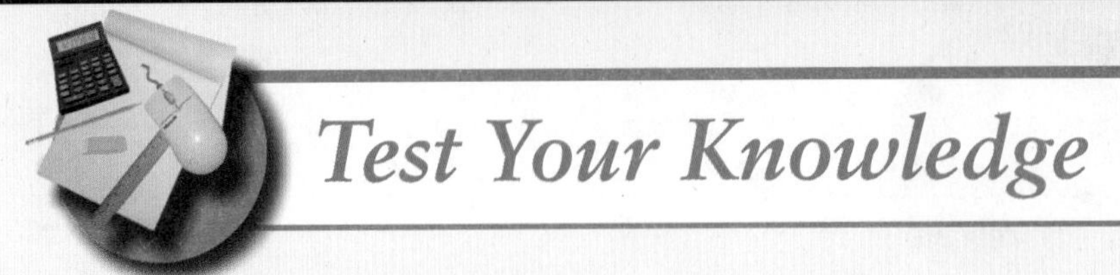

Test Your Knowledge

Multiple Choice *(continued)*

4. In JavaScript, which of the following symbols represents the operand, equal to?
   a. =
   b. !=
   c. *=
   d. = =
5. Which event handler performs an action when users click an associated button or link?
   a. onclick
   b. onsubmit
   c. onmouseover
   d. onload
6. Which event handler performs an action when a document is loaded?
   a. onclick
   b. onload
   c. onsubmit
   d. onfocus
7. In an If...Else statement, what statements are executed if the condition is true?
   a. the statements after the condition
   b. the statements after the else
   c. both statements
   d. neither; control is passed to whatever statements follow the last }
8. The parseFloat() built-in function returns a(n) __________ number.
   a. integer
   b. floating point
   c. absolute
   d. negative
9. The pow() method executes mathematical __________.
   a. exponents
   b. square roots
   c. rounding
   d. string conversions
10. Which window feature, in the open() window method, includes the URL bar?
    a. status
    b. title bar
    c. toolbar
    d. location

Test Your Knowledge

3 Understanding Event Handlers

Instructions: Fill in the blanks with the missing object or event handler names.

OBJECT	EVENT HANDLER
______________	onclick
______________	onload, onunload
form	______________, ______________
hyperlink	onclick, ______________, onmouseout
______________	onload, onabort
input box	onblur, ______________, ______________
submit button	______________
______________	______________, ______________, onblur, onfocus

4 Understanding Code Statements

Instructions: Carefully read each of the following descriptions. Write JavaScript code statements to accomplish these specific tasks. Record your answers on a separate sheet of paper. Number your answers to correspond to the code description.

1. Given the following form code, write the JavaScript statement to set focus on the Email text box.

```
<FORM Name="Form1">
      <INPUT Type="text" Name="BillingHours " value=" ">
      <INPUT Type="text" Name="Email" value=" ">
</FORM>
```

____

2. Using the same form as in question 1, write a JavaScript statement to assign the Email text box to a variable called TempEmail.

____

3. Using the same form as in question 1, write a JavaScript statement to assign the BillingHours text box to a variable and convert it to a floating-point number.

____

____

4. Given the following assignment statement: `var tempString="Test#12,Fall1999"`
write a JavaScript statement to extract the data before the comma and store it in tempTest and to extract the data after the comma and store it in tempDate.

____

____

5. Given the following geometry formulas, write the equivalent JavaScript statements.

area = s^2 ____

area =Πr^2 ____

1 Exploring Online Documentation

Instructions: Start your browser. Type the following in the Address text box: `www.scsite.com/js/p2.htm` and then click Project 2 Use Help 1. Using the Web site, answer the questions below.

1. Click Chapter 9, Events and Event Handlers in the left frame. Read about event handlers and answer the following: describe the onabort, onchange, onkeydown, and onmouseover event handlers.
2. Click Chapter 2, Capturing Event Handlers, in the left frame. Read about capturing events and answer the following questions:
   a. What does it mean to capture an event?
   b. What are the steps for capturing an event?
3. Return to the Project 2 Use Help 1 Web page. Click Frequently Asked Questions. Scroll down the page to find sections 2.4, 2.5, 4.6, 4.9, and 4.10 and then answer the following questions:
   a. How do you use the different substring functions to extract part of a string?
   b. How do you round numbers off to a certain number of decimal places?
   c. Why does a call to window.open() not display the window type and size specified?
   d. How do you create a modal window (one that cannot be minimized) using JavaScript?
   e. How do you control the placement of a new window using window.open()?
   f. How do you close a window without causing a confirm prompt to appear?
4. Hand in the answers to your instructor.

2 Exploring Links to Other JavaScript Sites

Instructions: Start your browser. Type the following URL in the Address text box: `www.scsite.com/js/p2.htm` and then click Project 2 Use Help 2. Perform the following tasks.

1. Click Microsoft's Marquee Statement. Read about the MARQUEE tag. Print the Web page.
2. Return to the Project 2 Use Help 2 Web page. Click JavaScript Statements. Click Chapter 3, Statements, in the left frame. Locate information on the If...Else discussion. Read and print this section.
3. Return to the Chapter 3, Statements, Web page. Locate information on the While statement. Read and print this section.
4. Click Chapter 4, Core, in the left frame. Click the Math link. Locate and click the pow link. Read and print this section.
5. Return to the left frame. Click Chapter 13, Global Functions, in the left frame. Locate information on the isNaN(), parseInt(), and parseFloat() functions. Read and print these sections.
6. Return to the Project 2 Use Help 2 Web page. Click Forms. Click Chapter 7, Form, and then click Form. Read and print this section.
7. Return to the Project 2 Use Help 2 Web page. Click Tutor. Scroll down to find Chapter 3 IF-THEN statements, in the left frame. Read the entire section and print the fourth page. Scroll down and click Chapter 4, While Loops and Text methods, in the left frame. Read the entire section. Print the fifth page.
8. Hand in the printouts to your instructor.

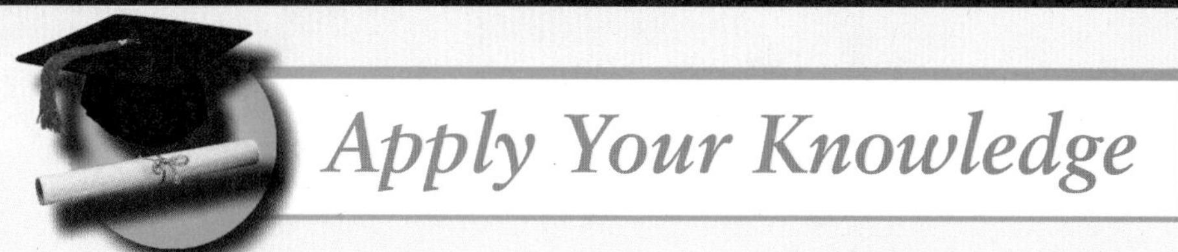

Apply Your Knowledge

1 Validating a Simple Registration Form

Instructions: Start Notepad. Open the Web page midwestrest.htm on the JavaScript Data Disk. If you did not download the Data Disk, see the inside back cover for instructions for downloading the JavaScript Data Disk or see your instructor. This Web page contains a simple registration form with three text boxes and one text area (Figure 2-50). The JavaScript code to validate the guest name and location already has been entered. You are to write the JavaScript code to validate the e-mail entered in the Your E-mail Address text box. Where appropriate, indent the lines of code. Perform the following tasks.

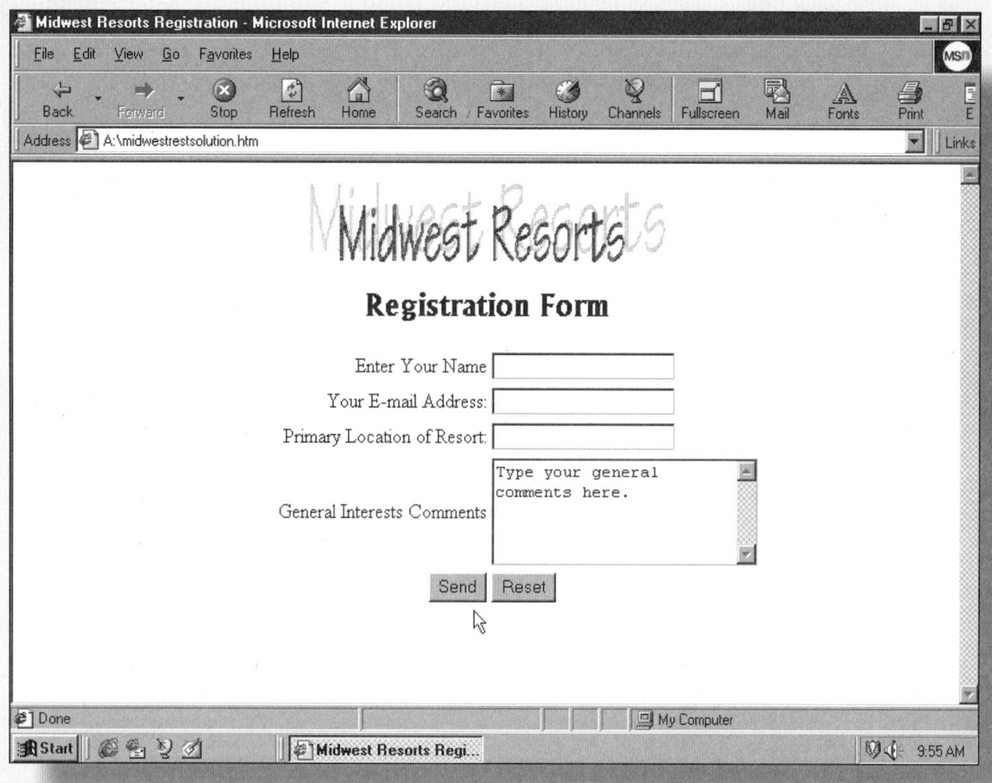

FIGURE 2-50

1. Locate the JavaScript tags and the validate() function in the HEAD section. Position the insertion point after the comment // validate the e-mail.
2. Enter `var RegeMail=document.Register.eMail.value`
3. Use the indexOf() function to determine if the e-mail address contains an @ sign. Enter `var atSign = RegeMail.indexOf("@")`
4. Enter `if (RegeMail == " " || atSign == -1) {`
5. Enter the following JavaScript statements under the If statement, indenting the statements where appropriate:

```
alert("Please enter your e-mail address")
document.Register.eMail.value=""
document.Register.eMail.focus()
}
```

6. Save the HTML file using the file name, midwestrestsolution.htm, on the Data Disk.
7. Start your browser. Open the a:\midwestrestsolution.htm Web page to test your JavaScript code. If any errors occur activate Notepad and double-check steps 1 through 6, save, and test again. If no errors occur, print the Web page, and activate Notepad and print the HTML file. Hand in the printouts to your instructor.

1 Calculating the Wind Chill Factor for a Ski Resort

Problem: You have a summer job as an assistant to the Webmaster at the Pine Peaks Ski Lodge. The Webmaster, Marian Shilling, asks you create a Web page that will allow guests and visitors to calculate the wind chill. Because the data is not fed directly to the computer, users must input the temperature and the wind speed in a form as shown in Figure 2-51. You then validate the data entered is numeric so it can be used in the wind chill conversion formula.

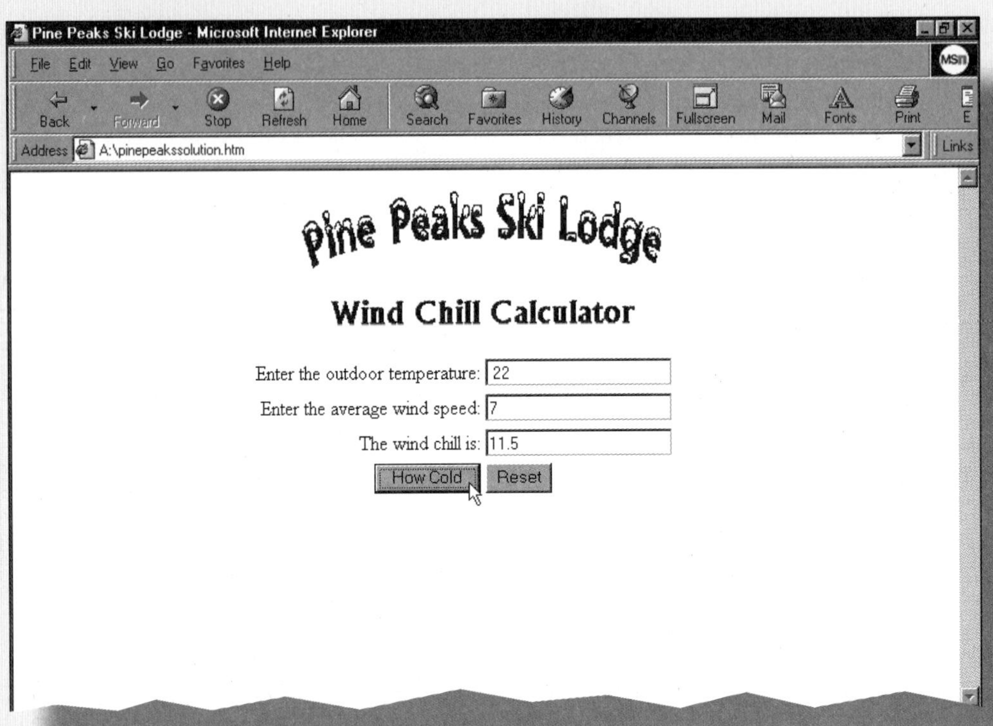

FIGURE 2-51

Instructions: Start your browser and Notepad. Using Notepad, open the pinepeaks.htm file from the JavaScript Data Disk. If you did not download the Data Disk, see the inside back cover for instructions for downloading the JavaScript Data Disk or see your instructor. Write a function called windChill() that accepts outside temperature and wind speed data from the user and displays the estimated wind chill by performing the following tasks.

1. Locate the SCRIPT tag in the HEAD section. Position the insertion point on line 6.
2. Enter the following code, indenting the lines of code, where appropriate:

```
function windChill(myform) {
         var Temp=document.Chill.OutTemp.value
         var Temp=parseInt(Temp,10)
```

3. Test that Temp is a number. If Temp is not a number, the statement will display a message, clear the OutTemp text box, and set focus to the OutTemp text box.
4. With the insertion point on line 8, enter the following code to test Temp and process for the True condition:

```
         if (isNaN(Temp)) {
                  alert("Enter the outdoor temperature")
                  document.Chill.OutTemp.value=" "
                  document.Chill.OutTemp.focus()
         } else {
```

5. With the insertion point on line 13, enter the following code to validate the value entered as the wind speed:

```
var Wind=document.Chill.windSpeed.value
var Wind=parseInt(Wind,10)
if (isNaN(Wind)) {
   alert("Enter the average wind speed")
   document.Chill.windSpeed.value=" "
   document.Chill.windSpeed.focus()
} else {
```

6. With the insertion point on line 20, enter the following code to calculate the wind chill temperature using the formula Temp-(1.5 * Wind) and assign the result to The wind chill is text box.

```
            windChillTemp=Temp-(1.5 * Wind)
            document.Chill.WindChill.value=windChillTemp
      }
   }
}
```

7. Locate the INPUT tag for the How Cold button. Insert the onclick event handler to call the windChill() function.
8. Save the HTML file using the file name, pinepeakssolution.htm, on the Data Disk.
9. Activate the browser and open pinepeakssolution.htm to test your JavaScript code. Use the following test data: Temp 22 and wind speed 7. The result 11.5 should display in The wind chill is text box.
10. If any errors occur, double-check steps 2 through 6 and test again. If no errors occur, print the Web page, activate Notepad, and print the HTML file. Hand in the printouts to your instructor.

2 Calculating a Percentage and Formatting the Result as a Percentage

Problem: You work part-time in the Online Development Group at Tri-County Community Hospital. The registered dietician, Tasha Barnes, requests that you develop a Nutrition Facts Web page that allows users to enter in the number of fat grams and total number of calories for a meal. Your Web page calculates the number of calories from fat alone and the percentage of the total calories. The results display in the text boxes. The nutritionist asks that you display the percentage of calories from fat as a percent value, not as a decimal value (Figure 2-52).

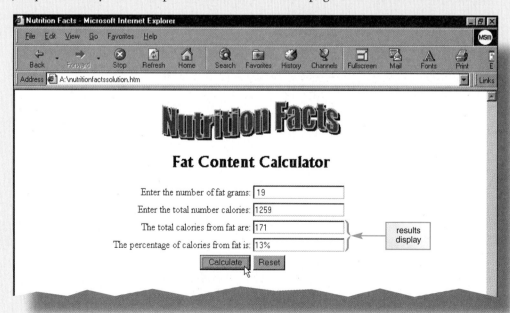

FIGURE 2-52

(continued)

Calculating a Percentage and Formatting the Result as a Percentage *(continued)*

Instructions: Start your browser and Notepad. Using Notepad, open the nutritionfacts.htm file on the JavaScript Data Disk. Perform the following tasks.

1. Locate the JavaScript section in the HEAD section and the comment, // calculate fat calories, on line 24. Position the insertion point directly beneath the first slash (/).
2. Complete the FatCal() user-defined function by entering the following JavaScript code. The JavaScript code calculates the total fat calories, assigns the TotalFatCal value to a text box, calculates the percentage of fat, and formats the result to display as a percentage.
```
var TotalFatCal = FatGrams * 9
document.Fat.Total.value = TotalFatCal
```
3. Enter the following after the // calculate percentage of fat comment and before the closing brace.
```
var TotalFatPerc = TotalFatCal/FatNumbCal
var TotalFatPerc = new String(TotalFatPerc)
document.Fat.FatPerc.value = makePerc(TotalFatPerc)
```
4. Write a function, called makePerc, which formats the result in the FatPerc text box as a percent. Position the insertion point on line 32 after the comment line, // Start makePerc function here, and enter the following code:
```
function makePerc(TotalFatPerc) {
      var valuein = TotalFatPerc
      strPercent = ""
      tPercent = valuein
      decimal = tPercent.indexOf(".")
      Percent = parseInt(tPercent.substring(decimal+1,decimal+3),10)
      strPercent = Percent+"%"
      return strPercent
      }
```
5. Locate the INPUT tag for the Calculate button. Insert the onclick event handler to call the FatCal() user-defined function.
6. Save the HTML file using the file name, nutritionfactssolution.htm, on the Data Disk.
7. Activate your browser. Open the nutritionfactssolution.htm Web page in the browser to test your JavaScript code. Use the following test data: fat grams – 19, total number of calories – 1259. The calories from fat are 171 and the percentage is 13%.
8. If any errors occur double-check steps 2 and 3 and test again. If no errors occur, print the Web page, activate Notepad, and print the HTML file. Hand in the printouts to your instructor.

3 Calculating Retirement Savings

Problem: You are an intern at Tri Star Investing. Jennifer Casey, the Webmaster, wants to develop a Web page that calculates this present value problem: Given an average annual interest rate, how much money should an individual save each month to be worth a certain amount, in a certain number of years? Jennifer's idea is that customers can use the page to enter in the years until retirement, the average annual interest expected, and their retirement amount goal. Jennifer wants you to create a form that will validate each text box and display the result as currency (Figure 2-53b). In addition, when you open the Web page, a pop-up window displays an advertising message (Figure 2-53a).

Instructions: Start your browser and Notepad. Use Notepad to open tristar.htm on the JavaScript Data Disk.

FIGURE 2-53a

FIGURE 2-53b

Perform the following tasks.

1. Locate the form and text box names.
2. Using the form and text box names provided, write a function to validate the years, interest rate, and goal text boxes using the techniques described in this project.
3. Write a function to determine the monthly investment. To calculate the monthly investment, use the formula:
   monthly = goal * rate / (1 - (1 / (1 + rate)^{deposits}))
   where goal is the retirement goal, rate is the estimated annual rate of interest, and deposit is the number of monthly deposits. Enter the rate as a percent and convert to a monthly amount using the following formula: rate = rate/1200
   Enter the monthly deposit and convert it to an annual amount as follows: deposits = years * 12
4. Pass the goal, years, and rate to this function.
5. Write a function that formats the result as currency, use the function developed in this project as a guide.
6. Add JavaScript statements that will open the file, tristarad.htm, on the JavaScript Data Disk as a pop-up window when the Tri Star Web page is opened.
7. Save the HTML file using the file name, tristarsolution.htm, on the JavaScript Data Disk.
8. Activate the browser. Open the tristarsolution.htm file to test your JavaScript code. Use the test data shown in Figure 2-53b.
9. If any errors occur, double-check steps 1 through 6 and test again. Look for matching variable names, missing quotation marks, parentheses, or braces. If no errors occur, print the Web page, activate Notepad, and print the HTML file.

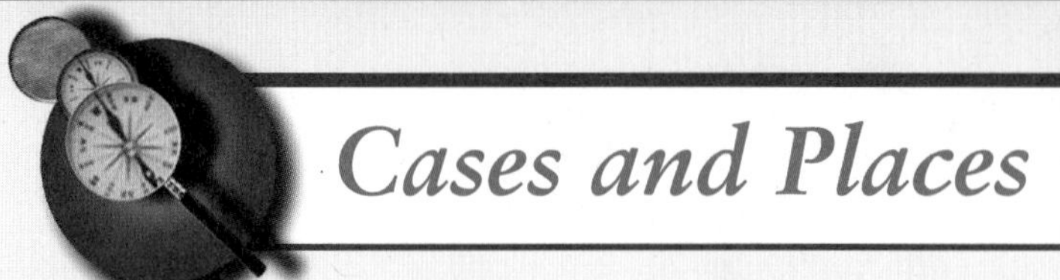

Cases and Places

The difficulty of these case studies varies:
▶ are the least difficult; ▶▶ are more difficult; and ▶▶▶ are the most difficult.

1 ▶ Your sister owns a travel agency, for which she has a Web page that features trips to 10 European nations. She wants you to add a pop-up window with a currency exchange form on the Web page. On the form, the user should enter the exchange rate and the number of dollars to be exchanged. To display the exchange rate in dollars in a text box, the user can click a button named "Exchange." Use the concepts and techniques presented in this project to create the Web page.

2 ▶▶ As captain of your fraternity bowling team, you have decided to create a Web page that displays the team standings. One of your teammates suggests that you add a pop-up window with a form that allows bowlers to enter game scores and calculate their bowling average. The form should accept input in a While loop that counts the number of scores. Use the concepts and techniques presented in this project to create the Web page.

3 ▶▶ As treasurer of your investment club, you are asked to create a Web page that calculates stock dividend reinvestments. The Web page should allow users to enter the current price of a stock; the number of shares owned; the amount of dividends the company pays on each share; and how often the company pays dividends. After validating the fields, the page should display the amount of time it will take to earn a new share of stock by investing the dividends. Use the concepts and techniques presented in this project to create the Web page.

4 ▶▶▶ To help entice moviegoers, the manager of the local movie theater wants to create a Web page to display a listing of currently running movies and show times. In addition, the manager wants to have a form that allows customers to order tickets online. The form should use option buttons or check boxes for data entry of the number of tickets, matinee discounts, and credit card number; and validate the data. Once they have ordered, users can pay for tickets at the window or via credit card online. Use the concepts and techniques presented in this project to create a form for the theater Web page (you do not have to build a form to transfer the data to, and store it in, a database).

5 ▶▶▶ A new subdivision developer has staked out an area for 4,500 homes and would like to have a Web page that displays a map with each lot numbered. In addition, he wants customers to be able to view any of nine basic floor plans on the Web page. The Web page should allow the customer to be able to pick a lot, pick a floor plan, and see a final cost. In addition, the developer wants a form to calculate and display the down payment needed from the customer to start construction (one-third the cost of the house). Use the concepts and techniques presented in this project to create the Web page.

JavaScript

PROJECT 3

Enhancing the Use of Image and Form Objects

OBJECTIVES

You will have mastered the material in this project when you can:

- Define rolling banner
- Create an image object
- Write a rolling banner function
- Define array
- Describe how to create an array instance
- Call the rolling banner function
- Create a dynamic greeting
- Describe the Switch statement
- Write a user-defined function that calculates the number of days to a future date
- Discuss the getMonth() and getTime()methods
- Describe the onmouseover event handler
- Write a user-defined function that changes an image when the mouse pointer passes over a related link
- Write a user-defined function that displays a menu of items and the price for an item that is selected from the menu
- Describe the onchange event handler
- Write a user-defined function that calculates the total cost of an item selected from a menu
- Write a user-defined function to format the total cost as currency

What a Doll!

Barbie® Doll Fans Are Tickled Pink About Custom Dolls

Walk down the doll aisle in any toy store, and you will find shelves brimming with hundreds of Barbie dolls and pink accessories. Happy Holidays Barbie. Dentist Barbie. Barbie Dream House. Barbie Motorhome. This merchandise is sold in more than 150 countries worldwide and accounts for more than 30 percent of Mattel's $4.8 billion annual revenues.

This ubiquitous doll has come a long way from her creation in 1959. At that time, Mattel cofounder Ruth Handler realized young girls wanted to play with teenage dolls, in addition to baby dolls. She bought a fashionable mature doll in Switzerland, made modifications, and named the creation after her daughter, Barbara. The original Barbie dolls sold for $3; they could be worth more than $5,000 today if they are in mint condition. Handler created the Barbie doll's boyfriend in 1961 and named him after her son, Ken.

More than one billion Barbie dolls and her family members have been sold since 1959 — enough to circle the Earth more than seven times if laid head to toe. The

average American girl between the ages of three- to ten-years-old now owns ten Barbie dolls.

Now each of these children can add a personalized friend of Barbie to her collection. The Barbie.com Web site (www.barbie.com) contains a My Design™page that uses JavaScript and allows users to customize a doll and see the results. For starters, the child names the doll. Then she clicks a button to choose a light, ivory, brown, or tan skin tone and either an open or closed mouth. Next come selections for eye color, hair color and style, outfits, and accessories. The last set of choices specifies the doll's birthday, career, hobbies, and friends.

The user can print a photo of the unique doll. In addition, adult users can place an order for Mattel to produce an actual doll based on these specifications. Even though the various combinations of features can result in thousands of unique dolls, Mattel has the production facilities to manufacture the doll in six to eight weeks.

The Barbie.com Web site developers used JavaScript in the My Design page. The onmouseover and onmouseout event handlers add simple animation to the page and change button colors to draw users' attention to their choices.

JavaScript also is prevalent in the Fashion Avenue™Fun page. With a "Girls have more fun with Barbie" theme, the page uses JavaScript arrays to display an image of Barbie, Ken, or her little sisters, Skipper and Kelly. A user selects one of these dolls, clicks forward and back arrows to view outfits for the doll, and then clicks Try It to see the outfit appear on the doll. After the user makes each selection, the JavaScript code executes to read the arrays and display the requested images on the screen.

In this project, you will use arrays and the onmouseover event handler to create a Web page for Midwest Caterers that features picnics, dinner parties, and weddings. Both your page and the Barbie page demonstrate JavaScript's powerful functions. JavaScript applications provide you with interactivity and variety and are limited only by your creativity.

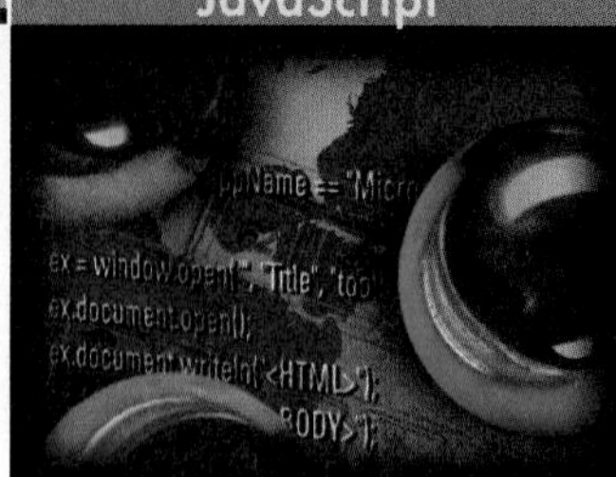

JavaScript

Enhancing the Use of Image and Form Objects

CASE PERSPECTIVE

Midwest Catering hired you as a part-time server when you started college last year. Your job is taking a new direction since you talked to the owner, Dennis Sullivan, and described the Web development course you just completed. Dennis knows that advertising on the Internet would expand his business. Most of the parties that Midwest caters center on holidays and three main specialties: picnics, dinner parties, and weddings. Dennis wants a Web page that highlights these catering services.

You have learned how to create a Web page that can display a greeting that counts down the number of days to any given holiday. If the holiday is more than a month away, you can design the Web page to display a generic greeting. Dennis likes these ideas. In addition, he wants the Web page to provide a way for clients to estimate prices before they place their orders. With these concepts in mind, Dennis tells you to start development of the Web page immediately.

Introduction

In Project 2, you learned about different object properties, methods, built-in functions, and event handlers. You used the If statement and If...Else statement to validate form text box values. You learned how to pass values to user-defined functions that executed mathematical expressions and returned a result. You learned about the While loop and how to open a second window to display a message. This project continues to emphasize these topics and introduces new ones.

The new topics in this project include using the Date() object's getMonth() and getTime() methods and the Math ceil() method to calculate the number of days to a specific date. You will learn how to use image objects and arrays to create an animated title called a rolling banner or image rollover. You will learn how to use the Switch statement and arrays to display prices based on a selection from an HTML Select drop-down list box. In Project 2, you wrote the dollarFormat() function to format output of one text box as currency. In this project, you will learn how to make any value a string object instance so it can be used with the dollarFormat() function from any text box. Finally, you will learn the onmouseover event handler to call functions to change the current graphic image to another graphic image. You use the onchange event handler to call functions associated with a Select drop-down list box.

Project Three — Creating the Midwest Catering Web Page

In your discussion with Dennis, you determined the following.

Needs: The Web page appears with the name of the company (Figure 3-1a).

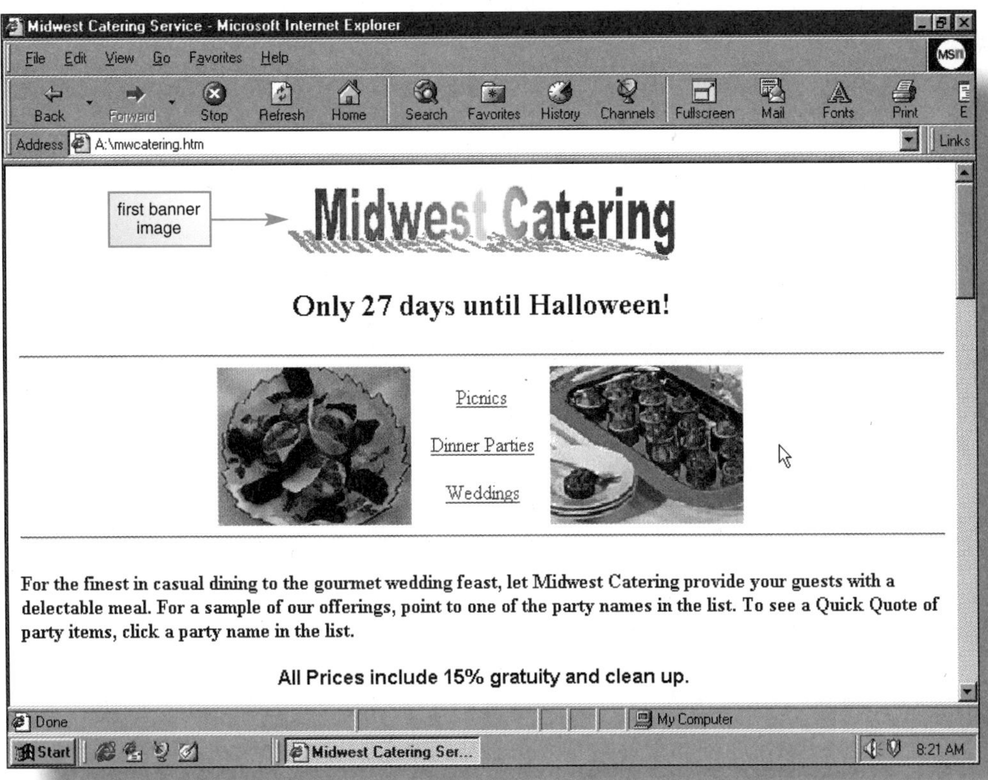

FIGURE 3-1a

After three seconds, the title changes and rolls through three more images (Figures 3-1b, 3-1c, and 3-1d). Beneath the banner is the dynamic greeting, which displays a countdown to selected holidays (Figure 3-1a). As shown in Figure 3-1d on the next page, Picnics, Dinner Parties, and Weddings display as links between two photos of food. When you drag the mouse over a link, the graphic images change and display food items normally associated with that type of food service.

FIGURE 3-1b

FIGURE 3-1c

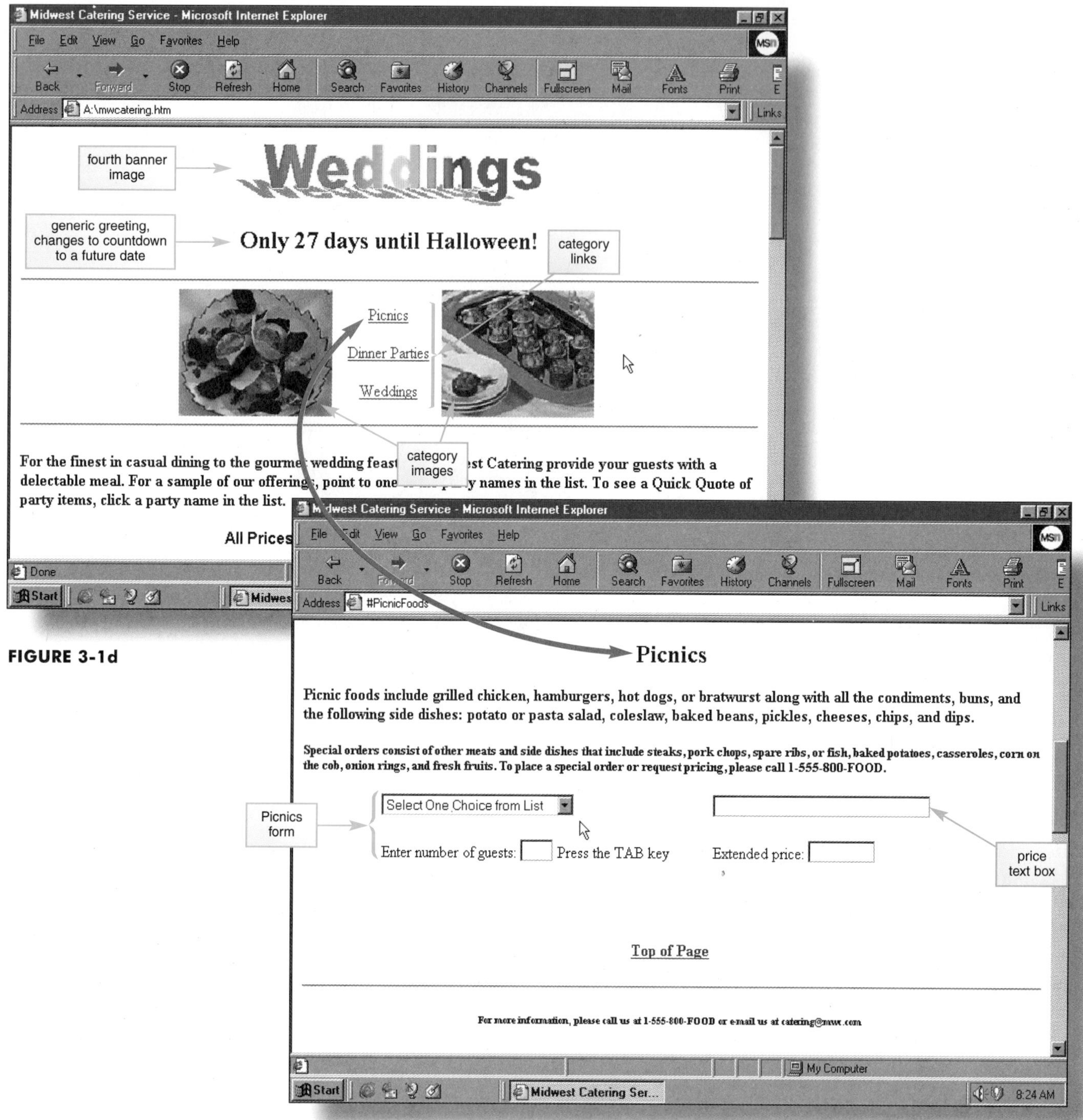

FIGURE 3-1d

FIGURE 3-1e

Forms: When you click a link, you jump to a section of the Web page that describes the type of food service available for that event. A select drop-down list provides a menu of meal choices (Figure 3-1e). When the you select an item, the price per person displays in a text box. You then can enter the number of guests in another text box, to view the total extended price.

Calculations: The calculation for determining the total price is the number of guests multiplied by the price.

Starting Notepad and Opening the Cater.htm File

The first step is to start Notepad and open the HTML file, cater.htm, on the JavaScript Data Disk as shown in the following steps.

TO START NOTEPAD AND OPEN THE HTML FILE

1. Start Notepad.
2. When the Notepad window displays, click the Maximize button.
3. Open the file, cater.htm, on the JavaScript Data Disk in drive A.

The cater.htm document opens in the Notepad window (Figure 3-2).

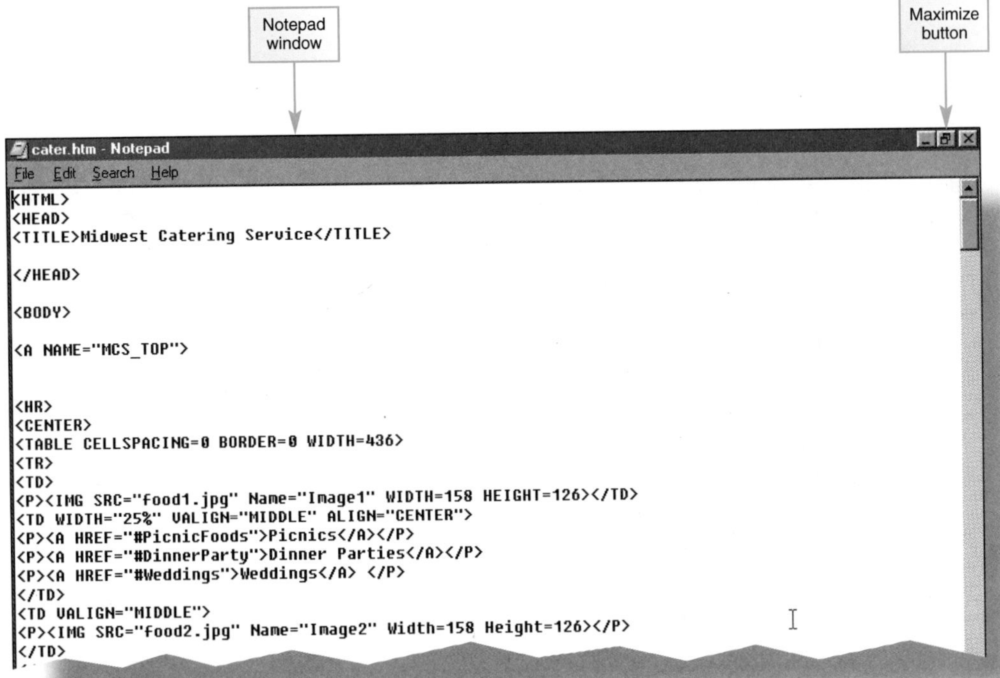


```
<HTML>
<HEAD>
<TITLE>Midwest Catering Service</TITLE>

</HEAD>

<BODY>

<A NAME="MCS_TOP">


<HR>
<CENTER>
<TABLE CELLSPACING=0 BORDER=0 WIDTH=436>
<TR>
<TD>
<P><IMG SRC="food1.jpg" Name="Image1" WIDTH=158 HEIGHT=126></TD>
<TD WIDTH="25%" VALIGN="MIDDLE" ALIGN="CENTER">
<P><A HREF="#PicnicFoods">Picnics</A></P>
<P><A HREF="#DinnerParty">Dinner Parties</A></P>
<P><A HREF="#Weddings">Weddings</A> </P>
</TD>
<TD VALIGN="MIDDLE">
<P><IMG SRC="food2.jpg" Name="Image2" Width=158 Height=126></P>
</TD>
```

FIGURE 3-2

Rolling Banners

The next step is to create the rolling banner. The page title, shown in Figure 3-1 (on pages J 3.5 and J 3.6), is similar to a rolling banner. A **rolling banner** is a set of images, all the same size, that display in the same location for a few seconds, one after the other. This banner includes the company name followed by the types of food service events Midwest Catering offers.

To create a rolling banner, perform the following three steps: (1) create an image object; (2) write the rolling banner function; and (3) add the event handler to call the function. The order in which you perform these steps is not critical, but all three steps must be completed before the banner will work.

Rolling Banners

Rolling banners also are called image rollovers and dynamic images. For more information, visit www.scsite.com/js/p3.htm and then click Rolling Banners.

Creating an Image Object

To create an image object, add the Name attribute to the HTML IMG SRC tag to allow the JavaScript code to reference the object. The Name attribute allows JavaScript to assign a new graphic image to the same location as the original image. Table 3-1 shows the general form of the IMG SRC tag with the name, width, and height attributes.

Table 3-1 – Image Object	
General form:	<IMG SRC = "Image_File_Name.Type" Name = "Object_Name" Width = pixels Height = pixels>
Comment:	where an initial image displays at the location where the tag appears. The name identifies the object for JavaScript. The Width and Height attributes define the image size in pixels.
Example:	`<IMG SRC = "banner1.jpg" Name = "Banner" Width = 350 Height = 65>`

Table 3-2 shows the general form of the statement to assign a new image to the defined location.

Table 3-2 – Assign New Image	
General form:	document.objectname.src = "new image file name"
Comment:	where the new graphic image displays in the same location as the original by assigning a new file name to the image object source (SRC) property. The object name in the JavaScript code that must match the object name in the IMAGE tag.
Example:	`document.Banner.src = "banner2.jpg"`

To create the location for the image object, which will display the rolling banner, perform the following steps.

Steps To Create the Location for the Image Object

1 Position the insertion point on line 10 (Figure 3-3).

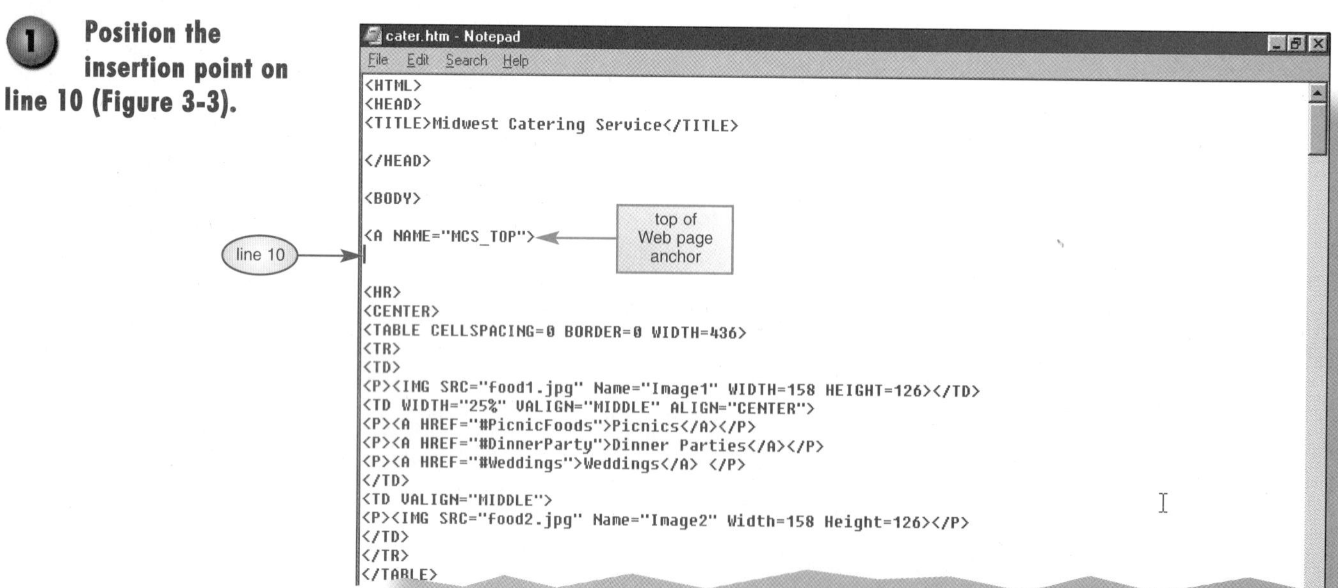

FIGURE 3-3

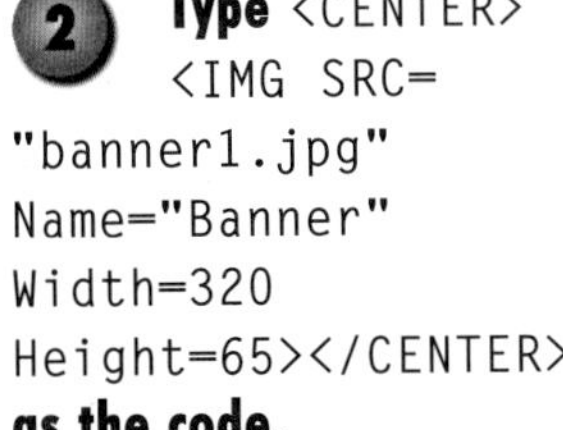

Type `<CENTER> <IMG SRC= "banner1.jpg" Name="Banner" Width=320 Height=65></CENTER>` **as the code.**

The image object is Banner and has a set width and height (Figure 3-4).


```
<HTML>
<HEAD>
<TITLE>Midwest Catering Service</TITLE>

</HEAD>

<BODY>

<A NAME="MCS_TOP">
<CENTER><IMG SRC="banner1.jpg" Name="Banner" Width=320 Height=65></CENTER>

<HR>
<CENTER>
<TABLE CELLSPACING=0 BORDER=0 WIDTH=436>
<TR>
<TD>
<P><IMG SRC="food1.jpg" Name="Image1" WIDTH=158 HEIGHT=126></TD>
<TD WIDTH="25%" VALIGN="MIDDLE" ALIGN="CENTER">
<P><A HREF="#PicnicFoods">Picnics</A></P>
<P><A HREF="#DinnerParty">Dinner Parties</A></P>
<P><A HREF="#Weddings">Weddings</A> </P>
</TD>
<TD VALIGN="MIDDLE">
<P><IMG SRC="food2.jpg" Name="Image2" Width=158 Height=126></P>
</TD>
</TR>
</TABLE>
</CENTER>
```

FIGURE 3-4

The width and height defined for the image source object is approximately the same size as a <H1> HTML tag to format text. The banner1.jpg image is the Midwest Catering logo. Because more than one image replaces the banner1.jpg image file, you must create a user-defined function, called bancycle(), to display the different images.

Writing the Rolling Banner Function

To write the rolling banner function, perform the following six steps: (1) define an array of images; (2) establish a counter; (3) increment the counter by 1; (4) test the counter against the number of items in the array; (5) assign the array element of the counter to the image object; and (6) call the function again using the setTimeout() method. Using the setTimeout() method in the function employs the recursive method discussed in Project 2. This recursive call continuously changes the images until the user closes the browser. The first step in creating the rolling banner is to create an array and store the image file names in the array.

An **array** is a collection of data items, represented by one variable name. A subscript references individual data items in the array. A **subscript** is a number that designates an individual item or occurrence in the array as shown in example 2 of Table 3-3 on the next page. The first item of a JavaScript array is element zero. Subscripts are placed after the array name in square [ ] brackets as shown in the examples in Table 3-3. A subscript is any valid JavaScript variable or numeric value.

Arrays are built-in objects. To use data in an array, create an instance of the object in which to store the data. Recall from the Introduction that an object instance is an object created from a built-in object. Table 3-3 shows the general form of creating an array object instance from the Array object using the *new* keyword.

More About

Arrays

Array objects are useful for storing large quantities of items. For more information on using arrays, visit www.scsite.com/js/p3.htm and then click Arrays.

More About

Subscripts

In JavaScript, the default first element is zero. If you create a simulated array instead of using the Array object, however, the element zero is used to indicate the number of items in the array. To store a value in the element zero would destroy the array. For more information, visit www.scsite.com/js/p3.htm and then click Subscripts.

Table 3-3 – Creating an Array	
General form:	var myarrayname = new Array()
Comment:	where Array is a built-in object and the new command creates a new object instance of the array. Assign data items to the array in one of two ways: (1) place data in the array object or (2) assign the items separately.

Examples:	`var banners = new Array("graphic1.jpg", "graphic2.jpg", "graphic3.jpg", "graphic4.jpg")`
	or
	`var banners = new Array()`
	`banners[0] = "graphic1.jpg"`
	`banners[1] = "graphic2.jpg"`
	`banners[2] = "graphic3.jpg"`
	`banners[3] = "graphic4.jpg"`

Once the array assigns the data elements, retrieve or use the data by referencing the array name with the subscript. The data in an array is stored sequentially as shown in Figure 3-5. For example, to reference the first item (graphic.jpg) use banners[0]. To reference the third element in the array use the contents of banners[2].

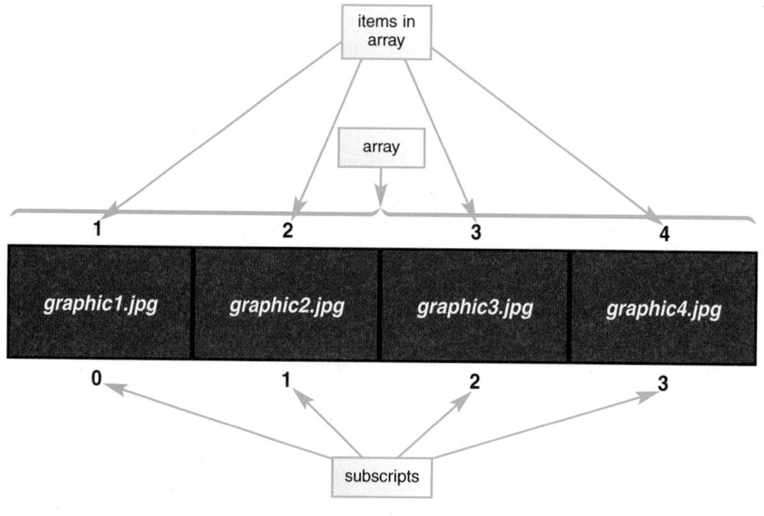

FIGURE 3-5

Table 3-4 shows the JavaScript code for the bancycle() function. Because this is the first function written in this project, it includes the code to create the JavaScript section in the HEAD section. Recall from previous projects that Web developers place user-defined functions in the HEAD section.

Table 3-4

```
LINE  CODE
 4    <SCRIPT  LANGUAGE="JAVASCRIPT">
 5    <!--  Hide from old browsers
 6         var banners = new Array("banner1.jpg","banner2.jpg","banner3.jpg","banner4.jpg")
 7         var bnrCntr = 0
 8         function bancycle() {
 9              bnrCntr = bnrCntr + 1
10              if (bnrCntr == 4) {
11              bnrCntr = 0
12              }
13              document.Banner.src = banners[bnrCntr]
14              setTimeout("bancycle()",3000)
15         }
16
17
18    //-->
19    </SCRIPT>
```

The bancycle() function begins in line 6 by creating an array of image file names. Line 7 initializes the counter variable named bnrCntr to zero, which serves as the subscript. Zero represents the first element in the array, which is the first banner image of the rolling banner displayed on the Web page. Line 8 defines the function name. Line 9 increments the bnrCntr by 1, and line 10 tests the counter against the number of items in the array, which is four. If bnrCntr is equal to four, line 11 assigns a zero (0) to bnrCntr. Line 13 assigns the contents of banners[bnrCntr] to the image object, so the new image displays. The function then calls itself with a three-second delay (line 14). The brace (line 15) completes the function. The blank lines at 16 and 17 reserve space for future user-defined functions, while lines 18 and 19 complete the JavaScript section.

To enter the bancycle() function to create a rolling banner, perform the following steps.

Steps To Enter a Function to Create a Rolling Banner

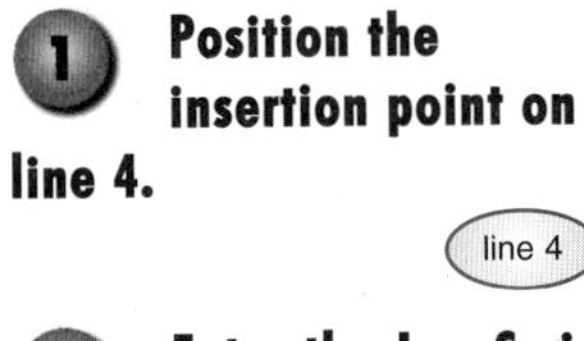

1 **Position the insertion point on line 4.**

2 **Enter the JavaScript code shown in Table 3-4.**

The bancycle() function displays (Figure 3-6).

FIGURE 3-6

Once the bancycle() function is called, the setTimeout() method on line 14 will continue to call the function until the user displays a new Web page or quits the browser.

Calling the Rolling Banner Function

The next step is to enter the event handler that calls the bancycle() function. In this project, place an onload event handler in the BODY tag using the setTimeout() method as you did in the bancycle() function. The setTimeout() method is used to delay changing the first image. A three-second delay is sufficient to allow the average user time to read the banner. To enter the onload event handler to call the bancycle() function, perform the following steps.

To Enter the onload Event Handler to Call a Function

1 Position the insertion point immediately to the right of the Y in BODY on line 22, inside the > symbol (Figure 3-7).

cater.htm - Notepad

File Edit Search Help

```
<HTML>
<HEAD>
<TITLE>Midwest Catering Service</TITLE>
<SCRIPT  LANGUAGE="JAVASCRIPT">
<!--  Hide from old browsers
     var banners = new Array("banner1.jpg","banner2.jpg","banner3.jpg","banner4.jpg")
     var bnrCntr = 0
     function bancycle() {
             bnrCntr = bnrCntr + 1
             if (bnrCntr == 4) {
                bnrCntr = 0
             }
          document.Banner.src = banners[bnrCntr]
          setTimeout("bancycle()",3000)
     }


//-->
</SCRIPT>
</HEAD>

<BODY>

<A NAME="MCS_TOP">
<CENTER><IMG SRC="banner1.jpg" Name="Banner" Width=320 Height=65></CENTER>

<HR>
```

line 22

FIGURE 3-7

2 Type `onload="setTimeout('bancycle()',3000)"` **and do not press the ENTER key (Figure 3-8).**

```
     }


//-->
</SCRIPT>
</HEAD>

<BODY onload="setTimeout('bancycle()',3000)">

<A NAME="MCS_TOP">
<CENTER><IMG SRC="banner1.jpg" Name="Banner" Width=320 Height=65></CENTER>

<HR>
<CENTER>
<TABLE CELLSPACING=0 BORDER=0 WIDTH=436>
<TR>
<TD>
<P><IMG SRC="food1.jpg" Name="Image1" WIDTH=158 HEIGHT=126></TD>
<TD WIDTH="25%" VALIGN="MIDDLE" ALIGN="CENTER">
<P><A HREF="#PicnicFoods">Picnics</A></P>
<P><A HREF="#DinnerParty">Dinner Parties</A></P>
```

onload Event Handler

Start | cater.htm - Notepad | 8:52 AM

FIGURE 3-8

The three steps for creating a rolling banner are complete. Recall that the three steps are (1) create an image object; (2) write the rolling banner function; and (3) add the event handler. The next step is to write the code to create the dynamic greeting for the holiday countdown.

Creating a Dynamic Greeting

The dynamic greeting in this project displays below the rolling banner on the Web page. The greeting notifies the user of the number of days until a given holiday. This project focuses on St. Patrick's Day, Independence Day, Halloween, and Christmas as the holidays.

The steps in writing a user-defined function to create a dynamic greeting include: (1) initialize a generic greeting; (2) create a Date() object instance; (3) determine the month number; (4) depending on month, set the holiday date; (5) subtract the number of days between the holiday and the current date; (6) test the current date, if before the holiday calculate the number of days until the holiday; and (7) assign a new message. Repeat steps 2 through 7 for each of the four holidays.

You need a variable to contain the new message assigned in step 7. Name this variable holidayCntMsg and use it to assign an initial generic greeting. The generic greeting does not reference any holidays. Use the holidayCntMsg variable to change the greeting in step 7 for the countdown to a specific holiday.

To test the current month and set the holiday date requires a set of multiple conditionals. The testing can be accomplished with nested If...Else statements. An easier way to test multiple conditions, however, is the Switch statement.

The Switch Statement

Recall in Project 2 that you used nested If...Else statements to test multiple conditions. The **Switch statement** is another way of testing multiple conditions as shown by the flowchart in Figure 3-9. The comparison begins with the first case statement, and continues until all conditions are tested. Table 3-5 on the next page describes the general form of the Switch statement.

More About

The Switch Statement

For more information on the Switch statement, visit www.scsite.com/js/p3.htm and click Switch. Then click Chapter 12, Overview of JavaScript Statements and locate the Switch statement.

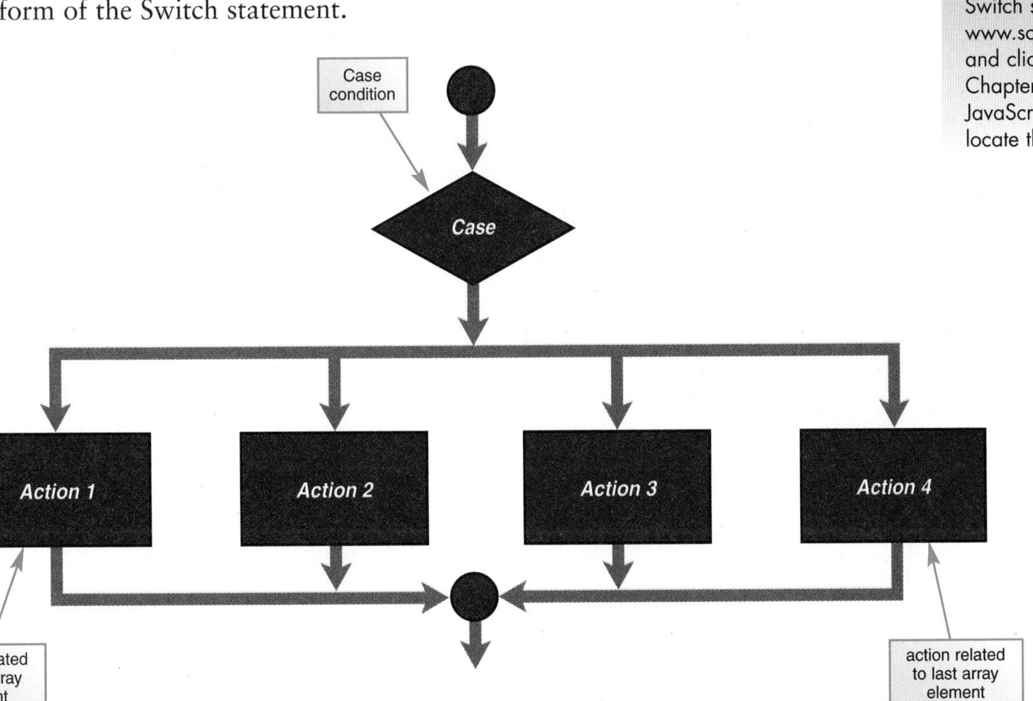

FIGURE 3-9

Table 3-5 – Switch Statement

General form:	Switch (expression) {
	case value :
	JavaScript statements
	break
	case value :
	JavaScript statements
	break
	default :
	JavaScript statements
	}

Comment:	where the expression is any valid JavaScript expression or variable and the case value is any valid JavaScript variable or constant. The condition compares the case value to the expression. If the condition is True, the JavaScript statements after the Case Condition statement execute. The Break statement passes control to the first statement after the closing brace for the Switch statement when a case condition is True. If the condition is False, the next case condition executes. The default statement is optional, and executes if none of the case conditions is True.

Example:	(the getDay() method returns the day of the week):
	`var curDay = new Date()`
	`var day = curDay.getDay()`
	`switch (day) {`
	`case 0 :`
	`document.write("Today is Sunday")`
	`break`
	`case 6 :`
	`document.write("Today is Saturday")`
	`break`
	`default :`
	`document.write("Today is a weekday")`
	`}`

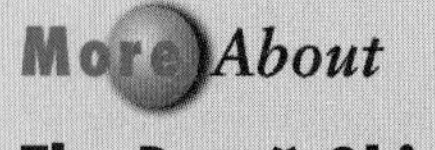

The Date() Object

A specific date can be set as Date("month, day, year hours:minutes:seconds") or Date(year, month, day) or Date(year, month, day, hours, minutes, seconds).

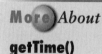

getTime()

You can divide by 86,400,000, but the expression 1000 * 60 * 60 * 24 is used to explain how the value is derived. For more information on the Date() object and the Date() method getTime(), visit www.scsite.com/js/p3.htm and then click getTime().

The getMonth() and getTime() Methods

To create the dynamic greeting, use the getMonth() and getTime() methods of the Date() object. Recall from Project 1 that the Date() object returns the current system date to an object instance. Using the new object with the current system date, the getMonth() method returns the number of the current month. Because the system starts counting from zero, the first month, January, is zero. February is one and so on through December, which becomes 11.

The getTime() method returns the number of milliseconds that have elapsed since January 1, 1970 at 00:00:00. Using the number of milliseconds is easier to use than counting the number of days between dates. To count the number of days between dates requires keeping track of the number of days in each month, because each month has a different number of days.

To determine the number of days, from the current date to a given holiday, divide the number of milliseconds by the product of 1000 * 60 * 60 * 24. This expression represents the 1,000 milliseconds in one second, the 60 seconds in a minute, the 60 minutes in an hour, and the 24 hours in a day. The name of the user-defined function that creates the dynamic greeting for the holiday countdown is HolidayDays(). The function creates the dynamic greeting, which determines the number of days until a given holiday.

Creating the HolidayDays() Function

The first holiday used in the function is St. Patrick's Day. The flowchart in Figure 3-10 shows the logic of the Switch statement used in the HolidayDays() function. Table 3-6 shows the JavaScript code for the function.

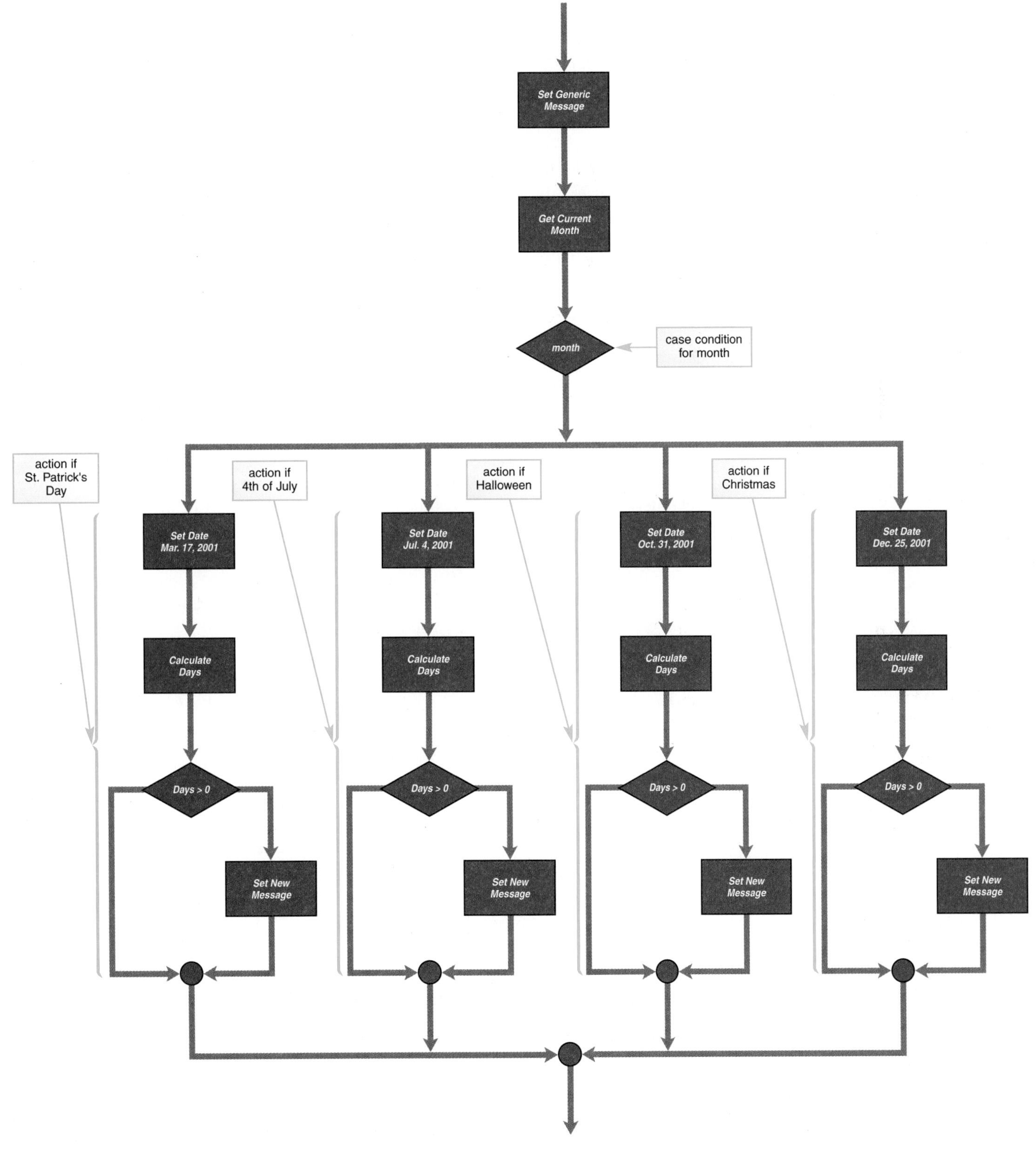

FIGURE 3-10

Table 3-6

LINE	CODE
17	var holidayCntMsg = "Leave the party to Midwest Catering"
18	var curDay = new Date()
19	var tMonth = curDay.getMonth()
20	function HolidayDays() {
21	switch (tMonth) {
22	case 2:
23	var tHoliday = new Date("March 17, 2001")
24	var curHoliday = tHoliday.getTime()-curDay.getTime()
25	if (curHoliday > 0) {
26	curHoliday = Math.ceil(curHoliday / (1000 * 60 * 60 * 24))
27	holidayCntMsg = "Only "+curHoliday+" days until St. Patrick's Day!"
28	}
29	break

Line 17 establishes the default greeting which displays if no holiday exists for a given month. Line 18 assigns curDay the current system date. Recall from project two that the Date() object returns the current system date, time, and time zone, and that specific information must be extracted from the string object. In line 19, the getMonth() method returns the number of the current month. Recall earlier that January returns a zero. Thus, the month of March returns a two. In line 22, the case statement (case 2) tests the month for March.

The Date() object sets a specific date (St. Patrick's Day) to an object instance in line 23. Line 24 subtracts the number of days of the current system date using the getTime() method from the assigned holiday date storing the result in curHoliday.

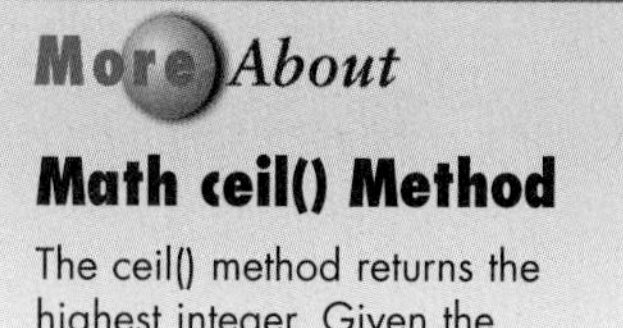

Math ceil() Method

The ceil() method returns the highest integer. Given the value -2.89, ceil(-2.89) returns -2. Given the value 3.02, ceil(3.02) returns 4.

The If statement in line 24 tests the value of curHoliday. If the value is greater than zero that means current system date has not passed the holiday. Divide the number of milliseconds by the product of (1000 * 60 * 60 * 24) as shown in line 26. The entire expression is rounded to the nearest highest integer using the Math ceil() method (line 26). Line 27 constructs the holidayCntMsg.

To enter the HolidayDays()function steps for St Patrick's Day, perform the following steps.

To Enter the HolidayDays() User-Defined Function Steps for St. Patrick's Day

1. **Position the insertion point on line 17.**

2. **Enter the JavaScript code shown in Table 3-6. For the date in line 23, enter the current year.**

The JavaScript code for the St. Patrick's Day displays a holiday message (Figure 3-11).

```
cater.htm - Notepad
File  Edit  Search  Help
<HTML>
<HEAD>
<TITLE>Midwest Catering Service</TITLE>
<SCRIPT  LANGUAGE="JAVASCRIPT">
<!--  Hide from old browsers
     var banners = new Array("banner1.jpg","banner2.jpg","banner3.jpg","banner4.jpg")
     var bnrCntr = 0
     function bancycle() {
             bnrCntr = bnrCntr + 1
             if (bnrCntr == 4) {
                bnrCntr = 0
             }
          document.Banner.src = banners[bnrCntr]
          setTimeout("bancycle()",3000)
     }

     var holidayCntMsg = "Leave the party to Midwest Catering"
     var curDay = new Date()
     var tMonth = curDay.getMonth()
     function HolidayDays() {
     switch (tMonth) {
         case 2:
            var tHoliday = new Date("March 17, 2001")
            var curHoliday = tHoliday.getTime()-curDay.getTime()
            if (curHoliday > 0) {
               curHoliday = Math.ceil(curHoliday / (1000 * 60 * 60 * 24))
               holidayCntMsg = "Only "+curHoliday+" days until St. Patrick's Day!"
            }
            break

//-->
</SCRIPT>
</HEAD>
```

line 17

replace 2001 with current year

Start | cater.htm - Notepad | 8:54 AM

FIGURE 3-11

The next section of the function completes the code for the Independence Day holiday and is shown in Table 3-7.

Table 3-7

LINE	CODE
30	case 5 : case 6:
31	var tHoliday = new Date("July 4, 2001")
32	var curHoliday = tHoliday.getTime()-curDay.getTime()
33	if (curHoliday > 0) {
34	curHoliday = Math.ceil(curHoliday / (1000 * 60 * 60 * 24))
35	holidayCntMsg = "Only "+curHoliday+" days until the 4th of July!"
36	}
37	break

To wait until July to begin the count down until the holiday, only three days are left. Because this is a popular summer holiday, the count down for Independence Day begins in June. The Case statement (line 30) is a multiple condition using the OR conditional operator (||) to test for months 5 (June) or 6 (July). Recall from the Introduction section before Project 1, that in an OR condition if either condition is True, the entire condition is True. Line 31 sets the date for July 4. The <SUP> tag on line 35 is the SUPERSCRIPT tag.

To enter the statements to count down the days to the Independence Day holiday, perform the following steps.

To Enter the HolidayDays() User-Defined Function Steps for Independence Day

1 **Position the insertion point on line 30.**

2 **Enter the JavaScript code shown in Table 3-7 on the previous page. For the date in line 31, enter the current year.**

The JavaScript code for the Independence Day holiday message displays (Figure 3-12).

```
cater.htm - Notepad
File  Edit  Search  Help
            document.Banner.src = banners[bnrCntr]
            setTimeout("bancycle()",3000)
      }

      var holidayCntMsg = "Leave the party to Midwest Catering"
      var curDay = new Date()
      var tMonth = curDay.getMonth()
      function HolidayDays() {
      switch (tMonth) {
           case 2:
               var tHoliday = new Date("March 17, 2001")
               var curHoliday = tHoliday.getTime()-curDay.getTime()
               if (curHoliday > 0) {
                   curHoliday = Math.ceil(curHoliday / (1000 * 60 * 60 * 24))
                   holidayCntMsg = "Only "+curHoliday+" days until St. Patrick's Day!"
               }
               break
           case 5 || 6:
               var tHoliday = new Date("July 4, 2001")
               var curHoliday = tHoliday.getTime()-curDay.getTime()
               if (curHoliday > 0) {
                   curHoliday = Math.ceil(curHoliday / (1000 * 60 * 60 * 24))
                   holidayCntMsg = "Only "+curHoliday+" days until the 4<SUP>th</SUP> of July!"
               }
               break

//-->
</SCRIPT>
</HEAD>

<BODY onload="setTimeout('bancycle()',3000)">

<A NAME="MCS_TOP">
<CENTER><IMG SRC="banner1.jpg" Name="Banner" Width=320 Height=65></CENTER>
```

replace 2001 with current year

line 30

Start | cater.htm - Notepad | 8:54 AM

FIGURE 3-12

The next section of the function code completes the count down for Halloween (Table 3-8).

Table 3-8

LINE	CODE
38	`case 9:`
39	`   var tHoliday = new Date("October 31, 2001")`
40	`   var curHoliday = tHoliday.getTime()-curDay.getTime()`
41	`   if (curHoliday > 0) {`
42	`      curHoliday = Math.ceil(curHoliday / (1000 * 60 * 60 * 24))`
43	`      holidayCntMsg = "Only "+curHoliday+" days until Halloween!"`
44	`   }`
45	`   break`

The count down begins in October, which the getMonth() method will determine as nine, as shown in line 38. The date for Halloween, is set in line 39.

To enter the function statements for Halloween, perform the following steps.

To Enter the HolidayDays() User-Defined Function Steps for Halloween

1 Position the insertion point on line 38.

2 Enter the JavaScript code shown in Table 3-8. For the date in line 39, enter the current year.

The JavaScript code for the Halloween holiday message displays (Figure 3-13).

```
cater.htm - Notepad
File  Edit  Search  Help
    switch (tMonth) {
        case 2:
            var tHoliday = new Date("March 17, 2001")
            var curHoliday = tHoliday.getTime()-curDay.getTime()
            if (curHoliday > 0) {
                curHoliday = Math.ceil(curHoliday / (1000 * 60 * 60 * 24))
                holidayCntMsg = "Only "+curHoliday+" days until St. Patrick's Day!"
            }
            break
        case 5 || 6:
            var tHoliday = new Date("July 4, 2001")
            var curHoliday = tHoliday.getTime()-curDay.getTime()
            if (curHoliday > 0) {
                curHoliday = Math.ceil(curHoliday / (1000 * 60 * 60 * 24))
                holidayCntMsg = "Only "+curHoliday+" days until the 4<SUP>th</SUP> of July!"
            }
            break
        case 9:
            var tHoliday = new Date("October 31, 2001")
            var curHoliday = tHoliday.getTime()-curDay.getTime()
            if (curHoliday > 0) {
                curHoliday = Math.ceil(curHoliday / (1000 * 60 * 60 * 24))
                holidayCntMsg = "Only "+curHoliday+" days until Halloween!"
            }
            break


//-->
</SCRIPT>
</HEAD>

<BODY onload="setTimeout('bancycle()',3000)">

<A NAME="MCS_TOP">
<CENTER><IMG SRC="banner1.jpg" Name="Banner" Width=320 Height=65></CENTER>
```


FIGURE 3-13

The code to finish the function for the Christmas holiday message is shown in Table 3-9. This case section follows the same logic as the code discussed in Table 3-8.

Table 3-9

```
LINE  CODE
46              case 11:
47                  var tHoliday = new Date("December 25, 2001")
48                  var curHoliday = tHoliday.getTime()-curDay.getTime()
49                  if (curHoliday > 0) {
50                      curHoliday = Math.ceil(curHoliday / (1000 * 60 * 60 * 24))
51                      holidayCntMsg = "Only "+curHoliday+" days until Christmas!"
52                  }
53                  break
54          }
55          return holidayCntMsg
56      }
```

The case condition for December tests for an 11 in line 46. The return command in line 55 sends the contents of the holidayCntMsg variable back to the calling function. If the current system month does not match any of the holiday months, the function returns the generic greeting originally set in line 17.

To enter the JavaScript code for the Christmas holiday, perform the following steps.

To Enter the HolidayDays() User-Defined Function Steps for Christmas

1 Position the insertion point on line 46.

2 Enter the JavaScript code shown in Table 3-9 on the previous page. For the date in line 47, enter the current year.

The final section of the function displays (Figure 3-14).

cater.htm - Notepad

File Edit Search Help

```
      case 5 || 6:
         var tHoliday = new Date("July 4, 2001")
         var curHoliday = tHoliday.getTime()-curDay.getTime()
         if (curHoliday > 0) {
            curHoliday = Math.ceil(curHoliday / (1000 * 60 * 60 * 24))
            holidayCntMsg = "Only "+curHoliday+" days until the 4<SUP>th</SUP> of July!"
         }
         break
      case 9:
         var tHoliday = new Date("October 31, 2001")
         var curHoliday = tHoliday.getTime()-curDay.getTime()
         if (curHoliday > 0) {
            curHoliday = Math.ceil(curHoliday / (1000 * 60 * 60 * 24))
            holidayCntMsg = "Only "+curHoliday+" days until Halloween!"
         }
          break
      case 11:
         var tHoliday = new Date("December 25, 2001")
         var curHoliday = tHoliday.getTime()-curDay.getTime()
         if (curHoliday > 0) {
            curHoliday = Math.ceil(curHoliday / (1000 * 60 * 60 * 24))
            holidayCntMsg = "Only "+curHoliday+" days until Christmas!"
         }
         break
      }
   return holidayCntMsg
   }

//-->
</SCRIPT>
</HEAD>

<BODY onload="
```

replace 2001 with current year

line 46

return message string

end of function

FIGURE 3-14

Calling the HolidayDays() Function

The next step inserts the JavaScript code in the BODY section that calls the HolidayDays() function and displays the appropriate greeting (Figures 3-1a through 3-1e on page J 3.5 and J 3.6). The dynamic greeting displays at the top of the page below the rolling banner images. Table 3-10 provides the code for the HolidayDays() function call and the write() method that displays the message.

Table 3-10

LINE	CODE
67	`<SCRIPT LANGUAGE="JAVASCRIPT">`
68	`<!-- Hide from old browsers`
69	`var holidayMsg = HolidayDays()`
70	`document.write("<H2><CENTER>"+holidayMsg+"</CENTER></H2>")`
71	
72	`//-->`
73	`</SCRIPT>`

Recall from previous projects that JavaScript code entered in the BODY section must be in a SCRIPT section. To enter the function call that displays the dynamic message on the Web page, perform the following steps.

To Enter a Function Call and Display a Message

1 **Position the insertion point on line 67.**

2 **Enter the JavaScript code shown in Table 3-10.**

The embedded HTML tags display the message center-aligned with the Heading 2 style.

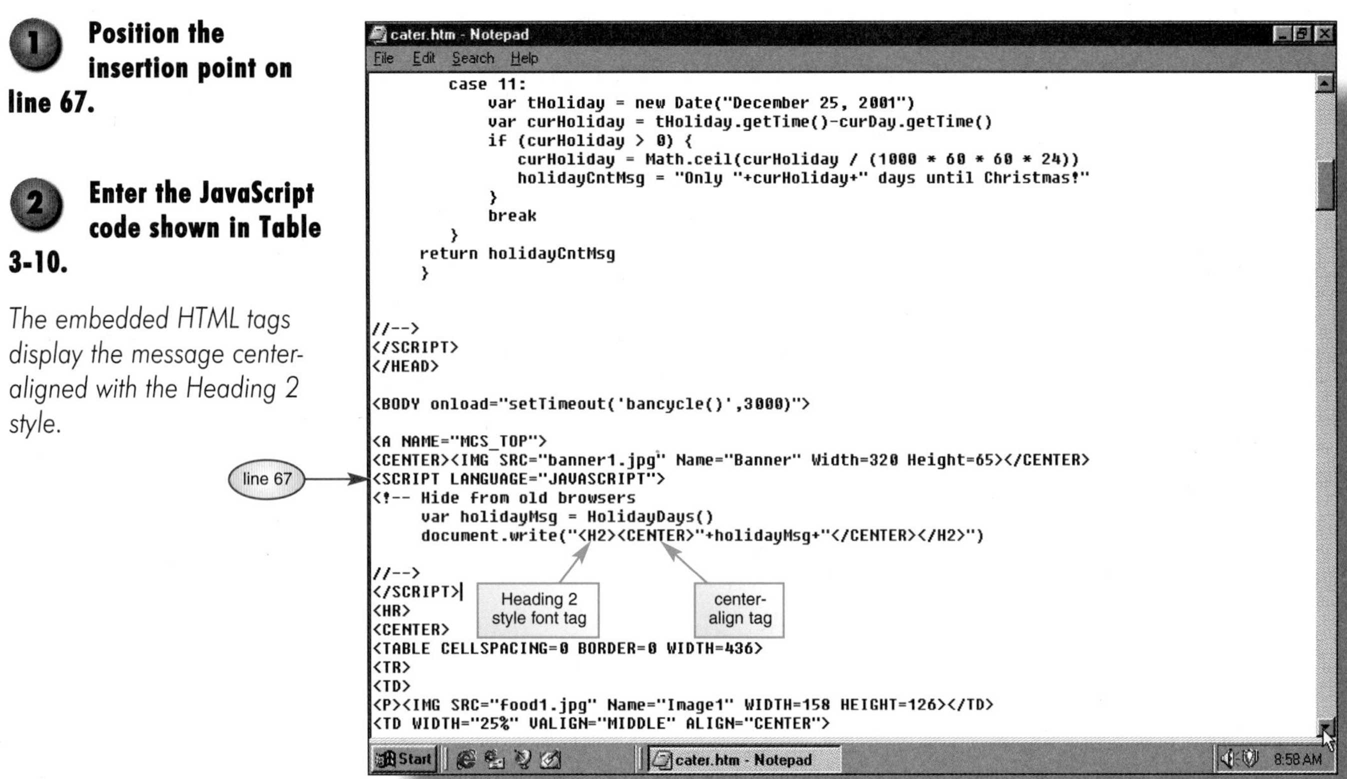

FIGURE 3-15

The JavaScript code to display the rolling banner and the greeting is complete. This is a good time to test the JavaScript code entered thus far.

Saving the HTML File and Viewing the Web Page

Save the HTML file with the JavaScript code using the name, mwcatering.htm, on the JavaScript Data Disk in drive A. Recall that you must add the .htm extension to the file name, because Notepad automatically saves all files with a .txt extension. To save and test the Web page, perform the steps on the next page.

TO SAVE THE HTML FILE AND TEST THE WEB PAGE

1. With the JavaScript Data Disk in drive A, click File on the menu bar and then Save As.
2. Type `a:\mwcatering.htm` in the File name text box and then click the Save button in the Save As dialog box.
3. Start your browser and open mwcatering.htm.

Figure 3-16 displays the first image of the rolling banner and the count down to Halloween message. The dynamic message that displays depends on the current system date.

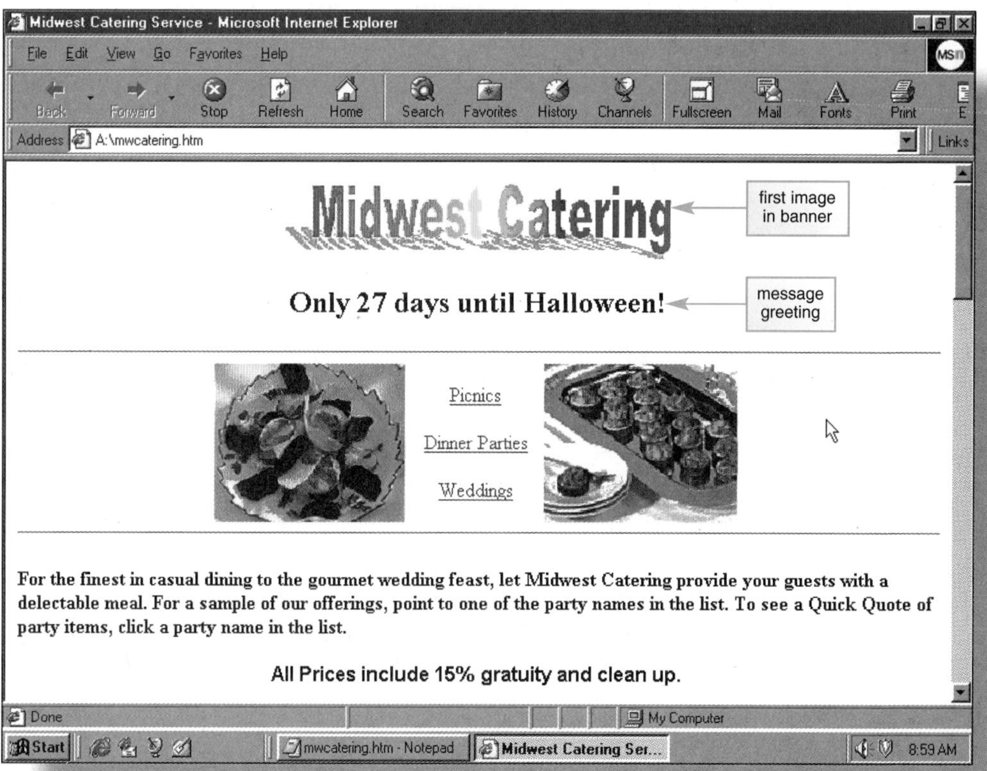

FIGURE 3-16

If the browser does not display the Web page correctly, close any error message dialog boxes and then click the Notepad button on the taskbar. Check the JavaScript code according to Figures 3-3 through 3-15 on pages J 3.8 through J 3.21. Correct any errors, save the file, activate the browser, and then click the Refresh button.

The onmouseover Event Handler

Recall from the requirements that the two images in Figure 3-1d (page J 3.6) change when the user places the mouse over one of the food service category links. To make these images change, assign a new image name to the image object. Each food service category link contains an onmouseover event handler that calls a function. The function assigns a new image to the image objects.

Web designers must be careful when writing onmouseover event handlers. While waiting for a Web page to load, a user might drag the mouse over an object associated with an event handler and trigger an action they were not expecting. Depending on the action, an error message may display, or the user may become lost or confused. If you get an error message associated with an onmouseover event handler, refresh the Web page, and make sure the page is completely loaded before moving the mouse.

In this project, the mouse event handler is associated with anchor links. A mouse event handler can be associated, however, with other objects such as buttons or graphics. Table 3-11 describes other mouse related event handlers.

Table 3-11

EVENT HANDLER	COMMENT
onmouseout	Triggers JavaScript code when the mouse pointer is dragged off an object
onmousedown	Triggers JavaScript code when the mouse button is pressed
onmouseup	Triggers JavaScript code when the mouse button is released
onmousemove	Triggers JavaScript code when a user moves the mouse pointer

Mouse Event Handlers

For more information, visit www.scsite.com/js/p3.htm, click Event Handlers, and then click Chapter 2, Handling Events.

Entering the onmouseover Event Handler

The user-defined functions for each of the food service categories are onPicnic(), onDinnerParty(), and onWedding(). For example, the link for Picnics in line 81 in Figure 3-17 reads <A HREF="#PicnicFood">. With the addition of the onmouseover event it will read <A HREF="#PicnicFood" onmouseover="onPicnic()">. To call the functions using the onmouseover event handlers, perform the following steps.

To Call the Functions Using the onmouseover Event Handler

1 **Position the insertion point immediately after the " and before the > on line 81.**

2 **Press the SPACEBAR once. Type** `onmouseover="onPicnic()"` **and do not press the ENTER key.**

The onmouseover event handler to call the onPicnic() function displays (Figure 3-17).

mwcatering.htm - Notepad

File Edit Search Help

```
<BODY onload="setTimeout('bancycle()',3000)">

<A NAME="MCS_TOP">
<CENTER><IMG SRC="banner1.jpg" Name="Banner" Width=320 Height=65></CENTER>
<SCRIPT LANGUAGE="JAVASCRIPT">
<!-- Hide from old browsers
     var holidayMsg = HolidayDays()
     document.write("<H2><CENTER>"+holidayMsg+"</CENTER></H2>")

//-->
</SCRIPT>
<HR>
<CENTER>
<TABLE CELLSPACING=0 BORDER=0 WIDTH=436>
<TR>
<TD>
<P><IMG SRC="food1.jpg" Name="Image1" WIDTH=158 HEIGHT=126></TD>
<TD WIDTH="25%" VALIGN="MIDDLE" ALIGN="CENTER">
<P><A HREF="#PicnicFoods" onmouseover="onPicnic()">Picnics</A></P>
<P><A HREF="#DinnerParty">Dinner Parties</A></P>
<P><A HREF="#Weddings">Weddings</A> </P>
</TD>
<TD VALIGN="MIDDLE">
<P><IMG SRC="food2.jpg" Name="Image2" Wi            ht=126></P>
</TD>
</TR>
</TABLE>
</CENTER>
```

line 81

mouse event handler

FIGURE 3-17

3 **Position the insertion point immediately after the " and before the > on line 82.**

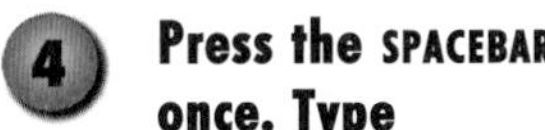

4 **Press the SPACEBAR once. Type** `onmouseover="onDinnerParty()"` **and do not press the ENTER key.**

The onmouseover event handler to call the onDinnerParty() function displays (Figure 3-18).

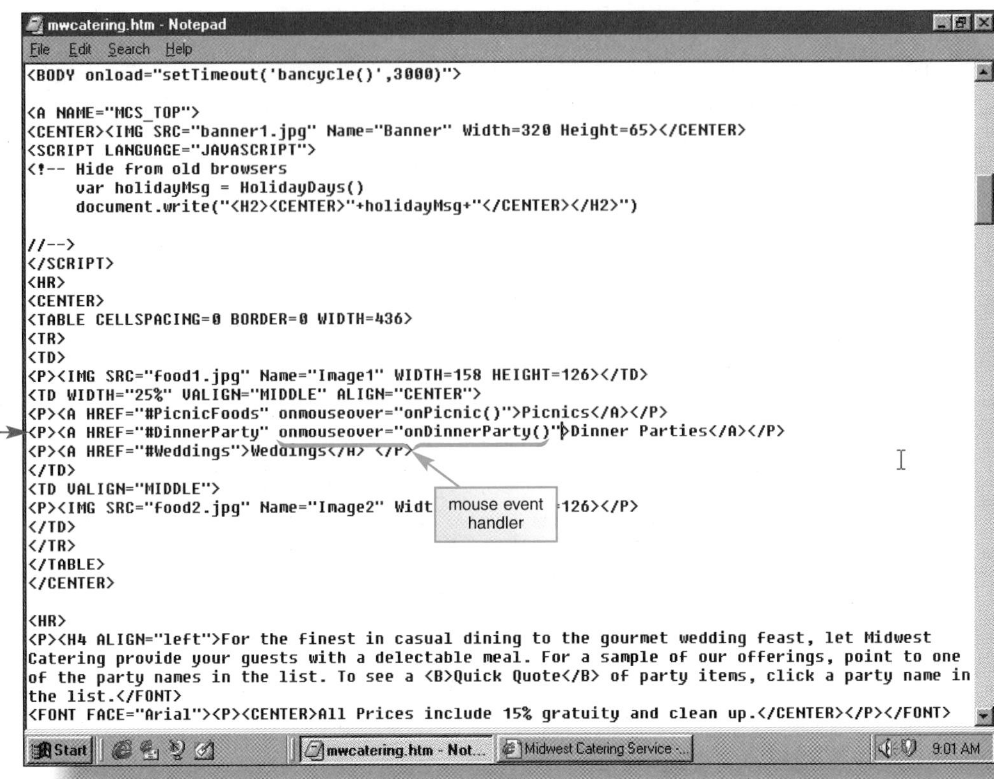


```
<BODY onload="setTimeout('bancycle()',3000)">

<A NAME="MCS_TOP">
<CENTER><IMG SRC="banner1.jpg" Name="Banner" Width=320 Height=65></CENTER>
<SCRIPT LANGUAGE="JAVASCRIPT">
<!-- Hide from old browsers
     var holidayMsg = HolidayDays()
     document.write("<H2><CENTER>"+holidayMsg+"</CENTER></H2>")

//-->
</SCRIPT>
<HR>
<CENTER>
<TABLE CELLSPACING=0 BORDER=0 WIDTH=436>
<TR>
<TD>
<P><IMG SRC="food1.jpg" Name="Image1" WIDTH=158 HEIGHT=126></TD>
<TD WIDTH="25%" VALIGN="MIDDLE" ALIGN="CENTER">
<P><A HREF="#PicnicFoods" onmouseover="onPicnic()">Picnics</A></P>
<P><A HREF="#DinnerParty" onmouseover="onDinnerParty()">Dinner Parties</A></P>
<P><A HREF="#Weddings">Weddings</A> </P>
</TD>
<TD VALIGN="MIDDLE">
<P><IMG SRC="food2.jpg" Name="Image2" Width=158 Height=126></P>
</TD>
</TR>
</TABLE>
</CENTER>

<HR>
<P><H4 ALIGN="left">For the finest in casual dining to the gourmet wedding feast, let Midwest
Catering provide your guests with a delectable meal. For a sample of our offerings, point to one
of the party names in the list. To see a <B>Quick Quote</B> of party items, click a party name in
the list.</FONT>
<FONT FACE="Arial"><P><CENTER>All Prices include 15% gratuity and clean up.</CENTER></P></FONT>
```

FIGURE 3-18

5 **Position the insertion point immediately after the " and before the > on line 83.**

6 **Press the SPACEBAR once. Type** `onmouseover="onWedding()"` **and do not press the ENTER key.**

The onmouseover event handler to call the onWedding() function displays (Figure 3-19).

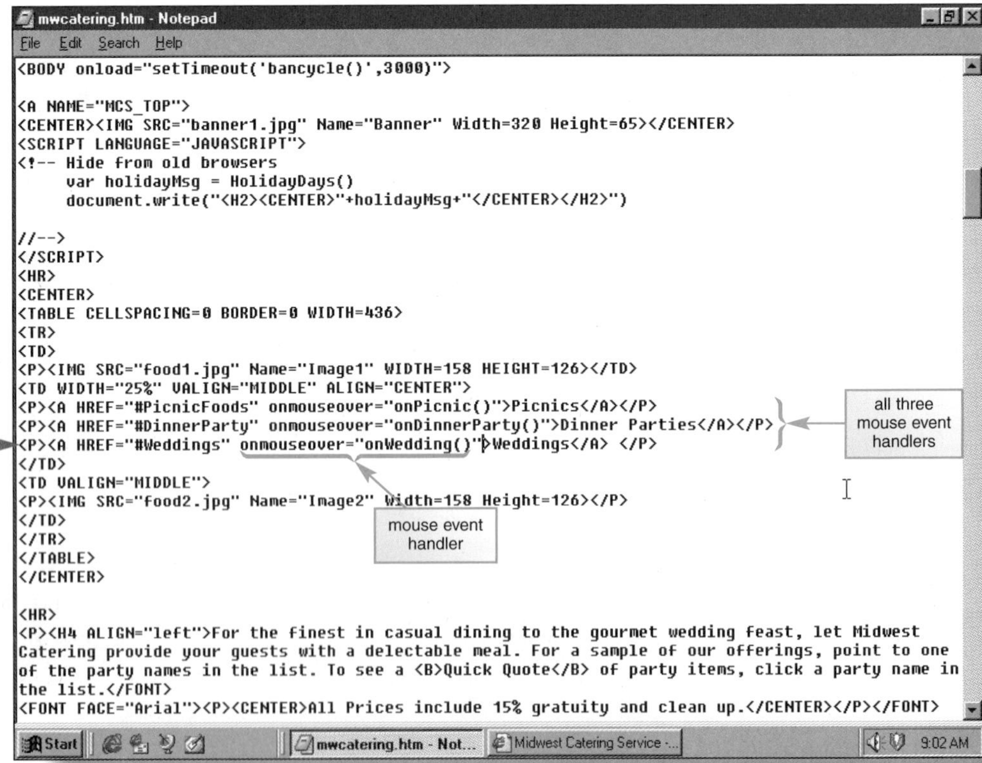


```
<BODY onload="setTimeout('bancycle()',3000)">

<A NAME="MCS_TOP">
<CENTER><IMG SRC="banner1.jpg" Name="Banner" Width=320 Height=65></CENTER>
<SCRIPT LANGUAGE="JAVASCRIPT">
<!-- Hide from old browsers
     var holidayMsg = HolidayDays()
     document.write("<H2><CENTER>"+holidayMsg+"</CENTER></H2>")

//-->
</SCRIPT>
<HR>
<CENTER>
<TABLE CELLSPACING=0 BORDER=0 WIDTH=436>
<TR>
<TD>
<P><IMG SRC="food1.jpg" Name="Image1" WIDTH=158 HEIGHT=126></TD>
<TD WIDTH="25%" VALIGN="MIDDLE" ALIGN="CENTER">
<P><A HREF="#PicnicFoods" onmouseover="onPicnic()">Picnics</A></P>
<P><A HREF="#DinnerParty" onmouseover="onDinnerParty()">Dinner Parties</A></P>
<P><A HREF="#Weddings" onmouseover="onWedding()">Weddings</A> </P>
</TD>
<TD VALIGN="MIDDLE">
<P><IMG SRC="food2.jpg" Name="Image2" Width=158 Height=126></P>
</TD>
</TR>
</TABLE>
</CENTER>

<HR>
<P><H4 ALIGN="left">For the finest in casual dining to the gourmet wedding feast, let Midwest
Catering provide your guests with a delectable meal. For a sample of our offerings, point to one
of the party names in the list. To see a <B>Quick Quote</B> of party items, click a party name in
the list.</FONT>
<FONT FACE="Arial"><P><CENTER>All Prices include 15% gratuity and clean up.</CENTER></P></FONT>
```

FIGURE 3-19

Entering the Functions

The next step is to enter the functions that the onmouseover event handlers trigger to change the images. Lines 79 and 86 contain the initial images, which display on the left and right sides of the links before the user drags the mouse over one of the links. The initial images display as shown in Figure 3-20.

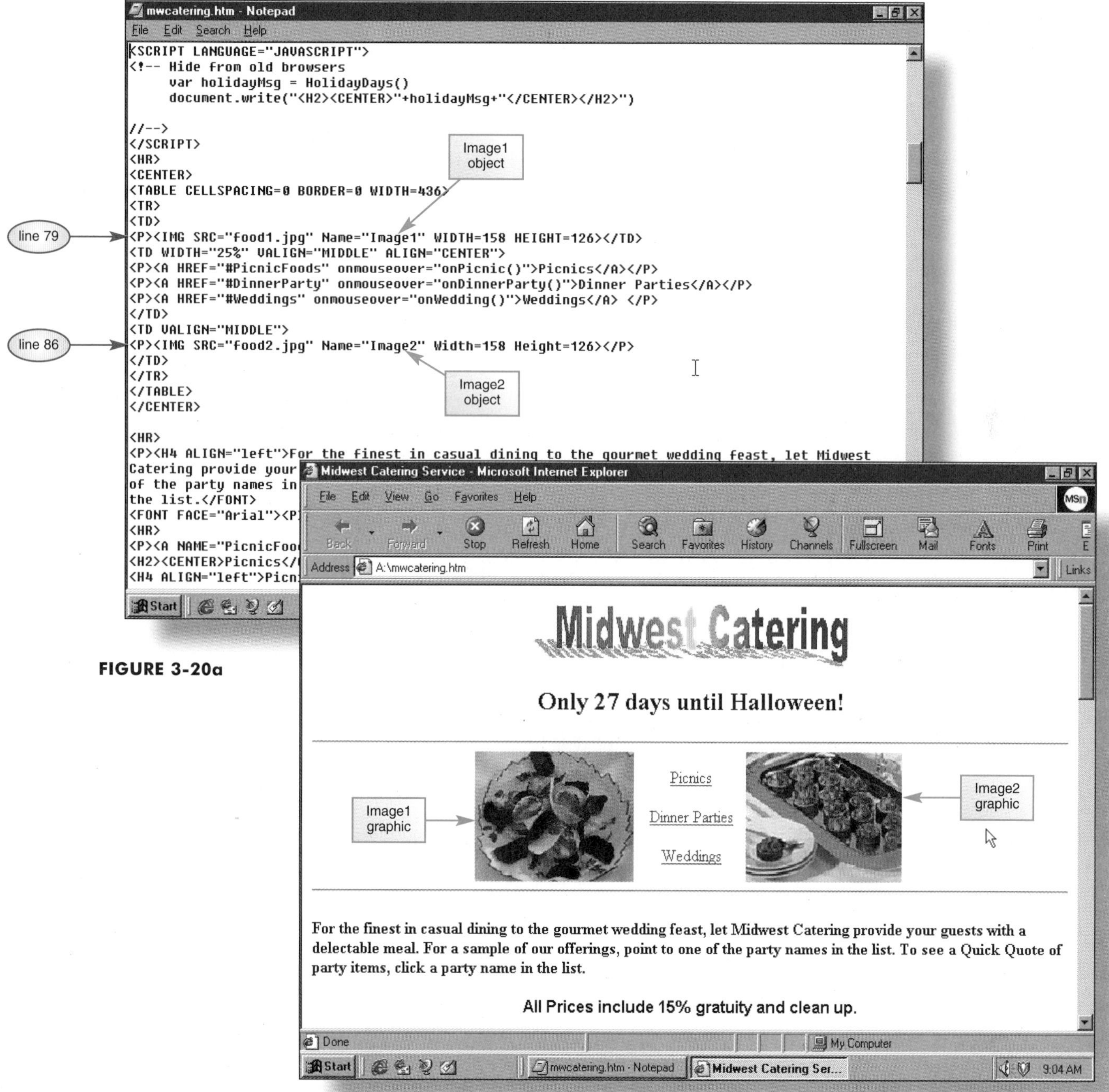

FIGURE 3-20a

FIGURE 3-20b

Table 3-12

LINE	CODE
58	`function onPicnic() {`
59	`document.Image1.src = "catering2.jpg"`
60	`document.Image2.src = "catering3.jpg"`
61	`}`

Table 3-12 shows the statements that assign the new images to the image object for the onPicnic() function.

In line 58, document.Image1.src contains the image on the left and in line 59, document.Image2.src contains the image on the right. To enter the onPicnic() function, which changes the images when the user drags the mouse over the Picnics Link, move to the HEAD section and then perform the following steps.

To Enter the onPicnic() Function

1. **Position the insertion point on line 58.**

2. **Enter the JavaScript code shown in Table 3-12.**

The onPicnic() function displays (Figure 3-21).

```
mwcatering.htm - Notepad
File  Edit  Search  Help
        case 9:
            var tHoliday = new Date("October 31, 2001")
            var curHoliday = tHoliday.getTime()-curDay.getTime()
            if (curHoliday > 0) {
               curHoliday = Math.ceil(curHoliday / (1000 * 60 * 60 * 24))
               holidayCntMsg = "Only "+curHoliday+" days until Halloween!"
            }
             break
        case 11:
            var tHoliday = new Date("December 25, 2001")
            var curHoliday = tHoliday.getTime()-curDay.getTime()
            if (curHoliday > 0) {
               curHoliday = Math.ceil(curHoliday / (1000 * 60 * 60 * 24))
               holidayCntMsg = "Only "+curHoliday+" days until Christmas!"
            }
            break
        }
     return holidayCntMsg
     }

     function onPicnic() {
         document.Image1.src = "catering2.jpg"
         document.Image2.src = "catering3.jpg"
        }

//-->
</SCRIPT>
</HEAD>

<BODY onload="setTimeout('bancycle()',3000)">

<A NAME="MCS_TOP">
<CENTER><IMG SRC="banner1.jpg" Name="Banner" Width=320 Height=65></CENTER>
<SCRIPT LANGUAGE="JAVASCRIPT">
```

line 58

Image1 object location reference

Image2 object location reference

Start | mwcatering.htm - Not... | Midwest Catering Service -... | 9:07 AM

FIGURE 3-21

Table 3-13 provides the code for the onDinnerParty() function.

Table 3-13

LINE	CODE
63	`function onDinnerParty() {`
64	`document.Image1.src = "catering4.jpg"`
65	`document.Image2.src = "catering5.jpg"`
66	`}`

Lines 64 and 65 assign the image file names to the image objects. To enter the onDinnerParty() function, perform the following steps.

To Enter the onDinnerParty() Function

1 **Position the insertion point on line 63.**

2 **Enter the JavaScript code shown in Table 3-13.**

The onDinnerParty() function displays (Figure 3-22).

```
    case 11:
        var tHoliday = new Date("December 25, 2001")
        var curHoliday = tHoliday.getTime()-curDay.getTime()
        if (curHoliday > 0) {
           curHoliday = Math.ceil(curHoliday / (1000 * 60 * 60 * 24))
           holidayCntMsg = "Only "+curHoliday+" days until Christmas!"
        }
        break
    }
return holidayCntMsg
}

function onPicnic() {
    document.Image1.src = "catering2.jpg"
    document.Image2.src = "catering3.jpg"
    }

function onDinnerParty() {
    document.Image1.src = "catering4.jpg"
    document.Image2.src = "catering5.jpg"
    }

//-->
</SCRIPT>
</HEAD>
```

line 63

Start | mwcatering.htm - Not... | Midwest Catering Service -... | 9:07 AM

FIGURE 3-22

Table 3-14 provides the code for the onWedding() function.

Lines 69 and 70 change the images. To enter the onWedding() function, perform the following steps.

Table 3-14

LINE	CODE
68	function onWedding() {
69	document.Image1.src = "catering6.jpg"
70	document.Image2.src = "catering7.jpg"
71	}

To Enter the onWedding() Function

1 **Position the insertion point on line 68.**

2 **Enter the JavaScript code shown in Table 3-14.**

The onWedding() function displays (Figure 3-23).

```
    case 11:
        var tHoliday = new Date("December 25, 2001")
        var curHoliday = tHoliday.getTime()-curDay.getTime()
        if (curHoliday > 0) {
           curHoliday = Math.ceil(curHoliday / (1000 * 60 * 60 * 24))
           holidayCntMsg = "Only "+curHoliday+" days until Christmas!"
        }
        break
    }
return holidayCntMsg
}

function onPicnic() {
    document.Image1.src = "catering2.jpg"
    document.Image2.src = "catering3.jpg"
    }

function onDinnerParty() {
    document.Image1.src = "catering4.jpg"
    document.Image2.src = "catering5.jpg"
    }

function onWedding() {
    document.Image1.src = "catering6.jpg"
    document.Image2.src = "catering7.jpg"
    }
```

line 68

Start | mwcatering.htm - Not... | Midwest Catering Service -... | 9:08 AM

FIGURE 3-23

Now is a good point to save the Web page and test the JavaScript code in the browser.

TO SAVE AND TEST THE WEB PAGE

1. With the JavaScript Data Disk in drive A, click File on the menu bar and then click Save.
2. Click the browser button on the taskbar and then click the Refresh button on the toolbar.
3. Point to the Weddings link and wait a few seconds.
4. Point to the Picnics link and wait a few seconds.

The images on both sides of the link change as you point to a link. Figure 3-24 displays the new images for the Picnics link.

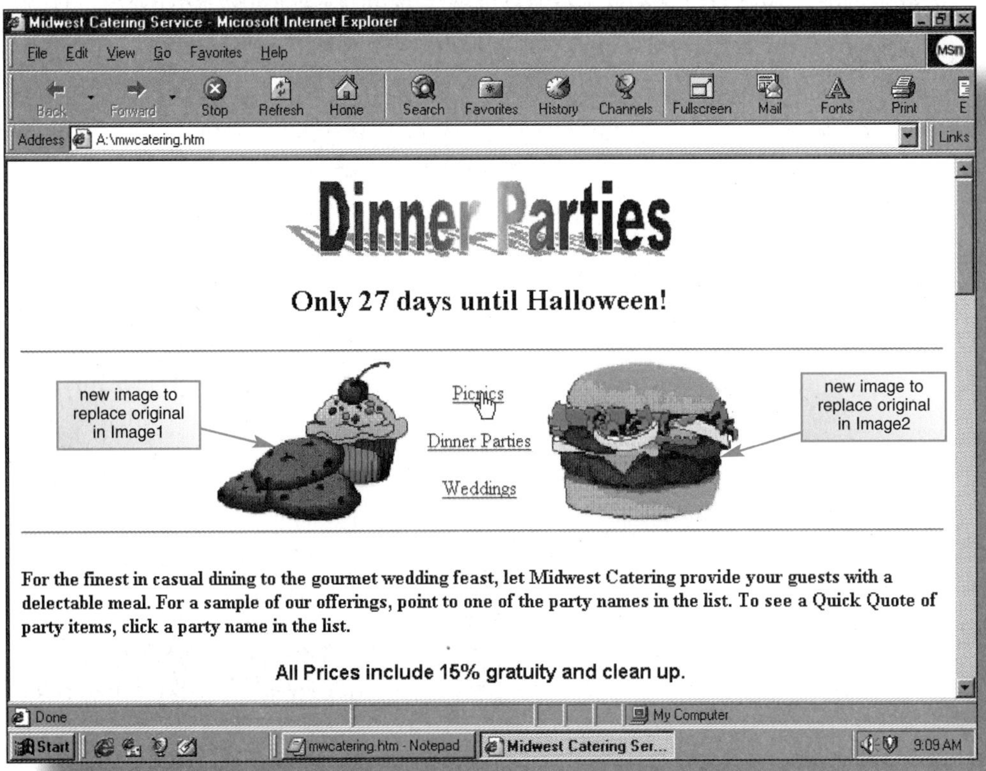

FIGURE 3-24

If the browser does not display the Web page correctly, close any error message dialog boxes and then click the Notepad button on the taskbar. Check the JavaScript code according to Figures 3-17 through 3-23 on pages J 3.23 through J 3.27. Correct any errors, save the file, activate the browser, and then click the Refresh button. The next step in the project is to display the per-person menu prices in a text box.

Using Selection Lists to Display Menu Items

Each of the three food service categories has a selection list that offers menu choices. Figure 3-25 shows the Picnics selection list. To display a price, the user clicks the down arrow associated with the upper-left list box (Figure 3-25). To select an item from the list, the user clicks the desired item. Each item in the list has a per-person price. An array object contains the corresponding per-person price to match the list.

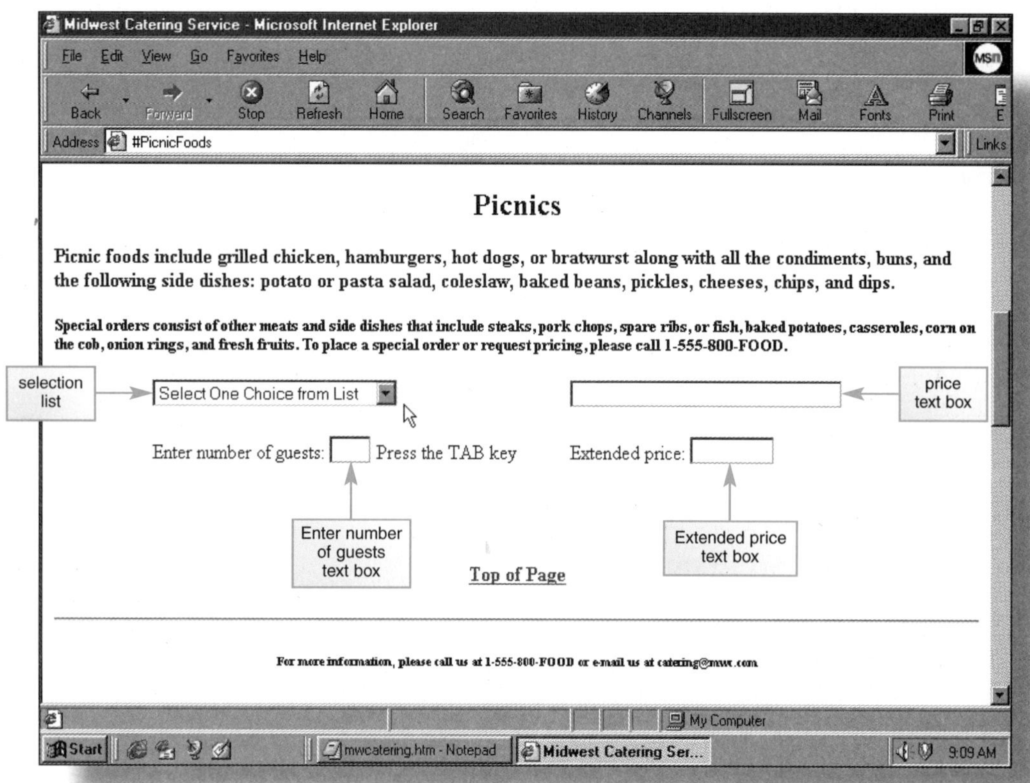

FIGURE 3-25

When the user selects an item, the price would display in the price text box shown in Figure 3-25. To obtain the correct price from the array, use the selectedIndex property. The **selectedIndex property** provides the position of the item selected in the list, which corresponds to the position of the price in the array. Figure 3-26 on the next page shows the function call from the PicnicMenu form and the relationship of the selectedIndex property to the array in the setPicnicPrice() function.

More About

Select Lists

For more information, visit www.scsite.com/js/p3.htm, click Select, click Chapter 7, Forms, and then click Select.

More About

Passing Form Names (this, form)

For more information, visit www.scsite.com/js/p3.htm and then click Functions.

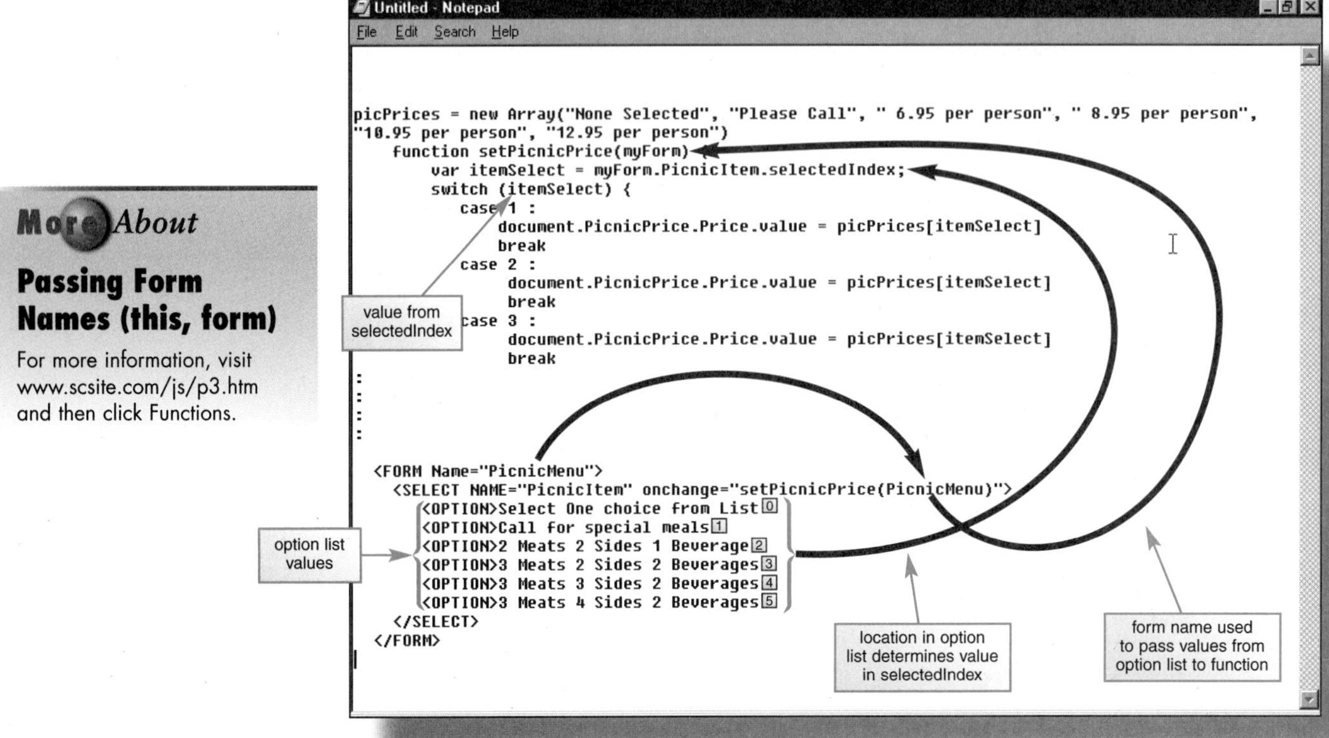

FIGURE 3-26

The onchange Event Handler

To display the price in the text box associated with the item, use the onchange event handler. The **onchange event handler** triggers an event whenever the object it is associated with changes. In this project, when a user selects an item, the list changes and triggers the onchange event handler.

For each of the price lists, the functions are setPicnicPrice(), setDinnerPrice(), and setWeddingPrice(). Associate each function with an onchange event handler in the SELECT tag. To call the setPicnicPrice(), setDinnerPrice(), and setWeddingPrice() functions for each option list form using the onchange event handler, move down into the BODY section and perform the following steps.

To Call the Functions Using the onchange Event Handler

1 Position the insertion point immediately after the right " and before the > on line 116.

2 Press the SPACEBAR once. Type onchange="setPicnicPrice(PicnicMenu)" **and do not press the ENTER key.**

The onchange event handler that calls the setPicnicPrice() function displays (Figure 3-27).

```
mwcatering.htm - Notepad
File  Edit  Search  Help
<HR>
<P><A NAME="PicnicFoods"></A></P>
<H2><CENTER>Picnics</CENTER></H2>
<H4 ALIGN="left">Picnic foods include grilled chicken, hamburgers, hot dogs, or bratwurst along
with all the condiments, buns, and the following side dishes: potato or pasta salad, coleslaw,
baked beans, pickles, cheeses, chips, and dips.</H4>
<H5 ALIGN="left">Special orders consist of other meats and side dishes that include steaks, pork
chops, spare ribs, or fish, baked potatoes, casseroles, corn on the cob, onion rings, and fresh
fruits. To place a special order or request pricing, please call 1-555-800-FOOD.</H5>
<P><CENTER><TABLE CELLSPACING=0 BORDER=0 WIDTH=599>
<TR>
  <TD>
  <FORM Name="PicnicMenu">
    <SELECT NAME="PicnicItem" onchange="setPicnicPrice(PicnicMenu)">
       <OPTION>Select One Choice from List
       <OPTION>Call for special meals
       <OPTION>2 Meats 2 Sides 1 Beverage
       <OPTION>3 Meats 2 Sides 2 Beverages
       <OPTION>3 Meats 3 Sides 2 Beverages
       <OPTION>3 Meats 4 Sides 2 Beverages
    </SELECT>
  </FORM>
</TD>
   <TD>
   <FORM Name="PicnicPrice">
     <INPUT Type="Text" Name="Price" Size=30>
   </FORM>
</TD>
</TR>
<TR>
<TD>
   <FORM Name="PicnicQuantity">
     Enter number of guests: <INPUT Type="Text" Name="PicQty" Size=3> Press the TAB key
</TD>
<TD>
```


FIGURE 3-27

3 Position the insertion point immediately after the right " and before the > on line 162.

4 Press the SPACEBAR once. Type onchange="setDinnerPrice(DinnerMenu)" **and do not press the ENTER key.**

The onchange event handler that calls the setDinnerPrice() function displays (Figure 3-28).

```
mwcatering.htm - Notepad
File  Edit  Search  Help
<A HREF="#TOP">Top of Page</A> </P>
<P><HR></P>
<H6 ALIGN="CENTER">For more information, please call us at 1-555-800-FOOD or e-mail us at
catering@mwc.com</H6><BR><BR><HR>
<P><A NAME="DinnerParty"></A></P>
<H2><CENTER>Dinner Parties</CENTER></H2>
<H4 ALIGN="left">Dinner party menus include seafood, rack of lamb, roast beef, chicken, and pasta
platters. Meals are served with choice of baked or mashed potatoes or rice pilaf, fresh
vegetables, green salad, rolls, beverage, and dessert.</H4>
<H5 ALIGN="left">Pasta dinners are available with fresh fruit garnish instead of potatoes or rice
and include garlic toast or Parmesan cheese bread sticks. </H5>
<CENTER>
<TABLE CELLSPACING=0 BORDER=0 WIDTH=599>
<TR>
<TD>
   <FORM Name="DinnerMenu">
   <SELECT NAME="DinnerItem" onchange="setDinnerPrice(DinnerMenu)">
      <OPTION>Select One Choice from List
      <OPTION>All Shrimp Dinners
      <OPTION>Rack of Lamb
      <OPTION>Prime Rib Beef Roast
      <OPTION>Baked Chicken
      <OPTION>Pasta
   </SELECT>
   </FORM>
</TD>
<TD>
  <FORM Name="DinnerPrice">
    <INPUT TYPE="Text" Name="Price" Size=30>
  </FORM>
</TD>
</TR>
<TR>
<TD>
   <FORM Name="DinnerQuantity">
```


FIGURE 3-28

5 **Position the insertion point immediately after the right " and before the > on line 216.**

6 **Press the SPACEBAR once. Type** onchange="setWedding Price(Wedding Menu)" **and do not press the ENTER key.**

The onchange event handler that calls the setWeddingPrice() function displays (Figure 3-29).

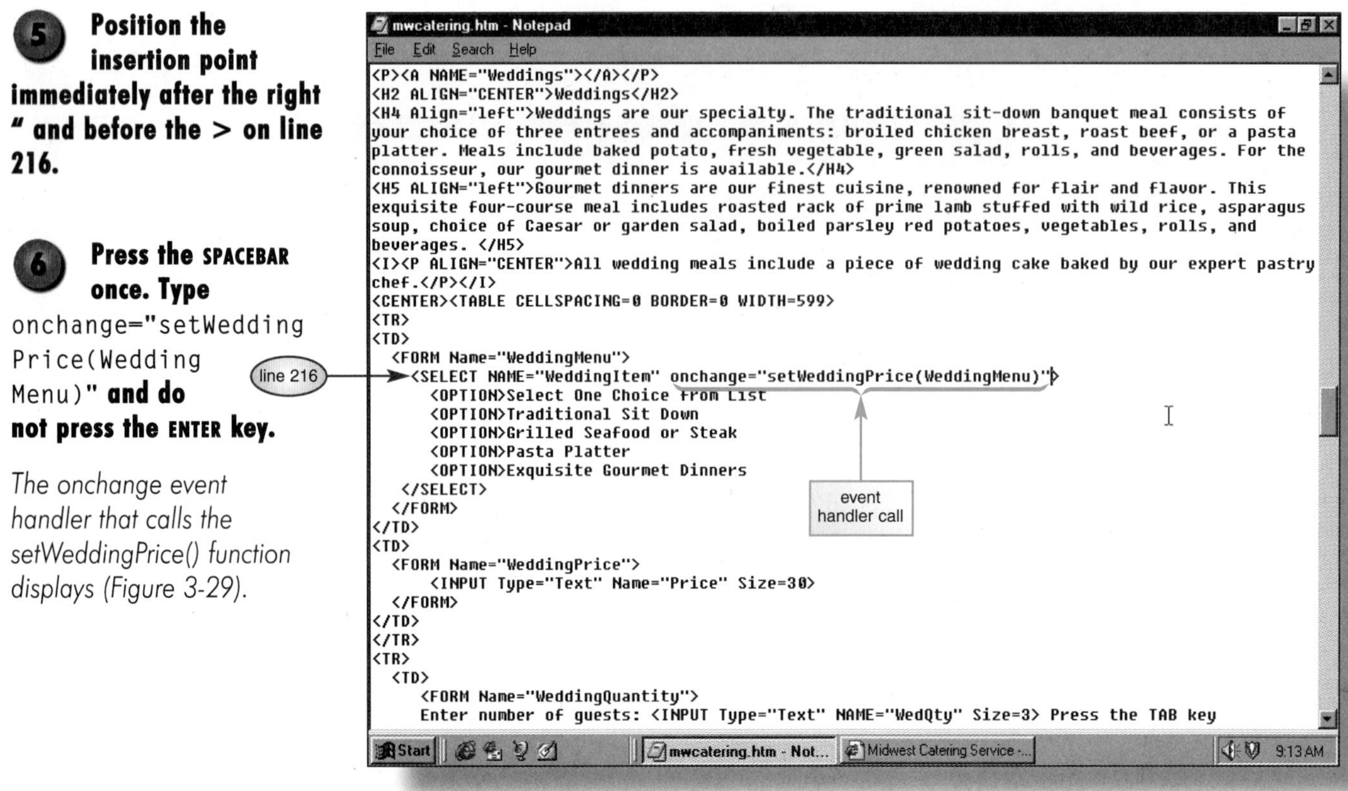

FIGURE 3-29

The next step is to write the user-defined functions to determine the item selected from the option list and display the price in the text box.

Entering the User-Defined Functions for the onchange Event Handler

The user-defined functions called by the onchange event handlers, display the price for the item selected in the option list. Each function performs the following steps: (1) defines an array for the prices; (2) clears the text boxes; (3) uses the selectedIndex property to set the subscript variable; and (4) sets the price to the price text box. Table 3-15 provides the code for the setPicnicPrice() function.

Table 3-15

```
LINE  CODE
73        picPrices = new Array("None Selected", "Please Call", "$10.95 per person", "$10.95 per
      person", "$11.95 per person", "$13.95 per person")
74        function setPicnicPrice(myForm) {
75            document.PicnicPrice.Price.value = ""
76            document.PicnicQuantity.PicExtPrice.value = ""
77            document.PicnicQuantity.PicQty.value = ""
78            var itemSelect = myForm.PicnicItem.selectedIndex;
79            switch (itemSelect) {
80               case 1 :
81                   document.PicnicPrice.Price.value = picPrices[itemSelect]
82                   break
83               case 2 :
84                    document.PicnicPrice.Price.value = picPrices[itemSelect]
85                    break;
86               case 3 :
87                    document.PicnicPrice.Price.value = picPrices[itemSelect]
88                    break;
89               case 4 :
90                    document.PicnicPrice.Price.value = picPrices[itemSelect]
91                    break
92               case 5 :
93                    document.PicnicPrice.Price.value = picPrices[itemSelect]
94               }
95             document.PicnicQuantity.PicQty.focus()
96        }
```

Line 73 defines the price array. The first item, None Selected, fills the zero element location, which is never used. Lines 75 through 77 clear out the text boxes each time the user selects a new item in the drop-down list. Lines 79 through 91 contain the JavaScript Switch statement. Line 78 shows the assignment of the index value from the selectedIndex property to the variable itemSelect. The index starts numbering the items in the list at zero. In the setPicnicPrice function, if the user selects the 2 Meats 2 Sides 1 Beverage choice, then the itemSelect value is 2 (Case Condition statement on line 83). The index value assigned to itemSelect becomes the subscript in lines 81, 84, 87, 90, and 93. These statements assign the corresponding price to the text box. Line 95 sets the focus to the number of guests text box to allow the user to enter the number of guests. To enter the function that assigns the picnic prices from the picnic menu to the text box, perform the steps on the next page.

To Enter the Function to Assign the Prices for Picnics

1. **Position the insertion point on line 73.**

2. **Enter the JavaScript code shown in Table 3-15.**

The setPicnicPrice() function displays (Figure 3-30).

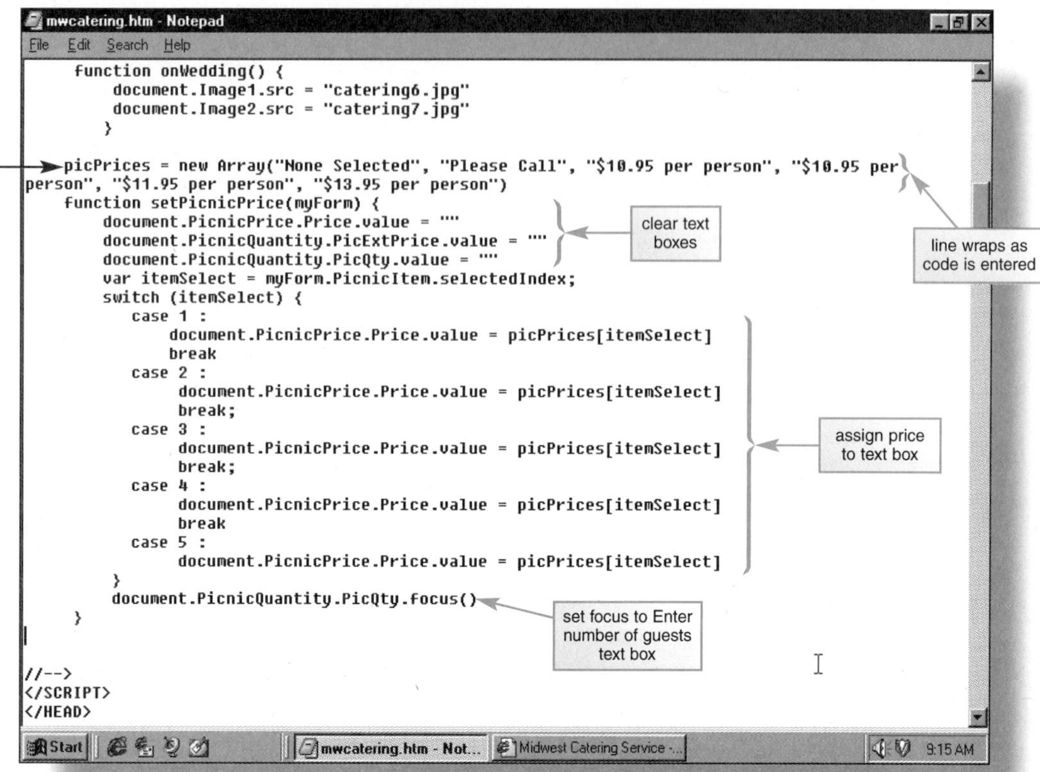

FIGURE 3-30

The user-defined function for dinner party prices is similar to the picnic function as shown in Table 3-16. The Switch statement tests the selected item and assigns the price to the price text box (document.DinnerPrice.Price.value) and the focus is set to the Enter number of guests text box.

Table 3-16

```
LINE  CODE
99        dinnerPrices = new Array("None Selected", "$13.95 per person", "$16.95 per person", "$18.95 per person", "$12.95 per person", "$12.95 per person")
100       function setDinnerPrice(myForm) {
101           document.DinnerPrice.Price.value = ""
102           document.DinnerQuantity.DinExtPrice.value = ""
103           document.DinnerQuantity.DinQty.value = ""
104           var itemSelect = myForm.DinnerItem.selectedIndex;
105           switch (itemSelect) {
106               case 1 :
107                  document.DinnerPrice.Price.value = dinnerPrices[itemSelect]
108                  break
109               case 2 :
110                  document.DinnerPrice.Price.value = dinnerPrices[itemSelect]
111                  break
112               case 3 :
113                  document.DinnerPrice.Price.value = dinnerPrices[itemSelect]
114                  break
115               case 4 :
116                  document.DinnerPrice.Price.value = dinnerPrices[itemSelect]
117                  break
118               case 5 :
119                  document.DinnerPrice.Price.value = dinnerPrices[itemSelect]
120                  break
121           }
122           document.DinnerQuantity.DinQty.focus()
123       }
```

Line 99 defines and fills the dinnerPrices array. The None Selected value fills the zero element in the array. Lines 101 through 103 clear the text boxes each time the function is called. The selectedIndex property (line 104) determines the item selected. Lines 105 through 120 set the corresponding price from the array to the text box. Line 122 sets the focus to the Enter number of guests text box to allow the user to enter the number of guests. To enter the function that assigns the prices for the dinner parties menu to the price text box, perform the steps on the next page.

To Enter the Function to Assign the Prices for Dinner Parties

1 Position the insertion point on line 99.

2 Enter the JavaScript code shown in Table 3-16.

The setDinnerPrice() function displays (Figure 3-31).

```
mwcatering.htm - Notepad
File  Edit  Search  Help
        case 5 :
            document.PicnicPrice.Price.value = picPrices[itemSelect]
        }
        document.PicnicQuantity.PicQty.focus()
    }
    dinnerPrices = new Array("None Selected", "$13.95 per person", "$16.95 per person", "$18.95
per person", "$12.95 per person", "$12.95 per person")
    function setDinnerPrice(myForm) {
        document.DinnerPrice.Price.value = ""
        document.DinnerQuantity.DinExtPrice.value = ""
        document.DinnerQuantity.DinQty.value = ""
        var itemSelect = myForm.DinnerItem.selectedIndex;
        switch (itemSelect) {
            case 1 :
                document.DinnerPrice.Price.value = dinnerPrices[itemSelect]
                break
            case 2 :
                document.DinnerPrice.Price.value = dinnerPrices[itemSelect]
                break
            case 3 :
                document.DinnerPrice.Price.value = dinnerPrices[itemSelect]
                break
            case 4 :
                document.DinnerPrice.Price.value = dinnerPrices[itemSelect]
                break
            case 5 :
                document.DinnerPrice.Price.value = dinnerPrices[itemSelect]
                break
        }
        document.DinnerQuantity.DinQty.focus()
    }

//-->
```


FIGURE 3-31

The third function required is for the wedding prices (Table 3-17). The process for setting wedding prices is identical to the process for setting picnic and dinner party functions.

Table 3-17

LINE	CODE
125	`weddingPrices = new Array("None Selected", "$13.95 per person", $16.95 per person , $18.95 per person", "$28.95 per person")`
126	`function setWeddingPrice(myForm) {`
127	`document.WeddingPrice.Price.value = ""`
128	`document.WeddingQuantity.WedExtPrice.value = ""`
129	`document.WeddingQuantity.WedQty.value = ""`
130	`var itemSelect = myForm.WeddingItem.selectedIndex;`
131	`switch (itemSelect) {`
132	`case 1 :`
133	`document.WeddingPrice.Price.value = weddingPrices[itemSelect]`
134	`break`
135	`case 2 :`
136	`document.WeddingPrice.Price.value = weddingPrices[itemSelect]`
137	`break`
138	`case 3 :`
139	`document.WeddingPrice.Price.value = weddingPrices[itemSelect]`
140	`break`
141	`case 4 :`
142	`document.WeddingPrice.Price.value = weddingPrices[itemSelect]`
143	`break`
144	`}`
145	`document.WeddingQuantity.WedQty.focus()`
146	`}`

To enter the function to assign the prices for wedding receptions, perform the following steps.

To Enter the Function to Assign the Prices for Weddings

1 Position the insertion point on line 125.

2 Enter the JavaScript code shown in Table 3-17.

The setWeddingPrice() function displays (Figure 3-32).


```
        }
        document.DinnerQuantity.DinQty.focus()
    }
weddingPrices = new Array("None Selected", "$13.95 per person", "$16.95 per person", "$18.95
per person", "$28.95 per person")
    function setWeddingPrice(myForm) {
        document.WeddingPrice.Price.value = ""
        document.WeddingQuantity.WedExtPrice.value = ""
        document.WeddingQuantity.WedQty.value = ""
        var itemSelect = myForm.WeddingItem.selectedIndex;
        switch (itemSelect) {
            case 1 :
               document.WeddingPrice.Price.value = weddingPrices[itemSelect]
               break
            case 2 :
               document.WeddingPrice.Price.value = weddingPrices[itemSelect]
               break
            case 3 :
               document.WeddingPrice.Price.value = weddingPrices[itemSelect]
               break
            case 4 :
               document.WeddingPrice.Price.value = weddingPrices[itemSelect]
               break
        }
        document.WeddingQuantity.WedQty.focus()
    }
```

FIGURE 3-32

The function for each category displays the price per person and positions the insertion point in the Enter number of guests text box. The next section calculates the extended price based on the number of guests entered.

Calculating the Extended Price Function

The instructions on the Web page, as shown in Figure 3-33 for the Picnic category, instruct the user to enter a number in the Enter number of guests text box and then press the TAB key.

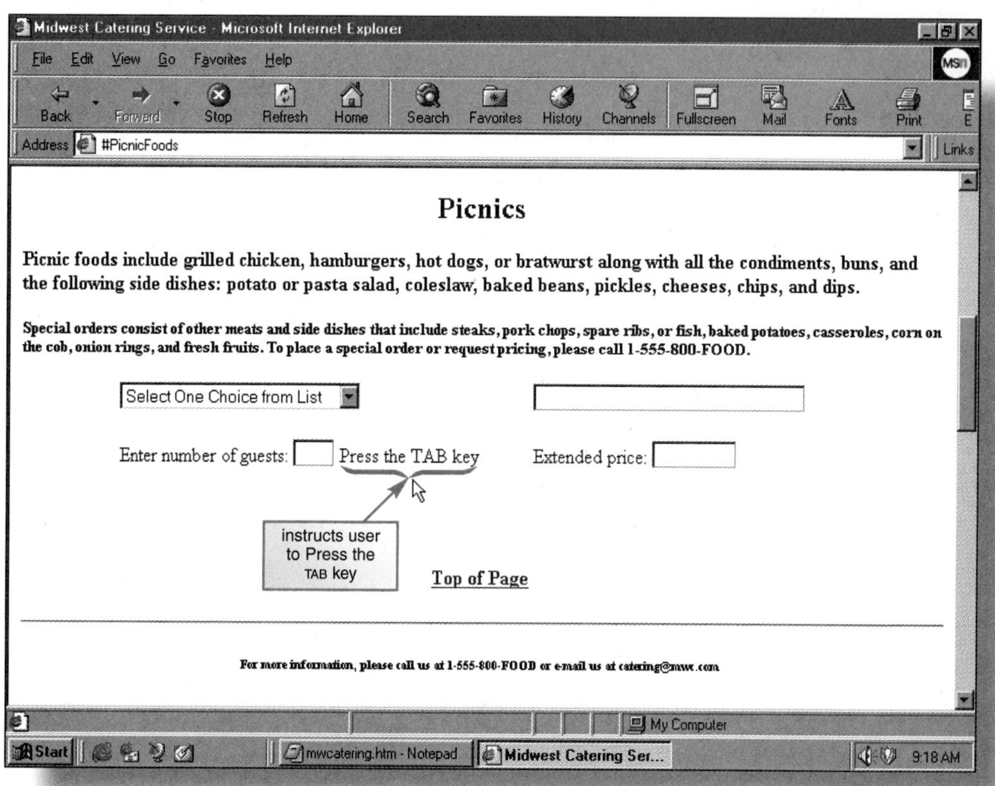

Midwest Catering Service - Microsoft Internet Explorer
Picnics
Picnic foods include grilled chicken, hamburgers, hot dogs, or bratwurst along with all the condiments, buns, and the following side dishes: potato or pasta salad, coleslaw, baked beans, pickles, cheeses, chips, and dips.
Special orders consist of other meats and side dishes that include steaks, pork chops, spare ribs, or fish, baked potatoes, casseroles, corn on the cob, onion rings, and fresh fruits. To place a special order or request pricing, please call 1-555-800-FOOD.
Select One Choice from List
Enter number of guests:
Press the TAB key
Extended price:
instructs user to Press the TAB key
Top of Page

FIGURE 3-33

When the user enters a number and presses the TAB key, the value of the Enter number of guests text box changes. This action triggers the onchange event handler and calls the appropriate function to calculate the extended price. Because each food service category has its own form and menu of prices, you cannot write a general-purpose function to calculate the prices.

The names of the three functions that calculate the extended price are picPrice(), dinPrice(), and wedPrice(). To call the functions that calculate the extended prices using the onchange event handler, perform the following steps.

To Call the Functions that Calculate the Extended Prices Using the onchange Event Handler

1 **Position the insertion point on line 221, immediately before the >.**

2 **Press the SPACEBAR once. Type** onchange="picPrice (PicnicQuantity)" **and do not press the ENTER key.**

Figure 3-34 displays the placement of the onchange event handler to call the picPrice function.

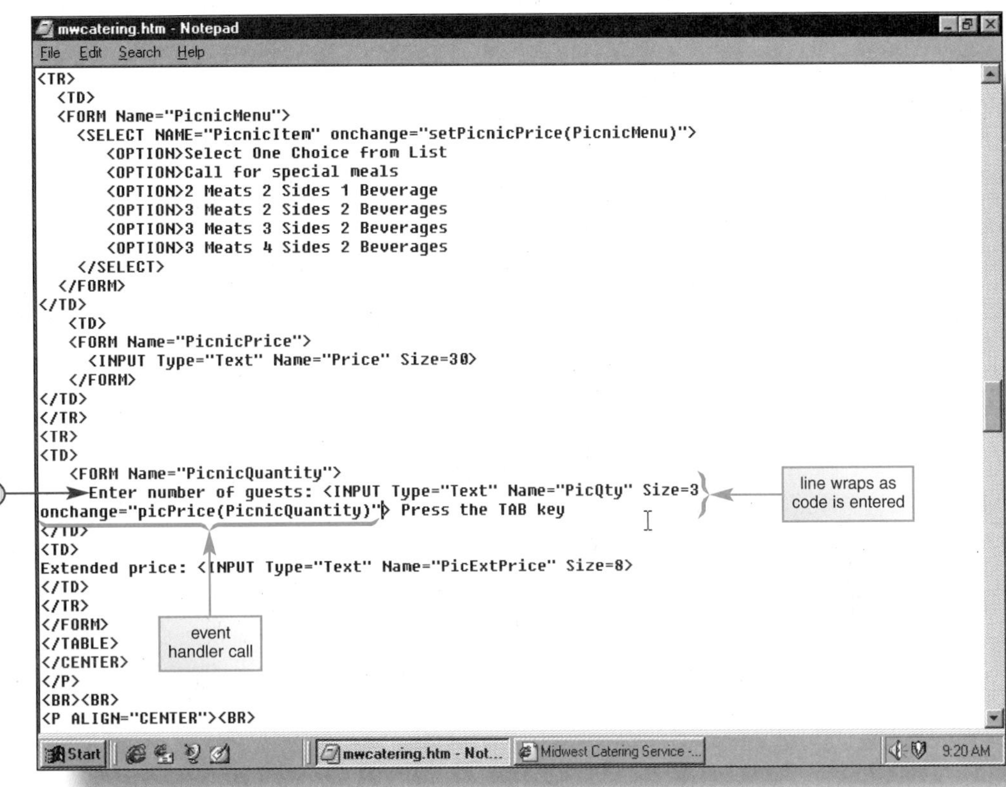
mwcatering.htm - Notepad
File Edit Search Help
<TR>
<TD>
<FORM Name="PicnicMenu">
<SELECT NAME="PicnicItem" onchange="setPicnicPrice(PicnicMenu)">
<OPTION>Select One Choice from List
<OPTION>Call for special meals
<OPTION>2 Meats 2 Sides 1 Beverage
<OPTION>3 Meats 2 Sides 2 Beverages
<OPTION>3 Meats 3 Sides 2 Beverages
<OPTION>3 Meats 4 Sides 2 Beverages
</SELECT>
</FORM>
</TD>
<TD>
<FORM Name="PicnicPrice">
<INPUT Type="Text" Name="Price" Size=30>
</FORM>
</TD>
</TR>
<TR>
<TD>
<FORM Name="PicnicQuantity">
Enter number of guests: <INPUT Type="Text" Name="PicQty" Size=3
onchange="picPrice(PicnicQuantity)"> Press the TAB key
</TD>
<TD>
Extended price: <INPUT Type="Text" Name="PicExtPrice" Size=8>
</TD>
</TR>
</FORM>
</TABLE>
</CENTER>
</P>

<P ALIGN="CENTER">
line 221
line wraps as code is entered
event handler call
Start
mwcatering.htm - Not...
Midwest Catering Service -...
9:20 AM

FIGURE 3-34

3 **Position the insertion point on line 266, immediately before the >.**

4 **Press the SPACEBAR once. Type** onchange="dinPrice (DinnerQuantity)" **and do not press the ENTER key.**

Figure 3-35 displays the placement of the onchange event handler to call the dinPrice function.

mwcatering.htm - Notepad

File Edit Search Help

```
  <FORM Name="DinnerMenu">
  <SELECT NAME="DinnerItem" onchange="setDinnerPrice(DinnerMenu)">
     <OPTION>Select One Choice from List
     <OPTION>All Shrimp Dinners
     <OPTION>Rack of Lamb
     <OPTION>Prime Rib Beef Roast
     <OPTION>Baked Chicken
     <OPTION>Pasta
  </SELECT>
  </FORM>
</TD>
<TD>
 <FORM Name="DinnerPrice">
   <INPUT TYPE="Text" Name="Price" Size=30>
 </FORM>
</TD>
</TR>
<TR>
<TD>
  <FORM Name="DinnerQuantity">
  Enter number of guests: <INPUT Type="Text" Name="DinQty" Size=3
onchange="dinPrice(DinnerQuantity)"> Press the TAB key
</TD>
<TD>
 Extended price: <INPUT Type="Text" Name="DinExtPrice" Size=8>
</TD>
</TR>
</FORM>
</TABLE>
</CENTER>

<BR><BR><BR><BR><BR>
```

line 266

line wraps as code is entered

event handler call

FIGURE 3-35

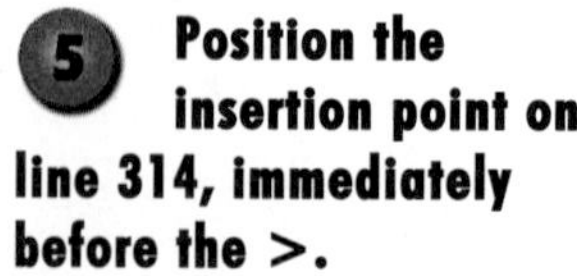

5 Position the insertion point on line 314, immediately before the >.

6 Press the SPACEBAR once. Type onchange="wedPrice (WeddingQuantity)" **and do not press the ENTER key.**

Figure 3-36 displays the placement of the onchange event handler to call the wedPrice function.

```
mwcatering.htm - Notepad
File  Edit  Search  Help
  <FORM Name="WeddingMenu">
    <SELECT NAME="WeddingItem" onchange="setWeddingPrice(WeddingMenu)">
      <OPTION>Select One Choice from List
      <OPTION>Traditional Sit Down
      <OPTION>Grilled Seafood or Steak
      <OPTION>Pasta Platter
      <OPTION>Exquisite Gourmet Dinners
    </SELECT>
  </FORM>
</TD>
<TD>
  <FORM Name="WeddingPrice">
      <INPUT Type="Text" Name="Price" Size=30>
  </FORM>
</TD>
</TR>
<TR>
  <TD>
    <FORM Name="WeddingQuantity">
    Enter number of guests: <INPUT Type="Text" NAME="WedQty" Size=3
onchange="wedPrice(WeddingQuantity)"> Press the TAB key
  </TD>
<TD>
  Extended price: <INPUT Type="Text" Name="WedExtPrice" Size=8>
</TD>
</TR>
</FORM>
</TABLE>
</CENTER>

<BR>
<P ALIGN="CENTER">
<A HREF="#TOP">Top of Page</A></p>
<P><HR>
<H6 ALIGN="CENTER">For more information, please call us at 1-555-800-FOOD or e-mail us at
```


FIGURE 3-36

The next section describes the JavaScript code for each of the user-defined functions that will calculate the extended price and set the formatted extended price in the text box with the call to the formatting function.

Calculating the Extended Price

After the user selects an item from the menu, the insertion point automatically is placed in the Enter number of guests text box. For each service category, a function calculates the extended price and displays in a text box. The onchange event handlers just entered call the appropriate functions. When the user presses the TAB key to move out of the Enter number of guests text box, the onchange event handler triggers and calls the function to calculate the extended price.

Table 3-18 provides the code for the picPrice() user-defined function.

Table 3-18

```
function picPrice(myForm) {
    var picnicQty =  myForm.PicQty.value
    var EstPrice = picnicQty * document.PicnicPrice.Price.value.substring(1,6)
    var EstPrice = new String(EstPrice)
    document.PicnicQuantity.PicExtPrice.value = dollarFormat(EstPrice)
}
```

Line 150 multiplies the picnicQty, which represents the number of guests, by the per-person price. The substring method extracts the numeric value from the per-person price. On line 151, the result is stored in EstPrice and converted to a string object. This procedure allows the dollarFormat() function to accept the EstPrice value as a string. Line 152 calls the dollarFormat() function. The dollarFormat() function returns the extended price to the text box formatted as currency. To enter the picPrice() function perform the following steps.

To Enter the picPrice() Function

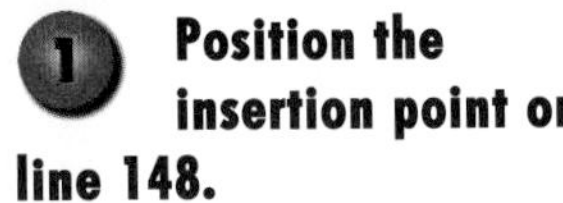

1 Position the insertion point on line 148.

2 Enter the JavaScript code shown in Table 3-18.

The picPrice() function displays (Figure 3-37).

mwcatering.htm - Notepad

File Edit Search Help

```
function setWeddingPrice(myForm) {
     document.WeddingPrice.Price.value = ""
     document.WeddingQuantity.WedExtPrice.value = ""
     document.WeddingQuantity.WedQty.value = ""
     var itemSelect = myForm.WeddingItem.selectedIndex;
     switch (itemSelect) {
          case 1 :
               document.WeddingPrice.Price.value = weddingPrices[itemSelect]
               break
          case 2 :
               document.WeddingPrice.Price.value = weddingPrices[itemSelect]
               break
          case 3 :
               document.WeddingPrice.Price.value = weddingPrices[itemSelect]
               break
          case 4 :
               document.WeddingPrice.Price.value = weddingPrices[itemSelect]
               break
     }
     document.WeddingQuantity.WedQty.focus()
}

function picPrice(myForm) {
     var picnicQty =  myForm.PicQty.value
     var EstPrice = picnicQty * document.PicnicPrice.Price.value.substring(1,6)
     var EstPrice = new String(EstPrice)
     document.PicnicQuantity.PicExtPrice.value = dollarFormat(EstPrice)
}

//-->
</SCRIPT>
</HEAD>

<BODY onload="setTimeout('bancycle()',3000)">
```

line 148

converts EstPrice to string object

Start | mwcatering.htm - Not... | Midwest Catering Service -... | 9:22 AM

FIGURE 3-37

The next step is to write the dinPrice() function shown in Table 3-19. This function uses the same logic and procedures as the picPrice() function.

Table 3-19

LINE	CODE
155	`function dinPrice(myForm) {`
156	`    var dinnerQty = myForm.DinQty.value`
157	`    var EstPrice = dinnerQty * document.DinnerPrice.Price.value.substring(1,6)`
158	`    var EstPrice = new String(EstPrice)`
159	`    document.DinnerQuantity.DinExtPrice.value = dollarFormat(EstPrice)`
160	`}`

To enter the dinPrice() function, perform the following steps.

To Enter the dinPrice() Function

1. **Position the insertion point on line 155.**

2. **Enter the JavaScript code shown in Table 3-19.**

The dinPrice() function displays (Figure 3-38).

mwcatering.htm - Notepad

File Edit Search Help

```
        switch (itemSelect) {
            case 1 :
               document.WeddingPrice.Price.value = weddingPrices[itemSelect]
               break
            case 2 :
               document.WeddingPrice.Price.value = weddingPrices[itemSelect]
               break
            case 3 :
               document.WeddingPrice.Price.value = weddingPrices[itemSelect]
               break
            case 4 :
               document.WeddingPrice.Price.value = weddingPrices[itemSelect]
               break
        }
        document.WeddingQuantity.WedQty.focus()
     }

     function picPrice(myForm) {
         var picnicQty =  myForm.PicQty.value
         var EstPrice = picnicQty * document.PicnicPrice.Price.value.substring(1,6)
         var EstPrice = new String(EstPrice)
         document.PicnicQuantity.PicExtPrice.value = dollarFormat(EstPrice)
     }

     function dinPrice(myForm) {
         var dinnerQty = myForm.DinQty.value
         var EstPrice = dinnerQty * document.DinnerPrice.Price.value.substring(1,6)
         var EstPrice = new String(EstPrice)
         document.DinnerQuantity.DinExtPrice.value = dollarFormat(EstPrice)
    }

//-->
</SCRIPT>
</HEAD>
```

line 155

Start | mwcatering.htm - Not... | Midwest Catering Service -... | 9:23 AM

FIGURE 3-38

The next step is to write the wedPrice() function. Table 3-20 shows the wedPrice() function, and it uses the same logic and procedures as the previous functions.

Table 3-20

LINE	CODE
162	`function wedPrice(myForm) {`
163	`    var weddingQty =  myForm.WedQty.value`
164	`    var EstPrice = weddingQty * document.WeddingPrice.Price.value.substring(1,6)`
165	`    var EstPrice = new String(EstPrice)`
166	`    document.WeddingQuantity.WedExtPrice.value = dollarFormat(EstPrice)`
167	`}`

To enter the wedPrice() function, perform the following steps.

To Enter the wedPrice() Function

1 Position the insertion point on line 162.

2 Enter the JavaScript code shown in Table 3-20.

The wedPrice() function displays (Figure 3-39).

mwcatering.htm - Notepad

File Edit Search Help

```
            case 4 :
                document.WeddingPrice.Price.value = weddingPrices[itemSelect]
                break
        }
        document.WeddingQuantity.WedQty.focus()
    }

    function picPrice(myForm) {
        var picnicQty =  myForm.PicQty.value
        var EstPrice = picnicQty * document.PicnicPrice.Price.value.substring(1,6)
        var EstPrice = new String(EstPrice)
        document.PicnicQuantity.PicExtPrice.value = dollarFormat(EstPrice)
    }

    function dinPrice(myForm) {
        var dinnerQty = myForm.DinQty.value
        var EstPrice = dinnerQty * document.DinnerPrice.Price.value.substring(1,6)
        var EstPrice = new String(EstPrice)
        document.DinnerQuantity.DinExtPrice.value = dollarFormat(EstPrice)
    }

    function wedPrice(myForm) {
        var weddingQty =  myForm.WedQty.value
        var EstPrice = weddingQty * document.WeddingPrice.Price.value.substring(1,6)
        var EstPrice = new String(EstPrice)
        document.WeddingQuantity.WedExtPrice.value = dollarFormat(EstPrice)
    }

//-->
</SCRIPT>
</HEAD>

<BODY onload="setTimeout('bancycle()',3000)">

<A NAME="MCS_TOP">
```

line 162

Start | mwcatering.htm - Not... | Midwest Catering Service -... | 9:24 AM

FIGURE 3-39

The wedPrice() function completes the three functions that display the extended cost. Each function makes a call to the dollarFormat() function.

The dollarFormat Function

Recall from Project 2 that the dollarFormat() function performs seven basic steps: (1) takes the string value passed to it and separates the dollars from the cents based on the position of the decimal point; (2) using the indexOf() method, determines the location of the decimal point; (3) establishes the value to the left of the decimal point as the dollar amount and the value to the right of the decimal point as the cents; (4) inserts commas in dollar amounts exceeding 999; (5) truncates cents to two decimal positions and not rounded; (6) reconstructs the string value with the commas and decimal values and inserts a dollar sign at the beginning; and (7) returns the completed formatted value. Table 3-21 on the next page provides the code for the dollarFormat() function.

Table 3-21

```
function dollarFormat(valuein) {
    var formatStr = ""
    var decipos = valuein.indexOf(".")
    if (decipos = = -1)
        decipos = valuein.length
    var dollars = valuein.substring(0,decipos)
    var Outdollars = ""
    var dollen = dollars.length
    if (dollen > 3) {
       while (dollen > 0) {
             tDollars = dollars.substring(dollen-3, dollen)
                    if (tDollars.length = = 3) {
                            Outdollars = ","+tDollars+Outdollars
                            dollen = dollen-3;
                    } else {
                            Outdollars = tDollars+Outdollars
                            dollen = 0
                    }
          }
           if (Outdollars.substring(0, 1) = = ",")
                   dollars = Outdollars.substring(1, Outdollars.length)
            else
                   dollars = Outdollars
    }
    var cents = valuein.substring(decipos+1, decipos+3)
    if (cents = = "")
        cents = "00"
    if (cents.length = = 1)
        cents = cents+"0"
    var formatStr = "$"+dollars+"."+cents
    return formatStr
}
```

To enter the dollarFormat() function, perform the following steps.

To Enter the dollarFormat() Function

1 Position the insertion point on line 169.

2 Enter the JavaScript code shown in Table 3-21.

The dollarFormat() function displays (Figure 3-40).

mwcatering.htm - Notepad

File Edit Search Help

```
function dollarFormat(valuein) {
    var formatStr = ""
    var decipos = valuein.indexOf(".")
    if (decipos == -1)
        decipos = valuein.length
    var dollars = valuein.substring(0,decipos)
    var Outdollars = ""
    var dollen = dollars.length
    if (dollen > 3) {
       while (dollen > 0) {
            tDollars = dollars.substring(dollen-3, dollen)
                   if (tDollars.length == 3) {
                           Outdollars = ","+tDollars+Outdollars
                           dollen = dollen-3;
                   } else {
                           Outdollars = tDollars+Outdollars
                           dollen=0
                   }
       }
           if (Outdollars.substring(0, 1) == ",")
                   dollars = Outdollars.substring(1, Outdollars.length)
            else
                   dollars = Outdollars
    }
    var cents = valuein.substring(decipos+1, decipos+3)
    if (cents == "")
        cents = "00"
    if (cents.length == 1)
        cents = cents+"0"
    var formatStr = "$"+dollars+"."+cents
    return formatStr
}

//-->
</SCRIPT>
```

Start | mwcatering.htm - Not... | Midwest Catering Service -... | 9:25 AM

FIGURE 3-40

The Web page now is complete. The next step is to save the Web page and test the JavaScript code in the browser. The data you must enter to test the Web page is provided in Table 3-22.

Table 3-22

CATEGORY	SELECTION	PRICE	GUESTS	EXTENDED PRICE
Dinner Parties	Rack of Lamb	16.95	15	254.25
Weddings	Traditional Sit Down	13.95	250	3,487.50
Dinner Parties	Pasta	12.95	10	129.50
Picnics	3 Meats 3 Sides 2 Beverages	11.95	30	358.50

Perform the steps on the next page to save and test the Web page.

TO SAVE AND TEST THE WEB PAGE

1. With the JavaScript Data Disk in drive A, click File on the menu bar and then Save.
2. Click the browser button on the taskbar and then click the Refresh button on the toolbar.
3. Enter the data shown in Table 3-22 on the previous page by clicking the link name under the category column. Select the meal type in the Selection column. Enter the number of guests in the Guests column. Click the Top of Page link to try the next category.

Figure 3-41 shows the test data results for the Picnics category. (Due to floating point math differences in some CPUs and browsers, your extended price may vary by one cent.)

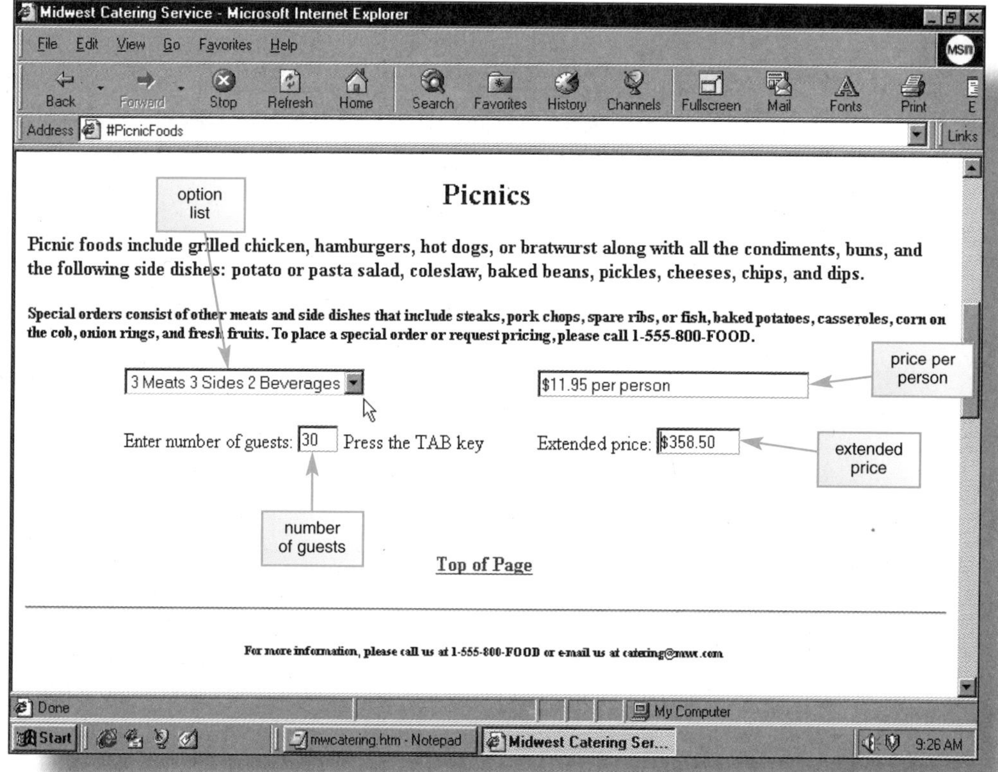

FIGURE 3-41

If the browser does not display the Web page correctly, close any error message dialog boxes, and click the Notepad button on the taskbar. Check the JavaScript code according to Figures 3-27 through 3-40 on pages J 3.31 through J 3.45. Correct any errors, save the file, activate the browser, and then click the Refresh button. The next step is to print the HTML file.

Printing the HTML Notepad File

After you have completed and tested the Web page, you may want to print it. Print the HTML file with Notepad. To print the mwcatering.htm Notepad file, perform the following step.

TO PRINT THE NOTEPAD FILE

 Make sure the Notepad window is active. Click File on the menu bar and then click Print.

A Notepad Print dialog box displays briefly with a message that indicates the file is being printed and informs you that to cancel printing, click the Cancel button. The dialog box closes after the file has been sent to the printer.

Project Summary

The Web page you created in this project is the home page for Midwest Catering. The Web page presents a rolling banner that acts as an additional advertisement. A greeting either displays a generic message, or indicates the number of days to one of four specific holidays: St. Patrick's Day, Independence Day, Halloween, and Christmas.

The main body has a link to each of the food service categories. When the user drags the mouse over a category link, the images on both sides of the category link change to reflect the type of entrée offered. Each food service category has a detailed explanation about the category. Each category has a form that allows users to obtain a cost estimate. To receive an estimate, the user selects a choice from a select drop-down list and enters the number of guests.

In creating this project, you learned how to create a rolling banner using the Array object. You learned more about the Date() object and the getTime() and getMonth() methods to construct a message that displays the number of days until a specific holiday. You learned the math ceil() method to round a number to the highest integer when calculating the number of days to a given date.

You learned how to use the onmouseover event handler to change images. You learned how to use the selectedIndex property to determine which item in an option list was selected. You used an array to store price data and associated that data with items in the option list. Finally, you learned how to pass form values to calculate and display an extended price formatted as currency.

What You Should Know

Having completed this project, you now should be able to perform the following tasks.

- Call the Functions Using the onchange Event Handler *(J 3.23, J 3.31)*
- Call the Functions that Calculate the Extended Prices Using the onchange Event Handler *(J 3.39)*
- Call the Functions Using the onmouseover Event Handler *(J 3.23)*
- Create the Location for the Image Object *(J 3.8)*
- Enter a Function to Create a Rolling Banner *(J 3.11)*
- Enter the Function to Assign the Prices for Picnics *(J 3.34)*
- Enter the Function to Assign the Prices for Dinner Parties *(J 3.36)*
- Enter the Function to Assign the Prices for Weddings *(J 3.37)*
- Enter the onload Event Handler to Call a Function *(J 3.12)*
- Enter the HolidayDays() User-Defined Function Steps for St. Patrick's Day *(J 3.17)*
- Enter the HolidayDays() User-Defined Function Steps for Independence Day *(J 3.18)*
- Enter the HolidayDays() User-Defined Function Steps for Halloween *(J 3.19)*
- Enter the HolidayDays() User-Defined Function Steps for Christmas *(J 3.20)*
- Enter a Function Call and Display a Message *(J 3.21)*
- Enter the onPicnic() Function *(J 3.26)*
- Enter the onDinnerParty() Function *(J 3.27)*
- Enter the onWedding() Function *(J 3.27)*
- Enter the picPrice() Function *(J 3.41)*
- Enter the dinPrice() Function *(J 3.42)*
- Enter the wedPrice() Function *(J 3.43)*
- Enter the dollarFormat() Function *(J 3.45)*
- Print the Notepad File *(J 3.47)*
- Save and Test the Web Page *(J 3.28, J 3.46)*
- Save the HTML File and Test the Web Page *(J 3.22)*
- Start Notepad and Open the HTML File *(J 3.7)*

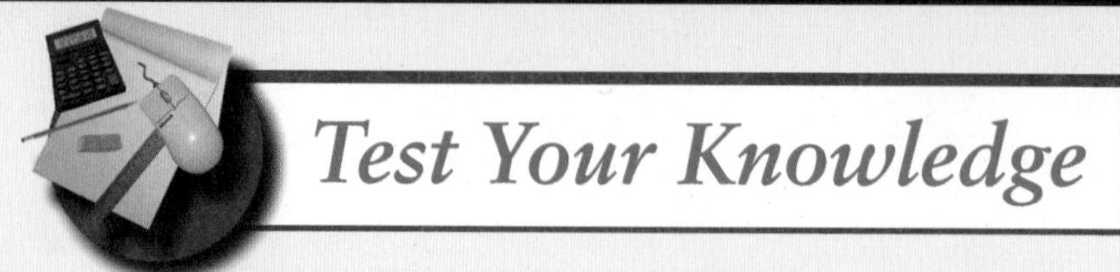

1 True/False

Instructions: Circle T if the statement is true or F if the statement is false.

T F 1. A rolling banner is a single graphic image created from several individual graphic image files.
T F 2. An array is a collection of data items represented by one variable name.
T F 3. A subscript is a number that designates an individual item or occurrence in an array.
T F 4. The getMonth() method returns the name of the month from the current system date.
T F 5. It is not possible to set a new date with the Date() object.
T F 6. The getTime() method returns the current time from the current system date.
T F 7. The Switch statement is another way of performing nested If...Else statements.
T F 8. The onmouseover event handler triggers the JavaScript code assigned to it when the user drags the mouse over the object associated with the event handler.
T F 9. The only disadvantage of the onmouseover event handler is that you must press the right mouse button for it to work.
T F 10. The selectedIndex is a string method that returns the actual data in a select list object.

2 Multiple Choice

Instructions: Circle the correct response.

1. To create an image object, you use the __________ attribute in the IMG SRC tag.
   a. Object
   b. Location
   c. Name
   d. Width
2. A(n) __________ is a collection of data items referenced by one variable name.
   a. subscript
   b. banner
   c. array
   d. object
3. The value that indicates which element in an array you are referencing is called a(n) __________.
   a. superscript
   b. subscript
   c. array
   d. object
4. The __________ object can return either the current system date or be used to set a different date.
   a. Time
   b. System
   c. Date
   d. Array

Test Your Knowledge

5. The getMonth() method returns the __________ the current month.
   a. name of
   b. number of days left in
   c. number of days in
   d. numerical equivalent of
6. The getTime() method returns the __________ since January 1, 1970.
   a. milliseconds
   b. microseconds
   c. number of days
   d. number of hours
7. In the JavaScript Switch statement, the Case statement is used to __________.
   a. execute the first statement outside of the Switch statement
   b. compare the value given to the expression stated in the Switch statement
   c. indicate the default statements to be executed
   d. terminate the Switch statement
8. Which of the following mouse event handlers triggers the JavaScript code when the user presses the mouse button?
   a. onmouseover
   b. onmouseup
   c. onmousemove
   d. onmousedown
9. Which of the following event handlers triggers the JavaScript code when the value in a text box or select list is altered?
   a. onload
   b. onfocus
   c. onclick
   d. onchange
10. Which JavaScript property of the form object is used to identify the item that is selected in a select list?
    a. value
    b. selectedIndex
    c. <Option>
    d. <Select>

3 Understanding JavaScript Code Statements

Instructions: Carefully read each of the following descriptions of writing code statements to accomplish specific tasks. Record your answers on a separate sheet of paper. Number your answers to correspond to the code descriptions.

1. Write a JavaScript statement that assigns the values “Freshman”, “Sophomore”, “Junior”, “Senior” to an Array object instance called ClassStanding.

(continued)

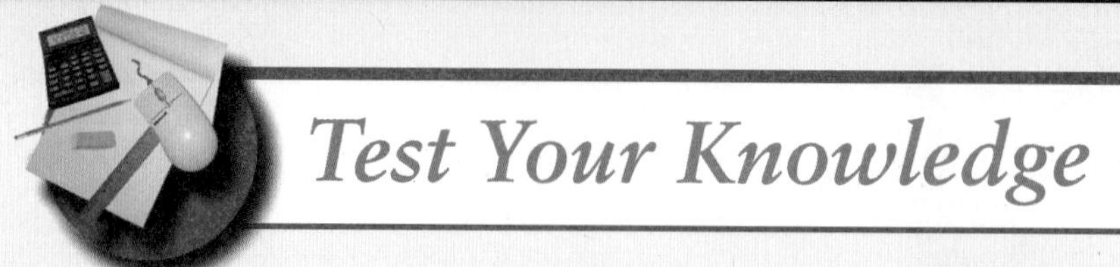

Understanding JavaScript Code Statements *(continued)*

2. Write a JavaScript statement that assigns the fifth element of an array called Course to an object named document.Schedule.Class.value.
3. Write a JavaScript statement that sets the date June 19, 2001 to an object instance named Anniversary.
4. Write a JavaScript statement that subtracts the current date from Anniversary and stores the result in AnnivReminder.
5. Using the variable AnnivReminder, write the JavaScript statements that test AnnivReminder for a result greater than zero. If the result is greater than zero, convert the milliseconds into the number of days.
6. Write a JavaScript statement that assigns the index value of an item selected from a list to a variable named itemNum. The form name is CategoryList and the select list name is Category.

4 Using onmouseover, onmouseout, onmousedown, and onmouseup to Simulate Animation

Instructions: Start your browser. Start Notepad. Maximize the Notepad window. Open the HTML file, mouse.htm, on the JavaScript Data Disk. The page has two images placed to the left and right of three lines of instructions (Figure 3-42). These images change through use of the mouse event handlers as explained in the instructions on the Web page. Enter the JavaScript code to change the images by performing the following tasks.

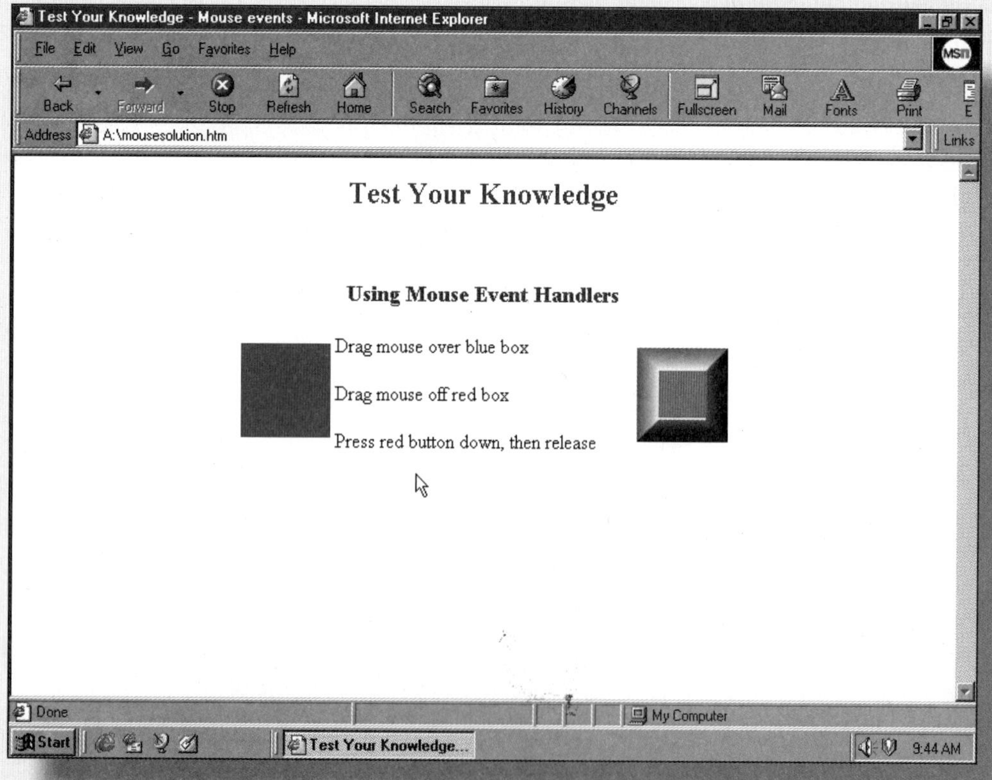

FIGURE 3-42

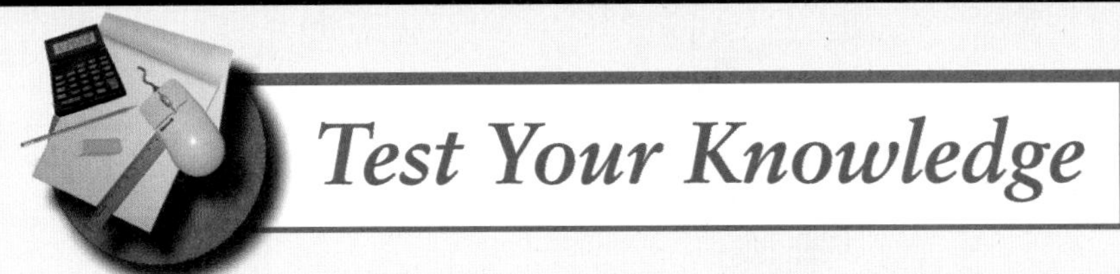

Test Your Knowledge

1. Enter the mouse event handlers to call the functions. Position the insertion point between the Name= "Location1" and Width="75" attributes in the IMAGE tag on line 21.
2. Type `onmouseover="chngColor1()" onmouseout="chngColor2()"` and do not press the ENTER key.
3. Move to the next IMAGE tag. Position the insertion point between the Name="Location2" and Width="75" attributes.
4. Type `onmousedown="pressDown()" onmouseup="Release()"` and do not press the ENTER key.
5. Position the insertion point in the SCRIPT section on the blank line (line 7). Enter the following code to create the functions called in steps 2 and 4.

```
function chngColor1() {
        document.Location1.src = "redbox.jpg"
}


function chngColor2() {
        document.Location1.src = "bluebox.jpg"
}


function pressDown() {
        document.Location2.src = "redbutton2.jpg"
}


function Release() {
        document.Location2.src = "redbutton1.jpg"
}
```

6. Save the file using the file name, mousesolution.htm, on the JavaScript Data Disk in drive A.
7. Start your browser. Open the file, a:\mousesolution.htm, in the browser. Follow the instructions on the Web page. If you have any errors, activate Notepad and check steps 2 through 7.
8. Save the Notepad file, activate your browser, and then click the Refresh button on the toolbar.
9. If no errors, print the Web page and return to Notepad to print the HTML file. Hand in the printouts to your instructor.

1 Exploring Online Documentation

Instructions: Start your browser and then type `www.scsite.com/js/p3.htm` in the Location text box. Click the link, Project 3 Use Help 1. Click Chapter 11, Predefined Core Objects and Functions. Complete the following tasks.

Read the Web page to find the answers to the following questions.

1. What are the predefined core objects?
2. What is an array?
3. What is the difference between defining an array in Navigator 2.0 and Navigator 3.0?
4. Describe the following Array object properties.
   a. concat
   b. pop
   c. push
   d. reverse
   e. sort
5. Describe how to refer to an array's elements and provide two examples. Scroll down to locate the Date object. Answer the following questions.
   a. Name the Date object properties.
   b. What is the limitation placed on prior dates?
   c. Describe the purpose of using parameters in the Date object and provide two examples.
   d. What are the general categories of the Date object's methods and what is their purpose?
6. Hand in the answers to your instructor.

2 Exploring Links to Other JavaScript Sites

Instructions: Start your browser and then type `www.scsite.com/js/p3.htm` in the Location text box. Click the link, Project 3 Use Help 2. Complete the following tasks.

1. Click Web Development. Read about Web development. Print the Web page.
2. Click the image link. Read about Image flipping or banners. Print the Web page.
3. Click the image rollovers link. Read the tutorial about image rollovers. Print the first page.
4. Click the date and time link. Read the about Time & Date. Print the first page.
5. Click the arrays and loops link. Read about arrays and loops. Print the first page.
6. Click the image changing link. Read how to accomplish image changing and cause a button to look repressed with onmousedown and up. Print the Web page.
7. Click the format link. Read how to add extra zeroes at the end of 2.2 to get 2.20 for an answer. Print the Web page.
8. Hand in the printouts to your instructor.

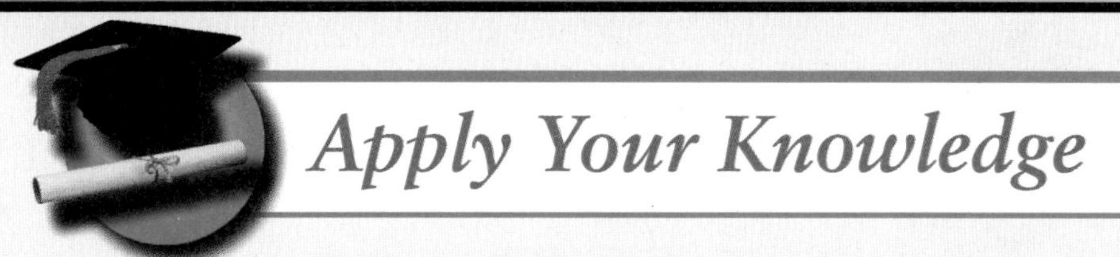

1 Using the onmouseover Event Handlers to Change Images

Instructions: Start Notepad. Open the Web page, travel.htm, on the JavaScript Data Disk. The High Flyers Travel agency Web page displays an image of a ship to the left of three vacation links, and a jet airliner to the right of the vacation links (Figure 3-43). Write three functions, called by onmouseover event handlers, that change the two images when the user moves the mouse pointer over each of the links. The names of the image objects are Image1 and Image2. To change the images, complete the following tasks.

FIGURE 3-43

1. Enter the onmouseover event handler to change the images for the Weekend Deals link.
   a. Locate the <A HREF="#Weekend"> link in the travel.htm file.
   b. Position the insertion point between the last " and >.
   c. Enter `onmouseover="Weekend()"` as the code.
2. Enter the onmouseover event handler to change the images for the Summer Vacations link.
   a. Locate the <A HREF="#Summer"> link in the travel.htm file.
   b. Position the insertion point between the last " and >.
   c. Enter `onmouseover="Summer()"` as the code.

(continued)

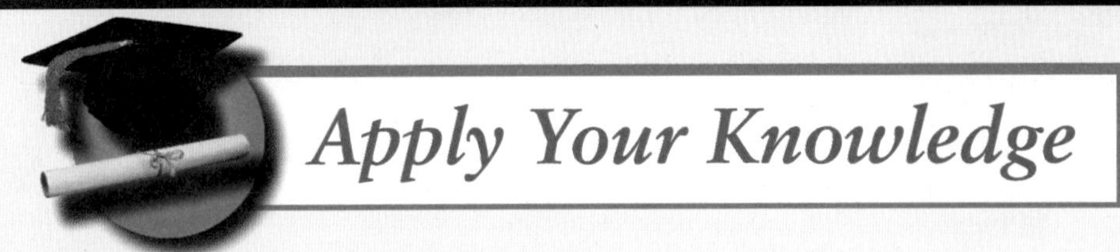

Using the onmouseover Event Handlers to Change Images *(continued)*

3. Enter the onmouseover event handler to change the images for the Winter Vacations link.
   a. Locate the <A HREF="#Winter"> link in the travel.htm file.
   b. Position the insertion point between the last " and >.
   c. Enter `onmouseover="Winter()"` as the code.
4. Move to the HEAD section to insert a SCRIPT section. (*Hint:* do not forget the SCRIPT tags.)
5. Position the insertion point on line 4 and then enter the following code for the Weekend() function:

```
function Weekend() {
        document.Image1.src = "Sanfran.jpg"
        document.Image2.src = "Vegas.jpg"
}
```

6. Using the function in step 5 as a model, write the Summer() function. Assign summer1.jpg to Image1.src, and summer2.jpg to Image2.src.
7. Using the function in step 5 as a model, write the Winter() function. Assign winter1.jpg to Image1.src and winter2.jpg to Image2.src.
8. Save the HTML file using the file name, travelsolution.htm, on the JavaScript Data Disk in drive A.
9. Start your browser. Open the file a:\travelsolution.htm to test the JavaScript code. Move the mouse pointer over the Weekend Deals link and stop. If no errors occur, move the mouse pointer over the Summer Vacations link and stop. If no errors occur, move the mouse pointer over the Winter Vacations link. If any errors occur, double-check steps 1 through 7 and then save and test again.
10. Print the Web page and the HTML file. Hand in the printouts to your instructor.

1 Using the Arrays Selection List Prices to Calculate a Total Price

Problem: As a Computer Science major, you are employed part-time at Campus Computers. While talking with the owner, Jermaine Wilson, you discuss your skills at developing Web pages. Jermaine would like a Web page that advertises his semester specials (Figure 3-44). He wants to display the basic computer specifications, then offer a few select upgrade options. Jermaine wants the user options to display in selection lists. The user clicks a Price button to display the total cost of the new computer.

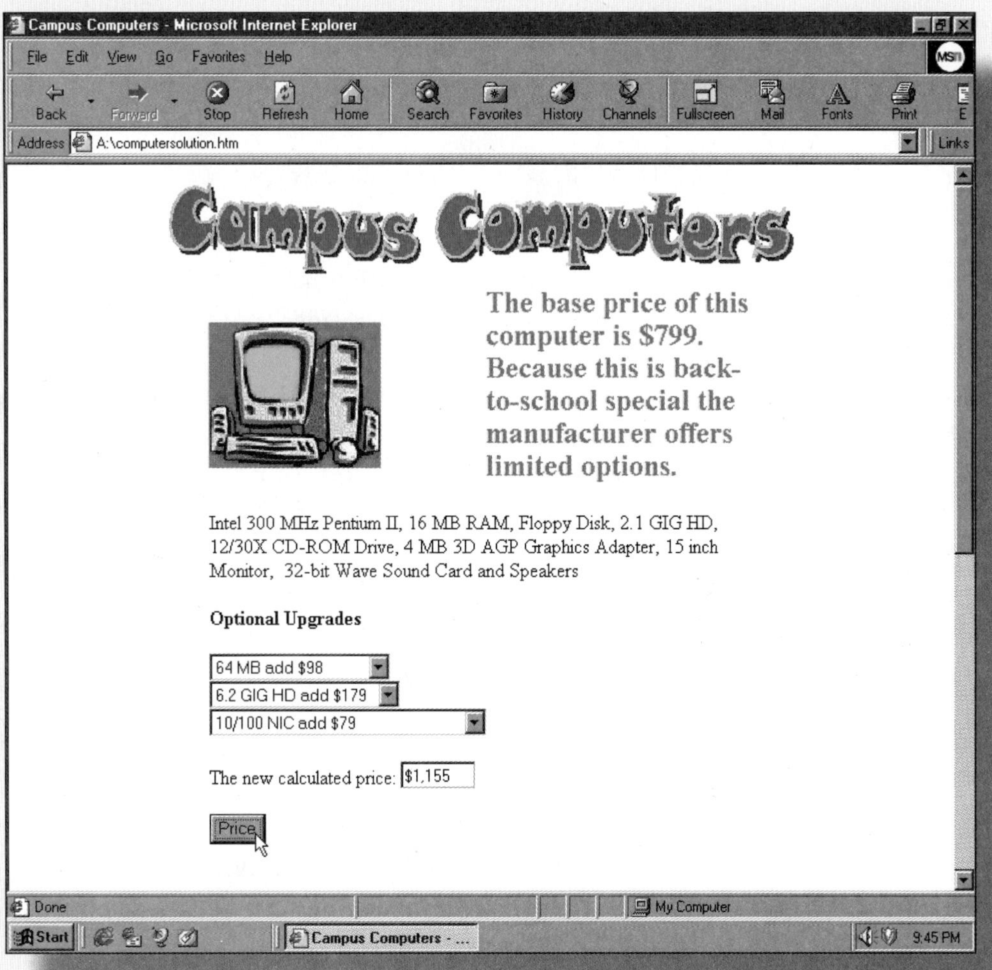

FIGURE 3-44

Instructions: Start your browser and Notepad. Using Notepad, open the computer.htm file on the JavaScript Data Disk. Perform the following tasks.

1. Enter the beginning SCRIPT section in the HEAD section by entering the following code on line 4:

```
<SCRIPT LANGUAGE="JAVASCRIPT">
<!-- Hide from old browsers
```

(continued)

Using the Arrays Selection List Prices to Calculate a Total Price *(continued)*

2. Create the arrays to store the prices for the RAM, hard disk, and communication device options. Position the insertion point on line 6 and enter the following lines of code:

```
    var Ram = new Array(0, 49, 98, 159)
    var Disk = new Array(0, 109, 179, 219, 299)
    var Comm = new Array(0, 109, 79, 279)
```

3. Write the function to determine the option prices, using the selectedIndex property for each drop-down list item by entering the following code on line 9:

```
  function Calc(myForm) {
    var ramItem = myForm.RAM.selectedIndex
    var diskItem = myForm.HardDrive.selectedIndex
    var commItem = myForm.CommCard.selectedIndex
    var totalPrice = 799+Ram[ramItem]+Disk[diskItem]+Comm[commItem]
    document.XOptions.PiecePrice.value = format(totalPrice)
  }
```

4. Be sure to complete the SCRIPT section and the ending SCRIPT tags.
5. To call the Calc() function when the user clicks the Price button, enter `onclick="Calc(Xoptions)"` in the INPUT tag where the Price button appears on line 87.
6. Save the HTML file using the file name, computersolution.htm, on the JavaScript Data Disk in drive A.
7. Activate the browser. Open the file, a:\computersolution.htm, to test the JavaScript code. If any errors occur, double-check steps 1 through 5 and test again. If no errors occur, print the Web page, and return to Notepad to print the HTML file. Hand in the printouts to your instructor.

2 Using Arrays to Create a Rolling Banner and Display Prices for a Selection List

Problem: You work part-time for your Aunt Jennifer at her floral and garden shop. She recently has signed up with an Internet service provider so she can advertise with a Web page. Because you recently completed a Web design course, she asks you to develop her Web site. She wants customers to see a selection list of different arrangements, and when the user selects an item from the list, the price displays. She also wants a simple rolling banner that continuously displays her floral shop offerings (Figure 3-45). This banner displays in the table cell under the store title.

FIGURE 3-45

Instructions: Start your browser and Notepad. Using Notepad, open the florist.htm file on the JavaScript Data Disk and perform the following tasks.

1. Place the onload event handler in the BODY tag before the > on line 6, which calls a function named roller() to start the rolling banner, by entering `onload="roller()"` as the code.
2. Position the insertion pointer on line 4 and enter the SCRIPT section in the HEAD section by entering:
```
<SCRIPT LANGUAGE="JAVASCRIPT">
<!-- Hide from old browsers
```
3. Create an array, called banner, to hold the banner file images, and initialize a variable for a subscript by entering the following code starting at line 6:
```
  var banner = new Array("florist1.jpg", "florist2.jpg", "florist3.jpg")
  var banctr = 0
```
4. Enter the function, called roller(), to roll the three images by entering the following on line 8 indenting where appropriate:
```
function roller() {
     if (banctr == 3) {
         banctr=0
     }
     document.Bannerspot.src=banner[banctr]
     banctr = banctr + 1
     setTimeout("roller()",3000)
}
```

(continued)

Using Arrays to Create a Rolling Banner and Display Prices for a Selection List *(continued)*

5. Place an onchange event handler to call the floralPrice() function in the SELECT tag on line 35 by entering `onchange="floralPrice(FloralMenu)"` between the double quote and the >.
6. On line 44, create an array, called floral, by entering `var floral = new Array ("Select a floral piece","Please call for special prices","18.95 a dozen", "7.95 a dozen", "25.95 a set")` as the code.
7. Complete the floralPrice function by entering the following JavaScript code:

```
function floralPrice(myform) {
        var itemSelect = myForm.FloralList.selectedIndex
        myForm.PiecePrice.value = floral[itemSelect]
}
```

8. Be sure to complete the SCRIPT section with a closing SCRIPT tag.
9. Save the HTML file using the file name, floristsolution.htm, on the JavaScript Data Disk in drive A.
10. Activate your browser. Open the floristsolution.htm file to test the JavaScript code. If any errors occur, double-check steps 1 through 8 and then save and test again. If no errors occur, print the Web page, return to Notepad, and then print the HTML file. Hand in the printouts to your instructor.

3 Creating Rolling Banners, Selection Lists, and Displaying Messages

Problem: While interviewing for a summer job with the owner of Three Rivers' Fencing, Yolanda Riveria, the discussion turns to your skills in Web page design. Being summer, Yolanda wants a Web site that focuses on deck prices. You suggest a selection list that displays the different deck offerings (Figure 3-46). The user selects an item from the list and then clicks a button to see a price. Yolanda wants a seasonal message that displays, mentioning different specials. Finally, because the company does more than fencing, she wants a rolling banner to remind people that Three Rivers' Fencing offers many services.

Instructions: Start your browser and Notepad. Using Notepad, open the fence.htm file on your JavaScript Data Disk and perform the following tasks. The Fence.htm file contains the HTML code for the drop-down list.

1. In the HEAD section, enter the SCRIPT tags for the functions.
2. Write the code for the rolling banner function. Name the function rollbanner(). The image files are "fence1.jpg", "fence2.jpg", and "fence3.jpg." The image object name is Banner.
3. Call this function with an onload event handler in the BODY tag.
4. Write the code for the drop-down list of deck prices function. Name the function displayPrice(). The prices are "$1,250.00", "$1,400.00", "$2,500.00", and "$1,395.00." Be sure to include a null price for the zero item in the list. The select list object name is DeckList.
5. Call this function with an onclick event handler when the user clicks the Price button in the DeckMenu form.
6. Write the code for the message display function. Name the function message().

FIGURE 3-46

7. Set the message using a Switch statement. The case condition tests the current month.
8. If the month is April or May, the message reads, See us for fence repairs from winter damage!
9. If the month is September or October, the message reads, Call us about fall landscaping specials!
10. If none of the conditions matches, display a generic message which reads, We have your seasonal supplies.
11. Call this function by placing the JavaScript code in the table cell below the select form. A SCRIPT section has been started, and a JavaScript comment says, // Place message function call here.
12. Save the HTML file using the file name, fencesolution.htm, on the JavaScript Data Disk in drive A.
13. Activate the browser. Open the fencesolution.htm file to test the JavaScript code. If any errors occur double-check steps 1 through 11 and then save and test again. If no errors occur, print the Web page, and return to Notepad to print the HTML file. Hand in the printouts to your instructor.

Cases and Places

The difficulty of these case studies varies:
◗ are the least difficult; ◗◗ are more difficult; and ◗◗◗ are the most difficult.

1 ◗ Your uncle has a used car lot. He has hired you to develop his new Web page. He wants to display pictures of the cars he has in stock, but he does not want customers to have to wait for thirty to fifty pictures to load. You tell him the easiest way to solve the problem is to use a drop-down list that shows the current models, and when the user selects a particular model, a picture displays along with the car's specifications. Use the concepts and techniques presented in this project to create the Web page.

2 ◗ A friend of your family is an antique dealer. She calls you for help on designing a Web page. As part of the basic layout, you suggest a title and logo that is a rolling banner. After discussing this basic layout, she tells you that every month she obtains about 10 to 12 items of high value. She wants to post the items on the Web page to get other dealer's attention. For these items, you suggest a drop-down list. You describe how the user could select an item from the list and in a section next to the list, a picture, description, and asking price for the item displays. Use the concepts and techniques presented in this project to create the Web page.

3 ◗◗ You are hired by a print shop to develop a Web page to advertise specials and promotions. Starting in late September, the owner wants to sell custom Christmas cards. She prints more than 20 varieties of Christmas cards. You realize it will take several minutes to download and display all the cards in a single Web page. You suggest using a simple description as a link, and when the user clicks the description, the card displays. To see the inside, you tell the user to drag the mouse over the picture, and the inside greeting displays. Use the concepts and techniques presented in this project to create the Web page.

4 ◗◗ As a parent of two children at the local elementary school, you volunteer to develop a Web page for the school. The principal wants the page to be a monthly calendar of events. Design a table of seven columns and five rows and place individual days in the table cells. To make the page more interesting, add a countdown to special events. For example, during the month of November, count down until Thanksgiving, where PTA members will provide dinner to less fortunate community members. In addition, on the days when no events are planned, you want random images to display in the table cells. Use the concepts and techniques presented in this project to create the Web page.

5 ◗◗◗ You volunteer to develop a Web site for your daughter's local Girl Scout troop. The troop raises money by organizing sporting events, and the Web page will promote the upcoming events. For example, to raise money, the troop organizes bowling, golfing, and fishing tournaments. Local businesses donate prize money or gifts for winners. While discussing the design of the Web page with troop leaders, everyone agrees that through links, each event will display on its own page, and that the page displays the number of days until that event. To show thanks for local business support, you suggest that the Web page display the logo of the businesses that support the event in a rolling banner. In addition, it is agreed that pictures of previous years' winners display in another rolling banner for each event. Use the concepts and techniques presented in this project to create the Web page.

JavaScript

Cookies, Arrays, and Frames

OBJECTIVES

You will have mastered the material in this project when you can:

- Create a cookie
- Use a cookie to store information from a Web page
- Set the expiration date on a cookie
- Read a cookie
- Explain the use of the escape() and unescape() functions
- Delete a cookie
- Determine the contents of a cookie
- Use the alert() method to debug JavaScript code
- Create an array of objects
- Populate an array of objects
- Describe the attributes of an object
- Use the **new** operator
- Explain the use of the **this** keyword
- Use a cookie to take action on a Web page
- Set a flag in a cookie
- Write information to a frame using JavaScript

One Sharp Cookie

Web Preferences Tracked and Saved

After eating your delicious Chinese dinner, you and your dining companion break open your fortune cookies and eagerly read what the future holds for you. "You will take a long trip to a small island." That sounds like a great spring break plan. "Patience is the path to prosperity." Guess you should stay in school and get that degree.

These fortune cookies peek into possible opportunities and expectations in your life. Likewise, cyber cookies peek into your Internet surfing habits and site selections.

WEB COOKIES WILL
SUIT YOUR TASTE

SPEED LIMIT 56K

In Project 4, you will create a Student Council Web site composed of three pages: a data entry page, a welcome page, and an intramural sports page. When students visit the first page, they enter their names and select the names of organizations that interest them. This data is stored in cookies, which are small text files that hold personal information about computer users. When they click the continue button, their names and hyperlinks to their organization choices display on a framed welcome page, which loads automatically when they subsequently visit the Student Council Web site. When they click one of the organization's hyperlinks, another page displays with the organization's information in one frame and the students' personalized preferences in another.

Likewise, custom pages display when you visit particular Web sites. Online newspapers, financial networks, airlines, and retailers use cookies to gather and store user names, passwords, page preferences, and previous buying habits. Their goal is to make site visits convenient and personalized. An estimated one-fourth of the most popular Internet sites use cookies.

Cookies are created using JavaScript code. The maximum size of cookie files is 4,000 bytes, although most are only a few characters. When Netscape was developing JavaScript, the programmers added the cookie instructions to reduce the transmission of data between users and the Web sites. A Web server sends a request to the user's computer to store particular information on the hard drive. In certain circumstances, this data is transmitted back to the Web site.

Some consumers object to this covert form of customer tracking. Web servers, however, cannot create cookies that will read an e-mail address, search a hard drive for personal information, or contain viruses. Personal data is captured only when users enter this specific information, such as credit card and Social Security numbers, home addresses, and telephone numbers, in HTML forms.

The name, cookie, possibly originates from the magic cookie program written several years ago. Unsuspecting computer users plagued with this program suddenly had the message, me want cookie, display on their screens. The only method of eliminating this persistent, annoying message was to type the word, cookie. If users refused to take this action, the magic cookie program damaged their work in progress.

Like fortune cookies, Internet cookies provide insight on your life and experiences. Perhaps the newest batch of cookies at the Chinese restaurant will contain the fortune, "Web cookies will suit your taste."

JavaScript

Cookies, Arrays, and Frames

PROJECT 4

CASE PERSPECTIVE

While attending a Student Council meeting, the secretary of the Student Council, Scott Walsh, approached you for help. He explained that recently, the number of student organizations with Web sites has increased rapidly. The Student Council believes that students feel overwhelmed by the number of places that they can gather information about the various clubs.

Scott wants a central Web site where students can obtain information about specific organizations, and a customized page for particular student needs. Student Council members want the ability to add new organizations easily. The page should include a header that remains static as the organization pages change.

Scott supplies you with six Web page addresses, appropriate artwork, and much of the HTML code necessary to get you started. His design includes three frames: a header frame, a link frame, and a display frame for the Web sites. Additionally, he supplies you with a default page to appear in the display frame when the user first enters the site. After reviewing his ideas, you decide to solve his problem using JavaScript.

Introduction

This project introduces you to three techniques that make Web pages more dynamic. You will learn how to store information about a user on his or her computer and how to retrieve that information at a later time. You also will learn how to make a Web page flexible and manageable for the Web page designer by extending the use of arrays. Finally, you will learn how to control the content of frames using JavaScript.

The ability to store information about the user and the user's actions allows for more exciting Web pages. Cookies allow you to accomplish this task. **Cookies** are small amounts of information that are stored on the user's computer by a Web page so the Web page can use that information in the future. Web page designers can take advantage of cookies in order to modify a page each time the user accesses the page. Cookies reside on the user's computer as long as desired by the Web page designer and are accessible by other Web pages if the Web page designer desires.

In Project 4, you will store the information in the Student Council Preferences Web page shown in Figure 4-1a into a cookie and then use that information to create the list in the left side frame in the Student Council Web page (Figure 4-1b).

Web page designers often use HTML frames to make Web pages more usable. JavaScript gives the Web page designer complete control of frames and the frames' contents. In Project 4, you will use JavaScript to control the content of the right frame shown in Figure 4-1b. Initially, the frame on the right of Figure 4-1b contains a welcome message to the student. As the student clicks links in the left frame, the right frame changes to the Web page of the organization selected. Figure 4-1c shows the page after clicking the Intramural Sports link. The student can change the list in the left frame of Figure 4-1b by clicking the Change Preferences hyperlink. This causes the Student Council Preferences Web page to again display.

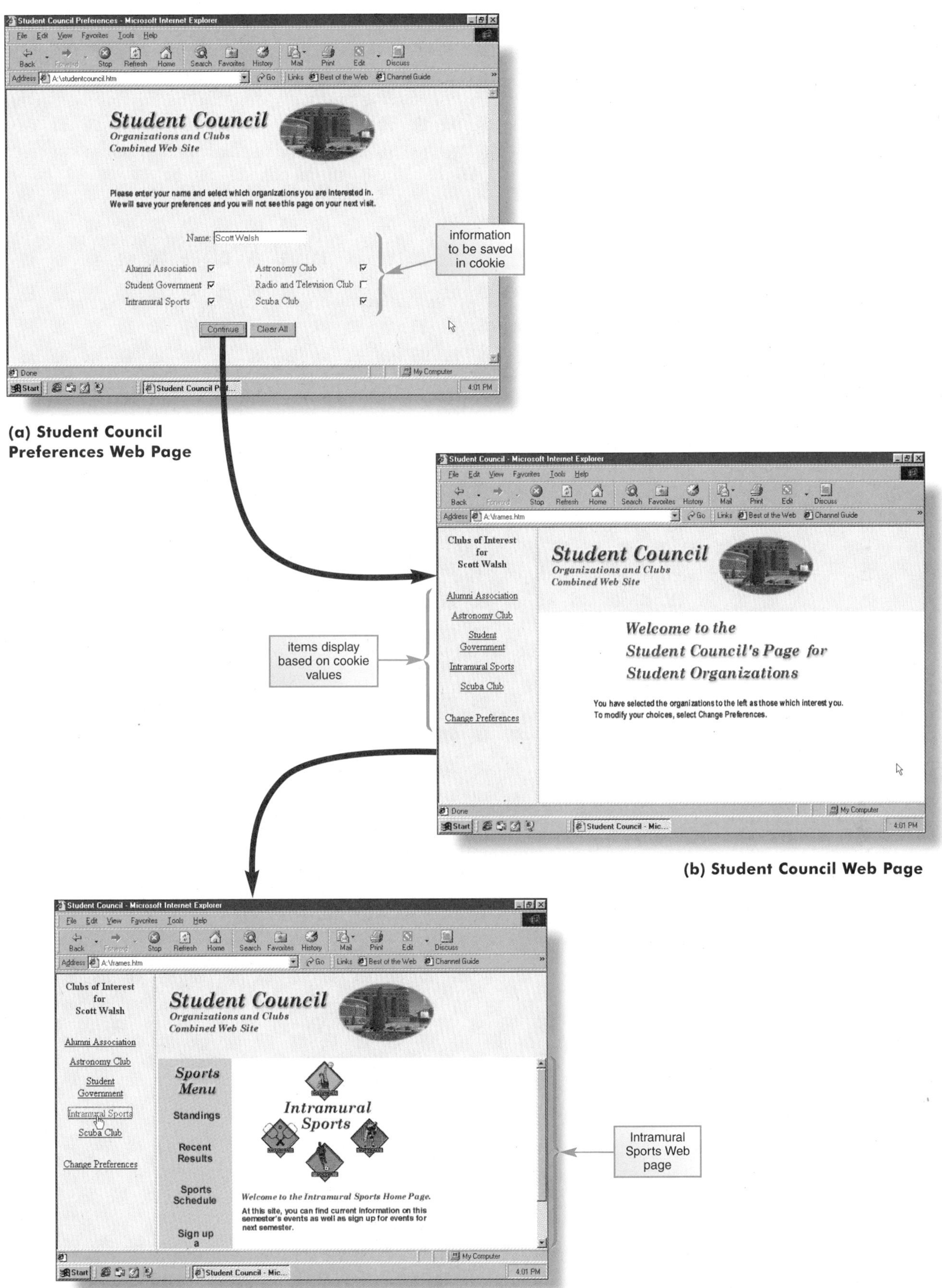

(a) Student Council Preferences Web Page

(b) Student Council Web Page

(c) Intramural Sports Web Page

FIGURE 4-1

Web page designers find that lists of items quickly become cumbersome to manage using traditional HTML. Arrays allow you easily to manage the items in a list. As you learned in Project 3, arrays are collections of similar types of data elements. Each item in a JavaScript array can have many attributes. One attribute describes whether the student has selected the organization for display in the list contained in the left frame. You will use an array to keep track of the list of organizations in the left frame shown in Figure 4-1b on the previous page.

Project Four — Student Council Web Site

After your meeting with Scott, you determine the following needs and data validation requirements.

Needs: The Student Council Preferences Web page shown in Figure 4-1a on the previous page allows the viewer to change the activities listed on the main Student Council Web page shown in the left frame in Figure 4-1b. The Web page viewer enters the student name. Check boxes allow the user to select the organizations that display on the Student Council Web page (Figure 4-1b). The Student Council Web page displays the student name and the organizations selected in the Student Council Preferences Web page (Figure 4-1a). The organizations display in the left frame of the Student Council Web page. When the user clicks an organization name, the browser loads the appropriate organization's Web page in the right frame of the Student Council Web page (Figure 4-1c on the previous page).

Data Validation Requirements: Scott indicated that when a student visits the Web site, the site should display the viewer's name in the left frame (Figure 4-1b). Because of this requirement, the Student Name field can not be empty on the Student Council Preferences Web page (Figure 4-1a).

Starting Notepad and Opening the Council.htm File

The first step is to start Notepad and open the HTML file, council.htm, on the JavaScript Data Disk as shown in the following steps.

TO START NOTEPAD AND OPEN THE COUNCIL.HTM FILE

1. Start Notepad.
2. When the Notepad window displays, click the Maximize button.
3. Open the file, council.htm, on the JavaScript Data Disk in drive A.

The council.htm document opens in the Notepad window (Figure 4-2).

file name

Notepad window

Maximize button

council.htm - Notepad

File Edit Search Help

```
<HTML>
<HEAD>
<TITLE>Student Council Preferences</TITLE>

</HEAD>
<BODY BGCOLOR="#FFFFCC" TEXT="#00384A">
  <CENTER>
    <img src="header1.gif" width="472" height="108">
    <p>
    <img src="please.gif" width="472" height="55"></p>
  </CENTER>

  <FORM NAME="StudentInformation">
  <CENTER>
    <TABLE BORDER=0>
        <TR>
            <TD>Name: </TD>
            <TD><INPUT TYPE="text" SIZE=20 NAME="StudentName"></TD>
        </TR>
    </TABLE>
    <BR>

    <TABLE BORDER=0 CELLPADDING=2>
        <TR>
            <TD>Alumni Association</TD>
            <TD><input type="checkbox" name="interest1"></TD>
            <TD WIDTH=50></TD>
            <TD>Astronomy Club</TD>
            <TD><input type="checkbox" name="interest2"></TD>
        </TR>
        <TR>
            <TD>Student Government</TD>
            <TD><input type="checkbox" name="interest3"></TD>
            <TD WIDTH=50></TD>
            <TD>Radio and Television Club</TD>
```

Start | council.htm - Notepad | 4:02 PM

FIGURE 4-2

Creating the Cookie

When the user enters his or her name and selects the activities of interest, a JavaScript function creates a special file called a **cookie** to store the information on the Web page viewer's computer. When the user visits the page again, another JavaScript function looks for the cookie and tells the browser what information to display based on the contents of the cookie. The browser handles the process of storing and finding the cookie; this process does not require any intervention by the user.

Web page designers find cookies useful because they can store information about the user's preferences or how often the user visits the page. A Web browser must have the capability of storing cookies in order for JavaScript to be able to create a cookie on the user's computer. Most modern Web browsers, including Internet Explorer and Netscape Navigator, allow cookies to be used. If you use multiple browsers on the same computer, however, and create a cookie using one browser, other browsers will not be able to read that cookie.

Because they reside on the user's computer, cookies can accumulate quickly if the user visits many Web sites that use cookies. To help reduce the number of cookies on a user's machine, every cookie includes an expiration date. When the **expiration date** on a cookie is reached, the browser automatically deletes that cookie from the user's computer. If no expiration date is specified when a browser creates a cookie, then the browser automatically deletes the cookie when the user leaves that Web page.

Cookies

Very old browsers do not support cookies. In addition, for security reasons, some users often turn off cookie functionality on their browsers. When designing a Web page, it is important to keep these facts in mind and be respectful of the users' situation. For more information about cookies, visit www.scsite.com/js/p4.htm and then click Cookies.

To create the cookie, perform the following two steps: (1) write the function that creates the cookie; and (2) add the JavaScript code that calls the function that creates the cookie.

Creating the addCookie() Function

To create the addCookie() function, perform the following two steps: (1) set a date variable for the cookie expiration date to a date that is one year from now; and (2) set the cookie value for the current document.

The browser stores the expiration dates for cookies as the number of milliseconds from January 1, 1970. A **millisecond** is one one-thousandth of a second. Recall from Project 3 that the getTime() method extracts the number of milliseconds from January 1, 1970 to the time when the method is called in a Web page. Therefore, to calculate the number of milliseconds for the expiration date, add the number of milliseconds in one year to the value returned by the getTime() method. Multiplying together the values in Table 4-1 results in the number of milliseconds in one year.

A browser stores cookies in a file or files located in a special directory on the user's computer. A separate file may exist on the user's computer for each cookie-storing Web page that he or she has visited. For security and privacy, by default the browser allows a Web page to have access only to the Web page's own cookies on the user's computer. The browser stores as many values as required by the Web page. The browser stores these values as name and value pairs. Table 4-2 gives some examples of name and value pairs.

More About

How Cookies Are Stored

Cookies are stored in special files by a browser. It is possible to find these files and read their contents on your computer. For more information about how cookies are stored, visit www.scsite.com/js/p4.htm and then click How Cookies Are Stored.

Table 4-1

VARIABLE	VALUE
Number of days in a year	365
Number of hours in a day	24
Number of minutes in an hour	60
Number of seconds in a minute	60
Number of milliseconds in a second	1000

Table 4-2

NAME	VALUE
StudentName	Steve Walsh
LastVisitDate	01/15/2000 01:15:00
NumberOfVisits	10
FirstVisitDate	12/15/1999 12:45:31
ZipCode	58382

The document object contains the cookie property for the Web page. A document contains only one cookie; however, many name and value pairs may be stored. To set the cookie of your document, you write the following JavaScript code:

```
document.cookie = "StudentName=Scott Walsh;"
```

Table 4-3 shows the JavaScript code for the addCookie() function. The function includes the JavaScript section in the HEAD section of the Web page.

The addCookie() function declared in line 6 requires two values as parameters: the name of the variable to save in the cookie (tag), and the value to store in that variable (value). The addCookie() function begins by initializing the variables expireDate and expireString. The setTime() method in line 9 sets the value of the expireDate variable with the current date and time. line 10 builds the string containing the expiration date by concatenating the variable name, expires, and the expiration date value. The method toGMTString() converts the expiration date to a date format that the browser understands when it later checks for the expiration date of the cookie.

Table 4-3

LINE	CODE

```
4   <SCRIPT LANGUAGE="JAVASCRIPT">
5   <!-- Hide from old browsers
6        function addCookie(tag, value) {
7           var expireDate = new Date()
8           var expireString = ""
9           expireDate.setTime(expireDate.getTime() + (1000 * 60 * 60 * 24 * 365))
10          expireString = "expires=" + expireDate.toGMTString()
11          document.cookie = tag + "=" + escape(value) + ";" + expireString + ";"
12       }
13
14
15  //-->
16  </SCRIPT>
```

Before storing a value in a cookie, the escape() method must be used to convert the value into a string that can be understood by all computers. The **escape() method** converts the string by changing all punctuation, spaces, accented characters, and other non-ASCII characters to a special hexadecimal notation. When storing a cookie that may contain such characters, you must use this method. Line 11 uses the escape() function and concatenates the values stored in the cookie. The browser stores the cookie as soon as line 11 executes.

To add the addCookie() function to council.htm, perform the following steps.

More About

The escape() Function

The escape() function has many uses. It can be utilized to process keystrokes from the user or to encode special display characters for a Web page. For more information about the escape() function, visit www.scsite.com/js/p4.htm and then click escape().

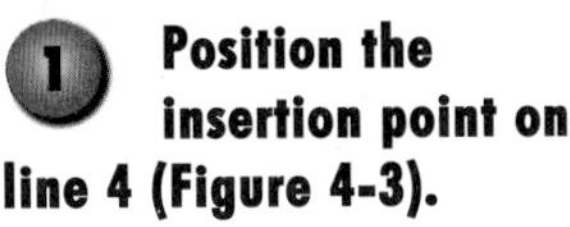

To Create the addCookie() Function

1 Position the insertion point on line 4 (Figure 4-3).

line 4

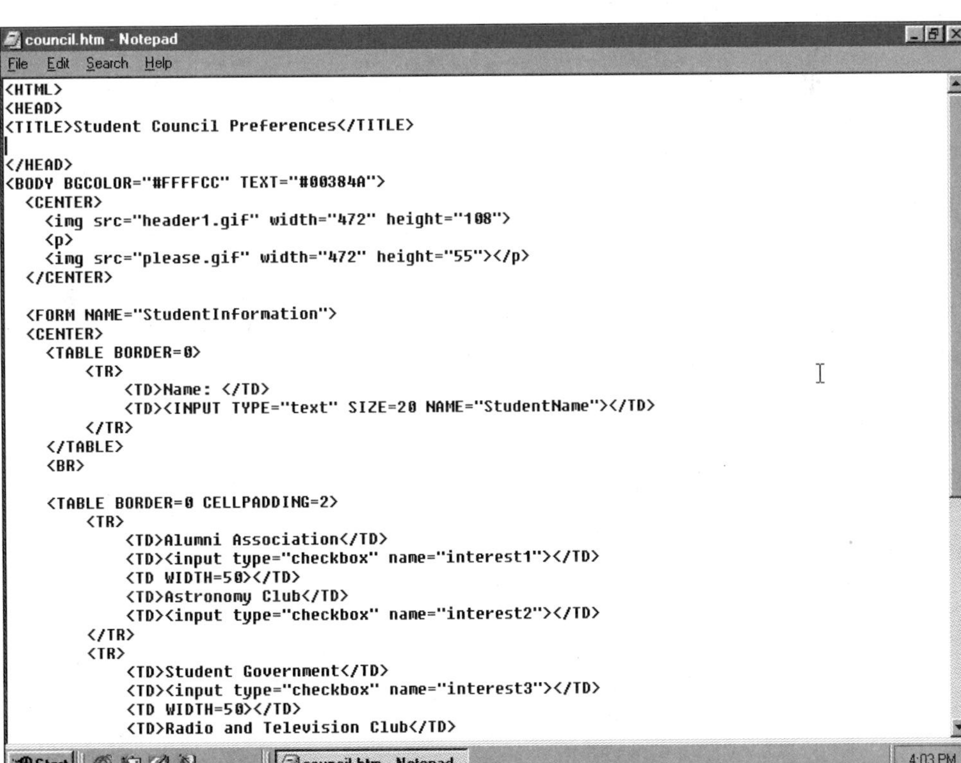
council.htm - Notepad
File Edit Search Help
<HTML>
<HEAD>
<TITLE>Student Council Preferences</TITLE>
</HEAD>
<BODY BGCOLOR="#FFFFCC" TEXT="#00384A">
<CENTER>
<img src="header1.gif" width="472" height="108">
<p>
<img src="please.gif" width="472" height="55"></p>
</CENTER>
<FORM NAME="StudentInformation">
<CENTER>
<TABLE BORDER=0>
<TR>
<TD>Name: </TD>
<TD><INPUT TYPE="text" SIZE=20 NAME="StudentName"></TD>
</TR>
</TABLE>

<TABLE BORDER=0 CELLPADDING=2>
<TR>
<TD>Alumni Association</TD>
<TD><input type="checkbox" name="interest1"></TD>
<TD WIDTH=50></TD>
<TD>Astronomy Club</TD>
<TD><input type="checkbox" name="interest2"></TD>
</TR>
<TR>
<TD>Student Government</TD>
<TD><input type="checkbox" name="interest3"></TD>
<TD WIDTH=50></TD>
<TD>Radio and Television Club</TD>
Start
council.htm - Notepad
4:03 PM

FIGURE 4-3

2 **Enter the JavaScript code shown in Table 4-3 on the previous page.**

The addCookie() function displays (Figure 4-4).

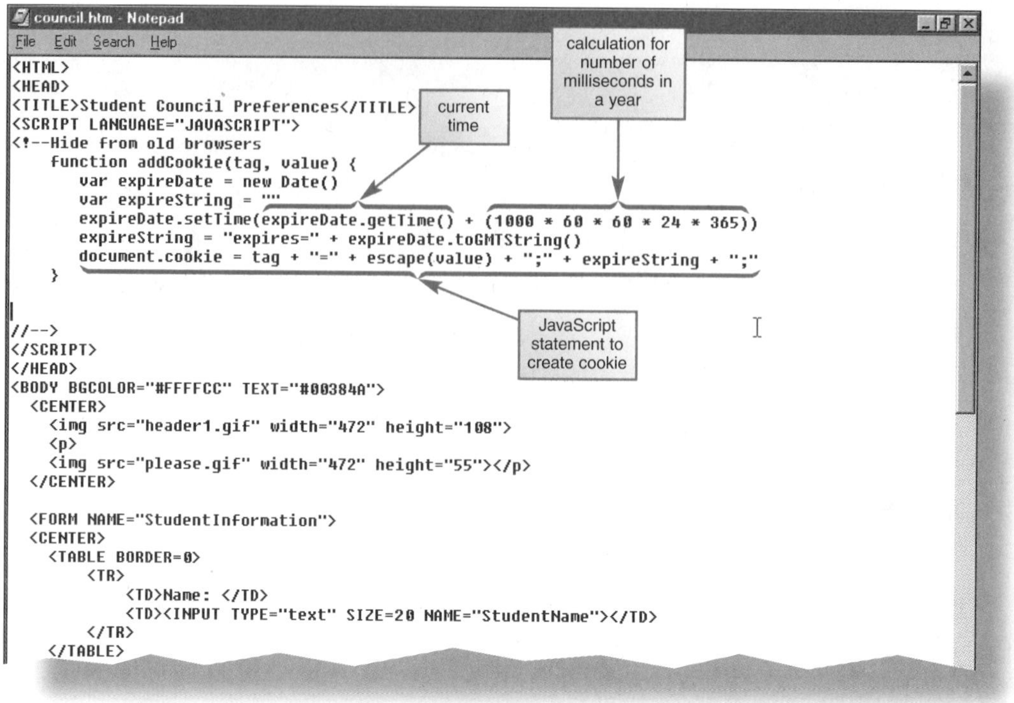

```
council.htm - Notepad
File  Edit  Search  Help
<HTML>
<HEAD>
<TITLE>Student Council Preferences</TITLE>
<SCRIPT LANGUAGE="JAVASCRIPT">
<!--Hide from old browsers
    function addCookie(tag, value) {
        var expireDate = new Date()
        var expireString = ""
        expireDate.setTime(expireDate.getTime() + (1000 * 60 * 60 * 24 * 365))
        expireString = "expires=" + expireDate.toGMTString()
        document.cookie = tag + "=" + escape(value) + ";" + expireString + ";"
    }

//-->
</SCRIPT>
</HEAD>
<BODY BGCOLOR="#FFFFCC" TEXT="#00384A">
  <CENTER>
    <img src="header1.gif" width="472" height="108">
    <p>
    <img src="please.gif" width="472" height="55"></p>
  </CENTER>

  <FORM NAME="StudentInformation">
  <CENTER>
    <TABLE BORDER=0>
        <TR>
            <TD>Name: </TD>
            <TD><INPUT TYPE="text" SIZE=20 NAME="StudentName"></TD>
        </TR>
    </TABLE>
```

calculation for number of milliseconds in a year

current time

JavaScript statement to create cookie

FIGURE 4-4

Other functions in council.htm may now call the addCookie() function by passing a tag, or variable name, and a value to assign to that tag.

Calling the addCookie() Function

The first variable to be stored in the cookie is the student name that the viewer enters on the first Web page. When the user clicks the Continue button on the page, the onSubmit event calls the updateValues() function. The **updateValues() function** makes certain that the user entered valid information and then calls the addCookie() function to save the information.

Table 4-4 shows the JavaScript code for the updateValues() function.

Table 4-4

LINE	CODE
14	`function updateValues() {`
15	`    if (document.StudentInformation.StudentName.value != null &&`
16	`        document.StudentInformation.StudentName.value != "")`
17	`        addCookie("StudentName", document.StudentInformation.StudentName.value)`
18	`}`

The updateValues() function first checks that the Student Name field contains a value. Lines 15 and 16 accomplish this by using an if statement to check the value in the field. It is good practice to always test for both blank and null values because variables are defaulted to the null value if you do not explicitly initialize them. Finally, line 17 calls the addCookie() function.

To enter the updateValues() function, perform the following steps.

To Create the updateValues() Function

1. **Position the insertion point on line 14.**

2. **Enter the JavaScript code shown in Table 4-4 and then press the ENTER key twice.**

The updateValues() function displays (Figure 4-5).

```
<HTML>
<HEAD>
<TITLE>Student Council Preferences</TITLE>
<SCRIPT LANGUAGE="JAVASCRIPT">
<!--Hide from old browsers
    function addCookie(tag, value) {
       var expireDate = new Date()
       var expireString = ""
       expireDate.setTime(expireDate.getTime() + (1000 * 60 * 60 * 24 * 365))
       expireString = "expires=" + expireDate.toGMTString()
       document.cookie = tag + "=" + escape(value) + ";" + expireString + ";"
    }

    function updateValues() {
       if (document.StudentInformation.StudentName.value != null &&
           document.StudentInformation.StudentName.value != "")
          addCookie("StudentName", document.StudentInformation.StudentName.value)
    }

//-->
</SCRIPT>
</HEAD>
<BODY BGCOLOR="#FFFFCC" TEXT="#00384A">
  <CENTER>
    <img src="header1.gif" width="472" height="108">
    <p>
    <img src="please.gif" width="472" height="55"></p>
  </CENTER>

  <FORM NAME="StudentInformation">
  <CENTER>
    <TABLE BORDER=0>
        <TR>
            <TD>Name: </TD>
```


FIGURE 4-5

Lines 15 and 16 of the updateValues() function validate that the user entered data in the Student Name field on the Web page. The addCookie() function is called in line 17 with the cookie name of StudentName and value of the Student Name field. The addCookie() function accepts the two parameters, stores a cookie with the parameters and the calculated expiration date, and calculates the expiration date of the cookie.

To save the values of the check boxes, a For loop is used in the updateValues() function to read each of the six possible values. The loop calls the addCookie() function once for each organization. Table 4-5 shows the JavaScript code that completes the updateValues() function.

Table 4-5

LINE	CODE
19	`var numElements = document.StudentInformation.elements.length`
20	
21	`for (var i=1; i<numElements - 2; i++) {`
22	`   if (document.StudentInformation.elements[i].value != null &&`
23	`       document.StudentInformation.elements[i].value != "")`
24	`      addCookie(document.StudentInformation.elements[i].name,`
25	`                document.StudentInformation.elements[i].checked)`
26	`}`

More About

The Elements Property

The Elements property is a very powerful object when executing forms processing on a Web page. It allows the JavaScript code to read a variable number of input items from a Web page and process them. For more information about the Elements property, visit www.scsite.com/js/p4.htm and then click Elements.

The updateValues() function first obtains the number of form elements in the StudentInformation HTML form. The **Elements property** of the form, referenced in line 19, refers to all of the HTML tags in the form that accept input or supply the data to the form. These elements include the Student Name field, the organizations' check boxes, and the Continue and Reset buttons. The **LENGTH attribute** of the elements property refers to the number of elements in the StudentInformation form. Therefore, line 19 assigns the number of elements in the StudentInformation form to the variable numElements. The For loop then begins at element number 1, or the first check box. The number of times the For loop executes is equal to the number of elements in the form minus two. The two that are subtracted, or not used, are the Continue button and Reset button form elements.

To enter the remainder of the updateValues() function, perform the following steps.

Steps To Enter the Remainder of the updateValues() Function

1. **Position the insertion point at the end of line 17 and press the ENTER key twice.**

2. **Enter the JavaScript code shown in Table 4-5 on the previous page.**

The remainder of the updateValues() function displays (Figure 4-6).

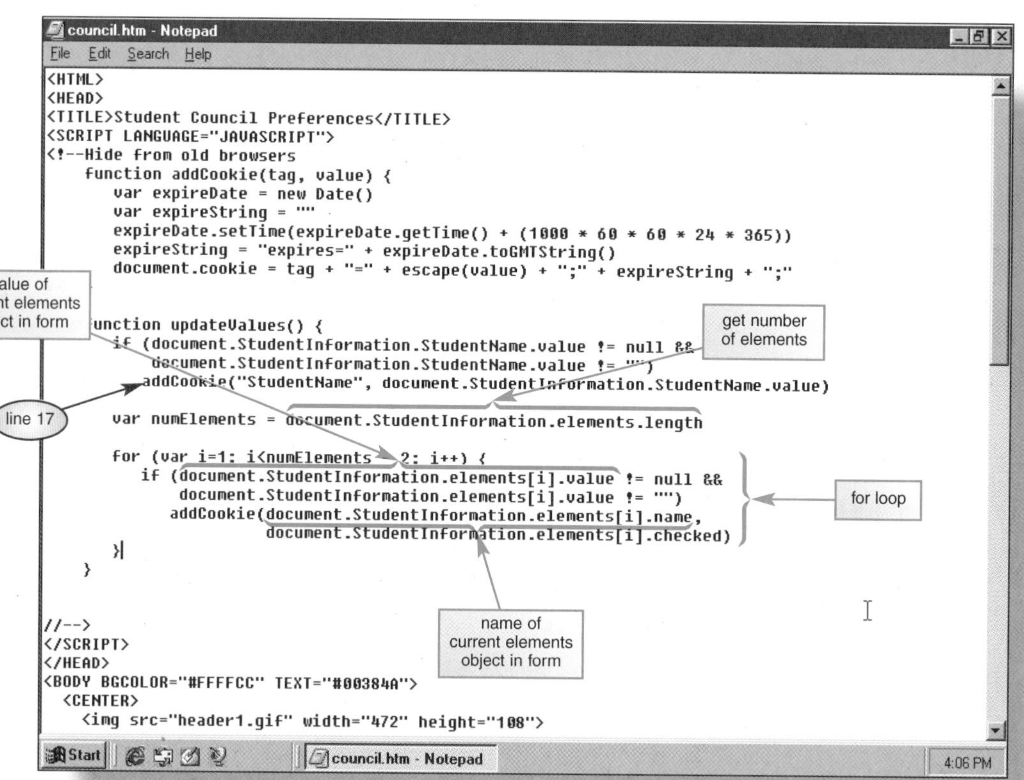


```
<HTML>
<HEAD>
<TITLE>Student Council Preferences</TITLE>
<SCRIPT LANGUAGE="JAVASCRIPT">
<!--Hide from old browsers
    function addCookie(tag, value) {
       var expireDate = new Date()
       var expireString = ""
       expireDate.setTime(expireDate.getTime() + (1000 * 60 * 60 * 24 * 365))
       expireString = "expires=" + expireDate.toGMTString()
       document.cookie = tag + "=" + escape(value) + ";" + expireString + ";"

    function updateValues() {
       if (document.StudentInformation.StudentName.value != null &&
          document.StudentInformation.StudentName.value != "")
          addCookie("StudentName", document.StudentInformation.StudentName.value)

       var numElements = document.StudentInformation.elements.length

       for (var i=1; i<numElements - 2; i++) {
          if (document.StudentInformation.elements[i].value != null &&
             document.StudentInformation.elements[i].value != "")
             addCookie(document.StudentInformation.elements[i].name,
                       document.StudentInformation.elements[i].checked)
       }
    }

//-->
</SCRIPT>
</HEAD>
<BODY BGCOLOR="#FFFFCC" TEXT="#00384A">
  <CENTER>
    <img src="header1.gif" width="472" height="108">
```

FIGURE 4-6

After the user enters a value in the Student Name field, he or she clicks the Continue button to proceed to the next Web page. The **Continue button** is defined as the submit button for the StudentInformation form on the Web page. A button that is defined as the submit button for a form causes the onSubmit() event for the form to execute when the viewer clicks that button. The next section of code adds the event handler to call the updateValues() function when the user clicks the Continue button. Perform these steps to call the updateValues() function.

To Call the updateValues() Function

1 **Position the insertion point on line 40 directly before the rightmost > bracket.**

2 **Press the SPACEBAR. Type** `onSubmit="return updateValues()"` **and do not press the ENTER key.**

The event handler associates the function updateValues() and the Continue button that is part of the StudentInformation form (Figure 4-7).

```
council.htm - Notepad
File  Edit  Search  Help
   function updateValues() {
      if (document.StudentInformation.StudentName.value != null &&
          document.StudentInformation.StudentName.value != "")
         addCookie("StudentName", document.StudentInformation.StudentName.value)

      var numElements = document.StudentInformation.elements.length

      for (var i=1; i<numElements - 2; i++) {
         if (document.StudentInformation.elements[i].value != null &&
             document.StudentInformation.elements[i].value != "")
            addCookie(document.StudentInformation.elements[i].name,
                      document.StudentInformation.elements[i].checked)
      }
   }


//-->
</SCRIPT>
</HEAD>
<BODY BGCOLOR="#FFFFCC" TEXT="#00384A">
  <CENTER>
    <img src="header1.gif" width="472" height="108">
    <p>
    <img src="please.gif" width="472" height="55"></p>
  </CENTER>

<FORM NAME="StudentInformation" onSubmit="return updateValues()">
  <CENTER>
    <TABLE BORDER=0>
        <TR>
            <TD>Name: </TD>
            <TD><INPUT TYPE="text" SIZE=20 NAME="StudentName"></TD>
        </TR>
    </TABLE>
    <BR>
Start    council.htm - Notepad    4:07 PM
```


FIGURE 4-7

When the viewer clicks the **Continue button**, the onSubmit() event executes and causes a cookie to be stored if he or she filled in the Student Name field. The next step is to read the cookie when the user visits the Web page and then to take an action based on the value of the cookie.

Reading the Cookie

Just as the addCookie() function saves any value that gets passed to it, the getCookie() function shown in Table 4-6 on the next page returns the value associated with any tag passed to it as a parameter. Programmers refer to functions such as addCookie() and getCookie() as **generic functions**, because they can be used over and over again in various applications with no modification.

Often, it becomes necessary to write JavaScript code that can test the accuracy of functions that you have written. You can test to ensure that a function you have written works in the way you intended it to work before writing more complex code that uses the function. The steps to read the cookie include (1) read the cookie that was created with the updateValues() function; and (2) test to make sure that the browser properly saved the cookie by displaying the value using the JavaScript alert() function.

More About

Generic Functions

If the users for whom you are writing are using current browsers, you can store generic functions in a single file on the server. You can place the generic functions in a file with a .js extension and then include it in the HTML source code. For example, if you stored several generic functions in a file called "myfunctions.js", you can include them in the HTML with the code <SCRIPT SRC="myfunctions.js"></SCRIPT>.

Creating the getCookie() Function

The **getCookie() function** accepts the tag name of the cookie that you want to read as a parameter. It then searches through all of the cookie's name and value pairs in the current Web page to find if that name exists in the cookie. If the name exists, the function returns the value of the cookie to the calling function. Table 4-6 shows the JavaScript code for the getCookie() function.

Table 4-6

LINE	CODE
29	`function getCookie(tag) {`
30	`    var value = null`
31	`    var myCookie = document.cookie + ";"`
32	`    var findTag = tag + "="`
33	`    var endPos`
34	
35	`    if (myCookie.length > 0) {`
36	`        var beginPos = myCookie.indexOf(findTag)`
37	`        if (beginPos != -1) {`
38	`            beginPos = beginPos + findTag.length`
39	`            endPos = myCookie.indexOf(";", beginPos)`
40	`            if (endPos == -1)`
41	`                endPos = myCookie.length`
42	`            value = unescape(myCookie.substring(beginPos, endPos))`
43	`        }`
44	`    }`
45	`    return value`
46	`}`

The getCookie() function reads the value of the Web page's cookie in line 31. After calling the document.cookie method, the variable myCookie contains all of the cookies names and values that have been saved in this Web page's cookie in the past. Semicolons (;) separate each name and value combination. Line 31 concatenates a semicolon to the end of the myCookie variable because the last cookie does not have a semicolon after it. Figure 4-8 gives an example of how the value of the myCookie variable appears after using the document.cookie method.

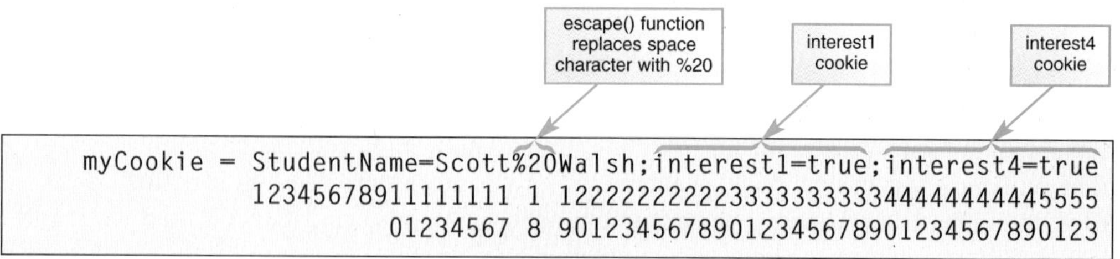

FIGURE 4-8

Line 32 concatenates the value of the tag being sought with an equal sign (=). The value of findTag will be searched for in the myCookie variable. The If statement in line 35 checks whether the cookie contains data. If the cookie contains data, then line 36 uses the indexOf() method that you used in Project 2 to find the variable name that the calling function requested. The value of beginPos is set to the starting position of the variable being sought. Line 37 checks that the variable being sought exists in the myCookie variable. If it does exist, then the beginPos variable gets set to the first character of the value part of the cookie being sought. For example, if the tag StudentName is being searched for in the cookie in Figure 4-8, then the beginPos now is set to 13.

Now that the starting position of the value being sought is known, the ending position must be identified. The function accomplishes this by searching for the next semicolon after the beginPos position in the cookie. The next semicolon will indicate the end of the value because semicolons delimit all of the values. In line 39, an alternate form of the indexOf() method finds the position of the next semicolon. This form of the indexOf() method accepts a second parameter, which is the position to begin searching for the value in the first parameter. The If statement in line 40 checks to see if the ending position was found. If it was not found, then line 41 sets the value of endPos to the last position in the cookie. Finally, line 42 uses the substring() method to extract the value from the cookie. The **unescape() function** makes certain that any special characters, such as spaces, are set back to their normal, viewable values. For example, the escape value, %20, replaced the space in the name Scott Walsh in Figure 4-8. The unescape() function changes this back to a space character when the value is set in line 42.

To enter the getCookie() function, perform the following steps.

To Create the getCookie() Function

1 Position the insertion point on line 29.

2 Enter the JavaScript code shown in Table 4-6 and then press the ENTER key twice.

The getCookie() function displays (Figure 4-9).

council.htm - Notepad

File Edit Search Help

```
    for (var i=1; i<numElements - 2; i++) {
      if (document.StudentInformation.elements[i].value != null &&
         document.StudentInformation.elements[i].value != "")
        addCookie(document.StudentInformation.elements[i].name,
               document.StudentInformation.elements[i].checked)
    }
  }
function getCookie(tag) {
    var value = null
    var myCookie = document.cookie + ";"
    var findTag = tag + "="
    var endPos

    if (myCookie.length > 0) {
      var beginPos = myCookie.indexOf(findTag)
      if (beginPos != -1) {
        beginPos = beginPos + findTag.length
        endPos = myCookie.indexOf(";", beginPos)
        if (endPos == -1)
          endPos = myCookie.length
        value = unescape(myCookie.substring(beginPos, endPos))
      }
    }
    return value
  }

//-->
</SCRIPT>
</HEAD>
<BODY BGCOLOR="#FFFFCC" TEXT="#00384A">
  <CENTER>
    <img src="header1.gif" width="472" height="108">
    <p>
```

line 29

get Web page's cookie

check for data in cookie

find cookie being sought

unescape() function deciphers contents of cookie

return cookie value

Start | council.htm - Notepad | 4:09 PM

FIGURE 4-9

The next step is to call the getCookie() function and take some action based on the value of the StudentName cookie.

Calling the getCookie() Function

If the StudentName cookie already contains a value, then the studentcouncil.htm Web page should not display. It is not necessary to have viewers enter their name once the name is stored in a cookie. Therefore, the studentcouncil.htm Web page redirects the viewer to the framed Student Council Web page shown in Figure 4-1b on page J4.5 without ever showing the Web page shown in Figure 4-1a on page J 4.5. Table 4-7 shows the JavaScript code for calling the getCookie() function.

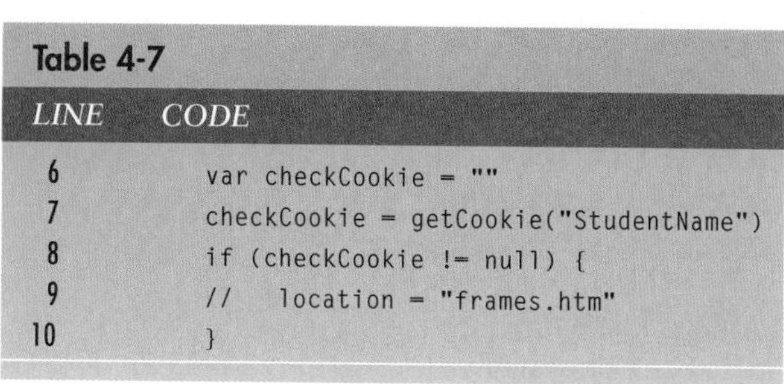

Table 4-7

LINE	CODE
6	`var checkCookie = ""`
7	`checkCookie = getCookie("StudentName")`
8	`if (checkCookie != null) {`
9	`//   location = "frames.htm"`
10	`}`

The getCookie() function call in line 7 sets the checkCookie variable declared in line 6. The call to the getCookie() function passes the name of the Student Name field on the HTML form to the function. Recall that the same name was passed to the addCookie() function in the updateValues() function. Line 8 checks if the cookie exists by testing the value of the cookie. If the value of the cookie is null, then the cookie does not exist. Otherwise, the Web page viewer has previously visited this site and set the StudentName cookie. In this case, Line 9 sets the location of the viewer's browser to the frames.htm Web page. The line is currently a comment, however, because it begins with two slashes (//) and, therefore, does not execute. This makes testing the Web page easier by not jumping to the frames.htm Web page at this time. After you are assured that the JavaScript code works as intended, then the line can be uncommented and activated.

To enter the call to the getCookie() function, perform the following steps.

Steps To Call the getCookie() Function

1. **Position the insertion point on line 6.**

2. **Enter the JavaScript code shown in Table 4-7 and then press the ENTER key twice.**

The code displays (Figure 4-10).

council.htm - Notepad

File Edit Search Help

```
<HTML>
<HEAD>
<TITLE>Student Council Preferences</TITLE>
<SCRIPT LANGUAGE="JAVASCRIPT">
<!--Hide from old browsers
   var checkCookie = ""
   checkCookie = getCookie("StudentName")
   if (checkCookie != null)   {
   //   location = "frames.htm"
   }

   function addCookie(tag, value) {
       var expireDate = new Date()
       var expireString = ""
       expireDate.setTime(expireDate.getTime() + (1000 * 60 * 60 * 24 * 365))
       expireString = "expires=" + expireDate.toGMTString()
       document.cookie = tag + "=" + escape(value) + ";" + expireString + ";"
   }
```

line 6

call getCookie() function

see if cookie exists

if cookie exists, load frames.htm page (line is a comment)

FIGURE 4-10

The Web page now can create and read a cookie. The next step is to give the viewer the ability to clear the value of the cookie by using the reset button.

Deleting a Cookie

The Web page in Figure 4-1a contains a **Clear All button** that deletes the contents of the Student Name field and clears all of the check boxes. When the viewer clicks the Clear All button, the value of the Student Name field must be deleted from the field on the screen and the StudentName cookie must be deleted as well. To delete a cookie, you set the cookie's expiration date to a date in the past. When the browser finds a cookie with an expiration date in the past, it deletes the cookie. Once the browser deletes a cookie, it no longer is accessible by the browser. Table 4-8 shows the JavaScript code for the deleteCookies() function.

Table 4-8

LINE	CODE
54	`function deleteCookies() {`
55	`    var Yesterday = 24 * 60 * 60 * 1000`
56	`    var expireDate = new Date()`
57	
58	`    expireDate.setTime (expireDate.getTime() - Yesterday)`
59	
60	`    document.cookie = "StudentName=nothing; expires=" + expireDate.toGMTString()`
61	`    document.StudentInformation.StudentName.value = ""`
62	`}`

The **deleteCookies() function** first determines how many milliseconds are in a day. Line 56 declares expireDate as a date. The calculation in line 58 subtracts one day's worth of milliseconds from the current date and time and assigns that value to the expireDate variable. Next, the value of the StudentName cookie is set to blank, and the expiration date of the cookie is set to the expireDate variable. It is necessary to set the expiration date on only one of the variables in order to expire all of the cookie values. Finally, the StudentName element of the StudentInformation form is set to blank in line 61.

To enter the deleteCookies() function, you first add and then call the function. Perform the following step to add the deleteCookies() function.

To Add the deleteCookies() Function

1 Position the insertion point on line 54.

2 Enter the JavaScript code shown in Table 4-8 and then press the ENTER key twice.

The code displays (Figure 4-11).

```
      var beginPos = myCookie.indexOf(findTag)
      if (beginPos != -1) {
         beginPos = beginPos + findTag.length
         endPos = myCookie.indexOf(";", beginPos)
         if (endPos == -1)
            endPos = myCookie.length
         value = unescape(myCookie.substring(beginPos, endPos))
      }
   }
   return value
}
function deleteCookies() {
   var Yesterday = 24 * 60 * 60 * 1000
   var expireDate = new Date()

   expireDate.setTime (expireDate.getTime() - Yesterday)

   document.cookie = "StudentName=nothing; expires=" + expireDate.toGMTString()
   document.StudentInformation.StudentName.value = ""
}

//-->
</SCRIPT>
</HEAD>
<BODY BGCOLOR="#FFFFCC" TEXT="#00384A" onLoad="InitializeValues()">
  <CENTER>
```


FIGURE 4-11

Then, perform the following steps to call the deleteCookies() function.

To Call the deleteCookies() Function

1 **Position the insertion point on line 75 directly before the rightmost > bracket.**

Press the SPACEBAR. Type `onReset="return deleteCookies()"` **and do not press the ENTER key.**

The event handler associates the function deleteCookies() and the Clear All button that is part of the StudentInformation form (Figure 4-12).

council.htm - Notepad

File Edit Search Help

```
    function deleteCookies() {
        var Yesterday = 24 * 60 * 60 * 1000
        var expireDate = new Date()

        expireDate.setTime (expireDate.getTime() - Yesterday)

        document.cookie = "StudentName=nothing; expires=" + expireDate.toGMTString()
        document.StudentInformation.StudentName.value = ""
    }


//-->
</SCRIPT>
</HEAD>
<BODY BGCOLOR="#FFFFCC" TEXT="#00384A">
  <CENTER>
    <img src="header1.gif" width="472" height="108">
    <p>
    <img src="please.gif" width="472" height="55"></p>
  </CENTER>
  <FORM NAME="StudentInformation" onSubmit="return updateValues()" onReset="return
deleteCookies()">
  <CENTER>
    <TABLE BORDER=0>
        <TR>
            <TD>Name: </TD>
            <TD><INPUT TYPE="text" SIZE=20 NAME="StudentName"></TD>
        </TR>
    </TABLE>
    <BR>

    <TABLE BORDER=0 CELLPADDING=2>
        <TR>
            <TD>Alumni Association</TD>
```

line 75

call deleteCookies() function

Start | council.htm - Notepad | 4:12 PM

FIGURE 4-12

When the user clicks the Clear All button, the onReset() event executes and causes the deleteCookies() function to be called. The deleteCookies() function clears the Student Name field and sets the expiration date of the Web page's cookie to yesterday's date. Because this causes the expiration date to be reached, the browser deletes the cookie.

Determining the Contents of a Cookie

To verify that the JavaScript code can create and read the cookie, it is helpful to add some code to test this functionality. As you learned in Project 2, the JavaScript alert() method causes a dialog box to be displayed during the execution of JavaScript code. Table 4-9 shows the general form of the alert() method.

Table 4-9 alert() Method	
General form:	alert(message)
Comment:	where message is the text to be displayed in the pop-up window
Example:	`alert("Thank you for visiting my Web site.") alert("The value of x is " + x + ".")`

You display the values of variables being used by JavaScript by placing an alert() method in the JavaScript code where you want to see the value. Perform the following steps to add an alert() method that displays the value of the StudentName cookie when the browser loads the Web page.

To Display the Value of the Cookie

1. **Position the insertion point on line 8.**

2. **Type** `alert("The Value of checkCookie is " + checkCookie)` **and then press the ENTER key. Press the SPACEBAR five times.**

The alert() method used to test the Web page displays (Figure 4-13).

```
<HTML>
<HEAD>
<TITLE>Student Council Preferences</TITLE>
<SCRIPT LANGUAGE="JAVASCRIPT">
<!--Hide from old browsers
    var checkCookie = ""
    checkCookie = getCookie("StudentName")
    alert("The value of checkCookie is " + checkCookie)
    if (checkCookie != null)   {
    //   location = "frames.htm"
    }

    function addCookie(tag, value) {
       var expireDate = new Date()
       var expireString = ""
       expireDate.setTime(expireDate.getTime() + (1000 * 60 * 60 * 24 * 365))
       expireString = "expires=" + expireDate.toGMTString()
       document.cookie = tag + "=" + escape(value) + ";" + expireString + ";"
    }

    function updateValues() {
       if (document.StudentInformation.StudentName.value != null &&
           document.StudentInformation.StudentName.value != "")
          addCookie("StudentName", document.StudentInformation.StudentName.value)

       var numElements = document.StudentInformation.elements.length

       for (var i=1; i<numElements - 2; i++) {
          if (document.StudentInformation.elements[i].value != null &&
              document.StudentInformation.elements[i].value != "")
             addCookie(document.StudentInformation.elements[i].name,
                       document.StudentInformation.elements[i].checked)
       }
    }
```


FIGURE 4-13

The JavaScript code beginning on line 6 executes when the Web page loads. The getCookie() function sets the value of the checkCookie variable. The alert() method then displays a message box that shows the value of the checkCookie variable. In the final Web page, the alert() method will be deleted. The alert() method, however, allows you to verify that the JavaScript code functions as intended.

The next steps are to save your file and test the Web page.

More About

Debugging JavaScript Code

Certain options built into modern browsers can help you debug code. In Internet Explorer versions 4 and 5, you can force the browser to tell you which line of code and which character in the line is causing a problem. For more information about debugging JavaScript code, visit www.scsite.com/js/p4.htm and then click Debugging.

Saving and Testing the Web Page

The JavaScript code that you created writes and reads a cookie. The alert() function informs you of the value of the cookie for your Web page. After successfully testing your JavaScript code, the alert() method should be removed.

Saving and Testing the Web Page in the Browser

Perform the steps on the next page to save and test your Web page.

To Save and Test the Web Page

1 With the JavaScript Data Disk in drive A, click File on the menu bar and then click Save As.

2 Type `a:\studentcouncil.htm` **in the File name text box and then click the Save button in the Save As dialog box.**

3 Start your browser and open studentcouncil.htm.

The Microsoft Internet Explorer dialog box displays containing the alert message indicating that the cookie is empty (Figure 4-14).

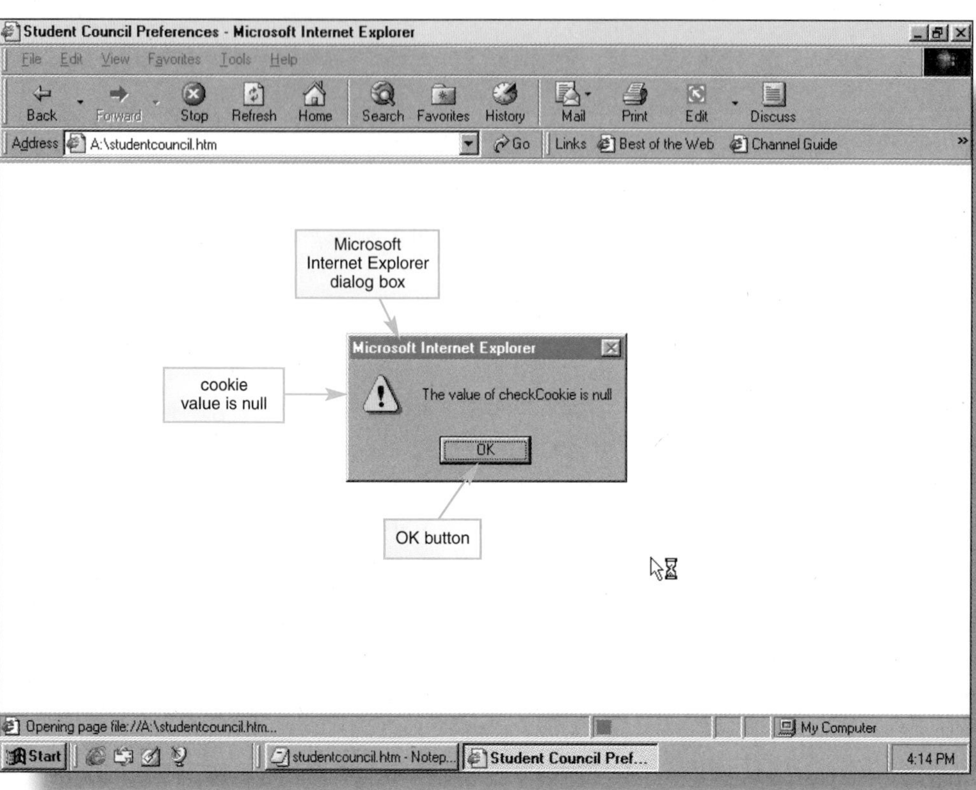

FIGURE 4-14

4 Click the OK button to remove the alert() message and then type `Scott Walsh` **(or your own name) in the Student Name field. Click the check boxes for the following organizations: Alumni Association, Astronomy Club, Student Government, Intramural Sports, and Scuba Club. Click the Continue button.**

The Web browser displays the alert message that indicates that the cookie contains the name Scott Walsh or your own name (Figure 4-15).

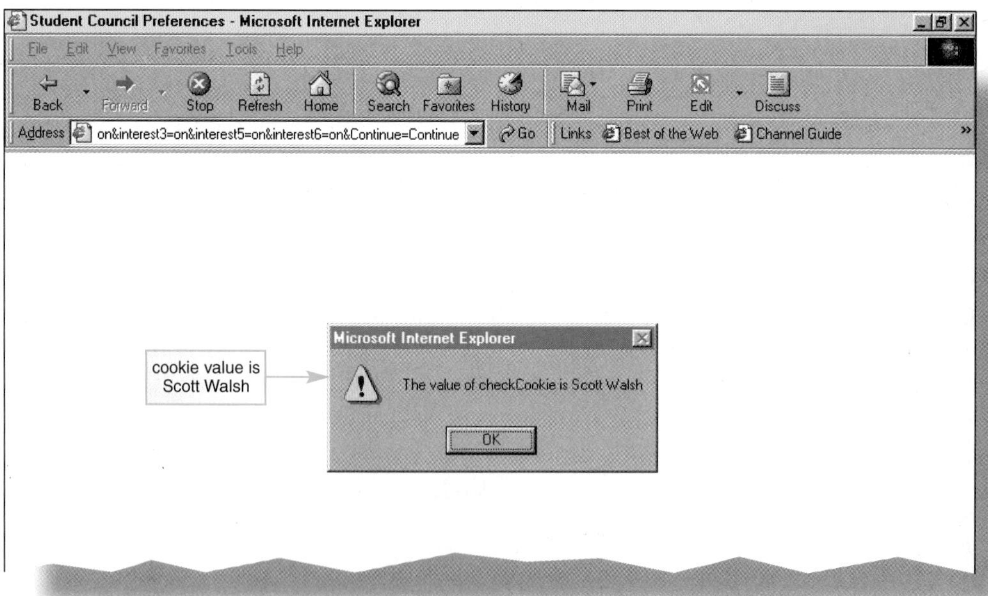

FIGURE 4-15

5 Open the studentcouncil.htm Web page again by clicking the appropriate Notepad button on the taskbar.

If the browser does not display the Web page and alert messages correctly, close any error message dialog boxes and then click the Notepad button on the taskbar. Check the JavaScript code according to Figures 4-2 through 4-13 on pages J 4.7 through J 4.19. Correct any errors, save the file, activate the browser, and then click the Refresh button.

Removing the Test Code

The alert() method served the purpose of letting you know that the Web page saved the cookie. The comment slashes (//) stopped the Web page from loading the frames.htm Web page. Now, you can remove the alert() method and the comment slashes from the JavaScript code so the viewer does not see the message and the frames.htm page loads. To remove the alert() method, perform the following steps.

To Remove the alert() Method

1. **Select the text on line 8 of the studentcouncil.htm file.**
2. **Press the DELETE key.**
3. **Position the insertion point on line 9 directly before the //.**
4. **Press the DELETE key twice.**

The JavaScript code displays without the alert() function and comment (Figure 4-16).

5. **With the JavaScript Data Disk in drive A, click File on the menu bar and then click Save.**

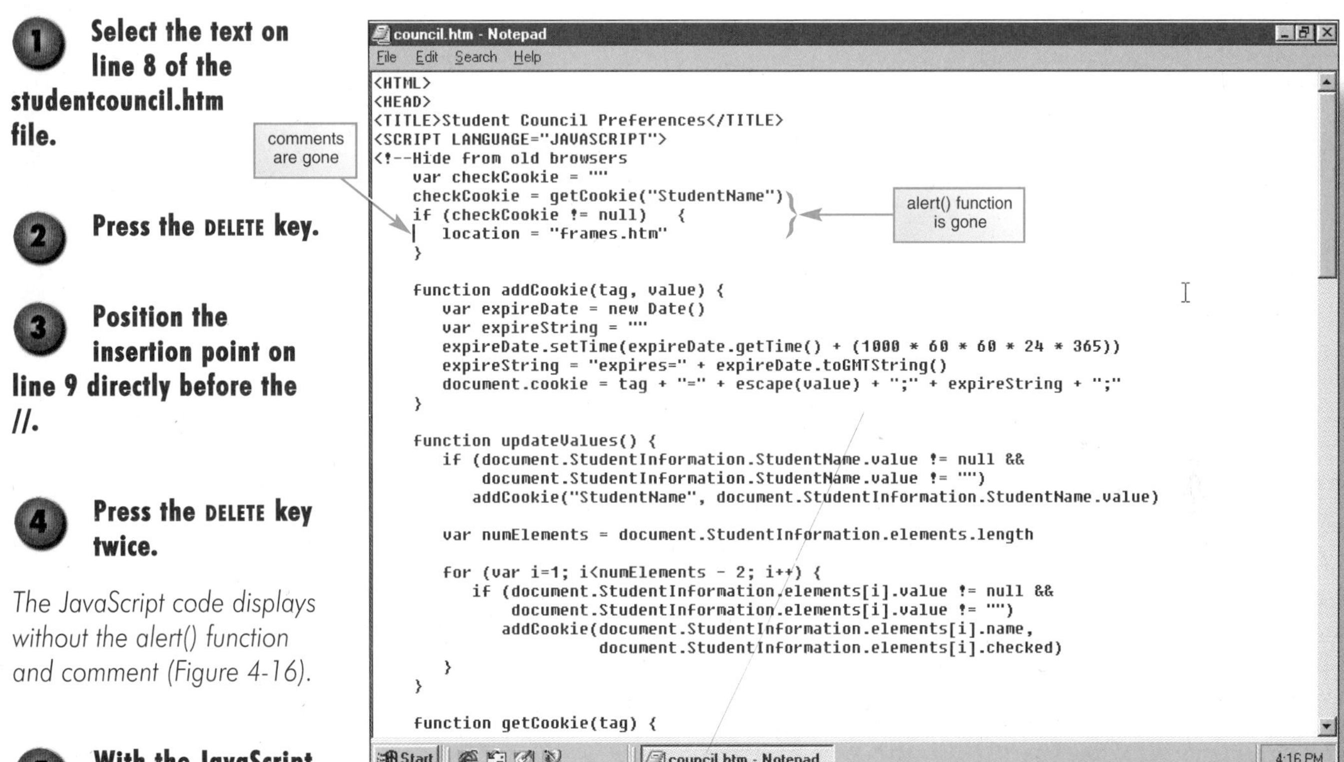

FIGURE 4-16

The next step in the project is to create an array that contains the list of various student organizations that display in the side frame of the Student Council Web page (Figure 4-1b on page J 4.5).

Creating the Array

Each student organization supplies a Web page or link for the Student Council. The Student Council allows these organizations to change their Web pages. The Student Council also adds new organizations. The Web page programmer's responsibilities include writing JavaScript code that is easy to maintain. An **array** can be used to store the information about each organization's Web page. As new organizations are added, the Student Council needs only to add a new array element for that organization, rather than write customized HTML for each addition. The array contains the information about the student's selected list of organizations (Figure 4-17). The array holds the information necessary to update the lower-right frame in Figure 4-17.

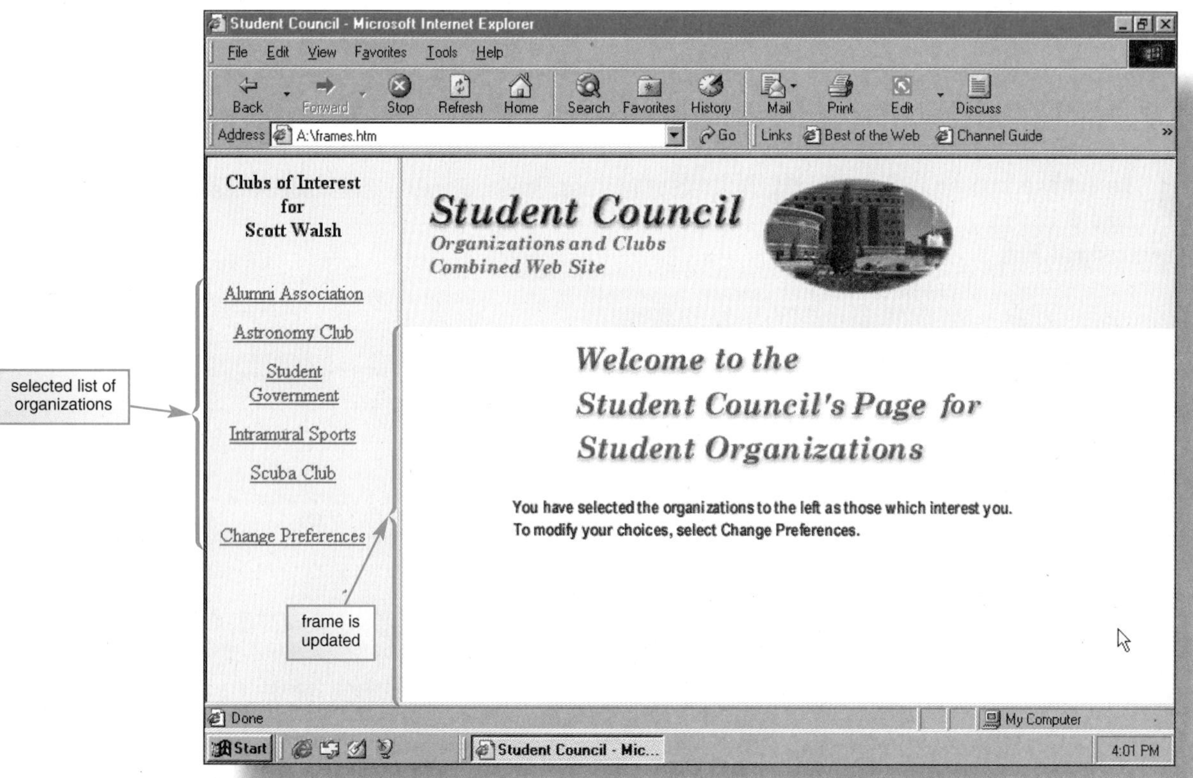

FIGURE 4-17

More About

Objects

Object-oriented programming is a powerful method for organizing how a program functions. JavaScript allows you to create and manipulate complex data for your Web page. For more information about objects, visit www.scsite.com/js/p4.htm and then click Objects.

Initializing the Array

The array used in Project 3 included one piece of information about each array element. With JavaScript, an array element may contain multiple pieces of information. You also can write special functions that act on array elements. When you create an array that contains multiple pieces of information and write special functions that act on the array elements, you are creating a custom object. A JavaScript **object** is a type of variable that contains several pieces of information.

The sidebar.htm file will populate the array by reading the values in the cookie created by the Student Council Preferences Web page. The first step is to start a second session of Notepad and then open the HTML file, sidebar.htm, on the JavaScript Data Disk as shown in the following steps.

TO START A SECOND SESSION OF NOTEPAD AND OPEN THE SIDEBAR.HTM FILE

1. Start Notepad.
2. When the Notepad window displays, click the Maximize button.
3. Open the file, sidebar.htm, on the JavaScript Data Disk in drive A.

The sidebar.htm document opens in the Notepad window (Figure 4-18).

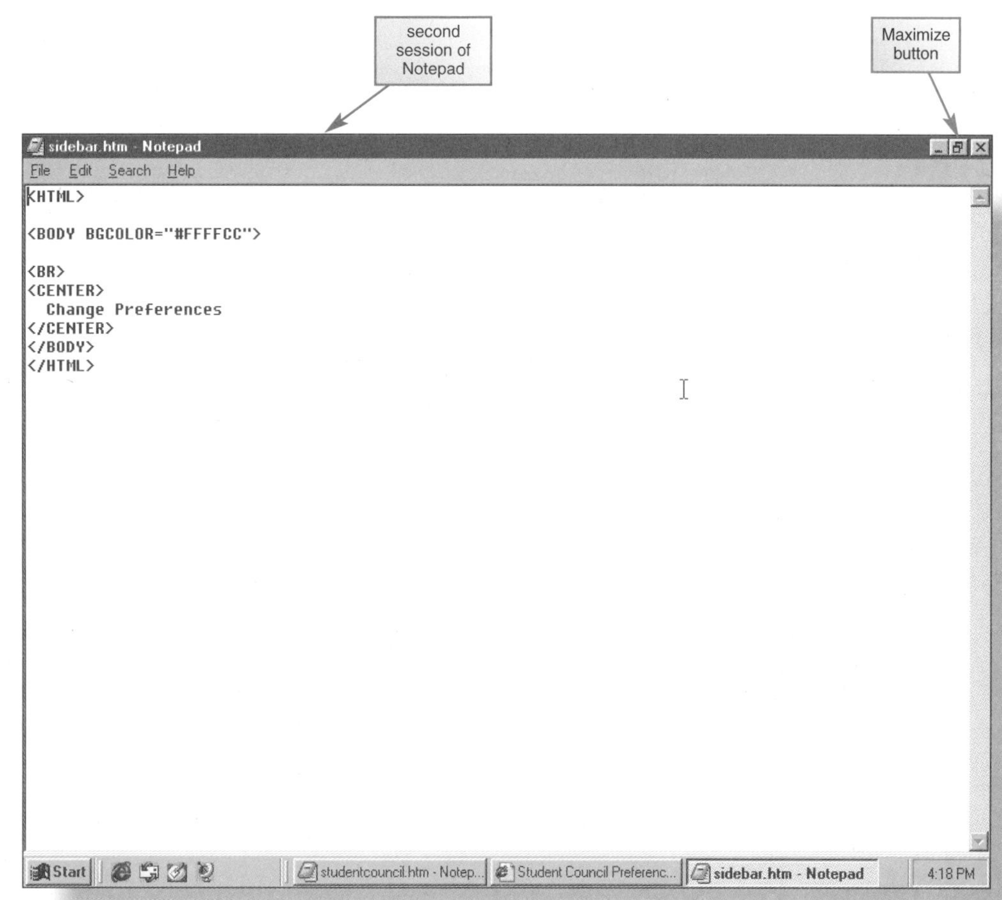

FIGURE 4-18

Each organization has multiple pieces of information that need to be stored in the Web page. This information includes the organization's name, the URL of the organization's Web page, and whether or not the user has selected the organization. The array must handle all of these pieces of information.

The first step to create an array with multiple attributes is to tell the browser to set aside the necessary memory required for the array. The ClubArray() function accomplishes this task. Again, the code in the ClubArray() function is a generic function that can be used again and again. Table 4-10 shows the JavaScript code for the ClubArray() function.

The **ClubArray() function** accepts a parameter that indicates how many elements will be in the array. Next, the For loop in line 7 loops through all of the elements and initializes each array element to 0.

The **this keyword** in line 6 refers to the array that the function is initializing. The ClubArray() function is called using the new operator that was introduced in Project 3. The this keyword tells JavaScript that you are referring to the current instance of that array currently being created with the new operator. In line 9, the calling function returns the current array that is referred to by *this*.

Table 4-10

LINE	*CODE*
2	`<SCRIPT LANGUAGE="JAVASCRIPT">`
3	`<!--Hide from old browsers`
4	`    function ClubArray(length) {`
5	`        var i = 0`
6	`        this.length2 = length`
7	`        for (i=0; i<length; i++)`
8	`            this[i] = 0`
9	`        return this`
10	`    }`
11	
12	
13	`//-->`
14	`</SCRIPT>`

To enter the ClubArray() function, perform the following steps.

To Add the ClubArray() Function

1. **Position the insertion point on line 2.**

2. **Enter the JavaScript code shown in Table 4-10 on the previous page.**

The code displays (Figure 4-19).

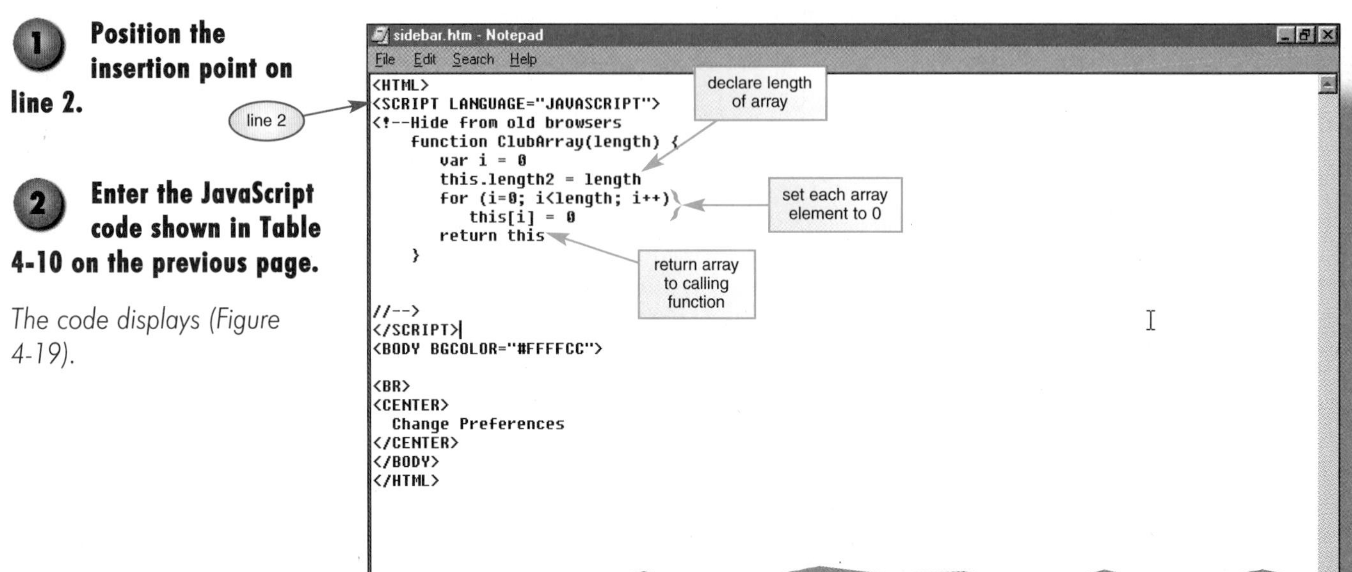

FIGURE 4-19

Multidimensional Arrays

While multidimensional arrays are not supported, you can simulate some of the usefulness of multidimensional arrays in JavaScript. For more information about simulating multidimensional arrays, visit www.scsite.com/js/p4.htm and then click Multidimensional Arrays.

JavaScript does not include the capability of multidimensional arrays as some programming languages do. JavaScript objects, however, allow you to store many attributes about each array item. The AddClub() function creates an object entry for the club that is passed to it. Table 4-11 shows the JavaScript code for the AddClub() function.

Table 4-11

LINE	CODE
12	`function AddClub(ClubName, URL, Cookie) {`
13	`this.ClubName = ClubName`
14	`this.URL = URL`
15	`this.Cookie = Cookie`
16	`return this`
17	`}`

The array initialized by the AddClub() function contains three attributes: the ClubName, the URL of the organization, and the cookie variable name for the organization. When the AddClub() function is called, it is called with the new keyword. The *this* keyword is used to define the three attributes of each array element in lines 13 through 15. The period (.) between the *this* keyword on the attributes is the JavaScript syntax for referring to attributes of an object. Finally, the AddClub() function returns the newly populated array element to the calling function in line 16.

To enter the AddClub() function, perform the following steps.

To Add the AddClub() Function

1 **Position the insertion point on line 12.**

2 **Enter the JavaScript code shown in Table 4-11 and then press the ENTER key twice.**

The code displays (Figure 4-20).

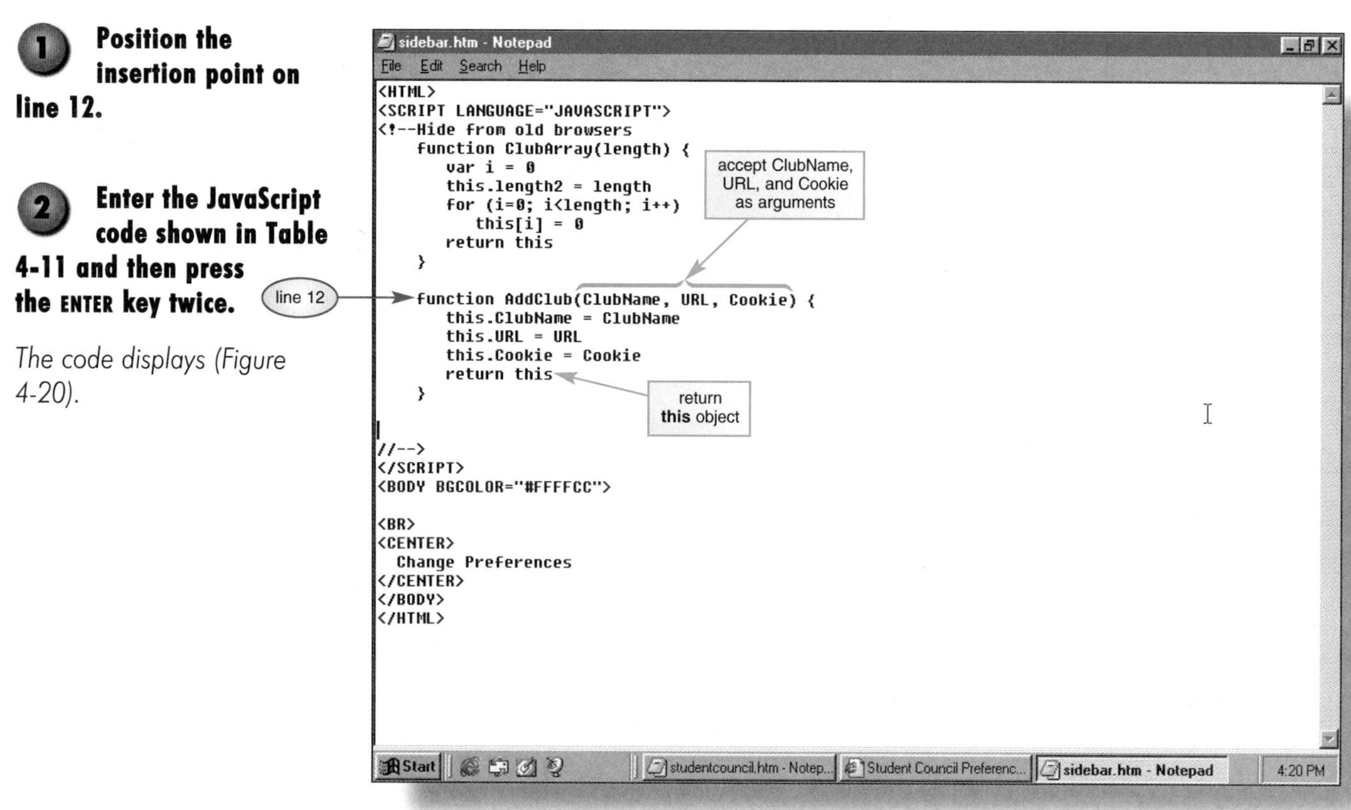
sidebar.htm - Notepad
File Edit Search Help
<HTML>
<SCRIPT LANGUAGE="JAVASCRIPT">
<!--Hide from old browsers
function ClubArray(length) {
var i = 0
this.length2 = length
for (i=0; i<length; i++)
this[i] = 0
return this
}
function AddClub(ClubName, URL, Cookie) {
this.ClubName = ClubName
this.URL = URL
this.Cookie = Cookie
return this
}
//-->
</SCRIPT>
<BODY BGCOLOR="#FFFFCC">

<CENTER>
Change Preferences
</CENTER>
</BODY>
</HTML>
accept ClubName, URL, and Cookie as arguments
line 12
return this object
Start
studentcouncil.htm - Notep...
Student Council Preferenc...
sidebar.htm - Notepad
4:20 PM

FIGURE 4-20

The next step is to call the ClubArray() and AddClub() functions in order to fill the array with data.

Populating the Array

To **populate the array**, the array first is declared with the ClubArray() function. At this point, you must know the number of organizations included on the Web page, because the ClubArray() function accepts the number of organizations as an argument. Next, the AddClub() function is called for each organization to be added. Table 4-12 shows the JavaScript code for populating the Clubs array.

Table 4-12

LINE	CODE
19	`var totClubs = 6`
20	`var Clubs = ClubArray(totClubs)`
21	
22	`Clubs[0] = new AddClub("Alumni Association", "alumni.htm", "interest1")`
23	`Clubs[1] = new AddClub("Astronomy Club", "astronomy.htm", "interest2")`
24	`Clubs[2] = new AddClub("Student Government", "studgovt.htm", "interest3")`
25	`Clubs[3] = new AddClub("Radio and Television Club", "radio.htm", "interest4")`
26	`Clubs[4] = new AddClub("Intramural Sports", "intramurals.htm", "interest5")`
27	`Clubs[5] = new AddClub("Scuba Club", "scuba.htm", "interest6")`

Line 19 sets the number of organizations currently being maintained by the Student Council Web page to six. Next, the ClubArray() function is called to set aside the memory for the array. Finally, in lines 22 through 27, the AddClub() function is called once for each organization. The AddClub() function is called with the organization name, organization Web page URL, and the organization's cookie name used in the studentcouncil.htm Web page. The Web page URL can be a local Web page or a remote Web page.

To populate the Clubs array, perform the following steps.

To Populate the Clubs Array

1. **Position the insertion point on line 19.**

2. **Enter the JavaScript code shown in Table 4-12 on the previous page and then press the ENTER key twice.**

The code displays (Figure 4-21).

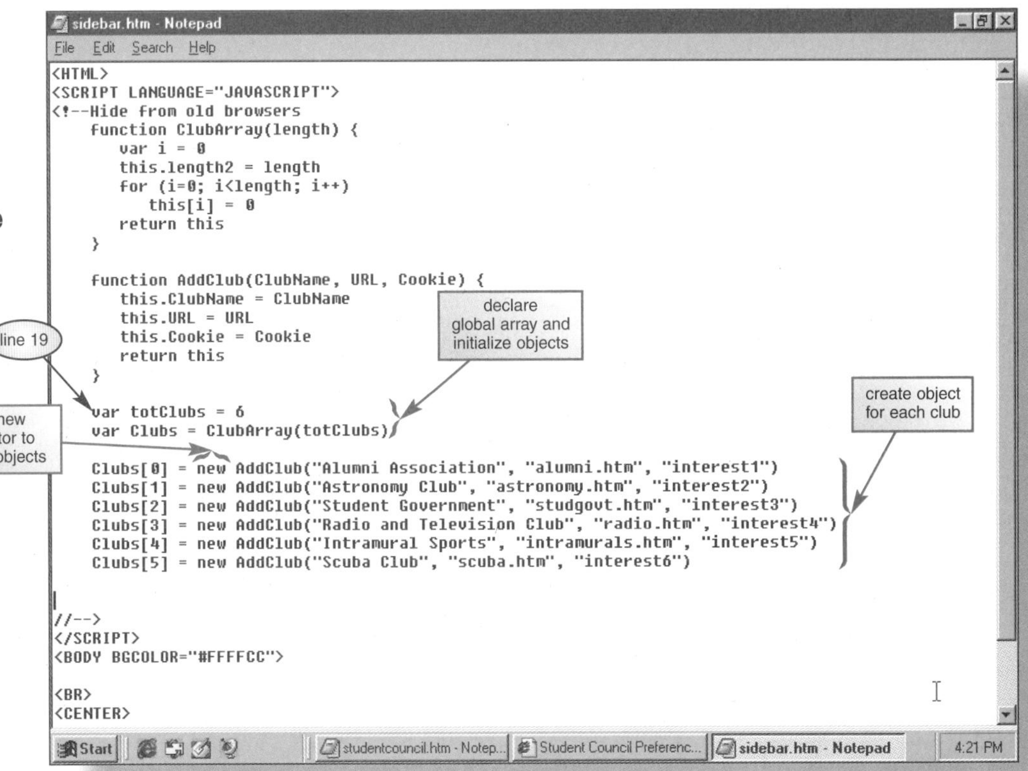

FIGURE 4-21

The array now contains the data describing the organizations. Figure 4-22 illustrates the contents of the array. Notice that each array index has three attributes associated with it.

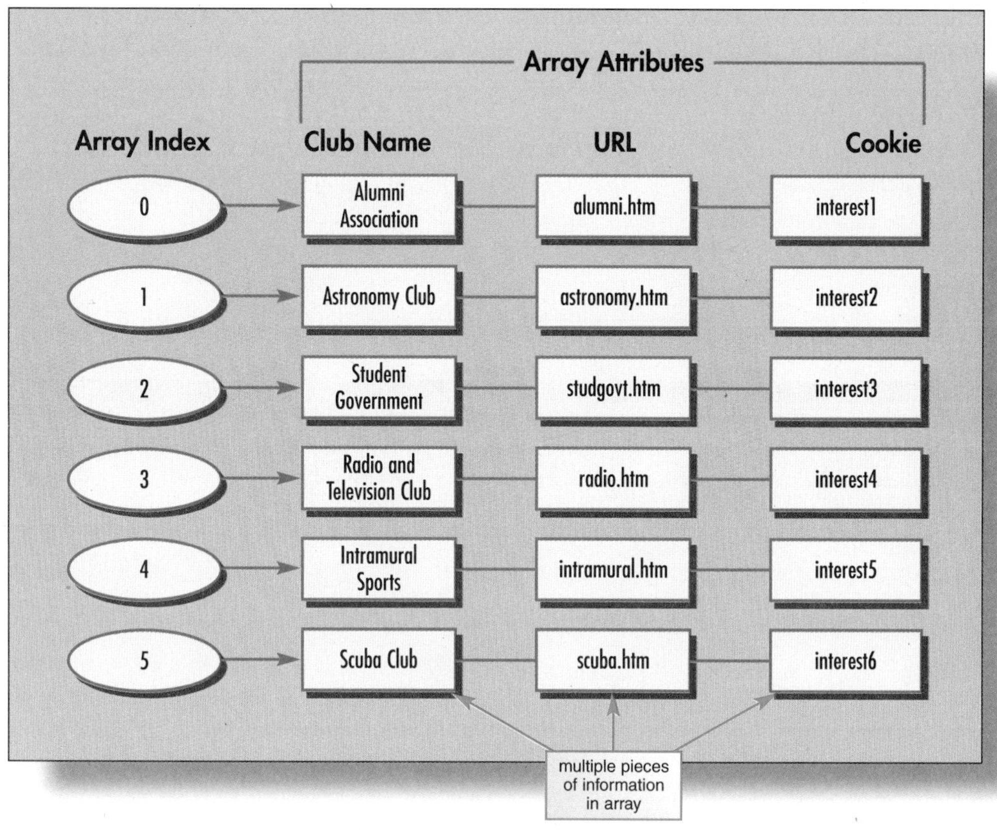

FIGURE 4-22

Displaying Data Based on a Cookie Value

The left frame in Figure 4-1b on page J 4.5 displays all of the data stored in the cookies by the studentcouncil.htm Web page. The browser populates this frame using JavaScript code, rather than with static HTML code. JavaScript code reads the cookies and then populates the left frame based on the value of those cookies.

Reading the Cookie

As previously stated, the getCookie() function is a generic function. You can use the function any time that you want to read a cookie for a Web page. The getCookie() function must be added to the sidebar.htm Web page just as it was added to the studentcouncil.htm Web page. Table 4-13 shows the JavaScript code for the getCookie() function.

Table 4-13

LINE *CODE*

```
function getCookie(tag) {
   var value = null
   var myCookie = document.cookie + ";"
   var findTag = tag + "="
   var endPos

   if (myCookie.length > 0) {
      var beginPos = myCookie.indexOf(findTag)
      if (beginPos != -1) {
         beginPos = beginPos + findTag.length
         endPos = myCookie.indexOf(";", beginPos)
         if (endPos == -1)
            endPos = myCookie.length
         value = unescape(myCookie.substring(beginPos, endPos))
      }
   }
   return value
}
```

The getCookie() function operates here just as it did in the studentcouncil.htm Web page. The function accepts a tag, or variable name, as a parameter and then returns the value of that variable from the Web page's cookie file if the cookie file and variable name exist.

To enter the getCookie() function in the sidebar.htm Web page, perform the following steps.

To Add the getCookie() Function

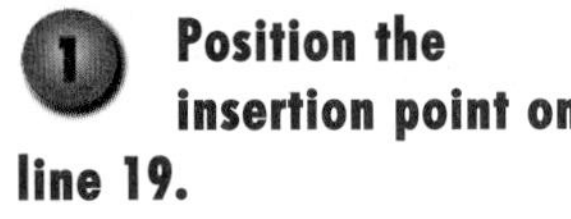

1 **Position the insertion point on line 19.**

2 **Enter the JavaScript code shown in Table 4-13 on the previous page and then press the ENTER key twice.**

The getCookie() function displays (Figure 4-23).

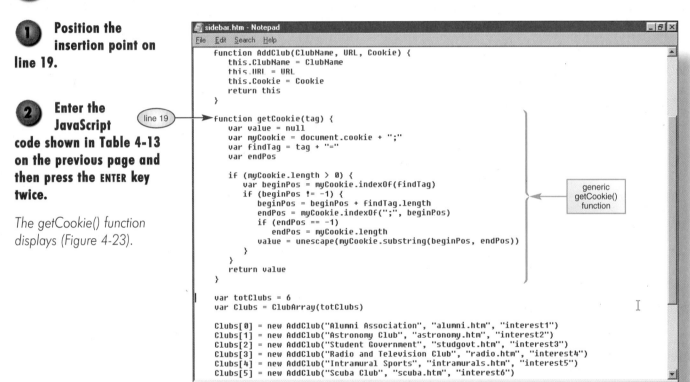

sidebar.htm - Notepad

```
function AddClub(ClubName, URL, Cookie) {
   this.ClubName = ClubName
   this.URL = URL
   this.Cookie = Cookie
   return this
}

function getCookie(tag) {
   var value = null
   var myCookie = document.cookie + ";"
   var findTag = tag + "="
   var endPos

   if (myCookie.length > 0) {
      var beginPos = myCookie.indexOf(findTag)
      if (beginPos != -1) {
         beginPos = beginPos + findTag.length
         endPos = myCookie.indexOf(";", beginPos)
         if (endPos == -1)
            endPos = myCookie.length
         value = unescape(myCookie.substring(beginPos, endPos))
      }
   }
   return value
}

var totClubs = 6
var Clubs = ClubArray(totClubs)

Clubs[0] = new AddClub("Alumni Association", "alumni.htm", "interest1")
Clubs[1] = new AddClub("Astronomy Club", "astronomy.htm", "interest2")
Clubs[2] = new AddClub("Student Government", "studgovt.htm", "interest3")
Clubs[3] = new AddClub("Radio and Television Club", "radio.htm", "interest4")
Clubs[4] = new AddClub("Intramural Sports", "intramurals.htm", "interest5")
Clubs[5] = new AddClub("Scuba Club", "scuba.htm", "interest6")
```


FIGURE 4-23

Displaying the Student Name

The <HEAD> section of the HTML in the sidebar.htm Web page contains the array functions and getCookie() function entered above. JavaScript, however, generates the display of the student's name and the organization list. This HTML must be placed in the <BODY> section of the HTML code. The JavaScript code that displays the student name and organization list first reads the appropriate cookie, then uses the write() method to create the proper HTML in the Web page. Table 4-14 shows the JavaScript code that displays the Student Name.

Table 4-14

LINE	CODE

```
52  <SCRIPT LANGUAGE="JAVASCRIPT">
53  <!--Hide from old browsers
54      var CookieValue = ""
55
56      CookieValue = getCookie("StudentName")
57      if (CookieValue != null) {
58         document.write("<TABLE BORDER=0 CELLPADDING=0 CELLSPACING=0 WIDTH=100%>")
59         document.write("<TR ALIGN=CENTER><TD><B>Clubs of Interest</B></TD></TR>")
60         document.write("<TR ALIGN=CENTER><TD><B>for</B></TD></TR>")
61         document.write("<TR ALIGN=CENTER><TD><B>" + CookieValue + "</B></TD></TR>")
62         document.write("</TABLE>")
63         document.write("<BR>")
64      }
```

The JavaScript code in line 56 assigns the value of the StudentName cookie to the CookieValue variable. If the CookieValue variable contains data; then an HTML table starts that includes the phrase, Clubs of Interest, in the first row, the word, for, in the second row; and the student name in the third row. Finally, line 62 closes the HTML table. Line 63 leaves some blank space in order to make the Web page more readable.

To enter the code to display the Student Name, perform the following steps.

To Display the Student Name

1. **Position the insertion point on line 52.**

2. **Enter the JavaScript code shown in Table 4-14 and then press the ENTER key.**

The code displays (Figure 4-24).

sidebar.htm - Notepad

File Edit Search Help

```
    var totClubs = 6
    var Clubs = ClubArray(totClubs)

    Clubs[0] = new AddClub("Alumni Association", "alumni.htm", "interest1")
    Clubs[1] = new AddClub("Astronomy Club", "astronomy.htm", "interest2")
    Clubs[2] = new AddClub("Student Government", "studgovt.htm", "interest3")
    Clubs[3] = new AddClub("Radio and Television Club", "radio.htm", "interest4")
    Clubs[4] = new AddClub("Intramural Sports", "intramurals.htm", "interest5")
    Clubs[5] = new AddClub("Scuba Club", "scuba.htm", "interest6")


//-->
</SCRIPT>
<BODY BGCOLOR="#FFFFCC">
<SCRIPT LANGUAGE="JAVASCRIPT">
<!--Hide from old browsers
    var CookieValue = ""

    CookieValue = getCookie("StudentName")
    if (CookieValue != null) {
       document.write("<TABLE BORDER=0 CELLPADDING=0 CELLSPACING=0 WIDTH=100%>")
       document.write("<TR ALIGN=CENTER><TD><B>Clubs of Interest</B></TD></TR>")
       document.write("<TR ALIGN=CENTER><TD><B>for</B></TD></TR>")
       document.write("<TR ALIGN=CENTER><TD><B>" + CookieValue + "</B></TD></TR>")
       document.write("</TABLE>")
       document.write("<BR>")
    }

<BR>
<CENTER>
  Change Preferences
```

line 52

get StudentName cookie

create HTML table with student's name

FIGURE 4-24

The student name now displays at the top of the side frame in the Student Council Web page, which gives the viewer a customized Web page. The next step is to display the list of organizations that the student has selected from the Student Council Preferences Web page.

Displaying the Organization List

When displaying the organization list, it is necessary to read each possible organization's cookie to see if the cookie exists. If the cookie exists, then JavaScript writes some HTML that includes the organization name. A For loop is used to process each of the organizations one at a time. Figure 4-25 shows the flowchart for this logic.

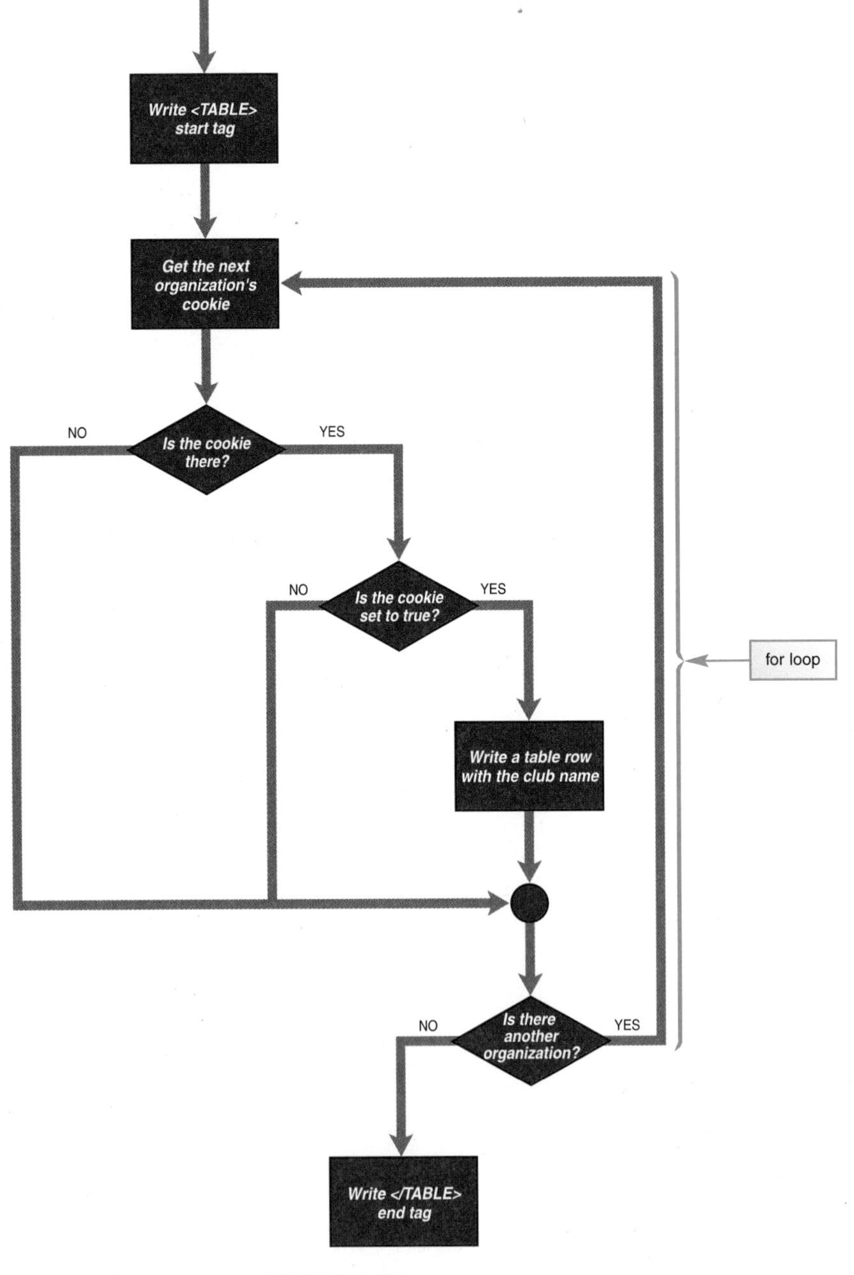

FIGURE 4-25

Table 4-15 shows the JavaScript code to display the organization list.

Table 4-15

```
LINE  CODE
65           document.write("<TABLE BORDER=0 CELLPADDING=0 CELLSPACING=12 WIDTH=100%>")
66           for (var i=0; i<=totClubs; i++) {
67               CookieValue = ""
68               CookieValue = getCookie(Clubs[i].Cookie)
69               if (CookieValue != null) {
70                  if (CookieValue == "true") {
71                     document.write("<TR ALIGN=CENTER><TD>" + Clubs[i].ClubName + "</TD></TR>")
72                  }
73               }
74           }
75           document.write("</TABLE>")
76       //-->
77       </SCRIPT>
```

The JavaScript code that displays the organization list first writes a beginning HTML TABLE tag in line 65. Next, a For loop executes once for each organization. The For loop checks for the existence of the next organization's cookie in line 68. If the cookie exists, then the JavaScript writes a table row in line 71 that displays the organization's name. In order to access the attributes of the Clubs array, the period notation is used again along with the array's subscript.

To enter the code to display the organization list, perform the following steps.

Steps To Display the Organization List

1. **Position the insertion point on line 65.**

2. **Enter the JavaScript code shown in Table 4-15.**

The code displays (Figure 4-26).

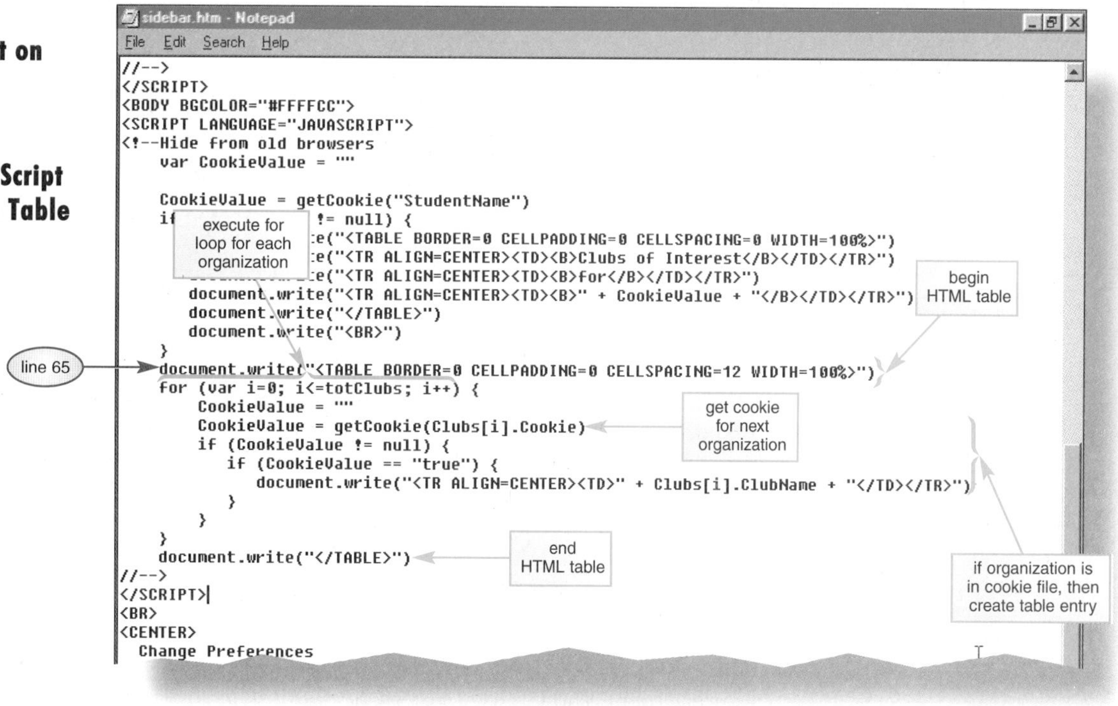

sidebar.htm - Notepad

File Edit Search Help

```
//-->
</SCRIPT>
<BODY BGCOLOR="#FFFFCC">
<SCRIPT LANGUAGE="JAVASCRIPT">
<!--Hide from old browsers
    var CookieValue = ""

    CookieValue = getCookie("StudentName")
    if             != null) {
                 :e("<TABLE BORDER=0 CELLPADDING=0 CELLSPACING=0 WIDTH=100%>")
                 :e("<TR ALIGN=CENTER><TD><B>Clubs of Interest</B></TD></TR>")
                 :e("<TR ALIGN=CENTER><TD><B>For</B></TD></TR>")
       document.write("<TR ALIGN=CENTER><TD><B>" + CookieValue + "</B></TD></TR>")
       document.write("</TABLE>")
       document.write("<BR>")
    }
    document.write("<TABLE BORDER=0 CELLPADDING=0 CELLSPACING=12 WIDTH=100%>")
    for (var i=0; i<=totClubs; i++) {
        CookieValue = ""
        CookieValue = getCookie(Clubs[i].Cookie)
        if (CookieValue != null) {
           if (CookieValue == "true") {
              document.write("<TR ALIGN=CENTER><TD>" + Clubs[i].ClubName + "</TD></TR>")
           }
        }
    }
    document.write("</TABLE>")
//-->
</SCRIPT>
<BR>
<CENTER>
  Change Preferences
```


FIGURE 4-26

At this point, the student's name and the student's selected organizations display in the left frame in the Student Council Web page. The next step is to save and test the Web pages to view the student name and organization list.

Saving and Testing the Web Page

Perform the following steps to save and test your Web page.

To Save and Test the Web Page

1. **With the JavaScript Data Disk in drive A, click File on the menu bar and then click Save As.**

2. **Type** `a:\side.htm` **in the File name text box and then click the Save button in the Save As dialog box.**

3. **Start your browser and open the studentcouncil.htm file.**

The three frames display. The left frame shows the student name and the selected organizations from the first time that the Web page was tested on page J 4.20. (Figure 4-27).

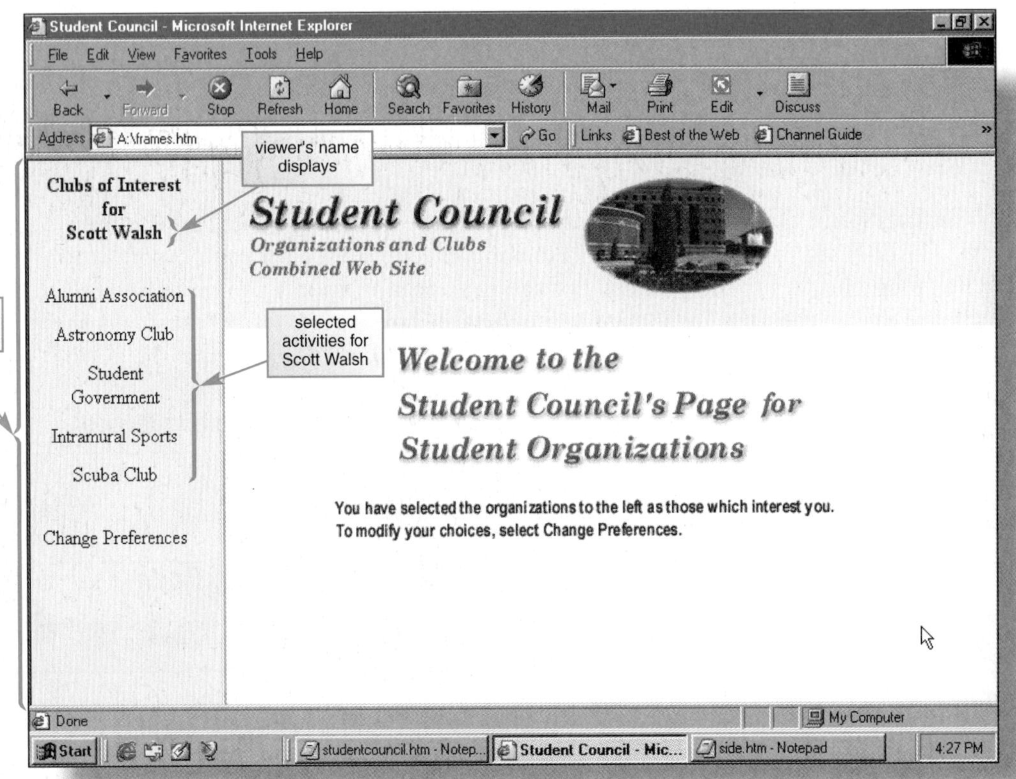

FIGURE 4-27

If the browser does not display the Web page correctly, close any error message dialog boxes and then click the Notepad button on the taskbar for the file that you suspect of causing the problem. Check the JavaScript code according to Figures 4-16 through 4-26 on pages J 4.21 through J 4.31. Correct any errors, save the file, activate the browser, and then click the Refresh button.

Setting a Flag in a Cookie

After students visit the Student Council Web page and select the organizations that interest them, the Change Preferences link shown in Figure 4-28 allows them to update their preferences. The JavaScript in the Student Council Web page, however, immediately jumps to the Student Council Web page shown in Figure 4-28 if the browser finds the StudentName cookie value. Therefore, it is necessary to let the Student Council Web page know that the user wants to update his or her preferences so the JavaScript does not automatically jump to the Student Council Web page.

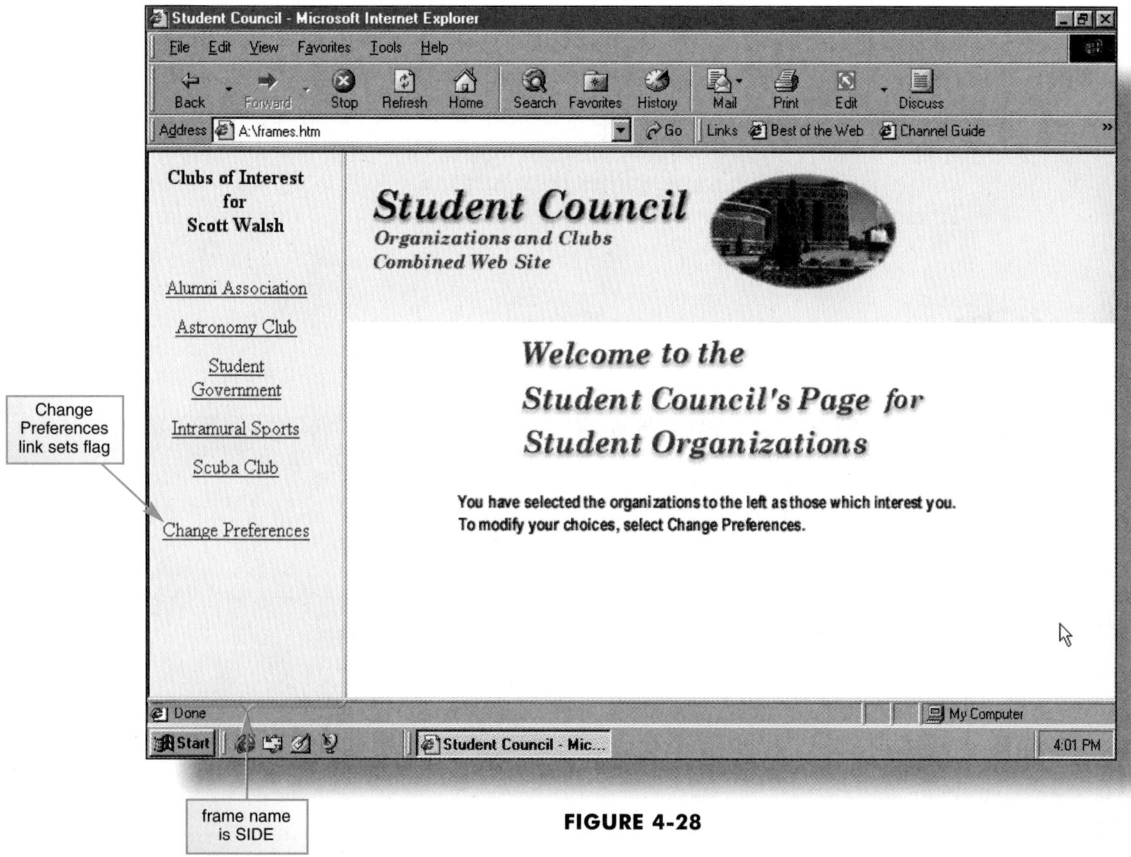

FIGURE 4-28

Setting the Value of the Flag

A flag will be set in a cookie by the Student Council Web page (Figure 4-28), and the Student Council Preferences page will read this flag. If the Student Council Preferences page finds this flag in the cookie, then the Student Council Preferences page will not load the Student Council Web page and will instead continue to load itself. The **setEditMode() function** adds the special cookie. Table 4-16 shows the JavaScript code for the setEditMode() function.

Table 4-16

LINE CODE

```
function setEditMode() {
   var expireDate = new Date()

   expireDate.setTime(expireDate.getTime() + (1000 * 60 * 60 * 24 * 365))
   document.cookie = "EditMode=" + escape("true") + "; expires=" + expireDate.toGMTString() + ";"
   top.location.href = "studentcouncil.htm"
}
```

Frames and JavaScript

For more information about frames in JavaScript, visit www.scsite.com/js/p4.htm and then click Frames.

The setEditMode() function first determines the expiration date of the flag cookie in line 41. Next, the cookie is written with the name EditMode and the value of true. Finally, the studentcouncil.htm Web page, which includes the Student Council Preferences Web page, becomes the new Web page in the browser. Normally, you call a hyperlinked Web page using location.href. The side.htm Web page, however, exists in a frame. If you use the location.href, then the Student Council Preferences page will load into the left frame of the Student Council Web page, rather than taking up the entire browser window. The **top property** of a Web page refers to the entire window of the browser. So in this case, the location.href specifies the location of entire window, rather than just the side.htm frame.

To enter the code to set the EditMode flag, perform the following steps.

To Set the EditMode Flag

1 **Position the insertion point on line 38.**

2 **Enter the JavaScript code shown in Table 4-16 and then press the ENTER key twice.**

The setEditMode() function code displays (Figure 4-29).

side.htm - Notepad

File Edit Search Help

```
function getCookie(tag) {
   var value = null
   var myCookie = document.cookie + ";"
   var findTag = tag + "="
   var endPos

   if (myCookie.length > 0) {
      var beginPos = myCookie.indexOf(findTag)
      if (beginPos != -1) {
         beginPos = beginPos + findTag.length
         endPos = myCookie.indexOf(";", beginPos)
         if (endPos == -1)
            endPos = myCookie.length
         value = unescape(myCookie.substring(beginP
      }
   }
   return value
}

function setEditMode() {
   var expireDate = new Date()

   expireDate.setTime(expireDate.getTime() + (1000 * 60 * 60 * 24 * 365))
   document.cookie = "EditMode=" + escape("true") + "; expires=" + expireDate.toGMTString() +
";"
   top.location.href = "studentcouncil.htm"
}

var totClubs = 6
var Clubs = ClubArray(totClubs)

Clubs[0] = new AddClub("Alumni Association", "alumni.htm", "interest1")
Clubs[1] = new AddClub("Astronomy Club", "astronomy.htm", "interest2")
Clubs[2] = new AddClub("Student Government", "studgovt.htm", "interest3")
Clubs[3] = new AddClub("Radio and Television Club", "radio.htm", "interest4")
```

line 38

set expiration date to one year from now

set cookie value of EditMode to true

load studentcouncil.htm Web page

Start | studentcouncil.htm - Notep... | Student Council Preferenc... | side.htm - Notepad | 4:29 PM

FIGURE 4-29

The Change Preferences hyperlink calls the setEditMode() function. An HTML anchor tag must be placed around the phrase, Change Preferences, in the side.htm Web page. Perform the following steps to call the setEditMode() function from a hyperlink.

To Call the setEditMode() Function

1. **Position the insertion point on line 88 directly before the C in the word Change.**

2. **Type** `<A HREF="JavaScript:setEditMode();">` **and do not press the ENTER key.**

3. **Position the insertion point on line 88 directly after the s in the word, Preferences.**

4. **Type** `</A>` **and do not press the ENTER key.**

A link is added from the phrase, Change Preferences, to the setEditMode() function (Figure 4-30).

```
side.htm - Notepad
File  Edit  Search  Help
//-->
</SCRIPT>
<BODY BGCOLOR="#FFFFCC">
<SCRIPT LANGUAGE="JAVASCRIPT">
<!--Hide from old browsers
    var CookieValue = ""

    CookieValue = getCookie("StudentName")
    if (CookieValue != null) {
       document.write("<TABLE BORDER=0 CELLPADDING=0 CELLSPACING=0 WIDTH=100%>")
       document.write("<TR ALIGN=CENTER><TD><B>Clubs of Interest</B></TD></TR>")
       document.write("<TR ALIGN=CENTER><TD><B>for</B></TD></TR>")
       document.write("<TR ALIGN=CENTER><TD><B>" + CookieValue + "</B></TD></TR>")
       document.write("</TABLE>")
       document.write("<BR>")
    }
    document.write("<TABLE BORDER=0 CELLPADDING=0 CELLSPACING=12 WIDTH=100%>")
    for (var i=0; i<totClubs; i++) {
        CookieValue = ""
        CookieValue = getCookie(Clubs[i].Cookie)
        if (CookieValue != null) {
           if (CookieValue == "true") {
              document.write("<TR ALIGN=CENTER><TD>" + Clubs[i].ClubName + "</TD></TR>")
           }
        }
    }
    document.write("</TABLE>")
//-->
</SCRIPT>
<BR>
<CENTER>
  <A HREF="JavaScript:setEditMode();">Change Preferences</A>
</CENTER>
</BODY>
</HTML>
```


FIGURE 4-30

The Change Preferences text is now a hyperlink. When a user clicks the Change Preferences hyperlink, JavaScript code sets the EditMode flag to the value true and the studentcouncil.htm Web page activates in the browser. The keyword JavaScript is a special way to call the setEditMode() function. Whenever an HTML anchor tag is used to call a JavaScript function, the word JavaScript followed by a colon (:) must be used before the name of the function.

The HREF Tag and JavaScript

The HREF tag is perhaps the most widely used means of executing JavaScript code. For more information about the HREF tag, visit www.scsite.com/js/p4.htm and then click HREF.

Reading and Using the Flag

Next, the Student Council Preferences Web page must determine the value of the EditMode flag and take action depending on the value. If this flag contains the value true, then the Web page should load, rather than loading the frames.htm Web page. This JavaScript code needs to be placed in the studentcouncil.htm file. Because this file is already open, perform the following step to bring the studentcouncil.htm Notepad session back into the foreground.

TO VIEW THE STUDENTCOUNCIL.HTM NOTEPAD SESSION

 Click the studentcouncil.htm Notepad button on the taskbar.

The studentcouncil.htm Notepad window display.

The studentcouncil.htm Web page needs to check the status of the EditMode flag immediately before it checks for the existence of the StudentName value in the cookie. Table 4-17 shows the JavaScript code to read the EditMode flag from the cookie and check its value.

Line 7 reads the EditMode flag from the cookie file. If the EditMode flag exists and the value equals true, then the StudentName flag is not checked and the frames.htm Web page is not loaded. Instead, the Student Council Preferences Web page (studentcouncil.htm) loads normally. Also, because the if statement is encapsulating some JavaScript code that already exists, that previous JavaScript should be indented to maintain the look of the source code.

To enter the code to use the EditMode flag and correctly indent the existing JavaScript code, perform the following steps.

Table 4-17

LINE	CODE
6	`var checkEditMode = ""`
7	`checkEditMode = getCookie("EditMode")`
8	`if (checkEditMode != "true") {`

Steps To Use the EditMode Flag

1. **Position the insertion point at the end of line 5 and then press the ENTER key.**

2. **Enter the JavaScript code shown in Table 4-17 and do not press the ENTER key.**

The code displays (Figure 4-31).

studentcouncil.htm - Notepad

File Edit Search Help

```
<HTML>
<HEAD>
<TITLE>Student Council Preferences</TITLE>
<SCRIPT LANGUAGE="JAVASCRIPT">
<!--Hide from old browsers
    var checkEditMode = ""
    checkEditMode = getCookie("EditMode")
    if (checkEditMode != "true")   {
    var checkCookie = ""
    checkCookie = getCookie("StudentName")
    if (checkCookie != null)    {
       location = "frames.htm"
    }

    function addCookie(tag, value) {
       var expireDate = new Date()
       var expireString = ""
       expireDate.setTime(expireDate.getTime() + (1000 * 60 * 60 * 24 * 365))
       expireString = "expires=" + expireDate.toGMTString()
       document.cookie = tag + "=" + escape(value) + ";" + expireString + ";"
    }

    function updateValues() {
       if (document.StudentInformation.StudentName.value != null &&
           document.StudentInformation.StudentName.value != "")
          addCookie("StudentName", document.StudentInformation.StudentName.value)

       var numElements = document.StudentInformation.elements.length

       for (var i=1; i<numElements - 2; i++) {
          if (document.StudentInformation.elements[i].value != null &&
              document.StudentInformation.elements[i].value != "")
             addCookie(document.StudentInformation.elements[i].name,
                       document.StudentInformation.elements[i].checked)
       }
```

line 6

get value of EditMode cookie

test value of EditMode cookie

Start | studentcouncil.htm - ... | Student Council - Microsoft... | side.htm - Notepad | 4:30 PM

FIGURE 4-31

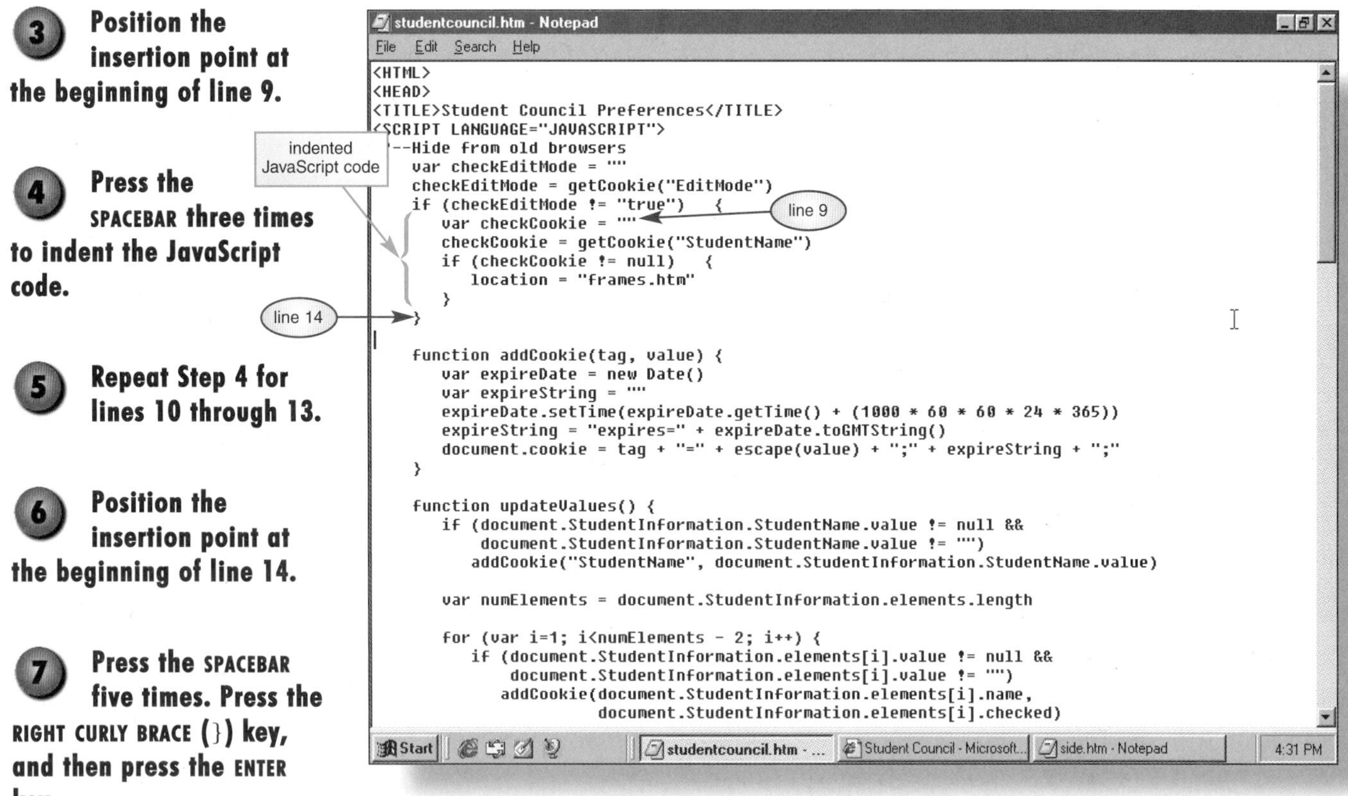

3 **Position the insertion point at the beginning of line 9.**

4 **Press the SPACEBAR three times to indent the JavaScript code.**

5 **Repeat Step 4 for lines 10 through 13.**

6 **Position the insertion point at the beginning of line 14.**

7 **Press the SPACEBAR five times. Press the RIGHT CURLY BRACE (}) key, and then press the ENTER key.**

The code displays (Figure 4-32).

FIGURE 4-32

The Student Council Preferences Web page displays when the user clicks the Change Preferences link on the Student Council Web page. The values of the Student Name field and the organization's check boxes must be properly initialized to the values contained in the cookie.

Initializing the Web Page

After the user clicks the Change Preferences hyperlink, the values of the student name and organizations' check boxes must be updated so the user can observe his or her previous choices. The InitalizeValues() function reads the existing cookies and sets the values on the Student Council Preferences Web page. Table 4-18 shows the JavaScript code for the first part of the InitializeValues() function that reads and displays the student name.

Table 4-18

```
function InitializeValues() {
   var CookieValue = ""

   CookieValue = getCookie("StudentName")
   if (CookieValue != null)
      document.StudentInformation.StudentName.value = CookieValue
}
```

The **InitializeValues() function** uses the getCookie() function to read the StudentName cookie and assign it to the CookieValue variable. This demonstrates the reusability of the getCookie() function. Next, if the StudentName tag in the cookie contains a value, then line 73 sets the StudentName element of the StudentInformation form to that value. The Web page viewer now sees the StudentName displayed in the Student Name field.

To enter the InitializeValues() function, perform the following steps.

To Add the InitializeValues() Function

1 Position the insertion point on line 68.

2 Enter the JavaScript code shown in Table 4-18 and then press the ENTER key.

The InitializeValues() function displays (Figure 4-33).

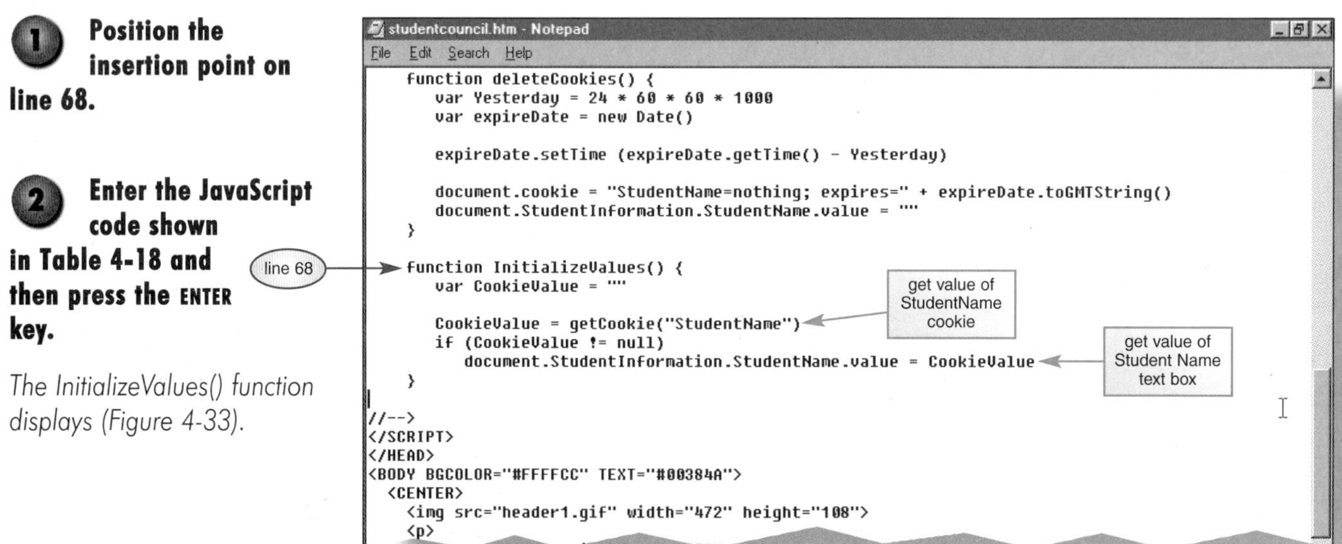

FIGURE 4-33

The next part of the InitializeValues() function reads the organizations' cookie tags and populates the check boxes if necessary. Finally, the InitializeValues() function makes certain that the EditMode flag contains the value of false. Table 4-19 shows the JavaScript code for the remainder of the InitializeValues() function.

Table 4-19

LINE	CODE
75	`var numElements = document.StudentInformation.elements.length`
76	
77	`for (var i=1; i<numElements - 2; i++) {`
78	`    CookieValue = ""`
79	`    CookieValue = getCookie(document.StudentInformation.elements[i].name)`
80	`    if (CookieValue != null) {`
81	`       if (CookieValue == "true") document.StudentInformation.elements[i].checked = true`
82	`       if (CookieValue == "false") document.StudentInformation.elements[i].checked = false`
83	`    }`
84	`}`
85	`addCookie("EditMode", "false")`

The InitializeValues() function determines the number of elements in the StudentInformation form using the length method on line 75. Just as in the updateValues() function on page J 4.11, the For loop in line 77 loops through the check boxes on the Web page. The function checks for a cookie for each organization on line 79. If the cookie exists and if the value of the cookie is true, then the JavaScript code places a check in the check box by setting the check box value to true. Otherwise, the check box remains unchecked and the code sets the check box's value to false.

The InitializeValue() function then initializes the EditMode flag to false. When the Web page loads, the JavaScript code at the top of the form in lines 6 through 13 executes and checks the EditMode flag. If the EditMode flag is true, then the page continues to load, rather then loading the frames.htm Web page. At this time, the onLoad event of the Preferences page initiates the call to the InitializeValues() function.

To enter the remainder of the InitializeValues() function, perform the following steps.

To Add the Remainder of the InitializeValues() Function

1 **Position the insertion point on line 74 and then press the ENTER key.**

2 **Enter the JavaScript code shown in Table 4-19 and then press the ENTER key.**

The remainder of the InitializeValues() function displays (Figure 4-34).

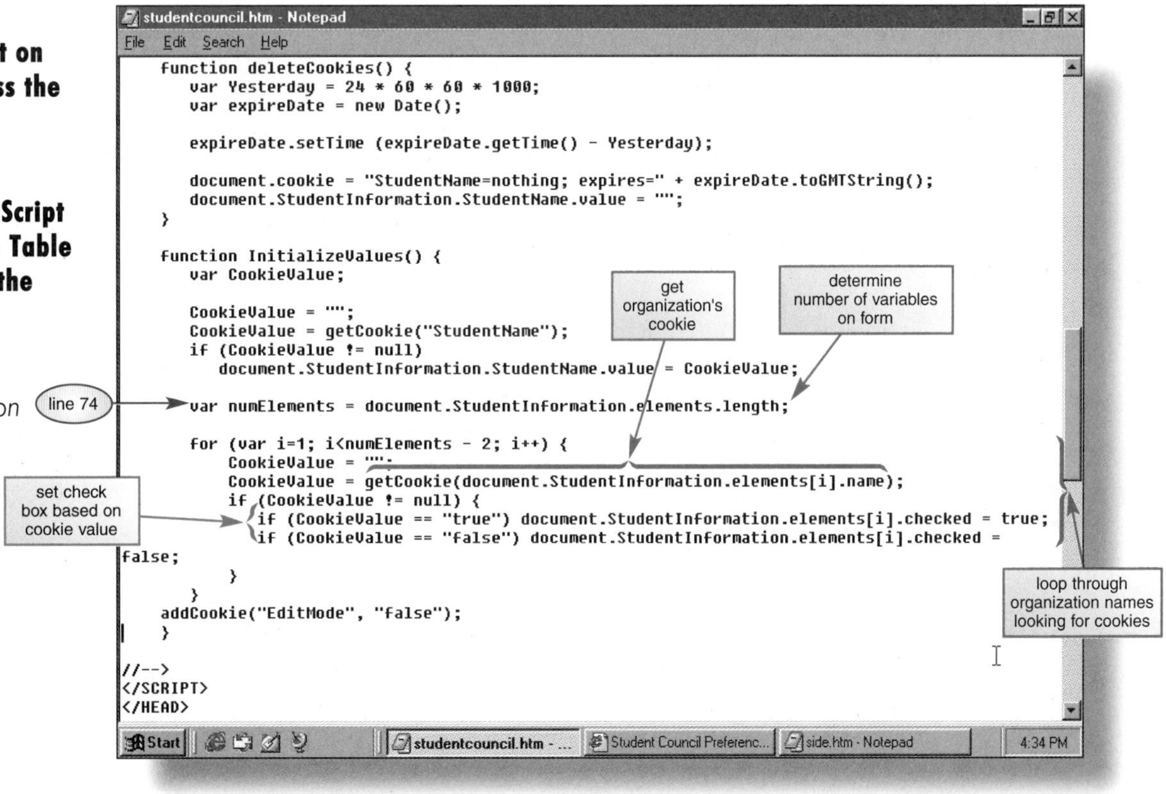

studentcouncil.htm - Notepad

File Edit Search Help

```
function deleteCookies() {
   var Yesterday = 24 * 60 * 60 * 1000;
   var expireDate = new Date();

   expireDate.setTime (expireDate.getTime() - Yesterday);

   document.cookie = "StudentName=nothing; expires=" + expireDate.toGMTString();
   document.StudentInformation.StudentName.value = "";
}

function InitializeValues() {
   var CookieValue;

   CookieValue = "";
   CookieValue = getCookie("StudentName");
   if (CookieValue != null)
      document.StudentInformation.StudentName.value = CookieValue;

   var numElements = document.StudentInformation.elements.length;

   for (var i=1; i<numElements - 2; i++) {
      CookieValue = "";
      CookieValue = getCookie(document.StudentInformation.elements[i].name);
      if (CookieValue != null) {
        if (CookieValue == "true") document.StudentInformation.elements[i].checked = true;
        if (CookieValue == "false") document.StudentInformation.elements[i].checked =
false;
      }
   }
  addCookie("EditMode", "false");
  }

//-->
</SCRIPT>
</HEAD>
```

line 74

get organization's cookie

determine number of variables on form

set check box based on cookie value

loop through organization names looking for cookies

Start | studentcouncil.htm - ... | Student Council Preferenc... | side.htm - Notepad | 4:34 PM

FIGURE 4-34

The InitializeValues() function must be called whenever the Web page is loaded; therefore, the onLoad event for the Web page makes the call to the InitializeValues() function. Perform the steps on the next page to add the call of the InitializeValues() function to the onLoad event of the body of the Student Council Preferences Web page.

To Call the InitializeValues() Function

1 **Position the insertion point on line 91 directly before the rightmost > bracket.**

2 **Press the SPACEBAR. Type** `onLoad="InitializeValues()"` **and do not press the ENTER key.**

The event handler associates the function InitializeValues() and the onLoad event that is part of the studentcouncil.htm Web page (Figure 4-35).

```
studentcouncil.htm - Notepad
File  Edit  Search  Help
   function InitializeValues() {
      var CookieValue = ""

      CookieValue = getCookie("StudentName")
      if (CookieValue != null)
         document.StudentInformation.StudentName.value = CookieValue

      var numElements = document.StudentInformation.elements.length

      for (var i=1; i<numElements - 2; i++) {
          CookieValue = ""
          CookieValue = getCookie(document.StudentInformation.elements[i].name)
          if (CookieValue != null) {
             if (CookieValue == "true") document.StudentInformation.elements[i].checked = true
             if (CookieValue == "false") document.StudentInformation.elements[i].checked = false
          }
      }
   addCookie("EditMode", "false")
   }

//-->
</SCRIPT>
</HEAD>
<BODY BGCOLOR="#FFFFCC" TEXT="#00384A" onLoad="InitializeValues()">
  <CENTER>
    <img src="header1.gif" width="472" height="108">
    <p>
    <img src="please.gif" width="472" height="55"></p>
  </CENTER>

  <FORM NAME="StudentInformation" onSubmit="return updateValues()" onReset="return
deleteCookies()">
  <CENTER>
    <TABLE BORDER=0>
        <TR>
```

line 91

call InitializeValues() function

FIGURE 4-35

When the Student Council Preferences Web page loads, the InitializeValues() function checks for the existence of the cookies and initializes the Web page for the view that includes the cookie values.

More About

Writing to Frames

In some cases, others may want to load your Web page into a frame on their own Web pages. If you can anticipate this, then you can write the JavaScript to detect the situation and react accordingly. For more information about writing to frames, visit www.scsite.com/js/p4.htm and then click Writing to Frames.

Working with Frames

The Student Council Web page (Figure 4-36e) consists of three frames. The frames.htm file (Figure 4-36a) defines the frameset. The top frame, named HEADER, (Figure 4-36c) consists of the header and maintains a consistent look as the viewer navigates through the site. The left frame, named SIDEBAR, (Figure 4-36b) contains a list of links that the viewer previously selected as those of interest. The right frame, named LOWERRIGHT, (Figure 4-36d) initially contains the welcome page. This page changes as the user clicks links in the left, or SIDEBAR, frame.

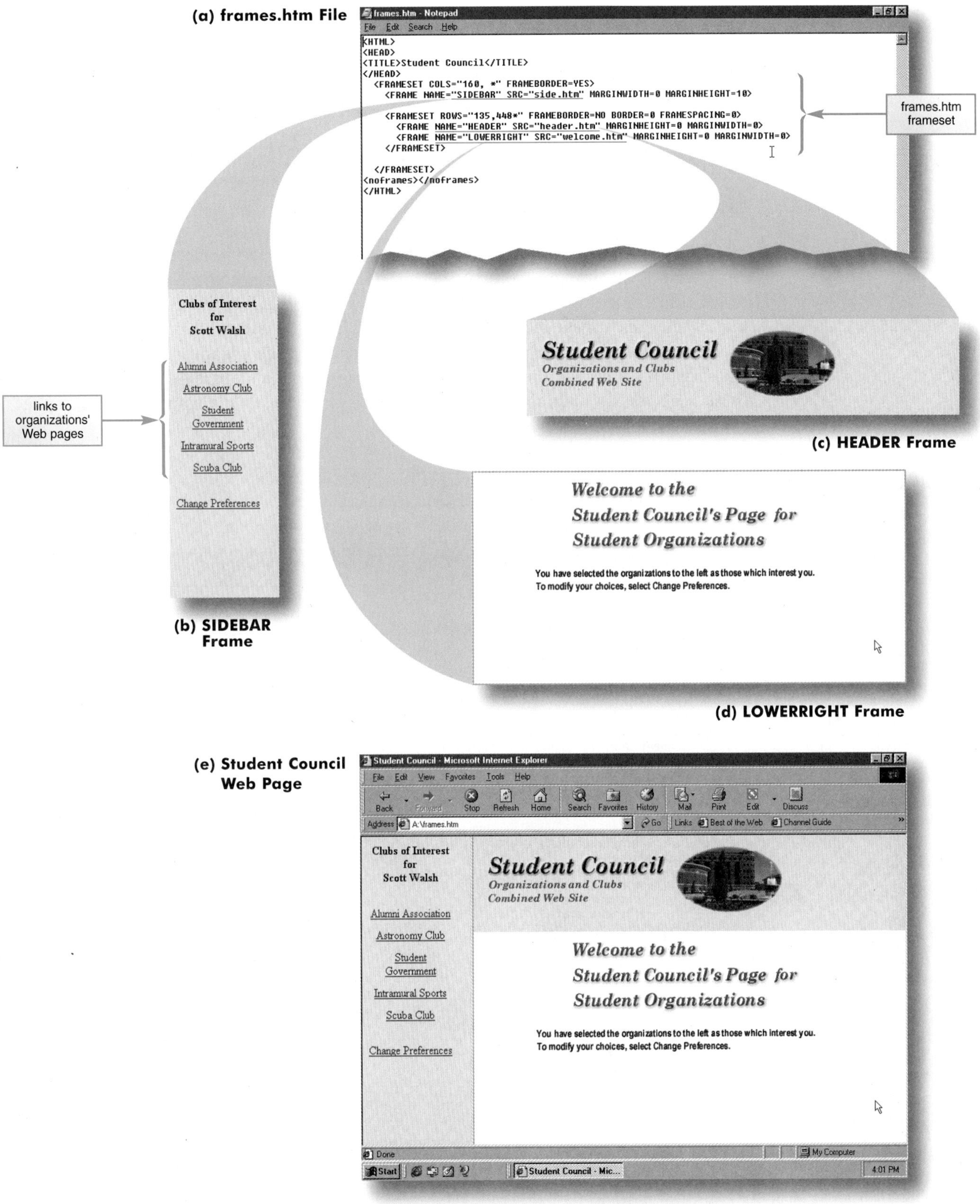

(a) frames.htm File
frames.htm - Notepad
File Edit Search Help
<HTML>
<HEAD>
<TITLE>Student Council</TITLE>
</HEAD>
<FRAMESET COLS="160, *" FRAMEBORDER=YES>
<FRAME NAME="SIDEBAR" SRC="side.htm" MARGINWIDTH=0 MARGINHEIGHT=10>
<FRAMESET ROWS="135,448*" FRAMEBORDER=NO BORDER=0 FRAMESPACING=0>
<FRAME NAME="HEADER" SRC="header.htm" MARGINHEIGHT=0 MARGINWIDTH=0>
<FRAME NAME="LOWERRIGHT" SRC="welcome.htm" MARGINHEIGHT=0 MARGINWIDTH=0>
</FRAMESET>
</FRAMESET>
<noframes></noframes>
</HTML>
frames.htm frameset
Clubs of Interest for Scott Walsh
Alumni Association
Astronomy Club
Student Government
Intramural Sports
Scuba Club
Change Preferences
links to organizations' Web pages
(b) SIDEBAR Frame
Student Council
Organizations and Clubs
Combined Web Site
(c) HEADER Frame
Welcome to the
Student Council's Page for
Student Organizations
You have selected the organizations to the left as those which interest you.
To modify your choices, select Change Preferences.
(d) LOWERRIGHT Frame
(e) Student Council Web Page
Student Council - Microsoft Internet Explorer
File Edit View Favorites Tools Help
Back Forward Stop Refresh Home Search Favorites History Mail Print Edit Discuss
Address A:\frames.htm
Go Links Best of the Web Channel Guide
Done
My Computer
Start
Student Council - Mic...
4:01 PM

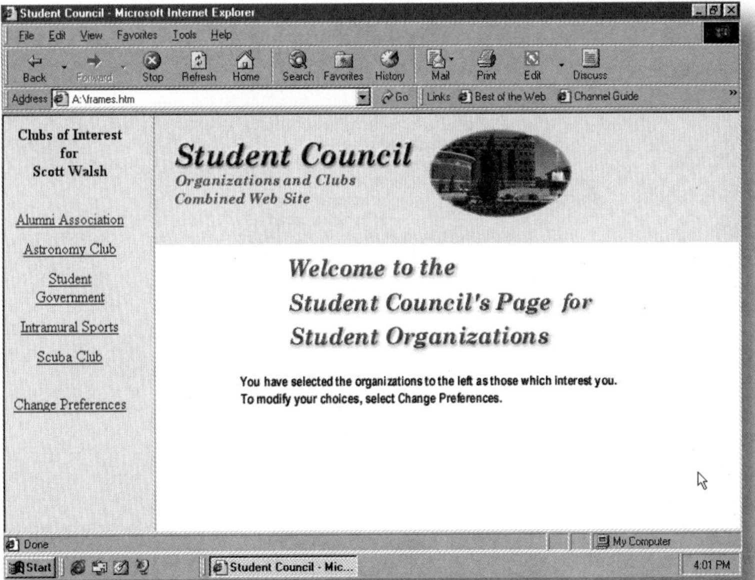

FIGURE 4-36

Each frame consists of a separate HTML file. The frames.htm file is the initial Web page that contains the links to the three HTML files that make up the three frames. Figure 4-36a shows the HTML used to display the frames. In order for you to use the frames with JavaScript, each frame must have a name.

Setting the Contents of the Display Frame

The side.htm file contains the JavaScript code for the frames. This file currently is in the background. Perform this step to bring the side.htm Notepad session to the foreground.

TO VIEW THE SIDE.HTM NOTEPAD SESSION

 Click on the side.htm Notepad button on the taskbar.

Recall that each organization that the Web page viewer selected displays in the left frame of the Student Council Web page. The JavaScript writes each organization's name in its own HTML table row. Now, an HTML ANCHOR tag needs to be added to each of these table rows. An **ANCHOR tag** links the organization's name in the left frame (Figure 4-36b on the previous page) to the organization's Web page. The organization's Web page displays in the right frame (Figure 4-36d). Perform these steps to add links that change the right side frame in the frames.htm Web page.

Steps To Add Links to Change the Frame

1. **Position the insertion point on line 78 directly after the <TD> tag.**

2. **Type** `<A HREF=" + Clubs[i].URL + "TARGET=LOWERRIGHT>` **and do not press the ENTER key.**

3. **Position the insertion point on line 78 directly before the </TD> tag.**

4. **Type** `</A>` **and do not press the ENTER key.**

An ANCHOR tag is added to the JavaScript code that links the name of each student organization to its Web page (Figure 4-37).

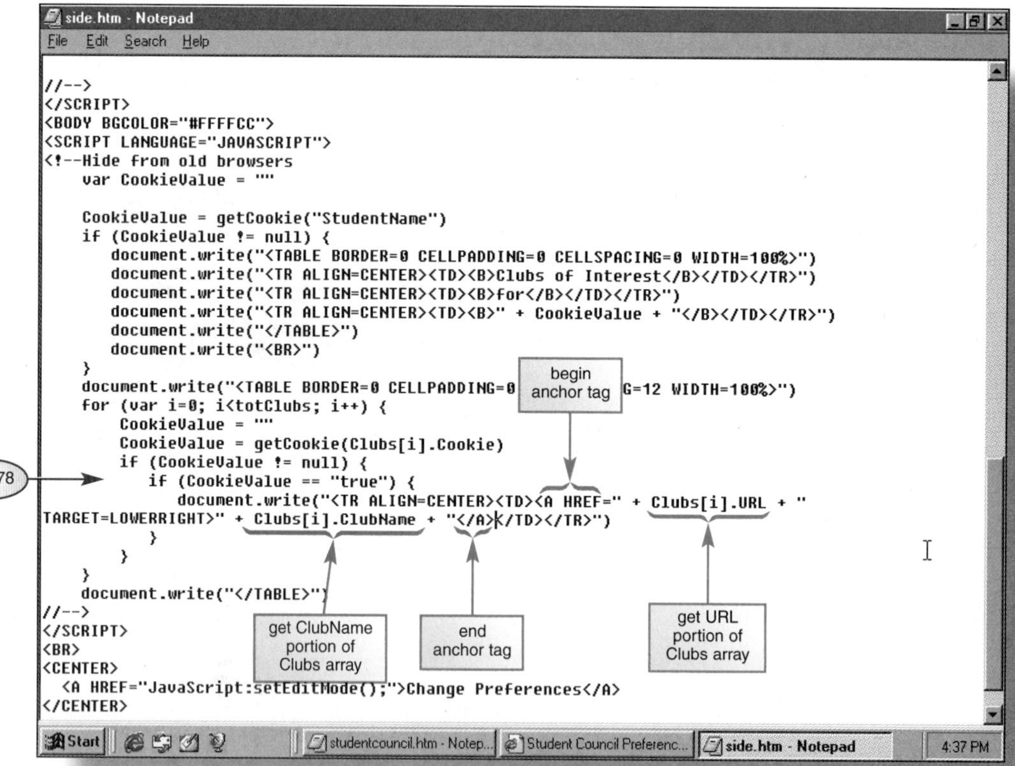

FIGURE 4-37

The URL being linked to in the ANCHOR tag is an attribute of the current array item named URL. The TARGET keyword in the ANCHOR tag tells the browser to link to the URL contained in the Clubs[i].URL variable and to display the Web page of the URL in the frame named, LOWERRIGHT.

Saving and Testing the Finished Web Page

Perform the following steps to save and test your Web page.

To Save and Test the Web Page

1. **With the JavaScript Data Disk in drive A, click File on the menu bar and then click Save.**

2. **Maximize the NotePad window containing the studentcouncil.htm file.**

3. **With the JavaScript Data Disk in drive A, click File on the menu bar and then click Save.**

4. **Start your browser and open studentcouncil.htm.**

The Student Council Web page displays with the information from the cookies displayed in the left frame (Figure 4-38).

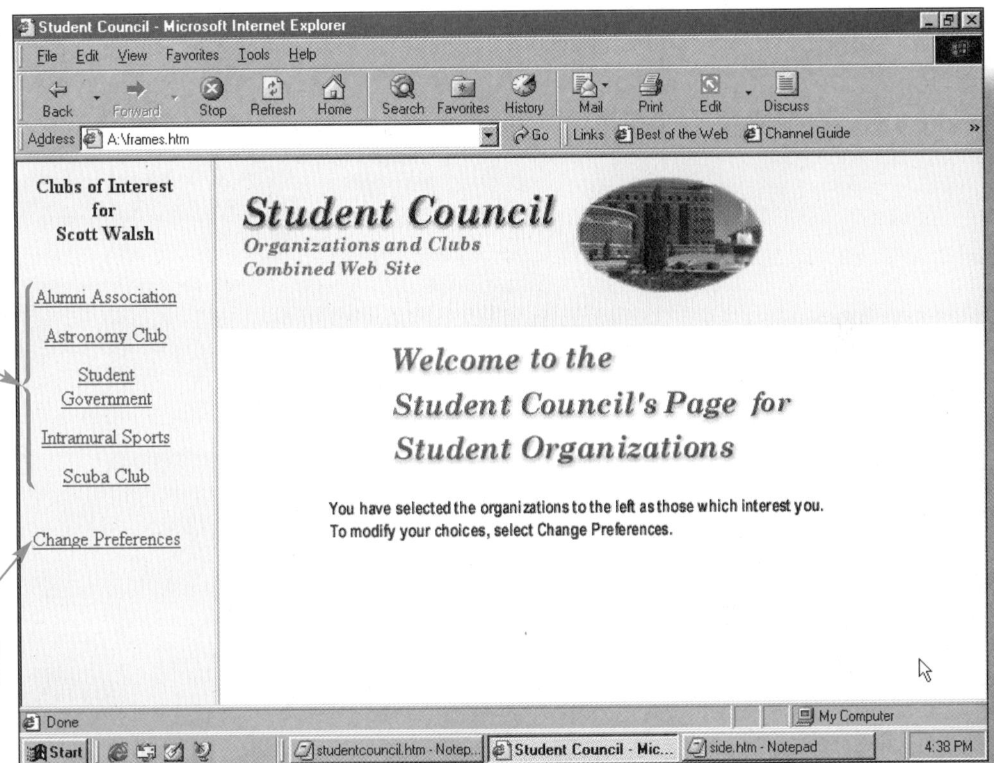

FIGURE 4-38

5 Click the Intramural Sports link.

The Intramural Sports Web page displays in the right side frame (Figure 4-39).

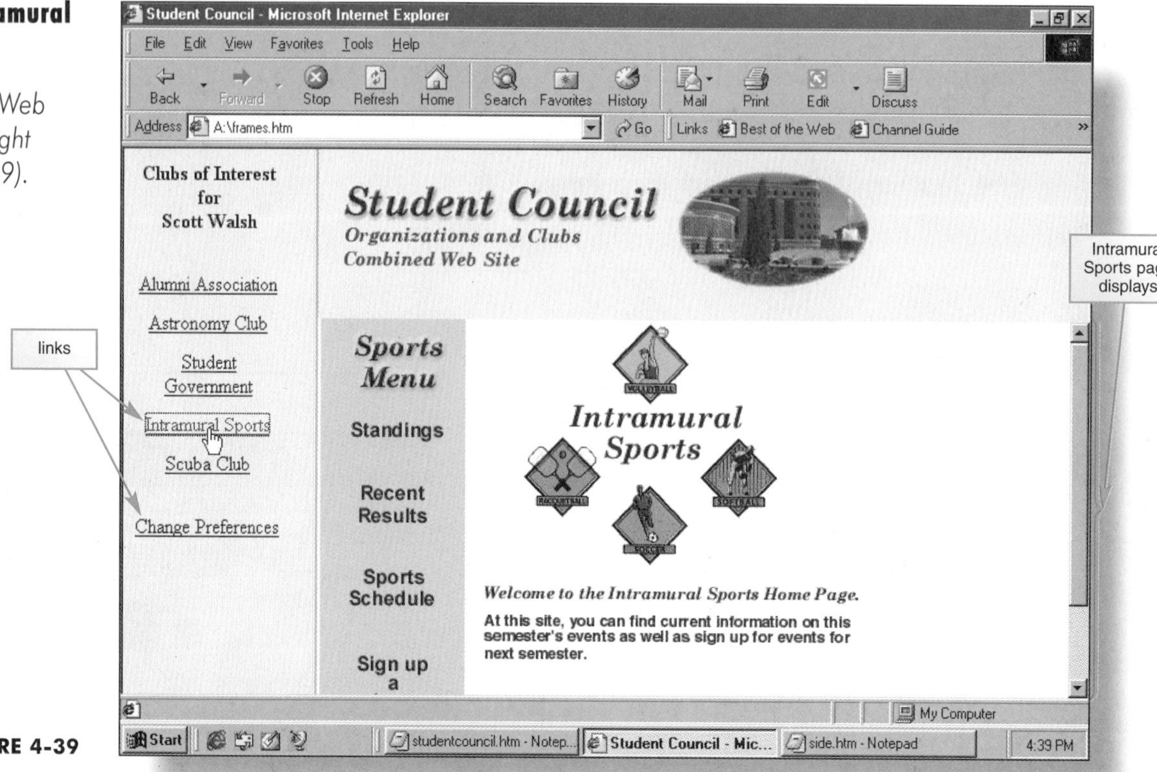

FIGURE 4-39

6 Click the Change Preferences link.

The Student Council Preferences Web page displays with the previously selected values loaded in the correct form elements (Figure 4-40).

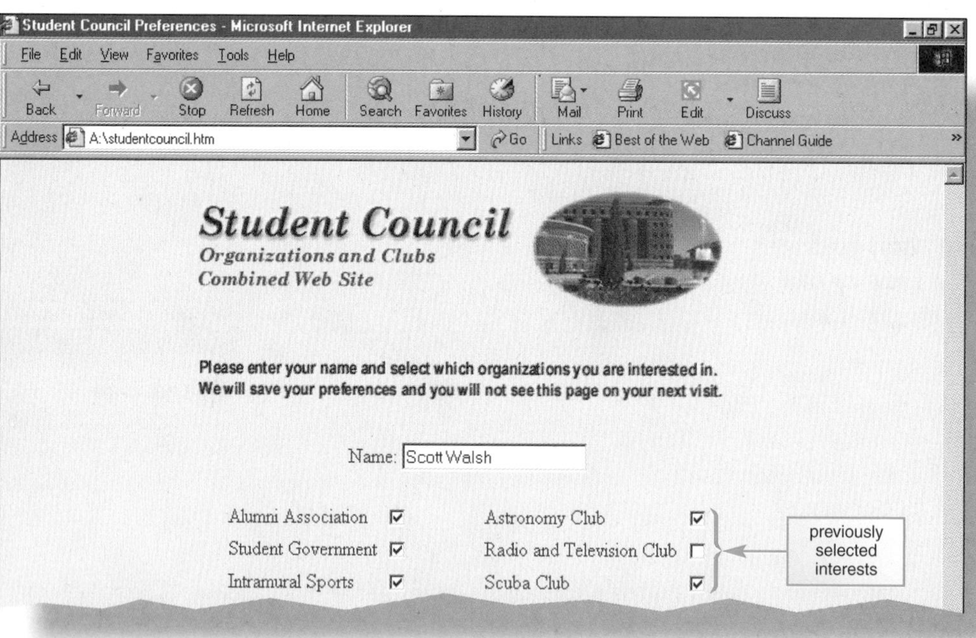

FIGURE 4-40

If the browser does not display the Web page correctly, close any error message dialog boxes and then click the Notepad button on the taskbar for the studentcouncil.htm file. Check the JavaScript code according to Figure 4-37 on page J 4.42. Correct any errors, save the file, activate the browser, and then click the Refresh button.

Project Summary

You now have created the Student Council Web page as specified by Scott Walsh. The first time users visit the page, they enter their name and select which organizations interest them. After clicking the Continue button, users view a customized version of the Student Council Web page that includes their name and a list of organizations in which they are interested. When they click a link to one of the organizations, that organization's home page displays in the right frame of the Student Council Web page. If users want to change the organizations they are interested in, they click the Change Preferences link, and they are allowed to update the information. If users want to clear the information on the Student Preferences Web page, they can click the Clear All button.

While creating the Web page, you learned how to create and read cookies using various JavaScript methods. You learned how to create and use special arrays called objects using the new and this keywords. You learned how to use JavaScript to communicate with frames using the TARGET keyword and the top object. Finally, You learned how to use the alert() method to debug your JavaScript code. You used the escape() and unescape() functions to store information correctly in a cookie.

What You Should Know

Having completed this project, you now should be able to perform the following tasks.

- Add Links to Change the Frame *(J 4.42)*
- Add the AddClub() Function *(J 4.25)*
- Add the ClubArray() Function *(J 4.24)*
- Add the deleteCookies() Function *(J 4.17)*
- Add the getCookie() Function *(J 4.28)*
- Add the InitializeValues() Function *(J 4.38)*
- Add the Remainder of the InitializeValues() Function *(J 4.39)*
- Call the deleteCookies() Function *(J 4.18)*
- Call the getCookie() Function *(J 4.16)*
- Call the InitializeValues() Function *(J 4.40)*
- Call the setEditMode() Function *(J 4.35)*
- Call the updateValues() Function *(J 4.13)*
- Create the addCookie() Function *(J 4.9)*
- Create the getCookie() Function *(J 4.15)*
- Create the updateValues() Function *(J 4.11)*
- Display the Organization List *(J 4.31)*
- Display the Student Name *(J 4.29)*
- Display the Value of the Cookie *(J 4.19)*
- Enter the Remainder of the updateValues() Function *(J 4.12)*
- Populate the Clubs Array *(J 4.26)*
- Remove the alert() Method *(J 4.21)*
- Save and Test the Web Page *(J 4.20, J 4.32, J 4.43)*
- Set the EditMode Flag *(J 4.34)*
- Start a Second Session of Notepad and Open the sidebar.htm File *(J 4.23)*
- Start Notepad and Open the council.htm File *(J 4.6)*
- Use the EditMode Flag *(J 4.36)*
- View the side.htm Notepad Session *(J 4.43)*
- View the studentcouncil.htm NotePad Session *(J 4.36)*

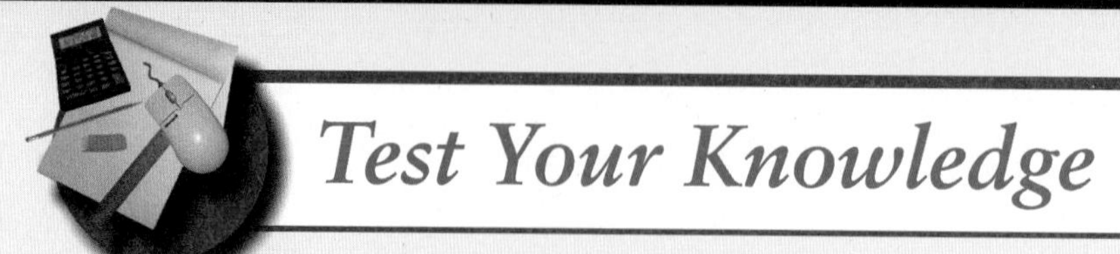

Test Your Knowledge

1 True/False

Instructions: Circle T if the statement is true or F if the statement is false.

T F 1. Cookies are stored on the Web page viewer's computer.
T F 2. A Web page can read any cookie on a user's computer.
T F 3. The escape() function causes JavaScript to exit.
T F 4. A generic function can be copied and used in other Web pages by a JavaScript programmer over and over again.
T F 5. To delete a cookie, set the expiration date of the cookie to a date in the past.
T F 6. The top property of a document refers to the top frame in the Web page.
T F 7. The number of elements in a form can be found by querying the LENGTH attribute of the form.
T F 8. The TARGET attribute of the HTML ANCHOR tag tells the browser where to send the Web page referenced in the HREF attribute.
T F 9. The this object must be used to initialize any array.
T F 10. JavaScript cannot be used to change the contents of the elements on a form.

2 Multiple Choice

Instructions: Circle the correct response.

1. If a cookie does not have an expiration date, the browser will expire the cookie __________.
   a. exactly one year from when the cookie is created
   b. as soon as the viewer leaves the Web page
   c. never; the cookie will be valid forever
   d. the next time the value of the cookie is set
2. Which JavaScript statement sets the nextWeek variable to the number of milliseconds until exactly one week from when it is executed?
   a. nextWeek.setTime(expireDate.getTime() + (7 * 60 * 60 * 24 * 365))
   b. nextWeek.setTime(expireDate.getTime() + (7 * 365 * 60 * 60 * 365 * 1000))
   c. nextWeek.setTime(expireDate.getTime() + (7 * 24 * 60 * 1000))
   d. nextWeek.setTime(expireDate.getTime() + (7 * 24 * 60 * 60 * 1000))
3. The __________ method is a useful tool for debugging JavaScript code.
   a. escape() b. alert() c. unescape() d. cookie()
4. The document.cookie property contains __________.
   a. all of the cookies stored for the current Web page
   b. all of the cookies ever stored by the browser that have not expired
   c. the cookie being sought by the TAG property
   d. the expiration date for the first cookie stored on the current Web page
5. In JavaScript, an array that has multiple pieces of data stored in each array element often is referred to as __________.
   a. this b. new c. a multidimensional array d. an object

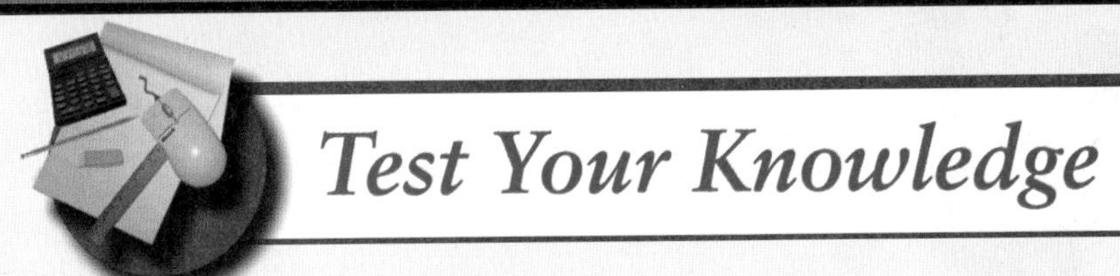

Test Your Knowledge

6. The __________ function must be used to format a date and time correctly for the expiration date of a cookie.
   a. addCookie() b. getTime() c. setDate() d. toGMTString()
7. JavaScript can delete a cookie by __________.
   a. using the document.cookie.delete method
   b. setting the expiration date to today's date
   c. setting the expiration date to a date in the past
   d. setting the value of the cookie to blank
8. The parts of a form that act as input to the form are referred to with the __________ property in JavaScript.
   a. TARGET b. index c. element d. top
9. If JavaScript code is in a frame named RIGHTSIDE and it needs to change the contents of another frame in the frameset named BOTTOM, which JavaScript code will allow the Web page viewer to update the BOTTOM frame with the HTML file named menu.html?
   a. <A HREF="menu.html" TARGET=RIGHTSIDE>Change Bottom Menu</A>
   b. top.location.href = "menu.html"
   c. RIGHTSIDE.href = "menu.html"
   d. <A HREF="menu.html" TARGET=BOTTOM>Change Bottom Menu</A>
10. Which JavaScript object references the entire current Web page?
   a. this b. TARGET c. top d. new

3 Understanding JavaScript Code Statements

Instructions: Carefully read each of the following descriptions of writing code statements to accomplish specific tasks. Record your answers on a separate sheet of paper. Number your answers to correspond to the code descriptions.

1. Write the JavaScript statements that set the cookie LastVisitDate to the current date and time, and expire the cookie in five years.
2. Write the JavaScript functions that can be used to initialize and populate an array containing the fields itemNumber, itemDescription, itemPrice, and quantity.
3. Given that a form on a Web page contains two elements at the top of the page named button1 and button2 followed by 10 check boxes named checkbox1 through checkbox10, write the JavaScript statements that read the values of the check boxes and send the values to a function named setCookieValue().
4. Given that a Web page contains two frames named TOP and BOTTOM, write the JavaScript statement in the TOP frame that creates links that change the contents in the BOTTOM frame to the pages index.htm, about.htm, and contact.htm.
5. Write the JavaScript code to test if a cookie value named Birthday exists for the current Web page. If the cookie does exist and equals today's date, then delete the cookie and use the JavaScript alert() method to write the message, Happy Birthday, in a pop-up window.

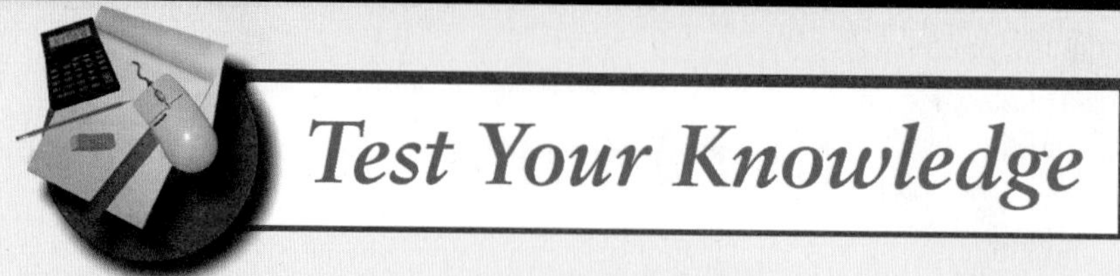

4 Using Cookies

Instructions: Figure 4-41 shows a Web page used to get the login and password for the user of a Web page. The field name for the login name is Login. The field name for the password is Password. The Login button is a submit button. The name of the check box is SavePassword. Write the JavaScript code to complete the following tasks. The HTML form name for the page is CustomerLogin. The generic functions addCookie() and getCookie() already exist in the Web page.

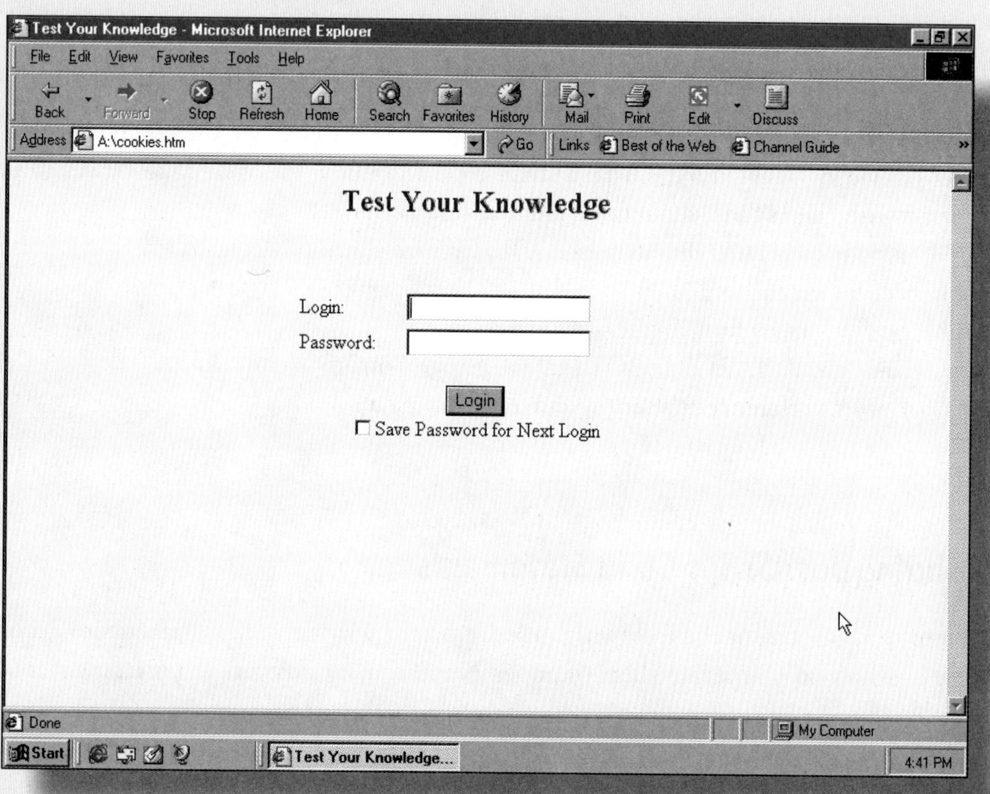

FIGURE 4-41

1. Write the event handler call in the FORM tag to a function named SaveLoginInfo() that executes when the user clicks the Login button.
2. Write the JavaScript statements in the SaveLoginInfo() function that saves the login and password fields in a cookie if the SavePassword check box is checked. Name the cookie values Login and Password.
3. Write the JavaScript statements that execute at the beginning of the Web page that looks for the cookies that you saved in step 2 and then populates the appropriate fields on the form.
4. Write the JavaScript statements in the SaveLoginInfo() function that save the value of the check box. Then, write the statements that execute when the Web page is loaded that look for this cookie and sets the value of the check box.

Use Help

1 Exploring Online Documentation

Instructions: Start your browser and then type `www.scsite.com/js/p4.htm` in the Location text box. Click the link, Appendix C, Netscape Cookies. Read the Web page to find the answers to the following questions.

1. Describe the domain attribute of a cookie and when you should use it.
2. What is the date string format for the EXPIRES attribute?
3. Describe the limitations on the size and number of cookies allowed by Netscape Navigator.
4. What happens when Netscape Navigator has reached the maximum number of cookies it will hold, and you try to add another cookie?
5. Describe the PATH attribute of a cookie and how the PATH attribute is used when retrieving a cookie.

2 Exploring Links to Other JavaScript Sites

Instructions: Start your browser and then type `www.scsite.com/js/p4.htm` in the Location text box. Complete the following tasks.

1. Click the frames link. On the first Web page, click the frames link and view the document titled, How can a script in one frame write text into another frame? Print the Web page.
2. Click the frame object link. Read about the syntax used to refer to frames. Print the portion of the Web page about the frame object.
3. Click the manipulating frames link. Use the links on the left side of the page to manipulate the other frames. Print each frame of the initial Web page.
4. Click the cookie link. Browse the Web page to learn more about cookies. Print the first page.
5. Click the arrays/objects link. Click the link to the first page of the tutorial. Read the tutorial about custom objects. Print the Web page.
6. Click the debugging link. Read about some techniques for debugging your JavaScript code. Print the Web page.
7. Hand in the printouts to your instructor.

1 Using a Cookie as a Counter

Instructions: Start Notepad. Open the Web page, newwave.htm, on the JavaScript Data Disk. If you did not download the JavaScript Data Disk, see the inside back cover for instructions for downloading the JavaScript Data Disk or see you instructor. The New Wave Furniture Company Web page has a welcome message for viewers (Figure 4-42). Write the JavaScript that displays different advertisement images on the on the welcome page on the visitor's first visit, and then every fourth visit thereafter. Use a cookie to count the number of visits to the page. The names of the advertisement images are newwave1.gif and newwave5.gif. The getCookie() and addCookie() functions already are included in the Web page.

FIGURE 4-42

1. Enter the call to the getCookie() function to get the cookie value for the VisitNumber variable.
   a. Locate the blank line after the closing curly bracket for the getCookie() function.
   b. Position the insertion point on the blank line. Press the ENTER key and then enter the following code:

```
var CookieValue = 0
CookieValue = getCookie("VisitNumber")
```

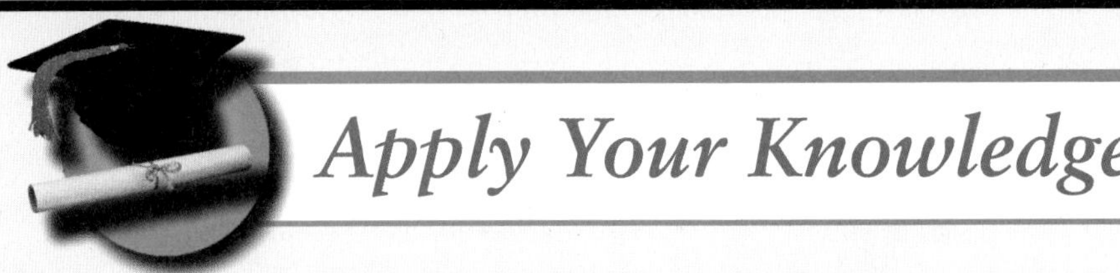

Apply Your Knowledge

2. Check the value of the VisitNumber cookie value and add 1 to it if it exists. Otherwise, set the value to 1.
   a. Position the insertion point at the end of the last line that you entered in step 1, then press the ENTER key and enter the following code (*Note:* the parseInt JavaScript function changes a string value into a numeric value):

   ```
   if (CookieValue != null) {
      CookieValue = parseInt(CookieValue) + 1
   }
   else {
      CookieValue = 1
   }
   ```

3. Enter the call to the addCookie() function that saves the CookieValue in a cookie.
   a. Position the insertion point at the end of the last line that you entered in step 1, press the ENTER key, and then enter the following code:

   ```
   addCookie("VisitNumber", CookieValue)
   ```

4. Move to the HTML BODY section and locate the <BR> tag that is located after the Welcome text on the Web page. Insert a SCRIPT section.
5. Inside the SCRIPT section from step 4, enter the following code to read the cookie and display the appropriate advertisement, if necessary:

   ```
   var CookieValue = ""

   CookieValue = getCookie("VisitNumber")
   if (CookieValue != null) {
      if (CookieValue == 1) {
         document.write("<IMG SRC=newwave1.gif>")
         }

         if (CookieValue == 5) {
            document.write("<IMG SRC=newwave5.gif>")
            addCookie("VisitNumber", 1)
         }
      }
   ```

6. Save the HTML file using the file name, newwavesolution.htm, on the JavaScript Data Disk in drive A.
7. Start your browser. Open the file a:\newwavesolution.htm to test the JavaScript code. The newwave1.gif advertisement should display the first time. Click the Refresh button on your browser toolbar several times. The newwave5.gif advertisement should display the fourth time you click the Refresh button. If any errors occur, double-check steps 1 through 7 and then save and test again.
8. Print the Web page and the HTML file. Hand in the printouts to your instructor.

1 Displaying Newsletter Item Links in a Frame Using an Array

Problem: Ravi Gupta writes a monthly newsletter for Stride Accounting Service about its services for small businesses. The company wants to put the newsletter on a Web page. Ravi has asked you to create a Web page that will allow easy updates for all of the news items in the newsletter each month. The Web page should display in frames, as in Figure 4-43. When the user clicks a news item in the left frame, the item displays in the right frame.

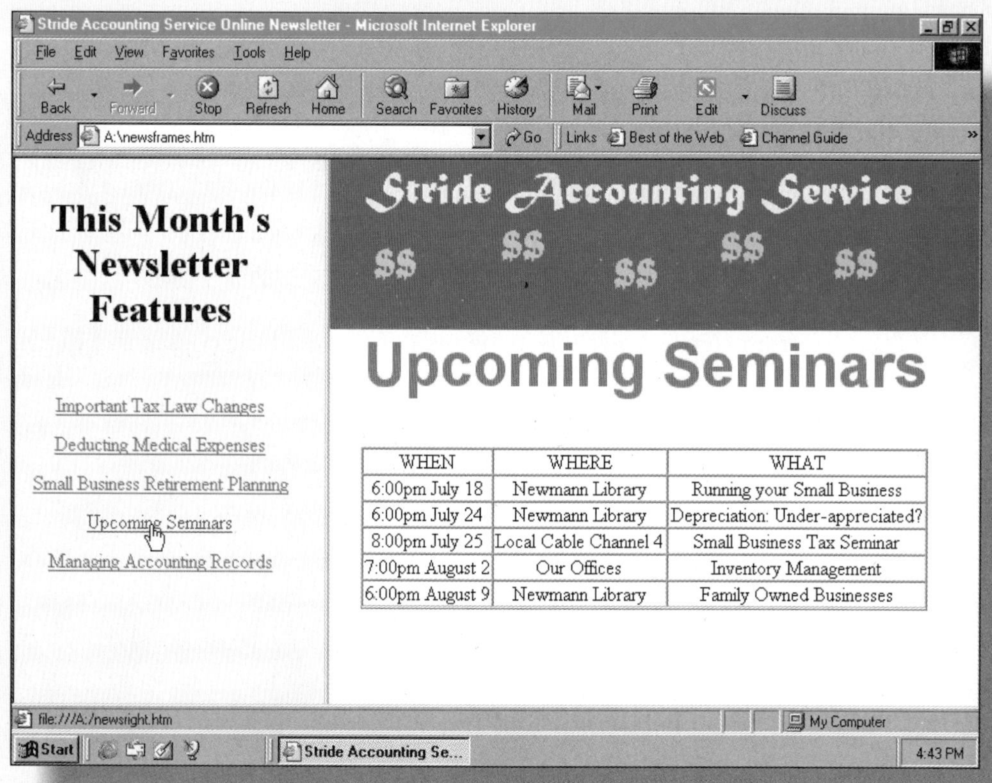

FIGURE 4-43

Instructions: Start your browser and Notepad. Using Notepad, open the news.htm file from the JavaScript Data Disk that is the HTML file for the left frame on the Web page. See the inside back cover for instructions for downloading the JavaScript Data Disk or see you instructor.

1. Create the function that will initialize a new array that will store each newsletter news item and its URL. Position the insertion point on line 2 and then enter the following lines of code:

```
function NewsArray(length) {
   var i = 0;
   this.length2 = length;
   for (i=1; i<length; i++)
     this[i] = 0;
   return this;
}
```

2. Create the function that will add a newsletter news item to the array. The function should accept a headline and associated URL. Position the insertion point on line 9 and then enter the following lines of code:

```
    <SCRIPT LANGUAGE="JAVASCRIPT">
 <!--Hide from old browsers
    function AddNewsItem(Headline, URL) {
       this.Headline = Headline;
       this.URL = URL;
       return this;
    }
```

3. Create the array that will store the news items by calling the functions created in steps 1 and 2 by entering the following lines of code on line 16:

```
    var totNewsItems = 5;
    var NewsItems = NewsArray(totNewsItems);

    NewsItems[0] = new AddNewsItem("Important Tax Law Changes", "construct.htm");
    NewsItems[1] = new AddNewsItem("Deducting Medical Expenses", "construct.htm");
    NewsItems[2] = new AddNewsItem("Small Business Retirement Planning", "construct.htm");
    NewsItems[3] = new AddNewsItem("Upcoming Seminars", "newsright.htm");
    NewsItems[4] = new AddNewsItem("Managing Accounting Records", "construct.htm");
//-->
</SCRIPT>
```

4. In the BODY portion of the Web page, enter the code that will display the array items constructed in step 3 by entering the following lines of code in the blank line after the </CENTER> HTML tag:

```
<SCRIPT LANGUAGE="JAVASCRIPT">
<!--Hide from old browsers
   document.write("<TABLE BORDER=0 CELLPADDING=0 CELLSPACING=12 WIDTH=100%>");
   for (var i=0; i<totNewsItems; i++) {
     document.write("<TR ALIGN=CENTER><TD><A HREF=" + NewsItems[i].URL + “ TARGET=LOWERRIGHT>"
+ NewsItems[i].Headline + "</A></TD></TR>");
   }
   document.write("</TABLE>");
//-->
</SCRIPT>
```

5. Save the HTML file using the file name, newssolution.htm, on the JavaScript Data Disk in drive A.
6. Activate the browser. Open the file, a:\newsframes.htm, to test the JavaScript code. If any errors occur, double-check steps 1 through 5 and test again. If no errors occur, print the Web page, then return to Notepad to print the HTML file. Hand in the printouts to your instructor.

2 Saving and Clearing Form Data in a Cookie

Problem: Shelly Franklin is the administrator of the prenatal services at County Hospital. Her program offers a variety of educational classes for expectant parents. Shelly has found that expectant parents have many appointments that they must keep regarding the coming baby. She would like to help the parents remember their appointments by letting them enter many of these dates on a Web page. Shelly plans to begin with the dates shown in Figure 4-44. The user is allowed to enter dates and also to clear the dates from the form.

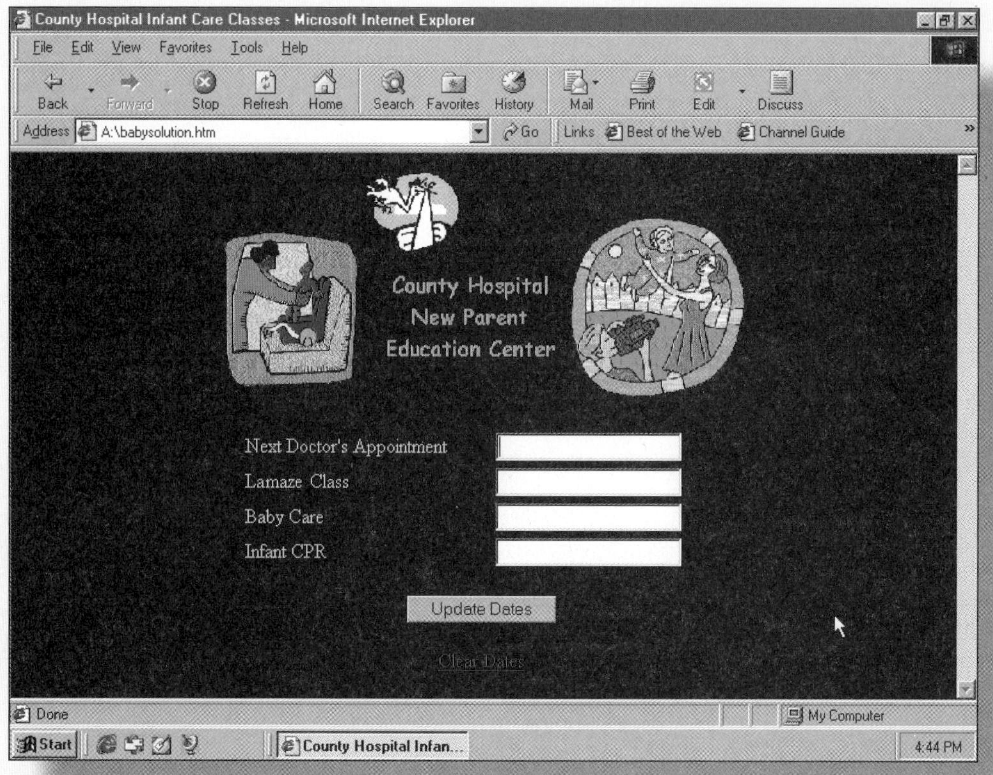

FIGURE 4-44

Instructions: Start your browser and Notepad. Using Notepad, open the baby.htm file from the JavaScript Data Disk. Perform the following tasks. The generic getCookie() and addCookie() functions have already been added to the Web page for you.

1. Place the onSubmit event handler in the FORM tag before the > on line 44, which calls a function named saveDates() to save the entered dates in a cookie, by entering onsubmit="return saveDates()" as the code.
2. Write the JavaScript that creates a line in an HTML table for each date that the Web page should save by entering the following code starting with the blank line of line 47.

```
<SCRIPT LANGUAGE="JAVASCRIPT">
<!--Hide from old browsers
   var currentCookie = ""
   document.write("<TR><TD>Next Doctor's Appointment</TD>")
   currentCookie = getCookie("DrAppt")
   document.write("<TD><INPUT TYPE=text NAME=DrAppt VALUE=" + currentCookie + "></TD></TR>")
   document.write("<TR><TD>Lamaze Class</TD>")
   currentCookie = getCookie("Lamaze")
   document.write("<TD><INPUT TYPE=text NAME=Lamaze VALUE=" + currentCookie + "></TD></TR>")
   document.write("<TR><TD>Baby Care</TD>")
   currentCookie = getCookie("BabyCare")
   document.write("<TD><INPUT TYPE=text NAME=BabyCare VALUE=" + currentCookie + "></TD></TR>")
   document.write("<TR><TD>Infant CPR</TD>")
   currentCookie = getCookie("InfantCPR")
   document.write("<TD><INPUT TYPE=text NAME=InfantCPR VALUE=" + currentCookie + "></TD></TR>")

//-->
</SCRIPT>
```

3. Write the function saveDates() that saves each date in the Web page when the user clicks the Update Dates button. Position the insertion point on line 36 and then enter the following code followed by pressing the ENTER key.

```
function saveDates() {
   addCookie("DrAppt", document.BabyDates.DrAppt.value)
   addCookie("Lamaze", document.BabyDates.Lamaze.value)
   addCookie("BabyCare", document.BabyDates.BabyCare.value)
   addCookie("InfantCPR", document.BabyDates.InfantCPR.value)
}
```

4. Create an HTML ANCHOR tag that calls a JavaScript function named clearDates(), which will clear out the date fields on the form by entering the following code in the blank line before the first </CENTER> HTML tag:

```
<A HREF="JavaScript:clearDates();">Clear Dates</A>
```

5. Write the function clearDates() that clears each date field in the Web page when the user clicks the Clear Dates link. Position the insertion point on line 42 and then enter the following code:

```
function clearDates() {
   document.BabyDates.DrAppt.value = ""
   document.BabyDates.Lamaze.value = ""
   document.BabyDates.BabyCare.value = ""
   document.BabyDates.InfantCPR.value = ""
   saveDates()
}
```

6. Save the HTML file using the file name, babysolution.htm, on the JavaScript Data Disk in drive A.
7. Activate the browser. Open the file, a:\babysolution.htm, to test the JavaScript code. If any errors occur, double-check steps 1 through 5 and test again. If no errors occur, print the Web page, and return to Notepad to print the HTML file. Hand in the printouts to your instructor.

3 Tracking Investments

Problem: You are an intern at Greene Financial Services, a small stock brokerage firm. You have been asked to create a Web page for the company's small investors to keep track of their stock holdings. The Web page must accept the users' stocks they want to track, the number of shares they own, the purchase date, the purchase price, and the current price. Users can track up to five stocks in their portfolio, and a total portfolio value is also displayed. Figure 4-45 shows the layout of the Web page. The Web page HTML already contains the generic getCookie() and addCookie() functions.

Instructions: Start your browser and Notepad. Use Notepad to open the greene.htm file on the JavaScript Data Disk. Perform the following tasks.

1. In the HEAD section after the getCookie() function, write a function that adds a cookie for each item in the stock table that the user must enter. Name the function saveStocks(). Name the cookie values Symbol0, Shares0, Price0, Symbol1, Shares1, Price1, Symbol2, Shares2, Price2, Symbol3, Shares3, Price3, Symbol4, Shares4, and Price4.
2. Call this function with the onSubmit event handler in the Stocks form.
3. Under the </TR> HTML tag, enter a new SCRIPT section for JavaScript code. Initialize variables Symbol, Shares, Price, Value, and totValue. Then write a For loop that reads each cookie and sets the values to blank or 0 if there is no cookie value. Calculate the Value variable based on the Shares variable and Price. Also, for each stock, add the Value to the variable totValue.
4. Within the For loop, write the code that writes an HTML table row for each stock. Each row should display the symbol, number of shares, price, and value of the stock.
5. After the For loop, write an HTML table row to display the totValue variable.
6. Save the HTML file using the file name, greenesolution.htm, on the JavaScript Data Disk in drive A.
7. Activate the browser. Open the file, a:\greenesolution.htm, to test the JavaScript code. If any errors occur, double-check steps 1 through 5 and test again. If no errors occur, print the Web page, and return to Notepad to print the HTML file. Hand in the printouts to your instructor.

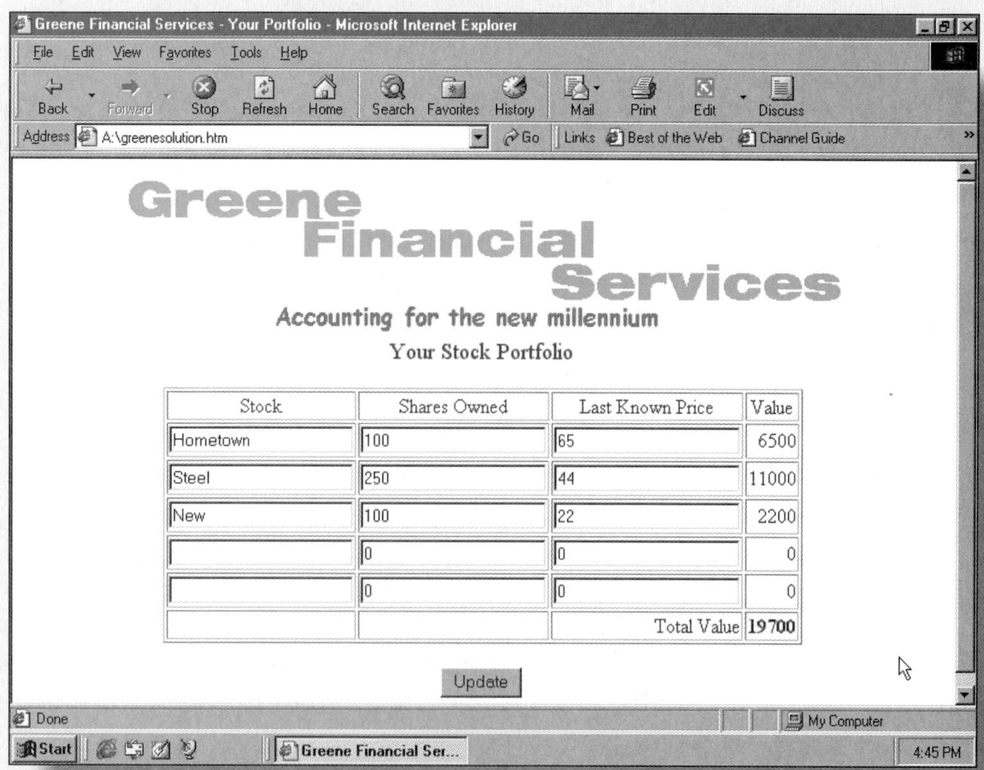

FIGURE 4-45

The difficulty of these case studies varies:
▶ are the least difficult; ▶▶ are more difficult; and ▶▶▶ are the most difficult.

1 ▶ Your friend owns a local computer store. His Web page has become very popular and several local merchants have purchased advertising on the page. He wants visitors to see different advertisements on each visit to the page. Each advertisement is a graphic image. You tell him that the easiest way to solve the problem is to use cookies to keep track of the last advertisement that the viewer saw, and then show the next advertisement the next visit. When the last ad has been seen, the cycle begins again with the first ad. Use the concepts and techniques presented in this project to create the Web page.

2 ▶ A local automobile dealer has a list of links to Web pages that link to the various car manufacturers' Web pages for each individual model that he sells. He wants you to create a framed Web page that contains a list of links for all the automobile models on the left side of the Web page. When the Web page visitor clicks a link, the Web page for that model displays in another frame on the right side of the browser. Use the concepts and techniques presented in this project to create the Web page.

3 ▶▶ The teachers at the local high school publish Web pages of the current day's assignments. Students or their parents can go online and view the current homework assignments for their classes. As of now, users must find each class in a large list every day in order to check the homework assignments. The principal has asked that you create a starting page for the parents where they can select all of the classes they want to monitor. After doing so, when parents visit the Web page, they would see a list of only the classes they have chosen. They also would have the option to edit this list. Use the concepts and techniques presented in this project to create the Web page.

4 ▶▶ Your professor has written an online study guide for her class. The study guide consists of 12 chapters of materials, each of which has its own Web page. She has asked you to write a table of contents Web page with links to each of the chapters. She would like the table of contents Web page to keep track of the last time the student went to each particular chapter and how many times the student visited that chapter, as well. The page should display a table including columns for the chapter title, the last date and time the student visited the page, and the number of times the student visited the page. The chapter title in the table should be a link to the Web page containing that particular chapter. Use the concepts and techniques presented in this project to create the Web page.

5 ▶▶▶ The local girls' softball league keeps Web pages that include statistics of all of the games in the conference. The head of the league would like you to design a Web page where a fan can monitor his or her favorite team. The viewer of the Web page needs to be able to select a favorite team and be able to change preferences, if desired. After the fan selects a preferred team, the Web page displays a list of games in a frame. The list includes links to games played only by the user's favorite team. When a link is clicked, the statistics for that particular game show in another frame on the page. Use the concepts and techniques presented in this project to create the Web page.

JavaScript

Using Objects to Create a Shopping Cart Application

OBJECTIVES

You will have mastered the material in this project when you can:

- Use a hidden frame for JavaScript code
- Explain why hidden frames are useful
- Explain the concept of a JavaScript object
- Create an object using the Object data type
- Write a method for an object
- Use the delete operator to delete an object
- Use the With statement to reference an object
- Use the For-in statement to loop through the elements of an object
- Use the history method of the document object to navigate to Web pages
- Write to a window object from a document
- Refer to windows from other windows
- Determine the browser being used with the navigator object
- Detect keystrokes in a Web page

Take an Order

Unordinary Dell Directs Online Computer Sales

Michael Dell was not an ordinary kid. When he was 8-years-old, he applied for a high school General Equivalency Diploma. When he was 9, he applied for his own checking account. When he was 12, he earned $2,000 creating a 12-page catalog and conducting a national mail order stamp auction. When he was 13, he invested successfully in stocks, gold, and silver.

As a freshman biology major at the University of Texas in 1983, Michael Dell had a vision: to sell computers directly to consumers without using dealers or stores. He started assembling computers in his dormatory, much to the chagrin of his parents and

roommate. His parents told him to "concentrate on your studies. Nothing will ever become of you if you don't get a degree." His roommate was so frustrated with seeing computer components everywhere that he stacked computers in front of the door to Dell's room — while Dell was sleeping inside.

So Dell took the hint and quit selling. This cold-turkey action lasted only one month. "I couldn't stand it," he says. With $1,000 in savings and unlimited passion, he channeled his energy into forming the Dell Computer Corporation in May 1984.

Dell expanded his vision to form one of the fastest-growing technology companies. In 1992, he was the youngest CEO to appear on the Fortune 500 list, and his computers and peripherals are found in two-thirds of America's Fortune 500 companies. Dell Computer Corporation is the world's leading direct computer systems company with nearly 30,000 employees worldwide.

The Dell Web site (www.dell.com) is part of the company's success. Since its inception in 1994, consumers have flocked to the site to configure, price, review, and order the precise custom computer system for their needs and budget. More than two million people visit the Web site each week, and they are spending more than $30 million per day online there, which accounts for nearly 40 percent of Dell's total revenue.

In JavaScript Project 5, you will create a similar Web page that allows Web page visitors to place custom orders with Val-U Computers for various systems and peripherals. Using objects, you will create a shopping cart application, and learn how to maintain the list of items that shoppers purchase.

Most Web pages created today with ordering capabilities use the shopping cart where individuals can build a list of items they want to buy from a company's Web site. As the customers make their selections, the components are added to the online shopping cart. When they are ready to place their order, they request a printable order form that lists the items in the shopping cart and the total cost.

Whether customers are shopping at Dell Computer Corporation or at Val-U Computers, they find their online experience convenient and informative. Certainly both these Web sites can take – and deliver – an order.

JavaScript

Using Objects to Create a Shopping Cart Application

CASE PERSPECTIVE

Val-U Computers sells personal computers to small- and medium-sized businesses. Jack Winters and his staff take orders for new computers by telephone. The company sells up-to-date system configurations that change as new computer chips are introduced. The prices also change on a regular basis. Most orders consist of several computers of various configurations. Customers choose from options such as the type of motherboard, amount of memory, size of the hard drive, and whether the computer has a network card or a modem.

As a new employee, you notice that the sales people spend too much time on the telephone taking orders and explaining options to the customer. You suggest to Jack that a Web page where customers can create orders online may lighten the burden on the staff. After creating the orders, the customers then submit them to Val-U Computers by fax or mail. The Web page should give the customers all of the options for the computers, pricing information, and a printable order form. Because of your experience with JavaScript, Jack asks you to do the programming to make this Web page a reality.

Introduction

In Project 5, you will extend your knowledge of the concepts presented in previous projects. The type of Web site you will produce is known as a shopping cart. **Shopping carts** allow users to build a list of items they want to purchase from a company's Web site. You will learn how to create and maintain the list of items that shoppers purchase.

In the previous project, you learned how to combine JavaScript with HTML. As a Web site becomes more complex with many windows and frames, it becomes difficult for the programmer to keep track of all of the JavaScript in the various HTML files. Hidden frames allow you to place all of your JavaScript in a single location for a Web site. They are hidden because the JavaScript is kept in a frame on the Web page that is not viewable by the user. Figure 5-1a shows the Val-U Computers Shopping Page. The Web page contains two frames, with only one visible. The hidden frame actually exists hidden above the page in Figure 5-1a and Figure 5-1b.

From your work in Projects 3 and 4, you learned that arrays allow you to store collections of similar types of data. Sometimes, however, you do not know ahead of time how many array items are needed. An object is a special type of data that is defined by the programmer. In this project, you will use an object to define each of the selected items that a user wants to purchase. You also will learn how to maintain the objects in the array. After users finish shopping, they display the contents of their shopping cart (Figure 5-1b) and if necessary, modify the contents.

Different Web browsers handle some HTML tags and JavaScript commands in different ways. You will learn how to identify which Web browser a Web page visitor is using. With this information, you will write the JavaScript code that will capture a keystroke on the shopping cart page (Figure 5-1a) and allow the user to view the shopping cart by using a shortcut key rather than a mouse click.

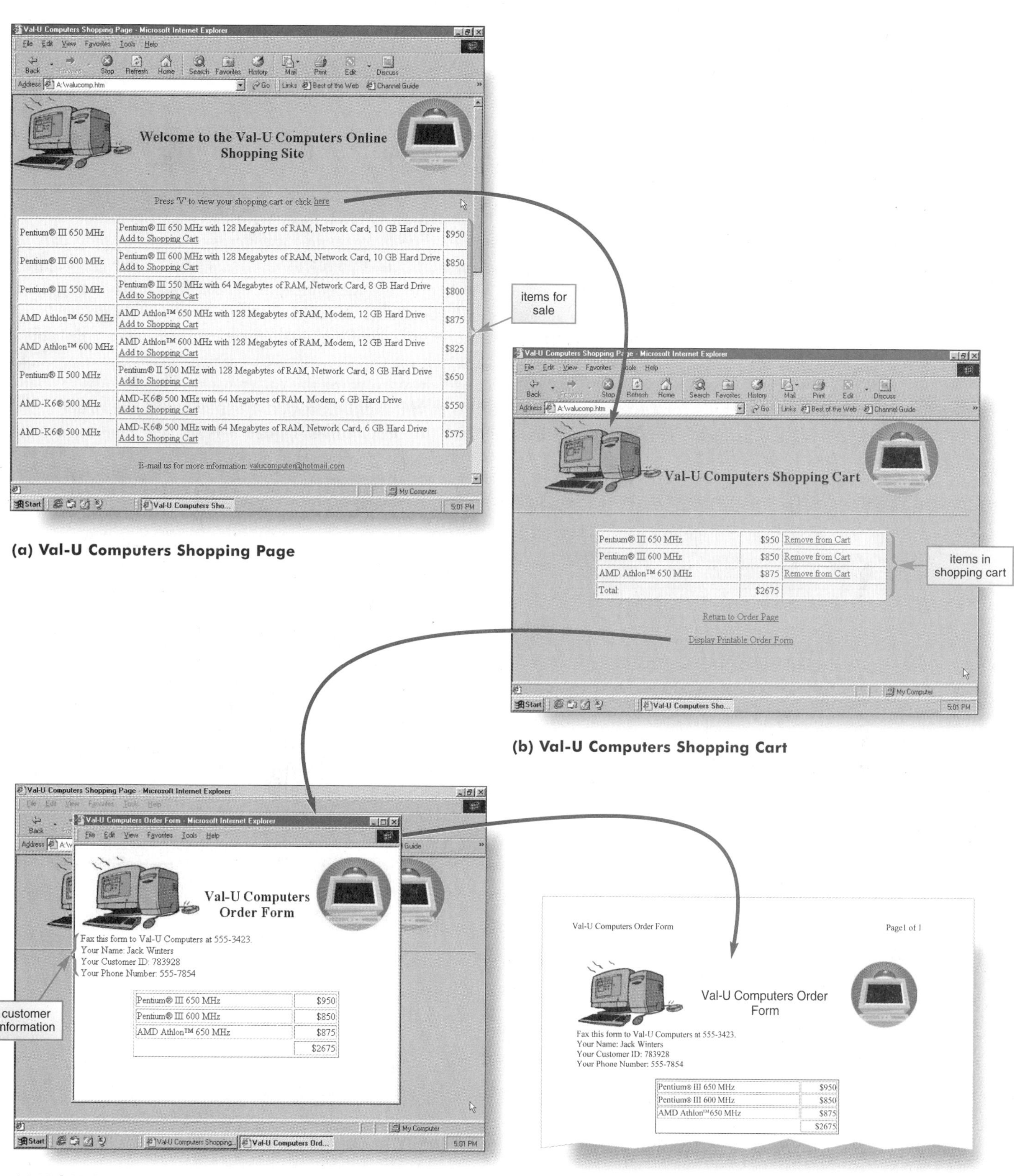

(a) Val-U Computers Shopping Page

(b) Val-U Computers Shopping Cart

(c) Val-U Computers Order Form

(d) Printed Order Form

FIGURE 5-1

Online Shopping

Some Web sites allow businesses to set up their own online shopping areas. This helps businesses keep down the cost of developing an online shopping area, and often gives customers a central area at which to shop. For more information about online shopping, visit www.scsite.com/js/p5.htm and then click Online Shopping.

In Project 2, you learned how to create a pop-up window. This project illustrates using JavaScript to communicate between the Web page and a pop-up window. In Figure 5-1c on the previous page, the pop-up window has been created using data stored in the hidden frame. After users display the window, they use the browser menu to print the order form (Figure 5-1d on the previous page).

Project Five — Val-U Computers Shopping Web Site

After your discussion with Jack, you determine the following needs.

Needs: Jack already has prepared an HTML page with the list of products that currently are sold by the company. The links to add the items to the shopping cart must be added (Figure 5-1a on the previous page). After users select their items, they view their shopping cart on another Web page (Figure 5-1b on the previous page). This Web page allows the users to delete items from the shopping cart or go back to the shopping page to make more selections. Finally, the users can obtain a printable copy of their order by clicking a link on the shopping cart page. When the user clicks this link, an alert box tells the user how to print the order form. The Web page then asks for customer information so that it can be properly displayed on the order form. The Web page then displays the order form (Figure 5-1c).

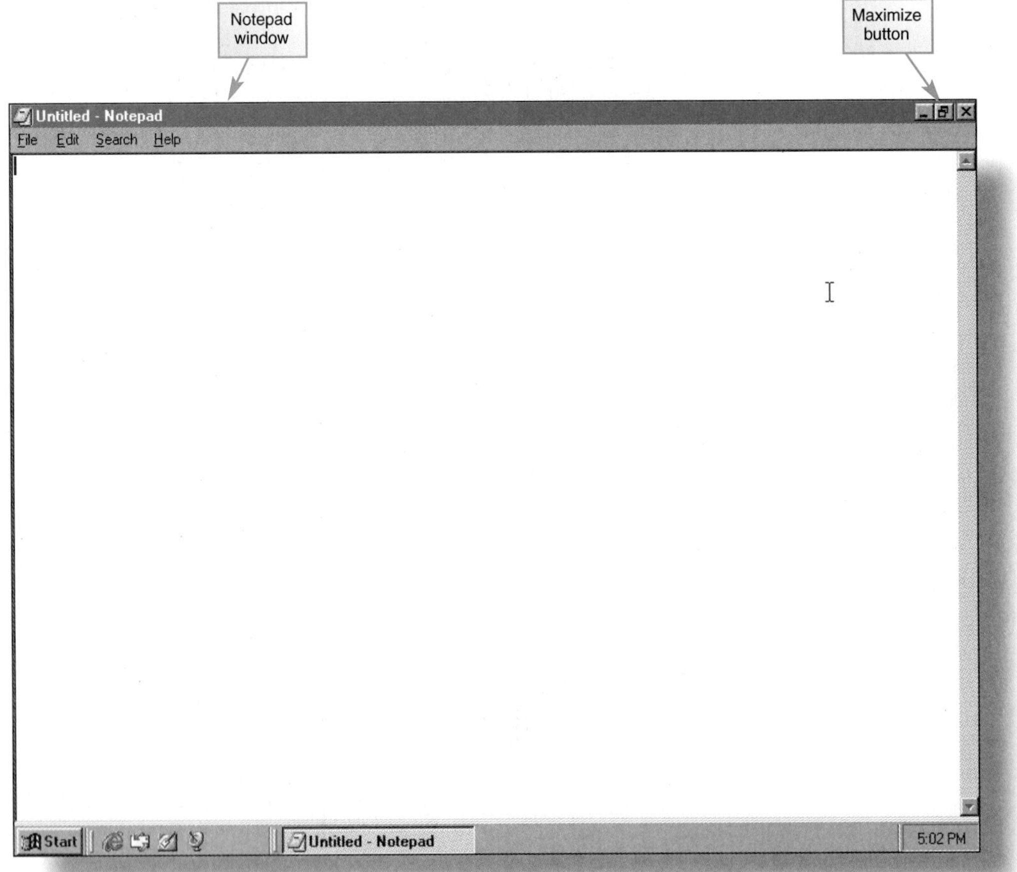

FIGURE 5-2

Starting Notepad

The first step is to start a new document in Notepad by following these steps.

TO START A NEW NOTEPAD DOCUMENT

1. Start Notepad.

2. When the Notepad window displays, click the Maximize button.

The Notepad window displays (Figure 5-2).

Creating an Object in a Hidden Frame

In the previous project, you learned how to store information in cookies for future use. As a user navigates around a Web site, it often is necessary to store information for short-term use. A **hidden frame** is an area of a Web page that is invisible to the user but can remain in place for use by JavaScript. JavaScript can be placed in hidden frames so common functions can be accessed from multiple Web pages within a Web site. In addition, data can be stored in the hidden frame and accessed by multiple pages within a Web site.

Storing data in hidden frames offers many advantages over the use of cookies. First, they are easier to use because each Web page does not need to read and write the cookie data each time the browser loads a Web page. The data remains intact in the hidden frame as the user navigates the Web site. Hidden frames also allow the Web page programmer to use complex data, such as objects, more easily. Data stored in hidden frames, however, is lost when the user visits another Web site or shuts down his or her browser.

Creating the Hidden Frame

You create a hidden frame in the same manner that you create any other frame. The only difference is that you set the size of the hidden frame to zero. You do not use JavaScript to create the hidden frame. It is only a matter of using the proper HTML to set up the frameset.

Table 5-1 shows the HTML tags used to create the frameset that includes the hidden frame, named HIDDEN, and the main Web page frame, named MAIN.

Hidden Frames

Hidden frames are useful for storing JavaScript code and data. They are not completely hidden from the user, however. Various ways exist for a Web page visitor to look at the JavaScript code that you store in a hidden frame. For more information about hidden frames and security, visit www.scsite.com/js/p5.htm and then click Hidden Frames.

Table 5-1

LINE CODE

```
<HTML>
<TITLE>Val-U Computers Shopping Page</TITLE>
  <FRAMESET ROWS="0,*", FRAMEBORDER=NO BORDER=0 FRAMESPACING=0>
    <FRAME NAME="HIDDEN" SRC="javascript.htm">
    <FRAME NAME="MAIN" SRC="order.htm" MARGINHEIGHT=0 MARGINWIDTH=0>
  </FRAMESET>
</HTML>
```

To add the HTML code for the frames, perform the steps on the next page.

To Add the HTML Code for the Frames

1. **Position the insertion point on line 1.**

2. **Enter the JavaScript code shown in Table 5-1 on the previous page.**

The HTML code displays (Figure 5-3).

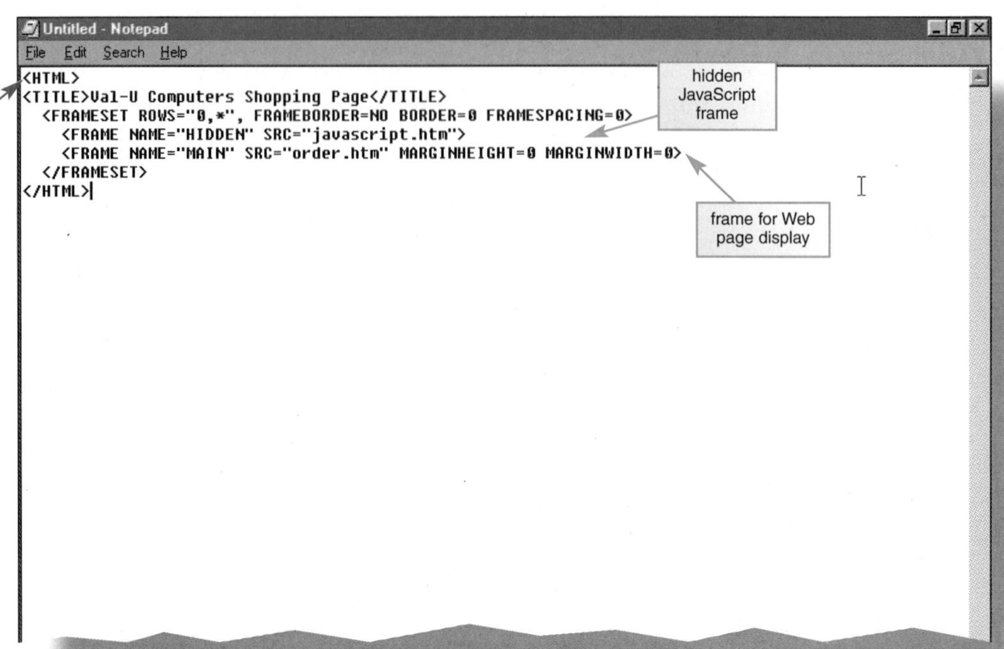

FIGURE 5-3

In line 3, the ROWS parameter in the frameset sets the top frame to 0 pixels in height. The second frame is set to a size of **asterisk** (*), meaning that it is allowed to take up the remaining portion of the browser window. In this case, the asterisk causes the browser to leave the entire browser window to the second frame. The frame named HIDDEN will not display, but it still will be available to contain JavaScript variables and functions.

Users access this HTML file as the main Web page for the Val-U Computers Web site. All of the Web pages for the Web site display in the frame named MAIN. The two frames remain in place as the user navigates around the Web site. The user does not perceive that the Web page is a framed Web page.

The next step is to save the frameset as an HTML file named valucomp.htm.

TO SAVE THE VALUCOMP.HTM FILE

1. With the JavaScript Data Disk in drive A, click File on the menu bar and then click Save As.
2. Type `a:\valucomp.htm` in the File name text box and then click the Save button.
3. Click the Close button on the Notepad title bar.

The valucomp.htm file is saved and the Notepad window closes.

Creating the ShoppingCart Object

In previous projects, you used arrays and arrays of objects to store similar types of data together. In addition to declaring a variable as an array, you can declare it as an object. An **object** is a type of variable that contains both properties and methods. Recall from the Introduction that a **property** is a value and a **method** is an action. Methods are assigned to objects the same way properties are assigned. Where a property is assigned a value, however, a method is assigned a function. JavaScript relies heavily on objects. Variables, functions, windows, and even arrays are all objects.

When declaring a variable as an object, usually it is suitable to declare the variable as an array as well. The only technical difference between declaring a variable as an object versus an array is that an array always has a length property. That is, you can always use the length property to find out how many items are in the array. The real difference between declaring something as an array versus an object is in how you will use the variable. Table 5-2 illustrates certain criteria that you can use to determine whether to declare a variable as an object or an array.

Object-Oriented Programming

While this book gives an overview of the concepts of objects and object-oriented programming, it is a complex but useful topic. JavaScript allows you to use concepts such as inheritance and operator overload in developing Web sites. Many Web sites and books are dedicated to object-oriented programming that can further enhance your knowledge of object-oriented programming.

Table 5-2 Determining Whether to Declare a Variable as an Object or an Array

IF YOU NEED TO...	DECLARE THE VARIABLE AS AN...
Add a method to the variable	Object
Know how many elements are in the variable	Array
Use identifiers other than integers to access the elements	Object
Add and delete an unlimited number of items from the variable	Object

As the user selects items to purchase, the Web page stores the items in the hidden frame in an object variable named ShoppingCart. Each item will itself be an object. These objects can be added to the ShoppingCart object or deleted from the ShoppingCart object. Each item in the shopping cart also will have the capability of displaying itself using the display method.

The first step in creating the ShoppingCart object and the shopping cart items is to start a new document in Notepad for the HIDDEN frame by following these steps.

TO START A NEW NOTEPAD DOCUMENT

1. Start Notepad.
2. When the Notepad window displays, click the Maximize button.

The Notepad window displays (Figure 5-4).

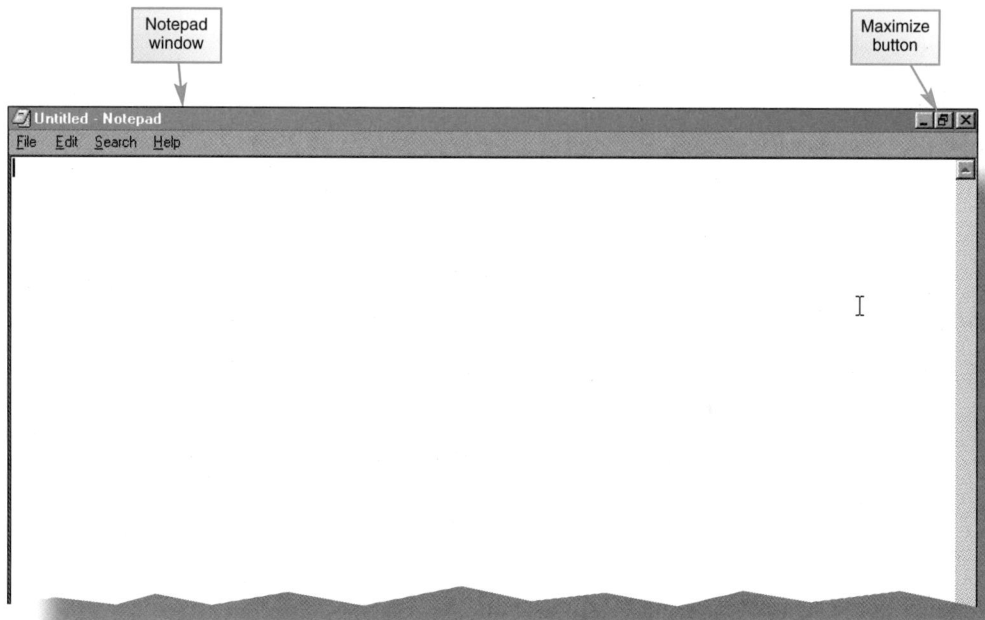

FIGURE 5-4

Table 5-3

LINE	CODE
1	<HTML>
2	<SCRIPT LANGUAGE="JAVASCRIPT">
3	<!-- Hide from old browsers
4	var numItems = 0
5	var ShoppingCart = new Object
6	
7	function addItem(Description, Price, ItemNum) {
8	this.Description = Description
9	this.Price = Price
10	this.ItemNum = ItemNum
11	this.display = printItem
12	return this
13	}
14	
15	//-->
16	</SCRIPT>
17	</HTML>

Table 5-4 Sample Object Indexes

INDEX	SAMPLE CODE
1	Names[1] = "Eric Thomas"
color	this["color"] = "blue"
itemnumber	Inventory["itemnumber"] = 3832

Table 5-3 shows the HTML code and JavaScript used to start a new document. This document exists in the hidden frame, named HIDDEN. The code contains the HTML and SCRIPT tags to begin and end the document.

The variable numItems in line 4 keeps track of the next index to use for adding a new item to the shopping cart. Each item in the shopping cart has a number associated with it to differentiate it from other items. When working with objects, it is not necessary to use a number as an index. Any unique string or number will suffice. Table 5-4 gives some examples of indexes that can be used to access the contents of an object. In line 5, the ShoppingCart object is declared as an object using the **new** operator.

The addItem() function adds an item to the ShoppingCart object. In this case, the addItem object contains three properties and one method. The properties are Description, Price, and ItemNum. The method is display. The three properties are all set to the appropriate values that are passed to the addItem() function.

While it is not possible to distinguish a property from a method in the code as shown, the difference occurs in how the variables are defined. Later, a function will be written named printItem() to match the method in line 11. This function will have the job of displaying an item in the cart on a Web page. When a property is associated with a function, as in line 11, the property becomes a method of the object with which it is associated. Later, the method can be called to perform an action.

To add the code to start the hidden frame and create the objects, perform the following steps.

Steps To Start the Hidden Frame and Create the Objects

1. **Position the insertion point on line 1.**

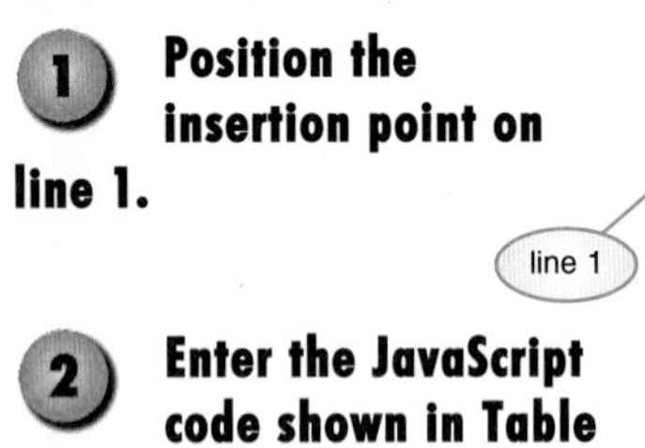

2. **Enter the JavaScript code shown in Table 5-3.**

The code to create the objects displays (Figure 5-5).

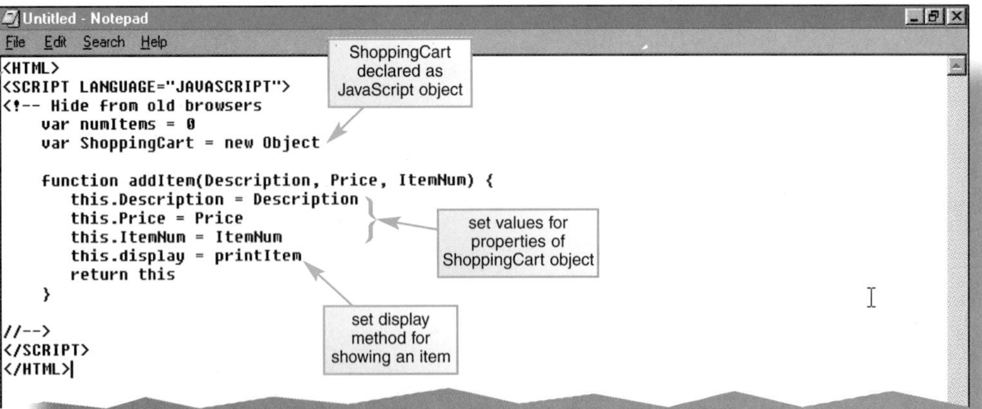

FIGURE 5-5

The next step is to create a function that can be called to add an item to the shopping cart. Table 5-5 shows the JavaScript function used to add a new item to the shopping cart. This function is called from the Web page when the user clicks one of the Add to Shopping Cart links.

Table 5-5

LINE	CODE
15	`function addtoCart(Description, Price) {`
16	`    ShoppingCart[numItems] = new addItem(Description, Price, numItems)`
17	`    numItems = numItems + 1`
18	`    alert(Description + " has been added to your shopping cart.")`
19	`}`

The addtoCart() function accepts the item description and price as parameters. It then adds a new addItem object to the ShoppingCart object in line 16. In line 17, the function updates the numItems counter so the next item added to the cart has a unique identifier associated with it. Finally, the function displays a message to the user confirming that the item has been added to the shopping cart.

To add the addtoCart() function, perform the following steps.

To Create the addtoCart() Function

1 **Position the insertion point on line 14 and then press the ENTER key.**

2 **Enter the JavaScript code shown in Table 5-5 and then press the ENTER key.**

The addtoCart() function displays (Figure 5-6).

Untitled - Notepad

File Edit Search Help

```
<HTML>
<SCRIPT LANGUAGE="JAVASCRIPT">
<!-- Hide from old browsers
    var numItems = 0
    var ShoppingCart = new Object

    function addItem(Description, Price, ItemNum) {
       this.Description = Description
       this.Price = Price
       this.ItemNum = ItemNum
       this.display = printItem
       return this
    }

    function addtoCart(Description, Price) {
       ShoppingCart[numItems] = new addItem(Description, Price, numItems)
       numItems = numItems + 1
       alert(Description + " has been added to your shopping cart.")
    }

//-->
</SCRIPT>
</HTML>
```

line 14

create new object with new index

Start | Untitled - Notepad | 5:06 PM

FIGURE 5-6

The delete Operator

Various browsers delete objects in different ways. The recovery of unused memory space is called garbage collection. The browser does garbage collection behind the scenes. When programming with large amounts of data, it is important to research how the browsers that you are targeting for development will handle memory management.

An item now can be added to the ShoppingCart object. The next step is to create a function that will allow you to delete an item from the ShoppingCart object.

Deleting an Object

When using an array, the only way to delete an item is to set all of its properties to a special value that you can test, such as null. When using an object, the **delete** operator tells JavaScript to delete all of the properties of an object. The delete operator uses the following syntax:

```
delete objectname
```

Using the delete operator is essentially the same as setting all of the objects properties to null. After using the delete operator, the object no longer takes up any memory space. The variable that was declared as an object no longer is available for use in JavaScript.

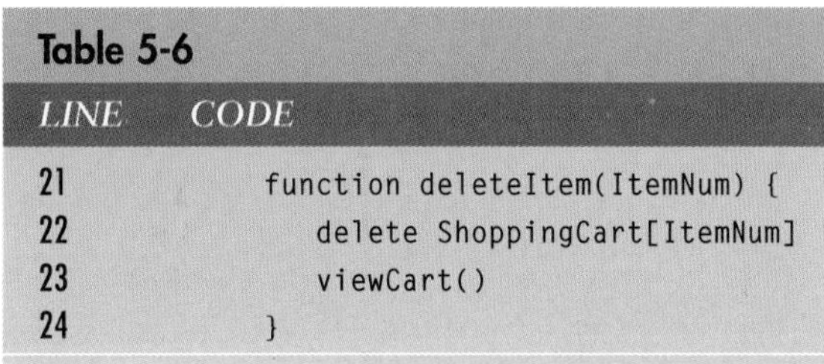

Table 5-6

LINE	CODE
21	`function deleteItem(ItemNum) {`
22	`    delete ShoppingCart[ItemNum]`
23	`    viewCart()`
24	`}`

Table 5-6 shows the **deleteItem()** function used to delete an item from the shopping cart. This code is called from the shopping cart Web page when the user clicks one of the Remove from Cart links.

The deleteItem() function first uses the delete operator to remove the shopping cart item with the ItemNum identifier, which is passed as a parameter. Next, the function calls another function, called viewCart(), that has not yet been written. The viewCart() function will re-draw the Web page for the shopping cart and the deleted item no longer will display. To enter the deleteItem() function, perform the following steps.

Steps To Add the deleteItem() Function

1 Position the insertion point on line 20 and then press the ENTER key.

2 Enter the JavaScript code shown in Table 5-6 and then press the ENTER key.

The deleteItem() function displays (Figure 5-7).

```
Untitled - Notepad
File  Edit  Search  Help
<HTML>
<SCRIPT LANGUAGE="JAVASCRIPT">
<!-- Hide from old browsers
    var numItems = 0
    var ShoppingCart = new Object

    function addItem(Description, Price, ItemNum) {
        this.Description = Description
        this.Price = Price
        this.ItemNum = ItemNum
        this.display = printItem
        return this
    }

    function addtoCart(Description, Price) {
        ShoppingCart[numItems] = new addItem(Description, Price, numItems)
        numItems = numItems + 1
        alert(Description + " has been added to your shopping cart.")
    }

    function deleteItem(ItemNum) {
        delete ShoppingCart[ItemNum]
        viewCart()
    }

//-->
</SCRIPT>
</HTML>
```


FIGURE 5-7

The final step to create the object for the items in the shopping cart is to create the printItem() method that will be used to display an item in the cart.

Creating the printItem() Method

The addItem() function includes the line this.display = printItem. The printItem() method will be declared as a function. Declaring printItem() as a function means the line in the addItem() function sets the display attribute of the addItem object as a method. Just as the Description, Price, and ItemNum properties are accessible when an object of type addItem is declared, the printItem() method is accessible. Whenever you want to display the object, you use the **display** method. Invoking the display method will call the printItem() function. For example, if you declare an object named myItem as addItem(), you access the Price property by using the syntax myItem.Price. To display the contents of myItem on a Web page, you call the display method using the syntax myItem.display().

Methods accept parameters just as functions accept parameters. In Figure 5-1b on page J 5.5, each shopping cart item displays in a table with the description, price, and a Remove from Cart link. In Figure 5-1c on page J 5.5, each item displays with only the description and price. The printItem() method accepts a flag that indicates whether it should display the Remove from Cart link. A second parameter tells the printItem() method which document to display the data in. Table 5-7 shows the printItem() method.

The function declaration in line 26 accepts the two parameters for the method. The **With** statement in line 27 provides a shortcut to some of the complicated syntax sometimes used in JavaScript. Whenever you need to work with an object's properties or methods in more than one line of code, you can use the With statement to save some coding. The With statement accepts an object as a parameter and several lines of code may follow the With statement enclosed in brackets. For the lines of code contained in the With statement, you do not need to type the object name that you passed as a parameter. If the With statement was not used in Table 5-7, then the write() statements in lines 28, 29, 31, and 32 would have to be preceded by the object name TargetDocument. TargetDocument is the name of the document that you want to display the contents of the shopping cart in. Table 5-8 describes the general form of the With statement.

More About

Methods

You may be familiar with the concept of public versus private methods. Public methods are accessible by other code outside of the object, while private methods are for internal use in an object. In JavaScript, all methods are public.

Table 5-7

```
LINE  CODE
26        function printItem(deleteFlag, TargetDocument) {
27           with (TargetDocument) {
28              write("<TR><TD>" + this.Description + "</TD>")
29              write("<TD ALIGN=RIGHT>$" + this.Price + "</TD>")
30              if (deleteFlag = true)
31              write("<TD><A HREF='JavaScript:top.HIDDEN.deleteItem(" +
          this.ItemNum + ")'>Remove from Cart</A></TD>")
32              write("</TR>")
33           }
34        }
```

Table 5-8 With Statement

General form:	with (object)
Comment:	where object is any valid JavaScript or user defined object
Example:	`with (window.document)`

Lines 28 and 29 display the item description and price in table cells. The If statement in line 30 checks to see if the Remove from Cart hyperlink displays in a separate table column. If so, then lines 31 and 32 display the Remove from Cart hyperlink. The Remove from Cart hyperlink calls the deleteItem() function and passes the unique ItemNum identifier of the current object in the shopping cart. To add the printItem() method, perform the following steps.

To Add the printItem() Method

1 Position the insertion point on line 25 and then press the ENTER key.

2 Enter the JavaScript code shown in Table 5-7 on the previous page and then press the ENTER key.

The printItem() method displays (Figure 5-8).

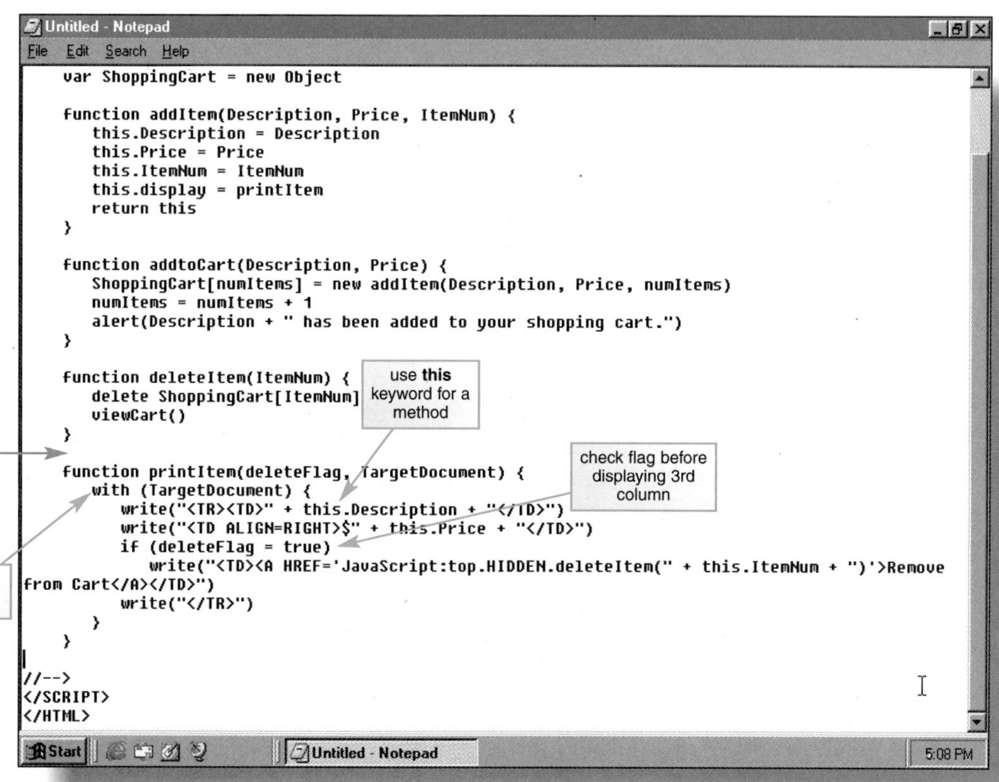

FIGURE 5-8

Shopping cart items display in two areas of the Web site. They display on the shopping cart page and on the printable order form. When an item needs to be displayed, you call the display method of the item. The next step is to write the function that will display the shopping cart items in the shopping cart Web page by invoking the display method.

Writing Object Data to the Web Page

The Web page in Figure 5-1a on page J 5.5 contains a link to view the contents of the shopping cart in Figure 5-1b on page J 5.5. Because the Web page content for the shopping cart changes depending on the user choices, the entire page needs to be generated dynamically by JavaScript. Table 5-9 shows the beginning of the viewCart() function that will display the shopping cart page in Figure 5-1b.

Table 5-9

LINE	CODE
36	function viewCart() {
37	var cartTotal = 0
38	
39	with (top.MAIN.document) {
40	write()
41	close()
42	write("<HTML><TITLE>Val-U Computers Shopping Cart</TITLE>")
43	write("<BODY BGCOLOR=#A0D0E0><CENTER>")
44	write("<TABLE BORDER=0><TR>")
45	write("<TD><IMAGE SRC=comp2.jpg></TD>")
46	write("<TD ALIGN=CENTER VALIGN=BOTTOM>")
47	write("<H2>Val-U Computers Shopping Cart</H2></TD>")
48	write("<TD><IMAGE SRC=comp3.jpg></TD></TR>")
49	write("</TABLE>")
50	write(" <HR> ")
51	write("<TABLE BORDER=1 CELLPADDING=3 CELLSPACING=1 WIDTH=500 BGCOLOR=LIGHTYELLOW>")

Line 37 declares the variable cartTotal that will be used to total the prices of the items selected by the user. The use of the With statement in line 39 makes lines 40 through 51 more readable and easier to code because the object reference top.MAIN.document does not have to be included on every line. Lines 40 and 41 are used to clear out the current contents of the frame named MAIN so the page can be updated with new information. To add the beginning of the viewCart() function, perform the following steps.

Steps

To Add the Start of the viewCart() Function

1 **Position the insertion point on line 35 and then press the ENTER key.**

2 **Enter the JavaScript code shown in Table 5-9 and then press the ENTER key.**

The beginning of the viewCart() function displays (Figure 5-9).

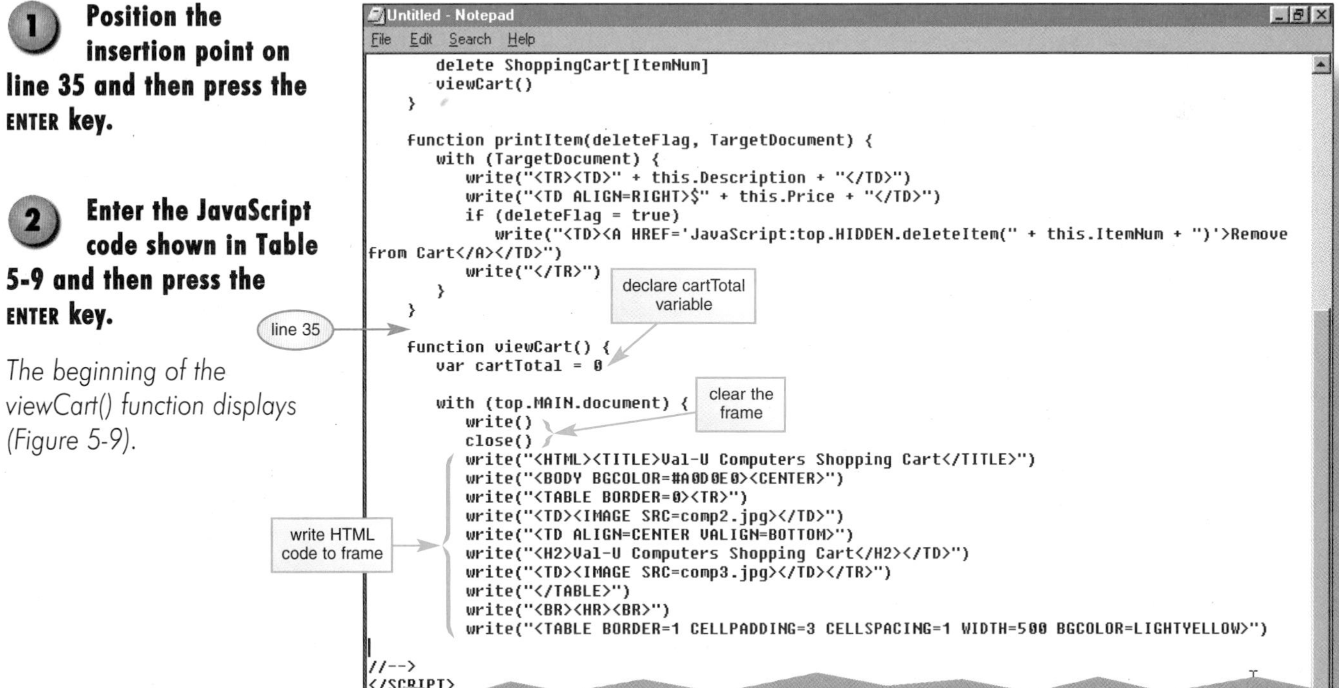
Untitled - Notepad
File Edit Search Help
delete ShoppingCart[ItemNum]
viewCart()
}
function printItem(deleteFlag, TargetDocument) {
with (TargetDocument) {
write("<TR><TD>" + this.Description + "</TD>")
write("<TD ALIGN=RIGHT>$" + this.Price + "</TD>")
if (deleteFlag = true)
write("<TD><A HREF='JavaScript:top.HIDDEN.deleteItem(" + this.ItemNum + ")'>Remove from Cart</A></TD>")
write("</TR>")
}
}
function viewCart() {
var cartTotal = 0
with (top.MAIN.document) {
write()
close()
write("<HTML><TITLE>Val-U Computers Shopping Cart</TITLE>")
write("<BODY BGCOLOR=#A0D0E0><CENTER>")
write("<TABLE BORDER=0><TR>")
write("<TD><IMAGE SRC=comp2.jpg></TD>")
write("<TD ALIGN=CENTER VALIGN=BOTTOM>")
write("<H2>Val-U Computers Shopping Cart</H2></TD>")
write("<TD><IMAGE SRC=comp3.jpg></TD></TR>")
write("</TABLE>")
write("
<HR>
")
write("<TABLE BORDER=1 CELLPADDING=3 CELLSPACING=1 WIDTH=500 BGCOLOR=LIGHTYELLOW>")
//-->
declare cartTotal variable
line 35
clear the frame
write HTML code to frame

FIGURE 5-9

The next step is to write the table rows for the HTML table that displays from the code shown in Table 5-9 on the previous page. Table 5-10 shows the JavaScript code required to write the table rows for the shopping cart items for the shopping cart Web page.

Table 5-10

LINE	CODE
53	`for (i in ShoppingCart) {`
54	`   cartTotal = cartTotal + ShoppingCart[i].Price`
55	`   if (ShoppingCart[i].ItemNum != null)`
56	`      ShoppingCart[i].display(true, top.MAIN.document)`
57	`}`

Line 53 uses the For-in statement to loop through the objects in the ShoppingCart object. The **For-in** statement is used to loop through all of the elements of an object or an array. The For-in statement is useful because sometimes it is impossible to tell how many elements are in an object. Recall that arrays include a length attribute that is automatically kept up to date by JavaScript, but objects do not. Table 5-11 shows the general form of the For-in statement.

Table 5-11	**For-in Statement**
General form:	for (variable in object)
Comment:	variable is any declared variable; object is any valid JavaScript or user-defined object
Example:	`for (vacantOffices in Building)`

Line 54 adds the Price property of the current ShoppingCart element in the loop to the cartTotal variable. In line 55, a test is made to make sure that the ShoppingCart item to be displayed is not empty or has not been deleted. Line 56 invokes the display method of the current ShoppingCart item, causing the printItem() function to be called with the parameters of true and top.MAIN.document. The true parameter tells the printItem() function to display the Remove from Cart link. The top.MAIN.document parameter tells the printItem() function to send its output to the frame named MAIN. To add the For-in loop to display the shopping cart items in the ShoppingCart object, perform the following steps.

Steps To Add the For-in Loop to Display the Shopping Cart

1 **Position the insertion point on line 52 and then press the ENTER key.**

2 **Enter the JavaScript code shown in Table 5-10 and then press the ENTER key.**

The For-in loop displays (Figure 5-10).

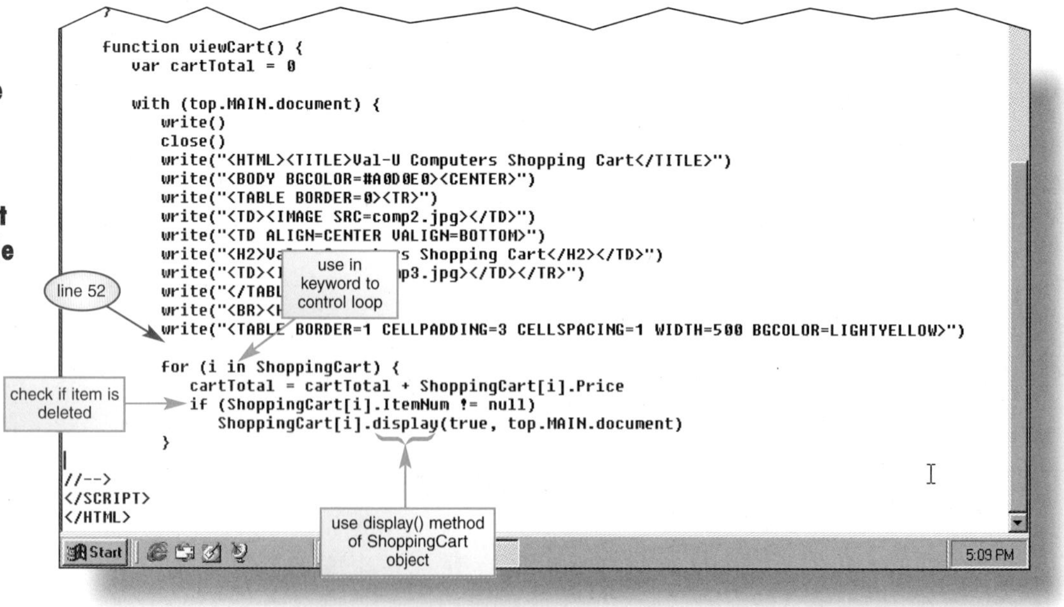

```
function viewCart() {
   var cartTotal = 0

   with (top.MAIN.document) {
      write()
      close()
      write("<HTML><TITLE>Val-U Computers Shopping Cart</TITLE>")
      write("<BODY BGCOLOR=#A0D0E0><CENTER>")
      write("<TABLE BORDER=0><TR>")
      write("<TD><IMAGE SRC=comp2.jpg></TD>")
      write("<TD ALIGN=CENTER VALIGN=BOTTOM>")
      write("<H2>Va        s Shopping Cart</H2></TD>")
      write("<TD><I        p3.jpg></TD></TR>")
      write("</TABL
      write("<BR><H
      write("<TABLE BORDER=1 CELLPADDING=3 CELLSPACING=1 WIDTH=500 BGCOLOR=LIGHTYELLOW>")

      for (i in ShoppingCart) {
         cartTotal = cartTotal + ShoppingCart[i].Price
         if (ShoppingCart[i].ItemNum != null)
            ShoppingCart[i].display(true, top.MAIN.document)
      }

//-->
</SCRIPT>
</HTML>
```


FIGURE 5-10

The shopping cart items now will print. Next, you will write the HTML code that writes the total price and finishes the HTML code for the shopping cart Web page. Table 5-12 shows the JavaScript code used to write HTML code used to finish the Web page.

Table 5-12

LINE	CODE
59	write("<TR><TD>Total:</TD><TD ALIGN=RIGHT>$" + cartTotal + "</TD>")
60	write("<TD> </TD></TR></TABLE> ")
61	write(" </CENTER></BODY></HTML>")
62	}
63	}

The code contained in the write statement on line 59 concatenates the necessary HTML with the cartTotal variable that was incremented in the For-in loop. Lines 60 and 61 finish the various HTML table tags and HTML tags. To finish the viewCart() function, perform the following steps.

More About

The For-in Statement

The indexes of objects can be numeric or text. When a For-in statement is looping through objects that have text indexes, it loops through the items in the order that they were added to the object. The For-in statement also can be used to loop through the properties of built-in JavaScript objects. For example, you can loop through all the properties of the document object by using the syntax for (element in document).

To Finish the HTML Code for the Shopping Cart Web Page

1 Position the insertion point on line 58 and then press the ENTER key.

2 Enter the JavaScript code shown in Table 5-12 and then press the ENTER key.

The remainder of the viewCart() function displays (Figure 5-11).

```
Untitled - Notepad
File  Edit  Search  Help
         }
      }

      function viewCart() {
         var cartTotal = 0

         with (top.MAIN.document) {
            write()
            close()
            write("<HTML><TITLE>Val-U Computers Shopping Cart</TITLE>")
            write("<BODY BGCOLOR=#A0D0E0><CENTER>")
            write("<TABLE BORDER=0><TR>")
            write("<TD><IMAGE SRC=comp2.jpg></TD>")
            write("<TD ALIGN=CENTER VALIGN=BOTTOM>")
            write("<H2>Val-U Computers Shopping Cart</H2></TD>")
            write("<TD><IMAGE SRC=comp3.jpg></TD></TR>")
            write("</TABLE>")
            write("<BR><HR><BR>")
            write("<TABLE BORDER=1 CELLPADDING=3 CELLSPACING=1 WIDTH=500 BGCOLOR=LIGHTYELLOW>")

            for (i in ShoppingCart) {
               cartTotal = cartTotal + ShoppingCart[i].Price
               if (ShoppingCart[i].ItemNum != null)
                  ShoppingCart[i].display(true, top.MAIN.document)
            }

            write("<TR><TD>Total:</TD><TD ALIGN=RIGHT>$" + cartTotal + "</TD>")
            write("<TD> </TD></TR></TABLE><BR>")
            write("<BR></CENTER></BODY></HTML>")
         }
      }

//-->
</SCRIPT>
</HTML>
Start    Untitled - Notepad    5:10 PM
```

line 58

write CartTotal variable

FIGURE 5-11

The steps on the next page save the file as javascript.htm. Recall that the valucomp.htm file uses the javascript.htm file as the Web page for the frame named HIDDEN.

TO SAVE THE JAVASCRIPT.HTM FILE

1. With the JavaScript Data Disk in drive A, click File on the menu bar and then Save As.
2. Type `a:\javascript.htm` in the File name text box and then click the Save button.

The javascript.htm file is saved.

Secure Transactions

Web sites that process financial information, such as credit card numbers, always should use secure transactions. Sites that use secure transactions often use a protocol called https, rather than http. After selecting links to secure areas of a Web site, you will see the Web address for the site preceded by https, rather than http, in your browser's address area.

Next, the link that allows the user to view the shopping cart needs to be added to the Shopping Page.

Calling the viewCart() Function

The shopping page will contain the link to the shopping cart. Jack Winters already supplied you with the list of items for sale on the shopping page in the file named order.htm.

To open the shopping page document, perform the following steps.

TO START NOTEPAD AND OPEN THE ORDER.HTM FILE

1. Start Notepad.
2. When the Notepad window displays, click the Maximize button.
3. Open the file, order.htm, on the JavaScript Data Disk in drive A.

The order.htm document opens in the Notepad window (Figure 5-12).

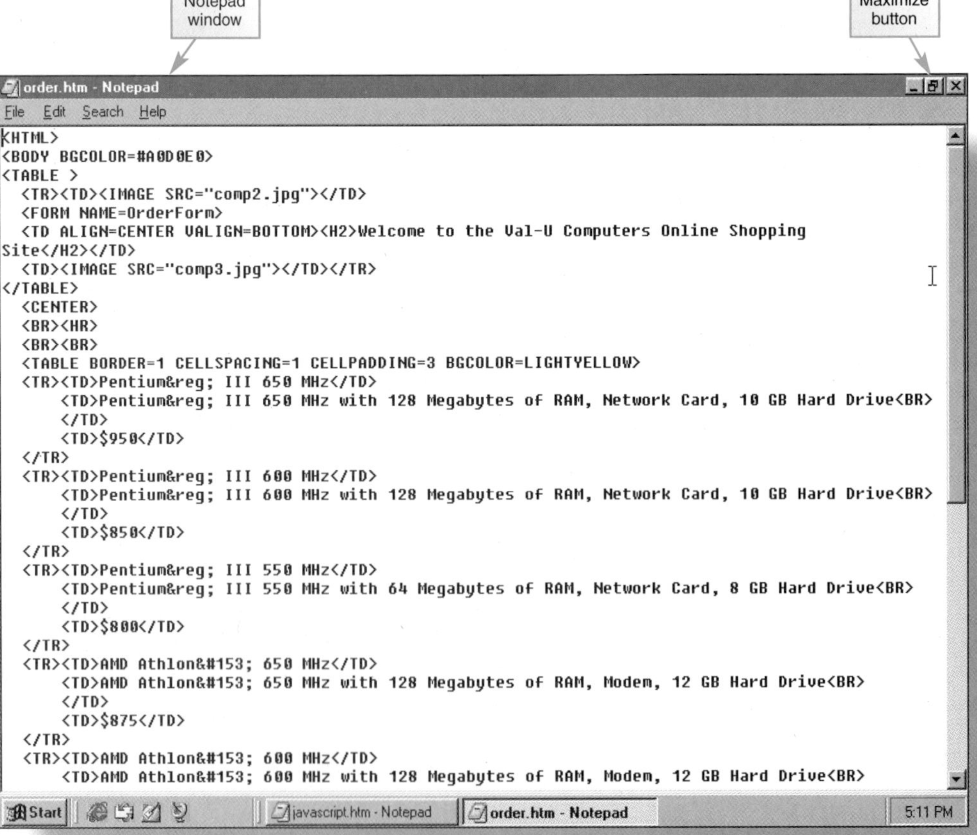


```
<HTML>
<BODY BGCOLOR=#A0D0E0>
<TABLE >
  <TR><TD><IMAGE SRC="comp2.jpg"></TD>
  <FORM NAME=OrderForm>
  <TD ALIGN=CENTER VALIGN=BOTTOM><H2>Welcome to the Val-U Computers Online Shopping
Site</H2></TD>
  <TD><IMAGE SRC="comp3.jpg"></TD></TR>
</TABLE>
  <CENTER>
  <BR><HR>
  <BR><BR>
  <TABLE BORDER=1 CELLSPACING=1 CELLPADDING=3 BGCOLOR=LIGHTYELLOW>
  <TR><TD>Pentium&reg; III 650 MHz</TD>
      <TD>Pentium&reg; III 650 MHz with 128 Megabytes of RAM, Network Card, 10 GB Hard Drive<BR>
      </TD>
      <TD>$950</TD>
  </TR>
  <TR><TD>Pentium&reg; III 600 MHz</TD>
      <TD>Pentium&reg; III 600 MHz with 128 Megabytes of RAM, Network Card, 10 GB Hard Drive<BR>
      </TD>
      <TD>$850</TD>
  </TR>
  <TR><TD>Pentium&reg; III 550 MHz</TD>
      <TD>Pentium&reg; III 550 MHz with 64 Megabytes of RAM, Network Card, 8 GB Hard Drive<BR>
      </TD>
      <TD>$800</TD>
  </TR>
  <TR><TD>AMD Athlon&#153; 650 MHz</TD>
      <TD>AMD Athlon&#153; 650 MHz with 128 Megabytes of RAM, Modem, 12 GB Hard Drive<BR>
      </TD>
      <TD>$875</TD>
  </TR>
  <TR><TD>AMD Athlon&#153; 600 MHz</TD>
      <TD>AMD Athlon&#153; 600 MHz with 128 Megabytes of RAM, Modem, 12 GB Hard Drive<BR>
```

FIGURE 5-12

An HTML anchor tag links users to the shopping cart page where they can view the current contents of the shopping cart. The HREF calls the viewCart() JavaScript function in order to generate the page dynamically in the frame named MAIN. The viewCart() function takes care of placing the HTML for the shopping cart page in the MAIN frame. Later, you will add code that allows the user to press the V key in order to view the shopping cart.

To add the call to the viewCart() function, perform the following steps.

To Enter the Link to the Shopping Cart Web Page

1 **Position the insertion point at the end of line 10 and then press the ENTER key. Press the SPACEBAR twice.**

2 **Type** `Press 'V' to view your shopping cart or click <A HREF="JavaScript:top.HIDDEN.viewCart();">here</A>` **and do not press the ENTER key (Figure 5-13).**

order.htm - Notepad

File Edit Search Help

```
<HTML>
<BODY BGCOLOR=#A0D0E0>
<TABLE >
  <TR><TD><IMAGE SRC="comp2.jpg"></TD>
  <FORM NAME=OrderForm>
  <TD ALIGN=CENTER VALIGN=BOTTOM><H2>Welcome to the Val-U Computers Online Shopping
Site</H2></TD>
  <TD><IMAGE SRC="comp3.jpg"></TD></TR>
</TABLE>
  <CENTER>
  <BR><HR>
  Press 'V' to view your shopping cart or click <A
HREF="JavaScript:top.HIDDEN.viewCart();">here</A>
  <BR><BR>
  <TABLE BORDER=1 CELLSPACING=1 CELLPADDING=3 BGCOLOR=LIGHTYELLOW>
  <TR><TD>Pentium&reg; III 650 MHz</TD>
      <TD>Pentium&reg; III 650 MHz with 128 Megabytes of RAM, Network Card, 10 GB Hard Drive<BR>

  </
  <T           eg; III 600 MHz</TD>
      <TD>Pentium&reg; III 600 MHz with 128 Megabytes of RAM, Network Card, 10 GB Hard Drive<BR>
      </TD>
      <TD>$850</TD>
  </TR>
  <TR><TD>Pentium&reg; III 550 MHz</TD>
      <TD>Pentium&reg; III 550 MHz with 64 Megabytes of RAM, Network Card, 8 GB Hard Drive<BR>
      </TD>
      <TD>$800</TD>
  </TR>
  <TR><TD>AMD Athlon&#153; 650 MHz</TD>
      <TD>AMD Athlon&#153; 650 MHz with 128 Megabytes of RAM, Modem, 12 GB Hard Drive<BR>
      </TD>
      <TD>$875</TD>
  </TR>
```

line 10

call viewCart() function in hidden frame

Start | javascript.htm - Notepad | order.htm - Notepad | 5:12 PM

FIGURE 5-13

Next, the links that add items to the shopping cart need to be added to the shopping page.

Calling the addtoCart() Function

The Web page in Figure 5-1a on page J 5.5 contains Add to Shopping Cart links for each of the items on the shopping page. These links execute the addtoCart() function when the user clicks one of them. The addtoCart() function accepts parameters for the item description and the item price.

To add all the calls to the addtoCart() function for the first item, perform the steps on the next page.

To Enter the Links to Call the addtoCart() Function

1 **Position the insertion point at the end of line 15 and then press the ENTER key.**

2 **Type** `<A HREF="JavaScript:top.HIDDEN.addtoCart('Pentium® III 650 MHz', 950)">Add to Shopping Cart</A>` **and do not press the ENTER key (Figure 5-14).**

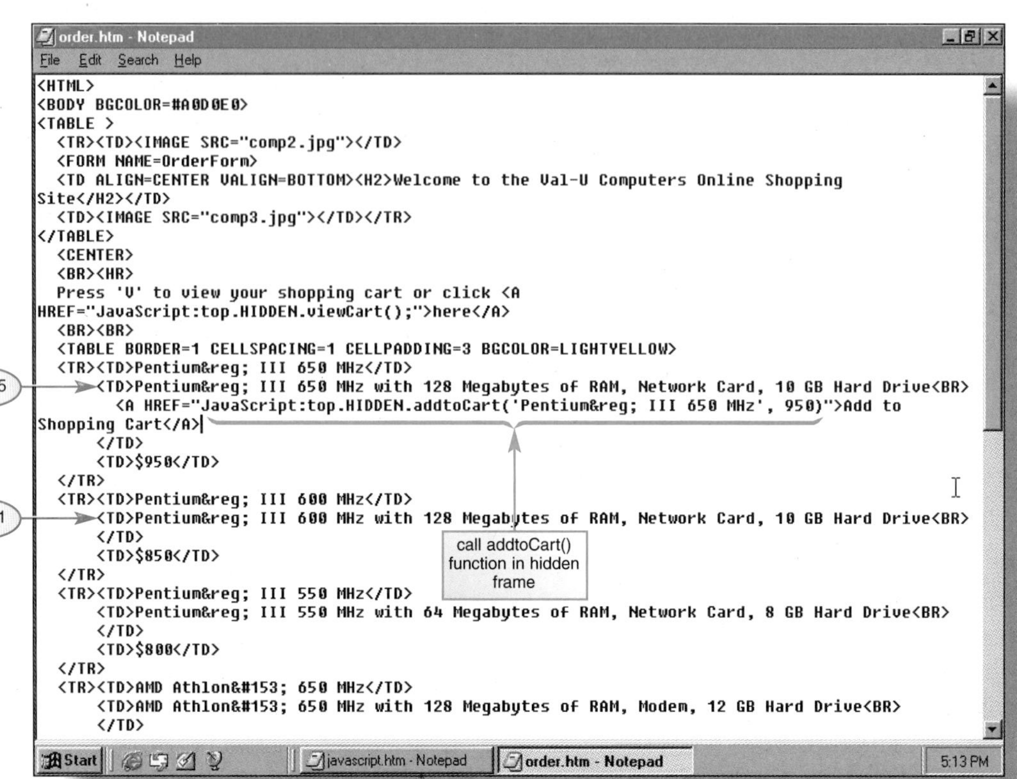


```
<HTML>
<BODY BGCOLOR=#A0D0E0>
<TABLE >
  <TR><TD><IMAGE SRC="comp2.jpg"></TD>
  <FORM NAME=OrderForm>
  <TD ALIGN=CENTER VALIGN=BOTTOM><H2>Welcome to the Val-U Computers Online Shopping
Site</H2></TD>
  <TD><IMAGE SRC="comp3.jpg"></TD></TR>
</TABLE>
  <CENTER>
  <BR><HR>
  Press 'V' to view your shopping cart or click <A
HREF="JavaScript:top.HIDDEN.viewCart();">here</A>
  <BR><BR>
  <TABLE BORDER=1 CELLSPACING=1 CELLPADDING=3 BGCOLOR=LIGHTYELLOW>
  <TR><TD>Pentium&reg; III 650 MHz</TD>
      <TD>Pentium&reg; III 650 MHz with 128 Megabytes of RAM, Network Card, 10 GB Hard Drive<BR>
        <A HREF="JavaScript:top.HIDDEN.addtoCart('Pentium&reg; III 650 MHz', 950)">Add to
Shopping Cart</A>
      </TD>
      <TD>$950</TD>
  </TR>
  <TR><TD>Pentium&reg; III 600 MHz</TD>
      <TD>Pentium&reg; III 600 MHz with 128 Megabytes of RAM, Network Card, 10 GB Hard Drive<BR>
      </TD>
      <TD>$850</TD>
  </TR>
  <TR><TD>Pentium&reg; III 550 MHz</TD>
      <TD>Pentium&reg; III 550 MHz with 64 Megabytes of RAM, Network Card, 8 GB Hard Drive<BR>
      </TD>
      <TD>$800</TD>
  </TR>
  <TR><TD>AMD Athlon&#153; 650 MHz</TD>
      <TD>AMD Athlon&#153; 650 MHz with 128 Megabytes of RAM, Modem, 12 GB Hard Drive<BR>
      </TD>
```

FIGURE 5-14

The remaining links contain similar calls to the addtoCart() function. The only differences are the parameters passed to the function. To enter the remaining links to the addtoCart() function, perform the following steps.

TO ENTER THE REMAINING LINKS TO THE ADDTOCART() FUNCTION

1. Position the insertion point at the end of line 21 and then press the ENTER key.
2. Type `<A HREF="JavaScript:top.HIDDEN.addtoCart('Pentium® III 600 MHz', 850)">Add to Shopping Cart</A>` and do not press the ENTER key.
3. Position the insertion point at the end of line 27 and then press the ENTER key.
4. Type `<A HREF="JavaScript:top.HIDDEN.addtoCart('Pentium® III 550 MHz', 800)">Add to Shopping Cart</A>` and do not press the ENTER key.
5. Position the insertion point at the end of line 33 and then press the ENTER key.
6. Type `<A HREF="JavaScript:top.HIDDEN.addtoCart('AMD Athlon™ 650 MHz', 875)">Add to Shopping Cart</A>` and do not press the ENTER key.
7. Position the insertion point at the end of line 39 and then press the ENTER key.
8. Type `<A HREF="JavaScript:top.HIDDEN.addtoCart('AMD Athlon™ 600 MHz', 825)">Add to Shopping Cart</A>` and do not press the ENTER key.

9. Position the insertion point at the end of line 45 and then press the ENTER key.
10. Type <A HREF="JavaScript:top.HIDDEN.addtoCart('Pentium® II 500 MHz', 650)">Add to Shopping Cart</A> and do not press the ENTER key.
11. Position the insertion point at the end of line 51 and then press the ENTER key.
12. Type <A HREF="JavaScript:top.HIDDEN.addtoCart('AMD-K6® 500 MHz/Modem', 550)">Add to Shopping Cart</A> and do not press the ENTER key.
13. Position the insertion point at the end of line 57 and then press the ENTER key.
14. Type <A HREF="JavaScript:top.HIDDEN.addtoCart('AMD-K6® 500 MHz/Network', 575)">Add to Shopping Cart</A> and do not press the ENTER key.

The remaining links to the addtoCart() function display (Figure 5-15).

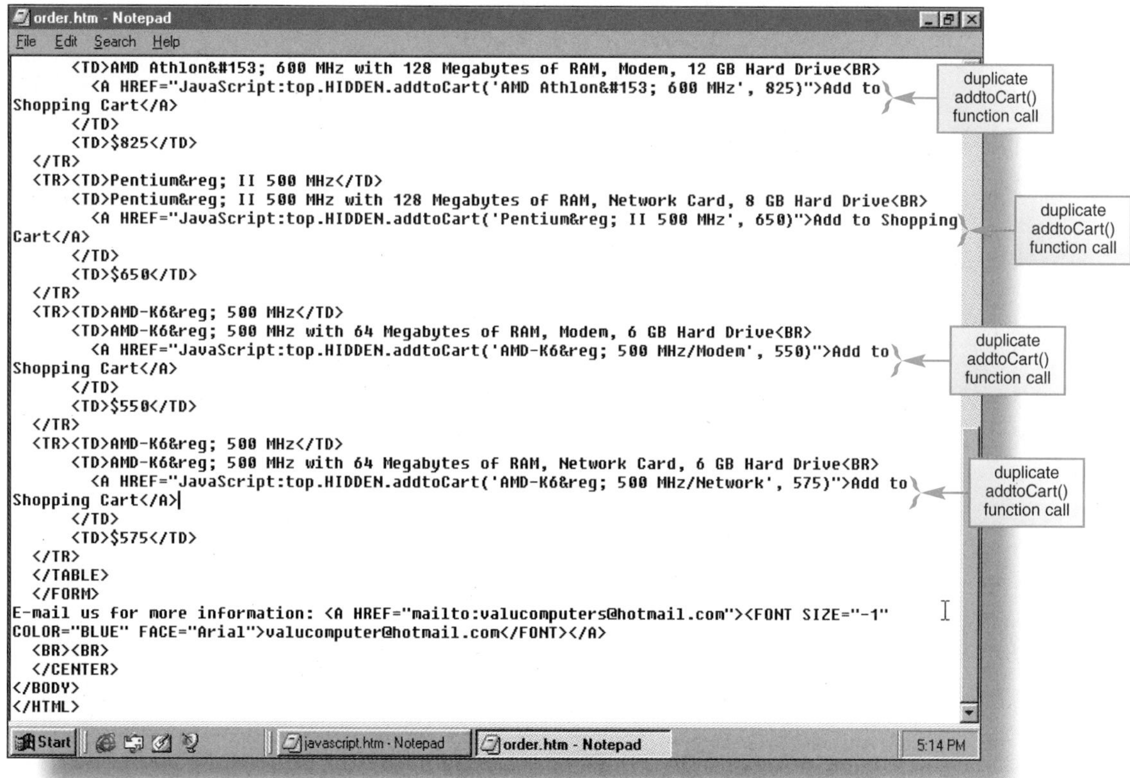


```
        <TD>AMD Athlon&#153; 600 MHz with 128 Megabytes of RAM, Modem, 12 GB Hard Drive<BR>
          <A HREF="JavaScript:top.HIDDEN.addtoCart('AMD Athlon&#153; 600 MHz', 825)">Add to
Shopping Cart</A>
        </TD>
        <TD>$825</TD>
    </TR>
    <TR><TD>Pentium&reg; II 500 MHz</TD>
        <TD>Pentium&reg; II 500 MHz with 128 Megabytes of RAM, Network Card, 8 GB Hard Drive<BR>
          <A HREF="JavaScript:top.HIDDEN.addtoCart('Pentium&reg; II 500 MHz', 650)">Add to Shopping
Cart</A>
        </TD>
        <TD>$650</TD>
    </TR>
    <TR><TD>AMD-K6&reg; 500 MHz</TD>
        <TD>AMD-K6&reg; 500 MHz with 64 Megabytes of RAM, Modem, 6 GB Hard Drive<BR>
          <A HREF="JavaScript:top.HIDDEN.addtoCart('AMD-K6&reg; 500 MHz/Modem', 550)">Add to
Shopping Cart</A>
        </TD>
        <TD>$550</TD>
    </TR>
    <TR><TD>AMD-K6&reg; 500 MHz</TD>
        <TD>AMD-K6&reg; 500 MHz with 64 Megabytes of RAM, Network Card, 6 GB Hard Drive<BR>
          <A HREF="JavaScript:top.HIDDEN.addtoCart('AMD-K6&reg; 500 MHz/Network', 575)">Add to
Shopping Cart</A>
        </TD>
        <TD>$575</TD>
    </TR>
    </TABLE>
    </FORM>
E-mail us for more information: <A HREF="mailto:valucomputers@hotmail.com"><FONT SIZE="-1"
COLOR="BLUE" FACE="Arial">valucomputer@hotmail.com</FONT></A>
    <BR><BR>
    </CENTER>
</BODY>
</HTML>
```

FIGURE 5-15

The user now can view the shopping cart by clicking the link on the underlined word, here, above the list of items. The user also can add items to the shopping cart by clicking the Add to Shopping Cart links that display with each item.

The next steps are to save your file and test the Web page.

Saving and Testing the Web Page

The JavaScript and HTML code you have written creates a frame set with a hidden frame. The ShoppingCart object will save an unlimited number of items in the Web page viewer's shopping cart. The links you have created on the shopping page allow users to add items to their carts and to view the shopping cart.

Saving and Testing the Web Page in the Browser

Perform the following steps to save and test your Web page.

To Save and Test the Web Page in the Browser

1 With the JavaScript Data Disk in drive A, click File on the menu bar and then click Save.

2 Start your browser and open valucomp.htm.

The Val-U Computers shopping Web page opens and the links to add the items to the shopping cart display (Figure 5-16).

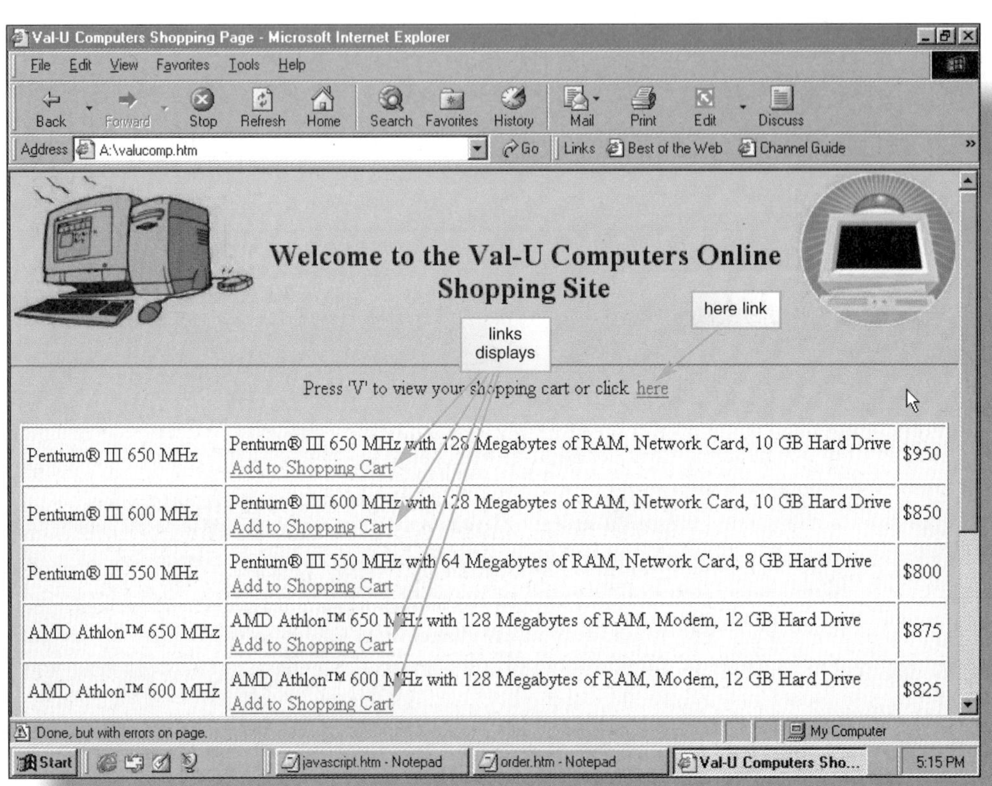

FIGURE 5-16

3 Click the Add to Shopping Cart link next to the Pentium III 650 MHz system.

The Web browser displays the Microsoft Internet Explorer dialog box with the alert message that indicates the item has been added to the shopping cart (Figure 5-17).

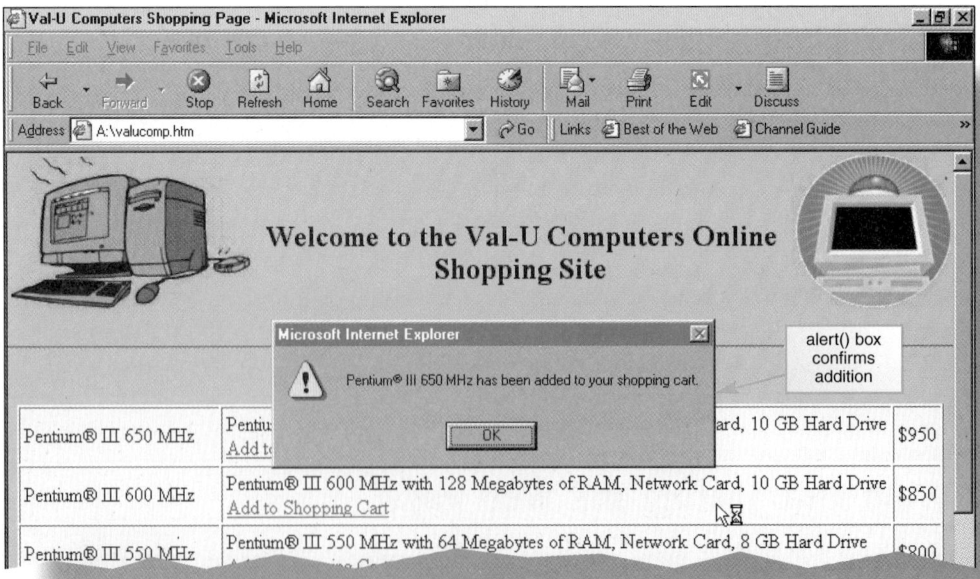

FIGURE 5-17

4 **Click the Add to Shopping Cart links next to the Pentium III 600 MHz system, the AMD Athlon 650 MHz system, and the AMD Athlon 600 MHz system.**

5 **Click the link on the underlined word, here, above the list of items that can be added to the shopping cart.**

The Web browser displays the items in the shopping cart (Figure 5-18).

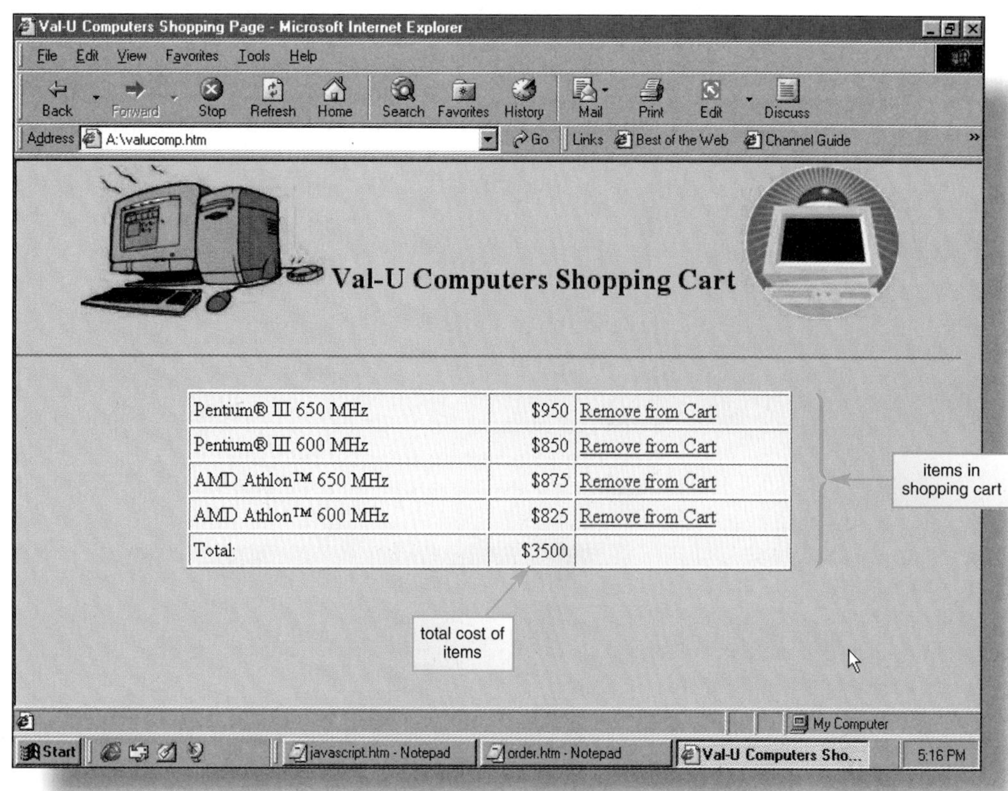

FIGURE 5-18

6 **Click the Remove from Cart link in the row that contains the AMD Athlon 650 MHz system.**

The Web browser displays the new shopping cart without the item just deleted (Figure 5-19).

7 **Close your browser. Open the javascript.htm Web page again by clicking the javascript.htm - Notepad button on the taskbar.**

FIGURE 5-19

If the browser does not display the Web pages and alert messages correctly, close any error message dialog boxes and then click the Notepad button on the taskbar. Check the JavaScript code according to Figures 5-3 through 5-15 on pages J5.8 through J5.21. Correct any errors, save the file, activate the browser, and then re-open the valucomp.htm Web page.

More About

The history Object

The history object is widely used in JavaScript programming for navigation. While seemingly simple, consider the many nuances when using the history object, particularly with frames. For more information about the history object, visit www.scsite.com/js/p5.htm and then click History.

Using the History Object

JavaScript contains a built-in object, called history, for every document. Every document has a **history** object associated with it that keeps track of the pages that have been visited. As you navigate the links in a document, you can use the Back and Forward buttons on your browser toolbar. The history object gives you the same freedom to navigate the browser among pages that have been viewed previously. Table 5-13 shows the properties and methods of the history object.

Table 5-13	Properties and Methods of the History Object
go(variable)	variable is a positive or negative number that instructs the browser to go back or forward variable number of pages in the current browser session
back()	Go back one page in the current browser session; same as clicking the browser Back button
forward()	Go forward one page in the current browser session; same as clicking the browser Forward button
length	Property tells how many pages have been visited in the current browser session

Adding the goBack() Function

When the user clicks the Return to Order Page link, the goBack() function returns the user to the shopping page from the shopping cart Web page. Table 5-14 illustrates the goBack() function.

Table 5-14

LINE CODE

```
function goBack() {
    top.MAIN.history.go(-2)
}
```

The goBack() function directs the document in the frame named MAIN to go back two pages. The reason that it goes back two pages is that when the shopping page was created, the page was cleared with the write() and close() methods. This effectively added a blank Web page between the shopping page and the shopping cart page. To add the goBack() function, perform the following steps.

To Add the goBack() Function

1 Position the insertion point on line 64 and then press the ENTER key.

2 Enter the JavaScript code shown in Table 5-14 and then press the ENTER key.

The goBack() function displays (Figure 5-20).


```
    var cartTotal = 0

    with (top.MAIN.document) {
       write()
       close()
       write("<HTML><TITLE>Val-U Computers Shopping Cart</TITLE>")
       write("<BODY BGCOLOR=#A0D0E0><CENTER>")
       write("<TABLE BORDER=0><TR>")
       write("<TD><IMAGE SRC=comp2.jpg></TD>")
       write("<TD ALIGN=CENTER VALIGN=BOTTOM>")
       write("<H2>Val-U Computers Shopping Cart</H2></TD>")
       write("<TD><IMAGE SRC=comp3.jpg></TD></TR>")
       write("</TABLE>")
       write("<BR><HR><BR>")
       write("<TABLE BORDER=1 CELLPADDING=3 CELLSPACING=1 WIDTH=500 BGCOLOR=LIGHTYELLOW>")

       for (i in ShoppingCart) {
          cartTotal = cartTotal + ShoppingCart[i].Price
          if (ShoppingCart[i].ItemNum != null)
             ShoppingCart[i].display(true, top.MAIN.document)
       }

       write("<TR><TD>Total:</TD><TD ALIGN=RIGHT>$" + cartTotal + "</TD>")
       write("<TD> </TD></TR></TABLE><BR>")
       write("<BR></CENTER></BODY></HTML>")
    }
 }

 function goBack() {
    top.MAIN.history.go(-2)
 }

//-->
</SCRIPT>
</HTML>
```

FIGURE 5-20

The next step is to add the write statements that write the links to the goBack() and printOrder() functions. The printOrder() function will display the contents of the shopping cart in a new browser window.

Calling the goBack() and printOrder() Functions

To call the goBack() and printOrder() functions, HTML code needs to be added to the shopping cart Web page with the links shown on the bottom of the Web page in Figure 5-1b on page J 5.5.

To add the hyperlinks to call the goBack() and printOrder() functions, perform the steps on the next page.

To Add the Calls to the goBack() and printOrder() Functions

1 **Position the insertion point at the end of line 62 and then press the ENTER key.**

2 **Press the SPACEBAR ten times and then type** `write("<A HREF='JavaScript:top.HIDDEN.goBack();'>Return to Order Page</A><BR><BR>")`

The call to the goBack() function displays (Figure 5-21).

```
javascript.htm - Notepad
File  Edit  Search  Help

      with (top.MAIN.document) {
         write()
         close()
         write("<HTML><TITLE>Val-U Computers Shopping Cart</TITLE>")
         write("<BODY BGCOLOR=#A0D0E0><CENTER>")
         write("<TABLE BORDER=0><TR>")
         write("<TD><IMAGE SRC=comp2.jpg></TD>")
         write("<TD ALIGN=CENTER VALIGN=BOTTOM>")
         write("<H2>Val-U Computers Shopping Cart</H2></TD>")
         write("<TD><IMAGE SRC=comp3.jpg></TD></TR>")
         write("</TABLE>")
         write("<BR><HR><BR>")
         write("<TABLE BORDER=1 CELLPADDING=3 CELLSPACING=1 WIDTH=500 BGCOLOR=LIGHTYELLOW>")

         for (i in ShoppingCart) {
            cartTotal = cartTotal + ShoppingCart[i].Price
            if (ShoppingCart[i].ItemNum != null)
               ShoppingCart[i].display(true, top.MAIN.document)
         }

         write("<TR><TD>Total:</TD><TD ALIGN=RIGHT>$" + cartTotal + "</TD>")
         write("<TD> </TD></TR></TABLE><BR>")
         write("<A HREF='JavaScript:top.HIDDEN.goBack();'>Return to Order Page</A><BR><BR>")
         write("<BR></CENTER></BODY></HTML>")
      }
   }

   function goBack() {
      top.MAIN.history.go(-2)
   }

//-->
</SCRIPT>
</HTML>
```


FIGURE 5-21

3 **Press the ENTER key. Press the SPACEBAR four times and then type** `write("<A HREF='JavaScript:top.HIDDEN.printOrder();'>Display Printable Order Form</A>")` **and do not press the ENTER key.**

The call to the printOrder() function displays (Figure 5-22).

```
javascript.htm - Notepad
File  Edit  Search  Help
      with (top.MAIN.document) {
         write()
         close()
         write("<HTML><TITLE>Val-U Computers Shopping Cart</TITLE>")
         write("<BODY BGCOLOR=#A0D0E0><CENTER>")
         write("<TABLE BORDER=0><TR>")
         write("<TD><IMAGE SRC=comp2.jpg></TD>")
         write("<TD ALIGN=CENTER VALIGN=BOTTOM>")
         write("<H2>Val-U Computers Shopping Cart</H2></TD>")
         write("<TD><IMAGE SRC=comp3.jpg></TD></TR>")
         write("</TABLE>")
         write("<BR><HR><BR>")
         write("<TABLE BORDER=1 CELLPADDING=3 CELLSPACING=1 WIDTH=500 BGCOLOR=LIGHTYELLOW>")

         for (i in ShoppingCart) {
            cartTotal = cartTotal + ShoppingCart[i].Price
            if (ShoppingCart[i].ItemNum != null)
               ShoppingCart[i].display(true, top.MAIN.document)
         }

         write("<TR><TD>Total:</TD><TD ALIGN=RIGHT>$" + cartTotal + "</TD>")
         write("<TD> </TD></TR></TABLE><BR>")
         write("<A HREF='JavaScript:top.HIDDEN.goBack();'>Return to Order Page</A><BR><BR>")
         write("<A HREF='JavaScript:top.HIDDEN.printOrder();'>Display Printable Order Form</A>")
         write("<BR></CENTER></BODY></HTML>")
      }
   }

   function goBack() {
      top.MAIN.history.go(-2)
   }

//-->
</SCRIPT>
```


FIGURE 5-22

The shopping cart Web page now contains two links at the bottom of the page. The Return to Order Page link executes the goBack() function that causes the browser to load the previous Web page, which is the shopping page. The Display Printable Order Form link will call the printOrder() function. The next step is to write the printOrder() function.

Writing HTML to Another Window

In a previous project, you opened a window and included an HTML document in the opened window. JavaScript also allows you to send HTML to a window. The printable order form in the pop-up window in Figure 5-1c on page J 5.5 contains the information for the items that the user selected. The HTML code for this window cannot exist in a static HTML document, but must be generated when the user clicks the Display Printable Order Form link.

When users view the printable order page, it is not obvious how they should obtain a copy of the order. A dialog box displays with an alert() message containing the printing instructions to the user.

Windows

When opening a window and assigning the new window to an object, the syntax newWindow = window.open ("", "WindowName") is used. The name of the object that you can use to reference the methods and properties of the window is newWindow. The name of the window that can be used to identify the window as a target from a link or form is WindowName.

Writing the printOrder() Function

The printOrder() function opens a new window and displays the items in the ShoppingCart object. The open() function, used to create the window, returns an object for the window that it opened. This document property of the object can be used to write HTML to the window. Table 5-15 shows the beginning of the print-Order() function.

Table 5-15

LINE CODE

```
72        function printOrder() {
73           var CartTotal = 0
74
75           alert("To print your order, click File on the menu bar and then click Print.
      When you are finished printing, you may close this window.")
76           order = window.open("", "orderWindow",
      "toolbar=no,width=550,height=400,status=no,menubar=yes,resize=yes")
77
78           with (order.document) {
79              write()
80              close()
81              write("<HTML>")
82              write("<TITLE>Val-U Computers Order Form</TITLE><BODY BGCOLOR=WHITE>")
83              write("<TABLE BORDER=0>")
84              write("<TR><TD><IMAGE SRC=comp4.jpg></TD>")
85              write("<TD ALIGN=CENTER VALIGN=BOTTOM>")
86              write("<H2>Val-U Computers Order Form</H2></TD>")
87              write("<TD><IMAGE SRC=comp5.jpg></TD></TR></TABLE>")
88              write("Fax this form to Val-U Computers at 555-3423.<BR>")
89              write("<CENTER><TABLE BORDER=1 CELLPADDING=1 CELLSPACING=3 WIDTH=350>")
```

Line 75 first displays the alert() message to tell the user how to obtain a hard copy of the order form. The window.open() statement in line 76 assigns the new window object to the variable named order. Line 78 uses the With statement to avoid the use of the order.window object name in lines 79 through 89. To add the start of the printOrder() function, perform the steps on the next page.

To Add the Start of the printOrder() Function

1 Position the insertion point on line 71 and then press the ENTER key.

2 Enter the JavaScript code shown in Table 5-15 on the previous page and then press the ENTER key.

The start of the printOrder() function displays (Figure 5-23).

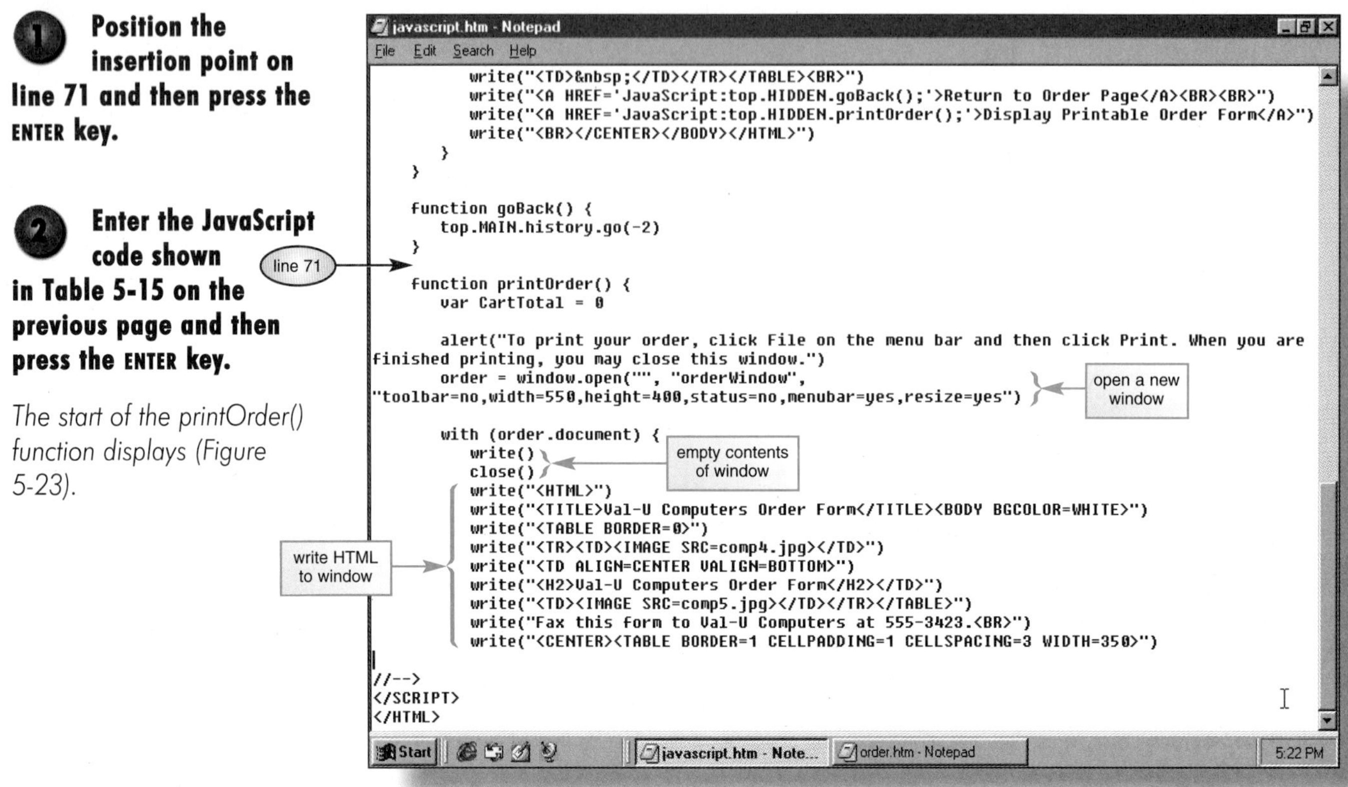
javascript.htm - Notepad
File Edit Search Help
write("<TD> </TD></TR></TABLE>
")
write("<A HREF='JavaScript:top.HIDDEN.goBack();'>Return to Order Page</A>

")
write("<A HREF='JavaScript:top.HIDDEN.printOrder();'>Display Printable Order Form</A>")
write("
</CENTER></BODY></HTML>")
}
}
function goBack() {
top.MAIN.history.go(-2)
}
function printOrder() {
var CartTotal = 0
alert("To print your order, click File on the menu bar and then click Print. When you are finished printing, you may close this window.")
order = window.open("", "orderWindow", "toolbar=no,width=550,height=400,status=no,menubar=yes,resize=yes")
with (order.document) {
write()
close()
write("<HTML>")
write("<TITLE>Val-U Computers Order Form</TITLE><BODY BGCOLOR=WHITE>")
write("<TABLE BORDER=0>")
write("<TR><TD><IMAGE SRC=comp4.jpg></TD>")
write("<TD ALIGN=CENTER VALIGN=BOTTOM>")
write("<H2>Val-U Computers Order Form</H2></TD>")
write("<TD><IMAGE SRC=comp5.jpg></TD></TR></TABLE>")
write("Fax this form to Val-U Computers at 555-3423.
")
write("<CENTER><TABLE BORDER=1 CELLPADDING=1 CELLSPACING=3 WIDTH=350>")
//-->
</SCRIPT>
</HTML>
line 71
open a new window
empty contents of window
write HTML to window
Start
javascript.htm - Note...
order.htm - Notepad
5:22 PM

FIGURE 5-23

The next step is to write the table rows for the HTML table that displays from the code in Table 5-15. Table 5-16 shows the JavaScript code to write the table rows for the shopping cart items for the printable order form.

Table 5-16

LINE	CODE
91	`for (i in ShoppingCart) {`
92	`CartTotal = CartTotal + ShoppingCart[i].Price`
93	`if (ShoppingCart[i].ItemNum != null)`
94	`ShoppingCart[i].display(false, order.document)`
95	`}`

Line 91 uses the For-in statement to loop through the items in the ShoppingCart object. The display method called in line 94 receives the parameters of false and order.document. The false parameter tells the display method not to display the Remove from Cart link in the table. The order.document parameter is the name of the document in the printable order page window. To add the For-in loop to display the shopping cart items in the printable order form window, perform the following steps.

Steps

To Add the For-in Loop to the printOrder() Function

1 Position the insertion point on line 90 and then press the ENTER key.

2 Enter the JavaScript code shown in Table 5-16 and then press the ENTER key.

The For-in loop in the printOrder() function displays (Figure 5-24).

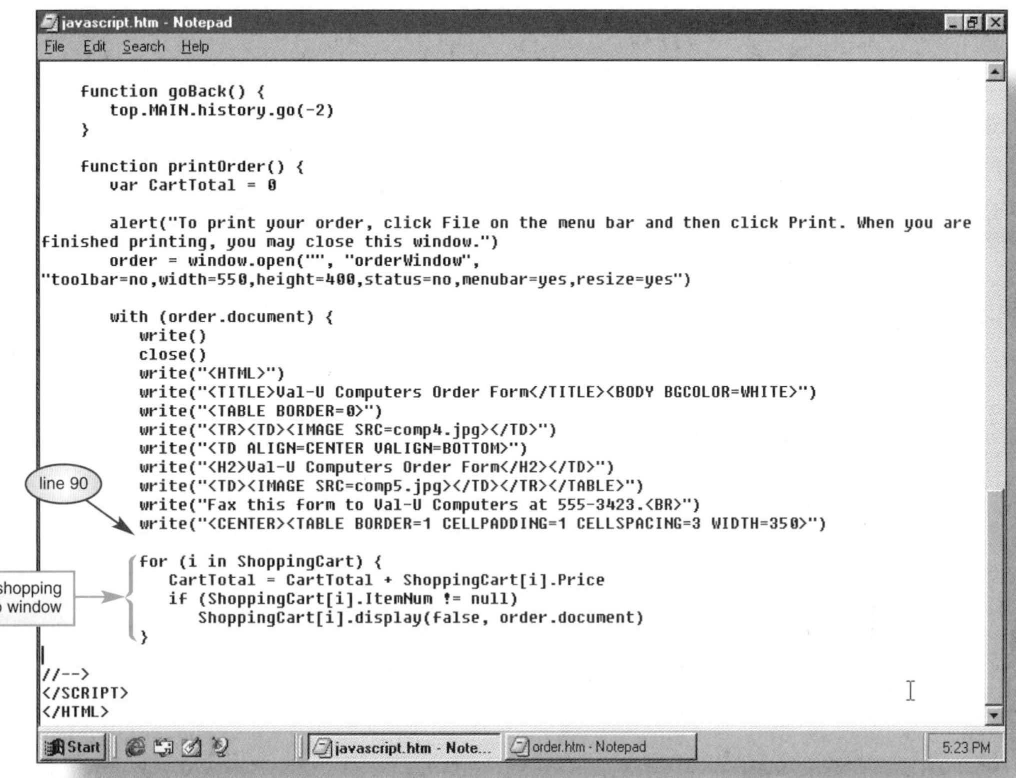
javascript.htm - Notepad
File Edit Search Help
function goBack() {
top.MAIN.history.go(-2)
}
function printOrder() {
var CartTotal = 0
alert("To print your order, click File on the menu bar and then click Print. When you are finished printing, you may close this window.")
order = window.open("", "orderWindow",
"toolbar=no,width=550,height=400,status=no,menubar=yes,resize=yes")
with (order.document) {
write()
close()
write("<HTML>")
write("<TITLE>Val-U Computers Order Form</TITLE><BODY BGCOLOR=WHITE>")
write("<TABLE BORDER=0>")
write("<TR><TD><IMAGE SRC=comp4.jpg></TD>")
write("<TD ALIGN=CENTER VALIGN=BOTTOM>")
write("<H2>Val-U Computers Order Form</H2></TD>")
write("<TD><IMAGE SRC=comp5.jpg></TD></TR></TABLE>")
write("Fax this form to Val-U Computers at 555-3423.
")
write("<CENTER><TABLE BORDER=1 CELLPADDING=1 CELLSPACING=3 WIDTH=350>")
for (i in ShoppingCart) {
CartTotal = CartTotal + ShoppingCart[i].Price
if (ShoppingCart[i].ItemNum != null)
ShoppingCart[i].display(false, order.document)
}
//-->
</SCRIPT>
</HTML>
line 90
write shopping cart to window
Start
javascript.htm - Note...
order.htm - Notepad
5:23 PM

FIGURE 5-24

The shopping cart items will display in the printable order form window. The next section adds the HTML code that writes the total price and finishes the HTML code for the order form window. Table 5-17 shows the JavaScript code that writes out the HTML code used to finish the Web page.

Table 5-17

LINE	CODE
97	`write("<TR><TD></TD><TD ALIGN=RIGHT>$" + CartTotal + "</TD></TR>")`
98	`write("</TABLE>")`
99	`write("</CENTER></BODY></HTML>")`
100	`close()`
101	`}`
102	`}`

The code contained in the write statement on line 97 concatenates the necessary HTML with the cartTotal variable that was incremented in the For-in loop. Lines 98 and 99 finish the HTML table and HTML tags. To finish the printOrder() function, perform the steps on the next page.

To Finish the HTML Code for the Printable Order Form Window

1 Position the insertion point on line 96 and then press the ENTER key.

2 Enter the JavaScript code shown in Table 5-17 on the previous page and then press the ENTER key.

The remainder of the printOrder() function displays (Figure 5-25).

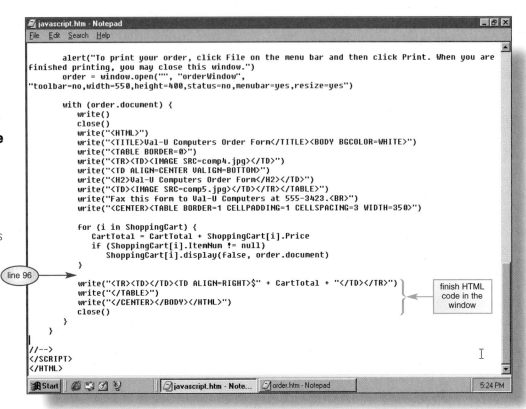

```
javascript.htm - Notepad
File  Edit  Search  Help

        alert("To print your order, click File on the menu bar and then click Print. When you are
finished printing, you may close this window.")
        order = window.open("", "orderWindow",
"toolbar=no,width=550,height=400,status=no,menubar=yes,resize=yes")

        with (order.document) {
            write()
            close()
            write("<HTML>")
            write("<TITLE>Val-U Computers Order Form</TITLE><BODY BGCOLOR=WHITE>")
            write("<TABLE BORDER=0>")
            write("<TR><TD><IMAGE SRC=comp4.jpg></TD>")
            write("<TD ALIGN=CENTER VALIGN=BOTTOM>")
            write("<H2>Val-U Computers Order Form</H2></TD>")
            write("<TD><IMAGE SRC=comp5.jpg></TD></TR></TABLE>")
            write("Fax this form to Val-U Computers at 555-3423.<BR>")
            write("<CENTER><TABLE BORDER=1 CELLPADDING=1 CELLSPACING=3 WIDTH=350>")

            for (i in ShoppingCart) {
                CartTotal = CartTotal + ShoppingCart[i].Price
                if (ShoppingCart[i].ItemNum != null)
                    ShoppingCart[i].display(false, order.document)
            }

            write("<TR><TD></TD><TD ALIGN=RIGHT>$" + CartTotal + "</TD></TR>")
            write("</TABLE>")
            write("</CENTER></BODY></HTML>")
            close()
        }
    }

//-->
</SCRIPT>
</HTML>
```


FIGURE 5-25

The contents of the shopping cart now display in a new browser window when the printOrder() function is called. The next step is to write the JavaScript code that checks for a keystroke on the shopping page.

Determining Browsers and Detecting Keystrokes

Different browsers often behave differently when running JavaScript. Most capabilities of JavaScript are the same across all browsers, but some important differences exist. The **navigator** object tells you which browser the Web page visitor is using. Based on this information, you can execute the appropriate JavaScript code.

One of the differences among the Netscape Navigator browsers and the Microsoft Internet Expolorer browsers is how they handle the onKeyPressed() event for a document. The **onKeyPressed()** event occurs when a user presses a key on a Web page. Sometimes, it is necessary to be able to capture a keystroke from a user on a Web page. The onKeyPressed() event passes a key code to the event handler assigned to the event.

Browser-Specific Issues

Many of the differences in browsers relate to how the browsers handle newer Web design techniques, such as dynamic HTML (DHTML). For more information about JavaScript and DHTML, visit www.scsite.com/js/p5.htm and then click DHTML.

Responding to a Keystroke Based on the Browser Type

The navigator object in JavaScript gives extensive information about the environment in which the Web page user is operating. Table 5-18 shows some of the properties of the navigator object. The appName property of the navigator object tells you which browser type the Web page visitor is using.

Once the browser type is determined, different JavaScript code can be executed for each browser. Table 5-19 illustrates the keyPressed() function executed on the onKeyPressed event and is used to test which key the user pressed.

Once the browser type is determined to be Netscape Navigator, the key that the user pressed is decoded in lines 108 and 109. Line 108 uses the **Which** property of the key that was passed to the function. The Which property returns the ASCII value of the key. The key.which value is forced to be a numeric value by making the result a new Number object. In line 109, the **toString**(16) method converts the KeyChar variable to hexadecimal. This hexadecimal value then is processed using the unescape() function and converted to a standard character that can be tested. To add the start of the keyPressed() function to detect a keystroke, perform the following steps.

Table 5-18 Some properties of the navigator object

PROPERTY	USE
appName	The product name of the browser
appVersion	The browser version number
cookieEnabled	Indicates if the user has enabled cookies in the browser
language	The language being used by the browser
platform	The operating system on which the browser is running

Table 5-19

LINE	CODE
104	`function keyPressed(key) {`
105	`   var sentString = ""`
106	
107	`   if (navigator.appName == "Netscape") {`
108	`      var KeyChar = new Number(key.which)`
109	`      sentString = sentString + unescape("%" + KeyChar.toString(16))`
110	`      if (sentString == "v" || sentString == "V")`
111	`         viewCart()`
112	`}`

To Detect a Keystroke in Netscape Navigator

1 Position the insertion point on line 103 and then press the ENTER key.

2 Enter the JavaScript code shown in Table 5-19 and do not press the ENTER key.

The start of the keyPressed() function displays (Figure 5-26).

javascript.htm - Notepad

File Edit Search Help

```
      write("<TITLE>Val-U Computers Order Form</TITLE><BODY BGCOLOR=WHITE>")
      write("<TABLE BORDER=0>")
      write("<TR><TD><IMAGE SRC=comp4.jpg></TD>")
      write("<TD ALIGN=CENTER VALIGN=BOTTOM>")
      write("<H2>Val-U Computers Order Form</H2></TD>")
      write("<TD><IMAGE SRC=comp5.jpg></TD></TR></TABLE>")
      write("Fax this form to Val-U Computers at 555-3423.<BR>")
      write("<CENTER><TABLE BORDER=1 CELLPADDING=1 CELLSPACING=3 WIDTH=350>")

      for (i in ShoppingCart) {
         CartTotal = CartTotal + ShoppingCart[i].Price
         if (ShoppingCart[i].ItemNum != null)
            ShoppingCart[i].display(false, order.document)
      }

      write("<TR><TD></TD><TD ALIGN=RIGHT>$" + CartTotal + "</TD></TR>")
      write("</TABLE>")
      write("</CENTER></BODY></HTML>")
      close()
   }
}
function keyPressed(key) {
   var sentString = ""

   if (navigator.appName == "Netscape") {
      var KeyChar = new Number(key.which)
      sentString = sentString + unescape("%" + KeyChar.toString(16))
      if (sentString == "v" || sentString == "V")
         viewCart()
   }
//-->
</SCRIPT>
```

line 103

navigator object

check for a Netscape browser

which property

call the toString() method

call the viewCart() function

FIGURE 5-26

The same logic can be used to detect the key that users press if they are using Microsoft Internet Explorer. Table 5-20 shows the JavaScript code that tests for the Microsoft Internet Explorer browser and finishes the keyPressed() function.

Table 5-20

```
LINE  CODE
113         if (navigator.appName == "Microsoft Internet Explorer") {
114            sentString = sentString + String.fromCharCode(top.MAIN.window.event.keyCode)
115            if (sentString == "v" || sentString == "V")
116               viewCart()
117            }
118      }
```

More About

Capturing Keystrokes

Many users prefer using the keyboard to the mouse for navigation and input. For more information about capturing keystrokes, visit www.scsite.com/js/p5.htm and then click Keystrokes.

Line 113 tests the appName property of the navigator object for the Microsoft Internet Explorer browser. In line 114, the **keyCode** property of an event occuring in the frame named MAIN is used. This property is available only in Microsoft Internet Explorer and is set when a key is pressed in a document. The property is passed to the fromCharCode method of the String variable type. The **fromCharCode** method converts the key to a readable character that can be tested in line 115. To add the end of the keyPressed() function to detect a keystroke, perform the following steps.

Steps To Detect a Keystroke in Microsoft Internet Explorer

1. **Position the insertion point at the end of line 112 and then press the ENTER key.**

2. **Enter the JavaScript code shown in Table 5-20 and then press the ENTER key.**

The rest of the keyPressed() function displays (Figure 5-27).

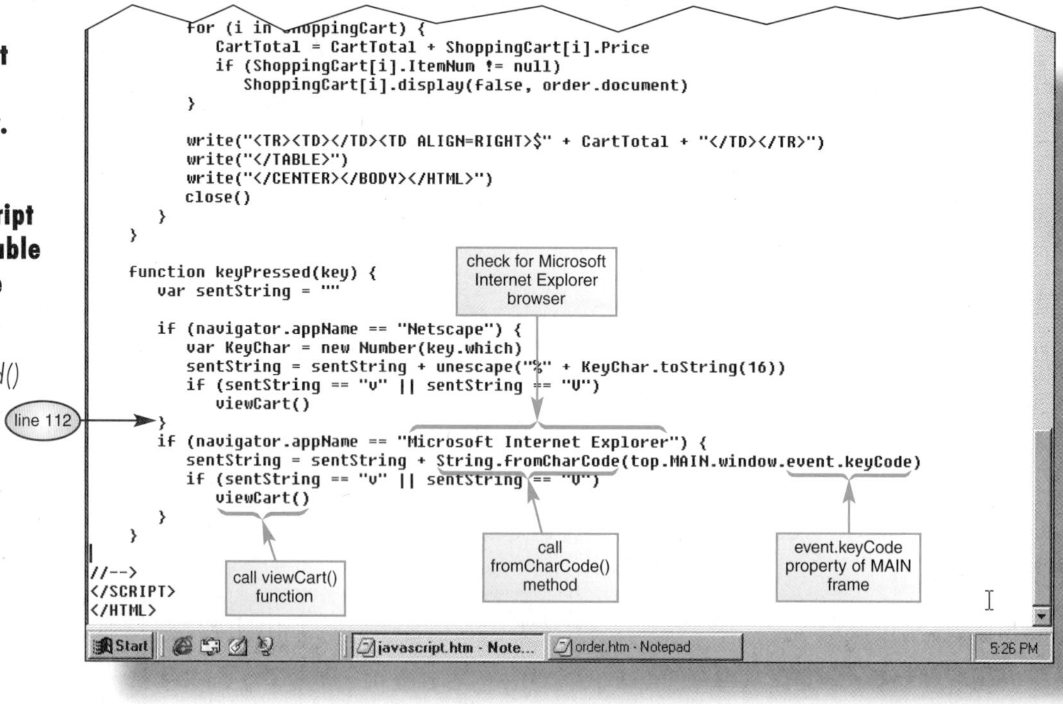

```
      for (i in ShoppingCart) {
         CartTotal = CartTotal + ShoppingCart[i].Price
         if (ShoppingCart[i].ItemNum != null)
            ShoppingCart[i].display(false, order.document)
      }

      write("<TR><TD></TD><TD ALIGN=RIGHT>$" + CartTotal + "</TD></TR>")
      write("</TABLE>")
      write("</CENTER></BODY></HTML>")
      close()
   }
}

function keyPressed(key) {
   var sentString = ""

   if (navigator.appName == "Netscape") {
      var KeyChar = new Number(key.which)
      sentString = sentString + unescape("%" + KeyChar.toString(16))
      if (sentString == "v" || sentString == "V")
         viewCart()
   }
   if (navigator.appName == "Microsoft Internet Explorer") {
      sentString = sentString + String.fromCharCode(top.MAIN.window.event.keyCode)
      if (sentString == "v" || sentString == "V")
         viewCart()
   }
}

//-->
</SCRIPT>
</HTML>
```

line 112

check for Microsoft Internet Explorer browser

call viewCart() function

call fromCharCode() method

event.keyCode property of MAIN frame

Start | javascript.htm - Note... | order.htm - Notepad | 5:26 PM

FIGURE 5-27

For Netscape Navigator, the onKeyPress event for the shopping page must be linked to the keyPressed() function using JavaScript. The browser must be instructed to execute the keyPressed() function in the hidden frame when a key is pressed in the frame named MAIN. Table 5-21 shows the JavaScript code used to tell the browser to link the onKeyPress event to the keyPressed() function.

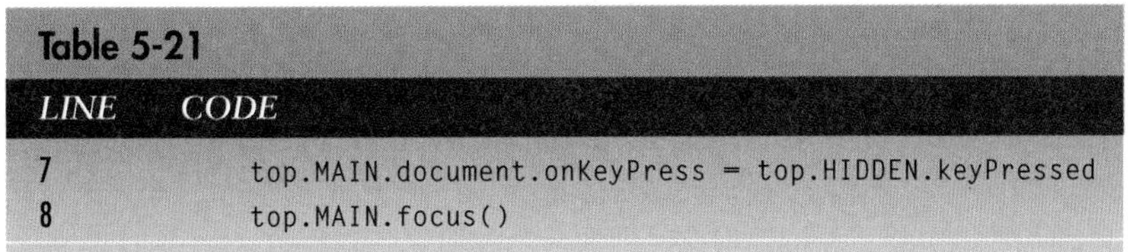

Table 5-21

LINE	CODE
7	top.MAIN.document.onKeyPress = top.HIDDEN.keyPressed
8	top.MAIN.focus()

Although this code always executes when the frame named HIDDEN is loaded, it is only meaningful to Netscape Navigator browsers. Line 8 forces the browser to give focus to the frame named MAIN when the Web page is loaded. Unless the browser is told explicitly to give focus to that frame, it is unknown which frame will have focus when the Val-U Computers Web page loads. By giving focus to the MAIN frame, any keys that the user presses will be captured by the onKeyPress event handler. To add the JavaScript code to set the onKeyPress event handler for Netscape Navigator, perform the following steps.

> **More About**
>
> **About fromCharCode**
>
> fromCharCode is a method of the built-in String object. The fromCharCode method can take several values as arguments and concatenate them together into a string. For more information about fromCharCode, visit www.scsite.com/js/p5.htm and then click fromCharCode.

To Detect a Keystroke in the Hidden Frame

1 **Position the insertion point on line 6 and then press the ENTER key.**

2 **Enter the JavaScript code shown in Table 5-21 and then press the ENTER key.**

The code displays (Figure 5-28).

```
<HTML>
<SCRIPT LANGUAGE="JAVASCRIPT">
<!-- Hide from old browsers
   var numItems = 0
   var ShoppingCart = new Object

   top.MAIN.document.onKeyPress = top.HIDDEN.keyPressed
   top.MAIN.focus()

   function addItem(Description, Price, ItemNum) {
      this.Description = Description
      this.Price = Price
      this.ItemNum = ItemNum
      this.display = printItem
      return this
   }

   function addtoCart(Description, Price) {
      ShoppingCart[numItems] = new addItem(Description, Price, numItems)
      numItems = numItems + 1
      alert(Description + " has been added to your shopping cart.")
   }

   function deleteItem(ItemNum) {
      delete ShoppingCart[ItemNum]
      viewCart()
   }

   function printItem(deleteFlag, TargetDocument) {
      with (TargetDocument) {
         write("<TR><TD>" + this.Description + "</TD>")
         write("<TD ALIGN=RIGHT>$" + this.Price + "</TD>")
         if (deleteFlag = true)
            write("<TD><A HREF='JavaScript:top.HIDDEN.deleteItem(" + this.ItemNum + ")'>Remove
From Cart</A></TD>")
```


FIGURE 5-28

The next step is to set the keyPressed event for Microsoft Internet Explorer. This is achieved with the BODY tag of the order.htm Web page. To add the event handler for the onKeyPress event in Microsoft Internet Explorer, perform the following steps.

Steps To Call the keyPressed() Function

1. **Click the order.htm – Notepad button on the taskbar to open the order.htm Web page.**

2. **Position the insertion point on line 2 just before the > character and then press the SPACEBAR once. Type** `onKeyPress="JavaScript:top.HIDDEN.keyPressed()"` **and do not press the ENTER key.**

   The call to keyPressed() function displays (Figure 5-29).

3. **With the JavaScript Data Disk in drive A, click File on the menu bar and then click Save.**

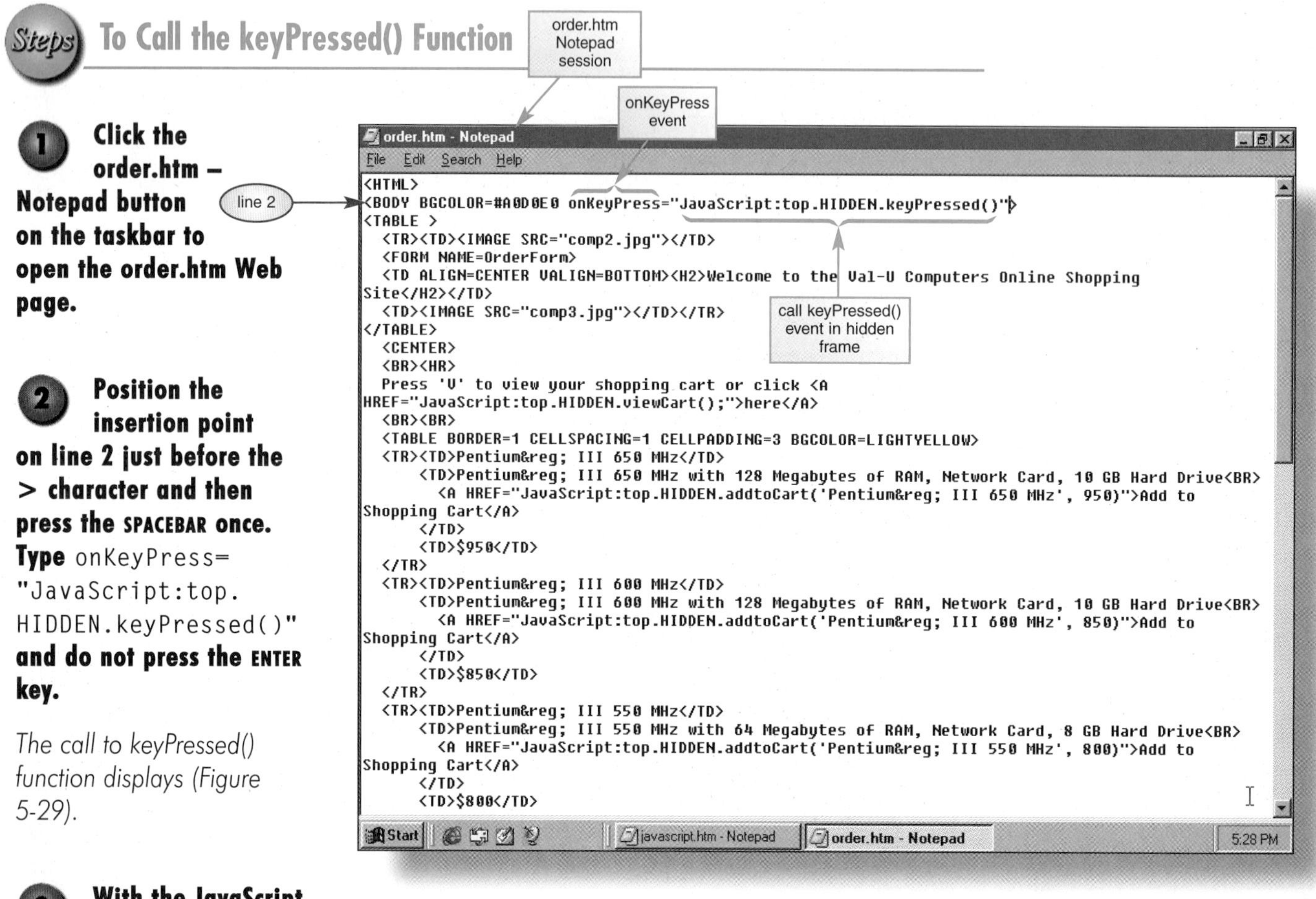


```
<HTML>
<BODY BGCOLOR=#A0D0E0 onKeyPress="JavaScript:top.HIDDEN.keyPressed()">
<TABLE >
  <TR><TD><IMAGE SRC="comp2.jpg"></TD>
  <FORM NAME=OrderForm>
  <TD ALIGN=CENTER VALIGN=BOTTOM><H2>Welcome to the Val-U Computers Online Shopping
Site</H2></TD>
  <TD><IMAGE SRC="comp3.jpg"></TD></TR>
</TABLE>
  <CENTER>
  <BR><HR>
  Press 'V' to view your shopping cart or click <A
HREF="JavaScript:top.HIDDEN.viewCart();">here</A>
  <BR><BR>
  <TABLE BORDER=1 CELLSPACING=1 CELLPADDING=3 BGCOLOR=LIGHTYELLOW>
  <TR><TD>Pentium&reg; III 650 MHz</TD>
      <TD>Pentium&reg; III 650 MHz with 128 Megabytes of RAM, Network Card, 10 GB Hard Drive<BR>
        <A HREF="JavaScript:top.HIDDEN.addtoCart('Pentium&reg; III 650 MHz', 950)">Add to
Shopping Cart</A>
      </TD>
      <TD>$950</TD>
  </TR>
  <TR><TD>Pentium&reg; III 600 MHz</TD>
      <TD>Pentium&reg; III 600 MHz with 128 Megabytes of RAM, Network Card, 10 GB Hard Drive<BR>
        <A HREF="JavaScript:top.HIDDEN.addtoCart('Pentium&reg; III 600 MHz', 850)">Add to
Shopping Cart</A>
      </TD>
      <TD>$850</TD>
  </TR>
  <TR><TD>Pentium&reg; III 550 MHz</TD>
      <TD>Pentium&reg; III 550 MHz with 64 Megabytes of RAM, Network Card, 8 GB Hard Drive<BR>
        <A HREF="JavaScript:top.HIDDEN.addtoCart('Pentium&reg; III 550 MHz', 800)">Add to
Shopping Cart</A>
      </TD>
      <TD>$800</TD>
```

FIGURE 5-29

The keyPressed() event triggers when the user presses a key while the MAIN frame is displaying the order.htm shopping page. When the user presses a key, the keyPressed() function in the top.HIDDEN frame executes. Recall that the top.HIDDEN frame always contains the javascript.htm Web page.

The next step is to capture the user's personal information for display on the printable version of the shopping cart.

Using the prompt() Function

The prompt() function, introduced earlier, is useful for capturing small amounts of information. The printable version of the shopping cart page requires that the customer name, customer ID, and telephone number be displayed so Val-U Computers can identify the customers when they order by fax or mail.

Table 5-22 shows the JavaScript code to declare the variables for the customer information and to prompt the user for the information.

Table 5-22

LINE	CODE
76	`var Name = ""`
77	`var CustomerID = ""`
78	`var PhoneNumber = ""`
79	
80	`Name = prompt("Enter your name:", "")`
81	`CustomerID = prompt("Enter your customer ID:", "")`
82	`PhoneNumber = prompt("Enter your phone number:", "")`

To add the JavaScript code that prompts the user for information, perform the following steps.

To Prompt the User for Customer Information

1 Click the javascript.htm – Notepad button on the taskbar to open the javascript.htm Web page.

2 Position the insertion point at the end of line 75 and then press the ENTER key.

3 Enter the JavaScript code shown in Table 5-22.

The JavaScript code that prompts the user for customer information displays (Figure 5-30).

javascript.htm Notepad session

line 75

prompt for customer information

```
javascript.htm - Notepad
File  Edit  Search  Help
    function printOrder() {
       var CartTotal = 0
       var Name = ""
       var CustomerID = ""
       var PhoneNumber = ""

       Name = prompt("Enter your name:", "")
       CustomerID = prompt("Enter your customer ID:", "")
       PhoneNumber = prompt("Enter your phone number:", "")

       alert("To print your order, click File on the menu bar and then click Print. When you are
finished printing, you may close this window.")
       order = window.open("", "orderWindow",
"toolbar=no,width=550,height=400,status=no,menubar=yes,resize=yes")

       with (order.document) {
          write()
          close()
          write("<HTML>")
          write("<TITLE>Val-U Computers Order Form</TITLE><BODY BGCOLOR=WHITE>")
          write("<TABLE BORDER=0>")
          write("<TR><TD><IMAGE SRC=comp4.jpg></TD>")
          write("<TD ALIGN=CENTER VALIGN=BOTTOM>")
          write("<H2>Val-U Computers Order Form</H2></TD>")
          write("<TD><IMAGE SRC=comp5.jpg></TD></TR></TABLE>")
          write("Fax this form to Val-U Computers at 555-3423.<BR>")
          write("Your Name: " + Name + "<BR>")
          write("Your Customer ID: " + CustomerID + "<BR>")
          write("Your Phone Number: " + PhoneNumber + "<BR><BR>")
          write("<CENTER><TABLE BORDER=1 CELLPADDING=1 CELLSPACING=3 WIDTH=350>")

          for (i in ShoppingCart) {
             CartTotal = CartTotal + ShoppingCart[i].Price
             if (ShoppingCart[i].ItemNum != null)
                ShoppingCart[i].display(false, order.document)
Start | javascript.htm - Note... | order.htm - Notepad | 5:30 PM
```

FIGURE 5-30

The Web page prompts the user for information just before the printing instructions display in the alert() box. Next, the customer information must be displayed on the order form. Table 5-23 shows the code that writes the HTML code that displays the user information on the printable page.

Table 5-23

LINE	CODE
98	`write("Your Name: " + Name + " ")`
99	`write("Your Customer ID: " + CustomerID + " ")`
100	`write("Your Phone Number: " + PhoneNumber + "  ")`

To add the JavaScript code that displays the customer information on the printable order form page, perform the following steps.

Steps To Display the Customer Information on the Printable Page

1 **Position the insertion point at the end of line 97 and then press the ENTER key.**

2 **Enter the JavaScript code shown in Table 5-23 and do not press the ENTER key.**

The code that writes the HTML to display the user information displays (Figure 5-31).

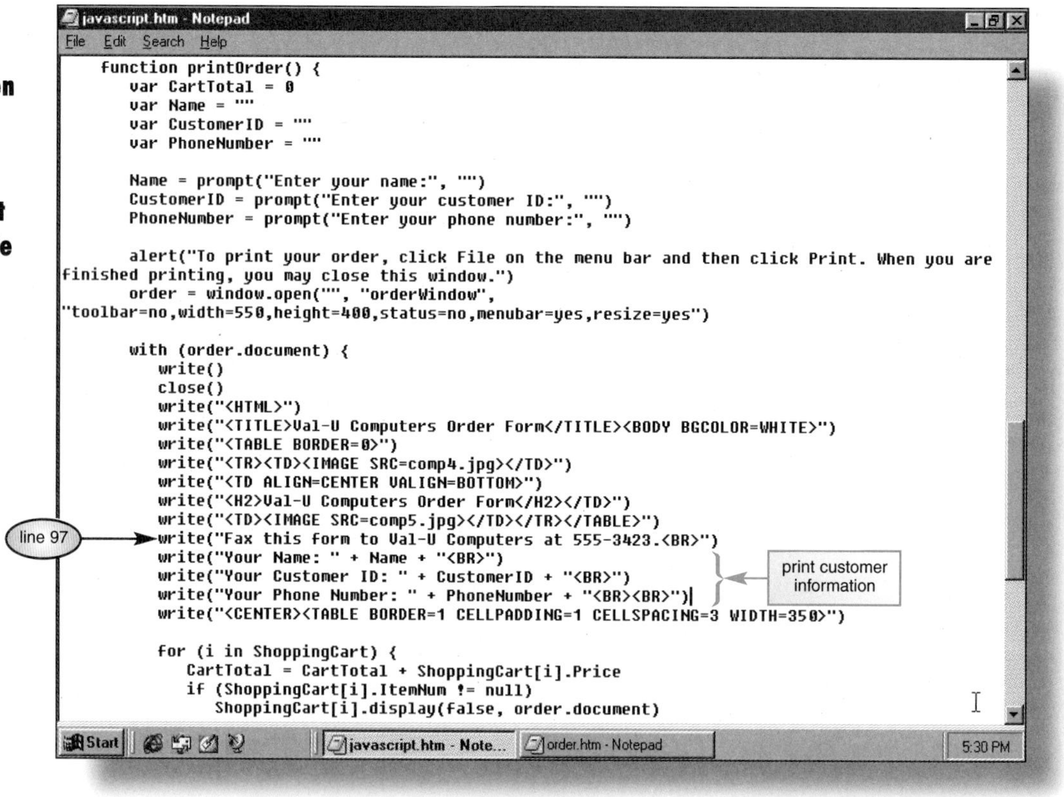

javascript.htm - Notepad

File Edit Search Help

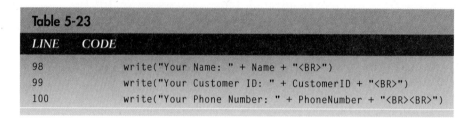

```
function printOrder() {
   var CartTotal = 0
   var Name = ""
   var CustomerID = ""
   var PhoneNumber = ""

   Name = prompt("Enter your name:", "")
   CustomerID = prompt("Enter your customer ID:", "")
   PhoneNumber = prompt("Enter your phone number:", "")

   alert("To print your order, click File on the menu bar and then click Print. When you are
finished printing, you may close this window.")
   order = window.open("", "orderWindow",
"toolbar=no,width=550,height=400,status=no,menubar=yes,resize=yes")

   with (order.document) {
      write()
      close()
      write("<HTML>")
      write("<TITLE>Val-U Computers Order Form</TITLE><BODY BGCOLOR=WHITE>")
      write("<TABLE BORDER=0>")
      write("<TR><TD><IMAGE SRC=comp4.jpg></TD>")
      write("<TD ALIGN=CENTER VALIGN=BOTTOM>")
      write("<H2>Val-U Computers Order Form</H2></TD>")
      write("<TD><IMAGE SRC=comp5.jpg></TD></TR></TABLE>")
      write("Fax this form to Val-U Computers at 555-3423.<BR>")
      write("Your Name: " + Name + "<BR>")
      write("Your Customer ID: " + CustomerID + "<BR>")
      write("Your Phone Number: " + PhoneNumber + "<BR><BR>")
      write("<CENTER><TABLE BORDER=1 CELLPADDING=1 CELLSPACING=3 WIDTH=350>")

      for (i in ShoppingCart) {
         CartTotal = CartTotal + ShoppingCart[i].Price
         if (ShoppingCart[i].ItemNum != null)
            ShoppingCart[i].display(false, order.document)
```

line 97

print customer information

Start | javascript.htm - Note... | order.htm - Notepad | 5:30 PM

FIGURE 5-31

The shopping cart page now prompts the user for customer information just before displaying the printable order form.

The next steps are to save your file and test the Web page.

Saving and Testing the Web Page in the Browser

The JavaScript code and HTML code you have written allows users to navigate backwards from the shopping cart page to the shopping page. The users can navigate to the shopping cart page with a keystroke or a mouse click. The user also can display a printable version of their order form in a new window. Perform the following steps to save and test your Web page.

To Save and Test the Web Page in the Browser

1. **With the JavaScript Data Disk in drive A, click File on the menu bar and then click Save.**

2. **Start your browser and open valucomp.htm.**

   The Val-U Computers shopping Web page opens.

3. **Click the Add to Shopping Cart links next to the Pentium III 650 MHz system, the Pentium 600 MHz system, the AMD Athlon 650 MHz system, and the AMD Athlon 600 MHz system.**

   The Web browser displays the dialog boxes containing the alert messages that indicate the items have been added to the shopping cart.

4. **Press the v key to view the shopping cart.**

   The Web browser displays the shopping cart page with the selected items (Figure 5-32).

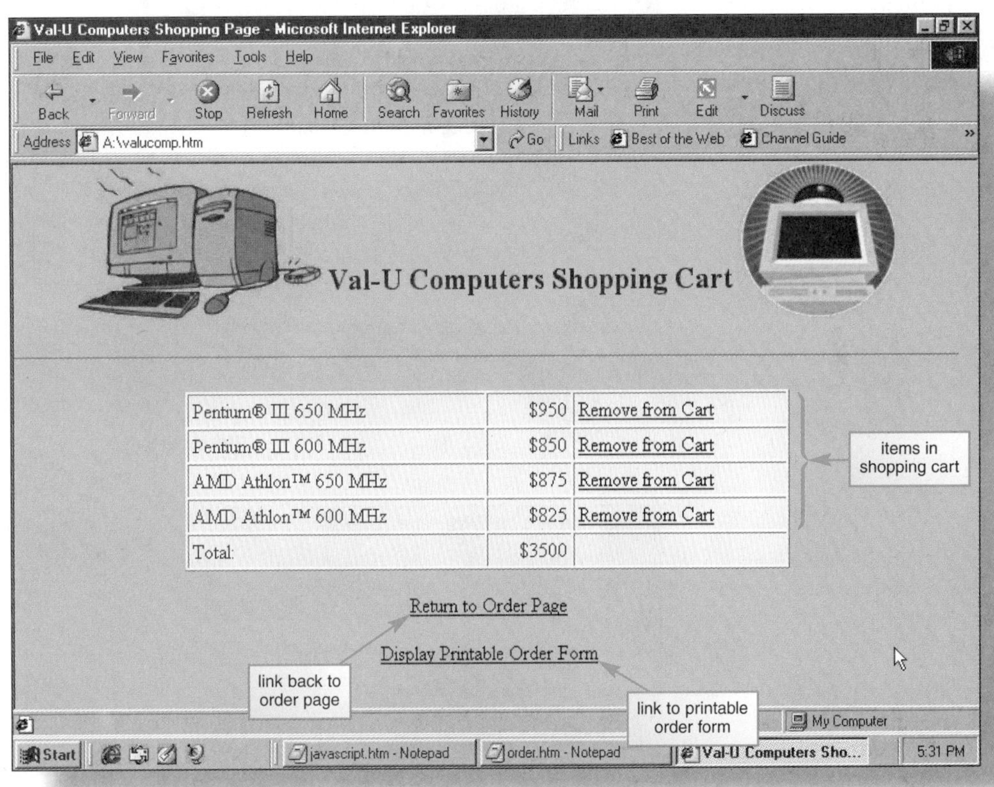

FIGURE 5-32

5 Click the Display Printable Order Form link to display the order form. Enter appropriate information for the name, customer ID, and telephone number.

The Web browser requests the customer information (Figure 5-33). Then, the Web browser displays the dialog box that contains the message informing the user how to print the order form (Figure 5-34).

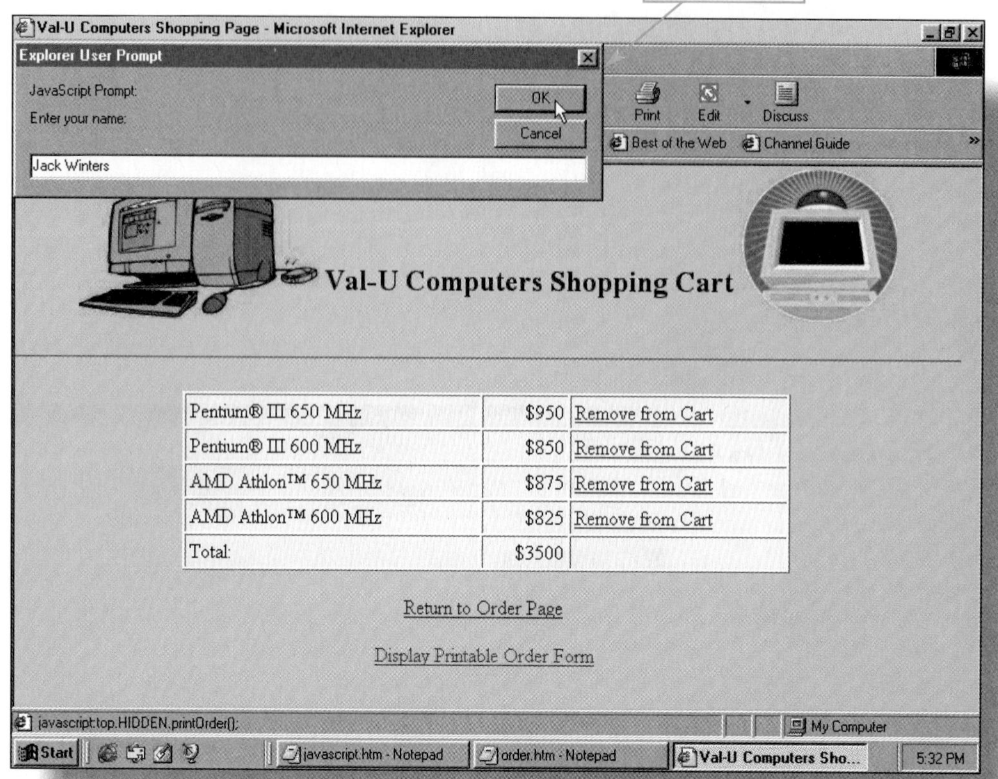

FIGURE 5-33

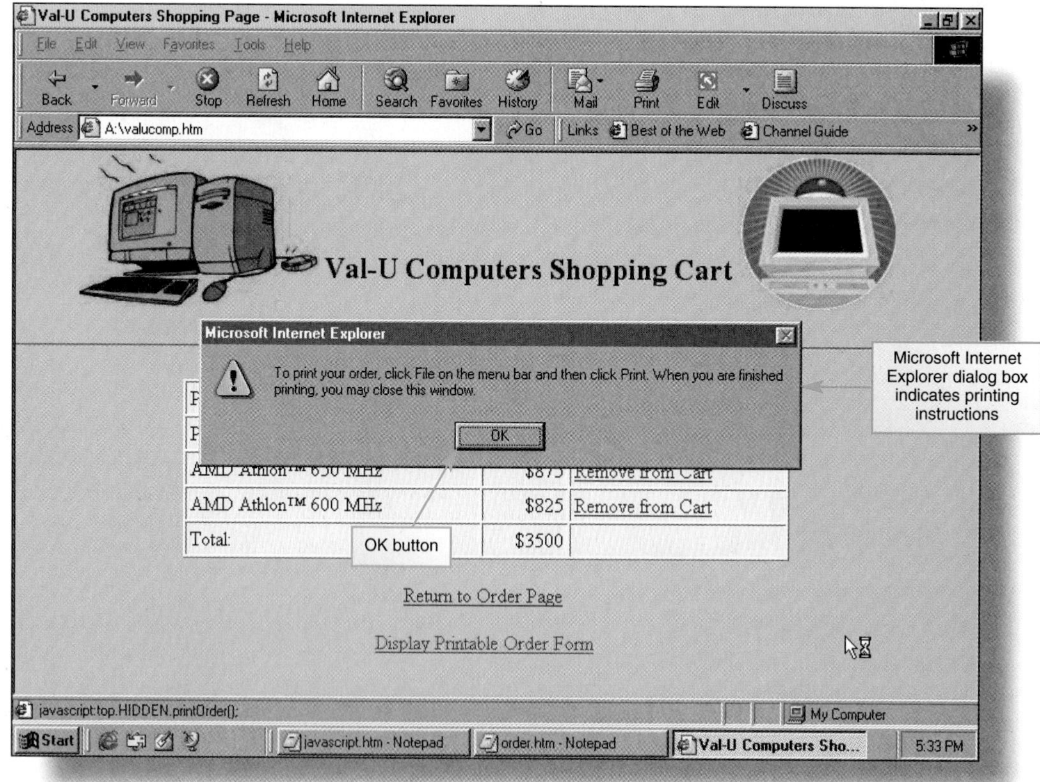

FIGURE 5-34

6 Click the OK button in the dialog box.

The Web browser displays the printable order form (Figure 5-35).

7 Click File on the browser menu bar in the printable order form window and then click Print.

The Web browser prints the order form.

FIGURE 5-35

If the browser does not display the Web page correctly, close any error message dialog boxes and then click the javascript.htm - Notepad button on the taskbar. Check the JavaScript code according to Figures 5-20 through 5-31 on pages J 5.25 through J 5.36. Correct any errors, save the file, close and reopen the browser, and then open the valucomp.htm Web page.

Project Summary

The Val-U Computers shopping page is complete. Users select computer systems to purchase. An object in a hidden frame keeps track of the user's selections. At any time, users can view their selections on what appears to be a separate Web page. If users decide to change their orders, they can click a Remove from Cart link to delete an item or they can return to the shopping page to make additional selections. When satisfied with their order, users can display a printable order form in a separate browser window. The order form includes customer information users enter when the order prints.

While creating the Val-U Computers Web page, you learned how to create and utilize hidden frames. You created an object that contained both properties and a method. The project illustrated how to use the For-in statement to loop through the elements of an object and the With statement as a shortcut to referring to object names. To determine the type of browser that a Web page visitor was using, you used the navigator object. You learned how to handle an onKeyPressed() event and handle the event differently, depending on the browser type. You opened a new window and wrote HTML code to the window. Finally, you used the prompt() function to gather user input and display the information in a Web page.

What You Should Know

Having completed this project, you now should be able to perform the following tasks.

- Add the Calls to the goBack() and printOrder() Functions *(J 5.26)*
- Add the deleteItem() Function *(J 5.12)*
- Add the For-in loop to Display the Shopping Cart *(J 5.16)*
- Add the For-in Loop to the printOrder() Function *(J 5.29)*
- Add the goBack() Function *(J 5.25)*
- Add the HTML Code for the Frames *(J 5.8)*
- Add the printItem() Method *(J 5.14)*
- Add the Start of the printOrder() Function *(J 5.28)*
- Add the Start of the viewCart() Function *(J 5.15)*
- Call the keyPressed() Function *(J 5.34)*
- Create the addtoCart() Function *(J 5.11)*
- Detect a Keystroke in Microsoft Internet Explorer *(J 5.32)*
- Detect a Keystroke in Netscape Navigator *(J 5.31)*
- Detect a Keystroke in the Hidden Frame *(J 5.33)*
- Display the Customer Information on the Printable Page *(J 5.36)*
- Enter the Link to the Shopping Cart Web Page *(J 5.19)*
- Enter the Links to Call the addtoCart() Function *(J 5.20)*
- Enter the Remaining Links to the addtoCart() Function *(J 5.20)*
- Finish the HTML Code for the Printable Order Form Window *(J 5.30)*
- Finish the HTML Code for the Shopping Cart Web Page *(J 5.17)*
- Prompt the User for Customer Information *(J 5.35)*
- Save and Test the Web Page in the Browser *(J 5.22, J 5.37)*
- Save the javascript.htm File *(J 5.18)*
- Save the valucomp.htm File *(J 5.9)*
- Start a New Notepad Document *(J 5.6, J 5.9)*
- Start Notepad and Open the order.htm File *(J 5.18)*
- Start the Hidden Frame and Create the Objects *(J 5.10)*

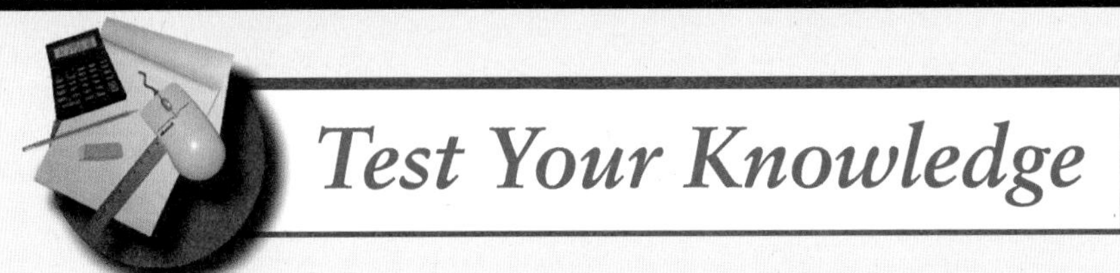

Test Your Knowledge

1 True/False

Instructions: Circle T if the statement is true or F if the statement is false.

T F 1. A Web page user can view formatted HTML code in a hidden frame.
T F 2. An object can have both a method and a property with the same name.
T F 3. An object variable always can be used in place of an array variable.
T F 4. The delete operator sets all of the properties of an object to null.
T F 5. The With statement usually should be avoided because it makes JavaScript code more unreadable.
T F 6. The For-in statement can be used to loop through the elements of an array or object.
T F 7. The go() method of the history object can be used only to move backwards through the history list for a document.
T F 8. Different versions of the same browser are indistinguishable by the navigator object.
T F 9. The keyPressed() event passes the key that the user pressed to its event handler.
T F 10. The prompt() function returns the number of characters entered by the user as well as the string that the user entered.

2 Multiple Choice

Instructions: Circle the correct response.

1. Which of the following does not apply to hidden frames?
   a. The user cannot view the contents of a hidden frame.
   b. The number of rows allocated for a hidden frame must always be zero.
   c. A hidden frame may contain only JavaScript code.
   d. Hidden frames are useful for storing data during a user's visit to a Web page.
2. A(n) ____________ is associated with an object and gives the object the ability to take an action.
   a. function b. property c. method d. array
3. The ____________ operator removes all references to an element of an object.
   a. null b. delete c. with d. new
4. If a window is named MYWINDOW and you are writing code inside of a With statement of the form `with (MYWINDOW)`, the proper way to use the close method for the window is ____________.
   a. close() c. close(MYWINDOW)
   b. MYWINDOW.close() d. close
5. The For-in statement can be used with ____________.
   a. only a variable declared as an object
   b. only a variable declared as an array
   c. a variable declared as an object or as an array
   d. any JavaScript built-in method
6. To return to the Web page that a user has just visited, use the ____________ statement.
   a. history.back() c. history.go(-2)
   b. history.back(1) d. history.forward()
7. Which of the following code returns the name of the browser that the Web page user currently is using?
   a. navigator.appVersion c. browser.version
   b. browser() d. navigator.appName

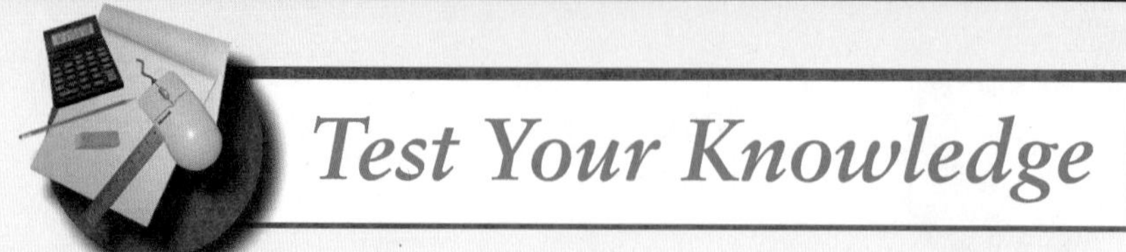

3 Understanding JavaScript Code Statements

Instructions: Carefully read each of the following descriptions of writing code statements to accomplish specific tasks. Record your answers on a sheet of paper. Number the answers to correspond to the code descriptions.

1. Write the HTML frame set that creates a hidden frame, a banner frame, and a main frame.
2. Write the JavaScript function that displays the browser name, browser version, and the operating system being used by the Web page visitor in a JavaScrtip alert() box.
3. Write the JavaScript statements that move the browser backward four pages in the current browser session.
4. Write the JavaScript function that initializes an object named car with the properties color, doors, and engine size, and the methods start, forward, and reverse.
5. Write the JavaScript statements that prompt a user for a ZIP code when the Z key is pressed on either Microsoft Internet Explorer or Netscape Navigator.
6. Write the JavaScript statement that initializes an object you created in Step 4 and then deletes the object.

4 Creating a New String Object

Instructions: Figure 5-36 shows a Web page containing a text box used to display the contents of an object that has a string value as a property. The two other text boxes are used to add text to the beginning and end of the string value property. The links next to those text boxes invoke methods that modify the string value property of the text box and redisplay the value in the top text box.

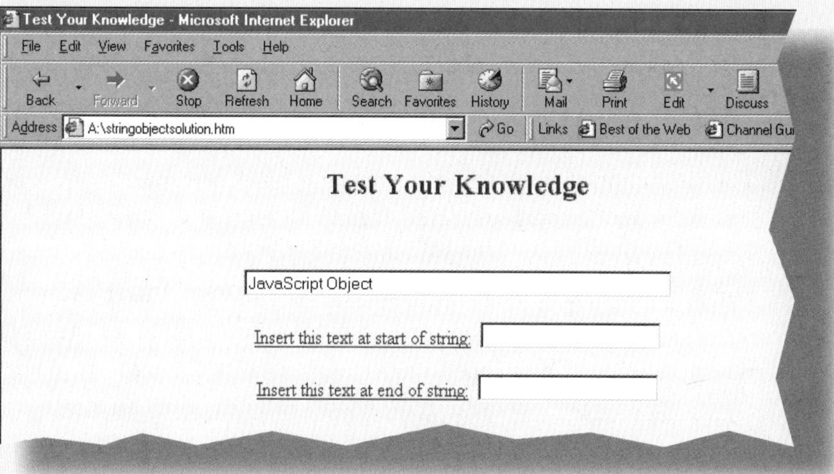

FIGURE 5-36

1. Write the function that creates an object named TextObject. The function should accept a parameter that sets the only property of the object. Name the property StringText. The object should have three methods: appendStart, appendEnd, and display. The methods should call the functions insertStart(), insertEnd(), and showText(), respectively.
2. Write the insertStart() function that is the appendStart method for the TextObject object. It should append the text in the text box named Beginning in the form named TestYourKnowledge to the beginning of the text in the StringText property. Insert a space between the new text and the existing text.
3. Write the insertEnd() function that is the appendEnd method for the TextObject object. It should append the text in the text box named Ending in the form named TestYourKnowledge to the end of the text in the StringText property. Insert a space between the existing text and the new text.
4. Write the showText() function that is the display method for the TextObject object. It should display the StringText property in the text box named TextBoxDisplay in the TestYourKnowledge form.
5. Write the JavaScript code that executes when the page loads to initiate an object named newString as a TextObject. Set the StringText property to "JavaScript Object".

Use Help

1 Exploring Online Documentation

Instructions: Start your browser and then type `www.scsite.com/js/p5.htm` in the Address text box. Click the link, Project 5 Use Help 1. Click Chapter 10, Object Model. Complete the following tasks.

Read the Web page to find the answers to the following questions.

1. What is a constructor function?
2. What is the arguments array of a function?
3. What are the rules regarding defining a property with an index versus defining a property by name?
4. Define the following object terms.
   a. method
   b. constructor
   c. property
   d. instance
5. What is an associative array?
6. Hand in the answers to your instructor.

2 Exploring Links to Other JavaScript Sites

Instructions: Start your browser and then type `www.scsite.com/js/p5.htm` in the Address text box. Complete the following tasks.

1. Click the Objects link. Read the overview of objects. Print the Web page.
2. Click the object support in a browser link. Read about how to detect which objects and methods are supported in a browser. Print the Web page.
3. Click the creating your own objects link. Read about creating custom objects. Print the Web page.
4. Click Creating Objects. Read more about creating your own objects. Print the Web page.
5. Click the history link. Read several of the answers to questions about the history object. Print the Web pages for two of the answers.
6. Click the adding methods to objects link. Read about multiple ways to add methods to an object. Print the Web page.
7. Click the screen resolution link. Read about how to display information based on the screen resolution of a Web page visitor's browser. Print the Web page.
8. Hand in the printouts to your instructor.

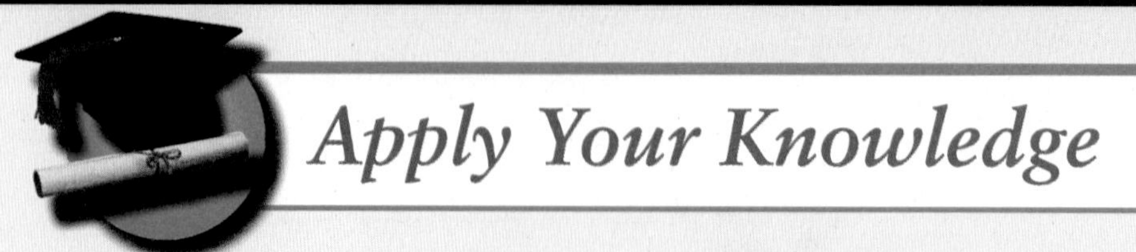

1 Using the For-in and With Statements to Display an Object

Instructions: Start Notepad. Open the Web page mycdsjs.htm on the JavaScript Data Disk. If you did not download the JavaScript Data Disk, see the inside back cover for instructions for downloading the JavaScript Data Disk or see you instructor. Grace Andreakis wants to list her CD collection on her Web page so her friends know which CDs they can borrow from her. She likes both classical and rock music, and eventually she wants the capability of adding a list of hundreds of CDs to the Web page and organizing them by musical type. She has started the list of the CDs and a JavaScript object. Complete the JavaScript that will display the list of CDs and allow visitors to screen the list based on the type of music on the CD.

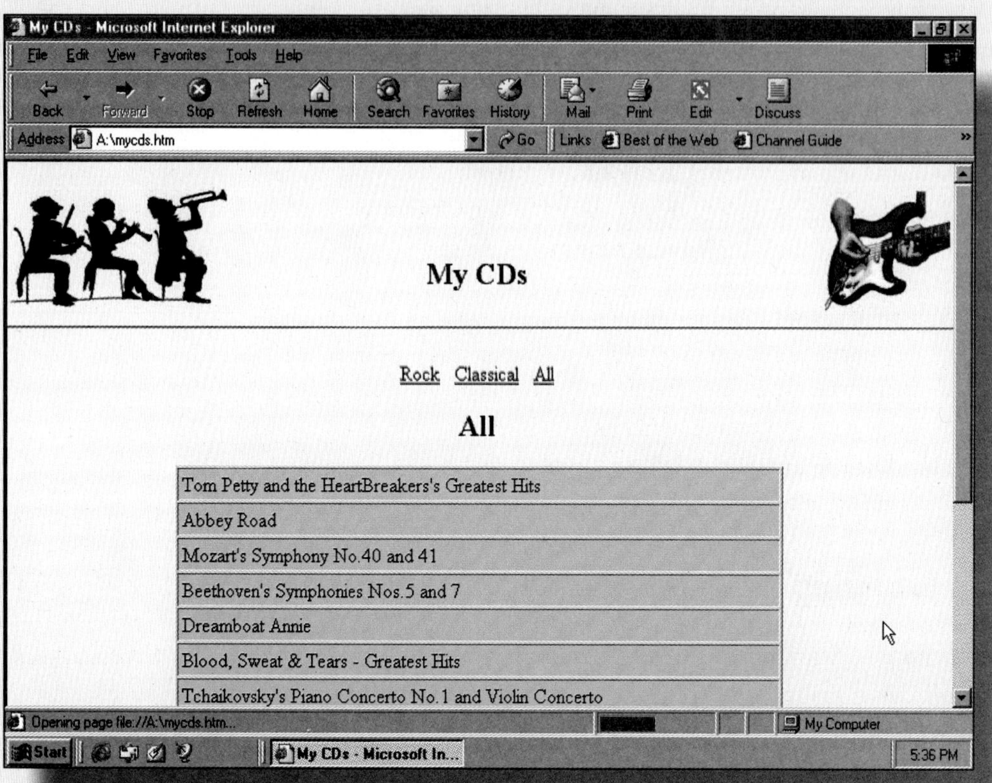

FIGURE 5-37

1. Enter the declaration for the object named CDList that will hold the list of CDs.
   a. Locate the blank line after the `<!—Hide from old browsers` comment.
   b. Position the insertion point on the blank line. Enter the following code followed by pressing the ENTER key:
   ```
   var CDList = new Object
   ```
2. Force the default Web page to show all of the CDs when the page initially is loaded by calling the Show method of the CDList object.
   a. Locate the blank line after the final addCD() call.
   b. Position the insertion point on the blank line. Press the ENTER key and then enter the following code:
   ```
   CDList.Show("All")
   ```
3. Enter the beginning of the function that is called for the Show method of the CDList object.
   a. Locate the blank line after the close of the addCD() function.
   b. Position the insertion point on the blank line. Press the ENTER key and then enter the following code:

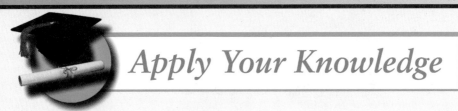

Apply Your Knowledge

```
function showCDs(Type) {
   with (top.MYCDS.document) {
     write()
     close()
     write("<HTML><TITLE>My CDs</TITLE>")
     write("<BODY BGCOLOR=LIGHTYELLOW><CENTER><BR>")
     write("<TABLE BORDER=0 WIDTH=100%><TR>")
     write("<TD WIDTH=30%><IMAGE SRC=cdclassical.jpg></TD>")
     write("<TD ALIGN=CENTER VALIGN=BOTTOM>")
     write("<H2>My CDs</H2></TD>")
     write("<TD ALIGN=RIGHT WIDTH=30%><IMAGE SRC=cdrock.jpg></TD></TR>")
     write("</TABLE>")
     write("<HR><BR>")
     write("<A HREF=JavaScript:top.HIDDEN.showCDs('Rock');>Rock</A>   ")
     write("<A HREF=JavaScript:top.HIDDEN.showCDs('Classical');>
Classical</A>   ")
     write("<A HREF=JavaScript:top.HIDDEN.showCDs('All');>All</A><BR><BR>")
     write("<H2>" + Type + "</H2>")
     write("<TABLE BORDER=1 CELLPADDING=3 CELLSPACING=1 WIDTH=500 BGCOLOR=#A0D0E0>")
```

4. Enter the remainder of the showCDs function using a For-in statement to loop through the CDList object. Position the insertion point at the end of the last line you entered in step 3, press the ENTER key twice, and then enter the following code:

```
     for (CDTitle in CDList) {
       if (CDList[CDTitle].Type != null)
         if (Type == 'All')
           write("<TR><TD>" + CDTitle + "</TD></TR>")
         else
         if (CDList[CDTitle].Type == Type)
           write("<TR><TD>" + CDTitle + "</TD></TR>")
     }
     write("</TABLE>")
     write("<BR></CENTER></BODY></HTML>")
   }
 }
```

5. Save the HTML file using the file name mycdsjssolution.htm on the JavaScript Data Disk in drive A.
6. Start your browser. Open the file a:\mycds.htm to test the JavaScript code. If any errors occur, double-check steps 1 through 4 and then save and test again.
7. Print the Web page and the HTML file. Hand in the printouts to your instructor.

1 Displaying Object Data in a Window

Problem: Frontier Equipment Rentals maintains a list of equipment for rent on its Web page. You have been hired to enhance the Web page so users can create a custom list of items they want to rent, and then print the list. The Web page should appear as shown in Figure 5-38. When the user clicks the Print your list link, the Web page displays a window with the items selected by the user.

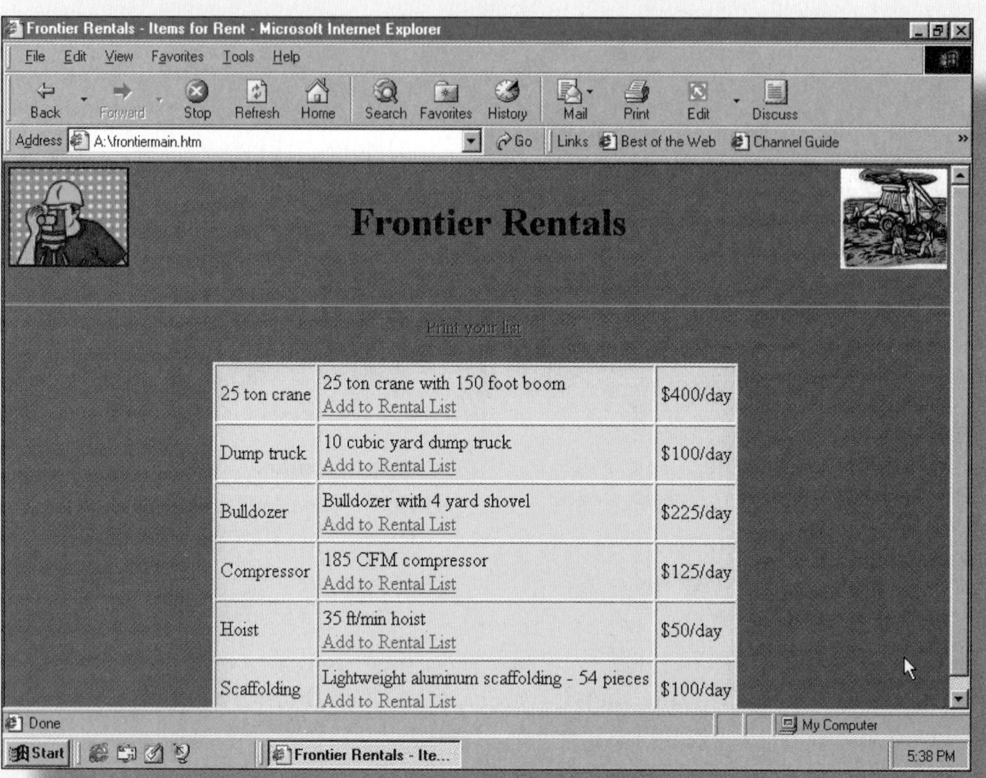

FIGURE 5-38

Instructions: Start your browser and Notepad. Using Notepad, open the frontierjs.htm file on the JavaScript Data Disk that is the HTML file for the hidden frame on the Web page.

1. Create the addtoCart() function that adds an item from the Web page to the rental list after the user clicks the Add to Rental List link. Position the insertion point on line 14, press the ENTER key, and enter the following code:

```
function addtoCart(Description, Price) {
  RentalList[numItems] = new addItem(Description, Price, numItems)
  numItems = numItems + 1
  alert(Description + " has been added to your rental list.")
}
```

2. Create the function that is the display method for the addItem object. Position the insertion point on line 20, press the ENTER key, and enter the following code:

```
function printItem(TargetDocument) {
  with (TargetDocument) {
    write("<TR><TD>" + this.Description + "</TD>")
    write("<TD ALIGN=RIGHT>$" + this.Price + "</TD>")
    write("</TR>")
  }
}
```

In the Lab

3. Start the printOrder() function that will open a window and display the contents of the RentalList object. Position the insertion point on line 28, press the ENTER key, and then enter the following code:

```
function printOrder() {
  var ListTotal = 0

  alert("To print your list, click File on the menu bar and then click Print. When you
are finished printing, you may close this window.")
  order = window.open("", "orderWindow",
"toolbar=no,width=550,height=400,status=no,menubar=yes,resize=yes")

  with (order.document) {
    write()
    close()
    write("<HTML>")
    write("<TITLE>Frontier Rentals Rental List</TITLE><BODY BGCOLOR=WHITE>")
    write("<TABLE BORDER=0>")
    write("<TR><TD><IMAGE SRC=frontier1.jpg></TD>")
    write("<TD ALIGN=CENTER VALIGN=BOTTOM>")
    write("<H2>Frontier Rentals Rental List</H2></TD>")
    write("<TD><IMAGE SRC=frontier2.jpg></TD></TR></TABLE>")
    write("Bring this form in with you to Frontier Rentals<BR>")
    write("<CENTER><TABLE BORDER=1 CELLPADDING=1 CELLSPACING=3 WIDTH=350>")
```

4. Enter the remainder of the printOrder() function by looping through the elements in the RentalList object. Position the insertion point on line 46, press the ENTER key, and then enter the following code:

```
    for (i in RentalList) {
      ListTotal = ListTotal + RentalList[i].Price
      if (RentalList[i].ItemNum != null)
        RentalList[i].display(order.document)
    }
    write("<TR><TD></TD><TD ALIGN=RIGHT>$" + ListTotal + "</TD></TR>")
    write("</TABLE>")
    write("</CENTER></BODY></HTML>")
  }
}
```

5. Save the HTML file using the file name frontierjssolution.htm on the JavaScript Data Disk in drive A.
6. Activate the browser. Open the file, a:\frontiermain.htm, to test the JavaScript code. If any errors occur, double-check steps 1 through 4 and test again. If no errors occur, print the Web page, and return to Notepad to print the HTML file. Hand in the printouts to your instructor.

2 Using the Navigator and History Objects

Problem: Dexter's Baby Toys sells products on a complex shopping Web page. Customers sometimes call the customer service area when they are experiencing problems using the Web page. As the Web page programmer for Dexter's, you have found that many of these problems are related to Web page visitors who are using older Web browsers. You decide to design a Web page to which customer service personnel can direct customers having problems. Because many users of the shopping site are beginners, the Web page must be very simple to use. The Web page will tell the user all of the information regarding which browser version they are running. Then, by clicking a link, the user will go back to the previous page.

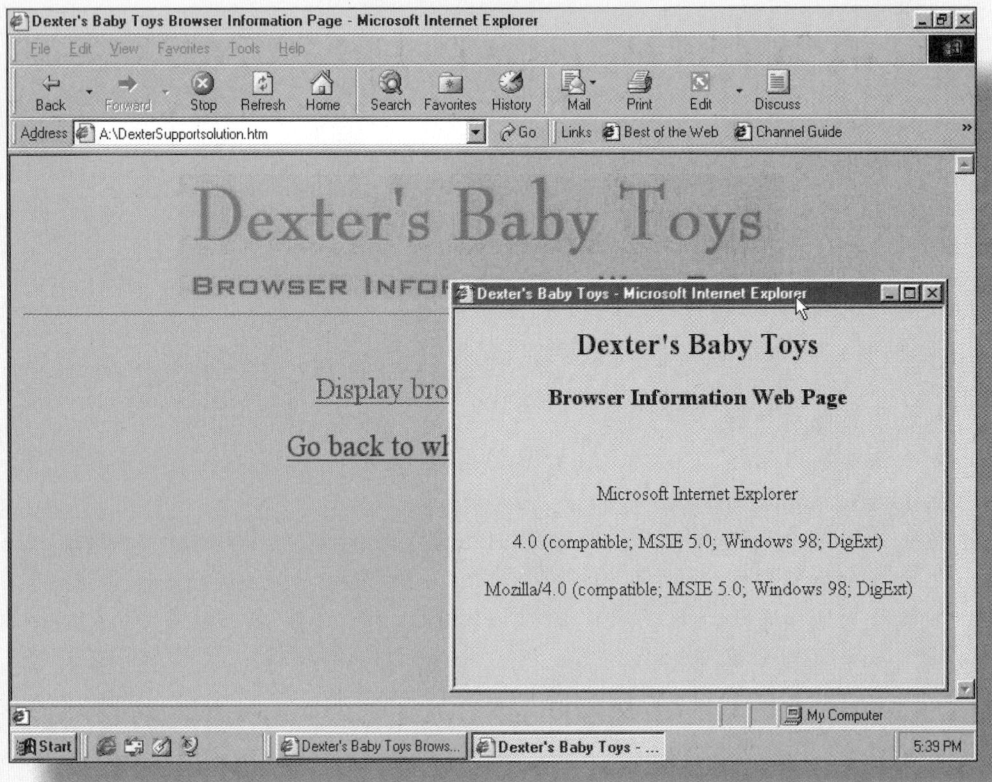

FIGURE 5-39

Instructions: Start your browser and Notepad. Using Notepad, open the DexterSupport.htm file on the JavaScript Data Disk. Perform the following tasks.

1. Write the showBrowser function that displays the the appName, appVersion, and userAgent properties of the navigator object in a new window by entering the following code starting with the blank line on line 4.

```
function showBrowser() {
 BrowserWindow = window.open("", "browserWindow", "toolbar=no,width=400,height=300,
status=no,menubar=no,resize=yes")
```

In the Lab

```
      with (BrowserWindow.document) {
         write()
         close()
         write("<HTML>")
         write("<TITLE>Dexter's Baby Toys</TITLE><BODY BGCOLOR=LIGHTBLUE>")
         write("<CENTER>")
         write("<H2>Dexter's Baby Toys</H2>")
         write("<H3>Browser Information Web Page</H3>")
         write("<BR><BR><CENTER>")
         write(navigator.appName + "<BR><BR>")
         write(navigator.appVersion + "<BR><BR>")
         write(navigator.userAgent)
         write("</CENTER></BODY></HTML>")
      }
   }
```

2. Write the function that will return users to where they started before the customer service agent directed them to this page by entering the following code immediately after the code you entered in step 1.

```
function goBack() {
  history.back()
}
```

3. Create the HTML ANCHOR tag that calls the showBrowser() function that you created in step 1 by entering the following line on a new line between the lines that reads

 and the end center tag, </CENTER>.

```
<A HREF="JavaScript:showBrowser();"><FONT SIZE=5>Display browser
information</FONT></A><BR><BR>
```

4. Create the HTML ANCHOR tag that calls the goBack() function to return users to their previous Web page by entering the following line on a new line immediately after the line you entered in step 3.

```
<A HREF="JavaScript:goBack();"><FONT SIZE=5>Go back to where you came from</FONT></A>
```

5. Save the HTML file using the file name DexterSupportsolution.htm on the JavaScript Data Disk in drive A.
6. Activate the browser. Open the file a:\DexterSupportsolution.htm to test the JavaScript code. If any errors occur, double-check steps 1 through 4 and test again. If no errors occur, print the Web page, and return to Notepad to print the HTML file. Hand in the printouts to your instructor.

3 Custom Computer Builder

Problem: You have been contracted by Sam Stern of Stern's Custom Computers to create a Web site where users can choose different computer components for a computer system and get a total price for a system including those components. The Web page has several drop-down lists of components from which users can choose. The Web page HTML code already contains the lists and a SCRIPT area for JavaScript.

(continued)

Custom Computer Builder *(continued)*

Instructions: Start your browser and Notepad. Use Notepad to open the compcost.htm file on the JavaScript Data Disk. Perform the following tasks.

1. In the SCRIPT section, define a new variable for an object named newComputer. Define a function that will initiate an object called ComputerObject and set the following properties to their corresponding SELECT list values: ProcessorCost, MonitorCost, HardDriveCost, and MemoryCost. Also, add a method called total that is set to a function named showTotal. Create a function named createComputer that can be called to set the newComputer variable to a new instance of the ComputerObject.
2. Call the createComputer from the onLoad event of the Web page body.
3. Create functions that can be called from the onChange events of each of the SELECT lists. The functions should set the appropriate properties of the ComputerObject with the value from the SELECT list and then call the total() method to update the total. Name the functions updateProcessor(), updateMemory(), updateHardDrive(), and updateMonitor().
4. Add the onChange event to each of the SELECT lists. When the onChange event occurs, call the appropriate function created in step 3.
5. Create the function named showTotal() that is the total method of the ComputerObject object. The function should add the values of all of the properties of the ComputerObject and then display the result in the input box named Total. Precede the amount with a dollar sign.
6. Save the HTML file using the file name compcostsolution.htm on the JavaScript Data Disk in drive A.
7. Launch the browser. Open the file a:\compcostsolution.htm to test the JavaScript code. If any errors occur, double-check steps 1 through 5 and test again. If no errors occur, print the Web page, and return to Notepad to print the HTML file. Hand in the printouts to your instructor.

FIGURE 5-40

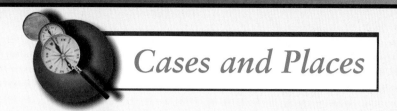

Cases and Places

The difficulty of these case studies varies:
◗ are the least difficult; ◗◗ are more difficult; and ◗◗◗ are the most difficult.

1 ◗ Web shopping carts come in a variety of designs. Visit the following Web based shopping sites and write a report on the differences and usability of each site: www.buy.com, www.amazon.com, and www.dell.com. Use the View Source feature on your Web browser to look at some of the JavaScript code being used to make these sites work.

2 ◗ Ask your instructor for the solution to the Val-U Computers Web site in this project. Add a feature to the site that keeps a running total of the number of items and total price for the items selected and display the information at the top of the shopping page. Make the addition and subtraction of these numbers a method of the shopping cart item. Use the concepts and techniques presented in the project to modify the Web site.

3 ◗◗ A local hardware store keeps a Web page of all of the items in the store. The owner has hired you to make an in-store kiosk out of the Web page where customers can look at lists of items by category. He wants to keep the kiosk simple to maintain, so he intends to use only a keyboard attached to the computer and no mouse. He would like you to modify the Web page so keystrokes can be used rather than mouse clicks to select items and navigate around the Web page. Use the concepts and techniques presented in the project to create the Web page.

4 ◗◗ A local computer training instructor uses a Web page filled with various links to help teach the students how to browse the Web. He would like to be able to keep track of which links the user has visited. Use a hidden frame to keep track of the which links have been visited and use and the rest of the Web page to display the page full of links and a button to press that reports in a window which pages have been visited and which have not. Use the concepts and techniques presented in the project to create the Web page.

5 ◗◗◗ A friend has an antique shop and shows many of her more unusual items on a Web page. She asks you to create an interactive page where users can create an order form and print it from their browsers. When the user clicks the first item, a window should pop up that contains the order. As items are added to the shopping cart, they show up in the pop-up window that was opened. Users should be able to select or delete an item simply by moving the mouse over the item and then pressing the A key to add or the D key to delete. Use the concepts and techniques presented in the project to create the Web page.

Index